D0930080

OFFICIALLY WITHDRAWN
NEW HAVEN FREE PUBLIC LIBRARY

AUG 3 0 2023

James Forten (The Historical Society of Pennsylvania, Leon Gardiner
Collection). This unsigned and undated watercolor may be the work of
African-American artist Robert Douglass Jr. Douglass, a Philadelphia
native and a close friend of the Forten family, enjoyed considerable
success as a portrait painter.

A Gentleman
of Color

A Gentleman of Color

The Life of James Forten

JULIE WINCH

OXFORD
UNIVERSITY PRESS

2002

OXFORD
UNIVERSITY PRESS

Oxford   New York
Athens   Auckland   Bangkok   Bogotá   Buenos Aires   Cape Town
Chennai   Dar es Salaam   Delhi   Florence   Hong Kong   Istanbul   Karachi
Kolkata   Kuala Lumpur   Madrid   Melbourne   Mexico City   Mumbai   Nairobi
Paris   São Paulo   Shanghai   Singapore   Taipei   Tokyo   Toronto   Warsaw

and associated companies in

Berlin   Ibadan

Copyright © 2002 by Julie Winch

Published by Oxford University Press, Inc.
198 Madison Avenue, New York, New York 10016

Oxford is a registered trademark of Oxford University Press

All rights reserved. No part of this publication may be reproduced,
stored in a retrieval system, or transmitted, in any form or by any means,
electronic, mechanical, photocopying, recording, or otherwise,
without the prior permission of Oxford University Press.

Library of Congress Cataloging-in-Publication Data
Winch, Julie, 1953–
A gentleman of color : the life of James Forten / Julie Winch.
p. cm.
Includes bibliographical references and index.
ISBN 0-19-508691-0
1. Forten, James, 1766–1842. 2. African Americans—Biography.
3. African American abolitionists—Biography. 4. African American soldiers—
Biography. 5. African American businesspeople—Pennsylvania—
Philadelphia—Biography. 6. Free African Americans— Pennsylvania—
Philadelphia—Biography. 7. Sailmakers—Pennsylvania—
Philadelphia—Biography. 8. Philadelphia (Pa.) —Biography. I. Title
E185.97.F717 W56   2002   326'.092—dc21   [B]   2001036215

3 5 7 9 8 6 4 2

Printed in the United States of America
on acid-free paper

FREE PUBLIC LIBRARY
133 ELM STREET
NEW HAVEN, CT 06510

B
FORTEN
J

In loving memory of my parents,
Doris Amelia Winch and Leslie Herbert Winch

CONTENTS

ACKNOWLEDGMENTS

I T IS DIFFICULT to know where to begin in expressing my gratitude to the many individuals and organizations that helped bring this project to completion. Each played a part, offering everything from funding to research materials, to house-room, to friendly advice, to knowledgeable criticism, to encouraging words. My thanks to all.

In terms of financial support, I received various grants from the Office of Graduate Studies and Research at the University of Massachusetts in Boston. I was also the recipient of a Paul Cuffe Memorial Fellowship from Mystic Seaport and an Albert J. Beveridge Research Grant from the American Historical Association. The National Endowment for the Humanities was particularly generous, awarding me a Travel to Collections grant and a year-long research fellowship, as well as sponsoring two fascinating summer institutes in maritime history.

Over the years I have worked in many libraries and archives in the United States, Canada, and England. Each has its own distinctive character, but I found staff members unfailingly helpful. I would like to single out for special mention three Philadelphia archives, each of which became a home away from home on my research trips. Through various renovations, the Historical Society of Pennsylvania has remained a superb place in which to work. Its neighbor, the Library Company of Philadelphia, proved equally valuable in terms of my research and just as welcoming. As for the Philadelphia City Archives, what can I say? City Archivist Ward Childs and his colleagues kept their sense of humor and their dedication to their patrons as they moved from one location to another across the city.

Two Philadelphia churches gave me invaluable assistance and helped me to uncover aspects of James Forten's religious life. Christ Church opened its archives to me, answered innumerable questions, and provided me with a comfortable place to work in. The members of the historical society of St. Thomas's Episcopal Church were truly gracious hosts. Arthur Sudler and his colleagues not only extended a warm welcome but spent a great deal of time searching through the church's archives for material on James Forten and his family. Closer to home, Cynthia Alcorn, the librarian of the Massachusetts Grand Lodge of Free and Accepted Masons, guided me through the intricacies of another facet of James Forten's spiritual life, his dedication to Freemasonry.

Jeff Bolster and William Fowler helped immensely with their knowledge of seafaring and maritime trade routes. Don Lucas, Howard Cooper, and "Spike" Thorrington shared with me some of the mysteries of the sailmaker's craft. Randall Burkett, David Brion Davis, W. M. P. Dunne, Todd Gernes, Earl Johnson, Charles K. Jones, Margot Melia, and the late Davidson Nicol pointed me to sources I would otherwise have overlooked. I would like to say a special word of thanks to Margaret Hope Bacon and Reg Pitts. My work was informed in so many ways by their research on the Forten and Purvis families. They saved me from many a false start and rescued me when I reached the inevitable dead end. They were unstinting in their generosity, ransacking their own files again and again on my behalf and sending me anything they thought I could use.

Two former students, Kevin Wall and Sally Stephenson, proved diligent research assistants. I would also like to pay tribute to the reference and interlibrary loan staff at UMASS-Boston's Healey Library. No request was too onerous. From tracking down treatises on sail-making to hunting for files of long-defunct newspapers, they tackled every one of my inquiries with grace and good humor.

Janet Harrison Shannon shared with me her knowledge of Philadelphia past and present, and she and her children, Jill and Larry, trekked with me through the city's churchyards in search of Forten family graves. Roy Finkenbine and his assistant at the Black Abolitionist Archives spent long hours searching through their superb collection of source material and copying items for me. My brother, Roy Winch, took time away from his own work to hunt down records for me in British archives. My partner, Louis Cohen, was always there, fixing my computer, ferrying me to libraries and museums, sharing with me his knowledge of navigation and ship-building and his enthusiasm for the sea, and offering me words of encouragement when the project seemed to be so far from completion. I would also like to thank Susan Ferber, my editor at Oxford University Press, for her help, her advice, her careful work on my manuscript at all its stages, and for her confidence that it would *eventually* be finished.

My book is dedicated to the memory of my parents, who urged me on in every endeavor. They taught me to love to read, to aspire to write, and to want to know more about the lessons the past can teach us.

A Gentleman
of Color

??

Ann Elizabeth Fortune
d. 1768

Thomas Fortune m. Margaret Waymouth
d. 1773/4   1722–1806

Abigail m. William Dunbar
1763–1846   d. 1805

Margaret   Nicholas   William   James
b. 1785   b. 1786   b. 1792   1799–1870

Martha Beatte m.   JAMES FORTEN m. Charlotte Vandine
1783/4–1804   1766–1842   1785–1884

Mary Wood m. Robert m. Mary Hanscone   Mary
1814–1840   1813–1864   c.1817–c.1876   1815–1842

Sarah m. Joseph Purvis   Thomas
1814–1884 1812–1857   1817–1897

                                                 William
                                                 1823–1909

Margaretta
1806–1875

Charlotte
1808–1814

Harriet m. Robert Purvis
1810–1875   1810–1898

James   m.   Jane Vogelsang
1811–c.1870 1819–1852

Introduction

O N A BLUSTERY Sunday afternoon early in March 1842 a funeral cortege set off from a house on Third and Lombard in Philadelphia's New Market Ward. It wound its way up Lombard to Fifth and then along Fifth to a church on Adelphi Street, within sight of Independence Hall. Behind the hearse walked the family of the deceased, his servants, his apprentices, his journeymen, and his closest friends. Behind them walked hundreds of ordinary citizens. Several thousand more stood in the streets and on the sidewalks to watch the solemn procession pass by.[1]

Such public displays of respect were hardly commonplace in Philadelphia. They were reserved for those individuals who had distinguished themselves in one way or another and won the admiration of their fellow citizens. Financier and city benefactor Stephen Girard had received this mark of honor, as had Episcopal bishop William White. And when Benjamin Franklin's funeral took place the entire city had come to a halt. But *this* funeral procession was different. Girard, White, Franklin, and the other Philadelphians who had been accorded a public funeral like this were all white men. James Forten, the man being honored on this occasion, was a man of color and, in what was an all-too-rare occurrence in a city that had been rocked again and again by racial violence, black and white citizens walked together to St. Thomas's African Episcopal Church to attend his funeral.

A visitor from England was amazed at the sight of black and white, rich and poor, coming together in this way. Sir Charles Lyell had not been in Philadelphia very long but he was already well aware of the contempt with which most white Philadelphians regarded their African-American neighbors. Why, he wanted to know, was a man of color being honored in this way? Who was he and what had he done?

Lyell's acquaintances explained that James Forten had been a very rich man. He had been one of the leading sailmakers in the port city, hence the numbers of white ships' captains and ship-owning merchants who had turned out to pay their last respects. He had been well liked, he had lived in Philadelphia virtually his entire life, he had a reputation for honest dealing, and all in all he had been an eminently respectable individual.[2] Lyell was evidently satisfied with that thumbnail sketch of the dead man, but it hardly did justice to the remarkable life James Forten had led.

On one level James Forten's story was pure Horatio Alger. A man of humble origins, he had risen to prosperity as a result of a combination of intelligence, hard work, and good fortune. He had proven himself an astute man of business who knew the value of a dollar and had a nose for a good investment. Shrewd and calculating but never rapacious, he had been well thought of by most members of Philadelphia's predominantly white business community, a fact that accounted for the hundreds of white "gentlemen of the pave" who left their homes that Sunday in March to follow his coffin to St. Thomas's Church.

But James Forten was much more than a black man who had succeeded against the odds and amassed a personal fortune. He had been one of the nation's most outspoken black critics of slavery. Although not born into slavery, he had been a fervent abolitionist, and the likes of William Lloyd Garrison, Benjamin Lundy, and Sarah and Angelina Grimké had been frequent visitors to his home. He had brought his children up to be abolitionists and they were already following in his footsteps.

James Forten's commitment to the cause of reform did not end with his decision to become involved in radical abolitionism. He had made his life's work the restructuring of American society. He had a vision of what the nation could be like if all its citizens abided by its founding principles. And he was confident he knew what those founding principles were, for he was, in a sense, a "founding father." He had fought in the conflict that had brought the United States into being.

James Forten had always prided himself on being a patriot. He had served in the Revolutionary War, not, as so many other black men had done, to gain his freedom—he was legally free already—but because he believed in the American cause. He had stood in the crowd on a hot day in July 1776 and had heard the Declaration of Independence read to the public for the first time. He had heard it and had believed in it. He had continued to believe in it when others seemed only too willing to ignore its promises of life, liberty, and the pursuit of happiness for all Americans. When he was urged to apply for a pension for his wartime service, he responded that he did not want money. What he wanted, and what he felt he deserved, was the title he would never in fact be given: American citizen.

James Forten's pursuit of the elusive goal of full citizenship—not for himself alone but for all Americans of African descent—propelled him into the role of spokesman for the entire black community. He wrote, he spoke, he agitated, and he made alliances with anyone, black and white, who shared his goals. Although he flirted briefly with the notion of racial separation, he quickly rejected it. To those who argued that the true homeland of black people was Africa he responded that *his* homeland was America. He had fought to create the United States and win its independence. Quite apart from considerations of natural justice, that fact alone had earned him the right to stay where he was and where he wished to remain. Besides, he reasoned, if black men and women who were legally free forsook America, who would help the millions still in bondage in the South? Freeborn though he was, he insisted that their struggle was his struggle, and to that struggle he dedicated his time, his energy, and his wealth.

Although never elected to political office, and effectively disfranchised, James Forten was a shrewd political operator. Year by year he grew in stature as a public figure. By the 1830s, his was one of the most powerful black voices, not just for men and women of color in his native city, but for many thousands more throughout the North. He knew how to use the press and the speaker's podium. He knew about building alliances, when to back down and when to press forward with his agenda. His rise to prominence, his understanding of the nature of power and authority, his determination to speak out and be heard are object lessons in the realities of community politics. Disfranchised he might have been, but voiceless he never was.

Not everyone appreciated the ways in which James Forten used his influence. He had his critics in the African-American community, people who did not share his vision or who resented his ways of getting what he wanted. His critics in the white community were even more vocal. He should use his influence, they insisted, to lead a mass exodus of free people of color to West Africa or to some other location far from America's shores. He should remind black people of their duty to be properly subservient to whites. He should caution them against aspiring to equality with whites, an equality they could never achieve. Strong-minded, independent, stubborn perhaps, James Forten ignored all his critics, black and white. He defined his goals and pursued them with single-minded determination. Nothing, not even the threat of violence, would deter him.

James Forten lived a life few African Americans of his generation could imagine. He enjoyed wealth and the privileges that came with it, but he did not use his wealth to insulate himself and his family from the realities of being black in America. At the same time, though, he expected and frequently received the deference of white Americans. He employed whites as well as blacks in his sail loft. He paid their wages and he expected them to do more than just labor diligently for him. He insisted they subscribe to his strict moral code and treat him with the respect he believed himself entitled to. As for the white men he did business with, he wanted them to recognize him as a true master of his craft who happened to be a man of color. By and large that was how they regarded him. They might gossip about him behind his back and comment on his ambitions for himself and his family, but they were pleased enough to give him commissions for sails, trade real estate with him, and discuss with him the state of the market. A man of color he might have been, but that he was something more— truly a *gentleman* of color, with all the respect that the term "gentleman" implied—many of them were prepared to concede. If he could not be recognized as an American citizen, the status he coveted more than any other, James Forten would surely have accepted "gentleman of color" as almost as good.

IT IS ONE of the ironies of James Forten's long life that his last years are by far the best documented. We know much more about him when he was in his sixties and seventies than when he was in his teens and twenties. Why that should be so is easily explained. The appearance in the 1830s of antislavery newspapers such as the *Liberator* and the *Pennsylvania Freeman* meant his activities, especially as they related to abolition, were meticulously chronicled.

But to see James Forten as he was toward the end of his life, a venerable patriarch, a dedicated abolitionist, and a wealthy "gentleman of the pave," is to see only a small part of who and what he was. He had lived through so much and had seen so many transformations in his own life and in the world around him. He had been born free at a time and in a place where the vast majority of black men and women were enslaved. He spent his early years as a British subject, owing at least nominal allegiance to a king in a distant country. He witnessed the dissolution of that bond of loyalty and he played a role in destroying it. Before he turned sixteen he had fought and suffered imprisonment in the name of a new nation that would ultimately never accept him as one of its citizens. As a young man still in his teens, he traveled as a common sailor to the seat of the British Empire and saw for himself the nation and the people from whom the United States had broken free. He eventually returned to his native city and to a remarkable opportunity—the chance to achieve the economic independence that was denied to so many of his contemporaries, irrespective of race.

James Forten witnessed the slow death of slavery in his home state and he fought to hasten its demise. As the institution that had once been commonplace in Philadelphia and elsewhere in the North was confined more and more with each passing year to the region of the country south of the Mason-Dixon line, he continued to fight it. It was a struggle he would never abandon. He would also fight to assert the rights of people like himself, people of color who were legally free but who still endured many of the indignities of slavery. There was scarcely any initiative relating to the advancement of African Americans in Philadelphia from the 1790s onward that did not benefit in some way or another from James

Forten's input. He was everywhere, speaking, drafting petitions, writing to the press, contacting anyone he thought might help his community. African Americans in other cities and towns throughout the North soon became aware of who James Forten was and how much power he wielded. By the time of his death he was one of the best-known men of color in the nation.

REGRETTABLY, FOR A man who lived so long and achieved so much, there is nothing that can really be called a James Forten archive. Researching Forten's history and trying to recreate the world in which he lived means hunting for individual pieces of the puzzle, often in the most unlikely places. James Forten left letters, but only a fraction of what he wrote has survived. Complicating matters is the fact that when he wrote to the press, as he did on many occasions and on many topics, he often adopted pen names. Identifying his letters involves searching for internal evidence to substantiate his authorship. (Happily, that is not quite as difficult as it sounds. James Forten had a fondness for two particular noms de plume, "A Man of Colour" and "A Colored Philadelphian," and he frequently included in his letters allusions to different episodes in his life that can be documented from other sources.) His business papers are scattered. His house is no longer standing. His church and even his grave site have long since been moved. As for the Philadelphia waterfront, it has changed out of all recognition from the collection of wharves, workshops, and warehouses that James Forten would have known. Fortunately, some things have survived. Papers have surfaced in various collections. Following James Forten's trail has taken me to archives across the United States, Canada, and Britain. The trail has been a long one and it has had more than its share of twists and turns, as well as the inevitable dead ends, but it has also had its unexpected rewards.

The paper trail has provided some of the answers as to who and what James Forten was, but there is another trail besides the one written with ink upon paper. James Forten's life was also a life written in canvas. The tools of his trade—one of the most technologically complex of his day—have hardly changed at all over the past two centuries. To practice the craft of traditional sailmaking is still to sit at a bench for long hours and work at sewing canvas with many of the same tools James Forten would have used. It is to smell the same smells and hear many of the same sounds that would have been so integral a part of his everyday life. Much of the research for this book was done in libraries and archives, but some of it was done in sail lofts and rigging lofts on two continents and on a variety of sailing vessels, large and small. To rediscover the world of the sail loft has been one of the challenges, and one of the unexpected delights, of writing about James Forten. Whatever else James Forten was, and in his long life he assumed so many different roles, he was a master of his craft. To try to tell James Forten's story by separating him from the sea and the sail loft is to miss a vital part of that story.

1

"BORN IN HIS MAJESTY'S DOMINIONS"

WHEN JAMES FORTEN was born on September 2, 1766, in his family's modest home on Third near Walnut in the section of Philadelphia known as Dock Ward, probably no one outside his immediate family bothered to take note of the event.[1] And yet the birth was significant, not just because of who James Forten would become, but because of what he represented. He belonged to the fourth generation of his family to live in British North America and the third to be born in the colony of Pennsylvania. The Fortens (or Fortunes, as the name often appeared in the early records) were colonists of long standing. Most of their neighbors were immigrants or the children of immigrants. Later in life, James Forten would take great pride in pointing out that his family had lived in Pennsylvania since the days of William Penn.[2] However, when they looked at him, what most white Philadelphians saw was not the scion of an old and deservedly proud family, but an "African."

In a sense, of course, James Forten *was* an African. That was the term whites in the colonial era and well into the nineteenth century applied to anyone with any discernible trace of African ancestry. It was also the title black men and women often used to describe themselves. African he might be, but James Forten's world was hardly the world his West African great-grandfather had known when he arrived in the small frontier settlement of Philadelphia as a slave in the 1680s.

James Forten's unnamed ancestor (if Forten knew his name he left no record of it) was not the only African in William Penn's fledgling colony. Black men and women lived along the Delaware decades before the arrival of Penn and his Quaker settlers. The Dutch and Swedish pioneers who had farmed and traded in the area for half a century before the creation of Pennsylvania owned African slaves. As for William Penn, whatever initial unease he may have felt about permitting human bondage in his new colony, he accepted the existence of slavery as a fait accompli and eventually became a slave owner himself.[3] His colonists were anxious to secure a labor force and few had any hesitation about buying Africans and holding them in servitude for life. In 1684 Philadelphia Quakers eagerly bid for the 150 men, women, and children brought up the Delaware aboard the slaver *Isabella*. The new arrivals were quickly put to work felling trees; building homes, stores, and warehouses; and performing a wide range of household tasks.[4]

Further "parcels" of Africans arrived over the next decade and a half. None was as large as the shipment on the *Isabella*. Most slaves came into Philadelphia in groups of a dozen or so because slave traders generally preferred to sell their cargoes in the West Indies, where sugar planters would pay high prices for quality "merchandise." Despite the complaints of white Pennsylvanians that they were getting only the "refuse" of the slave trade, the people that slaving captains could not market elsewhere, the population of enslaved colonists in Pennsylvania grew steadily. Some of the early white settlers to the Quaker colony came from Barbados and Jamaica and they brought their slaves with them. Others had friends and family in one or other of the British possessions in the West Indies. It was a simple matter to write and request that one's brother, cousin, or business agent look out for a few suitable "chattels" and send them to Philadelphia on the next available vessel. Some of the slaves who made the voyage up the Delaware had actually been born in the West Indies. Many more were Africans who had been "seasoned" for a few months, or possibly a year or two, in the Caribbean. By 1700 there were over 200 slaves in Philadelphia and more in the surrounding countryside.[5] Among that first generation of black Philadelphians was James Forten's ancestor.

Whether he came directly to Philadelphia from the Guinea Coast or via the West Indies, James Forten's great-grandfather found himself set down in the New World among an alien people. Separated from his owners by race, religion, language, and culture, he somehow managed to survive. That in itself was no mean feat. Africans did not fare well in Pennsylvania. As one white Philadelphian observed, they were "So Chilly they Can hardly stir from the fire."[6] Smallpox, respiratory diseases, malnutrition, and exposure to a far colder climate than they had been accustomed to claimed the lives of many Africans within months of their arrival.

Despite the paucity of written material about Forten's great-grandfather, we can deduce a few things about him. He was physically strong. Had he not been, he would hardly have survived the horrors of the "middle passage" or his first winter in Pennsylvania. He was also adept at mastering new skills. The white inhabitants of Penn's "green country town" demanded that their slaves be versatile. Although Philadelphia could hardly be described as a major urban center in the 1680s and 1690s, it was not the countryside, either. White Philadelphians expected their "chattels" to be able to perform a range of tasks, everything from fetching and carrying to building and maintaining their homes, loading and unloading their trading vessels, sailing those vessels, and in some cases helping to construct them. They also required of their bondsmen and women a facility with the English language, even if they only ever learned to speak broken English. As for the Africans' religious lives, there were precious few attempts to evangelize them. The English Friends complained about their slaves' "heathenism practices" but they did little to try to replace the Africans' belief systems with their own.[7]

In 1700, with the numbers of slaves in the colony growing, the Pennsylvania Assembly passed "an act for better regulation of servants in this province and territories." Lest there be any doubt about its legality—and a few whites had expressed such doubts—servitude for life was explicitly permitted and special courts were set up to try "Africans," including the handful who had somehow managed to gain their freedom.[8]

As for the enslaved, there is ample evidence that black men and women in and around Philadelphia were struggling to forge a sense of community. As early as 1693, Quaker masters expressed concern about "the tumultuous gatherings of the negroes in the towne of philadelphia, on the first dayes of the weeke."[9] While there may have been angry talk of rebellion at those gatherings, most black Philadelphians were just taking the opportunity to socialize and seek an hour or two for themselves, away from the watchful eyes of their owners.[10]

Perhaps James Forten's great-grandfather slipped away now and again to join in those "tumultuous gatherings." We know so little of his life in slavery. We have no record of the name his parents gave him, his slave name, or the name of his owner. We do not know how many times he might have been sold, whether he was considered a "good" slave, or whether he was regarded as a troublemaker. The one thing we do know is that at some point he took an enslaved African woman as his marriage partner. The practice in Pennsylvania, as in virtually every other slave-holding colony in British North America, was that children followed the condition of their mother. Had Forten's ancestor fathered a child with a white woman or an Indian woman, that child would have been free, even though he might have been forced to spend his early years working for a white master under some form of indenture.[11] However, James Forten was quite explicit. His grandfather had been born a slave and that meant that his great-grandmother had been a slave, too.

Whether Forten's great-grandparents and their son lived together for any appreciable length of time we have no way of knowing. Perhaps they were lucky enough to be owned by the same family or perhaps by neighboring families. In any event, as slaves, even if they did live in the same household, they always faced the possibility of separation through sale or the division of the estate when their owner died. Later commentators would talk of the "mild character" of slavery in Pennsylvania, and mild it might have been compared with its counterpart on the sugar plantations of the Caribbean or the rice plantations of South Carolina, but it was hardly mild to those who lived under it. Forten's great-grandparents might well have quarreled with assertions that they were happy with their lot.[12]

James Forten's great-grandfather would live out the rest of his days as a slave, but his son would eventually graduate to the ranks of the free. How he did it Forten never explained. He simply told a white friend: "My grandfather obtained his own freedom."[13] Perhaps he managed to accumulate enough money to be able to bargain with his master or perhaps he was promised his freedom in return for faithful service for a set term of years. Possibly he was set free by one of those rare individuals in the colony who was genuinely troubled by the existence of chattel slavery.

It goes without saying that becoming free was no easy matter. Nor did legal freedom confer anything approaching full civil rights. To begin with, the statute passed by the Pennsylvania Assembly in 1726 to supplement the law code of 1700 stipulated that slave owners must post a £30 bond when they manumitted a slave. If the bond was not paid, the slave remained a slave. Frankly, free "Africans" were considered to be a troublesome group of people, and most whites had no wish to see their numbers increase. Lawmakers stated outright that "'tis found by experience that free negroes are an idle, slothful people and often prove burdensome to the neighborhood and afford ill examples to other negroes."[14] Those who were deemed able-bodied could be bound out to labor without pay for a white master or mistress for a term of years if they would not work or if they were adjudged to be vagrants. Justices could also bind out free black children, with or without the consent of their parents, until the girls were twenty-one and the boys twenty-four.[15] Free blacks could not marry whites. Violation of that law would lead to their reenslavement, the binding out of their white spouse for a term of years, and a hefty fine for the minister who had married them. They could not travel as they wished or consume alcohol when and where they chose, and they were limited as to what they could trade and with whom. In short, freedom was precarious. James Forten's grandfather, legally free but "African" nonetheless, had to bear in mind that he could always be taken back into bondage if he became destitute or if he broke the law.[16] By a mix of sheer luck and determination, he managed to maintain his freedom and, just as important, find a free black woman to marry. Their children would be born into freedom in a city where the condition of most "Africans" was slavery for life and where whites were eagerly importing more slaves.

Facts about the lives of James Forten's parents are hardly more plentiful than they are about his grandparents and his great-grandparents. Forten was quite definite that his father was freeborn and "never wore the yoke."[17] The earliest accounts of James Forten's remarkable life identify his father as Thomas Forten, or Fortune, but they make no mention of his mother, beyond a brief acknowledgment that she was a virtuous and hard-working woman who possessed a "fine mind."[18] We would not even know her name if her son had not placed a death notice in the Philadelphia papers to mark her passing. That brief obituary reveals that her name was Margaret. It also hints at her background. Margaret was eighty-four when she died in 1806, hence she was forty-one in 1763, when her daughter, Abigail, was born, and forty-four when she gave birth to James.[19]

Why was Margaret Forten, or Fortune, so much older than most women in colonial Philadelphia, black or white, when she bore her first child? It is hardly likely that she would have had difficulty finding a marriage partner when she was in her late teens or early twenties, for the numbers of black men and women in the city were roughly even and Margaret's free status would have made her very attractive to a black man, regardless of his own condition, who did not wish his children to be born into bondage.[20] But perhaps she was not legally free. If Margaret was a slave, she would have known perfectly well that any child she bore would inherit her condition. She and Thomas Fortune may have delayed marriage and chosen not to begin a family until they had secured her freedom. Thomas "never wore the yoke" but Margaret may well have done so.[21]

Where Margaret was from, whose property she might have been, when and where she met Thomas Fortune, and what bargain they struck for her freedom are all questions on which the available sources are irritatingly silent. One cryptic reference indicates that her maiden name may have been Waymouth, but even that is vague and it does not connect her to any other family, black or white, in the Philadelphia area.[22] There is no marriage record for Thomas and Margaret that would supply the missing clues. Suffice it to say that Margaret had become a free woman before she bore Abigail in 1763 and she was able to leave both her children a legacy of incalculable worth—their legal freedom.

About Thomas Fortune we know rather more. According to Stephen H. Gloucester, who was a friend of James Forten's and wrote one of the earliest accounts of his life, Thomas had been born in the same neighborhood as his son.[23] Thanks to a stray receipt that has survived in a collection of business papers, we know that at some point Thomas learned to read and write, a remarkable achievement for the son of a slave and a rarity for any laboring man in colonial Philadelphia.[24] The family's religious affiliation offers a hint as to how Thomas might have acquired his formal education. He, his wife, and their children were Anglicans. Because their home was on Third and Walnut, they probably attended St. Paul's Church, which was just a block or two away. It was there, many years later, that Abigail Forten would be married.[25]

What would attract a family of "Africans," albeit free "Africans," to the Anglican faith? Surely this was the church of the white elite and those black people who went to Christ Church or St. Peter's or St. Paul's on Sundays did so only because they were slaves and had no choice in the matter. By the 1740s and 1750s a handful of Philadelphia's highly placed white Anglicans were making efforts to reach out to "Africans," both enslaved and free. The Quakers might be in the majority in Philadelphia, but the Anglicans were far more successful at connecting with black residents, including the Fortens.

Perhaps Thomas Fortune was converted to evangelical Christianity as a young man during the early stages of the Great Awakening. He and other members of his family may even have been among the "near fifty Negroes" who, according to George Whitefield, "came to give me thanks, under God, for what has been done to their Souls" when the Great Itinerant preached in Philadelphia in 1740.[26] If Whitefield's evangelism had not attracted Thomas to the Anglican fold, the quiet but kindly efforts of Rev. Robert Jenney might well have done so. Jenney, who became Rector of Christ Church in 1742, made a real effort to serve the black community, baptizing adults and children, officiating at weddings and funerals, and persuading the Society for the Propagation of the Gospel to appropriate £30 per annum to pay for an assistant minister to serve as "catechist for the Negroes." The man appointed was William Sturgeon.[27] In 1758 a British charity, the Associates of Dr. Bray, organized a school for free black children at Christ Church, with Sturgeon as its master.[28] The Forten family's adherence to Anglicanism could well have stemmed from tutoring Thomas received at the school, for Thomas was ambitious for himself and his family and probably shrewd enough to realize that literacy could enhance their status and improve their prospects.

JAMES FORTEN'S FATHER generally went by the last name "Fortune." James would modify that to "Forten," although in various documents it still appeared as "Fortune." There were good reasons for James Forten to wish to subtly alter the family name. Throughout the British colonies "Fortune" was a common slave name, almost as common as Cuff, Pompey, or Caesar. Perhaps "Fortune" had been the name his owners gave to James Forten's great-grandfather when they purchased him as a slave. No fewer than six Fortunes were involved in the 1741 New York City slave conspiracy. Nine slaves with "Fortune" as either their last or only name were listed as having fled to British lines during the Revolutionary War. To announce that one's name was Fortune was to invite the inquiry as to whose "boy" Fortune one was.[29] Even when it was applied to a white person, "Fortune" could have negative connotations. In 1789 the overseers of the Philadelphia Almshouse baptized a white foundling "Filius Fortunae, the child of Fortune."[30]

There were various free black families by the name of Fortune in Philadelphia in the eighteenth and early nineteenth centuries. Thomas and his family may have been related to them, but they may have shared nothing beyond a name. Primus and Jane Fortune lived in the part of the city known as Middle Ward in the 1770s and 1780s. Their daughter, Sarah, eventually married African-born Shandy Yard, a good friend of James Forten's.[31] The 1810 census listed two men of color named John Fortune. One, a sweep-master (a chimney-sweep with a gang of boys who worked for him), lived within a few blocks of James and his family. The other, a hairdresser, resided at various addresses over the years. In 1803 he lived just a block or two from a house Forten owned on Shippen Street in Southwark.[32] Then there was the mysterious Fortin Atus, or Fortune Ates, a free man of color who headed a household of six in 1800. He was probably the same individual as "Fortunatus," who, according to the 1790 census, had a total of ten people in his household on Race Street in Philadelphia's Middle Ward.[33]

There were also black people with the last name of Forten. In the 1820 census, for example, Mary Forten headed a household in Locust Ward. The list of the members of the African Lodge for the years 1797 to 1800 included a John Forten.[34] Again, these Fortens might have been relatives of James Forten and his family or they might simply have been other "Fortunes" who had changed their names or had their names changed for them by the census-takers and the compilers of city directories.

To add to the confusion, there were several white Fortens in Philadelphia when James was growing up. Anthony Forten (sometimes listed as "Fortune") kept the Three Tuns tavern in Middle Ward.[35] There were two George Fortens. One, a German-born tailor, also known as George Fadel, owned property on Front and Water Streets.[36] The other George Forten captained the ship *Ann* for the firm of William Fisher and Son and was a fairly well known figure on the Philadelphia waterfront. He died in 1784.[37] There is no evidence to suggest any ties, either of blood or ownership, to any of these men. By the time of James Forten's birth Philadelphia was a large and very cosmopolitan city. Shared names were not uncommon.

The one "Fortune" in Philadelphia who *was* related to Thomas was Ann Elizabeth Fortune. She was his sister. Young James probably grew up with no memory of his aunt, for she died before his second birthday, but he would obviously have heard about her. Ann Elizabeth Fortune was remarkable in several respects. Few women in colonial Philadelphia wrote wills, because most had nothing to leave. Upon marriage, a woman's property passed automatically to her husband. Most widows and spinsters did not go to the trouble and expense of drawing up a will when all they generally had to leave were a few personal items. As for African and African-American women, the vast majority were slaves. Those who were not enslaved enjoyed, at best, an uncertain freedom and almost all of them lived in poverty.[38] Ann Elizabeth was different. A "free Negroewoman born in his Majesty's Dominions," she was relatively well-to-do and a "Single-woman," so her property was hers to dispose of as she thought fit.

On August 10, 1768, when she made her will, Ann Elizabeth was close to death. Her signature was written in a shaky hand, probably indicative of both literacy acquired fairly late in life and bodily infirmity. She may have been dying, but her mind was clear. She knew what she wanted done with her estate. She named as her heir her brother's daughter, five-year-old Abigail Fortune. Her executor was instructed to keep a number of things for Abigail until she came of age—some pieces of furniture and Ann Elizabeth's collection of china, silver plate, and jewelry. Everything else was to be sold and the proceeds put "to Interest on Good Security" during Abigail's minority.[39] Abigail would be a moderately prosperous woman when she turned twenty-one.

Ann Elizabeth Fortune clearly had contacts in the white community as well as the black community. Quaker Hannah Cadwalader, who witnessed her will, was the mother of merchant Lambert Cadwalader, who subsequently employed Thomas Fortune. Another witness, Margaret Stevenson, was Hannah's niece.[40] Her executor was Anthony Benezet, a Quaker schoolmaster. The two men who appraised her estate were both Quakers. One, tanner Joseph Marriott, was a relative of Benezet's by marriage.

The choice of Anthony Benezet as executor was logical enough. His championing of the rights of the black community had earned him the affection of slave and free alike. His antislavery credentials were impeccable. For years he had been writing tracts arguing that slavery was immoral. He had no patience with whites who talked about "helping" benighted Africans by enslaving them and introducing them to a superior culture. He demanded that Africans be seen as fully human, with cultures of their own.[41] As for Cadwalader and the others, they may have been neighbors of Ann Elizabeth's. They may also have been motivated to help her because of their antislavery views. In 1755, in large part because of continual pressure from Benezet and other dissidents, the Society of Friends had adopted an antislavery testimony. Quakers were required to have no further involvement in the slave trade, to abstain from purchasing slaves, and to begin preparing to free those they already had.[42] Ironically, though, Benezet, Cadwalader, and the others might have opposed slavery, but the black woman they were helping to settle her earthly affairs was herself a slave owner. Ann Elizabeth Fortune was the legal owner of "Negroewoman Jane." Under the terms of her will she gave Jane her freedom, but Jane had obviously labored for her without recompense for some years. At first glance the ownership of one black woman by another is startling. To most white Philadelphians both mistress and slave were "Africans," but in reality a vast gulf separated the two. Ann Elizabeth might be descended from slaves but she had been born free in Pennsylvania. Jane had probably been born a slave in Barbados, for after Anthony Benezet completed the legal formalities to safeguard her freedom, that is where she went, presumably returning to a place where she had family and friends.

As for the rest of Ann Elizabeth Fortune's possessions, the inventory of her estate reveals a great deal about not only what she owned but her ties to her family, her status, and her knowledge of the business world. The formal appraisal of her estate began with the bed on which she had died. She had a feather bed at a time when many Philadelphians had mattresses filled only with rags or straw. In the living-room there were the trappings of a genteel middle-class existence—walnut tables, looking-glasses, pictures, and imported china. As for her silk and dimity gowns, they marked her out as a woman of means. The entire estate was appraised at £90, a considerable amount for anyone in late colonial Philadelphia, and all the more remarkable given Ann Elizabeth Fortune's race and gender.

Anthony Benezet drew on the estate for various charges. The first item, after the funeral expenses, was the sum of £1 2s 8d "paid Marg[are]t Fortane [sic] for Services & attendance." A working woman, who probably cleaned and cooked in the homes of whites to supplement Thomas's wages, Margaret had nursed her sister-in-law during her final illness and sacrificed her family's income to do so. It was right and proper that she be paid for her time.

The legal record of Ann Elizabeth's estate is very detailed but there is one glaring gap: Precisely what was the source of her wealth? A few facts are clear. She did not inherit her money from a husband, for she had none, or from her father, who had spent much of his life in slavery. Thomas, with a wife and children to provide for, could not have underwritten her comfortable lifestyle. Ann Elizabeth might have kept a store of some kind or a stall in the market, as a number of white women did, but there is no shopkeeper's stock in the inventory of her estate.[43] No tavern license was ever issued to her. If she sold beer and spirits in a small unlicensed establishment her estate would surely have included glasses and tankards. The fact that the appraisers found a length of fine "green sattin" among her possessions might suggest she was a dressmaker, but where are the tools of her trade? Surely scissors, pins, needles, and so on would have been left to Abigail? Ann Elizabeth's other options, cleaning and taking in washing, would hardly have netted her the income she evidently enjoyed.[44] The fine clothes, the furniture, the presence of a slave to keep her home clean suggest that Ann Elizabeth at some point might have had a wealthy lover. If he was in the West Indian trade, as so many Philadelphia merchants were, he might well have had a stake in the slave trade and have bought Jane for her as a cook and maid.

There is one other possibility that might explain Ann Elizabeth's affluence, her acquaintance with Benezet, and her ownership of a slave. On October 3, 1751, the *Pennsylvania Gazette* carried an intriguing advertisement. "TO BE SOLD, A Parcel of likely Negroes, very reasonable. . . . Said Negroes may be seen at a Free Negroe Woman, in Chestnut street, opposite to Mr. Anthony Benezet." Was Ann Elizabeth that "Free Negroe Woman" and was Jane in that "parcel" or one of the others she may have dealt in over the years?[45] If Ann Elizabeth Fortune was involved in some way in the slave trade—and clearly at least one "free Negroe Woman" was—then it complicates our understanding of the lines of separation between free and enslaved "Africans" in colonial Philadelphia.

Ann Elizabeth Fortune's funeral, which took place in August 1768, was a modest but respectable affair. Her body was decently laid out and a good coffin ordered. Most likely she was buried in the Negroes' Burying Ground, a section of the Strangers' Burial Ground in what is now Washington Square. It was carefully separated from the white graveyard, but it was by no means an unpleasant place. Affluent white Quakers like Elizabeth Drinker would sometimes stroll there. For the black community it functioned as a meeting place, to the intense annoyance of white authorities, who disliked the mix of Christian and "heathen" ceremonies that went on there as Africans and African Americans honored their dead in a variety of ways.[46]

A slave owner and successful businesswoman, Ann Elizabeth Fortune obviously had a shrewd understanding of how the economy functioned. The money put aside for Abigail was to be properly invested, while the fact that she left her estate to her niece rather than her nephew suggests a realization that Abigail's need was greater than James's. A decent dowry would get Abigail a husband with good prospects. James could learn his father's trade and become a craftsman.

Ann Elizabeth had every reason to believe that her young nephew would have little need of her money, for Thomas had a good trade to teach James. Thomas Fortune was a sailmaker, a valuable occupation in a city that was the location of several dozen flourishing shipyards. Vessels built in the yards along the Delaware had a deservedly good reputation throughout the British Empire, and it was not uncommon for a captain to receive an offer to buy his ship, as well as his cargo, in London or Barbados.[47] From the earliest days of English settlement, Philadelphia had been a center for shipbuilding. Penn himself had seen its potential. He had recognized the value of the timber stocks in the countryside around his new capital city. He had recruited shipwrights and personally financed the building of the first vessel.[48] By Thomas Fortune's day the small frontier settlement that his grandfather had known had been transformed into a major port. Philadelphia-built vessels, from three-masted ocean-going ships to small coasting brigs and sloops, carried down the Delaware the produce of the city's rich agricultural hinterland. Vessels of all sizes sailed up the Delaware from Europe, the West Indies, and ports in British North America. Philadelphia-built or foreign-built, those vessels needed new sails made and old ones repaired. Despite occasional downturns in trade, Philadelphia's seaport was flourishing and Thomas was well placed to take advantage of that fact.

Thomas knew that slaves as well as free men plied the sailmaker's trade.[49] Anyone who took a walk along the river would see gangs of slaves laboring in the shipyards, rope walks, sail lofts, and on the wharves. Black men were longshoremen and sailors. They caulked hulls and worked aloft in the rigging. Just possibly Thomas's father had worked along the waterfront and mastered one or other of the maritime trades. Perhaps it was his skill as a caulker or a rigger that had enabled him to strike a bargain for his freedom.

Whatever Thomas Fortune's father did as a slave and a free man, he was able to see to it that Thomas learned a good trade. As a young man, Thomas Fortune had probably been employed in a sail loft by the day or the week to sew canvas and make rope fittings. He may well have met his future employer, Robert Bridges, in the sail loft when Bridges was serving his apprenticeship. A young "African" without capital or influential connections, Thomas Fortune was not in a position to secure an apprenticeship and then graduate to owning his own loft. He could count himself lucky to have found steady employment in a skilled trade. Robert Bridges had inherited money from his father and he had friends who could get him an apprenticeship and eventually help him establish himself in business. Bridges's prospects were far brighter than Fortune's but Bridges knew the quality of the black sailmaker's work. When he completed his apprenticeship and opened his own sail loft he hired Thomas Fortune.[50]

Robert Bridges was a useful man to have as an employer and a patron. His Irish-born father, Edward, had done well as a merchant in the Philadelphia of the 1730s. From his house on the corner of Walnut and Front Streets he sold a variety of imported goods "at Reasonable Rates, for Ready Money or the Usual Credit." He was also the man to see to buy an indentured servant fresh off the boat from Ireland or arrange passage to London for oneself or one's cargo.[51]

The Bridges family was well on its way to joining the city's mercantile elite when disaster struck. In 1741 Edward fell ill and died.[52] His widow, Cornelia, set to work to realize as much capital as she could from Edward's estate. She disposed of the contents of his warehouse, collected various debts due him, and sold the family's slave, "a likely Negro Woman, fit for either Town or Country Work." An enterprising woman, she also made money taking in boarders, selling theater tickets, and running a dry-goods store. As soon as they were old enough, she and her children's guardian found employment for her sons. The two eldest joined the Royal Navy while Robert was apprenticed to a sailmaker.[53]

Once he was his own master, Robert Bridges had no shortage of business. Commissions flowed in for sails and other items, such as tents and floor coverings. One of the projects Thomas Fortune may have worked on was the fitting-out of the 1767 surveying expedition that determined the Mason-Dixon line. Robert Bridges secured the order to make several large tents or "marquees," sixteen smaller tents, and "Waggon clothes." His loft also repaired the telescope tents and constructed "2 speaking Trumpets."[54]

In the 1760s Robert Bridges was doing well financially. He owned a home, various pieces of real estate, and two slaves. He would eventually acquire a third slave. He also commanded the labor of several white indentured servants.[55] Like many craftsmen, Bridges acquired slaves as a sound investment. Few of Philadelphia's slave owners were aristocrats who used their slaves, as they did their carriages and their fine houses, to display their wealth. The typical slave owner was an artisan, a shopkeeper, a tavern-keeper, or a sea captain.[56] The ownership of slaves was something that crossed lines of class, gender, occupation, and, as the Forten family's own history reveals, race.

Slavery was woven into the fabric of social and economic life in colonial Philadelphia. Outside the ranks of the most zealous Quakers, virtually every moderately prosperous white person Thomas Fortune and his family knew owned a slave or had at least mulled over the pros and cons of slave ownership. If they did not own a slave, they probably employed a white servant who was bound to them by some form of indenture. In fact, it was the shortage of white indentured servants during the French and Indian War, and their tendency to run away to join the army, that had led to a sharp increase in the numbers of slaves imported into Philadelphia. For them, escape into the army was far more difficult, although it was not impossible. Between 1757 and 1766 some thirteen hundred slaves, many of them direct from Africa, were landed on the wharves along the Delaware. In 1762 alone, five hundred were auctioned off to eager bidders like Robert Bridges.[57]

The exploitation of unfree labor by those with the means to acquire that labor was simply a fact of life. Thomas Fortune was not Robert Bridges's slave. He had never been. Their interaction was that of employer and trusted employee. It is unlikely that Bridges made any objection to Fortune's plan to introduce his young son to the sailmaker's craft. He may have encouraged it or even suggested it.

His knowledge of his craft was one of the most valuable legacies Thomas Fortune could pass on to his son, and he probably set about doing so as soon as the boy could walk and talk and follow simple instructions. When young James first started accompanying Thomas to the loft on Willings' Wharf the lines between play and work were blurred. A large sail loft like Bridges's was a bustling place and there was no shortage of sights and sounds and smells to capture the imagination of an inquisitive child.

Like other sailmakers, Robert Bridges conducted his business on the upper floor of a warehouse. In his case it was one belonging to the firm of Thomas Willing and Co., one of the wealthiest in the city. If James ever asked his father why lofts were preferable to the lower floors of a building for sailmaking, Thomas would have explained that a sailmaker needed ample floor space for marking out the plans for each sail and laying down the canvas to be cut. It was only the upper story that could provide space free from the obstruction of supporting posts.

The staircases leading to most lofts were too narrow to allow any but the smallest sails to be carried up them for repair. The usual practice was to hoist furled sails up the outside of the building by means of a block and tackle and then haul them in through a window. Presumably James was warned to keep well out of the way when this delicate and potentially hazardous operation was going on. Still, the arrival of old sails could provide unexpected entertainment. James Franklin Briggs, himself a sailmaker's son, recalled being in the loft when sails came in from vessels plying the Caribbean trade. The spare sails stored in the ships' "lazaretes," or storage areas, had become nesting places for huge West Indian cockroaches, which would be shaken loose as the sails were hoisted into the loft. Briggs and the other boys in the loft would delight in chasing the roaches along the wharf.[58]

The workday started early at the sail loft, as it did in virtually all the city's various workshops. Thomas Fortune and the other men checked in with Bridges, carefully stowed away their food for the day, and changed from their street clothes into their canvas work outfits. This was not to save their clothes from wear and tear but to protect the sail cloth from any dirt and grime they might have tracked in from the streets. Generally they made their own work clothes— a blouse, like a fisherman's, that they pulled over their heads, and trousers that tied at the sides. So similar was this uniform to that of the common sailor that it often exposed sailmakers to the unwanted attentions of Royal Navy press-gangs. In fact, plenty of sailmakers had been to sea, willingly or unwillingly. Thomas Fortune may well have served his time before the mast, for black sailors, free and enslaved, were common in the Atlantic world of the eighteenth century.[59]

As the apprentices and journeymen began their day's work, Thomas would have ordered young James to settle down quickly and turn his hand to something productive. There was plenty of work that a young child was capable of doing. To begin with, the floor of the loft needed to be swept clean. No sailmaker wanted his expensive imported canvas dirtied or, even worse, snagged or torn. If James did nothing else in his first few months in the loft, he probably spent many hours wielding a broom.

As soon as he knew what to keep and what to throw out, he could be set to work "picking over the shakings." The "shakings" were the scraps of canvas and cordage that were discarded and swept into the corner as the sails were cut and shaped. Much of the "shakings" could be recycled. Off-cuts of canvas could be used for patches and fittings. As for the cordage, a child's hands were well suited to breaking down each piece of Russian hemp into separate strands. The resulting product, oakum, could then be sold for caulking.[60]

Also relegated to a child was the task of preparing the wax the apprentices and journeymen used for waxing their sewing thread. Young James would have heated up in an iron kettle a mixture of clear turpentine, tallow, and beeswax. The mixture had to be constantly tended so that it did not boil. As soon as the various ingredients were properly melted and blended, the mixture would be put into cold water and allowed to cool. When it was cold enough to handle, James would pick pieces out and work them into blocks small enough to fit into the palm of a man's hand. The sailmakers would run their thread through the wax before they began sewing to make the sewing easier and to prolong the life of the sails by making the stitching more waterproof. Like the "shakings," chips of wax could be salvaged. It was generally a child's work to gather up from around the various benches any fragments that had flaked off as the men sewed and then to take an old knife—woe betide him if he took one used for cutting canvas—and scrape off the floor any wax that had spilled from the kettle. The chips and scrapings would be melted down and reused.[61]

As his strength increased, there was other work James could do in and around the loft. He might well have returned home at night with his hands and arms sore and reeking after helping his father and some of the other men rub pungent Stockholm tar into the hanks of sewing twine. This task, one of the least pleasant in the loft, was important because, like the wax, the tar protected the twine from damp and mildew and ultimately prolonged the life of the finished sail.[62] He might also have been employed holding up the canvas as Robert Bridges or his foreman cut it to size for the various "cloths" or panels that would go into making up a sail. Generally regarded as "boy's work," this task gave a would-be apprentice the chance to see exactly how canvas was handled by a master and how sails were designed.[63]

Thomas Fortune gradually introduced James to the various tools of his trade. As soon as his fingers could grasp a needle, he was taught how to sew canvas. It was not light work by any means. The sailmaker's needle was far less easy to handle than those his mother and sister used to make and repair his clothes. It was much larger and, unlike an ordinary sewing needle, it was triangular in section, not round. There were also many different types of needles. As he became more familiar with his work environment, James would have learned to distinguish among the needles according to their size, shape, and function. There were "large marline, small marline, double bolt-rope, large bolt-rope, small bolt-rope, store, old work, tabling and flat-seam" needles. The "short square" or "lolley" was preferred for sewing the boltrope that went around the sides of the sail, while the "long square," with the blade longer than the shank, was the choice for seaming. Thomas would have impressed upon his son the need to keep these expensive precision tools in good repair, sharpening them on a water stone, greasing them with lard before he began sewing, and then cleaning them with polishing rouge before storing them in a leather or canvas needle-case, or perhaps in a more elaborate wooden case.[64]

Inevitably James stuck himself a few times before mastering the correct technique for forcing a needle through several layers of canvas. Depending on how sympathetic a parent Thomas was, he either comforted his son and tried to staunch the blood or warned him to be more careful in the future and not leave bloodstains on the canvas. James soon came to understand that as vital a part of the sailmaker's gear as his needles was his palm. The palm was a strip of leather shaped to encircle the hand, leaving the fingers free. There was a hole for the thumb and a metal disc or "eye" at the heel of the hand. The trick was to push the needle through the canvas with the "eye," in effect using the palm as a large thimble. The sailmaker generally made his own palm from a paper pattern, cut the leather, built up the post of leather or wood to hold the "eye," and then sewed all the pieces together.[65] Perhaps Thomas made James his own child-size palm or helped him make one so he could practice with it on odd scraps of canvas that were too small or too worn to be used for anything else.

The main item of furniture in the sail loft was the sailmaker's bench. Made of wood and some seven or eight feet in length, it was designed to provide both a seat and a work surface while keeping all the tools a craftsman needed close at hand. Sailmakers often added some kind of padding to make the bench more comfortable during their long hours of work. Attached to one end of the bench by a lanyard was a sail or bench hook to which the sailmaker fastened his canvas so he could keep it pulled tightly across his knees while he sewed. Also attached to the bench was a tray for loose items and a canvas bag for various fittings.[66]

There were slots cut into the bench for storing fids, the large tapered pins used for opening up the strands in lengths of rope ready for splicing. Fids were also used for forming the various rope fittings for the sails and forcing holes into canvas for those fittings. There were fids of various weights and sizes to conform to the various weights of cordage a sailmaker had to work with. Each one had to be stored in its appropriate place in the bench, within reach but clear of the floor. Made of imported lignum vitae, fids were expensive and it was essential that their points did not become blunt. A worn or damaged fid could pull out threads and even rip the canvas. Some of the very largest of the fids were too big to be stored at the benches and were kept in a special fid stool or table set high enough off the floor to keep the points sharp and clean.[67]

Apart from the fids, there was a whole array of marlin spikes, prickers, stabbers, and awls. Then there were the mallets of various kinds, ranging in size from the huge commander or driving mallet to the much smaller variety.[68] James Forten would have learned their names from his father and his workmates. He would also have learned the different kinds of stitching, the weight and feel of every kind of canvas and cordage Robert Bridges's workers used, and the names of each kind of sail and the parts of a sail. That knowledge, mastered in his childhood, would serve him very well indeed in the years to come.

Sailmaking was a good trade, one that could produce a steady income. A society where chattel slavery was commonplace and where those whites who preached the essential equality of blacks and whites were regarded as foolish in the extreme could still offer a talented "African" the chance to become self-supporting. While still working for Robert Bridges, Thomas Fortune began to branch out on his own. In August 1770, he got an order from merchant Lambert Calwalader, the son of his sister's acquaintance, Hannah Cadwalader. For making a sprit sail for Calwalader's boat and supplying the twine, grommets, and canvas, Thomas received the sum of £1 8s 8d. He was sufficiently literate to be able to keep his own accounts and to sign his name in acknowledgment of full payment.[69] Thomas had no sail loft of his own, but the commission from Cadwalader was modest enough that he could tackle it without all the space and equipment Bridges had in his loft. Gradually he built up his own small circle of customers. He was doing well and he was even able to accumulate a small sum of money to invest.

Thomas Fortune did not put his money in real estate. Like most Philadelphians of the colonial era, regardless of race, he rented his home.[70] What capital he did have he lent at interest. According to the Proprietary Tax of 1769, carpenter Israel Hallowell, a Quaker, paid tax on £11 belonging to "Negro Fortune." Hallowell was related to one of the men who appraised the estate of Thomas's sister. Another business acquaintance was James Cannon. In the 1774 tax list he had £10 belonging to "Thomas Fortune."[71]

How long their business relationship had lasted is unclear, but the links between Thomas Fortune and James Cannon are intriguing. Cannon, originally from Ireland, arrived in Philadelphia around the time James Forten was born. The holder of a degree from Edinburgh University, he began teaching night classes at his home in "Reading, Writing, Arithmetic, Navigation, Surveying, Algebra, and Geography," all the while studying for his master's degree at the College of Philadelphia, where he eventually became Professor of Mathematics. Cannon lived near the Fortens on the corner of Third and Walnut. He may also have worshipped with them, for he was an Anglican, too. Maybe he even taught Thomas or his son arithmetic and writing, if not formally at least on a neighborly basis. Like many of the white people the Fortens knew, Cannon acquired a slave to do domestic chores for himself and his wife as soon as he had the means to do so. As the political crisis with Britain deepened, Cannon would emerge as a leading radical and become one of the principal framers of the 1776 Pennsylvania Constitution.[72]

TOWARD THE END of 1773 or early the following year, Thomas Fortune's wife and children found themselves in need of help from Cannon and every other friend they could muster. Thomas fell ill and died, leaving Margaret to fend for herself and her children, both of them too young to support themselves. We know nothing of the circumstances of Thomas's death beyond the fact that it occurred when James was seven.[73] He may have suffered from a lingering ailment or he may have come down with a sudden fever. Much as the city fathers liked to boast of the healthfulness of Philadelphia, diseases of many kinds carried off hundreds of residents every year. In the winter there was pneumonia and a host of other respiratory illnesses. The summer months brought typhoid and fevers of various kinds. Philadelphia was appreciably cleaner than many other cities, but its streets were still filthy enough to serve as a breeding ground for disease and its water supply was far from safe. Margaret Fortune and her children were lucky that whatever killed Thomas did not kill them too. In small, cramped homes it was difficult to avoid contagion.

Thomas Fortune left no will and there are no records of his interment. Presumably he was buried in the Negroes' Burying Ground, perhaps with a white minister or assistant minister conducting a brief graveside service and offering a few words of consolation to the bereaved. With no income, Margaret had a difficult time making ends meet. She had to go to James Cannon to request the return of the ten pounds her husband had left with him. She may also have turned to Anthony Benezet and asked for an advance on the money he had invested for Abigail. It would do the child no good if she starved to death before she reached her majority. Margaret also wanted Benezet's advice on how to educate her son. James was too young to be apprenticed, even if he could find a master willing to take him on. Benezet apparently put Margaret in touch with the trustees of the Friends' African School. With his father dead, James Forten's practical training at the sail loft had ended for the time being and his formal schooling was about to begin.

In his account of James Forten's life, Stephen H. Gloucester made much of the crucial role Anthony Benezet played in helping him get an education. According to Gloucester, Forten attended the school for black children that Benezet operated from his home and "some of the first copies of writing that were ever done by Forten, and others, were sent to England" by Benezet "to show that coloured people could be taught to write." Gloucester was embellishing the truth here. So far as we know, Benezet never sent any of his students' writings to England. Philadelphia abolitionists did send over samples of work from the children at the Friends' African School but not until the late 1780s or 1790s, by which time Benezet was dead and James Forten had long since completed his schooling.[74] In fact, James Forten never attended Benezet's school because the abolitionist had closed it so that it would not draw students away from the Friends' School. However, although Benezet never taught James Forten, he did play a role in his education.

Anxious to undermine notions of black intellectual inferiority and a teacher by profession, Anthony Benezet had begun a night school at his home for black adults and children around 1750.[75] If Thomas Fortune did not learn with Rev. Sturgeon at Christ Church, it might well have been in Benezet's night classes that he mastered his letters and numbers. By 1770 Benezet's efforts had attracted the attention of prominent members of the Philadelphia Monthly Meeting of the Society of Friends. Quakers were moving ever closer to abolishing slavery, and to prepare their slaves for freedom they decided to establish what soon became known as the African School.[76] As a first step they hired a room in a house over the potash works on Pear Street (now Chancellor), next to St. Paul's Church. Eventually they built their own school on Willings' Alley, adjacent to their almshouse on Fourth and Walnut and barely a block from James Forten's home.[77] Satisfied that the black community no longer needed his night school, Benezet closed it.

Although he did not have charge of the Friends' African School, Benezet was one of its overseers and helped shape its curriculum. In the private day school he ran for white youths he emphasized useful skills, such as bookkeeping.[78] He may have suggested that at least some practical knowledge of mathematics be taught to students at the African School, and certainly at some point in his youth James Forten mastered bookkeeping and mathematics well enough to run his own business as an adult. The teachers at the African School probably also made use of Benezet's widely reprinted *Pennsylvania Spelling Book*, which taught reading skills by means of a series of moral lessons about such things as the iniquity of war, the evils of alcohol, and "the danger of delaying repentance."[79] Although, later in life, James Forten had many good reasons for stressing the need for peace, piety, and temperance, he may also have drawn on the moral lessons he learned from reading Benezet's primer as a child at the African School.

At the Friends' African School James Forten's instructor was Jacob Lehre, a pious man with considerable teaching experience. Under Lehre's tutelage Forten became proficient at reading and "ciphering" (basic arithmetic) and he learned to write in an elegant copperplate hand. However, the school ran into problems and after less than two years James Forten's lessons came to an end. To the dismay of the Board of Overseers, attendance at the school began to fall sharply. By January 1775 only nine pupils were attending regularly. In part this was the result of Jacob Lehre's failing health. Classes were often suspended for days at a time because he was too unwell to teach. The school was facing other difficulties as well. As Anthony Benezet explained to his fellow overseers, it was a considerable sacrifice for black families to keep a child in the classroom and out of the work force.[80] With trade disrupted because of the growing crisis with Britain, money was harder to come by, especially for laboring people.

The African School struggled on through the upheavals of the Revolutionary War, although it was often forced to close its doors. As for James Forten, he had to leave sometime in 1775. His mother and sister could no longer afford to underwrite his education. Their income from working as domestics in the homes of whites was insufficient to cover the essentials of rent, food, fuel, and clothing. They lived frugally enough but they needed the money James could earn. Apparently it was Anthony Benezet who helped him find work. He was too young to do much. Robert Bridges may have hired him from time to time, but the critical state of the economy meant he could not employ him on a regular basis. James went to work for a local storekeeper, keeping his shop clean and perhaps doing a bit of clerking. It was hardly what Thomas and Margaret had hoped their son would do but it was the best work he could get for now.[81] When economic "good times" returned, perhaps his prospects would improve, but in 1775 that seemed unlikely.

AN "AFRICAN" YOUNG James Forten might be, but he was also a British subject. His native city was a major commercial center, second only to London in a vast empire that stretched from Canada through the Caribbean to India. With the disintegration of the relationship between Britain and one part of its empire, James Forten's life would be changed forever, as would the lives of virtually every one of the king's subjects in the thirteen American colonies.

The change began slowly but it soon picked up momentum. The year before James Forten was born, the British Parliament had passed the Stamp Act. Before his first birthday the hated Townshend Duties had been passed, and colonists had responded with nonimportation agreements. Before James turned four, Crispus Attucks and his companions had been killed in the event that would become known as the Boston Massacre.

Forten was just seven when the Boston Tea Party took place. That there was no repetition in Philadelphia was due to the decision of the captain of the tea ship *Polly* to leave port rather than risk a showdown. Needless to say, news of events in Boston soon traveled down the Atlantic seaboard to Philadelphia. On May 19, 1774, Paul Revere rode into town with an appeal for help from the citizens of Boston. Britain had retaliated for the Tea Party by passing the Coercive Acts, a sharp reminder to the New Englanders of their duty to be obedient to their sovereign lord King George III. Two weeks later the British closed the port of Boston. It would remain closed until the tea was paid for. One diarist observed that on June 1, when the Boston Port Act went into effect, many Philadelphians, "to express their sympathy . . . had their shops shut up." The bells of Christ Church were muffled, with "a solemn peal" rung at intervals. Ships in the harbor flew their colors at half-staff, and churches were packed as people listened to "discourses, suitable to the occasion." Three days later, on the king's birthday, there was none of the customary bell-ringing and not a single bonfire.[82] The public celebrations that young James Forten had grown used to seeing were abandoned in favor of days of mourning and protest.

How much James Forten understood of what was going on around him is a matter of speculation, but he obviously knew something momentous was happening. There were mobs in the streets, heated discussions on street corners, and a growing sense of tension. The first Continental Congress convened at Carpenters' Hall, just a few yards from the Fortens' home, early in September 1774. James and his family must have seen the delegates arriving. What all this activity might lead to neither they nor their white neighbors knew for certain. However, they were aware of the rising tide of anger in their city and in many other communities. If that anger boiled over into armed rebellion, and if Britain sent in troops to restore order, they could hardly escape becoming caught up in the resulting turmoil.

By the time he celebrated his ninth birthday, James Forten was aware, if only dimly, of the many contradictions in his young life. He was legally free in a city where hundreds of those who shared his ancestry were slaves. He was literate at a time and in a place where few of his social standing knew their letters and their numbers. He had at least the elements of a skilled trade and perhaps some useful contacts, but he might never be able to graduate to doing anything beyond sweeping floors and stacking shelves. Although he knew he was the descendant of one of the first people to settle in Philadelphia, he was painfully aware that his great-grandfather had arrived in shackles. He was an "African" and he was a British subject "born in His Majesty's dominions." Before long he would have to decide whether or not to assume another identity and declare himself to be both an "African" and an "American."

2

IN THE SERVICE OF HIS COUNTRY

B Y THE SPRING of 1775, with the relationship between Britain and her
American colonies rapidly worsening and war seeming ever more likely,
most Philadelphians, regardless of age or condition, sensed something
was in the air. James Forten was no exception. A lively and inquisitive child, he
ranged about the city and the adjoining district of Southwark in search of work,
pausing to watch the ship traffic on the Delaware, picking up scraps of conversation, and glancing at anything—newspapers, pamphlets, or handbills—that
came his way. He was proud of his book-learning, anxious to put it to good use,
and ready to show it off whenever the chance arose.

That he read anything he could get his hands on is obvious. His prose style
as an adult, his love of the written word, and his experiments in honing language to move his audiences all testify to that. He took his words from two
main sources, the King James Bible and the great political theorists of the Revolution. So much for the adult James Forten. What the child James made of
what he read is another matter. Did the rhetoric about American colonists being "slaves" of their British masters get through to him? If so, how did he
respond to it?

He undoubtedly did seize on at least some of the subtle and not so subtle
messages, for they were voiced by people he much admired. In 1775 his friend
Anthony Benezet denounced slave-holding Patriot leaders for urging war in
the name of freedom and the rights of man, while routinely denying those
rights to others. That same year Benezet and other like-minded Philadelphians
united to establish the Society for the Relief of Free Negroes Unlawfully Held

in Bondage, the organization that would become the Pennsylvania Abolition Society. As the political crisis deepened, newspapers carried articles from the likes of Dr. Benjamin Rush and Thomas Paine arguing that slavery was "contrary to the light of nature," and linking its elimination to the success of the Patriot cause.[1] That the institution of chattel slavery was being questioned in Philadelphia and elsewhere can hardly have escaped James Forten's notice. True, his family was legally free, but the existence of a system of servitude based on race compromised their lives, their liberty, and most assuredly their pursuit of happiness.

With the clashes in and around Boston in April 1775, the convening of the Second Continental Congress a few blocks from his home the following month, and the mustering of troops in the city, James Forten knew something in his world was changing. How profound that change would be he had yet to learn. In the short term, if he needed a demonstration that events hundreds of miles away could have an economic impact on his city, he received it when Congress announced an embargo in response to the outbreak of hostilities in New England. Philadelphians might, in many cases, support the Patriot cause, but they were not necessarily prepared to sacrifice their profits in that cause. There was a mad dash to get cargoes shipped out. On September 10, the day before the ban on trade with Britain and her empire came into effect, "all the vessels . . . intended for sea (to the amount of 52) sailed from [Philadelphia] and . . . left . . . hardly a vessel in port."[2] There had been intense activity in the shipyards and sail lofts as caulkers, riggers, shipwrights, and sailmakers rushed to make the ships ready to sail. Perhaps there was casual work for James Forten in Robert Bridges's loft, even if it was only helping to mark out canvas, sweeping the floors, and keeping the journeymen well supplied with wax for their sewing twine. Overnight the wharves were deserted, the ships had sailed, and no one knew if or when they would return. Philadelphia depended on trade with the West Indies and Britain. What would happen to that trade, and all those, great and small, who derived a living from it, if Britain retaliated by permanently closing all the ports in her vast empire to shipping from North America?

It took time for the economic repercussions of the war to hit home. In fact, as the conflict entered its second year, Philadelphia was thriving. The British had stationed a couple of warships at the mouth of the Delaware, but goods continued to come overland. The city's workshops were humming with activity, for ammunition, clothing, and the like were much in demand by the military. In the words of merchant Robert Morris, Philadelphia was, "for . . . the extent of its commerce, the number of its artificers, manufactures and other circumstances . . . to the United States what the heart is to the human body." There was even a building boom, with well over a thousand new dwellings constructed in the city and the neighboring districts of Southwark and Northern Liberties between the start of the war and the fall of 1777. Much of the growth occurred in Dock Ward, where the Fortens lived. Short-term economic dislocation was proving exactly that—short-term. And there was plenty of employment. If Robert Bridges could not use him, James could always find work elsewhere. As for his mother and sister, like many other women in the city, they could earn money spinning yarn and weaving cloth at home.[3]

As the war escalated, James Forten and his family watched preparations taking place around the city. Regular military companies were being mustered to replace the ad hoc companies recruited before the outbreak of hostilities. So many men were under arms that the barracks were soon filled to overflowing and the military authorities took over the College of Philadelphia, churches, meetinghouses, and even private homes.

There was plenty of news for James Forten to mull over. To the south, in Virginia, British governor Lord Dunmore had done the unthinkable. While George Washington and his commanders wrangled over the expediency of arming even free men of color, Dunmore had offered freedom to the slaves and indentured servants of rebel masters who rallied to the king's standard. The response was overwhelming. Slaves made their escape on foot, commandeered boats, and even rode off on their masters' horses. And although Dunmore's invitation had been extended only to men of an age to bear arms, male runaways often took their families with them. Would this precipitate rebellions, as many whites feared? And what would the repercussions be in the North, where there were fewer slaves but where slavery existed nonetheless?

Philadelphia's slave population had been relatively quiet over the years, in comparison to the bondsmen and -women of New York, but there was no telling how slaves would respond if a British army threatened the city. Rumors were rife of "unruly" slaves uttering threats, refusing to yield the right of way to whites, and warning anyone who remonstrated with them that they had only to wait until "[L]ord Dunmore and his black regiment come, and then we will see who is to take the wall."[4] No rebellion occurred. Most of Philadelphia's slaves preferred to see how the war went and who made them the most attractive offer for their loyalty. Their goal was physical freedom, but for black Philadelphians like the Fortens, who already had their freedom, the choices were more complex. In so many ways they stood apart—not legally enslaved, but denied the rights other free people enjoyed. In years to come, when people expressed surprise at James Forten's fervent patriotism, and the intensity of his "interest . . . in any matter connected with his country," he would explain that he loved America because "'he had drawn the spirit of her free institutions from his mother's breast.'"[5] However, in the early stages of the War for Independence it was by no means clear which side a free man of color would or should choose. As the war dragged on and he reached the age at which he could bear arms, James Forten would have to resolve that dilemma for himself.

A CROWD GATHERING was generally the sign that something worth investigating was going on. On July 8, 1776, an inquisitive nine-year-old James Forten, alerted by the unexpected noonday ringing of the church bells, elbowed his way into a crowd "in the State House yard" and heard "the far-famed Declaration of Independence" read to the public for the first time by Sheriff John Nixon.[6] It was not, of course, Jefferson's original version, with its vigorous denunciation of the slave trade, but a document carefully phrased to unite the delegates from the various states. Yet, for all its shortcomings, it sounded well that humid summer day in the statehouse yard.

Within months, though, it seemed the high-sounding phrases of the Declaration of Independence counted for nothing against the military might of Great Britain. Washington suffered one defeat after another, and his army was driven back through New York and into New Jersey. By December things looked bleak indeed. In response to reports that the British were advancing on Philadelphia, the Continental Congress decamped to Baltimore. The military authorities imposed a curfew and subjected civilians to martial law. Hundreds fled Philadelphia, and, to make matters worse, smallpox and camp fever broke out among the troops stationed in the city. Many died, and James Forten would have seen parties of grave-diggers at work digging long burial trenches near the Walnut Street Prison. Hundreds more were buried in the Negroes' Burying Ground.[7] The disturbing of black graves was surely deeply distressing to James and his mother and sister, because Thomas Fortune, Ann Elizabeth Fortune, and probably other much-loved family members and friends were buried there. Gravesites that James and Abigail and Margaret had carefully tended were no longer places for private grieving.

An attack on Philadelphia seemed inevitable. It was the largest city in British North America, and the government in London insisted its capture was vital to the restoration of order and loyalty. Philadelphians of a Loyalist persuasion, and likely many in the slave community awaited the arrival of the British with keen anticipation, while the Patriots argued about the steps they should take to keep King George's forces out of Philadelphia. Panic subsided with Washington's victories at Trenton and Princeton in the last days of 1776, but this was only a respite.[8] The threat had receded. It had not been dispelled.

When the spring thaw came, the city authorities set to work to defend Philadelphia, hastily throwing up fortifications along the Delaware—Fort Mercer and Billingsport downriver on the Jersey shore, and Fort Mifflin on the western tip of Fort Island, roughly parallel to Fort Mercer. Additional protection was provided by the chevaux-de-frise, rows of iron-tipped spikes designed to hole any vessel that ran onto them. The forts constituted one line of defense, the chevaux-de-frise another, and a fleet of small armed vessels and fire ships a third.[9] Still, there were doubts about whether the city could be held.

Throughout the summer of 1777 fears of a British assault intensified. The members of the Continental Congress, back in Philadelphia after their sojourn in Maryland, were ready to flee again at a moment's notice. Quite apart from those with Loyalist sympathies, there were plenty who would rejoice to see them go. Congress had been giving orders for searches of private homes and

requisitioning essential goods with only the vaguest of promises about compensation.[10] Perhaps the Fortens suffered the terror and disruption of a search,
but most likely their poverty and lowly status spared them that. They had nothing
worth taking.

What they could not escape were the spiraling prices of everyday goods.
From January 1777 until the British marched in, prices of essentials like coffee
and flour rose by leaps and bounds. By July salt was virtually unobtainable.
Trade with the West Indies was almost completely cut off, paper currency was
falling in value, and people were hoarding goods.[11]

How badly the Patriot cause was faring became painfully obvious toward the
end of the summer. In a show of force on August 24 General Washington paraded his troops through Philadelphia. They hardly had the look of a conquering
army. To begin with, they had no uniforms. Each man was dressed in civilian
clothes, with a sprig of green in his hat "as an emblem of hope."[12] Like uniforms,
weapons, and food, hope was in short supply as the Patriots marched out of the
city to face the British army. Did James Forten watch the parade, scanning the
ranks to see black and brown faces? They were certainly there to be seen. The
general who at the beginning of the war had displayed such reluctance to enlist
Americans of African descent had changed his tune. Now he would take any
able-bodied men he could get, and count himself lucky to have them.

Washington had been ordered to Pennsylvania to prevent General Howe
from taking Philadelphia. He planned to halt the British at Chadd's Ford on
the Brandywine Creek. The roar of cannons could be heard in Philadelphia
throughout the evening of September 11, and the next day news of the battle's
outcome reached the city. Howe had been victorious. The delegates to the
Continental Congress gathered their belongings and fled, as did many of the
citizens. Worse was to follow. On the night of September 20 Anthony Wayne's
Pennsylvania Continentals were ambushed and slaughtered at Paoli.

On September 25 Philadelphia was alive with rumors that arsonists planned
to torch the city. The next morning, with military bands playing, General Sir
Henry Clinton marched his troops out of Germantown, where Howe had his
headquarters, through the Northern Liberties, and into Philadelphia. Hordes
of citizens came out to watch, with little evidence of discontent. In fact, according to one British observer, Clinton and his forces marched in "amid the acclamation of some thousands of the inhabitants[,] mostly women and children."[13]
Margaret Forten and her children stayed in the city and probably stood in the
street to see the British march by.

Gradually the British strengthened their hold on Philadelphia, securing outlying areas and opening the Delaware to shipping. The day after the British formally took possession of the city, the *Delaware*, the largest of the American vessels
assigned to keep the river closed to the enemy, was set ablaze by a shore battery
and run aground. The remaining vessels suffered desertions among their crews.
When the defenders of Billingsport spiked their guns, set fire to the fort, and

fled, the tiny Patriot fleet sailed upriver to a safer spot under the guns at Fort Mercer and Fort Mifflin.[14] The chevaux-de-frise proved more of a nuisance than a danger, and the British soon dredged it up and dismantled it.

A last-ditch effort by Washington to drive Howe out of Germantown ended in failure on October 4. Howe followed Clinton into Philadelphia and gave the order for the assault on the remaining rebel strongholds along the Delaware. The attempt to dislodge the defenders of Fort Mercer proved costly. The Hessian commander, Carl von Donop, was killed, along with more than 300 of his men. Two British warships were lost when they became stuck in the mud: One caught fire, and the other was ordered burned to prevent the rebels from taking her. As a result of their losses in the assault on Fort Mercer, the British changed their strategy, focusing instead on Fort Mifflin. On November 10 the British guns opened up on Fort Mifflin from Province Island. The barrage continued for five days, by which time the fort was a smoldering ruin and its defenders had retreated. Fort Mercer was evacuated and the Delaware was open.[15]

Eleven-year-old James Forten was well aware that a battle was raging. From his home or from vantage points along the Delaware he would have heard the great guns booming, seen the flames, and smelled the acrid smoke of a British warship or a Patriot fort ablaze downriver. He knew that black men had played a part in the defense of Fort Mercer because he had watched them march out of the city to garrison the fort and he learned from talk in the street that they had acquitted themselves like "brave Soldiers."[16] But they and their white comrades-in-arms had gone to join Washington in winter quarters at Valley Forge. Now the soldiers drilling in the streets and squares of his native Philadelphia were not Patriots but British regulars and Hessian mercenaries. The Walnut Street Prison, the old prison on Third and Market, and the statehouse were filled with American captives from the battles at Chadd's Ford and Germantown.[17] And the British were not slow to find employment for the city's black residents. A "Company of Black Pioneers," comprising almost a hundred men, women, and children, most of them the slaves of white Patriots who had fled the city, was organized to perform essential tasks such as keeping the streets clean. Clothed and fed by the British, many of these "Pioneers" left with them when the occupation of the city came to an end.[18] But that was months away. As the campaigning season of 1777 drew to a close, Howe was in firm control of Philadelphia.

How far the occupation changed the lives of the Fortens and their neighbors, black and white, can be only a matter of conjecture. There were many new faces to be seen in the streets, and old ones to be missed. Patriot merchants fled as the British moved in, but their places were taken by Loyalist merchants from New York, Boston, and even England. The influx of merchants, all of them eager to get their goods unloaded and their stores made ready for business, meant a demand for casual labor.[19] James Forten needed work—his family's survival depended on it—and work was certainly to be had as the British and their friends consolidated their hold on Philadelphia.

The first concern facing the British was how to accommodate and feed an army of almost 20,000 together with the hordes of Loyalists converging on the city. Howe instructed prominent Loyalist Joseph Galloway to take a census of vacant houses and stores where troops could be billeted, seize any citizens considered dangerous, and confiscate weapons. Almost all the churches were taken over and used as hospitals, riding schools, or stables. Galloway recruited other like-minded Philadelphians to spy on their neighbors and form volunteer companies to police the city.[20] Again the Fortens' poverty and humble status probably saved them. It made no sense to billet even one soldier on a poor black family that was barely eking out a living. Nor was it likely that the Fortens were actively conspiring with the enemies of Britain. Mere survival outweighed all other concerns and consumed every ounce of their collective energy.

As winter set in there were shortages of food and fuel. The availability of goods went in cycles. After the Delaware was cleared of American defenses, food was plentiful. Then there was a downturn, as the river froze and Washington did his best to prevent supplies from reaching the city by land. Merchants charged exorbitant prices for poor quality food, and many people went hungry.[21] However, as the ice on the Delaware melted, supplies came in again, only to dry up as the British prepared to evacuate the city. People complained that enterprising merchants were intercepting farmers bringing goods to Philadelphia, buying up their produce, and reselling it at inflated prices. Even when goods were in plentiful supply, most civilians had only devalued paper currency with which to buy them, and canny Loyalist shopkeepers demanded specie.[22] The struggle to feed her children must have taxed Margaret Forten's energy and imagination more than it had done at any time since the death of her husband and the family's descent into poverty.

Meanwhile, the British officers and the more socially prominent Loyalists were faring well and finding life in Philadelphia not totally devoid of amusement. Dances, dinners, and the like were given for the officers and offered by them in return. In May 1778 there was a celebration that surpassed all the rest. When news arrived that the king had finally acceded to Howe's request to be relieved of his command, his officers, headed by Major John André, organized the great "Meschianza" or jubilee in his honor. James Forten and his mother and sister would have seen the lavish preparations for the regatta, the tournament, the ball, and the supper, at which guests were served course after course by "[N]egroes in oriental garb."[23]

Howe's departure was soon followed by the departure of his forces under their new commander, General Clinton. London had determined the next assault should be far to the south, in Georgia and the Carolinas, where Patriot sentiment was believed to be weaker and where an attacking force could mobilize thousands of slaves. About one third of the citizens of Philadelphia had stayed through the occupation, some because they were Loyalists, but many, like the Fortens, because they had no alternative and because the city was their home. The British army marched out on June 18, and the British fleet left the next day, taking as many as 3,000 civilians to the Loyalist stronghold of New York City. There were the great ones, like Joseph Galloway and Chief Justice William Allen. And then there were the lesser folk—white artisans and tradesmen loyal to the king or fearful of the Patriots for one reason or another, and black men and women, most of them slaves with little reason to trust the Patriots' rhetoric about "liberty."[24]

Before they left, the British burned all the vessels under construction in the harbor. They also set fire to the stockpiles of shipbuilding materials in the warehouses in Southwark, near Gloria Dei Church, and in the Northern Liberties. The flames could be seen throughout the city. Fanned by high winds, the fires burned for two days, and windborne embers set fire to several houses.[25]

As he watched the warships set sail and the stockpiles of timber, pitch, tar, hemp, and canvas go up in flames, James Forten could reflect that the occupation had not proved completely disastrous. He and his mother and sister were alive and well. Their few possessions were safe. They were not among the unfortunate ones whose homes had been destroyed. Margaret and Abigail might even find work as Patriot families returned to see what had happened to their homes. There was plenty of cleaning to be done, for the British soldiers had been none too fastidious in their personal habits.[26] And the destruction of so much shipping might lead to employment for a sturdy youngster with a knowledge of the basics of sailmaking and the eagerness to learn more.

The restoration of Patriot control brought new prosperity to the city. Benedict Arnold was appointed military commander. There was a brief interlude of martial law, but that was allowed to lapse as peace (of sorts) was restored. Congress returned, as did many of the Patriot merchants. Now there were Patriot troops drilling in the same squares where Redcoats and Hessians had mustered only a few months before. There was an influx of French soldiers, the most tangible result of the French alliance that had followed Burgoyne's surrender at Saratoga. And there was the chance to combine patriotism with making money.

In the period after the British evacuation, Philadelphia emerged as a major privateering port. Fully one quarter of the letters of marque and reprisal issued during the war went to vessels sailing out of Philadelphia.[27] In his wanderings down by the Delaware James Forten probably paused from time to time to watch as ships' carpenters overhauled merchant vessels, piercing bulwarks for cannons, strengthening decks to bear their weight, and constructing powder magazines. Other vessels were being purpose-built as privateers, and the yards were filled with ships at various stages of construction, from keels and frames to ships awaiting only masts, sails, and rigging.

It seemed that anyone with money to invest wanted a stake in a privateering cruise. Robert Bridges was one of those who did well during the Revolution. He became the owner or part-owner of six vessels, ranging in size from the one-gun schooner *Hannah and Sally* to the ten-gun sloop *Comet*.[28] Quite possibly James Forten picked up casual work from him and his partners. There was certainly work to be had, and the needs of the Forten family were as pressing as ever. Prices of basic goods rose so dramatically in 1779 that rumors circulated about disloyal elements manipulating the economy to undermine the Revolutionary cause. Sophisticated explanations about supply and demand and the long-term impact of war on the economy did not lessen the suffering of Philadelphia's poorer inhabitants. All they knew was that they were hungry, their clothes were threadbare, and there was no prospect of improvement in the short term. Sailors struck for higher pay and there was a bloody riot when a mob attacked a suspected profiteer. Troops had to be deployed to quell the unrest.[29] And inflation continued to rise.

Even as the war dragged on, James Forten knew another war was being fought. Pennsylvania's lawmakers were debating the future of slavery. Far too poor to subscribe to a newspaper, Forten could still scavenge for papers that others had discarded. He may well have read about the debate, followed the arguments for and against emancipation, and rejoiced in March 1780 when an abolition law was passed. True, it came far short of a declaration immediately liberating every slave in the state. In fact, it did not free any slaves, only the children of slaves, and they would be in service to their mothers' owners until they reached the age of twenty-eight. As for people of African descent who were already legally free, it did not elevate them overnight to full citizenship. Still, the first step had been taken. And the new law explicitly linked abolition to the Patriot cause. Lawmakers spoke of abolition as a debt they owed for their deliverance from the British yoke. They expressed their joy "that it is in our power to extend a portion of that freedom to others, which hath been extended to us." In words that must have heartened James Forten they declared:

> It is not for us to inquire, why, in the creation of mankind, the inhabitants of the several parts of the earth were distinguished by a difference in . . . complexion. It is sufficient to know, that all are the work of an Almighty Hand. . . . Weaned by a long course of experience, from those narrow prejudices . . . we have imbibed, we find our hearts enlarged with . . . kindness and benevolence, towards men of all conditions and nations.[30]

Forten knew many men and women of color in Pennsylvania had not waited for white lawmakers to act. They had transformed the Revolutionary War into a war of personal liberation. They had fled from their masters, petitioned the legislature and the courts, and thrown in their lot with one side or the other in the contest for control of British North America. What the quality of citizenship might be for a black Patriot he would have to wait and see, but the abolition law, with its statements about justice and an end to prejudice, evidently convinced him that society was being reordered, and that merit, rather than complexion or condition, would be rewarded in the new republic.[31] He had made his choice of loyalties.

Gradually James Forten's desire grew to serve the country and the cause he had come to look upon as his own, to see more than the streets of his native city, and to make money into the bargain. Race was seldom an issue with privateering captains, as slave owners discovered to their intense annoyance when they tried to recover runaways. A tall, athletic fourteen-year-old, freeborn, eager to serve, and blessed with some knowledge of how to repair sails, James Forten was unlikely to be rejected by any captain because of the color of his skin.

Had he chosen service in the Pennsylvania Navy his race would not necessarily have disqualified him, either. Other black men were on the rolls. However, there were obvious advantages to opting for service on a privateer. First, the mission of the Pennsylvania Navy was only to patrol the Delaware, where relatively few prizes were to be met with. Privateers had the run of the seas. Second, it was not unknown for captains of privateers to neglect to report their prizes to the various Admiralty courts and instead divide the spoils among their crew. State and Continental captains understandably found it harder to escape the watchful eyes of the authorities.[32]

Stephen Decatur, the captain Forten chose to serve with, had compiled an impressive list of victories. In 1781, when he took command of merchant Francis Gurney's new vessel, the *Royal Louis*, named for America's ally, Louis XVI of France, Decatur was twenty-nine years old. A native of Newport, he was the son of a French naval officer who had fled to Rhode Island to escape a yellow fever epidemic in the West Indies, married, and stayed. Decatur spent his youth in Philadelphia and commanded his first vessel at age twenty. Although he was sailing for Gurney in 1781, he had captained two vessels for Robert Bridges, the *Retaliation* and the *Comet*, and had done well with both. He had also commanded Irish merchant Blair McClenachan's *Fair American*. Sailing in convoy with other privateers, he had taken a dozen prizes.[33]

Now, as master of the 450-ton, twenty-two-gun *Royal Louis*, Decatur and first mate George Duck set out to recruit 200 men and boys, the largest crew they had ever commanded.[34] By order of Congress, one third of the crew of a privateer had to be "landsmen," and not experienced sailors, so that the state and Continental navies would not be drained of manpower. Decatur's reputation for luck and skill proved a useful drawing card, but there were other captains in search of crews and he was competing with them. Even had he been inclined to do so, he was hardly in a position to turn away able-bodied and eager volunteers because they were black. He had lost vessels in the past by skimping on prize crews. He needed a large crew so that, as he took one prize after another, he could assign an adequate number of men to sail each captured ship into port without risking the prisoners regaining control of the vessel or seriously undermanning his own ship.[35]

James Forten had chosen his captain. Now he had only to persuade his mother to let him go to sea. According to Forten's son-in-law, Robert Purvis, Margaret Forten reluctantly gave her consent after "earnest and unceasing

solicitations" on James's part. His "young heart [was] fired with the enthusiasm
. . . of the patriots and revolutionaries of that day."[36] Forten told Purvis he
enlisted on the *Royal Louis* as a powder-boy in 1780, but, looking back over a
crowded life when he was in his sixties or seventies, he got the year wrong. The
Royal Louis did not get her letters of marque until July 23, 1781.[37]

Once the *Royal Louis* had her papers, Gurney ordered Decatur to set sail
immediately. After an emotional farewell, James Forten, three months short of
his fifteenth birthday, left his native city for the first time, confident he would
return covered in glory and with his pockets filled with prize money. Classed as
a "boy," because he was under sixteen, he was entitled to only one half of a full
share of the spoils. However, it was common practice to set aside a number of
shares for crew members who proved themselves particularly enterprising or
courageous, and Forten could always dream of being the first to spot a potential prize, board her, or distinguish himself in some other way.

His immediate concern, if he was spared the miseries of seasickness, was to
find a place to stow his belongings and swing his hammock. He wore the clothes
he normally worked in, with the addition of a hat and a thick coat. His few
possessions—a knife, a few items of sailmaker's gear, and perhaps a small Bible—
would have been packed in a canvas ditty bag he had made for himself.[38] The
ship, with her complement of 200 men and boys, rode low in the water, but
that would not be the case for long. As soon as they took a prize, a detachment
would be ordered off to sail her into port. A successful cruise could end with
barely enough men left on board the privateer to get her home.

Forten knew some of the crew members from the wharves, the streets, and
the workshops. The fact that he was black hardly set him apart. Another nineteen men and boys of color had volunteered for the voyage.[39] If anything set
James Forten apart, it was the fact that he was literate. He could sign his name
to the ship's articles and not simply make his mark. However, he was not an
experienced sailor, so he could be assigned to work only where he was supervised by older and more knowledgeable hands. Going aloft to reef or let out
the lighter sails, working at the capstan to raise or lower the anchor, swabbing
decks, and working in the galley were all tasks likely to fall to his lot. In the
event of a battle, he would stay on the gun deck to fetch powder and shot from
the shot locker, and generally keep out of the way of the gun crews. Humble
though his duties were, he could still expect his share of prize money at the end
of the cruise.

Despite his inexperience, Forten could make something of his surround-
ings. He had grown up close to the river and the shipyards. Unlike the true
landsman, he knew the names of most parts of the vessel and understood their
functions. He knew the standing rigging that supported the masts and bowsprit was blackened with tar to protect it from the elements, while the running
rigging, which had to be smooth enough to pass through the blocks, was left
untarred. Words like "reef," "buntline," and "cringle" came from a language

he had grown up hearing. He could name all the sails and their respective masts and yards. However, familiarity with terminology was no substitute for climbing the rigging to reef a topgallant with a gale blowing. It was a factor in Forten's later success as a sailmaker that he not only knew how to cut, seam, rope, and bend sails, but how to handle them at sea. His service with Decatur, and later with Thomas Truxtun, was as crucial as his formal apprenticeship with Robert Bridges.

On the *Royal Louis* Forten had to learn how to regulate his day according to the ship's bell and to respond to the bosun's whistle as it sounded the various commands. He would be assigned to a watch and learn to work with his fellows. He would be expected to make the best of his living conditions, to stumble around below decks in the half-light of lanterns, to sleep in a hammock swung alongside a six-foot-long carriage gun, to eat and drink whenever his watch was over, to stomach salt meat and grog, and to get along as best he could with officers and crew. He had exchanged his mother's home for a habitation that was constantly in motion and likely at any moment, day or night, to be attacked by the enemy or the forces of nature.

The first cruise of the *Royal Louis* was a great success. Decatur had instructions from Gurney to sail between the British-held ports of New York and Charleston. In company with an old ally, Blair McClenachan's *Holker*, the *Royal Louis* took four vessels. Then, sailing with another Philadelphia vessel, the much smaller three-gun *Governor Clinton*, she fell in with the sloop *Nancy* in Delaware Bay.[40] As each prize was taken, a prize crew was formed; its members gathered their belongings, clambered over the side into open boats, and boarded the captured vessel. Counting the prizes taken, and trying to estimate their worth, James Forten could speculate about the amount of prize money he would take home at the end of the cruise.

However, the cruise was far from over. Most vessels surrendered without firing a shot, or put up only token resistance when they saw the force ranged against them, but now and again an opponent would fight back. Many years after the event, James Forten recalled for Robert Purvis a bloody encounter with an English vessel he identified as the *Lawrence*. Purvis described the episode in his memorial address on Forten's life.

> [A]fter a severe fight, sustaining great loss on both sides, and leaving every man wounded on board the "Louis" but himself, they succeeded in capturing her, and brought her into port amid the loud huzzas and acclamations of the crowd that assembled upon the occasion.

The account family friend Stephen Gloucester gave in his memoir of Forten was even more graphic. He spoke of an encounter in which "Every man was killed at the gun at which [Forten] was stationed, but himself."[41] Apparently, after the passage of so many years, Forten's memory betrayed him again. Perhaps there *was* a battle with a merchant vessel called the *Lawrence*, but more likely the bloody clash he recalled was not with a merchantman, but with a Royal Navy vessel, the sloop of war *Active*. The *Royal Louis* was more than a match for her. The British vessel carried fourteen six-pounders to the privateer's twenty-two nine-pounders.[42] Nevertheless, the *Active* put up a fierce fight—and for a very good reason. She was on a special mission. On August 23, 1781, as the Philadelphia newspapers later reported, a prize crew from the *Royal Louis* brought into port the *Active*, "taken on her passage to New-York, with dispatches, from Antigua." She was carrying a message from Admiral Hood indicating "that a fleet of 12 or 13 . . . British ships of the line were to sail to the relief of New-York on or about the seventh inst."[43] The *Royal Louis* had also taken the sloop *Phoenix*, a British vessel that had been captured by a French frigate and recaptured by a British sloop, which was taking her to New York when Decatur intercepted her.[44]

There was no doubt about it. James Forten's first cruise had been a great success. He had returned to his mother and sister unscathed; he could take pride in having served his country by capturing a vessel carrying important dispatches; and he had money in his pockets. Robert Purvis's mention of the "loud huzzas" of the crowd on the wharves as the *Active* was brought into port—something he had obviously been told about by Forten—suggests that Forten had himself been a member of the prize crew and had shared in that heady moment of victory and public acclamation. "[S]haring largely in the feeling which so brilliant a victory had inspired, with fresh courage, and an unquenchable devotedness to the interests of his native land," he promptly signed on for another cruise.[45]

Even as Forten prepared for his second voyage, events were moving quickly, thanks, in part, to the loss of the dispatches aboard the *Active*. The dispatches Captain Delanoe had fought so fiercely to save contained information vital to the British naval commander in New York City, Admiral Graves. Graves had received reports that a large French naval force would sail from Saint Domingue to join up with the French fleet at Newport, Rhode Island. Together they would provide Washington with naval support for an attack on New York City. At the beginning of July, Graves had sent the *Active* to find the British fleet in the West Indies and request assistance. The reply—that Admiral Hood was aware of the danger, that he would sail to New York, and that he would look in on the Chesapeake Bay en route to see if the French fleet was menacing Lord Cornwallis's army in Virginia—was being carried aboard the *Active*. Captain Delanoe, although a prisoner in Philadelphia, did manage to get the gist of his dispatches to Graves, but only after considerable delay. For weeks Graves assumed a huge British force would overtake the French fleet and then sail to the rescue of New York.[46]

A British fleet—fourteen vessels and not the great armada Graves had hoped for—was on its way from the West Indies, but the British in New York did not know about it in time to make plans to rendezvous. Meanwhile, Cornwallis had allowed his army to become trapped on Virginia's Yorktown peninsula. He was awaiting a rescue by sea that never materialized. Abandoning plans for an assault on New York, Washington hastened south to cut off any retreat by land. On September 2 he marched his troops through Philadelphia. James Forten spent his fifteenth birthday watching the day-long parade. More than fifty years later he wrote: "I well remember that when the New England Regiments passed through this city on their way to attack the English Army under the command of Lord Cornwallis, there was [*sic*] several Companies of Coloured People, as brave Men as ever fought."[47] This did indeed seem to be a struggle that knew no lines of race. A few weeks later, buoyed up with patriotism, a desire for adventure, and thoughts of more prize money, Forten made his way back to the *Royal Louis*.

When Forten set sail at the beginning of October the siege at Yorktown was well under way. The British fleet en route from the Caribbean to New York had not spotted the French fleet in the Chesapeake for the simple reason that the French had not yet arrived. It was the hurricane season, and they had been delayed by rough weather on their way from Saint Domingue. Hood assumed that the French were ahead of him and that they had no designs on Cornwallis's army. Reassured, he sailed on. The French fleet arrived five days later. Cornwallis could not escape by sea. By the time Hood reached New York, realized what had happened, and spurred Graves into action, it was too late. In the Battle of the Chesapeake (September 5–13) the British failed in their bid to dislodge the French and resupply Cornwallis. Eventually a dispirited Graves set sail for New York to prepare for another rescue mission. The sea lanes to the south of the Delaware were full of British and French vessels, merchantmen, and warships. It was the luck of the draw whom the *Royal Louis* would encounter. And luck was not with her on this occasion.

The second cruise of the *Royal Louis* ended swiftly and disastrously. One day after leaving the relative security of the Delaware, she encountered a British warship, the *Amphion*.[48] Decatur knew before he left port that he was sailing into danger. He had received a report that "two British frigates [were] cruising off the Capes of Virginia," but he had a strategy worked out. The *Royal Louis* was part of "a large fleet" of cruisers and merchantmen sailing out of Philadelphia. Decatur and his fellow captains anchored well upriver and waited for the wind to change. If the British were lying in wait at the mouth of the Delaware, a northwesterly wind would force them out to sea. If they were simply heading back to New York, they would find it no easy matter to turn and pursue a flotilla of American vessels making for the south with the wind behind them. The first part of the plan worked. The wind changed, and under cover of night the Americans sailed down the Delaware and into the open sea. There were no enemy vessels in sight. It looked as though Decatur's gamble had paid off—until the dawn revealed two British warships uncomfortably close at hand.[49]

Although by no means the most fearsome of His Majesty's warships, the *Amphion* was more than a match for the *Royal Louis*. Built in the Chatham Dockyards on the Medway, and launched on Christmas Day, 1780, she had been classed as a fifth-rate ship of the line. A vessel of 679 tons, she carried thirty-two guns—twenty-six twelve-pounders and six six-pounders. She was sailing in company with *La Nymphe*, a thirty-six-gun French warship captured by the British in 1780 and pressed into service.[50] The *Amphion* and *La Nymphe* had joined forces off Sandy Hook, New Jersey, on October 1 for a cruise to the Upper South to spy on the French fleet. The French had spotted them and given chase. Now they were returning to New York to report to Graves.[51]

On October 7 the captains of the two British warships reported "Strong Gales with a heavy Sea"—precisely the conditions Decatur hoped to use to his advantage as he sailed the *Royal Louis* out of the Delaware, past Cape May and Cape Henlopen, and into the Atlantic.[52] The rough weather continued into the early hours of October 8. There was a "great sea," and the two warships were reducing sail to improve their handling. Then, at first light, a lookout on *La Nymphe* spotted a sail to the northwest. A quarter of an hour later two more came into view. The vessels were tentatively identified as two brigs and a ship—the *Royal Louis* and two more of the flotilla that had made their way out of the Delaware. John Ford, the captain of *La Nymphe*, sent a signal to John Bazely of the *Amphion*, and Bazely responded. *La Nymphe* would go after the small fry while the *Amphion* pursued the ship.[53]

Decatur was no novice at this game of cat and mouse. The *Royal Louis* quickly "put Before it" and tried to outrun the *Amphion*. But if Decatur was an experienced captain, so was his opponent. John Bazely had entered the king's service at age fifteen in 1755, and had served his apprenticeship as a lieutenant on cutters and sloops. With the outbreak of the American conflict advancement came quickly as he proved himself "a skillful and energetic officer." He had been put in command of the *Amphion* as soon as she was launched. In the spring of 1781 she had been employed transporting Hessian mercenaries to America. After arriving in New York in August, she had promptly been dispatched to support turncoat Benedict Arnold's raid on New London.[54] Now, with his ship through her sea trials, Bazely was ready to take on anything that came his way. The *Royal Louis* and her crew had run out of luck.

Bazely ordered his men to put on more sail, but the demands of the chase had to be combined with the limitations imposed by seas and winds. To the north *La Nymphe*, in pursuit of the other two American vessels, had her main topgallant yard carried away and the sail on the yard split by a sudden gust of wind.[55] No such calamity befell the *Amphion*. Gaining quickly on his quarry, Bazely identified her as a "Cruiser." As he had suspected, she was fair game. Still, he was willing to play with her, hoping to fool her captain into thinking the *Amphion* was a friendly vessel. He ordered the small chase gun fired to attract her attention and hoisted French colors. Decatur was not deceived; he knew a British ship of the line when he saw one. As the master of the *Amphion*, William Morris, Jr., reported it in his log, the *Royal Louis* "Hoisted American [colors] and Fir'd her stern Chace [*sic*] at us."[56] Decatur hurriedly put on more sail, his crew working feverishly to outrun the warship.

The pursuit continued, with the *Amphion* steadily bearing down on the privateer. By noon the two vessels were only half a mile apart. An hour later, off the Virginia coast, some forty miles due east of Hampton, the *Amphion* moved in for the kill. Bazely "Fir'd several shot" at the American vessel, which promptly "Brot. Too." Then, to leave no doubt in the enemy's mind, Bazely "Hoisted English Colours." Decatur knew when to acknowledge defeat; he promptly struck his colors and surrendered. Bazely learned his prize was "the Royal Lewis Privateer of Philadelphia."[57]

Exhausted after a chase that had lasted the better part of seven hours, the crew of the privateer awaited their fate. Bazely sent over a prize crew under the command of a mate and a midshipman to take charge of the *Royal Louis*. Then boats were lowered to ferry the Americans to the *Amphion*. To make matters worse, the seas were heavy and the captives were tossed about.[58] Meanwhile, *La Nymphe* had also had good hunting. When she rendezvoused with the *Amphion* she had two prizes in tow. The brig *Molly*, owned by merchant Robert Morris, had been on her maiden voyage, a cargo run to St. Thomas with tobacco. The eight-gun schooner *Raccoon* was bound for Havana with a load of flour and iron.[59]

The next day Bazely decided some shifting about of prisoners was necessary, and he ordered the transfer of about one third of them to *La Nymphe*. The *Molly* and the *Raccoon* had been lightly manned, so *La Nymphe* had ample room for more prisoners.[60] Their first night aboard the warship had been a wretched one for the privateers. To mental anguish and uncertainty about what lay ahead were coupled the physical discomforts of seasickness and poor sanitation. When some seventy-five of their fellows were ferried over to *La Nymphe* there must have been mixed emotions among those left behind—sorrow at parting with shipmates, but relief that there would be more room below decks. Bazely did what he could for his reluctant guests, ordering the ship "Clean'd below." Then, charting a course for New York, he gave the command to "wear," or turn the ship.[61]

Aboard the *Amphion*, James Forten's "mind was harassed with the most painful forebodings, from a knowledge . . . that rarely . . . were prisoners of his complexion exchanged; they were sent to the West Indies, and there doomed to a life of slavery."[62] However, a very different fate awaited him. Bazely had his two sons on board. The *Amphion*, like most other ships of the line, had her complement of boys barely in their teens training for careers in the Royal Navy. It was the responsibility of the captain "to see they [were] properly taught English grammar, writing, accompts [*sic*], and the elements of . . . mathematics, to lay the foundation for navigation." The actual teaching was done by schoolmasters, young men recruited from charity schools like Christ's Hospital and given the rank of midshipmen. The risks of shipboard life for "younkers" or "youngsters" ranged from unwelcome sexual advances from older members of the crew to falling through open hatchways when playing to the normal risks of active service—shipwrecks and enemy action.[63] Bored and full of mischief, they could easily become a danger to themselves and others.

John Bazely, Jr., fourteen years old, had plenty to keep him occupied. Already a midshipman, this was his second or third cruise. Henry Bazely, on the other hand, was proving something of a problem. He was twelve and this was his first cruise. Entered on the muster as his father's servant, he had few duties assigned him.[64] He needed a companion, someone to keep him out of trouble, but the *Amphion* was a warship, and Bazely could not spare any member of the ship's company for what amounted to playing nursemaid. Then he happened to notice a tall, dark-skinned youth among his prisoners. "[S]truck with [Forten's] honest and open countenance, he made him the companion of his son."

The forced association between James Forten and Henry Bazely deepened into a friendship in an unusual manner.

> During one of those dull and monotonous periods which frequently occur on ship-board, [they] were engaged in a game of marbles, when with signal dexterity and skill, the marbles were upon every trial successively displaced by the unerring hand of Forten. This excited the . . . admiration of his young companion, who, hastening to his father, called his attention to it.

Bazely asked Forten if he could repeat the feat, "and assuring the Captain that nothing was easier . . . the marbles were again placed in the ring, and in rapid succession he redeemed his word."[65] After that, Bazely took a friendly interest in the young Philadelphian, giving him greater freedom than his fellow prisoners. It was hardly likely to compromise the safety of the vessel to allow a teenage captive to roam about the ship. One can only wonder about the response of the crew and the prisoners to the elevation of Forten to the status of captain's favorite. Perhaps he became the object of jealousy and resentment, the target of snide remarks, but when all was said and done, he was under orders. It was his job to keep young Henry Bazely out of trouble. As for what might result from his privileged position, that was anyone's guess.

Prizes continued to come the way of the *Amphion* and *La Nymphe*. On October 11 another vessel was spotted. Bazely left the chase to *La Nymphe* and at nightfall she returned with the *Lexington*, a brig en route from Salem to Baltimore with a cargo of wine.[66] Then, just before noon on October 12, the *Amphion* and *La Nymphe* parted company. *La Nymphe* was to take her prisoners and the prize vessels straight to New York, while the *Amphion* continued her cruise and hunted out more prizes.[67] As for Forten and his companions, they would stay on board until the *Amphion* reached her destination. She was on active duty and could not cut short her patrol simply to transfer prisoners.

On October 14 there was a heavy squall. The *Amphion*'s master ordered the topsails clewed (fastened by their lower corners to the yards above them) and furled, and the courses, or lower sails, reefed.[68] Then, on October 15 there was a night chase lasting some four and a half hours in pursuit of the *Juno*, a privateer sailing from Havana to Philadelphia. Forten and the other Americans on the *Amphion* were reluctant witnesses, their sympathies with the *Juno*'s crew, and yet on the receiving end of her resistance. She fired on the British ship, and Bazely responded with a broadside. As the firing subsided, there came across the water, in the darkness, loud splashes as the *Juno*'s master ordered his men to jettison her carriage guns. Realizing he could not outgun his opponent, he hoped to lighten his load enough to outrun her. The strategy did not work. Bazely had his gun crews fire at the masts and rigging. The *Juno*'s foremast was hit, and flight was impossible. The captain surrendered, a prize crew boarded his vessel, and he and his men found themselves prisoners on the *Amphion*.[69]

The following afternoon the *Amphion* encountered a large convoy from Britain making for New York. The convoy, so Bazely learned from the captain of the lead ship, was on its way to join Admiral Graves for another bid to rescue Cornwallis. The *Amphion* joined the convoy, occasionally firing shots to signal straggling vessels to "fall in to their stations." On the morning of October 19 the convoy reached Graves's fleet "at Anchor outside the Bar."[70] It must have been an impressive and at the same time a rather fearsome sight to young Forten—the full might of the Royal Navy readying for an attack. What he could not know, any more than Bazely or Graves, was that this came too late. Cornwallis had already surrendered.

The *Amphion* joined Graves's fleet of twenty-six ships of the line and a number of smaller vessels as it got under way on the afternoon of October 20. She set a southerly course and remained with the fleet until noon the next day, serving as an escort ship.[71] Then, with the lighthouse at Sandy Hook in sight, the *Amphion* left the fleet and began working her way up to New York. Navigation was tricky, and the crew had to take regular soundings to avoid running aground. The next day there was a flurry of activity as a strong gust of wind split the main topsail and a new sail had to be bent to the yard. On October 22 the *Amphion* fell in with *La Nymphe*, which had discharged her prisoners a week before. A pilot was sent over, and by noon the following day the *Amphion* was safely moored in the East River. In his log her master reported that toward evening on October 23 his crew was "Employ'd Carr[y]ing our Prisoners to the Prison Ship."[72] James Forten, his name misspelled "Fortune," was entered on the muster of the prison hulk *Jersey* as prisoner number 4102.[73]

Had he chosen, Forten need never have set foot on a prison ship. As the *Amphion* neared New York, Captain Bazely sent for him. He had been impressed by his behavior, had approved of the growing friendship between his son and the young Philadelphian, and had a proposal to put to him. He offered to "send [Forten] home with his son to England." The captain stressed that Henry was the heir to a handsome estate and could do much for his friend. He "pointed out to [Forten] the road to return a wealthy and educated man under the protection of his son; and, of course, with freedom and equality." To Bazely's astonishment, Forten rejected the offer, insisting: "I have been taken prisoner for the liberties of my country, and never will prove a traitor to her interest."[74]

Had James Forten accepted Bazely's offer he would have been linking his future to that of a successful naval family. Captain Bazely ended his career as an admiral. His two sons also rose steadily through the ranks.[75] As it was, a disappointed and doubtless mystified Captain Bazely did what he could for his prisoner, keeping him on board until the last possible minute in case he changed his mind, and finally giving him, "as a token of his regard and friendship, a letter to the Commander of the prison ship, highly commendatory of him, and . . . requesting that [he] should not be forgotten on the list of exchanges." Forten never forgot the kindness of Bazely and his son, nor the strange twist of fate that had brought him to their notice in the first place. In later life he would often speak of the incident that had won him their favor and saved him from enslavement, observing that: "Thus . . . did a game of marbles save him from a life of West Indian servitude."[76]

In the short term, though, it must have seemed to James Forten that his position was little better than that of a slave. His chances of getting off the prison ship *Jersey* alive were not good. The British had prison hulks anchored in various ports throughout the empire—Charleston, St. Lucia, and the Leeward Islands. Some captives were even held on vessels off Portugal and Senegal. Had the *Royal Louis* been captured farther out into the Atlantic, Forten could have ended up in a prison in England—the Mill Prison near Plymouth or (ironically) the Forton Prison outside Portsmouth.[77] As it was, the *Amphion* operated out of New York, and so Bazely delivered his prisoners to the *Jersey*.

In her day the *Jersey* had been a proud vessel. Built in the Plymouth Dockyards in 1736, she had been a fourth-rate ship of the line, carrying sixty guns and a crew of 400. Converted to a hospital ship in 1771, that was her function when she was first moored in Wallabout Bay, in the East River off Long Island. By the winter of 1780 she had been pressed into service as a floating prison. She was stripped of her rudder, sails, and rigging, and virtually dismasted. Her portholes were sealed shut and her gunports had gratings put over them. The British left the flagstaff, bowsprit, and a spar amidships as a derrick to hoist supplies on board.[78]

Wallabout Bay was an ideal anchorage for the *Jersey* and the rest of the unwholesome flotilla of prison and hospital ships. It was fairly isolated, and that was an important factor, because contagious diseases were rife among the prisoners. There were other considerations as well. The bay was close enough for supplies and troops to be ferried out, but the vessels were not anchored in a spot where they could impede merchant shipping.[79]

Like Thomas Dring, a fellow prisoner, James Forten must have been appalled at the stench coming from the prison ship as he was rowed across to the *Jersey*. After clambering out of the longboat and up the side of the hulk, he was subjected to the usual treatment accorded American captives. He was searched for weapons, but allowed to keep his clothes and bedding. His name was entered on the list for exchanges. If he survived long enough, freedom would come when his name reached the top of the list and there were British prisoners available.[80]

Forten's first priority was to get himself accepted into the basic unit of social organization on the *Jersey*, the mess. The sooner he achieved this the sooner he would get to eat, for rations were distributed not to each prisoner but to each mess. A mess consisted of six men, and a newly arrived prisoner like Forten would have to seek out a mess where a member had recently been exchanged or had died. Forten apparently had no difficulty winning acceptance. The men from the *Royal Louis* who had been held aboard *La Nymphe* had already been on the *Jersey* over a week. Forten and the contingent from the *Amphion* were shipmates. Once they had accepted Forten, the old hands, who knew the routine of the ship, would help him find his way about. They would also become his most loyal friends, expecting from him complete devotion in return. The mess was a tight-knit little family in the larger community of prisoners. Escape attempts, which were not infrequent, invariably involved the members of one mess, with those who did not share the kinship of being messmates kept in complete ignorance.[81]

The first night on the *Jersey* was worse by far than Forten's first night below decks on the *Amphion*. For one thing, the prisoners were not allowed heat or light, presumably for reasons of safety. In the gloom Forten's messmates conducted him to his new sleeping quarters. Physical proximity strengthened his sense of solidarity with them; they used their chests and boxes to create partitions, separate themselves from the men in the adjoining mess, and secure some privacy. To combat theft by guards and fellow prisoners, one or more of the men would sleep on the boxes to protect the belongings of the mess. The others would swing their hammocks nearby, as close to the side of the deck as possible to get a little fresh air. As Forten tried to sleep—kept awake by hunger, for he had missed the day's handout of rations, and by the groans and delirious ravings of his fellow captives—he may have questioned his wisdom in rejecting Bazely's offer of a comfortable life in England.[82]

Morning meant the chance to escape the noise and stench belowdecks, look around, learn more about the floating prison and her inhabitants, and eat. Getting, preparing, and consuming food further strengthened the bonds among messmates. Every morning at nine o'clock a member of each mess was entrusted with the task of collecting the food ration from the steward.[83]

Standard British practice set the allowance at two thirds of the daily ration of a British sailor or soldier. This worked out to a weekly allotment of 4 pounds 10-2/3 ounces of bread, 3-1/2 pounds of meat, and peas, butter, and oatmeal when available. In fact, as a result of complaints, quantities had been increased by 1781 to slightly more than British servicemen received. However, the prisoners on the *Jersey* complained vociferously about cheating on the amount and quality of the food. Ebenezer Fox wrote of pounding the bread on the deck to dislodge the worms. Alexander Coffin, Jr., recalled that the *Jersey*'s officers kept hogs penned up on the gun deck. The hungry prisoners would "steal the bran from the hogs' trough, and go into the galley . . . boil it on the fire, and eat it."[84]

The members of the mess handed over their daily allowance of food to the cook to be cooked in a huge copper kettle divided in two. The rations for each mess were distinguished by a string "tally," and the food was deemed cooked when the cook—appointed from the ranks of the prisoners, and usually considered one of the most cantankerous individuals on board—said it was cooked. He boiled the peas and oatmeal in fresh water, and the beef in fetid sea water, unless messmates conspired to do a little better for themselves. To avoid food poisoning, the men in each mess would hoard fresh water from their daily ration and try to persuade the cook to let them hang their own small kettle over the fire, separate from the vast boiler.[85]

As Forten's messmates quickly informed him, one of the ways of securing better rations and coping with the tedium of the day was to serve on one or other of the work parties. Being in a work party entitled one to more food, half a pint of rum, and, of course, more time on deck. The prisoners in the work parties would wash the upper deck and gangway and unload the food and other supplies from the supply ships. They would then move the sick up on deck and search out the dead. It was also their job to empty the stinking "necessary" tubs. Some of them would be sent ashore under guard to get the 700 gallons of fresh water needed on the vessel every day. What was not doled out immediately or used in the copper kettle or in preparing the food for the guards was stored in the hold in butts. Forten soon learned not to slake his thirst at the butts, for they were never cleaned.[86]

During daylight hours the captives were allowed onto the spar deck. An awning that was stretched over the deck provided some shelter from the elements. They would put their belongings there while they cleaned their sleeping quarters. Thomas Dring recalled that recreation on the spar deck was regimented. "Owing to the great number of the prisoners . . . it was our custom to walk, in platoons, each facing the same way, and turning at the same time." The prisoners were permitted to stay on deck until sunset. Then, to shouts of "Down, rebels, down" from the guards, they were herded below for the night to get what rest they could amid the noise, the vermin, and the stench of close-packed bodies.[87]

James Forten quickly realized that the pattern of his captivity varied according to the composition of the guard. The vessel was under the command of a captain: His crew comprised two mates, a steward, a cook, and twelve sailors. There was also a guard of thirty soldiers, who were relieved weekly.[88] Thomas Dring was unlucky enough to be imprisoned on the *Jersey* twice, and he recalled the interaction between guards and prisoners. The Hessians were mercenaries; they had little reason to hate their captives, and the Americans knew that. As for the British regulars, there might be some trading of insults, but Dring and his fellow prisoners accepted that the Britishers were just following orders. However, tensions ran high when guards came on board from one of the Loyalist regiments. The prisoners heaped abuse on them, and they responded with violence.[89]

The prisoners filled their days as best they could, working if they had the strength, smoking if they could get tobacco and a light, carving their names into the planking, and speculating about how they could get off the *Jersey*. There was one way that actually had the approval of their captors. They could agree to enter the king's service. To make enlistment more palatable, the British offered them the option of garrison duty in Jamaica, where they would be serving not against fellow Americans but against Spanish and French troops. Then there was the possibility of making a break for freedom. However, escape attempts were invariably doomed to failure. Anyone able to get over the side undetected faced a two-mile swim, a barrier of mud flats, and the knowledge that Long Island was under British control. If they made it ashore, local residents would hand them back.[90]

James Forten had no intention of swimming to freedom. Imaginative and resourceful, he hit upon another method of escape. An officer of the Continental Navy was to be exchanged for a British officer, and Forten asked the man's permission to hide in his sea chest. At the last minute, though, he gave up his chance of freedom to Daniel Brewton, a white Philadelphian two years his junior, and "his companion . . . in suffering." Brewton took his place, and "Forten had the satisfaction of assisting in taking down 'the chest of old clothes' . . . from the sides of the prison ship." This was an act of kindness Brewton never forgot. The two became life-long friends. Years later, Brewton set down the facts of their service together in a sworn affidavit and told the story of his escape to Forten's son-in-law and biographer.[91]

Forten had no illusions about what he was giving up by ceding his place to Brewton. He was risking his life and he knew it. A poor diet, inadequate clothing, and close quarters took their toll on even the healthiest captives.[92] Some lost their reason. For those with physical ailments, medical treatment was at best rudimentary. Every day when the weather permitted, the surgeon would come over from the hospital ship *Hunter* to make his rounds. The sick were supposed to be taken to the hospital ships, but those vessels were soon packed to overflowing, and it became necessary to set up bunks on the *Jersey*'s upper deck and house the sick there.[93] Fleas, ticks, and lice infested the ship and her occupants. The *Jersey* was an ideal breeding ground for the smallpox bacillus. Some captives performed crude inoculations on themselves, using pus from the sores of those already infected. Scurvy, dysentery, yellow fever, pneumonia, and influenza were also serious threats. Little was done by the British in the way of disease prevention. Illnesses were generally neglected until they became serious. Occasionally an American physician was taken prisoner. He would do what he could with very limited resources, but he would usually soon be exchanged.[94]

Every day there were deaths on board. The dignity accorded the dead was almost nonexistent. If the dead man had a blanket, his comrades were permitted to sew him up in it. The burial party would then strap him to a board and lower him over the side into a small boat.[95] Men volunteered to serve in the burial party to get ashore for an hour or two, or to bury a friend. They rowed ashore under guard and headed for a hut where hoes, shovels, and handcarts were stored. They then dug a trench and laid in it the bodies of all those who had died the previous night. The graves were so shallow and so near the shoreline that it was not unusual for the dead to be washed out to sea during a storm.[96]

As the months passed, James Forten's name moved steadily up the list of prisoners. If he survived long enough, he would be released and sent home. Even though the surrender at Yorktown had left the Patriots with thousands of British prisoners on their hands, negotiations for prisoner exchanges were protracted, and men in the state and Continental forces were freed before privateersmen, who were technically civilians. The lot of the prisoner of war was seldom a comfortable one, but the peculiar nature of the American conflict made the situation far worse. From the British standpoint this was not a war of equals, where the fighting men on each side were treated as legitimate prisoners and soon exchanged. This was a rebellion, and any negotiations that treated American captives as prisoners of war invested that rebellion with the legitimacy of a war. Not until March 25, 1782, did Parliament pass a law defining American captives as prisoners of war.[97]

The status of men captured while serving on privateers was, at best, doubtful. Since the British did not recognize letters of marque issued by the Continental Congress and the individual states, privateers were technically pirates, and piracy was a capital crime.[98] The British did not execute any privateersmen out of fear of reprisals against their own men in Patriot hands, but they were unsure how to treat these civilian raiders. And Washington was unwilling to accede to British suggestions that privateers be exchanged for Redcoats. He argued that British troops were trained professionals, while privateersmen were, by and large, inexperienced sailors. Such exchanges would benefit the British more than the Americans. In truth, until Yorktown the Continental Congress had few prisoners at its disposal. Captured British sailors often opted to serve on American privateers. Those who refused were put under the supervision of the local community when they reached shore. Few towns were willing to bear the expense of jailing them, so they were generally released on parole. Ironically, privateering captains compounded the problem. Ignoring directives to deliver their prisoners to the Continental Commissioners, they set them ashore wherever was convenient and they promptly vanished into the general population.[99]

Nevertheless, as James Forten entered his seventh month of captivity, the pace of exchanges quickened. Finally, with most of those in the state and Continental forces free, the privateers had their turn. Forten and some of his companions were called on deck, told to get their belongings, and rowed ashore.

The last of the prisoners were freed a year later. On April 8, 1783, Forten's friend, Captain Bazely, boarded the *Jersey* and read the captives the king's proclamation that hostilities were at an end. Over the next few days everyone was released, and the *Jersey* was left to sink into the mud of the East River.[100]

BACK IN PHILADELPHIA, Margaret Forten had long since given up her son for dead. Philadelphians had learned the fate of the *Royal Louis* when the *Pennsylvania Gazette* reprinted a report from a New York newspaper that "one of his majesty's frigates" had sent into port "the Royal Louis, a privateer from Philadelphia, which had greatly annoyed the British trade." That news was bad enough, but Margaret had heard a rumor that James had been shot from the privateer's foretop.[101] The son who eventually came home to her was very different from the boy who had left Philadelphia so many months before. After his release he had walked barefoot from New York to Trenton, "where he was generously supplied" with shoes and with food. However, despite the kindness of the citizens of Trenton, he "reached home in a wretchedly bad condition, having, among other evidences of great hardship endured, his hair nearly entirely worn from his head."[102]

Back home, being nursed back to health by his mother and sister, how did James Forten interpret what the Revolution meant for him? In a sense, his months on the *Jersey* had been his "middle passage." Crammed into a dark, stinking hold, poorly fed, and with men around him dying of disease and neglect every day, he knew the suffering endured by his great-grandfather on his voyage into slavery a century before. In some respects Forten's lot was worse than that of the slave, for slavers took pains to keep enough of their captives alive to turn a profit. The British were simply warehousing their prisoners. Whether they lived or died was of no account. Forten never forgot the smell below decks on the *Jersey*. Years later, when he was one of Philadelphia's leading sailmakers, he was approached by a shipowner in need of a new suit of sails. As Forten boarded the vessel to take the measurements for his gore-book, he smelled again the telltale odor of close-packed bodies. The ship had been used as an illegal slaver; she was likely to be used again. A furious James Forten threatened the shipowner with the full force of the law and expressed in no uncertain terms his sense of personal outrage.[103]

But, when all was said and done, James Forten was not a slave in his months on the *Jersey*. Nor was he shunned or made to live apart from his fellows because of the color of his skin. The prisoners, most of them young men "induced by necessity or inclination to try the perils of the sea," banded together for mutual support and survival.[104] With his fellow Americans on board the *Jersey*, and most obviously with his messmates, Forten shared a sense of brotherhood so deep that he would give up his chance of freedom to a white messmate, and that messmate would respond with a lifetime of friendship.

In later years Forten would repeatedly draw on his wartime service to argue that he deserved the same rights as other Americans. When he was encouraged by "an honorable gentleman" to petition for a pension, he replied, "I was a volunteer, sir."[105] It was not a pension he wanted, but the status of "citizen" he believed he had earned. But the dreams of lasting brotherhood, of merit outweighing complexion and condition in the new republic, soon faded. If he needed proof, it came, ironically enough, on "the day set apart for the festival of Liberty." In 1776 the nine-year-old James Forten had stood in the crowd in the statehouse yard to hear the Declaration of Independence read to the people for the first time. Decades later the adult James Forten and his children had to stay at home on July Fourth or face the threat of physical violence if they ventured outside their home. As he sadly observed:

> It is a well known fact, that black people, on certain days of publick jubilee, dare not be seen after twelve o'clock in the day, upon the field to enjoy the times, for no sooner do the fumes of that potent devil, Liquor, mount into the brain, than the poor black is assailed like the destroying Hyena or the avaricious Wolf. . . . Is it not wonderful, that the day set apart for the festival of Liberty, should be abused by the advocates of freedom, in endeavouring to sully what they profess to adore?[106]

3

MR. BRIDGES'S APPRENTICE

WITH HIS RELEASE from the *Jersey* and his painful trek back to Phila-delphia, the war came to an end for James Forten. Once the joy of reunion was over, Margaret and Abigail must have taken a good look at him and been shocked at what they saw. He was pitifully thin. Great clumps of his hair had fallen out as a result of scurvy; his skin was ashy and unhealthy-looking, his feet cracked and swollen. The care and affection his mother and sister lavished on him, decent food, rest, and his own robust constitution combined to repair the ravages of sickness and malnutrition. His recovery *had* to be a speedy one. Money was as scarce as ever in the Forten household. James Forten was soon back at work, most likely sewing and repairing canvas in Robert Bridges's sail loft, and learning more of the sailmaker's craft.

The next major event for the family was Abigail's marriage. Her husband's name was William Dunbar, he was a sailor, and he was described in the marriage register as a "Free African." The records reveal nothing about where and when he had been born, whether or not he had been a slave, and how he met Abigail. He was just one of many hundreds of black mariners who drifted into the port of Philadelphia and made their homes there.[1]

At the time of Abigail's marriage she and her mother and brother were still living in Dock Ward, in or near the house where James had been born. Resisting the growing appeal of Methodism within the African-American community, the Fortens remained loyal Episcopalians. (Now that the break with Britain was complete, the Anglican Church in America had been reconstituted as the Episcopal Church.) The church they attended was the one closest to their home,

St. Paul's, and it was there, on April 10, 1784, with Rev. Samuel Magaw, a white minister, officiating, that twenty-one-year-old Abigail married William Dunbar.[2] There was little by way of a wedding celebration. The Forten household was not exactly awash with money, and if there was anything at all left of Abigail's inheritance from her aunt, it would be best spent setting up a home. And there was scarcely any time for celebrating. William Dunbar had already signed on for another voyage, and he had persuaded his new brother-in-law to sail with him. They were bound for London on Thomas Truxtun's ship, the *Commerce*.[3]

As a privateer during the war, the 250-ton *Commerce* had carried fourteen guns and a crew of fifty.[4] But the Treaty of Paris had brought hostilities with Britain to an end. The crew of fifty had shrunk to at most two dozen. The heavy carriage guns were gone from the deck. The shot locker and powder magazine had been converted to cargo space, and provisions had been made for passengers. As for veteran privateersman Thomas Truxtun, he was now a merchant. He and partner James Collins owned a dry-goods store on Water Street, which they aimed to stock with the British-made goods Philadelphians had been hankering after for so long. Collins stayed home to manage the store while Truxtun made one voyage after another to London. Speed was of the essence if he was to beat out the other captains plying the London route. He needed a reliable crew, and matters such as race were far outweighed by considerations of skill and reliability.[5] Perhaps Dunbar had sailed with Truxtun on earlier voyages and was able to introduce Forten to him. Perhaps the two had simply gone down to the docks looking to ship out and found the *Commerce* making ready to sail. Whatever the case, Truxtun could count himself lucky to have secured the services of two good men, one a seasoned seafarer and the other something of a green hand but knowledgeable when it came to repairing canvas.

In many ways Truxtun was a good captain to serve under. Left an orphan, he had gone to sea when he was twelve with the intention of carving out a career for himself as a merchant and a master mariner. He had survived clashes with the enemy, come close to losing his ship in a hurricane, and been press-ganged into the Royal Navy.[6] He would turn each of these experiences to good use, writing a treatise on weathering hurricanes and "tuffoons" and drawing on his intimate, if unlooked-for, knowledge of the Royal Navy to shape the republic's new navy when he was appointed one of its first commodores in 1794. A stickler for discipline, he scoffed at the notion some naïve people entertained that common sailors were nature's gentlemen. In his opinion, they were a set of "abandoned miscreants, ripe for any mischief or villainy." But he insisted a good captain must get to know his crew, respect their skills, punish "Skulking and Loitering," and yet recognize when a man was genuinely sick and in need of "humanity and Care."[7] Forten and Dunbar could have chosen a much worse captain to sail with.

The *Commerce* cleared the port of Philadelphia on April 21, late enough in the season for the Delaware to be free of ice.[8] She made her way down to New Castle, Delaware, where she took on seven passengers—Quakers from the socially prominent Emlen and Dillwyn clans, and acquaintances of Philadelphia diarist Elizabeth Drinker.[9] These were affluent men and women, and Truxtun took pains to accommodate them comfortably. As for his crew, they swung their hammocks in their own quarters in the forecastle.

Truxtun the merchant captain regulated the crew of the *Commerce* as he would later regulate his United States Navy crews, assigning the more experienced men to control the lines or climb aloft to manage the sails, while the less experienced kept the vessel clean and in good repair. Conditions on the *Commerce* bred closeness. On a voyage that could reasonably be expected to last six or seven weeks, captain, crew, and passengers came to know each other well. Indeed, they could hardly avoid it.

Truxtun had made the voyage to London many times before and doubtless had his favorite route, one that enabled him to take full advantage of ocean currents and winds. Once out of the Delaware, the *Commerce* most likely bore north, past the Long Island Sound, and clear of the busy shipping lanes into New York. Later in the sailing season she might have headed as far north as Newfoundland and Prince Edward Island. However, for an April sailing, speed had to be weighed against safety. Icebergs and fogs off the Grand Banks probably obliged Truxtun to take a more southerly route than he would have done had the *Commerce* been making the crossing in August or September. Most likely he kept south of Nantucket and the Grand Banks, even though it made for a longer voyage by several hundred miles.[10]

Once out in the North Atlantic the *Commerce* sailed on for days without sight of land. This was a new and rather disquieting experience for James Forten, whose privateering cruises had been largely confined to American coastal waters. Because she was making for London rather than Liverpool, the *Commerce* kept well to the south of the southern tip of Ireland. The first land her lookout spotted was the Scilly Isles, off the Cornish coast. Soon they were working their way through the southwestern approaches to England, past Land's End and the Lizard, past Eddystone Light, past Portland Bill, with its treacherous race, past the Isle of Wight and the great naval installation at Portsmouth, and on past Beachy Head, Dungeness, and the Goodwin Sands, the scene of many a maritime disaster.[11] The volume of shipping was increasing with every mile, and the Channel was narrowing all the time. As they maneuvered through the Straits of Dover Truxtun never left the helm, and his crew was constantly employed trimming the sails, taking soundings, and watching the movements of other vessels.

The *Commerce* sailed east and then north into the Thames Estuary. This stretch of water, with its picturesquely named hazards, the Nob, the Girdler, and Oaze Edge, was a challenge in the art of seamanship even for someone of

Truxtun's expertise, but the *Commerce* continued on her way without incident to enter the lower reaches of the Thames. All along the route James Forten would have seen small ports, riverside villages, and isolated farms. He would have caught glimpses of the dockyards at Tilbury, the arsenal at Woolwich, and the observatory at Greenwich. Then it was on into London proper, to anchor in the Pool of London just below London Bridge and in sight of the Tower.[12]

This, then, was the great metropolis Forten could have visited as the protégé of Captain Bazely and his son. He could have accepted their promise of a comfortable life, a chance to further his education and master a trade, establish himself with their patronage, and make a future for himself in England. Now here he was, a few months short of his eighteenth birthday, a common sailor on an American vessel, knowing no one in London. And yet he decided to take his chances and stay, at least for a while. Was this a sudden whim, or had he set out with that thought in mind? After all, what was waiting for him back home? William Dunbar was certainly not about to linger. He would want to hurry back to Abigail, and with a steady fellow like Dunbar now a member of the family, Forten need feel no anxiety about his sister and mother. The burden he had borne for so many years was easing. Why should he not stay and see what London had to offer?

So long as Forten stayed to get the vessel unloaded, Truxtun probably made no difficulties about paying him off. There were plenty of sailors in London looking for a berth. In the short term, though, Truxtun had to discharge his cargo and load up with English goods for the return voyage, and that was no easy matter. The congestion on the Thames was a source of much complaint. Even with outports like Liverpool and Bristol, most imports and exports still went via London. Cargoes from all over the world—West Indian sugar, Virginia tobacco, East Indian tea and spices—were off-loaded into barges and ferried to one of the twenty legal quays to clear customs. Truxtun knew the risks of delay. The wharves might not be well organized, but the pilfering was. Practitioners of the various refinements of thievery had their own names. River Pirates, Scuffle Hunters, Night Plunderers, Light and Heavy Horsemen, and Mud Larks would all take their share if a captain and his crew were not on the alert, and even then they might manage it, for pay was low and theft a desperate necessity for many.[13]

The *Commerce* did not leave for Philadelphia directly from London but from the Kentish port of Deal, a dozen or so miles from Dover, where the Bazely family lived.[14] It is tempting to imagine Forten leaving London on board the *Commerce*, helping maneuver her down the Thames, being put ashore with the pilot as she made ready to sail, watching her until she was out of sight, and then making his way along the coast road to Dover to turn up on the Bazelys' doorstep, renewing the friendship with father and son and reclaiming their patronage. It is a nice picture, but there is not a scrap of evidence to suggest Forten ever met the Bazelys again after he left the *Amphion* in Wallabout Bay.

Most likely Forten stayed behind in London, looking to earn his living along the wharves and in the shipyards of the great port. For a young man without friends and without a skill that might be no easy matter. But James Forten did have a skill. Someone who could sew canvas quickly and neatly would not be long without work where there were sails to be made and repaired. True, he had not served an apprenticeship with an established master of the craft, but he was a more than competent sailmaker, and if he had to earn his first few shillings laboring on the docks as a porter, he would soon do better for himself.

London's shipyards might be losing ground to the newer yards of the northeastern ports, like Newcastle and Whitby, but there was no shortage of work along the Thames. In a score of yards great and small downriver from the Tower of London vessels of various sizes were under construction, from 700-ton East Indiamen and warships to fishing sloops and wherries. As James Forten sailed up the Thames aboard the *Commerce* in the early summer of 1784, Barnard's Yard, Wells' Yard, and Adams and Co. in Deptford were all fitting out seventy-four-gun ships of the line, as was Batson's in Limehouse. The Blackwall or East India Yard, described at the time of Forten's arrival in London as the "most capacious private dockyard in the Kingdom," was humming with activity, as was its rival, Randall and Brent.[15] From gossip in the riverside taverns and from his own observations, Forten soon learned that the London yards were facing a shortage of skilled workers. Shipwrights, riggers, caulkers, and, most important for his purpose, sailmakers, were in great demand.[16] Why not stay when there was the prospect of good wages and valuable work experience?

What did James Forten make of the city in which he had been set adrift by his own request? He was no naïve country boy, uneasy if he could not see trees and green fields. He was city-bred, accustomed to cobblestones and crowds. Even so, nothing could prepare him for London. Philadelphia had been the second largest city in the British Empire, but the difference in scale between Philadelphia and London was unimaginable. Philadelphia was a city of some 50,000 people. London's population was ten or twelve times greater. Philadelphia was a new city, at the time of Forten's birth not even a hundred years old. As he walked around London he could trace its many centuries of growth in stone and bricks and mortar, from the new houses built during the period of prosperity after the Seven Years' War, back to the handiwork of Christopher Wren and Inigo Jones, the Tudor splendors that had escaped the Great Fire of 1666, the medieval churches, the great abbey of Westminster and the Tower of London, and in places the old Roman wall breaking through the various layers.

Both Philadelphia and London were "walking cities," but whereas a leisurely stroll soon took one beyond the boundaries of Philadelphia, London was physically much larger. The old walled city had long since burst its confines, spreading south of the Thames to Southwark and beyond, and west to

Westminster, still technically a separate city. Yet London remained, in some
ways, a rural city. Each day fresh fruit and vegetables, milk and cheeses, meat and
poultry were brought in from the surrounding countryside and sold in the markets or in the streets. The city itself had its cow sheds and chicken coops, and in
St. James's Park one could buy a mug of milk fresh from the cow for a penny.

As for the physical environment, the Philadelphia Forten had left might
not exactly live up to William Penn's dream of a "green country town," but it
was sweet and clean in comparison to London. The London of 1784 was a
dirty, crowded metropolis, its streets congested, its gutters full of mud and
filth. It was summertime when Forten arrived, and the city stank in the heat.
The Thames was an open sewer running through its heart. The king and his
court had left for one of the royal estates. Anyone else with the leisure and the
means to do so had followed suit and escaped from the city, but the majority of
Londoners stayed put, taking their chances with typhoid and dysentery. As
winter approached, the stench was replaced, or at least masked, by coal smoke,
for Londoners preferred burning coal to wood. Pollution from coal smoke had
defaced many of the buildings, including the great dome of St. Paul's, and a
dingy yellow-gray pall hung over the city for days at a time, irritating the lungs
and the eyes of those not inured to it.

Then there was the sheer human misery. Even as Forten gawked at the
pageantry of the city—the Lord Mayor's procession, the progress of a nobleman or the king himself—he could not ignore the poverty, for it was all around
him. Beggars abounded on a scale he had never seen back home. Prostitutes
plied their trade everywhere, in fashionable thoroughfares and dark alleys, in
riverside taverns and more select places of entertainment. Gin drinking had
declined since the days of Hogarth's "Gin Lane," but scenes of public drunkenness were still more prevalent than in staid and relatively sober Philadelphia.

Violence was never far below the surface in eighteenth-century London.
Forten had witnessed the power of the mob in Philadelphia both before and
during the Revolution, but the London mob was different. To begin with, it
was larger and apt to be more violent. It could be summoned out into the
streets seemingly at a moment's notice to rally behind a hero like John Wilkes
or to protest a rise in the price of bread. Two parliamentary elections took
place while Forten was in London, neither noted for their riotousness, but
neither free from disruption and very vocal expressions of partiality. As for
everyday violence, thanks to the efforts of Henry Fielding and his half-brother,
the blind magistrate John Fielding, the city was a safer place than it had been,
but it still held its terrors, for crime went hand in hand with want.[17]

The part of London Forten became most familiar with lay south of the
Thames and east of the Tower. Neighborhoods like Wapping and Limehouse,
Shadwell, Stepney, Rotherhithe, Poplar, and Blackwall were not known for
their tranquility. Here, close to the wharves and shipyards, were the areas where
sailors from around the globe congregated. Life was tough here; work was hard

and poverty never far away. The denizens of these riverside communities had a taste for less genteel, or at least cheaper, entertainments than their fellow Londoners in the West End. But interspersed with the grog shops, cheap lodging-houses, and brothels were the homes of merchants, captains, and craftsmen who earned their living in one or other of the maritime trades.[18] It was here, among the rope walks and warehouses, the ship chandleries and the sail lofts, that James Forten found employment and companionship.

In the dockside communities, as in most of the rest of the capital, his complexion did not mark him out as an oddity. Indeed, he quickly discovered that few white Londoners gave him a second glance on account of the color of his skin, except perhaps to notice that he did not wear servant's livery and was obviously not a pauper or a beggar. There had long been a black presence in London. For more than two centuries black "servants," the vast majority of them slaves, had been imported to labor in the homes of aristocrats and wealthy merchants. Planters visiting from the West Indies often brought their house slaves with them. Some succumbed to the climate and to maladies such as smallpox, while others, to the annoyance of their masters, made their escape. In 1768, for instance, magistrate Sir John Fielding charged that the white mob often protected black runaways.[19]

In 1772, when Lord Mansfield handed down his decision in the much-lauded Sommersett case—a judgment that did not free every slave in Britain, as so often assumed, but did curtail the power of a slave owner over his slave—there were between 15,000 and 20,000 black men, women, and children in the country. Many of them lived in London as slaves, servants, sailors, or common laborers. They were scattered throughout the city, but there were sizable black enclaves in the riverside communities and in poor areas like Paddington and Mile End.[20] On the south bank of the Thames, where he most likely lived and worked, James Forten would have rubbed shoulders with Africans and West Indians, black Britishers, and Americans like himself. Many were former slaves. Some were freeborn. The London of Dr. Johnson was also the London of Johnson's black servant and valued companion, Francis Barber, and of African-born writers and antislavery advocates Olaudah Equiano and Ottobah Cugoano. Ignatius Sancho, who had been born on a slave ship and risen from obscurity to become the friend of author Laurence Sterne and actor David Garrick, and a London "personality" in his own right, had died just a few years before Forten's arrival.

In the poorer quarters of London, blacks and whites lived in a harmony born of shared poverty and desperation. Black men far outnumbered black women. The demand for male domestics, such as footmen and coachmen, had traditionally outpaced that for female domestics, thus many more men than women had been brought over from Africa and the Caribbean. Black men often married or cohabited with English women, especially those in service like themselves, to the annoyance of genteel observers, who commented on the existence of "a little race of mulattoes, mischievous as monkeys and infinitely more dangerous." Some black men had secured apprenticeships and entered the skilled trades. They were crossing sweepers and vendors, sailors and house servants, street entertainers and beggars. Black women were cooks and maids and hucksters. Like the majority of the city's laboring poor, black Londoners, whether native-born or newcomers, worked when work was to be had and turned to crime when there was no work, or when honest labor yielded less than thievery or prostitution.[21]

Men and women of color had their friends and allies outside the ranks of the white poor. Being a pious young man, James Forten might well have found his way to the chapel of Dr. Johnson's friend, Dr. Mayo, in Nightingale Lane, Stepney. Mayo was "particularly kind to the Blacks and uninstructed men of Colour who, employed generally on board of ship, occasionally resided in his parish, which is full of seafaring people." He educated and baptized them, and generally showed a great concern for their welfare. That concern drew forth an outpouring of affection. Black sailors from around the world would visit Mayo and worship at his church every time their ships docked in London.[22] In addition to Mayo there were individuals like Granville Sharp, the man who had helped secure at least a partial victory for England's enslaved black men and women in the Sommersett case. However, to most white Britons of the middle and upper classes black people were included in that part of the population— the poor and the laboring classes—they instinctively distrusted.

James Forten arrived in England at a time when attitudes toward black people were undergoing a crucial shift. Racism had never been far below the surface. Ignatius Sancho had complained of "the national antipathy and prejudice" of whites in Britain "towards their wooly headed brethren." He was frustrated that, despite all the evidence to the contrary, many whites resorted to stereotyping their black neighbors: "from Othello to Sancho the big—we are foolish—or mulish—all—all without a single exception."[23] But Sancho had died before racial lines had hardened and before the authorities gave legal sanction to personal antipathies. When Forten reached London, racial antagonism was intensifying, and the reason lay in large part in Britain's defeat in America's War for Independence.

In 1784 the British capital was full of American Loyalists. Clinging together in exile, they frequented the same taverns and coffeehouses, swapped the latest news from across the Atlantic, and laid bets on how long the new "United States" would endure. Above all, they complained. They had not been adequately compensated for their loyalty. London was full of thieves and whores and scoundrels. The food was dreadful and the climate worse. In short, England might be the "motherland," but it was not "home."

But if the white Loyalists were given at best a lukewarm welcome, their black counterparts were most definitely not wanted. The influx of black refugees led to increased racial prejudice, at least among those in positions of power. There were reports that "the city of London, and the country about it [was] . . . infested with American negroes."[24] The black Loyalists "had no prospect of subsisting in this country but by depredations on the public, or by common charity."[25] A more sympathetic observer wrote that "great numbers of Blacks and People of Colour, many of them refugees from America and others who have by land or sea been in his Majesty's service, were . . . in great distress."[26] The officers of the various London parishes drove black mendicants from place to place, unwilling to afford them any relief.[27]

Several hundred black Loyalists, perhaps as many as a thousand, had been evacuated to Britain at the end of the war. Some had been prosperous in America, with homes and trades and a legal right to freedom. A number managed to become self-supporting in their new homeland. George Peters was "attending at a Gentleman's house," while Samuel Burke worked in London's "Artificial Flower Garden at 1s. per Day." William Snow had been a tailor in Charleston and had found work in his trade in London. He stated that he had no wish to return to South Carolina. John Robinson had been a cook with his own shop in Charleston; now he ran a similar shop in Newmarket Street in London.[28]

There *were* success stories, but by and large, black Loyalists did not prosper. Some were pressed into service in the Royal Navy.[29] A few turned to crime, while others begged in the streets. About forty men filed claims for compensation for losses suffered on account of their loyalty. A handful, like Shadrach Furman, were able to produce character witnesses or otherwise document their service, and they received small pensions.[30] Furman had lost his sight fighting for the king in America; he got a pension which he supplemented by playing the fiddle in the streets. However, most claimants found securing compensation from the British authorities was well nigh impossible. The government of George III contended that they should count themselves lucky to be in England. Had they not been slaves in America? Only if an individual could furnish irrefutable proof that he had been free would he have any hope of getting a pension.[31]

What was to be done with these black Loyalists? Could they somehow be removed from the country? If so, where could they be sent to? Perhaps the Sierra Leone project was already being talked of while James Forten was in Britain. He may even have met another freeborn Philadelphian, Richard Weaver, who would play a role in founding the African colony.[32] However, plans for the colony did not really begin to crystallize until after Forten sailed for Philadelphia. In January 1786 a group of London businessmen organized the Committee to Aid the Black Poor. Their aid took the form of opening a hospital and giving daily cash handouts, although the amount given was too little to support an adult.[33] Obviously, a more permanent solution was needed. A solution of sorts was found in the Sierra Leone scheme. At least it satisfied the government by diminishing the number of black paupers in London. Although abolitionist Granville Sharp later took a hand in the scheme, he did not initiate it, and his humanitarian impulses did not shape it.[34]

The idea of establishing a British colony on the west coast of Africa had obvious appeal. It would make the British presence there far stronger, and the ideal people to colonize the settlement would be those who had been born in the region or who were descendants of Africans. Surely they would be better able to resist the diseases that made the West African coast the "white man's grave." They would know how to make the colony economically viable. It would be an act of simple justice to return the "children of Africa" to the land of their ancestors—and get them out of Britain. Settlers were to get land, free passage, and basic supplies until they could support themselves. Almost 700 people agreed to go, but death and second thoughts thinned their ranks. By the time the ships sailed, only 350 black people—some American refugees and others West Indians and Africans—left. Sixty whites joined them, most of them the wives of black men. Granville Sharp, who was in a good position to know, thought half the men were Americans—"chiefly seamen, that had served in the Royal Navy . . . or as Rangers with the Army in the American Woods." Most black Loyalists preferred to take their chances in England.[35]

Whether or not he knew of talk of an African colony when he was in London, James Forten would later take a keen interest in Sierra Leone. He would follow its early struggles, come to see it as a refuge for newly liberated slaves from America, and help to recruit settlers. He would also correspond with some of the most ardent supporters of the Sierra Leone venture in Britain, in the United States, and in the colony itself.

And what of the abolition cause that would eventually consume so much of his energy? According to Robert Purvis, while James Forten was in England he took "no small interest in the discussions both in and out of Parliament. . . . It was among the many pleasing reminiscences of his life to refer to those scenes so strikingly analogous to the trials and persecutions of the friends of freedom here."[36] Purvis surely embellished the truth, or perhaps his venerable father-in-law did it for him when he recalled his time in England. When James Forten arrived in London the abolitionist crusade was only just beginning. In 1783 London Friends had responded to news that Parliament was about to authorize the resumption of the slave trade after suspending it during the War for Independence. At the request of a committee of six appointed by London Friends, Forten's old benefactor, Anthony Benezet, sent over a manuscript copy of his *The Case of Our Fellow Creatures, the Oppressed Africans*, a work Philadelphia Friends were reluctant to print because they considered it too radical. The London committee funded the printing of 2000 copies, one of which they presented to Parliament with 258 signatures. The remaining copies, and a second and third printing, were sent to people who it was believed could advance the cause.[37]

The Quakers were aided in their campaign by popular revulsion over the news of the barbarous treatment of the captives aboard the *Zong*, whose captain in 1782 had drowned 131 slaves to collect insurance money. The non-sectarian

Society for the Abolition of the Slave Trade did not come into existence until 1787, but, in the words of one historian of race in Britain, "the initial—and quite unexpected—public response to abolition suggests a reservoir of antipathy waiting to find expression."[38] A host of spiritual and cultural concerns, from respect for "traditional" English freedoms to a desire to help the less fortunate to views about the "noble savage," were fusing together into an antislavery campaign. Whether it was a reverence for the tenets of the Enlightenment or a commitment to the Golden Rule that one should do as one would be done by, it all tended in the same direction.[39] However, freeing slaves in Britain's far-flung empire was one thing. According all the rights of Englishmen to black people in Britain was another matter entirely.

WHY DID JAMES Forten leave England in 1785 and return to Philadelphia? Had the deteriorating racial climate made London a less attractive place than it had seemed at first glance? Had he felt out of place as a black American who was not a Loyalist but an ardent supporter of American independence? Or had he simply always intended to go back to Philadelphia? Had his year abroad been the result of a young man's wish to see the world before settling down? And while he was overseas had he taken the chance to become acquainted with more than the dockyards and port communities of London? Had he traveled within England, or even crossed the Channel to France? He left no record of what he did during his time overseas. His son-in-law noted simply that he spent a year in London before sailing back to Philadelphia.

Getting back to Philadelphia posed few problems. With the war over, and Americans once more importing British goods, there were plenty of vessels plying the London to Philadelphia route. He need only ask around in the taverns and on the docks to find out which masters needed to take on an extra hand. He may even have sailed with Thomas Truxtun again, for in 1785 Truxtun was sent over to London on his new vessel, the *London Packet*, to ferry the venerable Dr. Benjamin Franklin back to the United States after his sojourn in Europe.[40] Forten's return voyage was uneventful. At least he found no reason to comment on it.

He came home to find there had been changes during his absence. He had a baby niece, whom Abigail and William had named Margaret in honor of her maternal grandmother. The following year the Dunbars had another child, a boy, Nicholas.[41] Other developments were less joyful. Forten's beloved mentor, Anthony Benezet, was dead. He had died soon after Forten's departure for England, and his simple Quaker funeral had been attended by many members of the black community.[42]

Once back in Philadelphia, Forten soon found work. He "was apprenticed, with his own consent," to Robert Bridges.[43] The arrangement was an excellent one in that it suited the needs of both men. Bridges had known Forten since he had come to work with his father and had picked up a few pennies doing simple errands around the sail loft. Bridges had hired Forten over the years and watched him master one skill after another, from seaming to working the various rope and leather fittings for sails. He knew him to be a careful workman and he saw the younger man's eagerness to learn more, to truly master the craft.

How much did James Forten know about his future role in the sail loft when he signed his indentures? What promises were made, either verbally or in writing? Did he understand that he would be treated differently from the other apprentices? How would he interact with the other men and boys in the loft? Robert Bridges had a large work force of journeymen and apprentices, but Forten was apparently the only free man of color he employed. What did Forten know about Bridges's plans for him?

At the time James Forten began his apprenticeship, Robert and Jemima Bridges had seven children. Another child would be born to them in 1788.[44] In the normal course of events, Forten could expect to remain, at best, a trusted journeyman as young Culpepper Bridges and his brothers came of age and assumed control of the business. Even if his sons pursued other careers, Bridges had daughters who would marry and bring him sons-in-law to learn his trade and eventually take over the sail loft. In fact, though, prospects were better for James Forten than might have been supposed. He would graduate from apprentice to foreman, from foreman to junior partner, and from junior partner to owner of the loft, partly as a result of his own drive and ability, and partly because Robert Bridges had other plans for his children.

So much about James Forten's future was rooted in Robert Bridges's past. Bridges had become a sailmaker because of his father's untimely death. By dint of hard work and good luck, he had done well for himself, but not as well as he would have done had his father lived, and had the mercantile firm of Edward Bridges and Co. survived to become Edward Bridges and Son. In 1785, at age forty-six, Robert Bridges had a thriving business on South Wharves and a home on Front Street. His wartime investments in privateering had paid off. He had substantial real estate interests.[45] And he wanted his children to do better than he had. He expected his sons to become merchants or professional men, not artisans, to have the careers and the social status he had been denied.[46] As for his daughters, he intended that they should marry merchants and lawyers, not craftsmen. James Forten was well acquainted with the Bridges family, and very likely with Robert Bridges's plans for his children. With his potential competitors out of the running because they were destined for other things, a hard-working, intelligent, and ambitious young man in the Bridges sail loft could justifiably look to a day when he might be the master where he had once been the apprentice—always provided that his race did not disqualify him.

As for Robert Bridges, had he spotted in James Forten a worthy successor when the young man's indentures were drawn up? His treatment of him suggests very strongly that he had, and that he may even have promised Forten rapid promotion in return for faithful service. In his memorial address Robert

Purvis cast Forten in the role of the faithful apprentice who won his master's favor by his "great skill, energy, diligence, and good conduct."[47] But James Forten seems never to have been just one apprentice among many. That he was their employer's designated right-hand man became abundantly clear to the other men in the sail loft when, barely a year after he began his period of indenture, Forten became their foreman.[48] Bridges was putting a young, highly skilled black craftsman in a position of authority over a score or more of white workers and indicating that if they did not care for the arrangement they could seek employment elsewhere.

The relationship between Robert and Jemima Bridges and James Forten was apparently a very close one. The entry for the Bridges household in the 1790 census indicates that the couple may well have taken James Forten into their home. This was, of course, customary in the case of apprentices, who expected to board with their masters. But Forten was no ordinary apprentice. He was marked out for greater things. He was also a free man of color in a household that contained other black people who were far from free. The subtleties of the interactions between Forten and the Bridges family constitute just one piece in the complex pattern of racial relations in the Philadelphia of the 1780s and 1790s. Race was a factor in everyday life. There was no denying it. But condition was equally important. Robert Bridges obviously never looked upon James Forten as a slave, even though he held other black people as property. The two were employer and employee, or perhaps it is more accurate to say they were protégé and patron. As for Forten's attitude toward Bridges's various bound laborers—his white indentured servants as well as his slaves—and their attitudes towards him, that is something about which we can only speculate.

LONG BEFORE HE began his apprenticeship with Bridges, James Forten had acquired the rudiments of the sailmaker's art from his father. Handy with needle and twine while still a young boy, he had been able to earn good money seaming. As a hired hand in the loft during and immediately after the war, he probably graduated to making reef points and sewing on reef bands, but that was very likely the extent of his skills. Now he learned the full range of the sailmaker's craft, and, just as important, with Bridges's help, he forged the contacts with captains and shippers that would eventually enable him to run his own loft.

There was much that he did not need to be told, for he knew the vocabulary. As a child he could name the various sails on the vessels he saw in the harbor. A sail took its name from the mast, yard, or stay to which it was attached. A square-rigged vessel had courses—lower sails, like the main and the foresail. Above them were the topsails, and above those the topgallants. Some rigs had added refinements to catch every puff of wind—royals above the topgallants, skysails above them, and, even higher, the quaintly named moonsails. In addition to the square sails, attached to the masts and yards, which reefed, there were staysails, triangular in shape, hoisted on stays set between the masts, which furled. There were also studding sails, quadrilateral sails spread beyond the "leeches" or edges of the forecourse and topsails and royals in moderate and steady breezes by means of stays and booms. As for the parts of a sail, the top edge of a square sail was (logically enough) the "head," the lower edge the "foot," and the sides the "leeches." The bottom corners were "clews," and the top corners "earings." Forten also knew the names and the uses of most of the tools on the sailmaker's bench. However, as an apprentice, and an ambitious one eager to become a master craftsman, he needed a far more sophisticated knowledge than that. He had the rudiments, but he knew he had to master the refinements, understanding every aspect of sailmaking from purchasing canvas to bending a sail to its yard.

To begin with, Forten needed to know how to judge the quality of the materials he would be working with. Bridges had his regular suppliers, but there was always the possibility someone would try to unload inferior canvas or cordage on him or his foreman. That would lead to a poorly made sail, a canceled order, or even the loss of a vessel at sea. If, as often happened, the owner of the vessel undertook to supply the canvas, the craftsman who was to make it up had to know when to reject it as being of poor quality. A cheeseparing merchant could endanger his ship and her crew if he chose, but a sailmaker would not risk his reputation if he hoped to remain in business.

James Forten knew from his earliest years working in the loft that canvas came in various grades, from the coarse no. 1 to the fine no. 8 and higher. The lower the number, the heavier the canvas. Canvas duck (from the Dutch word *doek*) was made of flax, and by far the best sailcloth came from the Baltic. That was a problem in itself, and Forten would have heard much from Bridges about the fact that the United States could not produce high-quality duck in sufficient quantity. Bridges remembered only too well what had happened during the Revolutionary War, when supplies of canvas had been drastically reduced, prices had risen, and the various committees of Congress had squabbled over the need for canvas for tents versus the need for canvas for sails.[49] Grumbling and dire predictions notwithstanding, the United States simply was not able to develop an industry to manufacture high-quality sailcloth. No self-respecting sailmaker would use American sailcloth because it was of such inferior grade. There was speculation that this had much to do with the processing of the flax. There were plenty of serfs in the Baltic to "ret" or break down the sticky fibers in the cut flax by constantly changing the fresh water in which it was soaking. Added to this was the reputation the Russians had for strict quality control.[50] Labor was far more expensive in the United States. No one had yet thought to use slaves to do what serfs did. American flax was cut and left on the ground to be "dew retted." There was no doubt about which method was better.

The lack of a domestic source of supply put the new nation at a distinct disadvantage. How could a merchant fleet put to sea if canvas was in short supply?

As for warships—and the United States was developing a navy even as Forten was mastering his trade—what would happen if a major sea power, like Britain or France, decided on a blockade? The United States would be starved of its vital supplies of Baltic canvas. How could the independence of the new nation be defended if its warships could not leave port because they had no sails?

Increasingly, American politicians and promoters would turn their attention to the problem, and their solutions to this critical shortage would involve the nation's slave population, but that was at least two decades away when James Forten began his apprenticeship. He had to learn how to judge the quality of the sailcloth that was available. As Bridges showed him, there were various quality checks a sailmaker could make, from the simple (forcing a fid into the canvas to see how easily the threads broke) to the complex (taking two pieces of the same grade made by different manufacturers, cutting a slit in each, knotting them together and hanging weights on the loose ends to see which 'gave' first).[51] He might be asked by a captain to recut a used sail. He needed to know when that could be done, and when the canvas was simply too badly worn to work with.

There were other supplies that needed to be bought for the loft, and always there was the possibility of being tricked into buying substandard goods. The boltrope—of the best Baltic hemp—that was sewn around the head, foot, and leeches of a sail had to be strong enough to take the strain, but not spun so tightly that it was difficult to sew. Again, the sailmaker learned by experience how to judge the quality of the cordage offered him by the operators of the various rope walks. The sewing twine had to be of the finest quality, whether it was for roping or seaming. The beeswax and turpentine that went into the concoction young James had boiled up in the sail loft for waxing the twine had to be the genuine articles. Smell and feel would help James Forten the apprentice sailmaker judge their quality.

As a young day laborer in the sail loft, Forten had sewn together "cloths" or panels of canvas as they were handed to him. He had watched sails being designed, but he had played no role in that process. Now, as an apprentice, an important part of his education was learning how to measure for sails, whether for a single sail or a whole suit.[52] For a vessel that Bridges worked on regularly that was relatively simple. A sailmaker kept a gore book with the measurements of each of the sails. He could fill an order for a new fore-topsail or mizzen-topgallant while the ship was still at sea and have it ready when she came into port.[53] Once he was promoted to foreman, James Forten did what any other aspiring craftsman would do: He compiled his own gore book for the vessels he had charge of.

When it was a question of fitting out a new vessel, or one that the sailmaker had not previously worked on, it was necessary to take precise measurements, and that entailed climbing aloft to gauge, for instance, the precise distance between the cleats on the yardarm to determine the width of the "head" of a topsail.[54] Of course, this task could be left to a seaman, who could climb the rigging and call down the measurements, but it made more sense for the sailmaker or his assistant to do it. After all, any mistakes would cost the firm money. Here Forten was invaluable to the older Bridges. He had been aloft on the *Commerce* as she pitched and rolled in the North Atlantic. Climbing the rigging of a vessel, with yardstick, pencil, and notebook at the ready, as she lay at anchor in the Delaware was child's play for an agile young man in his twenties. And he understood the nature of his task. The "depth," "hoist," or "drop" of a sail was of critical importance. Too little and it would be stretched so tightly it would rip. Too loose and it would "bag" or become slack, depriving the captain of the chance to use the wind to full advantage. Forten learned how to measure not only lengths and widths and diagonals but also how to calculate angles and make careful scale drawings for use in the loft.[55]

Once the sailmaker had his measurements, he could begin designing the sail. Forten learned the use of drafting tools. There were the small ones that were used for the paper plan, and the much larger ones used on the loft floor—a wooden square with legs six feet long, a cord with a pencil at one end, a tape line, and a yard stick. The scale drawing would be made on paper and carefully tacked to the drawing board. The design would then be transferred full-scale to the floor of the loft, drawn out in chalk, and awls driven into the floor at strategic points like huge dressmaker's pins, with sewing twine stretched from one to another to mark out the pattern. In all stages of design the sailmaker had to factor in the allowances for seams and "tabling" (the hem that ran all around the sail and strengthened it so the boltrope could be sewn on). With all these allowances, the sail as it was drawn on the loft floor would be significantly larger than the finished sail. With the sail chalked out, the craftsman would draw in the corners ("tacks," "clews," or "earings" according to their position or the type of sail). The corners would then be marked by driving "prickers" (wooden-handled spikes some six to ten inches in length) into the floor of the loft. The sailmaker would also mark the position of linings, patches, and various other fittings.[56]

Courses were cut straight across at head and foot, but all the sails above them were cut with a "roach" in the foot. In other words, the cloths had to be carefully cut and assembled so that the lower edge of the sail curved upward at the center. The center cloths in the sail would be shorter than those at the sides or leeches. The curve, or roach, would be drawn in on the loft floor, as would the "gore," the slopewise angle cut in the leeches of a sail to shape it. In working out the gore one could use gore tables, like those compiled by English sailmaker David Steel, but Steel himself admitted that for some gores "no strict rule can be given; they can only be determined by the judgment of the sailmaker."[57]

Eventually the bolts of canvas, each a standard width of 24 inches, would be unrolled in strips on the floor, cut with a knife (scissors, so it was believed, damaged the weave), and marked to indicate where each panel belonged in the composition of the sail.[58] Because several sails were probably being made in the loft at the same time, it was necessary to avoid confusion. A sail might well be larger than the available floor space. In that case it was designed in one piece in a scale drawing, laid down in units, and then assembled. Each section would be meticulously set out in the plan.[59] No sail, however small, was made out of just one piece of canvas. In fact, it would have reduced the sail's strength if it had been. It was the seams joining the various cloths together that helped give a sail its strength.

In designing any sail, and especially in looking over the entire sail plan for a new vessel, a sailmaker had to ask himself a series of questions. What use would a particular sail be put to? What was the overall size of the vessel, and how long might she remain at sea? What weather conditions might she encounter? This was especially important as Philadelphia merchants ventured into the China trade. A sail that was to withstand a typhoon in the South China Sea might need to be constructed differently from a sail that was expected to cope with a freezing gale in the North Atlantic. However it was treated, canvas retained water, and that water could freeze in cold weather, making the sails more difficult to handle. The action of salt and sunlight hastened the deterioration of the canvas, as did the leaching out of its natural oils. Natural fibers were highly susceptible to mildew, and seldom did a sail last longer than five years.[60] And then there was the issue of the efficiency of the whole sail plan. It was a great advantage if a sailmaker had an aptitude for mathematics, especially geometry. With that knowledge, he could determine both the center of gravity of a sail and the "center of effort" of the entire sail plan—"the point in which, if a single force were applied equally, and directly opposed to the force of the wind, it would destroy its effect, or produce the same result as when uniformly distributed."[61] Top-heavy or badly placed sails could put a vessel at risk and would certainly impede her progress. Again, practical knowledge of how sails handled under different conditions was crucial, for then the sailmaker could combine theory and practice. A master sailmaker also needed to be a competent rigger. True, a rigger would rig the vessel, but the sailmaker had to know what would happen to his sails at the hands of the rigger and his journeymen.

Once a sail had been cut, and the tabling neatly creased with a seam rubber (a wooden tool rather like a chisel but without a sharp point), the journeymen and apprentices would set to work sewing one cloth to another.[62] Each seam was double-stitched. When one row of stitching was finished, it would be smoothed down and the second row of stitching done.

With plenty of orders on hand—and Robert Bridges was one of the most successful sailmakers in the city—the sail loft was a hive of activity. Suppliers and ships' captains would be in and out all day long. As for the work force, several dozen men and boys might be employed in the loft at any one time. Some would be apprentices and others journeymen who had completed their apprenticeship but had not yet found the means to open their own lofts. A good number would be sailors. When a loft was particularly busy it was usual to hire sailors, most of whom had a basic knowledge of how to sew canvas, to do some of the simpler tasks. These men were paid by the yard. They needed to be able to sew quickly and neatly. Every different kind of workplace had its own peculiar sounds, and the sounds of the sail loft were quite distinctive. Accompanying the constant buzz of conversation was the clicking of metal on metal as the men used their palms to push their needles through the canvas.

As a sail grew, it became more and more unwieldy, and required more skilled attention. A big square main-course for a ship would bear the brunt of the wind. It needed to be made of thick canvas, no. 1 or 2, and could easily comprise thirty separate cloths, with a middle band, reef bands, leech pieces, and buntline cloths.[63] The more modest mizzen royal, which bore less strain and could be made of far lighter no. 8 canvas, was composed of half a dozen or more cloths.[64]

When the basic sail had been assembled, the real work of making it function properly began. Different parts of a sail needed additional strengthening. The sailmaker might have his men reinforce the flat seam with a middle seam done in a "sticking" stitch.[65] He had to add linings to the leeches and the middle points of sails to help them withstand the elements and the constant chafing they would undergo once they were bent to the masts and yards. Linings were usually made from the same bolts of canvas used for the sail. They had to "give" in exactly the same way. Even on relatively calm days at sea, chafing was a constant problem. Sails would flap and rub against the rigging. Chafing gear was intended to remedy this. The sailmaker would judge from the various sails he had repaired where a new sail was likely to sustain the most damage. He would design chafing gear, construct it from canvas, rope, spun-yarn, marlin, or leather, and sew it on to the sail.[66] Strong wrists and fingers were essential. A sailmaker could be sewing through as many as a dozen thicknesses of canvas with tablings, linings, patches, and chafing gear.[67]

Then there was the ropework. The first stage was the addition of reef points and reef bands—three and occasionally four bands—to square sails. These rows of carefully worked strings or laces would be used to reduce or increase the extent of a sail as the wind varied. In a gale, for instance, no captain wanted his sails fully extended; they would make the vessel unwieldy and even overset her. His crew would have to go aloft to tie all or part of each square sail to the yard using the reef points. When the storm subsided, the command would be given to "out reefs" and the weary crew would go aloft again to unfasten the reef points. Working on reef bands and points, Forten knew from personal experience how they would be used on shipboard.

It was the boltrope sewn around the leeches of a sail that gave it its shape and transformed it from a two-dimensional to a three-dimensional object. Roping was a highly skilled job. As Robert Kipping observed in his treatise on sailmaking: "Many a well-cut sail is spoiled by the roping."[68] One had to know what weight of rope to use, what thickness of twine to sew it on with, and how much of a twist to put in it. Again, there were tables one could use—Kipping's treatise included them—but the master sailmaker knew by instinct and experience what was wanted.

There was more to be done than measuring the boltrope and sewing it on. As Kipping noted, in preparing the boltrope the sailmaker would need to splice different pieces of rope together and protect portions of it by "worming" (filling the spaces between the strands with marline), "parceling" (wrapping strips of old canvas around the rope), and "serving" (tightly wrapping marline around the strips of canvas).[69]

There were cringles and earings to be added—loops worked in the boltrope by doubling it back on itself. They would be used for fastening the end of a line and hauling the sail up to the yard. There were grommets to be inserted into the sail for lines and fittings. The sailmaker made the grommet, a small wreath worked in rope. He carefully worked a hole in the canvas by inserting a stabber or pegging-awl into the weave, and pushed in the grommet, using a fid to stretch it and ensure it retained its shape. He then stitched around it, in effect creating something that resembled a large buttonhole.

The task of completing a suit of sails for an oceangoing ship could keep a team of sailmakers employed for many weeks. Thousands of square feet of canvas and many hundreds of yards of rope would be used. The sails were the most expensive fitting on the vessel and arguably the most crucial. "The stretching of sails when only natural fiber cloths were used was most important. Many sailmakers insisted on being the first to hoist the new sails, and gave strict instructions on how the sails were to be run in. Otherwise they might not accept any responsibility whatever."[70] The true test of the quality of a particular loft's work would come not when the sails were bent to the yards but when the ship returned from Europe or Asia with her sails intact and wearing well. That was the sailmaker's most valuable advertisement.

IN THE THIRTEEN years he trained him, Robert Bridges taught James Forten to work with a wide variety of rigs—schooners (for the vital trade in flour and wheat with the West Indies), brigs for coasting, oceangoing square-riggers for the trade with Europe—in fact, with just about any vessel, large or small, that required sails. He needed to know how to make or repair all the types of sails that might come his way, from a sloop's save-all topsail to a flying jib, a skyscraper, a royal staysail, and a storm mizzen. A new sail or rig, one the sailmaker had not seen before, presented a professional challenge. Contemporary sailmakers are not above taking a sail to pieces and reassembling it to discover the trade secrets of a rival in a distant port. The sailmakers of Forten's day were probably no different from their twenty-first-century successors.

Forten learned to make more items than conventional sails. Like other sailmakers, he would be expected to know how to measure for and manufacture windsails. In an era before air conditioning, these devices were essential for shipboard ventilation. Windsails were large canvas tubes that were given their shape by wooden hoops sewn into the canvas. At the top of each windsail would be canvas wings to direct the air flow. At sea, particularly in hot climates, the windsails would be lowered through the hatches into the hold to provide air for both men and cargo.[71] Smoke sails were another item in the sailmaker's repertoire. They were canvas sails hung near the forecastle to prevent the smoke from the galley chimney from coming aft. Sailmakers also made awnings, sometimes with curtains, to be stretched over the decks to protect crew and cargo from the elements. They made tarpaulins to keep victuals dry when they were being transported in small boats to the ship and stored on deck in the boats, and hammock cloths to protect hammocks from water damage when they were folded into the hammock nettings during the day.[72] Bridges taught Forten how to make canvas "coats" to protect the masts and rudder. There were other canvas items that were not intended for shipboard use. Sailmakers made tents, large and small. Forten would even try his hand at a piano cover for an esteemed customer and canvas bags for the city's volunteer soldiers during the War of 1812. In short, if something could be made from canvas, a sailmaker would try to make it.

As he came to play a more prominent role in the loft's dealings with masters and owners of vessels, James Forten engaged in professional exchanges. Sailmakers and captains had their own ideas about exactly how a sail should be cut, sewn together, or tabled. How much "bag" or "belly" should be allowed in this sail? How should that sail be bent to the yard? Could an old sail be reroped or a new reef band added? How much "peak" should there be in a fore-and-aft sail? What looked good didn't always handle well. How low should the clew on a jib be?[73] It was in his conversations with masters and shipowners, all of them white men, that James Forten seized the opportunity to show that he knew his craft, that Bridges had taught him well, and that he would prove a worthy successor.

The partnership between Robert Bridges and James Forten was a mutually productive one. Bridges taught Forten all he knew, and introduced him to the merchants and shipowners who gave the firm its commissions. In return, Forten contributed an important perspective to Bridges's business. Bridges had probably never been to sea. Forten had, in peace and in war. He had learned a great deal about handling canvas under sail. He understood, for instance, that sails were often split as they were being reefed. He knew, in a way Bridges could not, the difficulties of working a vessel in different weather conditions, in gales, against adverse tides, when the ship was in danger of being run ashore or overset because her sail area was too great. He had also seen much larger vessels than Bridges had ever set eyes on. As she sailed up the Thames to her mooring, the *Commerce* had been dwarfed by 700-ton monsters employed in the East India trade. Ships of that size were simply not seen in American ports in the 1780s and 1790s.[74] Above all, James Forten understood the rigors of a sailor's life. He knew about canvas as someone who worked with it on the loft floor and in the rigging of a trans-Atlantic trader. In the words of one Royal Navy captain, a man after Forten's heart because he was interested in the better design of sails:

> Some well-meaning People might be apt to suppose that the honest Tars, as they call them, are fond of Reefing the Courses on a dark Stormy Night, when the Ship might be Rolling the Yard Arms under Water, and perhaps consider it as one of the favorite amusements of a Sea Life, particularly on a Lee Shore in a Gale of Wind; but what would be their opinion . . . if they were themselves admitted to partake of the Diversion, and favored with an Outside Birth [*sic*] on the Yard?[75]

James Forten was a successful sailmaker in large part because he had been a sailor.

He was interested in developments in his craft, and one of the stories often told about him is that he was an inventor. That may or may not have been true. According to Anna Julia Cooper, who apparently relied on the work of white abolitionist author Lydia Maria Child, Forten "invented an improvement in the management of sails the patent for which netted him a substantial income as it rapidly came into general use."[76] Unfortunately, there is nothing to substantiate this. During the late eighteenth and early nineteenth centuries there were many refinements being developed in the making and managing of sails, both to improve the handling of a vessel and to cut down the appalling loss of life resulting from such routine operations as reefing topsails by having men "lay out" on the yards to reef them by hand.[77] Forten may have studied a certain problem of sailmaking or sail-handling and devised a new technique or piece of machinery, but if he did he never secured a patent for it. No patent was registered to him, to Bridges, or to the firm of Willing and Francis, who became his patrons after Bridges retired.[78]

In 1792, in a singular act of trust in his foreman, or perhaps a sense that he was making a good investment, Robert Bridges purchased a house for James Forten. On November 13, 1792, he paid £250 Pennsylvania money to Emanual and Barbara Priest for a two-story brick house and a lot on the south side of Shippen Street, near George Street, in Southwark, about four blocks from the sail loft. The understanding was that Bridges was buying the property "for and on account of . . . James Forten," and that "on his paying the said sum he the said Robert Bridges . . . would . . . convey the same . . . premises unto the said James Forten."[79] James Forten had thus secured a home for himself and his family, while Bridges had bound his foreman more closely to his business. Presumably there was some informal arrangement for the purchase price to be paid back in installments. There was never any doubt in the tax-collector's mind as to who owned the property. Forten paid all the taxes on it from 1793 onward.[80] The house at 50 Shippen Street was modest enough and probably rather crowded. It sheltered Forten, his mother, his sister, her husband (when he was not at sea), and the growing brood of young Dunbars. Still, crowded and modest, it put James Forten into a class apart. In a city where many working men and women, black and white, remained renters all their lives, he was a homeowner.

Southwark, one of the city's unincorporated districts, was growing rapidly. Its population rose from 5500 in 1790 to 9500 in 1800. Most of its inhabitants were white, but at least 200 were free people of color and in 1790 twenty-nine were slaves. A decade later there was not a single slave in Southwark West, the district where Forten lived.[81] Many of the residents of Southwark were transients, either immigrants from Europe or migrants from various states. The neighborhood might be less desirable than Philadelphia itself. "Houses were more ramshackle, streets were less often paved, public water pumps were scarcer, and garbage collection was less common, while doctors, pharmacists, churches, and charities were all rarer than in the city proper."[82] However, for now, it suited Forten. It was the center of Philadelphia's shipbuilding industry. Some of his neighbors were, like himself, craftsmen in the maritime trades. Others were sailors, at least a few of whom would go on to become masters of vessels. Southwark was "home" and would remain so for the next fourteen years.

In 1798 Robert Bridges prepared to retire from business. He was fifty-eight years old, he had made ample provision for his family, and he could look to enjoy the years remaining to him in comfort. For his trusted foreman and chosen successor everything had been leading up to this—the careful training he had received, the growing dependence on him by Bridges in the day-to-day running of the loft, the introductions to old established customers.

What actually changed hands when the firm of Robert Bridges and Co. became James Forten and Co.? Obviously there was the gear in the loft, the tools that belonged to the firm rather than to individual workmen, the stocks of canvas and twine, beeswax and cordage. Then, of course, there were Bridges's gore books and the goodwill he had established in more than three decades in business. As for the loft itself, Bridges did not own that. It was in a building owned by the mercantile firm of Willing and Francis, and they leased it to him. Such arrangements were not uncommon, and shippers who had shares in as many vessels as Willing and Francis did could appreciate the usefulness of having a sailmaker, a rigger, and the like as tenants.[83]

So much for the property that changed hands, but what of Bridges's work force? When the two dozen workers in the loft realized the business was about to be taken over by Forten, they split into two camps. In the case of the apprentices, he received what amounted to a vote of confidence when "they all, with one consent, agreed to take [him] as their new master." Their indentures had been drawn up with Robert Bridges. He was to impart to them the mysteries of his craft. Now they were judging James Forten skilled enough to train them. And there were other young men eager to indenture themselves to him. By

1805 he had twenty-five apprentices, the majority of them white, working in the sail loft.[84]

The situation with regard to the journeymen was different, though. The apprentices had invested long years with Bridges learning their craft. The journeymen had finished their period of indenture. They were free to come and go as they wished, and seek other employers if they scorned the idea of working for a man of color. For them, issues of race were intertwined with questions of financial solvency. Forten had been supervising them for some time as Bridges gradually loosened his ties to the business, but it was Bridges who paid their wages. What they were dubious about was Forten's ability to retain Bridges's customers, get more customers, keep the sail loft a going concern, and pay them on a regular basis. After all, there was no other economic enterprise in the city of this size and complexity being run by a black man. If they feared a loss of status at the notion of being given orders by a man of color, what they feared far more was that their wages would not be forthcoming.

Robert Bridges came to the rescue, although how he did so is not clear. Perhaps he won over the journeymen with a ringing endorsement of Forten and assurances of full order books and more orders to come. Perhaps he arranged a loan for Forten. A friend of Forten's observed simply that "the person of whom he learned his trade, pleased with his intelligence, honesty, and enterprise, enabled him to hire for long terms, and make punctual payments. This system gradually obviated his difficulties."[85]

Then there was the patronage of Willing and Francis. Probably because they had already employed Bridges and knew the quality of the work his loft produced, the partners gave Forten some of his first orders.[86] This was indeed a coup, and there is ample evidence to substantiate the crucial role Willing and Francis played in Forten's career. His obituary in the *North American* says he "was established in business by Thomas Willing, and afterwards patronized by Willing and Francis."[87] There was also Forten's very personal acknowledgment of thanks. He named his third son Thomas Willing Francis Forten.

The partners in the firm were invaluable patrons to have, and their acknowledgment that James Forten was a worthy successor to Robert Bridges undoubtedly earned him more orders. Thomas Willing, one of the city's richest and most astute men of business, became president of the newly organized Bank of North America in 1781. A decade later he was a director of Alexander Hamilton's Bank of the United States, serving as its president until he retired in 1807. Willing was in partnership with various men over the years, including financier Robert Morris, but eventually he became the patriarch of a family firm. In 1794 Thomas Willing Francis, Willing's nephew, married Willing's daughter, Dorothy, and the firm of Willing and Francis was born. When Willing's son, Thomas Mayne Willing, joined the firm, it became Willings and Francis. Thomas Willing may have been a model for James Forten. He believed that "the proper object of a reasonable man [is] the pursuit of riches."

Wealth had come to him because of his "steady application" to every endeavor, his "civil and respectful deportment to all fellow citizens, and an honest and upright conduct in every transaction of life."[88] That Willing, like many other Philadelphia merchants, had traded in slaves before the Revolution Forten knew or guessed. That he was a friend and patron Forten never forgot.

ROBERT BRIDGES DIED on January 18, 1800. James Forten almost certainly attended his funeral at Christ Church and probably closed the sail loft for a few hours as a mark of respect. When Bridges's will was read there was no mention of his former apprentice.[89] Most likely Forten expected none. Robert Bridges had done what he could for him. He had treated him, if not as a son, at least as a trusted junior partner and a friend. James Forten never forgot that. Now he was on his own, to make his way as best he could among Philadelphia's master craftsmen and "gentlemen of the pave." Would they regard him as Bridges had done, as a skilled craftsman and a knowledgeable man of business who happened to be of African descent? Or would they see him first and foremost as a man of color, an interloper in their midst? Time alone would tell.

4

"A GENTLEMAN OF THE PAVE"

TRYING TO PUT virtually any aspect of James Forten's business career into perspective is like trying to assemble a jigsaw puzzle with many of the most important pieces missing and only a vague sense of what the finished picture should look like. The paper trail is woefully inadequate. The records of the firm of James Forten and Sons were presumably destroyed when the sail loft was sold. The family carefully preserved personal correspondence—there is a touching account in his granddaughter's journal of her poring over his letters and reflecting on the high regard in which he was held—but receipts, ledgers, rent books, and so forth were most likely consigned to the kitchen fire or the sail loft stove.[1]

Regrettable though the loss of Forten's business papers is, some pieces of the puzzle have survived. There are the records of some of his customers. There are stray letters that people found worth keeping for one reason or another. One recipient noted on the back of a letter that he had kept it as a curiosity because "it was from a Negro-man; —a Negro-gentleman, I may say. He was in possession of a fortune made by his own industry."[2] Forten bought and sold real estate, and those transactions generated deeds and mortgages. He sued people and so, buried in the dockets of the Philadelphia Court of Common Pleas, the District Court, and the Pennsylvania Supreme Court are at least the outlines of those cases. The dockets provide names, and the censuses and directories provide biographical data to attach to those names. Tax records indicate who some of Forten's tenants were. The wills Forten witnessed and those in which he was appointed an executor offer additional insight into his reputa-

tion. Who trusted him enough to have him take care of their estate and safeguard the rights of their heirs? Finally, though the records of *his* sail loft have
not survived, those of several other lofts up and down the eastern seaboard
have. Allowing for different local and regional conditions, and for the very
significant fact that none of those lofts was operated by a man of color, we can
learn something of how a successful sailmaker ran his business.

ANY ASSESSMENT OF Forten's career has to take into account the economic back-
drop against which he was struggling to succeed. It is fair to say that the economy
of the nation and of Philadelphia in the years from his takeover of the sail loft
to his retirement was volatile. Good times were all too often followed by sharp
downturns. He began his career with Robert Bridges in the midst of economic
uncertainty. He ended it with the nation's banking system in a shambles and
many businesses fighting to stave off failure. On a local and a regional level, he
witnessed the eclipsing of Philadelphia by her rivals. The city in which he had
been born was the second largest in the British Empire. By the time of his
death, three quarters of a century later, it was far from a commercial backwater,
but its heyday was over.

    Some problems, of course, were beyond mere human control. Anyone in-
volved in the maritime trades knew Philadelphia was the victim of topography
and climate. Although a seaport, it is a hundred miles from the ocean. Ships'
captains had to navigate up and down the Delaware, and even for experienced
river pilots that was no easy task. Because Philadelphia was so far from the sea,
it tended to become ice-bound. One never knew from year to year when, if, or
how severely the Delaware would freeze. In February 1815 Forten described
to a friend a picturesque winter scene, with the river iced over so thickly it
could bear the weight of sleds.[3] In early 1818 it was closed for almost a month.
It iced up again at year's end, but the following winter it was relatively clear. In
1821 both the Delaware and the Schuylkill froze, and shipping literally came to
a standstill. The Delaware froze to such a depth in the winter of 1823–24 that
Philadelphians were able to roast an ox on it. The winter of 1825 was relatively
mild, with Valentine's Day compared to a balmy day in May. In 1826 Philadelphians were skating on the Delaware on February 3, but the river was safe for
shipping by February 8.[4]

    The knowledge that the Delaware could and did freeze combined with
other factors, such as the Atlantic hurricane season and the course of the Gulf
Stream, to influence sailing patterns. Clearances rose in late spring and early
summer, declined around midsummer, and rose again in the fall, peaking in
December as ships' captains escaped before the ice trapped them. Of course,
when a vessel was kept in port by adverse weather conditions that might be the
ideal time for an overhaul. New York sailmaker Stephen Allen recalled that
"the fall and winter months . . . was always the most busy season."[5] Very likely
the same situation prevailed in Philadelphia.

So much for nature. What of economics and politics? During the months when the Founding Fathers were working behind closed doors in the Pennsylvania state house, ostensibly amending the Articles of Confederation but in reality hammering out a new constitution, James Forten was some ten blocks away on South Wharves mastering the complexities of his trade in Robert Bridges's sail loft. An avid newspaper reader, someone who liked to keep abreast of the latest developments, he was well aware that the nation's economy was in crisis. He knew the flag of the new republic merited little respect abroad, and that boded ill for American traders. He had heard of Shays' Rebellion, the uprising of financially hard-pressed farmers in Massachusetts, and the rumblings of discontent elsewhere. He could see for himself the shuttered stores of failed businesses in Philadelphia. Would the new framework of national government he heard talked about in the streets and on the wharves bring stability? He had every reason to hope that it would.

Good government and a promise of security at home and abroad was generally pleasing to Philadelphia's merchants and craftsmen. They had had enough of uncertainty. It was bad for trade. In the short term their hopes for peace and prosperity seemed justified. In 1790 Philadelphia exported more than any other port in the new nation. Her rich hinterland provided many commodities, most notably wheat and flour, to fill the holds of her vessels.[6] Philadelphia was a bustling, prosperous city, the capital of the state and the nation. The citizens' sense of confidence was displayed in bricks and mortar. Writing to her father in London in 1792, a young Philadelphia Quaker observed: "[T]hee would hardly know the upper ends of Market, Chestnut, Walnut, and Arch Streets, they are so built up with new houses—a Theatre, a Library, a Philosophic Hall and a Court House have all been built within a small distance from the State House, and they are building a large house for the President G. Washington, far up Market Street."[7]

The devastating yellow fever epidemic of 1793 brought commerce and construction to a halt, but Philadelphia soon bounced back, weathering the 1793 outbreak and further outbreaks over the next decade. The removal of the state capital to Lancaster and then to Harrisburg was a severe blow, as was the loss of the federal capital, but Philadelphia had always been more than an administrative center. Waterborne trade was its lifeblood, and during much of the 1790s trade was flourishing. For Robert Bridges and his foreman times were good. Plenty of vessels entering and leaving the port meant full order books. "Scarcely a vessel which had made the long run from Europe, Africa or the West Indies, not to mention the Orient, did not require reprovisioning, refitting or repairs of some kind."[8] And there were vessels being built in Philadelphia yards that needed new suits of sails. Shipbuilding had declined immediately after the Revolution, as Britain, France, Spain, and the Netherlands had all passed regulations forbidding their nationals from buying American-built ships and instead ordering them to get their vessels from within their respective empires. Prices of American ships had fallen precipitously until a domestic market emerged. However, what really saved American shipbuilding was the outbreak of war in Europe. Europe needed American produce, and much of that produce reached Europe in American-built ships.[9]

At least in the early 1790s trade was good. Traditional markets were kept open and new ones explored. Cuba remained a major trading partner through much of the time Forten was in business. Philadelphia shippers took to Havana and other ports such as Matanzas and Cárdenas flour, meat, fruit, vegetables, fish, and a range of manufactured goods. In Cuba they loaded up with sugar and specie.[10] Despite British attempts to keep American traders out of their West Indian ports, they found their way there, as they did to Saint Domingue before, after, and even during the great slave uprising. Of course, one had to keep abreast of the rapidly changing diplomatic situation. A once friendly port could become decidedly less welcoming and more interested in seizing a foreign vessel, cargo, and crew, but, at least for the shipowners, who often stayed safely at home, the returns warranted the risks.

The Philadelphians followed the lead of the New Yorkers and entered the China trade. Between 1784 and 1804 as many as seven ships per year left Philadelphia for China. Bridges and Forten fitted out China traders, made extra sails for the year-long voyage, and did essential repairs as vessels limped back with valuable cargoes and badly worn sails.[11]

The economic picture was not one of unchecked growth, however. The economy experienced a series of upheavals, largely as a result of the European conflict. It stumbled in 1796, and Philadelphia's banks, like those elsewhere, began calling in loans. By 1797 the nation was in a depression, and it did not help that America seemed to be pitted against France in an undeclared naval war. The crisis deepened when Napoleon's forces took the major European entrepôts for American goods, Amsterdam and Leghorn, and threatened others, such as Hamburg and Bremen. American capital was tied up in those places and could not be transferred to London to settle bills of exchange, many of which were returned protested. There were also losses at sea. In just six weeks during the winter of 1796–97, 150 businesses in Philadelphia failed. They included that of merchant prince Robert Morris, who dragged down many smaller men whose interests were bound up with his.[12] Fortunately, recovery soon came.

In 1798, when James Forten assumed control of the sail loft, Philadelphia was slowly losing ground to New York. As yet, though, that trend was barely perceptible. It was certainly not apparent to anyone who took a stroll along the Delaware and observed the vessels from all over the globe moored there. Ships from France and the German Hanseatic ports rode at anchor alongside those from England and the Netherlands. In 1800 there were over 400 arrivals from American ports and more than 500 from overseas.[13] Many of those vessels came into port needing repairs to their sails, or even just extra canvas and twine for their stores. And new vessels were being built along the Delaware, resulting in orders for complete suits of sails.

By and large, his first eight or nine years in business were good ones for James Forten. The city's export trade reached all-time highs in 1806 and 1807.[14] That meant profits for anyone involved in the fitting-out of vessels. The sail loft was thriving, and Forten's role as a phenomenon, a successful black businessman, was soon well established. Wrote painter and dramatist William Dunlap to his wife while visiting the city in 1806: "In Philadelphia, where the emancipation of the Blacks originated[,] there are more free people of that colour than in any other place in the union. Most of them are degraded & vicious but there are many useful and respectable" individuals. He singled out "a rich sail maker, having many journimen & apprentices under him."[15]

Word of Forten's growing wealth and his reputation for probity spread. In 1807 a London journal, the *Monthly Repository of Theology and General Literature*, published *Brief Memoirs of the Life of Capt. Paul Cuffee*, prepared by the Delaware Society for Promoting the Abolition of Slavery. Annexed to the account of the remarkable career of Forten's New England friend were a few lines about Forten himself, although the authors managed to misspell his name.

> As a tribute due to merit it may be stated, that there is now resident at Philadelphia, James Torten, a man of colour, who received an education at the school established by the Society of Friends in that city, where he carries on the sail-making business with reputation to himself and satisfaction to his employers, and is engaged in that branch more extensively than any other person at Philadelphia. He possesses considerable property, acquired by his own industry . . . and is very much respected by the citizens generally.[16]

However, Forten's prosperity was tied to that of his home port, and in 1807 disaster loomed. Jefferson's embargo, the response to British and French assaults on neutral American vessels—assaults most shipowners accepted as the price of doing business—brought overseas trade to an abrupt halt. Foreign clearances from the port of Philadelphia were impressive before the embargo—617 in 1805, 730 in 1806, and 712 in 1807.[17] Now shipowners were obliged to employ their vessels in the far less profitable coasting trade. Their earnings plummeted and they skimped on items such as new sails and rigging. Shipyards stood idle as orders for new vessels were canceled. Ships were transformed overnight into worthless hulks. Sails rotted on masts and yards. James Forten could see his hard-won prosperity decaying with them.

There was a glimmer of hope in the spring of 1809 when Congress replaced the embargo with the Non-Intercourse Act, but since the act still forbade trade with Britain and France, America's two largest trading partners, recovery was a long way off. Not until May 1810, and the passage of Macon's Bill No. 2, which lifted virtually all restrictions on foreign trade, did things really begin to pick up. The easing of restrictions "changed sailing ships from liabilities to assets" almost overnight.[18] Merchants wanted them fitted out and ready for overseas voyages as soon as possible. James Forten and many more craftsmen along the waterfront began to hope that "good times" were back.

Two years later, in June 1812, the nation found itself embroiled in a second war with Great Britain. The conflict brought gains and losses for Philadelphians. During the War of 1812 there would not be the profits from privateering that shipowners and merchants had enjoyed during the Revolutionary War. In early 1813 the Royal Navy commenced a tight blockade of the Delaware, effectively closing the port of Philadelphia. With only 74 and 43 foreign arrivals, respectively, 1813 and 1814 were lean years.[19] However, there were other opportunities for profit. Philadelphia became a huge supply depot. Goods were channeled through the city, west to Pittsburgh, and from there to the armies in the Indiana Territory and on other battlefronts. In the early months of the war government money flowed into the city. The result was a real estate boom. Reportedly, more houses were built in the summer of 1814 than at any point in the city's history.[20] According to one merchant: "Real Estate in Town & Country has in general considerably advanced since the war. Lands are at least 1/3 higher & many plantations have sold for double what they would have brought three years ago."[21] James Forten had already begun making forays into the real estate market. Now he stood to reap substantial profits. However, problems lay ahead for him and for the rest of the business community.

By the fall of 1814 the boom had turned into a slump. The Bank of the United States had been dissolved in 1811, and across the nation a crop of local banks had sprung up to take its place. In 1814 alone forty-two banks received charters from the Pennsylvania legislature. In many cases they were unstable and underfunded. With news of the British advance on Washington and fears of an attack on Philadelphia, bank directors anticipated a run on specie. They agreed, effective August 30, 1814, to suspend specie payments. Banks across the state followed suit. To make matters worse, in November 1814 the government defaulted on the national debt.[22]

The latter stages of the war and its immediate aftermath saw a wave of business failures. James Forten was luckier or perhaps more prudent than many, although he referred to "the losses I have met with." Still, he was not above moralizing over the misfortunes of others. Merchant John James had been bedridden for ten weeks and was "threw greef almost worn to a skeleton." As Forten wrote a mutual friend: "[C]ould you have thought it that a man who a few years ago could command recorses to the amount of a hundred thousand Dollars, has not now nor cannot command anuff to subsist on . . . he has told me himself that he has been for weeks without a Dollar in his house, nor n[e]ither did he know w[h]ere to command one (wonderfull are thy afflictions o Lord)."[23]

Despite his losses, the end of the war saw James Forten firmly in control of his growing business empire. His sail loft was flourishing. He had real estate he could sell or rent out. He had money loaned at interest. Of course, like any man of business, he could become caught up in financial crises beyond his control, but he was cautious about overextending himself.

The postwar period brought economic upheavals to Philadelphia, as it did to communities large and small throughout the United States. Cheap British goods flooded the market. Inflation, and then the efforts of the banks to rein in the economy, led by the Second Bank of the United States, headquartered in Philadelphia, helped precipitate the Panic of 1819.[24]

The panic led to widespread bankruptcies. Land values in Pennsylvania plummeted from $150 an acre in 1815 to $35 per acre in 1820. In Philadelphia, during the worst of the crisis, over 1800 people languished in debtors' prison.[25] In this uncertain climate even the soundest firms could fail.

The steady decline of Philadelphia as a port and a shipowning and shipbuilding center continued. The trend was more noticeable than it had been before the war, but it could not as yet be described as dramatic or as a true crisis. Although foreign arrivals had decreased from the peak years of the 1790s, they still enriched the city and provided work for Forten and others in the maritime trades. Only three times between 1818 and 1830, for instance, did the number drop below 450.[26] The vast majority of the vessels entering from foreign ports were American-owned. Of foreign-owned vessels, the largest contingent came from Britain. In terms of destinations, Britain ranked first, closely followed by "British American possessions" and Cuba. By 1815 the once important China trade had dwindled to almost nothing. There had, however, been an overall increase in the coasting trade.[27] Forten worked not only on vessels that belonged to local merchants but on vessels from up and down the eastern seaboard, from the Caribbean, South America, and Europe.

By 1815 Philadelphia was of only "secondary importance" as a shipbuilding center. Its yards produced one vessel in 1816 and none at all in 1817.[28] Things eventually began to pick up, but they did so slowly. In 1824 Philadelphia took third place behind New York and Boston in tonnage owned by local merchants. By 1826 the city had slipped into fourth place behind Baltimore. That year Philadelphia yards turned out fifty-one vessels, most of them under a hundred tons.[29] Still, large or small, locally owned or not, vessels needed sails. There might be a preference for fitting out a vessel in her home port, but if she could not safely make the return voyage then repairs must be done in her port of call. As long as trade was coming into Philadelphia, James Forten had orders.

By the early 1820s some of the more perceptive of Philadelphia's merchants and politicians began to realize that their city was no longer the economic powerhouse it had once been, but why New York had forged ahead of Philadelphia they were not quite sure. In fact, there was no one easy explanation. It was a matter of topography, cooperation between businessmen and lawmakers, and a willingness to take chances. Although farther north than Philadelphia, the port of New York was very much closer to the open ocean and hence far less likely to ice up. Favorable legislation and marketing techniques won New York the bulk of British trade. Her shippers also took a calculated gamble and commenced a packet service with Liverpool in 1817. Vessels would leave on a regular day each month, regardless of whether their holds were full. They would not remain in port for days and even weeks awaiting more cargo. Merchants and passengers quickly realized they could rely on the packet service and that a sailing date constituted a firm commitment—weather permitting. Further packet services were soon operating to Le Havre and London. Not until 1821 did Thomas P. Cope begin a transatlantic packet service from Philadelphia.[30]

New York also increased its role in the coasting trade. The Erie Canal, completed in 1825, gave the city access to the West. Grain shipments flowed along the canal to New York and from there to points up and down the East Coast and abroad. Manufactured goods flowed back to the farmers. In 1829 Philadelphia struck back with the opening of the Chesapeake and Delaware Canal, but it was of limited use and very expensive to construct and operate. The Erie Canal had been built over far less challenging terrain.[31]

Despite the occasional upturn, Philadelphia's economy was far from sound during the 1820s and 1830s. There were recessions in 1824, 1829, and 1833. In 1829 the state of Pennsylvania literally ran out of money and the governor was obliged to ask financier Stephen Girard for a loan.[32] In 1837 an economic crisis swept the nation in the wake of President Jackson's war with the Second Bank of the United States. An avalanche of bank failures and business collapses swallowed up the fortunes of many thousands of people in trade and commerce. Lower down the socioeconomic ladder tens of thousands of workers found themselves unemployed. Not until 1842 did the situation improve. James Forten's last years in business were difficult ones, as trade declined and old customers went bankrupt. His sons found themselves struggling against almost insuperable odds to try to keep the firm solvent and their father's business empire intact. For James Forten and his sons the factor of race was clearly significant and no assessment of their careers can or should minimize the impact of prejudice in the calculation of commercial success or failure, but the Fortens were also members of Philadelphia's business community, and their fortunes rose and fell with the economy of the city and the nation.

BY THE 1830s James Forten's loft was a showplace of his industry and his values. Abolitionists, reformers, politicians, and sometimes the just plain curious came to call at South Wharves, intrigued by reports of Forten's wealth and the all-too-rare sight of a racially integrated work force presided over by a man of color. In 1834, for instance, the author of a piece in the *Anti-Slavery Record* visited James Forten in his place of business, which he noted occupied several adjoining lofts.

> [H]is workmen, twenty or thirty in number, were industriously at work. . . . All was order and harmony. . . . My friend took great delight in pointing out to me various improvements that he had introduced . . . and spoke very kindly of his workmen. Here was one who had been in his employ twenty years, who owned not a brick when he came, but now was the possessor of a good brick house; here was another who had been rescued from ruin. These were *white*

men, but not so all. As far as I can recollect, about one-half of them were colored. My friend remarked to me that both colors had thus been employed together for more . . . than 20 years, and always with the same peace and harmony which I then saw. "Here," said he, "you see what may be done and ought to be done in our country at large."[33]

Another visitor was fascinated by what he saw. "There appears to be the utmost order and regularity in conducting his business, and among his workmen." The loft was completely free of alcohol, and Forten proudly informed his guest "that he never drank a single glass in his life." The visitor was introduced to other black men in managerial jobs: foreman Joseph Waterford, "a colored gentleman, [who] has been with him twenty-five years," and James Forten's sons, James Jr. and Robert.[34]

That Forten was proud of what he had achieved, in terms of both wealth and racial harmony, was evident in the information his daughter, Sarah, passed on to white abolitionist Angelina Grimké in April 1837.

My Father bids me tell you that white and colored men have worked with him from his first commencement in business. One man (a white) has been with him nearly thirty seven years; very few of his hired men have been foreigners; nearly all are natives of this country; the greatest harmony and good feeling exists between them; he has usually 10 or twenty journeymen, one half of whom are white; but I am not aware of any white sailmaker who employs colored men; I think it should be reciprocal—do not you?[35]

Sarah was probably correct in her perception of employment practices. In 1827 thirty men sought incorporation as the Journeymen Sailmakers' Benevolent Society of Philadelphia. Membership was open to all "men of good morals . . . of the full age of twenty-one years [who] have served a regular apprenticeship in the sailmaking business or are considered journeymen sailmakers."[36] A check of the names against the censuses and directories indicates that no black men were members.

The glowing reports in the antislavery press and from Forten's reform-minded friends are useful, but they have their limitations. To begin with, almost all of them date from the 1830s, the last decade of his career. They tell us little about his early struggles, his search for customers, or his interactions with his workers. They also reveal little of day-to-day life on the Philadelphia waterfront. We see James Forten at the height of his prosperity, preparing to retire and hand over the business to his sons. We do not see the ambitious young craftsman, competing with white men for commissions, buying supplies, confronting technological and commercial challenges, fighting to succeed in a market where there was no shortage of rivals, and where failure was an ever-present possibility. It is that aspect of James Forten's life that must be teased out of a mass of evidence, ranging from stray comments in journals to newspaper articles, ships' papers, bills, and receipts. Only then do his achievements as a black "gentleman of the pave" really begin to emerge.

Life in the sail loft was seldom dull. Philadelphia merchant Abraham Ritter managed to convey in his reminiscences a lively sense of the waterfront at the time James Forten was starting out on his own. Ritter might have romanticized about some things. The ships were "floating castles of the mighty deep," and every sailor was a "merry mariner," but some things ring true. He noted the presence of black longshoremen, "the swarthy operator[s] of the derrick." He also captured the mingling of black and white voices, with "the negro song at the capstan or the derrick, echo[ing] from wharf to wharf."[37] There was the feeling of excitement, for fortunes rode quite literally on the safe and timely arrival of a vessel. "The booming of a 'big gun'" five miles downriver "was the sure announcement" that an East Indiaman had been sighted. "And men and boys, from all quarters, flew to the wharf to see the smoke and the flash as the 'big ship' turned the point, and inquire 'What ship is that?'"[38]

There were also the hazards of life on the waterfront. Men fell from the rigging, lost limbs in horrific accidents, and were killed as derricks collapsed or heavy loads fell and crushed them. As Ritter and Forten knew all too well, drownings were distressingly frequent, for few people could swim, even if they were sober when they missed their footing and fell into the Delaware. "Being on the banks of the river, [Forten] had several opportunities of exercising benevolence at the risk of his life. With his *own* hands, he saved twelve persons from drowning."[39] Perhaps he was a strong swimmer, or perhaps he kept a small boat for getting out to vessels he was working on and used that on occasion to save lives. Several of his rescues took place during the winter months, when he risked hypothermia as well as drowning. On May 9, 1821, Joseph Crukeshank, president of the Humane Society of Philadelphia, presented him with a certificate in recognition of his heroism.[40] Forten was justifiably proud of it. He had it framed and hung in his sitting-room. When English reformer Edward Abdy dined with the Fortens in 1834 and asked about the certificate, James Forten told him he would not take a thousand dollars for it.[41]

James Forten spent much of his working life, and much of his leisure time, in the company of sailors. Some of his journeymen and apprentices, black and white, had been to sea. He hired sailors to work in the loft when he had a lot of orders on hand. The average sailor could sew a straight seam in canvas, even if he could not be trusted with more complex tasks, and for a man ashore between voyages, payment of a few cents per yard for sewing canvas was better than no pay at all. Forten had been to sea and he had family members who were sailors. He worshipped alongside sailors and their families at St. Thomas's African Episcopal Church. His sense of sympathy was something a sailor in trouble could rely on. Any sailor, irrespective of race, faced hardships, low pay, and brutal treatment. An African-American sailor faced the additional danger of enslavement.[42]

In March 1817, Forten wrote his old friend Captain Paul Cuffe about a young West African, Cuffee Johnson. Johnson had sailed with Cuffe and then shipped out of Boston on a brig bound for Charleston. The captain of the brig took him to New Orleans and sold him into slavery. By chance, his master had brought Johnson to Philadelphia, but how long they would be in town Forten had no idea. The young man claimed his papers were on file in New Bedford. Could Cuffe help?[43]

When *he* was in trouble, William Wright turned to James Forten as someone he believed had both the inclination and the ability to help him. In July 1822 Wright sailed out of Philadelphia on the brig *George*, captained by James Gaul, for a voyage to the West Indies. They were on their way back in October, but when the vessel called at New Castle, in the slave state of Delaware, Gaul put Wright in prison, "he says for Safe keeping." Wright, sensibly enough, was taking no chances. He feared Gaul meant to sell him. As soon as he could secure pen and paper, he composed a brief note explaining his plight to "Mr. James Fortune, Sailmaker," of Philadelphia. Perhaps a sympathetic fellow sailor took it upriver for him. In his estimation of Forten's readiness to take his part Wright was correct. Forten passed the note on to Pennsylvania Abolition Society officer Isaac Barton, and Wright was restored to his family.[44]

James Forten also counted captains and shipowners among his friends. Again and again in his letters he referred to a particular individual, such as iron merchant Thomas Ash, or to unnamed friends among the seafaring fraternity who supplied him with news of happenings in distant ports. From his many acquaintances Forten amassed a wealth of information about the world of business in general, which enabled him to make sound decisions about the effective running of the sail loft and about his various investments. Again, he was following in Robert Bridges's footsteps. Bridges had impressed upon him the importance of listening to his customers when they spoke about matters beyond sails.

What of James Forten's work force? From the first he determined it would be a racially integrated one. He retained Bridges's workers, all of whom were white. He also employed white men who came to him in search of apprenticeships. He paid his workers and he expected them to defer to him in certain matters. That deference went far beyond arriving for work on time and sober, and laboring faithfully at their assigned tasks. If Forten's assessment of his influence is to be believed, he governed other aspects of their lives as well. For instance, he considered himself perfectly justified in telling his white journeymen how to vote.[45]

It would be valuable to know more about these white men who labored for James Forten, accepted his pay, and followed his orders, even to the extent of voting for political candidates of his choosing. Unfortunately, the available records tell us almost nothing about Forten's white workers, other than that there *were* white men in his employ, and that they interacted well with him and with his black workers. Names would have been useful for determining precisely who worked for him and for how long. Sadly, that is an aspect of James Forten's career that we simply cannot recover.

The records are more telling about his African-American employees. Some were family members—his nephews, his niece's husband, his sons. Others were friends, or the sons or brothers of friends. Pennsylvania-born Charles Anthony, whom Forten had known since infancy, eventually collaborated with another sailmaker to buy the Forten loft. Like Forten, his parents, Charles Sr. and Pleasant, had attended St. Paul's Church back in the days before the founding of St. Thomas's African Episcopal Church.[46] Delaware native James Cornish, a longtime employee, was the younger brother of Samuel E. Cornish, a Presbyterian minister, newspaper editor, and one of Forten's closest friends in the 1820s and 1830s.

Forten's ties with black New England shipper Paul Cuffe and the members of his extended family brought two new apprentices to the loft. When Cuffe's daughter, Ruth, married New Bedford merchant Richard Johnson, they both had children from previous marriages, and when it came time to find good trades for their various offspring, they contacted a man they both knew well, James Forten. Ezra Rothschild Johnson and his stepbrother, Shadrach Howard, were sent to Philadelphia to board with the Forten family and learn the "mysteries" of sailmaking.[47] On Ezra Johnson's death decades later, the editor of the *Pacific Appeal*, who had spent his youth in Philadelphia, wrote: "[W]e vividly recollect him [Johnson] as one of the many young colored men who were sent from the surrounding cities to learn the sailmaking trade with the late James Forten. After learning that trade, he returned to New Bedford, and subsequently devoted his attention to fitting out whaling ships, chandlery, etc."[48]

In an obituary of James Forten's longtime foreman, Joseph Waterford, readers of the *Pacific Appeal* got a review of his life, as well as a brief account of what it was like to be an apprentice "in the great sail-making establishment of James Forten . . . the best representative business establishment of colored men in the United States." The loft was described as a sort of professional academy. "The best class of colored youth of Philadelphia and surrounding States were sent to this firm."[49] As for Waterford, he had done well, and in time his son, Joseph Jr., had joined him in the Forten loft.[50]

As for other black journeymen and apprentices, in 1838 the *Register of Trades* listed nineteen African-American sailmakers in Philadelphia. Three were members of the Forten family—James and his two eldest sons. Of the remaining sixteen, most worked for Forten. Only one, James Crummill, clearly did not; his place of business is listed as Almond Street Wharf. A number of the black sailmakers lived fairly close to one another. Charles Anthony lived at 23 Little Pine and Joseph Waterford and his family lived nearby at no. 8. (Little Pine ran from Seventh to Eighth Streets between Pine and Lombard.) George Thomas and Nathaniel Fox lived on the same street. James Cornish was not far away on Pine below Tenth. John Emerson resided several blocks away in Currant Alley. Then there was a family group—Edward Johnson, who lived at 21 Hurst, and Edward Jr. and Robert in Giles' Alley, just off Lombard. John Jones lived in Pryor's Court, which ran from Ninth to Tenth Street, south of Walnut.

John Moore's home was on Lombard near Eighth, John Scott's on Passyunk Road below Fifth, William Valentine's at Perry below Spruce, and William Middleton's in Freytag's Alley, just off Shippen Street.[51]

The brief descriptions of these men provided by the Pennsylvania Abolition Society's census of the city's free black community reveal that some of Forten's employees had done quite well financially. Robert Spence, who resided at 152 South Eighth, had $1000 in personal property in 1838. James Cornish and his wife had also prospered. Several of them enjoyed especially close ties with Forten outside the sail loft. Anthony, Cornish, Emerson, and Spence all worshipped with him and his family at St. Thomas's African Episcopal Church.[52]

To work for James Forten meant, at least outwardly, to adhere to his moral code. At the time of his death Forten owned a gold watch worth $75, with which he presumably enforced punctuality.[53] As for more serious transgressions than arriving late for work, some of his employees wisely hid those from him. A temperance advocate himself, Forten did not permit the use of alcohol in his home or in his workplace. Of course, there were good practical reasons for insisting on sobriety. A workman who spent his lunch break in a local tavern or kept a bottle in his lunch pail was unlikely to do careful work. A poorly sewn seam or a badly cut sail could cost Forten money. However, it was more than a question of preventing costly mistakes. James Forten believed that drinking was a sign of moral weakness and he simply would not tolerate it.[54]

He was even stricter when it came to sexual improprieties. Robert Spence and John Jones both fathered illegitimate children as the result of extramarital affairs, and both needed friends to stand surety for them when they were issued with support orders by the Guardians of the Poor. Many men in that situation asked their employers for help. Spence and Jones knew better than to approach Forten, who would probably have lectured them on the need for sexual restraint and on the sanctity of the marital bond.[55]

So much for James Forten's workers. What of his customers? Without complete business records there is no way of knowing precisely for whom he worked, or how he sought out commissions. It was common for sailmakers, like others in the maritime trades, to own a few shares in a vessel. That ensured them the business of making her sails.[56] Forten may have owned shares in one or more vessels at various times in his long career, but there is no evidence from surviving ships' papers that he did so, and the inventory of his estate does not mention any such investments. Perhaps he relied on word of mouth to get orders.

Clearly James Forten's earliest patrons were the partners in the firm of Willing and Francis. He acknowledged their help and trust by naming one of his sons in their honor. But who were his other customers in his first few years in business? Robert Purvis referred simply to his being "indebted to some few staunch friends, for whose encouragement and kindness he was ever wont to speak in terms of gratitude," but he named no names.[57]

According to another writer, Forten "was a friend of the late Louis Clopier [*sic*] and Stephen Girard."[58] As an active member of the business community, he obviously would have known both Girard and Clapier by sight, as well as by reputation, and they would have heard of Robert Bridges's black protégé. Clapier was in the French trade and was kept in touch with affairs across the Atlantic by his brother, who lived in Marseilles, "but besides this his commercial interest connected him with China, East India, Havanna, Vera Cruz, etc. . . . He owned many ships, all paying their way profitably." He was a couple of years older than Forten and was in business almost as long as him.[59] He may well have given Forten work, but his business records have not survived. As for Forten's supposed links with Stephen Girard, before one conjures up a picture of the two walking arm in arm along Front Street discussing sail plans for Girard's newest ship, a word of caution is in order. An examination of disbursements on Girard's vessels from 1797 onward reveals he never employed Forten. He ordered his sails from William Wright, then from the firm of Wright and Williamson. Wright died in 1805 and the sail loft passed to William Williamson, as did Girard's orders. Eventually Girard employed another of Forten's rivals, Jacob Dunton.[60] Perhaps Girard deliberately passed over Forten on account of his race, or perhaps he had simply never given Robert Bridges any work and saw no reason to employ his successor.

One can guess from circumstantial evidence who some of Forten's friends in the mercantile community were. There was merchant William Deas, after whom Forten named his youngest son. There were also the various members of the Bridges family. Robert Bridges had sent his son Culpepper into the countinghouse of John Leamy on Walnut and Third to learn the art of buying and selling.[61] Culpepper did well, and in 1809 he, his sister Emily's new husband, Robert Murdock, and Murdock's business partner, John Duffield, became the owners of the brig *Aurora*. Her master, James Murdock, was a co-owner. The following year Bridges, Duffield, and Robert Murdock acquired the brig *Catharine*.[62] Given that Culpepper Bridges had known James Forten most of his life, and had had ample opportunity to see the quality of his work, it would have been surprising if Forten had *not* received commissions from him. Another Bridges connection may also have resulted in business for Forten. In 1814 Culpepper's sister Sarah married Robert Ritchie, the owner of the brigs *Assistance* and *Two Friends*.[63]

According to Abraham Ritter, a contemporary of Forten's and a chronicler of Philadelphia's mercantile community, one of Forten's neighbors when he was starting out in business was M. H. Messchert, "an eminent Hollander in the German trade." His brother-in-law, Jacob Gerard Koch, lived nearby and dealt in German linens. Another neighbor was merchant Samuel Rhoades.[64] Perhaps one or all three of these men gave Forten business, but again there is no proof that they did.

One intriguing possibility is that James Forten did work for the navy. International tensions disrupted trade in the 1790s, but those same tensions led to the creation of the United States Navy. Warships needed sails, and two of the commanders of the fledgling navy, Stephen Decatur and Thomas Truxtun, were Philadelphians, at least by adoption. They were also men Forten had served under. It was just possible that they were able to put work his way. He may also have reaped some benefits from the appointment of William Jones as the nation's fourth Secretary of the Navy. A Philadelphia merchant and captain who had sailed with Truxtun during the Revolution, Jones almost certainly knew Forten, because the firm of Jones and Clark had its offices at 225 Front Street and the Bridges family lived at 259.[65] The network of patronage and influence may have reached out to embrace Forten during Jones's time in office (1813–16). Civilian sailmakers, like Forten's contemporary in Boston, Charles Ware, did get work from the navy before and immediately after the War of 1812.[66] In the 1830s Forten's friend, merchant and abolitionist Lewis Tappan, gave a rather misleading description of the kinds of commissions Forten received. "It was said by the secretary of the navy, 'Mr. Forten can undertake to rig a seventy-four-gun ship, and not call for any money until the job is done.'"[67] If Tappan was implying that Forten was doing work for the United States Navy in the 1830s he was almost certainly mistaken. By then it was navy policy to replace civilian sailmakers with warrant officers.[68] However, Forten might have been supplying sails for naval vessels a decade or two earlier. Unfortunately, the records of the Philadelphia Navy Yard—and they are far from complete—contain no mention of James Forten.

Without his ledgers and daybooks, tracking Forten's business year by year is virtually impossible. Luckily, the picture is not a complete blank. The records of one of his customers have survived, and those records illuminate a relationship between Forten and an influential shipper that spanned more than a decade.

Patrick Hayes, the nephew of Commodore John Barry, had extensive interests in the China trade and in commerce with Cuba. Barry had brought his orphaned nephew over from Ireland around the time Forten became the foreman of Bridges's sail loft. With his uncle's patronage and his own very considerable talents as a captain and a merchant, Hayes did well for himself. By the 1820s he concentrated on supervising his business ashore, while his son, Thomas, captained his vessels, the brig *Emma* and the ship *Tontine*. James Forten and his sons made sails for both vessels.

During the winter of 1821–22, for instance, Forten fitted out the *Tontine* with an expensive new main topsail for a spring voyage to Nice.[69] Her sails continued to be made and refurbished in his loft for the next decade. In June 1831 Forten billed Hayes $226.18 for five new sails, repairs to two more, sundries, and canvas for the vessel's stores.[70] The following spring he presented his bill for "middle stitching" to strengthen two sails, repairs, oddments of twine and canvas, and the making of a tarpaulin for covering cargo. The settlement of the account is interesting. Hayes traded a box of "Segars" valued at $17.50, the results of a voyage to Cuba, perhaps. Forten gave him credit for just over $4, and eventually only a few dollars changed hands.[71] Both men were satisfied. Hayes was a good customer. Forten knew him, knew his vessels, and knew there would be more work. As for Hayes, he recognized good craftsmanship when he saw it.

In November 1832 Forten billed Hayes for work on the *Emma*—repairs to the jib, a new main topsail and fittings, a new pump coat—and for four bolts of first-quality Russia Duck and thirty yards of cotton duck for the stores.[72] At the end of another sailing season the brig was back for a more substantial refit. In October 1833 Forten charged Hayes almost $400 for four new sails, repairs to seven more, bolts of canvas of various weights for the ship's stores, sewing twine, metal thimbles, reef points, and thirteen yards of second-hand canvas to make a cover for Hayes's piano. Hayes paid Forten $200 on account.[73] In July 1834 there was another bill for new sails, more repairs, another tarpaulin, and more Russian Duck and Raven's Duck for the stores. Hayes and Forten had also been in consultation about an improvement in the *Emma*'s sail plan. Under Forten's direction, the workers in the sail loft set about the complex task of altering the topgallant sail in preparation for another sailing season.[74]

The African-American master-craftsman and the Irish-born shipper seem to have developed a great respect for one another in the years they did business together. As far as James Forten was concerned, it did not hurt that Hayes had substantial mercantile interests, that he was a Warden of the Port of Philadelphia, and that his son was married to Commodore Bainbridge's daughter. The Hayes papers are intriguing for the glimpse they give us into the racially and ethnically diverse world of the Philadelphia waterfront. How many of James Forten's other commissions, and how many of his relationships with members of the predominantly white shipowning fraternity, are lost, perhaps buried in the business papers of various firms?

As FOR THE technology of sailmaking, there were some significant changes in sail plans during the decades Forten operated his loft. With the War of 1812 over, speed could be sacrificed to cargo space. No longer were ships being built as blockade-runners or privateers. Hulls became broader and more full-bodied, and sail plans reflected that. The typical vessel employed in the transatlantic trade was "the deep, burdensome, full-rigged ship, which carried three masts . . . and . . . usually had three decks. . . . These vessels required a large amount of canvas to drive them, but because they were still relatively small, the size of the individual sails was such that the vessels were handy with small crews."[75] In the West India trade and on longer coasting voyages, topsail schooners and brigantines predominated. For shorter voyages in shallower waters, there was a preference for schooners with fore-and-aft rigging. The vessels were relatively small—those trading with the Caribbean were rarely over 100 feet long, and few in the coasting trade over 80 feet. Until the late 1830s few American vessels were larger than 500 tons, because "Large ships had difficulty in quickly filling their holds with cargo partly because merchants were not organized in this direction and partly because port facilities were poor."[76]

The new developments in sail plans, the preferences of this or that captain, and the need to adjust as vessels were powered by steam as well as sails were all things James Forten would have understood. His success depended on being astute, versatile, and well informed. That he brought all these attributes to bear was obvious, for he prospered, "and before many years he employed more hands, and did a greater amount of business than all the other sail-makers in Philadelphia."[77] Antiquarian Charles A. Poulson noted that Forten was "A most reliable business man, [and] had command of the best custom in his line, and among colored people stood undoubtedly 'A no. 1.'"[78] Poulson, the son-in-law of merchant Francis Gurney, was in a fairly good position to judge.

By the early 1820s, though, James Forten's pursuit of wealth clashed with his antislavery principles in an unlikely way. As a sailmaker he had had his brushes with slavers. "A ship that had been engaged in the slave trade, and was likely to be thus employed again, was in need of sails, and applied to him to furnish them; but he indignantly refused."[79] For one thing, fitting out a slaver was illegal in Pennsylvania. Anyway, with a full order book, Forten could safely adhere to his principles, although one senses he would have done so whatever the circumstances. But when the interests of the Southern cotton planters and their friends fundamentally changed the nature of sail-making, he had to meet the economics of slavery head-on. Much as he detested slavery, by the 1820s he had no choice but to use slave-produced cotton to make his sails.

Like his father before him, James Forten had learned his craft working with flaxen sail duck imported from the Baltic and the Netherlands. Robert Bridges used nothing else. There was prejudice on the part of sailmakers and sailors against anything but the traditional article. "The American sailor . . . thought twice—and twice again—before he took any craft without Russian rigging, cables, and sails beyond the harbor mouth."[80] However, there were obvious dangers for a country that could not put a merchant fleet or a navy in the water without dependence on an imported commodity. Those dangers had come to the fore during the Revolutionary War, and they intensified during the 1790s. Enemy blockades that prevented the importation of sailcloth or a war thousands of miles away that cut off supplies at their source posed grave threats to the United States. The Anglo-French conflict, the crises in American relations with the warring superpowers, Napoleon's invasion of Russia, and eventually the outbreak of the War of 1812 drove home to anyone concerned about trade and national defense the seriousness of not having a domestic source of supply for sailcloth and cordage.[81]

Textile manufacturers in New England in the early years of the nineteenth century did experiment with homegrown flax, but the price of the finished cloth was too high to make it very attractive to potential purchasers. During the

War of 1812 New England duck hauled overland to Baltimore sold for one dollar a yard. Shippers and sailmakers resorted to various stratagems to get Baltic canvas. It was not uncommon for privateers to take the sails from their prizes and have them recut and reroped. Speculators also ran the British blockade.[82]

If the United States could not produce adequate amounts of flax, it could produce cotton, and under the pressure of Jefferson's embargo some manufacturers of sailcloth had begun experimenting with homegrown cotton. Baltimore's Union Mills were turning out cotton duck before the start of all-out war with Britain, and a few schooners ventured out on cruises during the war with cotton sails. Some masters insisted cotton sails "held their shape better, were lighter, and required less wetting down to catch a wind than flaxen sails."[83] But could cotton cloth be produced cheaply enough and efficiently enough, and would it win acceptance among captains and shipowners?

With the end of the War of 1812 and the final defeat of Napoleon in Europe, stocks of foreign sailcloth were once more available. The Russians scurried to recover their old markets, and for a while the price of Baltic duck fell. However, the wartime disruption had served as a wake-up call. Added to that was the patriotic appeal of "buying American." Thanks to some successful industrial espionage, the United States now had the technology to manufacture textiles. And, with more cotton-producing states entering the Union, there was a reliable domestic source of raw cotton. That slave labor was used to produce it was just a fact of life as far as most white Americans were concerned. But for abolitionists it raised the specter that slavery would not die within a generation of the closing of the overseas slave trade, as many had confidently predicted. The growing market for cotton gave the institution a new lease on life. For Forten, a vociferous opponent of slavery, who made his living supplying sails, this meant a painful choice.

He could follow in such publications as *Niles' Weekly Register* the growing enthusiasm for cotton duck. By 1822 John Colt and Co.'s Passaic No. 1 Mill in Patterson, New Jersey, was producing cotton canvas. As business increased, and power looms were introduced, Colt's product carved out a sizable niche in the market.[84] Forten had an opportunity to see Colt's sail duck for himself. In February 1822 *Relf's Gazette* announced to "Merchants, Sailmakers, and others interested in shipping" that William Craig, of 8 Chestnut Street, Philadelphia, had it available for sale.[85] Others followed Colt's lead. By late 1823 Charles Crook, Jr., and Brother of Baltimore was producing canvas that was "judged by experts to be superior to Russian sail-cloth." *Niles' Register* declared proudly: "It is *American* canvass, made by *American* hands, and of *American* cotton."[86]

Soon the navy was taking notice. In 1826 the Navy Board had ordered enough cotton duck to fit out five vessels. "This canvas appears now to have been fully tested, both as to its strength and durability, in severe gales . . . and long voyages, and the prospect is that its use will become general." *Niles' Register* concluded: "This matter is . . . important to the cotton planters . . . for it will mightily increase the demand for their product."[87]

As cotton production rose, prices of canvas fell. By 1826, cotton canvas and flaxen canvas sold for the same price, 48 cents per yard for the same weight. In the merchant marine the transition to cotton came fairly rapidly. The navy was more conservative and, despite the Navy Board's tests, continued to opt for flaxen sails for decades. Of course, foreign vessels still arrived in American ports with flaxen sails that had to be repaired.[88]

By the early 1830s "free labor" was an important plank of the antislavery platform. In December 1830 black Philadelphians organized the Colored Free Produce Association of Pennsylvania, whose members vowed not to use any commodity—sugar, rice, cotton, tobacco—that had been produced by slaves. James Forten's daughter, Harriet, and her husband were active in the Colored Free Produce Association. Although he himself never muted his opposition to slavery, he used and sold cotton duck. Some individuals, like white Philadelphia merchant James Mott, had stopped dealing in cotton because of the morality issue, but if James Forten had qualms about using slave-produced cotton that is not reflected in his business practices.[89] Perhaps expediency won out over morality, or perhaps he reasoned that slavery was more than a matter of cotton.

THE SAIL LOFT was at the center of James Forten's business empire. His prosperity was based upon the fitting-out of vessels. He described himself first and foremost as a sailmaker. He trained his sons as sailmakers. However, his commercial interests extended far beyond South Wharves. Like any shrewd man of business, he was averse to having his money lying idle. Always looking out for a good investment, by the early 1800s he had begun to divert some of his capital into moneylending. Under-capitalized as the economy was, and without adequate banking facilities, merchants, artisans, and others needed credit. Sometimes it was a case of getting a short-term loan to buy supplies or pay the wages of one's employees. Sometimes it was a long-term loan. A businessman might need capital to expand or to develop a potentially lucrative sideline.

James Forten had the necessary prerequisites for moneylending—capital to spare and a shrewd knowledge of the market. He also had a sound grasp of the unwritten rules for successful moneylending. In bad times, restrict credit and try to get personal notes from creditors. A note could be deposited in a bank, which, if necessary, would collect. It was also irrefutable evidence of how much the debt was for and what the repayment terms were.

In addition to making loans, Forten discounted notes—a common practice in an era when the banking system was not very sophisticated. In principle the system was fairly simple. Merchant A gave a note to Merchant B for the full amount and face value of the debt he owed for goods or services. The note might be payable in sixty days. If Merchant B needed cash before the sixty days were up, he would try to sell that note to a bank, a broker, or Merchant C, another businessman. Since the note had not matured, it had to be sold at a discount. Thus C might pay $90 for A's note for $100. Of course there were risks. Merchant A might default. Merchant C had to rely on his judgment, and on that of Merchant B.[90]

Those who drove others into the ground by demanding excessively high profits and discounting notes by more than the market average were known as "note-shavers." James Forten was proud of his reputation for honest dealing. His son-in-law, a shrewd man of business himself, recalled that "he never had, as I have often heard him declare, been guilty of that genteel kind of swindling, which all sorts of professedly good people practice under the gloss of the name of note-shaving."[91] What rates of interest Forten charged and precisely what kind of discounting of notes he did we cannot know without his business records.

Certainly, had he gone in for note-shaving—and we only have his word for it that he did not—he would not have been alone. His longtime friend, African-American hairdresser Joseph Cassey, grew very wealthy indeed on note-shaving, as did plenty of white businessmen.[92] Without his ledgers and his files of business correspondence, James Forten's various loans come to light only by chance. However, when they do, they illustrate the intimacy of Philadelphia's business community, an intimacy that reached out across lines of race to embrace a black "gentleman of the pave" with money to lend at interest.

Some of Forten's loans are easily explained. They were made to assist his friends. In 1818, for instance, Forten was serving on the vestry at St. Thomas's African Episcopal Church when the church's venerable minister Absalom Jones died. A childless widower, Jones left some of his estate to his nephews and other members of his extended family, but he also left a generous legacy to the church, with the usual stipulation that his "just debts" and funeral expenses should be deducted first. The vestrymen were calculating just how much money the church would receive and how it should be spent when James Forten spoke up. He produced a note signed by Jones promising to pay back a loan of $191.20 with interest. The other vestrymen examined the signature, declared it genuine, and voted (perhaps somewhat reluctantly) that Forten should get his money. He promptly "Made the Church a present of [the] Interest," which amounted to $11.84.[93]

There may well have been other loans to members of the African-American community. There were certainly loans to white businessmen. For instance, merchant Joseph Sloan was indebted to Forten for $608. Sloan died at age thirty-three in the fall of 1809, caught up in a tangled web of debts and credits. People owed him money, among them the firm of Murdock and Duffield, and Forten's friend, iron merchant Thomas Ash. Sloan hoped his executors would collect on his debts and use that money, together with an inheritance he had received, to pay Forten and his other creditors. In Sloan's case it is possible to see how a loan was arranged. Sloan had his business premises at 90 South Wharves, close to Forten's loft. One of his executors, and a man with whom he may at one time have been in business, was Culpepper Bridges. Incidentally, Bridges's brother-in-law, Robert Murdock, had secured a personal loan from Sloan. It was a small world indeed, and smaller still when one discovers that Sloan's other executor was Culpepper Bridges's neighbor, factor William Maris.[94]

Another business relationship came to light when it turned sour, but it illustrates how a loan was negotiated. At some point in 1828 Norristown lawyer Philip S. Marckley approached James Forten and asked for a loan for a couple of days.[95] Forten did not know Marckley, but Marckley referred to a mutual acquaintance, the eminently respectable and influential Samuel Breck, with whom he had served in the Pennsylvania Senate. As Forten explained to Breck: "[A]n inducement to loan Mr. M. the money was the fact that he mentioned . . . in our first interview, that he was connected by marriage with your family." Forten made the loan, received only empty promises, gave Marckley time and more time, and then probably threatened legal action. Breck, who had taken a hand in sorting out Marckley's muddled finances, wrote Forten. Forten replied with a deft mix of tact and directness: "Weeks have elapsed—Under these circumstances my claim may perhaps be considered as entitled to a preference and to be immediately paid." Still, he was willing to do what Breck said other creditors had done and give Marckley yet more time, "if you or some other equally responsible Gentleman would guarantee the payment."[96] The money was important and he expected to recoup it, or at least most of it, but it did not hurt to have a powerful man like Breck beholden to him.

Some appreciation of the extent of James Forten's dealings as a money-lender can be gained from other instances in which those indebted to him either could not or would not pay up. Hardly a rapacious man, Forten gave people time to settle, but he had to draw a line somewhere. When faced with nonpayment he was ready to go to court. Possibly the realization that he was in earnest induced some to make good on their debts. For instance, in April 1810, attorney Richard Rush commenced an action on Forten's behalf against one Henry Powers. A summons was issued, but before the return of the summons was due, the case was discontinued.[97] This is the earliest record of an action initiated by Forten. By having his lawyer obtain a summons against the recalcitrant Powers he was not only attempting to get what he was owed but at the same time sending a not-too-subtle message to others in the business community that he was not to be trifled with.

It is worth noting that Forten could and did employ first-rate legal counsel. His business concerns were considerable. There were real estate transactions, questions of title, actions for debt, and the like. He needed sound legal advice and he could pay for it. Richard Rush, son of abolitionist and famed physician Benjamin Rush, became Attorney-General of Pennsylvania the year after he represented Forten in the Powers case and, to his father's chagrin, went on to carve out a career for himself in politics in Washington. The lawyers Forten retained after Rush's departure were a father and son, members of one of the city's most influential families. Richard Peters was a close friend of Chief Justice John Marshall. He handled one or two cases for Forten, but it was his son who had greater contact with the sailmaker. At least as late as 1820, Richard Peters, Jr., was a prominent abolitionist, even if he did limit his involvement in the Pennsylvania Abolition Society and in antislavery activities in general in the wake of the Missouri Compromise. Perhaps not coincidentally, he was married to Abigail Willing, the daughter of Forten's old patron.[98]

The elder Peters handled the case Forten brought against grocer Jacob Vanderslice, who, as Powers, was a victim of the economic upheavals that followed Jefferson's embargo. Forten had loaned Vanderslice a substantial sum of money and had received only vague promises when the loan became due. He had no alternative but to instruct Peters to proceed against Vanderslice. On the face of it, Vanderslice did not have much of a defense to offer. On June 29, 1812,

> Defendant's Attorney comes & Defends the force and injury . . . and saith that he cannot gainsay the writing obligatory aforesaid nor but the same is his deed nor but that he owes to the said James Forten the sum of five hundred and ten dollars in manner and form as he against him hath declared &c.

In plain English, Vanderslice owed Forten the money, but he could not pay it because he did not have it. Peters secured various writs on his client's behalf in an attempt to attach Vanderslice's assets. Then, in the midst of the proceedings, Vanderslice died. Forten had to try to recover what he could from the man's estate. Finally, after four years, he got about half of the sum owed him, with interest.[99]

In the uneasy period during the war with Britain, Forten was doing far better than merchant Jonathan Jenks, who was in debt to him for almost $120. In July 1814, unable to collect the money, Forten instructed Richard Peters, Jr., to bring suit. A week later Forten and Jenks appeared in court to settle on arbitrators. They were to meet at Strembeck's Tavern on August 10. However, court proceedings were at the mercy of the British, who were reported to be advancing on Philadelphia. Presumably the arbitrators had other things on their minds. Forten certainly had. He was busy rallying the black community to work on the city's defenses. In February 1815 the case resumed. Forten got a judgment in his favor, but it took him three years to secure payment.[100]

The war brought hard times for many in the business community. The firm of Murdock and Duffield failed in the early months of 1814 and the partners were obliged to assign their real estate to pay off their creditors. James Forten was one of their creditors. He never brought suit against them, and he eventually signed a deed releasing their property from any further claims he might have, but he reserved the right to all his existing liens. Eventually he acquired Robert Murdock's home on Front Street at a bargain price at a sheriff's sale.[101]

Robert Murdock and John Duffield were not the only people who had borrowed money from James Forten and then fallen victim to the wartime financial upheavals. In 1815 Miles H. Hughes, proprietor of a lottery and exchange office, had a judgment rendered against him and in favor of Forten in the District

Court.[102] Merchant George L. Seckel was also in trouble, in part because Hughes owed *him* $6500. In January 1816 Forten initiated an action to recover over $400 from Seckel. He got the money due him, along with attorney's fees.[103]

In the uneasy postwar period James Forten kept Attorney Peters busy recovering sums of money due him. In 1819 he sued a group of four merchants for an undisclosed amount.[104] That same year he got a judgment against shipsmith John R. Mullin for $247.45. Once more he had recourse to arbitrators, all of them neighbors, to get what was owed him.[105] A few months later tavernkeeper Henry Witmer was ordered to pay him $146.20.[106] Then it was the turn of Edward Tilghman, a merchant with extensive interests in overseas trade who had borrowed $112. Tilghman was in serious trouble by the time Forten began proceedings, but, as usual, Forten had managed to get in ahead of the pack. Tilghman's case was not strengthened by his failure to appear in court when arbitrators were selected. Forten did show up. The arbitrators recommended Forten receive the full amount of the debt, interest, and attorney's fees. Forten was wise to act quickly. Tilghman declared bankruptcy a few months later and many of his creditors were left with worthless notes.[107]

Another luckless member of the business community was Thomas Ellis. Ellis kept a livery stable in Drinker's Alley and in 1821 he was indebted to Forten in the amount of $150. After an appearance in the District Court, and some months spent haggling, the two reached an agreement. Forten paid Ellis $5 and forgave all his debts in return for a house and lot on Lombard, between Tenth and Eleventh Streets.[108]

Some of Forten's loans were relatively small. Thomas Hope, a lottery and exchange broker of 63 Chestnut Street, and William McPherson, occupation unknown, owed less than $50. Even so, proceedings dragged on for months. Forten got an initial judgment in 1821, but not until 1825 did he get the sum due him.[109] James and Henry Brady, dry-goods merchants, owed $58. Peters secured a writ against them on Forten's behalf in Common Pleas in September 1823 and had their property attached.[110]

Other cases involved substantial sums of money. In the early 1820s Forten had loaned $700 to three merchants, Joseph Beylle and Joseph Severlinge, who were involved in the wine trade, and Andrew Curcier, who was simply listed in the directory as a "merchant." The link with Forten was probably a maritime one. Curcier was part-owner of the brig *Adeline*. He also owned the schooners *Atlas* and *Commodore*, and the ship *Cordelia*.[111] All three men lived or did business fairly close to Forten. Beylle's business premises were at 63 South Second. Severlinge (who was Beylle's godson) lived at 62 South Third, and Curcier at 5 Minor. In December 1825 Forten secured writs in the District Court authorizing the sheriff to take the three into custody, although bail was set aside on the understanding that they appear in court. Presumably they paid up, or at least reached an agreement to do so, since there is no further record of proceedings against them.[112]

Like other men of business, sometimes Forten was too trusting and waited too long to try to recover money owed him—with the predictable result. In 1824 he had a summons issued against merchant Thomas Reily. However, the officer charged with serving the writ reported "nihil habet." In other words, Reily was nowhere to be found and the writ could not be served.[113] With a pack of creditors at his heels, he had fled the city.

The case against "gentleman" William R. Boyer may have involved a dispute over unpaid rent, since Boyer leased a home, 111 South Ninth, from Forten. The suit commenced in the District Court on June 7, 1826, with a request from Forten's attorney for arbitrators to be chosen. The presiding magistrate agreed, and three men were selected. One, merchant William Patton, Jr., was Robert Bridges's grandson. The three conferred at a local tavern and reported back that the plaintiff should be awarded $263.69. Unable to pay immediately, Boyer was given nine months' grace, and he found a friend to stand surety for him.[114]

Forten was also embroiled in a dispute with merchant Joseph Head, "a well bred gentleman who [had] inherited a considerable fortune from his father" and gone into trade. Head was not a very good businessman, and at some point he borrowed money from Forten, which he neglected to pay back. In 1826 Forten instructed Attorney Peters to take the matter to court. Head's defense was that he *had* paid. Plaintiff and defendant both filed formal "narratios" stating their case. How Forten fared in court is not recorded, but Head salvaged something from the ruins of his business career. He became the proprietor of the Mansion House Hotel, "knowing by the experience of his former luxurious life how to furnish a good table."[115]

Forten and his attorney also had recourse to the Pennsylvania Supreme Court. During the December 1823 term, Richard Peters brought suit against Philadelphia merchants Andrew and William L. Hodge. Andrew could not be found, so the writ was delivered to his last known address.[116] Unfortunately, a five-year gap in the Appearance Docket makes it impossible to discover how the case ended.

Rarely did Forten find himself in the role of defendant. In only one case was he summoned—by the widow of merchant John Diamond. Exactly what the link was between Forten and Diamond is not clear from the cryptic notes on the case in the records of the Court of Common Pleas. Diamond had lived at 204 South Front, Robert Murdock's old home. Forten had owned the property for a number of years until he sold it, although not to Diamond. The case came to court in April 1832 and was soon settled. The amount involved is not recorded, nor is the nature of the dispute, but the fact that the case was commenced in Common Pleas, where sums at issue were generally smaller than in the District Court, suggests Forten did not owe Diamond's estate very much.[117]

Forten continued suing creditors, usually with success.[118] The last record of a case brought by him involves a debt of $47 owed by blacksmith Elias Wolohon. Forten initiated the action in Common Pleas and in the summer of

1833 received a judgment in his favor for the sum in dispute, with interest and attorney's fees.[119] Is it significant that there were no further cases? Did Forten fear that in an increasingly hostile racial climate he would not get a fair hearing? One thing is clear. For over two decades he was a reasonably well-known presence in the District Court and the Court of Common Pleas. Most actions were handled by his attorney, but Forten was often in court to advance his side of the case and simply to keep a watchful eye on his affairs. That he should not have been there, that he had no right to sue white debtors, was never suggested. After all, if *his* rights were not secure, then no one else's were, and the whole debtor–creditor network was threatened.

IN ADDITION TO his moneylending activities, James Forten speculated in real estate. The Philadelphia property market was a flexible one, and he realized early on in his career how to take advantage of that flexibility. He could buy ground rents for a steady 6 percent per annum yield. He could purchase vacant lots and build on them. He could buy houses and rent them out. He could watch the market, acquiring real estate when prices were low and selling when land values rose.

Within five years of taking over the Bridges sail loft James Forten had amassed sufficient capital to invest in real estate, albeit on a modest scale. He already owned the house at 50 Shippen Street that Robert Bridges had purchased for him back in 1792. In 1803 he acquired a lot and frame stable at 67 George Street in Southwark from "gentleman" Thomas Bowen for $200, with the intention of improving it. He did what other speculators did. He hired a house carpenter, settled on costs and a timetable, and then left the man to complete the job. It was the carpenter's responsibility to purchase materials, subcontract with various craftsmen, and build the house within the time and for the amount stated in the contract.[120] Living on Shippen, and working just a few blocks away, Forten could check on the site every day if he chose. The development of the George Street property was a clear sign that he had patronage to give. Already, at least in a minor way, he was a presence on the business scene.

Then came the purchase of the house on Third and Lombard that would become the Forten family home for the next eight decades. On October 29, 1806, merchant John M. Soullier sold James Forten a three-story brick house and lot on Lombard, between Third and Fourth. The price was $3400, and Soullier gave Forten a one-year mortgage on payment of half the purchase price.[121] The house was well located. It was just a four-block walk to the sail loft.

During the embargo Forten was understandably cautious, but by December 1809 he was doing well enough to buy his first piece of investment real estate in the city proper. African-American waiter William Jefferson sold him a house and lot on Lombard, between Tenth and Eleventh, for $459.17.[122] Forten probably intended to rent it out. He was already renting his two properties in Southwark.

More transactions followed as Forten took advantage of rising real estate prices.[123] On the eve of the war with Britain he made one substantial investment and a much smaller one. The smaller one was the purchase of a lot on James Street in Blockley Township, just outside the city. The property, in an area he considered ripe for development, cost him $230.[124] The larger investment must have taken a sizable share of his capital, but he was doing far better than house carpenter Ebenezer Osbourne, who had several judgments against him and needed cash in a hurry. On July 13, 1812, Forten paid him $3,400 for a house and lot, 111 South Ninth Street, just off Walnut. Two days later he paid Edward Burd, an Osbourne creditor, $1,500 to relinquish his claims to the property and a further $1,233.33 to extinguish a ground rent. Then he made a token payment of $1 to merchant Robert Ralston, who had won a judgment against Osbourne.[125] The expenditure of over $6,000 was a calculated gamble, but the house remained in the Forten family for over three decades and proved one of the most profitable of Forten's rental properties.

On March 2, 1813, Forten's lawyer sold him a house and lot on Lombard, between Ninth and Tenth.[126] Five months later he bought a house and lot on Little Pine. The price, $400, was a rather low one. Perhaps the seller had overextended himself or had had the piece of real estate wished on him in some way. Bricklayer Lewis H. Foote had gained title to the property only two days before he sold it to Forten.[127] Both properties were soon rented out. Forten was consolidating his position as a landlord in the Pine and Lombard neighborhood.

For those who survived the War of 1812 with their fortunes intact and weathered the postwar crisis, there were some good real estate bargains to be had. In September 1816 Forten bought a ground rent of £6 per year on a lot in George Street in Southwark, near his other property.[128] In December he acquired a house on Lombard and Sixth adjoining the property he had bought from Foote.[129] Marriages, deaths, and business failures among Robert Bridges's heirs had prompted Forten several months earlier to seek confirmation of his right to the Shippen Street home Bridges had bought on his behalf so many years before. He had long since paid the purchase price in full. Now he paid Jemima Bridges, her surviving children, and the heirs of her deceased children, $1 apiece to relinquish any claims they might have.[130]

Over the next few years more real estate bargains came his way at sheriff's sales. In February 1820 he bought twelve and three-quarter acres, a frame house, kitchen, barn, and carriage house in Oxford Township for $2000.[131] As with the Blockley purchase, he knew the value of land on the outskirts of Philadelphia. A growing city needed to be fed, and small farms like those in Blockley and Oxford could be leased to tenants in dairying or market-gardening.

Occasionally Forten sold property, but he tried to do so in a manner that ensured a steady income. For instance, in October 1817 he sold the house and lot on Lombard he had bought from William Jefferson back in 1809. The selling price to distiller Joseph Kenton was five shillings down, and a rental payment of $50 per year.[132] Sometimes he disposed of real estate at a handsome profit. He sold Robert Murdock's house on South Front Street, the one tangible thing he had salvaged from his dealings with the troubled firm of Murdock and Duffield, to Captain Peter Anderson in 1824 for more than a thousand dollars over what he had paid for it.[133]

Although the pace of his buying and selling slowed in the late 1820s, Forten continued making deals. In March 1829, for instance, he paid Jacob G. Morris $200 for a lot on Barley and Eleventh that adjoined property he already owned.[134] Sometimes he entered into a transaction to help a friend. By the mid-1820s Mary Bridges, Robert's daughter, was unmarried, her mother and all of her siblings were dead, and she derived a living from the property she had inherited from her parents. In January 1827 Forten gave her a mortgage on the Bridges's home at 259 South Front. Over the next three years he gave her three more mortgages, and then, in August 1833, he paid her $1,800 outright for the house in which he had probably lived many years before when he had been her father's apprentice.[135]

In the early 1830s Forten disposed of a number of pieces of real estate. Given the unhealthy state of the market, he did not reap the kind of profits he had done in the past. In December 1833 he sold Robert Coburn a £6 ground rent for $208, $20 less than it had cost him.[136] The sale of the Blockley farm to Silas Evans for $250 netted Forten only $20 more than he had paid for it, but perhaps he was looking to gain more through interest payments. He gave Evans a four-year mortgage. It was common practice to allow extra time on mortgages and not to push for full payment unless it seemed the purchaser would default.[137] In March 1832 he sold his Oxford property at a considerable loss to surveyor John Foulkrod.[138] Perhaps the sail loft needed an infusion of cash and this was a way of raising it quickly.

Throughout his long career in business James Forten bought property for resale. He also bought property to be rented out. At the height of his prosperity he had homes for rent in various wards of the city, as well as in Philadelphia County. Although his rent books have not survived, it is possible, using tax records, directories, and censuses, to reconstruct a partial list of his renters. The roster of his tenants indicates he leased his properties to black and to white Philadelphians, to men and to women, to the well-to-do and to those of more modest means.

The house at 50 Shippen was apparently a desirable residence. In 1810 Forten leased it to white teacher Joseph Hutton and in 1814 to accountant Lewis Miles.[139] In the period from 1816 to 1819 the tenant was sea captain Charles Erwin.[140] In 1831, and for several years thereafter, Forten let it to another captain, Robert M. Wilson. At the time of Forten's death it was occupied by "gentleman" James Veacock.[141] Nearby, 38 George was rented to African-American carter Jonathan York from 1817 to 1819. When he died, his widow, Mary, sublet it to James Lee, a black laborer.[142]

James Forten's properties in Cedar Ward, on the southern fringe of the city, had a series of tenants, all of them African Americans. In 1814 John Hart was running an "intelligence office," or employment bureau, from the home he leased from Forten on Washington Court.[143] Carter Samuel Porter rented a home from Forten on Lombard above Ninth in 1817. John Blake rented a nearby property from Forten in the same year.[144]

As for Forten's other properties, in 1809 a white soapboiler, Robert Kennedy, was living at 94 South Fourth. Ann Wereet occupied another of Forten's homes in New Market Ward. The following year a Miss Deranby or Daneby was renting one of the houses, possibly the one previously rented by Kennedy, since the valuation in the tax ledger was exactly the same.[145]

Of course, what the records do not reveal are the interactions between James Forten and his tenants. We cannot tell from individuals' names and occupations how and where rents were paid, what kind of bargaining went on, and what degree of deference Forten expected and received from the men and women who lived in his properties. It is the minutiae of these tenant-landlord relationships, complicated as they may well have been by factors of race and class, that continue to elude us and leave a vital part of the story untold.[146]

Equally elusive is the attitude of the white business community toward James Forten. Well-to-do Quaker Susanna Emlen knew something of Forten. In 1809 she sent a relative in England a copy of "a Letter written by a black man of Philad[a] to one of the friends of his oppressed brethren." She added a few words about the letter's author. He "is a person of good character and considerable property employing at his sail loft many white persons. [O]n his marriage a few years ago it was said a number of the most respectable merchants in Philad[a] called to congratulate him and drink punch with him."[147]

Merchant Abraham Ritter indicated something of the mixed response to James Forten.

> Mr. Forten was a gentleman by nature, easy in manner, and affable in intercourse; popular as a man of trade or gentleman of the pave, and well received by the gentlemen of lighter shade. He was very genteel in appearance, good figure, prominent features, and upon the whole rather handsome than otherwise.[148]

Beyond Ritter's thumbnail sketch there are stray references to white businessmen greeting him in the street. "Though he belonged to a proscribed race, it was no uncommon thing to see him shaking hands, or walking arm in arm, with merchants of the first respectability."[149] As his various court cases suggest, they were not reluctant to borrow money from him, either. Nor did they simply set their prejudices aside when it came time to ask for a loan. The inventory of Forten's estate proves that white merchants and shippers also loaned him money on occasions. How his various business relationships began and progressed, who visited Forten at his home and who called on him at his place of business, who took him by the hand and who greeted him in the street—these are the dimensions of his life as a "gentleman of the pave" on which the records are silent.

The attitude of many members of the African-American community was that James Forten was definitely a man to be trusted, a man whose business abilities and knowledge of how to get things done could be relied upon. Joseph Head (not to be confused with the luckless white merchant Forten sued) was a fellow member of St. Thomas's Church. Like Forten, he was a freeborn native of Philadelphia. He also had at least the elements of literacy. In 1803, when he shipped out to China aboard the *George Washington*, he was one of the few crew members, black or white, who could sign his name to the ship's articles. Before he embarked on another voyage, this time to Calcutta and Madras aboard the *China Packet*, he made his will, appointing his wife, Hannah, and his "friend James Forten" his executors. The will was drawn up on April 17, 1807, the day before he sailed. Joseph Head was all too aware of the frailty of life. He had already buried one wife and a baby son. He and his second wife had been married barely a month. However, he had other kin in Philadelphia and he wished to provide for them, as well as for Hannah. Joseph did not return from India, and it fell to Forten and Hannah to settle the estate.[150]

When oysterman George Jones, minister Absalom Jones's nephew, wrote his will, he appointed his wife, Sarah, Forten, and fruit-seller Robert C. Gordon as executors.[151] In 1818 Haitian-born confectioner John Appo named Forten not only as an executor of his estate but also as guardian of his minor children.[152]

African-American organizations elected James Forten to their boards. He served on the vestry of St. Thomas's Church many times from its founding to his death. He was a man who knew how to take care of "business," in all its facets, whether it was arranging a loan or advising on the investment of funds. He was an officer of the African Lodge, whose records are replete with references to his handling of finances. He helped coordinate the raising of funds to support black schools and colleges. He gave white abolitionists advice on handling the marketing of antislavery publications. In short, what he did not know about the making and investing of money was probably not worth knowing.

In addition to his real estate interests and his moneylending, Forten held stocks and shares in various enterprises, including insurance companies and banks. For instance, he owned shares in the Mount Carbon Railroad Company, in the anthracite region of Pennsylvania's Schuylkill County. The brainchild of a consortium of businessmen in Philadelphia, Berks, and Schuylkill Counties, the company was incorporated in 1829. It opened books at a number of places, including the Philadelphia Coffee House. Shares cost $50 apiece. Like other rail lines in the region, it was intended to transport coal from the coal fields to the Schuylkill Canal. From the canal it would be transshipped to the Delaware, and eventually taken to Philadelphia for export. By 1827 more than 3,000 vessels per year were leaving Philadelphia loaded with coal.[153] James Forten knew a good investment when he saw one.

Precisely how wealthy James Forten was at any one point in his career is difficult to gauge. Most accounts indicate that the sail loft did a thriving business. An obituary noted that "for many years" until his death, Forten was "the leading sailmaker in this city."[154] A white visitor in the 1830s marveled at the number of orders he had. He paid $10,000 per year in wages (a figure that seems impossibly high given what journeymen sailmakers earned), and had at one time the sails for ninety-five vessels engaged.[155] Evidence like this is useful. Account books and ledgers would be even more useful.

In 1838, in a bid to defeat the proposal to disfranchise people of color in Pennsylvania, white abolitionist Benjamin C. Bacon and African-American minister Charles W. Gardner went from house to house in Philadelphia's black community gathering data on schooling, home ownership, employment, and the like, for a massive census the Pennsylvania Abolition Society was undertaking to prove the general worthiness of black citizens. James Forten opposed disfranchisement, and spoke up loudly for equality before the law, but he withheld the details of his personal fortune, which must have been considerable. In 1832 he was paying tax on "Bonds, Mortgages, Bank Stock and Ground Rents."[156] However worthy the cause—and he was clearly in sympathy with the aims of the Pennsylvania Abolition Society—there were some things an astute businessman kept to himself.

IF THE NARRATIVE of James Forten's life as a "gentleman of the pave" has many more loose ends than, for example, the story of his involvement in the antislavery crusade, or his relationships with various family members, it is largely because of the nature of the evidence. His business interests were many, and it was as a businessman that he would often define himself. For example, when he wrote his friend, abolitionist William Lloyd Garrison, he alluded again and again to his need to attend to "business." "Business prevents more at this time."[157] "I would have answered your Letter earlier had it not been owing . . . to a multiplicity of business."[158] "You know I am a man of business, and have not always time at my disposal."[159] Perhaps these were polite excuses for his delay in answering the editor's letters but, when all was said and done, he *was* "a man of business." Sadly, the records that should enable us to get to the heart of his success in business have simply not survived. Pulling together the scattered pieces of the puzzle, the loose threads of half a century spent in the amassing of an impressive fortune, is a task that intrigues even as it ultimately frustrates. In matters of business James Forten did as any good "gentleman of the pave" would do. Aware that idle talk about one's affairs could prove costly, he kept his counsel . . . and he keeps it still.

5

"OUR HAPPY FAMILY CIRCLE"

B Y THE STANDARDS of his contemporaries, James Forten delayed marriage a long time. There was no reluctance on his part to marry, nor was there any shortage of potential partners. The delay was forced upon him. Becoming a master craftsman and setting up in business on his own account left precious little money or time to spare for a wife and children. And then there were his existing obligations. Margaret Forten had been haunted by the specter of poverty most of her life. She had labored long and hard when Thomas was alive, supplementing his modest income by doing domestic work. After she was widowed, the burden on her had become much greater. But for her, the family would have been destitute. Her son would certainly have received no formal education and would probably have spent the rest of his life among the ranks of the laboring poor. As James Forten prospered, he was concerned to make sure his mother had the security she had struggled to provide for him and his sister.

Then there was Abigail and her family. Forten knew from personal experience how meager a sailor's pay was. William Dunbar was away for months at a time.[1] Even if he could get an advance on his wages, Abigail and the children would barely be able to make ends meet while he was at sea. James Forten did what he could for Abigail and William, offering them a home until the Dunbar brood simply outgrew the small house on Shippen Street.[2] When they moved into lodgings he continued to help with gifts and loans. In 1799 Abigail gave birth to yet another child, her fourth and last. She named him James Forten Dunbar in acknowledgment of past favors and in the hope that his uncle might take a special interest in him.

JAMES FORTEN'S FIRST wife was Martha Beatte, seventeen years his junior, from Darby Township, some seven miles downriver from Philadelphia. Perhaps Martha (or Patty, a popular diminutive of "Martha") left Darby to find work in Philadelphia, or perhaps Forten had business in Darby and met her by chance. As for her background, that remains a mystery. Darby Township records do not mention any family, black or white, by the name of Beatte.[3] Assuming Martha Beatte was a woman of color and a native of Pennsylvania, she would not have been a slave. The Gradual Abolition Law was passed in 1780, and she had been born in 1783 or 1784. Still, if her mother had been a slave, she would have been indentured to whoever owned her mother until age twenty-eight. Unless she had been released from her obligations, James Forten would have had to pay for the time remaining on her indenture.

The difficulties, if any, that may have stood in the couple's way were taken care of, and on the evening of November 10, 1803, "Patty" Beatte and James Forten were married at St. Thomas's African Episcopal Church in a ceremony performed by Forten's friend, Absalom Jones. A proud bridegroom announced his marriage to his growing circle of acquaintances, black and white, throughout the city, in *Poulson's American Daily Advertiser*. Less than seven months later those same acquaintances read in *Poulson's* of the death of "Mrs. Martha Forten." She died on May 31, 1804. The brief notice said nothing about the cause.[4]

Forten family friend Stephen H. Gloucester knew little about James Forten's first marriage, other than that his wife was "an interesting lady" and that "this happy union was soon dissolved . . . by death."[5] Forten seldom spoke of his first wife, perhaps out of a deep and abiding sorrow that she had died so young, but more likely because the marriage was of such short duration and it produced no children.

The next year and a half seemed to bring nothing but gloom to James Forten, his kin, and his circle of friends. In January 1805 came news of the death of Robert Bridges's son, Edward. Twelve years younger than Forten, he had been studying law when he was diagnosed with tuberculosis. He set out for the warmer climate of Spain, only to die in Gibraltar.[6] Forten lost not only a friend but also a potential ally in the business world. Had he survived and been admitted to the Pennsylvania Bar, Edward Bridges might well have handled James Forten's legal affairs.

A couple of months later word reached Philadelphia that William Dunbar was dead. Abigail had probably learned from his shipmates that he had been left behind sick in New York Hospital when his ship sailed. The stark announcement in *Poulson's* listing the names of Philadelphians who had died in New York City over the previous few weeks confirmed her worst fears.[7] At age forty-two she found herself a widow.

The news came as a bitter blow to James Forten, not just because he was fond of his brother-in-law and had a warm regard for his sister but because he was contemplating a second marriage. Now he was faced with the need to provide for Abigail and her family. William's estate was negligible. The couple had never owned any real estate, and without help Abigail would simply not be able to manage.

He did what he could for his sister and her children. They would have a home with him as long as they needed one. Abigail and her youngest child lived with him for more than a decade. Then, with the last of her children grown, and James's household becoming overcrowded with his own children, his servants, and his apprentices, she moved into lodgings. However, James took steps to ensure that whatever happened, she would always have a roof over her head. In the mid-1820s he moved Abigail into one of the houses he owned on Washington Court, close to his own home. She lived there rent-free for the rest of her life.[8]

As for his niece and three nephews, he accepted the responsibility for seeing them decently settled. On June 20, 1806, very likely given away by her uncle, Margaret Dunbar married twenty-four-year-old George Lewis at Gloria Dei Church. Lewis, the son of Paris and Elizabeth Lewis, was a free man of color and a native of Delaware.[9] Like so many others before him, he had come to Philadelphia in search of work. Pennsylvania's southern neighbor was gradually divesting itself of its slaves, and every year brought a new crop of manumissions, as slaveholders responded to criticism of the institution of slavery, or as soil exhaustion and slumping tobacco prices made it less profitable. However, freedom was not translated into greater economic mobility for men and women of color. If George Lewis stayed in Delaware, the best he could hope for was to rent or buy a parcel of land and eke out a precarious existence as a smallholder. More likely he would be relegated to laboring on someone else's land.[10] In Philadelphia prospects seemed far brighter. Lewis was more fortunate than most other migrants in that he married into the family of a successful black entrepreneur. Perhaps he was working in Forten's sail loft when he met his employer's niece, or perhaps Forten offered him work as a way of helping Margaret. Whatever the case, within months of his marriage, George Lewis was working for his wife's uncle and mastering a skilled trade.[11]

James Forten also found room in the sail loft for his nephews. Nicholas proved something of a disappointment. Probably against his uncle's advice, he married young. By 1810 he was heading a household of six in Moyamensing.[12] Though seafaring did not agree with him, in time he went to sea, perhaps to escape the demands of family life back in Philadelphia. In 1816 he deserted from the brig *Mary* in St. Croix. After that he disappeared from the records, abandoning his wife and children and leaving his uncle with yet more family obligations to discharge.[13]

William was a worthier object of his uncle's benevolence. Thirteen years old when his father died, he went to work in the sail loft and in time became a competent sailmaker. Like his older brother, he also went to sea, making voyages to Cuba, England, and India. The skill he had mastered under his uncle's tutelage meant higher pay and more status. On the year-long voyage to India, for instance, William shipped out not as a common sailor but as the ship's sailmaker, an especially valuable crew member in the eyes of any captain.[14]

The youngest of the Dunbars, James, was only six when his father died. He stayed with Abigail as his siblings married and moved out. However, when he turned eleven his uncle decided it was time he, too, began to earn his living. On July 12, 1810, James Forten took his nephew to the office of Alderman Alexander Tod at 221 South Front Street to get his seaman's protection certificate. As Forten realized, this was not simply a formality. Desperately short of manpower, the British were impressing into the Royal Navy any sailor who lacked proof that he was not a British citizen. Young James also needed to be safeguarded from unscrupulous Americans who might try to sell him into slavery, a fate that befell so many unwary black sailors. The brief description on his protection certificate indicates he was a sturdy child. He stood 4 feet 7 inches with his shoes on, he had a "Yellow complexion, [and] Black hair," and bore scars from a smallpox inoculation and a dog bite. He was illiterate.[15]

Whether or not his uncle signed him up as a crew member immediately is not clear, but what is clear is that by the time he was forty James Dunbar had seen a great deal of the world. Like James Forten, he made his first overseas voyage on a vessel trading between the United States and Britain. In the spring of 1819, when the ice on the Delaware melted, he set sail for Liverpool on the *William Savery*. A year later he was off to China. More voyages followed—to Cuba, England, China, and the East Indies. Sometimes he sailed with men his uncle knew, masters of vessels who had ordered sails from the Forten loft and discussed matters of trade with James Forten. When he signed on for a voyage to Havana aboard the schooner *George Hand, Jr.*, one of his shipmates was twenty-three-year-old Daniel Brewton, Jr., the son of Forten's friend and fellow prisoner from the *Jersey*.[16]

Perhaps on the strength of his pay from one of his year-long voyages to China, James Dunbar married. On April 20, 1823, at Christ Church, the twenty-four-year-old sailor wed Mary Welsh.[17] Marriage and a family kept him closer to home. There were more voyages, but they were of shorter duration, and he also found shore-based work in his uncle's loft. He and Mary and their children lived for a while with his mother in Washington Court.[18] They briefly rented a home of their own in Pine Ward—they were living there in 1830—but by 1833 they had moved back in with Abigail, probably to cut down on expenses. Soon afterward, sensing, perhaps, that Philadelphia was being eclipsed as a seaport by her neighbor to the north, they moved to New York. It was from New York that James made his next voyage in 1838. After a year-long venture to the East Indies, he left the merchant service, returned to Philadelphia, and joined the United States Navy. As he aged, the appeal of shipboard life increased, or perhaps it is more accurate to say that the attractions of shore life diminished. The Navy offered security of sorts—pay, a place to sleep, three meals a day, and companionship. No sooner would one term of enlistment end than Dunbar would reenlist. He was still in the navy when the Civil War broke out.[19]

THE DEATH OF his brother-in-law and the desperate plight of his sister and her children forced James Forten to postpone his wedding plans, but he did not cancel them. On December 10, 1805, Absalom Jones joined in marriage James Forten, age thirty-nine, and Charlotte Vandine, age twenty. Once more Forten announced his marriage in *Poulson's*.[20] This time, however, his bride outlived him, bearing nine children and dying just days short of her hundredth birthday.

The historical record is far more revealing about Charlotte Vandine's background than about Martha Beatte's. To begin with, we know something of her racial identity. A photograph taken of her in old age shows unmistakably that she was of Native American as well as African and European extraction. A Pennsylvania native, Charlotte could well have been of Lenni Lenape descent and have had family members who were living in the Delaware Valley at the time of William Penn's arrival. The name "Vandine," "Vandyne," or "Vanduyen" suggests some of her African forebears had been owned by one of the families of early Dutch settlers in the region. Most likely she had at least some Dutch ancestors as well.[21]

Charlotte had family in and around Philadelphia. George and Alice Vandyne, probably her parents, were members of St. Thomas's Church in 1794. Perhaps James Forten met his future bride at church. George Vandine's name appeared in the city directories for almost three decades. He bought and sold real estate. He was variously a sugar refiner, a carter, a "dealer," and a sailmaker. His racial designation changed over the years. Some directories listed him as a man of color and others as white. The census takers were similarly befuddled. In 1790 George "Vandell," a free man of color, lived on North Fifth Street, in the city's Middle Ward. In 1810 George "Vandyon" headed a family of six free persons of color in Southwark. That same year a George Vandine, sailmaker, lived at 246 Lombard. In 1820 his household at 65 George Street in Southwark (the property adjoining Forten's) comprised three white persons. As a sailmaker, George Vandine was in partnership in the late 1810s and early 1820s with John Massac in a loft on South Wharves.[22] He may have learned his trade from his son-in-law, or he may already have been operating a loft when his daughter married Forten.

There were other Vandines, also of mixed race, in the Philadelphia area. Ruth Vendine, described as a "free mulatto," married Francis Mitchel, a "free black," at Gloria Dei on November 12, 1792.[23] On October 10, 1798, George Vandine, "a black child," died of yellow fever and was buried in the burial ground of the City Hospital. In 1800 Garret Vandine, a free man of color, headed a household of six in Bucks County. Samuel Vandine lived in the Northern Liberties between 1802 and 1804 and worked as a carter. He and his wife,

Catherine, were members of St. Thomas's.[24] George Vandine, a native of Bucks County, born around 1786, made at least three voyages as a sailor in the 1820s. His protection certificate described him as a dark-complexioned white man. He was probably the same George Vandine, classified as a white man between the ages of sixteen and twenty-six, who headed a household of three in Philadelphia in 1810. Two decades later the census taker in Middletown Township, Bucks County, listed him as a man of color.[25] Like George, Charles Vandine, another "dark complexioned white man," born in 1800, received a sailor's protection certificate from the authorities in the port of Philadelphia. These two men were almost certainly Charlotte's brothers. Various sources indicate she had at least two brothers, George, a year her junior, and Charles.[26] There may have been other siblings. A Garrett Vandim was baptized at St. Paul's Church in Philadelphia in 1789 and a Rachel Vandine in 1791.[27]

James Forten moved his new bride into the house on Shippen Street that he shared with his mother, but Margaret Forten died on May 27, 1806, before the birth of James and Charlotte's first child. True, her death was not unexpected; she was eighty-four. Still, her presence as the matriarch of the family was sadly missed. Forten's father, dead some thirty years, was a shadowy memory. His mother had been the principal caregiver and provider during most of his childhood, struggling to keep a home together for him and his sister, and encouraging him to get an education. Later, as he worked to carve out a place for himself in Philadelphia's business community, she ran his household for him. Now she was gone, just as he looked to provide her with another grandchild to fuss over. He did not let her passing go unnoticed. The brief announcement in *Poulson's* described how her "virtues endeared her to her Relations, and a numerous acquaintance of friends, who will sincerely regret her loss."[28]

Margaret died as her son was quite literally taking his place among Philadelphia's well-to-do merchants and master craftsmen. Less than six months after his mother's death James Forten completed the purchase of his new home on Lombard Street. It was a very visible sign of just how well he was doing. The house was also in the city proper, rather than in Southwark. City streets were better lit, better paved, and generally cleaner than those in the outlying areas. On Shippen Street, Forten's neighbors had been sailors, ship's carpenters, and small craftsmen in the maritime trades.[29] On Lombard he lived alongside merchants and substantial men of business like himself. It was in the Lombard Street home on September 11, 1806, that James and Charlotte's first child was born. A girl, she was christened Margaretta, or "little Margaret," in memory of her grandmother.[30]

Other children followed in fairly rapid succession. On November 4, 1808, Charlotte gave birth to a second daughter. Baptized Charlotte after her mother, she died on March 24, 1814, at age five of "Dropsy in [the] Brain," or hydrocephalus.[31] On February 1, 1810, a third daughter was born. She was named

Harriet Davy Forten, a tribute to someone who had meant a great deal to James Forten. Back in the days when he had been Robert Bridges's foreman, and probably lived in Bridges's home, he had befriended little Harriet Bridges. Born in 1784, she was a toddler when he first met her. He had watched her grow up and had seen her marry well. In 1804, at age nineteen, she had wed John Broome Davy, scion of a wealthy merchant family. Five years later she died. Forten named his third daughter in her memory. Perhaps he hoped to ingratiate himself with her husband and his family. After all, the Davys were shipowners. But it seems to have been personal considerations, rather than mercenary ones, that weighed with him.[32]

On November 15, 1811, Charlotte presented James with a long-awaited son and heir. There was no hesitation about whom to honor in naming *this* child. He was James Forten, Jr.[33] Another son, born on May 12, 1813, was baptized Robert Bridges Forten in memory of James Forten's friend and benefactor.[34]

A fourth daughter was born in 1814, although the precise date of her birth was not recorded in the register of St. Thomas's Church. She was baptized Sarah Louisa, possibly to honor another Bridges daughter.[35] On April 2, 1815, James and Charlotte's seventh child was born. She was named Mary Isabella, perhaps for yet another Bridges daughter, Mary.[36]

On October 13, 1817, Charlotte gave birth to a third son, Thomas Willing Francis Forten.[37] "Thomas" may have been a belated nod to James's father. It also acknowledged, as did the rest of the name, a debt of gratitude. Although by 1817 the firm of Willing and Francis was past its zenith, Forten did not forget that the partners had placed their trust in him at a time when other merchants were doubtful about the ability of a man of color to run his own business.

The Fortens' ninth and last child, another son, was born in 1823 when Charlotte was thirty-nine and James fifty-seven. James named him for another man, by then long dead, who had helped him in those difficult early years in business. A couple of years younger than Forten, William Deas had been a partner in the firm of Knox and Deas, and part owner with David Knox of the ship *Ariana* and the schooner *Charles*. Deas's life had been a short and tragic one. He had died at age thirty-seven in 1806. His wife outlived him by just a year and a half, and their children were left with precious few resources. In memorializing their father, Forten was hardly trying to win the favor of people who could help him. Rather, he was showing his gratitude for trust and confidence given at a critical time two decades before. James Forten was not one to forget his friends.[38]

If not an overly indulgent parent, James Forten was very much attached to his children, protective of them, and concerned about their future. In his *Letters from a Man of Colour*, written in 1813, by which time he had three daughters and two sons, he issued a challenge to legislators who were considering a package of laws that would erode the legal status of people of color: "[A]re you a parent? Have you children around whom your affections are bound, by those delightful bonds which none but a parent can know? Are they the delight of your prosperity, and the solace of your afflictions? If all this be true, to you we submit our cause. The parent's feelings cannot err."[39]

By all accounts, the younger Fortens enjoyed a happy, supportive childhood. In 1833, Sarah, who had emerged as an accomplished poet, turned for a moment from writing about the plight of the slave to reflect on her own "Hours of Childhood." Her memories were happy ones, tinged with sadness only by the inevitable losses brought about by death and separation.

> Dear cherished hours, how much ye tell
> Of all we've known, and loved so well!
> On memory's page there is a leaf,
> Bearing a trace of pleasure brief;
> Of schoolday mirth, of pasttime gay,
> With which we whiled those hours away.[40]

Sarah readily acknowledged that in "our happy family circle" she and her siblings had been given privileges denied to so many other young people of color.[41]

The Forten family home at 92 Lombard was crowded, but far less so than the miserable tenements of Hog Alley and other poor quarters of the city. The home was a typical Philadelphia town house—three floors, each divided into two rooms; an attic and basement similarly divided; a "piazza"; and a two-story back building split into four rooms.[42] There were always people around—an aunt and cousins, apprentices, and servants. In 1810 James Forten presided over a household of fifteen. There was James himself, Charlotte, their three eldest children, Abigail, and young James Dunbar. The other eight people were individuals Forten employed in one capacity or another.[43] A decade later there were eighteen people in the home. Apart from Forten, his wife, and their children (they had seven by then), and possibly Abigail, there were eight boarders of various sorts. By 1830 the household had grown to twenty-two. Eight of the eleven black boys and men between the ages of ten and twenty-four were Forten employees. In addition to Charlotte and her four surviving daughters, there were four female residents. By 1838, when the Pennsylvania Abolition Society conducted its ambitious survey of the black population of the city and county of Philadelphia, three of Forten's children had married and moved away, but there were still seventeen people living at 92 Lombard. The household size remained stable at seventeen in 1840. James Jr. had married and he and his wife and son lived with his parents. However, there were still half a dozen apprentices and domestics.[44]

Who were these unrelated men and women who lived under Forten's roof? We know about a couple of them, because they were formally indentured to James Forten through the Pennsylvania Abolition Society's Committee on Indentures. On July 25, 1805, fifteen-year-old Maryland native Samuel Elbert was bound to Forten for five years and five months. He was a minor, and the indenture had been made with the consent of his mother, Wealthy Hill. Most likely Forten took him on to work in the sail loft. As the boy's master, it was Forten's responsibility to house him. Samuel would have lived with Forten and his mother at 50 Shippen, and then moved with the household to 92 Lombard.[45] On November 29, 1811, Judy, an African-American woman whose age and last name were not recorded on the indenture, was bound to Forten's service for eleven years. With four young children to care for and busy supervising the live-in apprentices and journeymen, Charlotte Forten needed help around the house. Then there was the question of status. Forten was doing well and it was right and proper that his wife should have a servant. Another consideration was the sense that, by taking in a woman who was most likely a recently liberated slave, and someone new to the city, he and his family could assist her while assisting themselves.[46] Over the years Samuel Elbert and Judy would have their successors—domestics, apprentices, and journeymen who all formed part of James Forten's extended family, and over whom he expected to have a great degree of authority.[47]

Without evidence from journals and personal letters, the maintenance of physical and social boundaries in the Forten home is something that can only be guessed at. Domestics such as Judy almost certainly spent most of their lives in the kitchen area. But what of the apprentices? How much interaction did Forten encourage between his sons and the men they would one day employ? As for his daughters, what did the presence of young men who were at once members of the extended family but not actual family members mean? There is no evidence that Forten either sanctioned or forbade friendships, and possibly courtships. After all, some of the apprentices were related to old friends such as New England merchants and shipowners Paul Cuffe and Richard Johnson. Likely to inherit substantial sums of money and property, and become successful businessmen in their own right, apprentices Shadrach Howard and Ezra Johnson would presumably have been acceptable to James Forten as sons-in-law. Of course, not every young man who lived at 92 Lombard had *their* prospects.

Over the years the Forten children formed many friendships. They socialized with their cousins, the various Dunbars, Lewises, and Vandines. They mixed with the sons and daughters of other affluent free people of color. They were active in their church and found companionship there. They also enjoyed friendships with white children. For instance, Robert found a playmate in future Congressman William D. ("Pig Iron") Kelley. They were the same age, but the Kelleys were poorer than the Fortens. William was the youngest child of jeweler and watchmaker David Kelley. In the panic that followed the War of 1812 the older Kelley endorsed a note for a relative, who defaulted and bankrupted him. The shock killed him. His widow, Hannah, opened a boardinghouse to support herself and her children. Years later Congressman Kelley recalled Robert Forten as "one with whom I played in the earliest days of my childhood." He "grew to manhood an elegant gentleman; he was skilled in art and gifted with a rare voice, and a proficient in music. His education was liberal, and his manners and tone those of a gentleman."[48]

Charlotte and James Forten were determined to give their children a good education, one they hoped would match their prospects. They could teach them their letters and numbers at home, but they wanted more for them than that. The issue they had to confront was the same one faced by other well-to-do African-American parents. How could they get their children an education that would train them to be more than "hewers of wood and drawers of water"? There were no publicly funded schools for black children in Philadelphia until 1822.[49] Private academies invariably refused to admit black pupils, while the charity schools for blacks generally offered only a basic education. James and Charlotte Forten refused to give up. They joined forces with another African-American couple who was struggling with the same problem.

James Forten had probably known Grace Bustill Douglass from childhood. She was the daughter of Cyrus Bustill, a man who was very much a presence in the African-American community in the 1780s and 1790s. Bustill, the child of an English-born lawyer and a slave, had secured his freedom and made money as a baker and brewer. His wife, Elizabeth Morey, was the daughter of an English aristocrat and a Native American woman. Grace was the fifth of their seven children. Cyrus Bustill's concern that his children get an education had eventually extended to a concern for the wider community of color, and after his retirement he operated a school from his home. In 1803 Grace Bustill married Robert Douglass, a prosperous barber from the Caribbean island of St. Kitts. Douglass was a member of St. Thomas's Church and served on the vestry with Forten, although he eventually left to join First African Presbyterian. Despite repeated rebuffs from white Friends, Grace, like her parents, remained in fellowship with the Quakers.

Grace and Robert had a high regard for education, and both agonized over their children's schooling. They had six children—two daughters, Elizabeth and Sarah, and four sons, Robert, James Forten (named for their friend), Charles Frederick, and William Penn.[50] The struggle to find a school that would accept their eldest, Elizabeth, was especially traumatic. Finally, in 1819 the Fortens and the Douglasses pooled their resources and began a school of their own, "in order that their children might be better taught than they could be in any of the schools then open to our people." They hired a teacher, a white man, Britton E. Chamberlain. When he left in 1826 or 1827, his place was taken by Sarah Douglass.[51] Other prosperous black parents enrolled their children in the school, and it was rather exclusive, or at least that was how it was perceived. Philadelphia reformer Elliott Cresson described it as "supported by the more wealthy blacks for their own children."[52]

With the possible exception of Mary Isabella, who seems to have been an invalid much of her life, the Forten daughters attended this school until they were in their mid-teens. Their father then hired tutors to teach them music and French at home. They also read extensively, devouring novels, poetry, theological works, and histories. They studied advice books such as Hannah More's *Strictures on the Modern System of Education with a View of the Principles and Conduct Prevalent Among Women of Rank and Fortune*, and reflected in their writings on what they had read. The result was everything their parents could have hoped for. White abolitionist Samuel J. May, for instance, was delighted to be introduced to James Forten's daughters, whom he found to be "lovely [and] accomplished." He added: "I learned from him [Forten] that their education, evidently of a superior kind, had cost him very much more than it would have done, if they had not been denied admission into the best schools of the city."[53]

Like their sisters, the Forten boys were educated at the school their parents and the Douglasses had established, but eventually Forten transferred them to the Pennsylvania Abolition Society's new Clarkson School. He may also have arranged for private tutoring. In the 1850s young Charlotte Forten, James's granddaughter, referred in her journal to a meeting with one "Mr. Coffin," whom she identified as "the former tutor of my father and uncles" and "a radical abolitionist." Joshua Coffin, a graduate of Dartmouth College, had taught for a short time at the Clarkson School in the early 1830s under the direction of Quaker abolitionist Evan Lewis. Perhaps Forten had hired Coffin to teach his sons privately. When Lewis's death left the school without a permanent head teacher, Coffin applied to the Abolition Society for the post, citing his extensive teaching experience, his "vigorous constitution," and his "interest . . . for that class of our fellow-citizens for whose improvement your Society has so long . . . laboured." He got the appointment and took charge of the Clarkson School on February 11, 1834. James Jr. and Robert had left to work in the sail loft by then, but both Thomas and William were in Coffin's classes.[54]

The household at 92 Lombard was a musical one, and the Forten daughters became accomplished musicians. Young Charlotte Forten noted in her journal that "Scotch airs" always transported her back to her childhood, when she would listen to her father, Robert, and her uncles sing those same songs.[55] One gets a glimpse of genteel social life in the homes of well-to-do black Philadelphians from Joseph Willson's *Sketches of the Higher Classes of Colored Society*. Willson, a wealthy young man of color from Augusta, Georgia, moved to Philadelphia with his family in the early 1830s. The Willsons worshipped at St. Thomas's with the Fortens and moved in the same social circles. In 1841 Joseph Willson observed:

> It is rarely that the visitor in the different families where there are two or three ladies, will not find one or more of them competent to perform on the piano-forte, guitar, or some other appropriate musical instrument. . . . The love of music is universal; it is cultivated to some extent . . . by all; so that it is almost impossible to enter a parlor where the ear of the visitor is not . . . greeted therewith.[56]

In addition to the large household that James Forten presided over, there was a steady stream of guests, for the Fortens had the reputation for being very hospitable. There were also wards of one sort or another who enjoyed the Fortens' care and protection. On one occasion James Forten brought home to a surprised Charlotte a young West African prince who had been entrusted to him. The eight-year-old prince, renamed "George Sherker," stayed for only a few days, but another child lived with the Fortens as James's ward for several years.[57] Forten's business know-how, his reputation for honesty, and his proven loyalty to his friends induced some in the African-American community to seek him out when they settled their estates. He witnessed their wills, agreed to act as their executor, and was sometimes asked to become the guardian of their minor children. That was how young Ann Appo joined the household at 92 Lombard.

Confectioner Jean Baptiste, or John Appo, and his wife, Ann, were members of Saint Domingue's community of *gens de couleur*. Wealthy and very obviously of European as well as African descent, they found it prudent to pack their belonging and leave for Philadelphia during the upheavals of the 1790s. They never returned. Thanks to some astute investments, and Ann's recipe for ice cream, they did well in their new home. They acquired real estate, some of which they rented out, and they also made loans at interest. When Appo wrote his will shortly before his death in 1818, he named the eldest of his four children, Ellen, as executrix. Ellen was of age, but his three other children, Joseph, William, and Ann, were minors. Appo's will specified that his two executors, Forten and oyster-seller Richard Howell, would become their guardians in the event that their mother remarried or died.[58]

John Appo's widow died in 1825. By then Joseph and William were of age, but Ann was still in her teens, and she apparently moved in with the Fortens. It may well have been the connection with the Appos that gained for the Forten children their musical education. All four Appo children were talented musicians. Ann was the organist at St. Thomas's Church until her tragic death from consumption in 1828.[59] Back in 1819 Ellen Appo had married composer and bandleader Francis Johnson. Johnson was a member of St. Thomas's and the couple lived just a few blocks away from the Fortens. Joseph and William were members of Johnson's band, and both taught music.[60]

THE LINKS BETWEEN the Fortens and Robert and Joseph Purvis were ties of affection rather than legal ties, but in a sense the brothers were, at least informally, wards of the Forten family. The relationship between the two families was a complex one that deepened over time. Robert and Joseph would both marry into the Forten family and Robert would become James Forten's closest ally in the last decade and a half of his life. The ties forged through friendship and marriage would become every bit as powerful as if the two were indeed father and son.

James and Charlotte had probably met the father of Robert and Joseph, Englishman William Purvis, on one of his visits to Philadelphia. Four years older than Forten, Purvis came from the tiny village of Ross, in Northumberland, close to the Scottish border. His parents had been blessed with a superfluity of sons. The eldest stood to inherit the bulk of what was evidently a fairly modest estate, while William and his brothers were left to fend for themselves. One became the captain of a privateer, while the others decided to try their luck in the newly independent United States. Their destination was as different as possible from the bleak, windswept coast of Northumberland. One by one, they made their way to South Carolina. John, Alexander, and Robert went into business as cotton brokers.[61] William and Burridge formed a partnership with one Ainsley Hall, possibly a relative. Burridge and Hall ran their store in Columbia, and William took charge of the Charleston end of the operation. The partners dealt in pretty much anything at first, importing manufactured goods and taking whatever they could get in return. Eventually, with the growing profitability of cotton, they became cotton brokers.[62]

All the brothers prospered. John made his fortune and retired to New England, apparently in search of a healthier climate. Alexander sold up around 1809 and moved to Scotland, where he bought an estate. Burridge married in Charleston and eventually relocated to Scotland with his wife and children, buying an estate near Alexander's.[63] As for William, he made his home in South Carolina and became an American citizen in 1799. With Burridge back in Britain, he ran their entire business, dividing his time between Columbia and Charleston.[64]

It was during one of his trips to Charleston that William met Harriet Judah, a free woman of color many years his junior. Her mother, Dido Badaracka, was a native of Morocco. Kidnapped into slavery at the age of twelve in 1766 and brought to Charleston, Dido had been purchased by an elderly white woman, Harriet Deas, as a maid and companion. Harriet Deas treated Dido fairly well, freeing her in her will and leaving her a pension of $60 per year. According to her grandson, Dido married a German Jewish flour merchant, "Baron" Judah, and the couple had at least three children, including a daughter, whom Dido named Harriet in memory of her former mistress.[65]

William Purvis never married Harriet Judah. Their son, Robert, insisted they had been married, but William's will indicates otherwise. Harriet was not his wife, but she was his "beloved friend." The couple lived together in Charleston and it was there that their three children were born—William Jr. in 1808, Robert in 1810, and Joseph in 1812. Robert remembered his father with deep affection and reverence. Not only did he insist his parents had been legally married, but he reacted angrily to suggestions that William had been involved in slave-trading. When in 1853 Frederick Douglass charged that the older Purvis had amassed "blood-stained riches," Robert was furious. His father had denounced slavery, taught his sons to hate it, "and was known . . . as a friend and benefactor of the free and enslaved colored man."[66] On another occasion he insisted his father had been "instinctively and practically an abolitionist." He himself had become an antislavery activist because of his father. "My first impression of the evils of slavery was derived from the books he placed in our hands, viz: 'Torrey's Portraiture of Slavery' and 'Sandford and Merton.'"[67]

Robert might not have cared to admit it, but his father *had* owned slaves. In 1819, for instance, he purchased an entire family from Susan Hipkins of Charleston.[68] Nor was this his only purchase. Under the terms of William Purvis's will, Robert and his brothers actually became slaveholders, although the fate of their slaves was complicated by a legal battle with two cousins who were rival claimants to the estate.[69] As for Harriet Judah, she also bought and sold slaves. And it was not the case that she purchased friends and relatives out of bondage. She dealt in slaves, as did so many of her neighbors in Charleston's free colored community. In the space of one month in 1812 she sold "a Country born Negro Girl about ten years old named Betty" and purchased "an [A]frican [N]egro wench named Bella" and "a negro Girl named Jenny."[70] Apparently she had no qualms about these transactions. After all, she herself had never been a slave. She was freeborn, light-skinned, and had a wealthy white lover.[71]

In 1819 William Purvis began making plans to retire and return to Britain. It was time to follow the example of Burridge and Alexander and buy an estate somewhere in the north of England or in Scotland. He had his family to consider. Married or not, Harriet was his wife, his lifelong partner, but there would be difficulties as long as they remained in a community where her ancestry was known. And then there were their sons. He could leave them his fortune, but he could not educate them as gentlemen in South Carolina. The family must move.

As a first step, William sent Harriet and the children to Philadelphia while he settled his affairs in South Carolina. In January 1820 he enrolled William and Robert in the Pennsylvania Abolition Society's Clarkson School. Their younger brother joined them the following year.[72] Harriet and her sons lived at various addresses in Philadelphia. Sometimes she was listed as white in the city directories and sometimes as a woman of color.[73] She and her children knew the Forten boys through the Clarkson School. The families also met every Sunday at St. Thomas's Church.

Although his various business activities forced William Purvis to spend a great deal of his time away from his family, he visited whenever he could. In the fall of 1826 he was staying with Harriet and the children when he fell ill with typhus. He died on October 3. The funeral took place the next day. The nature of typhus demanded a quick interment and left little time for mourning. The family placed a brief notice in *Poulson's* announcing the death, giving details of the funeral (at Second Presbyterian), and inviting acquaintances, especially those visiting from Charleston and Columbia, to attend.[74]

Two years earlier William had made a trip to Britain, intending probably to prepare for his family's move. Before he left America, he took the sensible precaution of settling his estate in case he died on the voyage. That will now came into effect. Apart from a modest bequest to a niece, he left his entire fortune to his "beloved friend" and his three sons. Harriet received a hundred shares of United States Bank stock, worth $10,000. William, Robert, and Joseph shared an estate valued at a quarter of a million dollars.[75]

Within two years of her lover's death Harriet Judah married a leading African-American cleric, William Miller. Miller had been born free in Queen Annes County, Maryland, in 1775 and had moved to New York when he was in his late teens. A cabinetmaker by trade, he had done well.[76] However, it was not as a craftsman but as a religious leader, albeit something of a maverick, that he distinguished himself. A Methodist by upbringing, he was a close associate of African Methodist Episcopal Zion founder James Varrick. In fact, it was in Miller's house at 36 Mulberry Street that Varrick and his followers first met for worship. In 1814 Miller broke with Zion (some alleged because of his "unstayable ambition") and helped found the Asbury Church. Still, he enjoyed considerable respect and was a driving force for education within New York's African-American community. For many years he ran a school at his home. In 1817 he became president of the New York African Bible Society. The organization had its headquarters in his home. It was Miller's aim to put Bibles in the hands of people of color and make sure they had the necessary schooling to read them. Over the years he wavered back and forth from the AME Zion Church to "regular" Methodism, then to Richard Allen's AME denomination. A deacon of the AMEZ in 1808, he became an AME elder in 1823, and then a minister, before returning to the AMEZ fold and being consecrated a bishop in 1840.[77]

There are no letters or journal entries to indicate how her sons reacted to Harriet's marriage or how they got along with their stepfather. Rev. Miller was very active as a community leader. His friends included Christopher Rush, Peter Williams, and Samuel Cornish—in fact, the champions of "reform" within New York City's African-American community.[78] There must surely have been a meeting of minds, at least between Miller and the intellectually inclined Robert. However, quite possibly Harriet's two younger sons saw little of their stepfather. They were packed off to Amherst Academy, a private preparatory school in Massachusetts affiliated with nearby Amherst College.[79] While they were there, another tragedy befell the family. William had not joined them at school because his health was failing. By the spring of 1828 he knew he was dying of tuberculosis and he drew up his will. He left his estate to his mother in trust for his brothers. He died in Philadelphia on April 5, 1828, and was buried at St. Thomas's Church.[80]

In the space of two years Robert and Joseph had lost their father and elder brother. Their mother had married and, although she owned a home in Philadelphia, she spent much of her time in New York with her husband. Was it so surprising that the two young men should have seized the chance to become "adopted" members of the Forten family, a family they had known for over a decade? James and Charlotte were prepared to treat them like sons. They attended the same church. Their own sons had been schoolfellows of the Purvises. Their four surviving daughters were handsome and accomplished young women. Who knew what might develop?

JAMES FORTEN COULD secure many advantages for the members of his extended family. He could buy his children an education and look for wealthy marriage partners for them. He could house his sister comfortably and provide for his mother in her old age. He could give the young men who worked for him over the decades the opportunity to master a trade and move out of the ranks of unskilled laborers. He could take in his friends' orphaned children and give his servants a stable life, albeit one lived under his watchful eye, amid the snares and dangers of the urban environment. What he could not do for any one of these individuals was to insulate them from the consequences of being black in America. Admittedly some were so light-skinned that whites did not always perceive their African ancestry. But when they did it exposed them to everything from a snub or a muttered epithet to violent assault or enslavement. No member of his household, from the lowliest of his servants to Forten himself, was spared, and he knew it.

In 1834 English reformer Edward S. Abdy called on James Forten, met his family, and heard from Forten the remarkable story of his life. Abdy reported that Forten told him his family "does not, so far as he has been able to ascertain, number one slave among its members."[81] But Forten knew better than to assume that slavery could not reach out to threaten his family. A decade earlier he had been brought face to face with the reality of slavery in an episode that spoke, paradoxically, both to the vulnerability of any person of color and to the strength of his own reputation as a black man of means and influence.

Amos Dunbar was most likely the son of Forten's wayward nephew, Nicholas. Left to cope as best she could with the burden of supporting her family after Nicholas jumped ship in St. Croix, Jane Dunbar turned to the Guardians of the Poor in 1820 to help place her ten-year-old son. Amos was indentured to Samuel Chapin, on Christian Street, until he turned twenty-one, to learn "the art & mystery of a House Servant." For whatever reason, the indenture was canceled and Amos returned to the Guardians after a few months.[82] A subsequent placement proved even more disastrous.

At some point in the early 1820s Jane Dunbar married again. She had either learned of Nicholas's death or had given up waiting for his return and cut her losses.[83] Her new husband, porter Abraham Morton, tried to do his best for his stepchildren. In the summer of 1824 Pennsylvania Abolition Society member Thomas Shipley reported that Morton had been to see him about Amos. The youth had been bound to one Henry Moore of Pittsburgh, and it now appeared that Moore had sold him, "As information has been received from two different persons, that he is now held as a slave in New Orleans."[84]

Amos had indeed been sold into slavery in New Orleans. His purchaser was Robert Layton, a dealer in ship chandlery. At some point Amos spoke up about his situation and dropped the name of his rich and influential great-uncle back in Philadelphia. As Layton confessed to James Forten, he had been angry. He could not understand why Amos had not said something earlier, "as he was some time in my Family on trial, and ought to have mentioned his situation and had no restraint upon him to prevent him." It never crossed Layton's mind that Amos was scared. Layton considered Amos "intelligent and artful" and believed he "certainly aided the man who sold him to me."[85]

Still, an enslaved free black was a potential troublemaker, and one with powerful friends a positive menace. Layton, as someone involved in the maritime trades, had heard of the wealthy black sailmaker James Forten and was inclined to follow up on Amos's allegations of unlawful enslavement, instead of just beating the youth into silence and submission. Forten was influential enough to make trouble. He was also reputedly rich enough to afford to be generous to anyone who helped a member of his extended family.

Layton pursued the matter when he traveled north near the end of 1824. He met with members of the Pennsylvania Abolition Society, and perhaps with Forten and the Dunbars. He mentioned an "interview with the Boy's friends," and he took back to Amos a letter from his stepfather. On his return to New Orleans he found Amos "well and . . . quite hearty," but he was not best pleased by other developments. As he explained in a letter to Forten, Amos had hired a lawyer! Layton endeavored to be tactful. If Forten and his friends had advised that course of action, it was one thing. If Amos had acted on his own initiative, it "must mean expenses which must be paid." Layton had "lodged [Amos] in jail for safe keeping," and someone would have to pay the jail fees. Layton was anxious, so he said, about two things—that Amos should recover his liberty "in a Legal manner," and that he (Layton) should have "proper recourse on the man who sold him to me . . . should I ever have the opportunity." Frankly, he was aggrieved, out of pocket, and tired of the whole business.

> I have divested myself of all claims upon the Boy unless through the Honour and Gratitude of his Friends to reimburse me . . . after his return home. As the friend of this Boy, and as a man, who I believe will consider . . . the claims I have on him in equity and justice, I . . . beg your attention to the same.[86]

By November 1825 there was good news. The New Orleans law firm of Watts and Lobdell, whose partners had cooperated with the Abolition Society in the past, wrote Thomas Shipley that they had secured Amos's freedom, "and he is now Engaged on Board one of our Steam Boats as a hired servant, well satisfied; and not wishing to go back to his mother."[87] Had he not had a relative with the ability to both make trouble and help pay for his freedom, Amos Dunbar would almost certainly have lived out his life as a slave.

Amos Dunbar's case was not the only one in which slavery reached out to touch the Forten family. A relative of Charlotte's also fell victim to the "peculiar institution." In 1827 the Pennsylvania Abolition Society learned that "Garrett Vandyne[,] a free man of Color born in this city, has been lately discovered to be in Slavery in . . . Mississippi." Members authorized the expenditure of $25 to cover the cost of securing his freedom.[88]

JAMES FORTEN'S FAMILY was a tremendous source of strength in his life. Happy in his marriage, proud of his children, he enjoyed his role as husband and father. His "family" also embraced those who were not related to him but lived under his roof or enjoyed his protection in one way or another. He expected deference from his servants and his apprentices, and by and large he received it. A man of means, an astute and farsighted businessman, he could have made his home and his sail loft the two centers of his life. And, of course, in a sense, that is exactly what he did. It was from his home and family that he drew emotional strength, and from his place of business that he derived both his sense of pride as "a gentleman of the pave" and the very tangible power that came with the possession of wealth. But James Forten reached out beyond his home and his workplace. By the 1820s he was one of the most influential men of color in the United States. Understanding how he achieved that status, what causes he championed, what battles he won and lost, and what friends and enemies he made is as vital to a sense of who James Forten was as his flair for business and his ability to command the respect of his household.

6

BROTHER FORTEN

I N 1785, WHEN he returned from his year-long sojourn in England and apprenticed himself to Robert Bridges to learn the "mystery" of the sailmaker's craft, James Forten was one of some 1500 black people who counted themselves as residents of Philadelphia and its surrounding districts."[1] In certain respects he was an anomaly. Freeborn, and a Philadelphia native, his experiences were unlike those of the vast majority of black Philadelphians, who had known physical bondage and who were, in so many cases, relatively new arrivals to the city. His almost two years of formal education also set him apart, not just from black citizens but from many working people in the larger white community. However, when all was said and done, James Forten *was* a member of the black community, and to understand his growing influence within that community entails understanding the world black Philadelphians were struggling to make for themselves as the eighteenth century drew to a close.

"Africans" was how most white citizens, even the champions of abolition, referred to their black neighbors. Some uttered the term with more than a hint of contempt, but others employed it with a feeling that it was accurate and appropriate. After all, were these men and women not the scattered children of Africa? Nor was the term one that black people themselves found offensive, although they put a subtly different construction on it. For them it signified both a common descent and a shared heritage of suffering. No shame was attached to being "African." Far from it. The 1780s and 1790s would see the creation in Philadelphia by black people of the Free African Society, the African Lodge, and the African Church. A black minister, one of James Forten's closest friends, would urge his congregation to "constantly *remember the rock whence we were hewn.* . . . [I]t becomes us . . . to acknowledge, that an African slave, ready to perish, was our father or our grandfather." And Forten himself, separated by three generations from his West African great-grandfather, would speak up on behalf of "Africans and descendants of that unhappy race" in the United States, identifying himself as one of their number.[2]

Fraught with meaning though the term "African" was for both black and white Philadelphians, it was problematic in terms of describing the composition of the city's black population in the 1780s and 1790s, for it downplayed the diversity of that population with respect to ethnicity, language, education, job skills, and experience of enslavement. "Africans" black Philadelphians might be, but identical because of a shared African ancestry they most definitely were not.

James Forten certainly knew men and women who had first-hand knowledge of the cultures and peoples of West Africa. Among his parents' generation there were plenty of Africans. Slave traders had imported significant numbers of slaves direct from the Guinea coast into the colony of Pennsylvania during the French and Indian War to remedy the critical labor shortage brought about by the dwindling supply of European indentured laborers. However, once the wartime crisis was over, white Philadelphians resumed their normal patterns of acquiring workers, preferring indentured servants from Europe and slaves from the American mainland or the Caribbean to disease-prone, non-English-speaking "saltwater Negroes."[3] In the 1790s the survivors of that influx of the 1750s and early 1760s were well into their forties and fifties, but there were other Africans besides them. One of Forten's most trusted friends, Shandy Yard, a grocer and sometime mariner, had been born in West Africa around 1772. Forten knew others from the African continent, among them the Senegalese ex-slave Antoine Servance, whom he eventually befriended.[4] And even after the passage of Pennsylvania's Gradual Abolition Act, Africans continued to arrive in Philadelphia. In August 1800 the *Phoebe* and the *Prudent* docked at the Lazaretto, or quarantine hospital, with more than a hundred naked Africans on board. The illegal slavers had been intercepted in the Delaware by the warship *Ganges*. Their reluctant passengers were clothed by benevolent Philadelphians, their names were recorded by the officers of the Pennsylvania Abolition Society, all with "Ganges" as a last name, and then they were bound out as servants for different periods of time according to their ages.[5] The name "Ganges" would crop up again and again over the next half-century, as the men, women, and children who had made up the human cargo from the *Phoebe* and the *Prudent* completed their periods of indenture and carved out lives for themselves, socializing, worshipping, and intermarrying with long-time black residents of Philadelphia.

The port city's longstanding commercial ties with the Caribbean brought in a steady stream of West Indian immigrants. Some arrived as sailors on trading vessels, liked what they saw, and stayed. Forten's friend Anthony Cain, originally from Bermuda, fell into that category.[6] Others came in service to white masters or employers, took one look at Philadelphia, and promptly absconded, losing themselves within the rapidly growing black community.[7] Still others arrived with their legal freedom assured, with skilled trades, and with cash in their pockets, determined to make better lives for themselves in this new setting than they thought they could back home. Barber Robert Douglass from St. Kitts, grocers Robert and Sarah Gordon from Barbados, and perfumer Joseph Cassey from one of the French islands, all four of them Forten family friends, added their distinctive customs, their accents, and their perspectives to the diversity of the city's black population.[8] The upheavals on Saint Domingue would contribute yet more elements to the mix of cultures, languages, and lifestyles that was the black Philadelphia of the 1790s.

Many American-born black residents of the city were migrants, and many, unlike Forten, strangers to urban life. As neighboring states like Delaware, Maryland, and Virginia loosened the restrictions on private manumissions, hundreds of newly liberated people headed north to a city where they believed they would find both a warm welcome and the chance to earn a decent living.[9] A thriving mercantile center, and the nation's capital until 1800, Philadelphia held out the chance to the industrious person of color of gainful employment. Sailors and cooks, carters and sweeps, laundresses and laborers, hucksters and waiters—black men and women seized all those jobs and more, anxious to become financially independent after years, perhaps decades, of laboring in bondage for the benefit of others.

Black people poured in from New Jersey, where slavery was taking a very long time to die, and from Philadelphia's rural hinterland.[10] New York masters complained about runaway slaves making for Philadelphia in the belief that they would be free once they got there.[11] Even though they could feel more secure in their freedom, given the passage of manumission laws in their home states, a sprinkling of New Englanders settled in Philadelphia. Among these "black Yankees" were sailor turned clothier John Bowers from Boston, who would worship alongside James Forten at the African Church, and Rhode Islander Peter Gardiner, a self-trained "botanic physician" and preacher, who would collaborate with Forten in various initiatives over the years.[12]

So many of the men and women who made up Philadelphia's rapidly growing black population had been enslaved. That was true of most of James Forten's associates in the 1790s. His friend and future minister, Absalom Jones, had worked long and hard to raise the money to free himself and his wife. Richard Allen, separated from most of the members of his immediate family through sale, had finally prevailed on his master to let him and his brother earn the price of their freedom. New Jersey native Cyrus Bustill, the son of a well-to-do English lawyer and a slave, had also bargained and toiled for his liberty. William Wilshire had been set free by his owner.[13] The list went on and on. Although he had certainly feared enslavement during his time as a prisoner of the

British, James Forten had never known what it was to be the property of another human being.

In a sense, of course, even he was not technically free. Upon his return from England he had apprenticed himself to Robert Bridges, voluntarily entering into a legally binding indenture. But he was bound only to the extent that a white youth was bound to a master, and his prospects were so much more promising than those of the average teenage apprentice. Hundreds of nominally free black Philadelphians lived under much more onerous types of indenture, while scores more were still enslaved.

While the Gradual Abolition Act of 1780 had been hailed by Pennsylvania's white antislavery activists and by many in the African-American community as the beginning of the end for slavery in the state, it *was* only a beginning. Not a single slave alive on the day the act was passed was legally entitled to his or her freedom. Only the children of enslaved women benefited—and only at age twenty-eight, after a lengthy period spent laboring without pay for their mothers' owners. Technically apprentices, the reality was that they were little better than slaves. Moreover, their indentures could be sold or bargained away, and they could be separated from their families. Admittedly, the 1780 Act contained provisions intended to protect slaves and "apprentices" from abuse, but they were flouted so often and so flagrantly that additional legislation was needed.

Much of the pressure for a change came from the revitalized Pennsylvania Abolition Society, whose members were all too aware that the spirit of the 1780 law, if not strictly speaking the law itself, was being violated.[14] A package of provisions passed by the Pennsylvania legislature in 1788 plugged some of the loopholes. Sojourners from other states intending to reside permanently in Pennsylvania had to free any slaves they brought with them within six months. Slaves could not be removed from the state and sold. Knowing that the offspring of slave women born outside Pennsylvania did not have to be treated as apprentices and set on the path to freedom, owners routinely shipped expectant mothers off to neighboring Delaware to give birth. That practice was now outlawed. All children liable to indenture had to be registered. In 1788 it also became unlawful to separate spouses or parents and children by more than ten miles without their consent.[15] The revised abolition law passed the legislature, but not without opposition, and there were plenty of slave owners prepared to fight it. The Pennsylvania Abolition Society was kept very busy following up on violators.[16]

Slavery died much more rapidly in Philadelphia than in the state as a whole, but that did not mean all black residents were legally free. Some were still enslaved. The 1790 census recorded the presence of 301 slaves in Philadelphia and its surrounding districts. A decade later there were 55.[17] Why the decline? After all, the 1780 and 1788 laws had left the status of slaves unchanged. While some Philadelphia slave owners had moral qualms about their human property and freed their slaves unconditionally, others were responding to different imperatives. In light of fundamental changes in the urban economy, and the fear that a bondsman or woman could all too easily slip away, they made the best deal they could for themselves. They opted to manumit their slaves, but they did so with strings attached. The individual slave might find him or herself set free, but with the obligation to labor for a master and his heirs for many years to come.[18]

Then there were the children born to slave women after the passage of the Gradual Abolition Act. They stood to benefit from the law, provided they survived their period of indenture. In Philadelphia in the 1780s and 1790s there were significant numbers of these young men and women toiling away in private homes and in workshops of one kind or another. Some were fortunate enough to be working for caring employers. Others were bound to masters and mistresses whose sole concern was to get as much labor out of their apprentices as they could before the term of indenture expired. The earliest any of the apprentices could claim their full freedom was March 1, 1808.

There were other bound workers besides the apprentices. Indigent free people of color bound out their children and sometimes themselves for food, a roof over their heads, and (in the case of their children) the chance of an education. The Pennsylvania Abolition Society did what it could to safeguard those living under indentures, but its officers could not be everywhere and supervise every such arrangement.[19]

Even where there was no formal indenture, hundreds of black Philadelphians continued to live in an uneasy half-freedom as domestic servants in the households of whites. Admittedly, they worked for pay as well as board and lodging, and sometimes bonds of friendship formed between employer and employee, but such arrangements retarded the growth of the black community, limiting the development of independent households, and keeping alive at least some of the vestiges of slavery. James Forten had only to look around him and see how others lived to know that he was among the freest of the free. He had been born free. By the time he was twenty-six he headed his own household in a home he owned. And his indenture, instead of being a restrictive agreement binding him to a harsh taskmaster, was a promise of an even better life. He was fortunate indeed and grateful for his good fortune.

Despite the less-than-complete freedom so many black people actually enjoyed in Philadelphia, the image of the city as a haven of liberty persisted among free and slave alike throughout the Union. To the annoyance of many white Philadelphians, the "African" population increased dramatically in the waning years of the eighteenth century, and much of that increase was due to migration. The 2,150 black men, women, and children living in the city proper, Southwark, and the Northern Liberties in 1790 accounted for 4.9 percent of the total population, an increase from 2.1 percent a decade earlier. By 1800 the 6,083 people of color in the city and neighboring "liberties" made up 9 percent of the total. That figure would rise to 10 percent a decade later, with angry and fearful whites insisting it was actually far higher if one counted all the runaway slaves who were lying low and escaping the notice of the census-takers.[20] As for residential distribution, at least in the 1780s and 1790s black families were to be found in every ward of the city and in all of its suburbs. As time went on, though, significant clusters would develop in North and South Mulberry, Cedar and Locust Wards, and in the districts of Southwark and adjacent Moyamensing on the city's southern fringe.[21]

The black migrants who headed to Philadelphia from all points of the compass did so because they perceived it as offering so much more than they were leaving behind. Whether they were escaping bondage, poverty, threats of violence, the bitter memories of the past in a region where they had been enslaved, or simply the loneliness and isolation of existing as members of a tiny minority in an overwhelmingly white neighborhood, they believed things would be better in Philadelphia. For many the perception was belied by the reality. True, the Quaker influence was still fairly strong and the Quakers had adopted an antislavery testimony. True, the Pennsylvania Abolition Society, moribund since 1775, had been reborn in 1784 and was working to see that the state's Gradual Abolition Act was enforced. However, prosperity was hard to achieve and whites often made it abundantly clear that they resented the growing black presence in "their" city. Even so, the picture was not one of unrelieved gloom. Not all black Philadelphians found themselves mired in poverty. Black craftsmen and small-scale entrepreneurs made a decent living for themselves and their families. They bought real estate and made investments.[22] They sought education for themselves and their children. And they looked with hope toward a brighter future. The City of Brotherly Love might not have been everything they hoped for, but they felt confident enough to build on what they had found there and what they had already achieved. The churches, the schools, the African Lodge, and the benevolent societies they created in the 1780s and 1790s spoke of optimism, not despair.

INTERACTING WITH "AFRICAN" men and women from many different backgrounds in the Philadelphia of the 1780s and 1790s was one dimension of James Forten's life. Being caught up in momentous events that impacted on all of the city's residents, regardless of race, was another. It is actually more accurate to see these not as separate dimensions of his life as much as parts of a seamless whole. Forten, like his black friends and neighbors, was an "African," but he and they were also Americans. Moreover, they were Americans living in one of the most vibrant cities in the nation at a turbulent point in the nation's history. James Forten, who had seen in the American Revolution a promise of liberty and full citizenship that transcended lines of race, would come of age in a society that was grappling with the implications of that revolution. While he left no personal record of the events to which he was witness in the Philadelphia of the late 1780s and 1790s, his later writings and reflections indicate he was deeply influenced by them. Silent he might have been, but unseeing and uninterested he certainly was not.

To begin with, he was in Philadelphia when the Founding Fathers were busy restructuring the whole framework of government. Like other residents of the city, he may well have known something was happening in the summer of 1787 when so many notables gathered at the statehouse day after day. He might even have seen Washington, Franklin, Madison, Randolph, and other lesser lights walking or riding to their lodgings, going to dine at the various taverns, or socializing with old friends in the hours when they were not closeted behind locked doors and shuttered windows debating who knew what—although Forten and his fellow citizens probably had an inkling that some revision of the Articles of Confederation was being contemplated. He certainly knew what the outcome had been by the fall. His home state became the second, after Delaware, to ratify the new Constitution, a document about which he would have a great deal to say in later years.

He could hardly have missed the festivities that took place on July 4, 1788, to celebrate both the anniversary of independence and the implementation of the new Constitution. The necessary nine states out of thirteen had ratified it. The nation now officially had a new form of government. (A tenth, Virginia, ratified between the planning of the celebrations and July 4.) The day of rejoicing began at sunrise, with the bells of Christ Church pealing and a blast of cannon from the *Rising Sun* moored in the harbor. (The vessel had been christened anew in honor of Benjamin Franklin's musings about the likely success of the new Constitution.) The grand procession that wound its way through the city was fraught, almost top-heavy, with symbolism. There was the float with the "grand federal edifice" of Union, complete with ten seated delegates. There was the carriage in which rode "Peter Baynton, esquire, as a citizen, and colonel Isaac Melchor as an Indian chief . . . smoking the calumet of peace together." There were horns symbolizing Plenty, ploughs Agriculture, and beehives Industry. On the blacksmiths' float they were busy hammering swords into ploughshares. The sailmakers carried a flag "representing the inside view of a sail loft, with masters and men at work; on the top thirteen stars; in the fly five vessels.—Motto, '*may commerce flourish, and industry be rewarded.*' Followed by a number of masters, journeymen and apprentices." Just possibly James Forten was among them. Tobacconists and tanners, coopers and cushion-makers, brewers and barber-surgeons, all had their place in the mile-and-a-half long train that wound its way through the city. Might not Forten reasonably conclude that the new nation embraced him as well as his white neighbors? After all, the orator of the day, James Wilson, urged:

> Let no one . . . harbour . . . the mean idea, that he is and can be of no value to his country. . . . Every one can, at *many* times, perform, to the state, *useful* services; and he, who steadily pursues the road of patriotism, has the most inviting prospect of being able . . . to perform *eminent* ones.

One of the toasts that day was to "The whole family of mankind."[23]

If Forten or anyone else expected harmony to prevail with the adoption of the new Constitution, they were sadly mistaken. Bickering broke out almost immediately, soon to be formalized in the growth of distinct political parties. Over the next decade—and especially after 1790, when the city once more became the nation's capital, following the federal government's removal from New York—Philadelphia would all too often be the scene of mob violence. A highly partisan press centered in the city would indulge in an orgy of character assassination. Federalists and Republicans would denounce one another as traitors to the national interest and lackeys of a foreign power—Britain in the case of the Federalists and France in that of the Republicans. On March 18, 1794, for instance, there was a huge and very noisy rally to protest what many Philadelphians viewed as the spineless United States foreign policy.[24] In the summer and fall of 1794 Philadelphia was alive with rumors about the Whiskey Rebellion in the western part of Pennsylvania. The rebellion, sparked by Secretary of the Treasury Alexander Hamilton's tax on whiskey, threatened to bring about the collapse of the Union. Americans were treated to the sight of the nation's president leading an army not against a foreign foe but against tax rebels, a strange sight indeed in a republic that had come into being as the result of outrage over the payment of taxes! What started off as a July 4 celebration in 1795 rapidly degenerated into a violent demonstration as citizens responded with outrage to Jay's Treaty with Great Britain. They insisted that John Jay had sold out on American rights of free trade in return for a vague promise of limited access to Britain's West Indian colonies. He had done nothing to secure British recognition of America's rights as a neutral nation or to save American vessels from search and seizure by the Royal Navy. An effigy of the luckless Jay was paraded through the streets and then burned, amid cries of "traitor."[25] The upheavals seemed to go on and on.

The first major crisis to overtake the new nation began, ironically enough, with news of a freedom movement an ocean away. In 1789 Philadelphians, in common with New Yorkers, Charlestonians, and people across the new nation, were ecstatic to learn of the storming of the Bastille in Paris. Quite possibly the news evoked for James Forten, as it did for so many of his contemporaries, the vision of "liberty" spreading from the New World to the Old. As the uprising in France grew in intensity, sweeping from power America's old ally, Louis XVI, and all that he stood for, Forten may have hoped for great things. After all, did the revolutionaries not speak of "Liberty, Equality, and Fraternity"? What might that not mean for France, for her colonies, for the rest of Europe, and indeed for America, whose own revolution he considered far from complete? Later, he would come to take a very dim and thoroughly Federalist view of the excesses of the French Revolution. In 1813, when he wrote of the barbarity of the Jacobins, it was in the light of the Terror and the rise of Napoleon.[26] However, in the abstract, "revolution" was something to be welcomed rather than feared.

While there are obvious dangers in attributing to an individual in one phase of his life views he expressed many decades later, James Forten's writings suggest that he generally approved of revolutions, especially if violence could be kept to a minimum. Again and again he lamented the betrayal of the full promise of the American Revolution. So much could have been achieved had the principles of the Declaration of Independence been adhered to. Even so, his optimism about the future never quite faded. Delighted by the revolutionary movements that had broken out across Europe in 1830, for instance, the old revolutionary anticipated that they would bring sweeping changes at home and abroad. He was downcast at times, but he never abandoned the hope that a time would come when "all tyrants, and the tyrants of this country, must tremble."[27] He might deplore excessive bloodletting as anathema to the true revolutionary spirit, but revolution itself was most assuredly a "good thing."

Forten knew all too well that revolutions had a way of impacting on places and people far from the scene of unrest. Living in Philadelphia in the early 1790s, he witnessed the turmoil caused in his native city as the French Revolution proceeded on its bloody course. Just possibly he was in the crowd that gave such a rapturous reception to Citizen Edmond Genêt in May 1793, when the envoy of the new revolutionary government arrived in Philadelphia to urge the United States to make good on its 1778 treaty with France. If he was not on the wharves to welcome Genêt, he obviously saw and heard enough to know how many of his fellow citizens felt. He was also well aware of the outrage that ensued when Genêt, rebuffed by George Washington, tried to appeal over the head of the president to the American people.

The French Revolution was not the only revolution to impact on Americans, James Forten among them, in this volatile period. Hardly had they assimilated the reports of what was going on in France than a revolution far closer to home transfixed them. Toward the end of 1791 the first rumors of momentous happenings in the French West Indian colony of Saint Domingue reached Philadelphia. In the following months the rumors were confirmed as a steady trickle of refugees began arriving, lucky to have made it out of Saint Domingue alive. The colony's slaves had risen up and were slaughtering their masters. This news had an even more profound effect in Philadelphia than events in Paris, for the French colony was far closer to Philadelphia, and it was a major trading partner.[28] Working away in Robert Bridges's sail loft on the banks of the Delaware, James Forten may have been one of the first Philadelphians to hear of the rebellion. He may even have spoken with sailors, black and white, who had actually seen the rebels.

The insurrection on Saint Domingue changed the composition of Philadelphia society, as it did the populations of communities up and down the Atlantic seaboard. The trickle of refugees soon became a flood. In the summer of 1793, when the stronghold of Cap François fell, a huge flotilla of vessels set sail for America carrying thousands of refugees. They made for cities from Boston southward. Some 2,000 French men, women, and children crowded into Philadelphia.[29] Quite a few of them brought at least a handful of their slaves with them. *Their* arrival was a lesson to white Philadelphians that not all "Africans" were alike. These newcomers looked different. They did not dress like most black people in the city. They certainly did not speak like they did. These "Africans" spoke French or Creole or Yoruba or Ibo. And they seemed restless, discontented with their lot. In a city where slavery was rapidly dying, magistrates found themselves dealing with a rash of cases in which slaves with names like Silvain, Delphine, and Pierre were defying the authority of their owners, people with names like Mme. Bordie and Fiette la Garde.[30] Try as they might to retain their human property by gaining exemption from the residency restrictions imposed by the Gradual Abolition Act, the colonists from Saint Domingue were unable to do so, although they found various ways of keeping their slaves bound to them by indenture.[31] Still, slaves or servants, the likes of Silvain and Delphine and Pierre mixed with black Philadelphians, demanded their freedom, fled when the chance arose, and showed in many ways, some subtle and others not, that they deeply resented their servitude. They saw free "Africans" in Philadelphia and craved that freedom for themselves.

The open warfare between the planters and their slaves on Saint Domingue not only brought to Philadelphia slave owners and some of their bondsmen and women. It also brought people like Antoine Servance. Born in Senegal, captured by slavers, and sold to a French planter, Servance had not stayed to find out who would prevail on Saint Domingue. He had made a break for freedom. He was almost certainly the "Antoine" who appeared in the Prisoners for Trial docket for Philadelphia County in 1795. His "crime" was that he had stowed away aboard the vessel *Minerva* out of Saint Domingue and landed illegally in Philadelphia. Apparently the magistrates decided to dismiss the case.[32] How could they send Antoine back to Saint Domingue when no one but he knew who his master was? He settled down in Philadelphia, married, learned to read and write, and met with a modest degree of success in his new home. Eventually James Forten used his impressive network of contacts to help Servance return to West Africa.

Besides Servance, who was escaping from bondage on Saint Domingue, people from the colony's small but influential free community of color found their way to Philadelphia. James Forten worshipped at the African Church with *gens de couleur* such as John and Ann Appo and members of the Depee and Duterte families. He heard from them about their lives on Saint Domingue as people in between, neither black nor white. Of course, white Philadelphians left the Depees and other *gens de couleur* in no doubt that in Philadelphia they were "Africans." And many whites were upset that their city had become home to so many "French Negroes," whatever their condition had been on Saint Domingue. The demographic impact was considerable. During the 1790s as many as 848 people of African descent, some free and others enslaved, arrived in Philadelphia from Saint Domingue, increasing the black population by 25 percent.[33]

If James Forten was more than casually interested in events in France, he was fascinated by what was going on in Saint Domingue. Distressed though he was by reports of atrocities, whoever the victims were, he told anyone who would listen that violence was inevitable when a people were oppressed and brutalized.[34] When the rebellion on Saint Domingue culminated in 1804 in the creation of the Haitian republic, he was delighted. A white visitor to Philadelphia in 1817 reported that Forten was profoundly optimistic, believing that the achievements of the Haitians were somehow bound up with those of "Africans" elsewhere in the diaspora. He "was animated. . . . He said [his] people would become a great nation: he pointed to Hayti, and declared it as his opinion that [his] people could not always be detained in their present bondage."[35] Several years later another white man who called on Forten at his home confessed to being rather upset by what Forten had to say about the black republic. "He thinks he sees in the great men of Hayti the deliverers and the avengers of his race."[36]

THE 2,000 REFUGEES who turned up in Philadelphia in the summer of 1793 stirred up strong emotions. While scores of white citizens reached into their pockets and donated to the relief fund that was set up to help the white émigrés, some grumbled about the threat posed by the sullen and potentially rebellious slaves they had brought with them. What would happen, they asked, if they got loose and started infecting Philadelphia's slaves, its black servants, and even its white poor with the contagion of rebellion? They had no idea that the real danger of contagion came from an enemy that they could not see.

James Forten never mentioned the yellow fever epidemic of 1793 and his role, if any, in relieving the sufferings of its victims. Quite possibly he was one of those recruited from among the African-American community to nurse the afflicted or carry them to the plague hospital at Bush Hill, or perhaps he simply watched, horrified, from the sidelines. He was certainly in the city when the first cases were reported. In the late summer of 1793 he and Robert Bridges were busy refitting the sloop *Fair American* for Andrew Clow and Co. in anticipation of a fall voyage. As they oversaw the bending of the new sails to the *Fair American*'s masts and spars and collected the payment for their work, they knew something was seriously wrong in Philadelphia.[37]

August tended to be a sickly time. The humid air seemed to breed illnesses that carried off the very young, the old, and those already in poor health. On average there were three to five burials a day. But in August 1793 the mortality rate seemed higher. As the month drew to a close, twenty graves per day were being dug in the various burial grounds. By the end of the month 325 people were dead.[38] After a thirty-year absence, the dreaded yellow fever had returned, brought by the Saint Dominguan refugees.

Dr. Benjamin Rush, the city's most eminent physician, blamed the outbreak on the noxious "miasma" from a cargo of coffee rotting on a wharf on Water Street. Other observers cited poor sanitation and ventilation, too many cemeteries within city limits, the lack of rainfall, or the sluggishness of the Delaware in consequence of the construction of new docks. Some did actually identify the refugees as the source of the epidemic, noting that outbreaks of yellow fever were rare indeed in northern climes, but all too common in the West Indies.[39] Debate raged over the best cure—Rush's bloodletting or the use of quinine bark, wine, and cold baths. Partisan bickering intensified as the Federalists blamed the French, the allies of their hated Republican rivals, for the sickness, and the Republicans blamed the city, with all the evils, physical and moral, they insisted urban life brought with it.[40] Arguing over causes and cures did nothing to lessen the toll the disease was taking.

As the death rate rose, people fled the city in droves, often taking the sickness with them. The nation's government all but collapsed as President Washington, most of his cabinet, and scores of clerks from the various government departments left the capital. City and state officials joined the exodus, along with many hundreds of lesser folk.[41] In an awful twist of fate, the Pennsylvania Abolition Society had finally prevailed on the legislature to draft a law to free all the remaining slaves in the state. A bill was under consideration when the epidemic forced a hurried adjournment.[42] On Shippen Street, where James Forten, his mother, his sister, and her family lived, a total of nineteen houses were shut up and forty-four remained open. As for the residents, by the end of November twenty-seven had died. Altogether, eighty-six residents—eighty-five white and one black—had fled. The Fortens and the Dunbars stayed put.[43]

Inevitably, the disease struck close to home. Forten knew of many neighbors and friends who had succumbed. Among those fortunate enough to survive both the yellow fever and Dr. Rush's "heroic" treatment, which involved draining massive amounts of blood from a patient's body, was one of Robert Bridges's sons.[44] Not until the third week of October did the number of burials begin to decline. Only when the first frosts came did the epidemic loosen its grip on the city, and by then 4,000 people were dead.[45] No one who lived through it ever forgot that dreadful summer and autumn, with dead carts carrying away victims, men and women lying where they had fallen in the streets, the shrieks of the bereaved, and the stench that hung over Philadelphia.

Ironically, in the early stages of the outbreak it appeared there was one segment of the population that was spared. As of September 8, according to diarist Elizabeth Drinker, no black residents had contracted the sickness.[46] Benjamin Rush insisted none *would* contract it. Their African origins conferred on them near-total immunity. As he told his friend, ex-slave turned preacher Richard Allen, based on his own observations and accounts he had read of other outbreaks, the "fever . . . passes by persons of your color."[47] To the abolitionist Rush this well-known "fact" suggested a remarkable, indeed, a heaven-sent, initiative. Through the medium of the *American Daily Advertiser* he recommended to white citizens that they hire black nurses. At the same time he offered a "hint to the black people, that a noble opportunity is now put into their hands, of manifesting their gratitude to the inhabitants of that city which first planned their emancipation . . . and who have since afforded them so much protection and support, as to place them, on point of civil and religious privileges, upon a footing with themselves."[48] In the midst of the crisis Rush envisaged that good might emerge from the suffering of so many. Black Philadelphians, safe from infection, could win the love of the whites by relieving their distress. When the epidemic finally ran its course, Philadelphians would be a united people, with grateful whites eager to repay every kindness shown to them by their black neighbors by helping them build schools and churches, employing them, treating them as they themselves would wish to be treated. It was a wonderful vision. Unfortunately, it was based on mistaken beliefs—that white gratitude would outlive the crisis and, more fundamentally, that black people were immune from yellow fever. By late September Rush was forced to admit he had been mistaken on the question of immunity. Black people "took the disease, in common with the white people, and many of them died."[49] One of those who succumbed was grocer Caesar Cranchall, a stalwart of the African-American community and a man James Forten would have known quite well. Cranchell declared he would not take a penny for nursing the sick. To do so would be to "sell his life." In the end that noble gesture killed him.[50]

If James Forten and the various members of his family were among those who responded to Rush's initial call for help, they had good reason to "feel themselves injured" by the aspersions cast on the characters of the black nurses by Mathew Carey. The white publisher asserted that they took advantage of their patients, robbing them of their belongings and demanding unrealistically high payments for any services they rendered.[51] Outraged, Richard Allen and Absalom Jones, two men James Forten knew and respected, published a rebuttal. Carey had actually praised *them*, but they were speaking for the rest of their community. They insisted that at first black citizens had asked nothing for their help, other than what individual families had been ready to pay.[52] Most of the nurses were poor. People offered them high wages, and they were hardly at fault in accepting what was freely offered, "especially under the loathsomeness of many of the sick, when nature shuddered at the thoughts of the infection." If there were some few blacks who neglected or robbed their patients, there were plenty of whites who had done the same. And there were many selfless people like Caesar Cranchell.[53]

The yellow fever returned in 1794 and again in 1797, when it claimed almost 1,300 victims.[54] James Forten was among those who believed that the surest way to prevent yet another recurrence was for Philadelphians to practice "virtue" in all its forms. But to do so they would need help. In January 1798 he and Absalom Jones, as representatives of the recently established African Church, joined members of fifteen white religious bodies, from Baptists to Catholics, in a petition to the Pennsylvania legislature. They insisted that "the sore calamity under which this city has lately and renewedly suffered" was a wake-up call, "a solemn intimation to them not to relax, but to increase their efforts." They explained that they and the people on whose behalf they spoke had "been long and greatly aggrieved by the prevalence of certain evil practices, which they conceive to be equally contrary to the moral law of God, [and] to the peace and welfare of society." There was a law on the books "for the prevention of vice and immorality" passed after the 1793 epidemic, but no one seemed to want to enforce it.[55]

Their chief concern was that too often, while they were trying to worship on Sunday mornings, they were "disturbed by the noise and confusion occasioned by the passage of carriages," almost all of which were "employed in worldly business." This had to stop. They wanted permission "to extend . . . chains across the . . . streets, opposite to our several places of public worship, during the hours of its continuance."[56]

They had other violations of the Sabbath to complain of.

> [A]musements have been publicly advertised for the Lord's day and admission to them offered at a reduced price, with a view to entice the young and unthinking to violate their duty both to God and man. . . . [C]hildren and youth are allowed to engage in the public streets and on the commons . . . in the most boisterous and unlawful sports and diversions, to use the most profane and unseemly language, and by going into the river to bathe . . . not only to offend against all law, but to disregard and violate all the sentiments of decency.[57]

The city was truly a pit of sin. Brothels and "places of lewd resort" abounded. Taverns operated freely on the Sabbath, offering not only drink but gambling. "Your memorialists are at a loss to conceive how these and many other contraventions . . . of the act for the prevention of vice and immorality, (passed . . . shortly after our city had been delivered from that awful visitation of heaven, by which thousands were suddenly swept into eternity) can have passed unnoticed . . . by those who are set to enforce the laws." They demanded action, insisting that they spoke for the respectable element in society, "that part of the community (it is not vanity to assert it) which best deserves encouragement and protection."[58]

Permission *was* given to chain off the streets on the Sabbath, but nothing the legislature could do was sufficient to prevent further outbreaks of yellow fever. The disease returned to Philadelphia with dreadful regularity. In the summer of 1798 its toll was almost as great as in 1793. Before it had run its course, over 3500 were dead. The following year just over a thousand died. Another 835 people succumbed in 1802.[59]

Ineffective though it was in achieving its major goal, the petition from the churches is interesting for what it reveals about the understanding of the na-

ture of epidemic disease, and for its assertion that the state must help the guardians of moral purity. As for the involvement of the African-American community in the petitioning effort, it was a bold assertion that the members of the
new African Church viewed themselves as upholders of virtue, and the equals
of their white brothers and sisters who worshipped God and tried to live righ-
teously. In regard to James Forten's growing prominence, it indicates that someone who scarcely figured in community affairs a few years previously had now
risen to become a man of moral weight and authority.

JAMES FORTEN CAME fairly late to the African Church, but within a few years he
was one of its most influential members. Around the same time he emerged as
an officer of the African Lodge. However, charting Forten's growing visibility
within the African-American community is far from easy. For the period before 1796, when he first made his appearance as a vestryman at the African
Church, there is a great lack of evidence. The paper trail is nonexistent and
conjecture is no substitute for solid documentation. Forten may, for instance,
have added his name to the "petition from a number of persons of the African
race, praying that they may be permitted to enclose a part of the lott . . . com-
monly called the Negroes burial ground, for the purpose of burying their dead
exclusively." The Supreme Executive Council considered the petition at its
February 10, 1786, meeting but neglected to record the names of the petitioners.[60] Decades later, when Forten came to settle his estate, he set money aside
to ensure that African-American men and women had a decent place in which
to bury their dead.[61] He might have been involved in the 1786 initiative, but at
this early stage in his life he could well have had issues of more immediate
concern to occupy his attention.

James Forten might have been a member of the Free African Society, the
mutual benefit society founded in the spring of 1787 by a group of men led by
future ministers Absalom Jones and Richard Allen. Intended to function as a
relief organization and a religious society, it also sought to inculcate sound
moral principles among its members and among people of color throughout
the city. His later statements and actions suggest Forten would certainly have
been in sympathy with the society's goals. However, he was not yet twenty-one
when it was founded, and at no point was he named as one of its officers.[62] If he
was a member, he was a very lowly one.

Jones and Allen had far-reaching plans for the Free African Society. What
had begun as a mutual benefit society would, they hoped, grow into a fully-
fledged interdenominational church for Philadelphia's African-American population. Freed from slavery in Delaware in 1780, Allen had already made a name
for himself as a Methodist preacher when he was invited to come to Philadelphia in 1786 to preach to the growing body of black Methodists who worshipped at St. George's Methodist Episcopal Church. Impressed by the number
of black people in the city in general, and by the fact that while hundreds were

scattered among the various congregations, many belonged to no church what-soever, Allen and Jones envisaged the creation of a church that would come closer to meeting the spiritual needs of "Africans" than any white church could possibly do. Supported and encouraged by abolitionist Benjamin Rush, Allen, Jones, and a small group of associates forged ahead with their plans.[63]

James Forten may have been among the dozen or so free black men who met with Rush at the home of William Wilshire on July 25, 1791, to hear the doctor "read to them sundry articles of faith and a plan of church government which [he] had composed for them."[64] However, there is nothing to indicate that Forten was there, or that he took part in any of the fund-raising initiatives to build the African Church. He may have been aware of growing anger on the part of various white churchmen at talk of the new church. Bishop William White, the leader of Pennsylvania's Episcopalians, stopped Rush in the street one day and let him know in no uncertain terms what he thought of the pro-posed African Church. White was convinced it "originated in pride." Why were black people not content to keep attending predominantly white churches? The Quakers were equally annoyed.[65] Emboldened by this opposition, and more than ever convinced of the wisdom of their plan, Jones, Allen, and Rush pushed ahead.

James Forten was not with Jones, Allen, and their friends Dorus Jennings and William White (another black Philadelphian) one Sunday in 1792 when they attended morning service at St. George's. Like many other black Phila-delphians who believed that Methodism was a truly egalitarian denomination whose ministers were "no respecters of persons," the foursome had been wor-shipping at St. George's for some time, as had scores of other people of color. Admittedly, some of the white members of St. George's seemed to resent their presence, but that did not lessen their attachment to the basic tenets of Methodism. Presumably they hoped that tensions within the congregation would ease with the passage of time. However, the growing numbers of black wor-shippers were something the church elders contemplated with disquiet, rather than delight. African Americans were accommodated, but separately from their white brothers and sisters. After the church was enlarged—with black worship-pers contributing their mite to the renovation—they were assigned to a suit-ably remote part of the building. Whether by accident or design, Allen, Jones, and the others made for the "wrong" part of the church that Sunday morning. Pulled from their knees during prayer by two of the white trustees, the four walked out, vowing never to return.[66] It was a dramatic event with far-reaching implications, and doubtless James Forten heard it discussed over and over again, but he was not there to witness it, for a very good reason. While Jones, Allen, and many others were drawn to Methodism (at least initially) as a liberating faith, Forten had found *his* religious home in the Episcopal church. His Sun-days were spent at St. Paul's Episcopal Church, where his sister had been mar-ried and where Rev. Joseph Pilmore presided. The evangelical Pilmore had proven himself most sympathetic to the needs and concerns of his black parishioners. He also officiated regularly at the services the Free African Society held.[67] Frankly, at least in the early 1790s, James Forten saw no reason to abandon Rev. Pilmore and St. Paul's for the dubious spiritual comforts of St. George's and the Methodists.

In time, though, Forten would leave St. Paul's. Just possibly he had become a convert to the idea of a separate African church by 1793. If so, maybe he was present at the roof-raising on August 22. Benjamin Rush wrote eagerly to his wife to describe it.

> This day . . . I dined a mile from town, under the shade of several large trees, with about a hundred carpenters and others. . . . We were waited upon by nearly an equal number of black people. I gave them the two following toasts: "Peace on earth and good will to men," and "May African churches everywhere soon succeed to African bondage." After which we rose, and the black people . . . took our seats. Six of the most respectable of the white company waited upon them. . . . Never did I witness such a scene of . . . such virtuous and philanthropic joy.[68]

Even if Forten was there for the roof-raising—and there is nothing to suggest he was—his involvement was still minimal. In November 1793 it was Absalom Jones, William Gray, and William Gardner who identified themselves to English abolitionist Granville Sharp as the "Acting Officers of the African Church of Philadelphia."[69] Nowhere was Forten's name mentioned.

After many months spent trying to persuade white Philadelphians, and whites elsewhere, to loosen their purse strings and contribute to an eminently worthy cause, the members of the African Church were finally able to finish the building.[70] On July 17, 1794, several hundred people gathered to see it dedicated. *Dunlap and Claypoole's American Daily Advertiser* reported: "On Thursday last Divine Worship [was] performed for the first time in the African Church in this city. Prayers and passages of scripture suited to the occasion were read by the Rev. Abercrombie and afterwards an excellent sermon was delivered by the Rev. Dr. Magaw from the following text—'The people that walked in darkness have seen a great light.'"[71] The chances are good that James Forten was there that day, for the church records make it clear that he had, at long last, left St. Paul's and joined the African Church.[72]

As yet, though, James Forten was simply a member of the congregation. On August 12, less than a month after the dedication, the officers of the new church set forth their rules and an explanation of "the causes and motives for establishing" it. Forten was not one of those officers. Perhaps, at twenty-seven, he was not considered senior enough. Absalom Jones was twenty years older than him, and William Gray twenty-five years older. They and most of the other church officers were members of a different generation, truly the "elders."[73] Still, Forten presumably approved of the statement they issued to the public and shared their pious hopes for the future. They were confident "God has marked out our way with blessings" and opened "the hearts of our white friends and brethren." They spoke of God's help "to encourage us to arise out of [the] dust and shake ourselves and throw off that servile fear that the habit of oppression and bondage trained us up in weakness and fear." It was God's will that "we would walk in the liberty wherewith Christ has made us free."[74]

They named their church St. Thomas's for St. Thomas the Apostle, the "doubting Thomas" who eventually became the first of the disciples to acknowledge the divinity of the risen Christ. They also put themselves firmly under the jurisdiction of the Protestant Episcopal Church, "*provided* . . . we and our successors shall always retain . . . the power of choosing our minister and assistant minister."[75] Officers, including a twenty-man vestry, would be chosen every Easter Monday by a ballot of all duly admitted church members of one year's standing.[76] The powers of the vestry were considerable. Vestrymen were to receive all payments due the church, balance the books, "regulate the minister and assisting minister's salary," and keep the building and churchyard in good repair.[77] In a significant provision they required "that none . . . but men of colour, who are Africans, or the descendants of the African race, can elect, or be elected into any office . . . save that of a minister, or assistant minister; and that no minister shall have a vote at our elections."[78]

Bishop White had finally turned from foe to friend and had given his support to the African Church, probably because it was no longer to be an interdenominational undertaking. Rebuffed by the Methodists at St. George's, and encouraged by the Episcopalian Rush and by other white members of the denomination, the majority had decided to affiliate with the Episcopal Church. Perhaps that, as much as anything else, won Forten over. However, in the short term the decision precipitated a crisis. Neither Allen nor Jones would go along with it at first. They were Methodists, and Methodists they intended to remain. To objections that the Methodists had cast them out from St. George's they answered that one group of Methodists might have treated them badly, but they believed Methodism, with its emphasis on humility and spiritual equality, was the faith for "Africans" to follow. In the end, Allen remained resolute, but Jones was converted. Allen would go on to establish Mother Bethel, a black church within the Methodist fold, and eventually found the African Methodist Episcopal denomination. Jones would seek ordination as an Episcopal priest.[79]

With Bishop White's backing, acceptance of St. Thomas's into the Episcopal denomination was soon forthcoming. The Council of Advice and Standing of the Diocese of Pennsylvania met at White's home on Walnut Street on September 9 and approved the request. On October 12, Rev. Blackwell appeared in the pulpit at St. Thomas's and formally announced the church's admission to the denomination. A week and a half later the trustees of St. Thomas recommended Absalom Jones for ordination. The Council approved, pending a vote by the State Convention on the language requirement. Meanwhile, White gave Jones permission to read services.[80]

At its 1795 meeting the Convention of the Protestant Episcopal Church recommended that "in the examination for Holy Orders of Absalom Jones . . . the knowledge of the Latin and Greek languages be dispensed with." This was a concession to Jones's limited education, but he was not the only applicant granted such a dispensation. What was unusual was the resolution "that the same be granted, provided it is not to be understood to entitle the African Church to send a Clergyman or deputies to the convention . . . this condition being made, in consideration of their peculiar circumstances at present."[81] Possibly the "peculiar circumstances" that barred St. Thomas's from representation in the convention stemmed not so much from the dispensation as from the unusual degree of autonomy the church insisted upon for itself and from its policy of racial exclusion.[82] Whatever the case, Jones's ordination went ahead. Bishop White raised him to the diaconate on August 6, 1795, and to the priesthood in 1804.

To further strengthen its legal position, St. Thomas's sought and was granted formal incorporation in 1796.[83] It was now a legally recognized corporation, with the power to initiate and defend itself against lawsuits, to enter into contracts, to administer its funds, and so forth. The work of organization and consolidation was complete. Finally, on March 28, 1796, Easter Monday, it elected its first vestry. Among the vestrymen was twenty-nine-year-old James Forten.[84]

The church soon became a major focus of James Forten's life. He served regularly on the vestry. He joined Absalom Jones in representing the church in the 1798 Sabbath observance petition. He brought his business expertise to bear when church members died and left money or property to St. Thomas's. Real estate had to be sold or rented out, and cash invested so that it yielded a good return.[85] Various legal matters needed to be dealt with. Again, with his solid business background as Robert Bridges's junior partner, James Forten was the ideal person to consult on a whole range of issues, from prosecuting a dishonest churchwarden to dealing with a botched fund-raising endeavor. He would become a trustee of the church's new school and one of the founders of the church's Society for the Suppression of Vice and Immorality. He would also discover that vestry politics could be very murky indeed. More than once over the years he crossed his fellow vestrymen, and more than once he tangled with the majority of the congregation. In the 1790s, though, his relationship with the church was a harmonious one.

In 1801 Forten was elected the president of the Friendly Society of St. Thomas's, a sure sign of his growing influence within the church. Established sometime between 1794 and 1797, the Friendly Society effectively superceded the Free African Society. In their preamble the subscribers, all of them members of St. Thomas's, observed that, as a result of "frequently conversing on that most amiable of all the social virtues, Charity, and feeling a desire to promote it . . . as far as our circumstances in life will admit," they had determined to organize a society.[86] Each month every member would pay a quarter into the common fund. The Society would aid its sick and indigent members (after the committee had determined their claims were valid), bury "in a plain and decent manner" any whose families were too poor to pay for a funeral, and relieve the wants of deceased members' widows and orphans.[87] Although Forten might hope to do well enough never to need to draw on the society's funds, he knew it would be the means of saving many of its members and their families from destitution. Being chosen its president was a singular honor, and an unmistakable sign of his standing within the church. By then, though, he had already achieved recognition in another organization at the heart of African-American community life.

ON JUNE 24, 1797, white Quaker Elizabeth Drinker witnessed something quite new in her experience. "There was to day a procession of white, and another of black Free-Masons—Absalom Jones, the black Bishop, walked before his brethren to the African Church[,] the others to St. Pauls—tis the first I have heard of negro masons—a late thing I guess."[88] Among the black Masons Drinker saw heading to the African Church for the observance of the feast of St. John the Baptist, one of the most solemn days in the Masonic calendar, was James Forten.

What attracted Forten to the "mysteries" of Freemasonry? On one level, it was those very same things that appealed to others in the Masonic brotherhood, irrespective of race—an appreciation of sound morality and religious principles, a reverence for learning, a conviction of the need for men of good repute to band together for the common welfare, and a desire for fellowship. It was those same goals and values that had brought into the Masonic fold so many of the luminaries of the Revolution, chief among them George Washington. Indeed, many Masons saw their "craft" as one of the pillars of the new republic. In 1793, with all due Masonic ceremony, and attired in his Masonic apron, President Washington gave the new United States Capitol a truly fraternal blessing.[89] Not for nothing did the great seal of the republic have emblazoned on it the pious Masonic hope for a *novus ordo seclorum*, along with the Masonic symbols of the pyramid and the mystic eye of spiritual enlightenment. The iconography was something Brother Forten would have recognized instantly.

Brother Washington and Brother Forten would have seen in Freemasonry many of the same things, but for Forten and other aspiring black Masons there were even more attractions. To be a Freemason was to be a *free* Mason, a man whose essential liberty was recognized. There was also the implied union that came with membership of the fraternity—union with black Masonic brothers in other communities and with white Masons, who would surely extend the hand of friendship to a fellow Mason, whatever the color of his skin.[90] Sadly, as James Forten and his brothers soon learned, cooperation among black Masons was more easily achieved than a bonding across racial lines.

African, also known as Prince Hall, Masonry originated in Boston in 1775 in the months before the bloody clashes at Lexington and Concord. Prince Hall and a number of his friends, skilled artisans and men of influence in Boston's small but vibrant free black community, had been meeting together for some time and adhering to Masonic principles before they sought formal incorporation into a lodge. They found unlikely allies among the British soldiers sent to keep them and their unruly white neighbors in check. Hall and his brothers were "tried," found worthy, and given permission to assemble as a lodge by British Traveling Lodge No. 58. There was only one problem. When the fighting began, most of the black Masons declared themselves Patriots. According to tradition, at war's end they applied for a charter to the Provincial Grand Master of Modern Masons in Massachusetts, only to have their application rejected on the grounds of race. However, Hall's own words suggest that was not in fact the case. In 1784 he approached the Grand Lodge of England for a warrant of constitution, noting, "We have had no opportunity to apply for a Warrant before now." Evidently, no application had been made to any Masonic body on either side of the Atlantic. The English Lodge granted Hall's request and he and his brothers eventually received their warrant in 1787.[91]

Meanwhile, Philadelphia's African-American Masons were grappling with the question of how they could gain some kind of legitimacy for themselves, but here things start to get rather confused. Freemasonry is and was essentially a secret organization, and over the past two centuries Prince Hall Freemasonry has been repeatedly condemned by many in the white brotherhood as uncanonical and essentially illegitimate. Documents have been lost (deliberately in some cases) and "histories" fabricated to validate one or other viewpoint. Hence, one must pick one's way through a maze of conflicting "evidence" to try to arrive at something approaching a coherent account of the growth of Philadelphia's African Lodge.

According to Grimshaw's *Official History*, Prince Hall, not only master of the lodge in Boston but a redoubtable presence in community affairs, was in contact with the Free African Society of Philadelphia. On September 16, 1789, he wrote that he had heard of their society from Henry Stewart, who was visiting Boston, and he wished them every success. He added, "Your brother Stewart will inform you by word of mouth of some Masonic proposals we made to him, which I do not care to write at this time."[92] The suggestion is that the Philadelphians had as yet no lodge of their own and that Hall spurred them into action, prompting them to organize. Significantly, when Rev. William Douglass came to write his *Annals of St. Thomas* in 1862, he transcribed the early records of the Free African Society, including the letter from Hall. Douglass's transcription does not include the word "Masonic."[93] Either Grimshaw added it or Douglass removed it.

In his *History of Negro Freemasonry*, Harry E. Davis asserts that the Philadelphians were in fact already operating a lodge and approached Hall for help and advice at a later stage. Davis cites a tradition that Peter Mantore, master of the Philadelphia Lodge, had applied to England for a warrant and had been referred to Hall. Accordingly, on March 2, 1797, Mantore composed a letter to Hall.[94] Davis supplies a transcription of the letter, but it varies in several important respects from the letter that actually appears in the records of the African Lodge of Boston. That letter begins with a warm expression of fraternal greeting and then implores the help of the Bostonians. "We in Philadelphia are all ready for to go to work. We have all but a Warrant." The letter goes on to explain their progress and the problems they had encountered. "We have now been try'ed by five Royal Arch Masons." However, "[t]he White Masons hear [*sic*] say they are afraid to grant us a warrant for feare the black men liv[ing] in Virginia would get to be free masons too." Even if the white masons should have a change of heart, "we had rather be under our Dear Brethren in Boston than the Pennsylvania Lodge[. I]f we are under you then we shall always be ready to asseast one of you." There were eleven individuals in the lodge, five of whom were masters. Mantore himself, a "super excellent" and Royal Arch Knight Templar, was "Master of the Whole." The others had various degrees, several of them from a lodge in London.[95] Grimshaw's account of the approach to Hall is slightly different. According to him, the initiative came from Absalom Jones and "other leading colored citizens," among them Mantore, William Harding, Peter Richmond, Richard Parker, and James Forten.[96]

Hall replied in a letter to Mantore dated March 22, 1797. He understood that "there are a number of Blacks in your city who have Recved the Light of Masonry" and he expressed the hope that "they got it in a duly and lawful manner." If that was indeed the case, "I think we are willing to set you at work under our charter . . . under the atheroty and by the Name of the African Lodge." Accordingly, "We hear by and hear on give you license to a sembel and work."[97] He advised them "not to take in aney at present till [you] chuse your officers and your Master be instorl'd." He promised them his aid, "and we may give [you] a full Warrant instead of a promitt [permit]."[98] True to his word, Hall traveled to Philadelphia later that year and on September 22 he installed their officers.[99] However, there is some question whether he ever gave the Philadelphians a warrant, and the dispatch of various individuals to Boston seems to have been intended to secure one.[100]

The original minute book of the African Lodge of Philadelphia for the years 1797–1800 disappeared at some point during the middle of the twentieth century, but fortunately someone had the foresight to microfilm it. What it reveals on one level is the ongoing deliberations of the Philadelphia Lodge over their warrant. More to the point for this study, the minute book bears out the pivotal role of Brother Forten. Very little of the lodge's business escaped his attention.

There is nothing in the records to indicate when exactly James Forten became a Mason. One source suggests he had been admitted to the brotherhood during his time in England, but, given his lowly status, his lack of connections, and the fact that he was well below the age of twenty-one when he went to England, that seems unlikely. His youth alone would have made his admission highly irregular.[101] However, by December 27, 1797, the feast of St. John the Evangelist and another solemn day of celebration for Freemasons, the thirty-one-year-old Forten was not only a brother in good standing in the Philadelphia African Lodge but also its outgoing Senior Warden.[102]

Over the next two years the minutes of the lodge are replete with mentions of the doings of Brother Forten, usually in connection with matters of business. On March 10, 1798, perhaps in the absence of Peter Richmond, who had volunteered to go to Boston in pursuit of the elusive warrant, Forten acted as master. Not surprisingly, he concerned himself with the lodge's financial stability. "Brother James Forten made a move that the Members accompt of Quarterage should be sent in to them." A few weeks later, on April 7, Forten, William Harding, and William McConnel were "Chosen as A Committee to Settle the Treasurers Book."[103]

Faithful member of the lodge though he was, there was a limit to how much of his time and energy Forten was prepared to devote to it. On April 9 Absalom Jones proposed Forten for the vacant post of treasurer, and he was unanimously elected. Forten had been absent from that meeting. When he learned of his election he was not at all pleased. "Brother James Forten being informed that he was Chosen Treasurer would not Accept of it. But said he would rather pay his fine than serve." Nicholas Marks, a grocer, was chosen in his place.[104]

Despite his refusal to serve as treasurer, James Forten continued to do his utmost to sort out the lodge's finances. On May 5, presiding as Senior Warden, he "Made a Move that A Committee of three be Chosen to Call on the Members With their dues Which was Carried and himself and M[atthew] Black and Wm. Harding was Chosen." A week later he was authorized to help settle the lodge's unpaid rent. In this instance he dipped into his own pocket, trusting his brothers to repay him. On June 2 "Brother James Forten reported . . . he [had] waited upon Mr. Appleby and given him his Note for the Rent payable in Eight days and he was Authorized to Draw on the Treasurer [for] the Sum of £3." It was not an enormous amount, but it was significant—a laborer's hire for many weeks—and the fact that his note was accepted by Appleby, presumably a white man, was also revealing about his financial standing. On another occasion members resolved that the Masonic "society" should seek a loan of $30. George Bampfield, Peter Richmond, and James Forten were "appointed as a committee to Borrow the money."[105] Again, Forten was among the handful of black Masons in a position to approach a member of the white business community and negotiate a loan. He commanded respect and his brothers acknowledged that.

Forten was also resourceful and imaginative when it came to financial matters. Collecting unpaid dues was not a pleasant task. It involved tracking down delinquents and listening to a variety of excuses, from the heart-rending to the highly suspect. Brothers were reluctant to undertake the task—until Forten came up with a tempting arrangement. "[I]t was moved by Brother Forten that a member be chosen to collect the dues from the members and such member should be allowed 2/6 in every pound that he collect." With the prospect of a very tangible reward for their efforts, two volunteers immediately stepped forward.[106] Over the next few months they were able to recoup at least some of the money owed the lodge, along with something to cover their time and trouble. Clearly, Brother Forten was a shrewd man who understood that a cash incentive could make a distasteful job more appealing. He knew "business" and he also knew human nature.

Besides concerning himself with financial matters, James Forten took an active part in the other business of the lodge, investigating applicants for admission and "see[ing] in to the Conduct of Some Brethren." On one occasion, as Worshipful Master, he gave a St. John's Day oration on the principles of Masonry, and the minutes record it "was Reseavd [with] Pleasure." As one of its most literate members, he wrote letters for the lodge, and helped in the complex business of getting the warrant from Hall. On January 26, 1798, for instance, he "brought forward an address to be Presented to the Brethren of the Lodge of Boston which met the approbation of the Brothers." Getting the warrant was a protracted affair. On June 10, 1799, it was "Resolved by the lodge that [the] warrant should be Sent on to Boston by post and . . . that Brother Harding and Brother Forten be appointed a committee to Write the letter."[107]

Though he might shirk the onerous office of Treasurer, James Forten apparently enjoyed his involvement in the lodge. The Masons embodied so many of the principles he already adhered to—the practice of charity, devotion to religion, and a profound respect for learning. A generous man, he had an opportunity through the lodge to help the needy. Supporting the widows and orphans of deceased brothers was one of the prime duties of every lodge. Forten could socialize with his brothers. Indeed, dining together, providing it was not done to excess and was not seen as an end in itself, was an important part of Masonic ritual. Sitting at table with one's brothers was a true sign of virtuous fellowship.[108] A bachelor, Forten found a network of friends among his brethren. And a diverse group they were. Freeborn and slave-born, Philadelphians and newcomers to the city, they were drawn from various walks of life. Sailors rubbed shoulders with artisans and shopkeepers. However, they all shared certain characteristics. They might be relatively poor, but none was destitute. It cost money to be a Mason. As for respectability, a man had to withstand the scrutiny of the lodge when he sought admission. And Masons could be and were expelled for misconduct. In terms of aspirations and self-identification, these men constituted Philadelphia's black "better sort." Masonry in effect created a brotherhood among a group of black Philadelphians whose one common characteristic was "worthiness." The lodge was a religious body, but it was nonsectarian. Whatever church they attended on the Sabbath, black Methodists and Episcopalians and Baptists could offer the fraternal hand to one another. Sadly, it was all too rare to see a white fraternal hand offered to a black brother.

Despite the apparent display of unity Elizabeth Drinker witnessed on St. John's Day, and despite the mentions in the correspondence with Prince Hall of meetings between black Masons and individual whites, the white lodges of Philadelphia were not always prepared to accept black Masons as brothers. In 1797 Israel Israel reported to the white Grand Lodge that he and others had visited a black lodge on Front Street and that its members were not acquainted with the mysteries of the craft. The white lodge forbade further visits on pain of expulsion.[109] How long the ban remained in effect is unclear. On at least a few occasions several white Masons did defy it, and now and again the African Lodge was included in Masonic observances. On February 10, 1800, for instance, the members of the African Lodge were gratified to receive a proposal from a white Mason, Hiram Levenstein, that they should join in the birthday parade for their departed brother, George Washington.[110]

There is no way of knowing how long James Forten continued his involvement with the lodge. The records of the Philadelphia African Lodge for the years 1801–13 have not survived, and there is not a single mention of him in the minutes for 1813–15.[111] Why, after achieving high office in the lodge, did he choose not to continue his involvement? Was he deterred by the kind of feuding that sometimes arose among black Masons as it did among whites, resulting in disownments and expulsions?[112] Did marriage, family, and the demands of his business limit the time available for involvement in the lodge? There is no evidence of a breach with his brothers, but then, given the missing records, there is no evidence of anything whatsoever. One thing is clear, though. Whatever the reason for his break with the lodge, James Forten remained on good terms with his Masonic brothers, prime among them his much-loved and respected minister Absalom Jones.

IN SO MANY respects the decade and a half from 1785 to 1800 was one of the most momentous periods in James Forten's life. He moved from teenage apprentice to master craftsman, from a dependent in his employer's home to the head of his own household. White men labored under his direction and received their pay from his hands. White captains and merchants learned to treat him if not as they themselves would wish to be treated, at least as a man of integrity and common sense, someone who knew his trade and knew the value of a dollar. But James Forten grew not merely in wealth and respectability. He had a life beyond the sail loft, away from white merchants and white workmen. He was drawn into the growing community of "Africans." Wealth and status— at least status in the eyes of whites—did not isolate or insulate him. In part that was because, for all his prosperity, he would never be white. In large part, though, it was because he did not seek to be. He was the great-grandson of an African. He knew it and felt no distress or embarrassment on that account. But he was an American, too, and he had fought for the country that he felt instinctively was his.

What James Forten was working out for himself—his identity as a person of African descent in America—was what every member of his community was working out. Beyond the community of color, it was also what Americans of European descent were working out. Would the nation, founded on a promise of equality, live up to that promise? James Forten and so many of the black men and women in the new nation's capital city hoped it would. He and they worked to build churches, schools, benevolent societies, and other community institutions in the expectation that it would. Their allies in the white community shared their optimism. In the decades that followed, though, that optimism would be put to the test, and James Forten would have to grapple again and again with the question of whether an "African" could ever truly be an "American."

(*Right*) Charlotte Vandine Forten (Francis J. Grimké Papers, Moorland-Spingarn Research Center, Howard University). This photograph of James Forten's second wife was treasured by her granddaughter and namesake, Charlotte Forten Grimké. It was preserved among the papers of the younger Charlotte's husband, Rev. Francis J. Grimké.

(*Below*) Robert Purvis and Fellow Members of the Pennsylvania Anti-Slavery Society (The Historical Society of Pennsylvania, Society Print Collection). James Forten's son-in-law and collaborator is the young bearded man in the center of the front row. To his left are Forten family friends Lucretia and James Mott.

East Prospect of the City of Philadelphia, by N. Scull and G. Heap, 1756 (Library Company of Philadelphia). This view shows the city James Forten would have known as a child. The bustling ship traffic on the Delaware indicates why the sailmaker's trade was such a profitable one.

Charlotte Forten Grimké (Schomburg Center for Research in Black Culture, The New York Public Library, Astor, Lenox and Tilden Foundations). Diarist, author, and educator Charlotte Forten Grimké was the daughter of James Forten's son, Robert Bridges Forten.

Captain Stephen Decatur, Sr. (The Historical Society of Pennsylvania, Gratz Collection, C5 B27). Decatur was James Forten's captain on the privateer *Royal Louis* during the Revolutionary War.

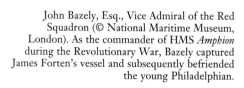

John Bazely, Esq., Vice Admiral of the Red Squadron (© National Maritime Museum, London). As the commander of HMS *Amphion* during the Revolutionary War, Bazely captured James Forten's vessel and subsequently befriended the young Philadelphian.

The Prison-Ship *Jersey*, from Edgar S. Maclay, *History of the United States Navy* (photograph courtesy Peabody Essex Museum). The *Jersey* was the British prison-ship on which James Forten was held for seven months in New York Harbor.

Captain Thomas Truxtun
(The Historical Society of
Pennsylvania, Stauffer
Collection, v. x, p. 684).
Truxtun was James Forten's
captain when he sailed to
England in 1784 on the
Commerce.

A View of London from the Thames, 1794 (Library Company of Philadelphia). This panorama shows the city of London much as James Forten would have seen it in 1784.

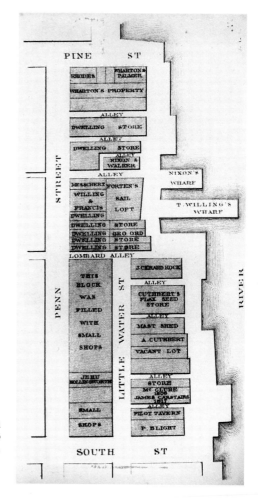

James Forten's Sail-Loft, from Abraham Ritter, *Philadelphia and Her Merchants*, 1860 (Library Company of Philadelphia).

Arch Street Ferry, Philadelphia, from W. Birch & Son, *The City of Philadelphia As It Appeared in 1800* (The Historical Society of Pennsylvania, Bd 61 B531.1 pl. 4). Here, as elsewhere along the Philadelphia waterfront, black and white workers toiled side by side.

(*Facing page*) Sail-Plan, from Darcy Lever, *The Young Sea Officer's Sheet Anchor* (photograph courtesy Peabody Essex Museum). Lever's illustration shows how complex a sail-plan was for a fully rigged ship. As both a sailor and a sailmaker, James Forten would have been very familiar with the name and function of every sail: (a) foresail, (b) fore topsail, (c) fore topgallant, (d) fore topgallant royal, (e) fore studding sail, (f) fore topmast studding sail, (g) fore topgallant studding sail, (h) mainsail, (i) main topsail, (k) main topgallant, (l) main topgallant royal, (m) main topmast studding sail, (n) main topgallant studding sail, (o) mizzen topsail, (p) mizzen topgallant sail, (q) mizzen topgallant royal, (r) spritsail, (s) spritsail topsail, (t) jib, (u) fore topmast staysail, (v) fore staysail, (w) main staysail, (x) main topmast staysail, (y) middle staysail, (z) main topgallant staysail, (aa) mizzen staysail, (ab) mizzen topmast sail, (ac) mizzen topgallant staysail, (ad) driver or spanker.

Fig. 291.

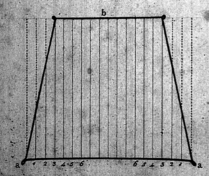

Fig. 293.

Fig. 292

Bending the Foresail, from Lever, *The Young Sea Officer's Sheet Anchor* (photograph courtesy Peabody Essex Museum). This complicated and potentially hazardous operation was something James Forten took part in as a sailor and later supervised as a sailmaker.

Representation of a Sail Loft, from David Steel, *The Art of Sail-Making* (photograph courtesy Peabody Essex Museum). This is a depiction of a sailmaker at his bench, circa 1796.

The Plummer Sail-Loft, Searsport, Maine, 1884 (Maine Maritime Museum, Bath, Maine). Although this photograph was taken more than four decades after James Forten's death, it shows a scene that would have been very familiar to him.

Rev. Richard Allen (The Historical Society of Pennsylvania, Society Collection). James Forten's sometime friend and sometime adversary, Allen was the founder of the African Methodist Episcopal Church.

Rev. Absalom Jones (The Historical Society of Pennsylvania, Leon Gardiner Collection, B76). The minister of St. Thomas's African Episcopal Church, Jones was one of James Forten's oldest friends.

(*Facing page, top*) The A. Dunton Sail-Loft, Boothbay Harbor, Maine, 1892 (Maine Maritime Museum, Bath, Maine). The interior of a busy sail-loft. The one innovation since Forten's day was the sewing machine, but much of the sewing was still done by hand.

(*Facing page, bottom*) Certificate from the Humane Society of Pennsylvania (The Historical Society of Pennsylvania, Certificate Flatfile). James Forten's certificate from the Humane Society, awarded in recognition of a number of river rescues he made over the years, was one of his prized possessions.

"A Sunday Morning View of the African Episcopal Church of St. Thomas in Philadelphia, taken in June 1829," lithograph by William L. Breton (The Historical Society of Pennsylvania, Bb862 B56#44). James Forten attended this church for almost fifty years.

Dr. Benjamin Rush (Library Company of Philadelphia). James Forten knew Rush well as a result of their shared antislavery activities. He praised Rush as one of the best representatives of the Revolutionary generation.

Captain Paul Cuffe (New Bedford Whaling Museum). Cuffe was James Forten's friend and collaborator in the African emigration scheme.

"A Black Tea Party," from Edward W. Clay, *Life in Philadelphia*, ca. 1833 (Library Company of Philadelphia). Edward Clay's cartoon series mocking well-to-do African Americans like the Fortens and the Purvises sold very well and helped reinforce negative racial stereotypes

William Lloyd Garrison, 1835 (The Historical Society of Pennsylvania, Society Portrait Collection). This portrait of James Forten's friend William Lloyd Garrison was painted by another friend, Robert Douglass Jr.

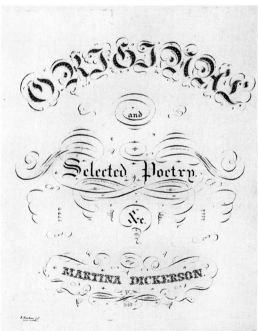

Artwork by James Forten's children (Library Company of Philadelphia). James Forten Jr. and Margaretta Forten were both accomplished artists, who decorated their friends' albums with examples of their artwork. Margaretta Forten's flowers, along with a four-line verse, appeared in Amy Matilde Cassey's album, and James Forten Jr.'s calligraphy decorated the title page of Martina Dickerson's album of poetry.

"Destruction by Fire of Pennsylvania Hall" (The Historical Society of Pennsylvania, Bb 107 B786). The burning of Pennsylvania Hall during an antislavery convention in 1838 demonstrated to James Forten and other abolitionists just how unpopular and how controversial their cause had become.

7

REFLECTIONS OF
"A MAN OF COLOUR"

I N THE DECADE and a half after his return from England in 1785 James
Forten not only made the transition from apprentice to master craftsman
but established himself as a man of influence within Philadelphia's free
community of color. During the next decade and a half, from 1800 to the end of
the War of 1812, he would build on those foundations. In terms of his business
career, these were the years when he began to branch out, buying real estate,
extending loans, forging ties with white businessmen. During this period he would
also gain the recognition of his community as a figure of real authority, an individual capable of articulating the hopes and fears of black Philadelphians. Inevitably the two worlds intersected. His increasing prosperity and business know-how
contributed to his influence. Here was a man who could get things done, a man
who could chair committees, write petitions, and approach white men in positions of power in state and city governments, the court system, and the church.
James Forten had had the formal education most people of color had not. Moreover, he worked in a world few of them could imagine. As an employer of white
men, a partner in trade with white men, his experiences diverged from theirs in a
number of ways. But when all was said and done, his concerns were their concerns, and with so many of the white citizens of Philadelphia expressing a growing unease about their black neighbors, James Forten assumed a larger and larger
role in defending black Philadelphians, himself included, from hostile legislation, harassment, and open violence. In crafting a defense of his community, he
would prove himself not merely a shrewd representative of that community but a
formidable debater and a political theorist of no mean ability.

TO GET A sense of James Forten's activism in the period after 1800 it is necessary to step back briefly to the 1790s when he was just beginning to make his presence felt among Philadelphia's free people of color. The year 1793 was a momentous one in many respects for all the city's residents. It saw street demonstrations over the French alliance, the arrival of the Saint Dominguan refugees, and the deaths of some 4,000 Philadelphians in the yellow fever epidemic. For black people it saw, on top of everything else, the passage of the Fugitive Slave Law. When they learned what its provisions meant in everyday terms, they were bitterly resentful and in many cases deeply afraid. Under the new law, escaped slaves could be seized and returned to bondage. As black Philadelphians and their white allies pointed out, the same law could give cover to kidnappers. Willing to testify before a magistrate that the individual in question was indeed the same "boy" or "wench" who had absconded years before, and required to present as evidence only a vague description of the missing "chattel" and some proof of ownership, a slave owner or his agent could carry off into slavery a freeborn man or woman. Some claimants never even went near the courts, quite literally taking the law into their own hands and hustling an alleged runaway back to the South. In effect, no black person was safe anywhere in the Union. And Philadelphia, with its rapidly growing black population, soon became a hunting ground for everyone from the indignant slaveholder in search of his human property to the unscrupulous slave catcher and the professional kidnapper.[1]

The leaders of the African-American community, and their friends in the Pennsylvania Abolition Society, petitioned again and again for the repeal of the Fugitive Slave Law, the emancipation of Pennsylvania's remaining bondsmen and women, and, as a long-range goal, the outlawing of slavery throughout the Union. Only when slavery was gone forever, they argued, could black people truly feel secure. The initiative in the Pennsylvania legislature in 1793 for total abolition at the state level died with the outbreak of the yellow fever epidemic. Undeterred, black and white foes of slavery redoubled their efforts, bombarding both Congress and the Pennsylvania legislature with petitions.

In the first weeks of 1797 four ex-slaves from North Carolina submitted their petition to Congress. All four, "liberated under the hand and seal of humane and conscientious masters," had been compelled by a state law devised by "men of cruel disposition, and void of just principle," to leave North Carolina or face reenslavement. Separated from loved ones and hunted like animals, they had come at last to Philadelphia. Yet even there they and many like them were not safe. It was pathetically easy to seize a free person of color, claim him as a slave, and drag him into lifelong bondage. Would Congress not listen to their stories and repeal, or at least amend, the Fugitive Slave Law? The matter occasioned a lively, indeed, an acrimonious debate, but it ended with a vote of 50 to 33 against receiving the petition.[2]

Refusing to abandon the struggle, black residents of Philadelphia launched another assault on slavery in general and the Fugitive Slave Law in particular.

In 1799, probably with the active encouragement of the Pennsylvania Abolition Society, Absalom Jones and some seventy other men of color living in the
city and its outlying districts embarked on a bold initiative to assert their rights
as "freemen" and secure an improvement in the treatment of black people, free
and slave, nationwide. Identifying themselves unequivocally as citizens, they
petitioned Congress for redress of grievances.

"The Petition of the People of Colour, Freemen within the City and Suburbs of Philadelphia" expressed the petitioners' gratitude that they had been
spared "the oppression and violence [to] which so great a number of like colour
and National Descent are subjected." At least they were not slaves. However,
in the midst of their happiness they could not forget the sufferings of those less
fortunate than themselves. "We . . . humbly conceive ourselves authorized to
address . . . you in their behalf, believing them to be objects of representations
in your public Councils, in common with ourselves and every other class of
Citizens." They had two requests, one relating to their own situation and the
other to the plight of all people of color. In the short term they begged Congress to act to prevent the wholesale kidnapping that was taking place under
the Fugitive Slave Law. "Can any Commerce . . . so detestably shock the feelings of Man, or degrade the dignity of his nature equal to this, and how increasingly is the evil aggravated when practised in a Land, high in profession of the
benign doctrines of our blessed Lord." They acknowledged, though, that only
when black people were no longer considered commodities anywhere in the
United States would kidnapping cease. They longed to see slavery ended once
and for all, but they were realistic. "We do not wish for the immediate emancipation of all, knowing that the degraded state of many . . . would greatly disqualify for such a change; but humbly desire you may exert every means in your
power to . . . prepare the way for the oppressed to go free."[3]

On January 2, 1800, Representative Robert Waln of Pennsylvania presented
the petition to Congress. Immediately, it became the subject of heated debate.
South Carolina's John Rutledge, Jr., was appalled. "Already had too much of this
new-fangled French philosophy of liberty and equality found its way . . . among
these *gentlemen* in the Southern States."[4] Massachusetts Federalist Harrison Gray
Otis was equally hostile. Such petitions should not be encouraged. "It would
teach them the art of assembling together, debating, and the like, and would
soon, if encouraged, extend from one end of the Union to the other." James
Jones of Georgia painted a fearsome picture of what members of Congress could
expect if they considered the petition. Give black people an inch and they would
take a yard. "I would ask gentlemen whether, with all their philanthropy, they
would wish to see those people sitting by their sides, deliberating in the councils
of the nation?" Gabriel Christie of Maryland did not believe that men of color
were capable of independent thought. They had been put up to this petitioning
effort by "a certain society," the Pennsylvania Abolition Society, which had been
bothering Congress every year with its own petitions.[5]

A few members were sympathetic. John Smilie of Pennsylvania felt black people should at least be able to petition for redress of grievances. They were "a part of the human species, equally capable of suffering and enjoying with others, and equally objects of attention." Samuel W. Dana of Connecticut thought their petition deserved a hearing. The language was "very decent."[6] However, their most outspoken champion was George Thacher of Massachusetts, a Harvard-trained lawyer, a Federalist, and a former member of the Continental Congress. His support on this occasion was hardly surprising, for he had been one of those who had urged that the petition of the North Carolina freedmen be heard back in 1797.[7] Now he went on the offensive, not just defending the right of the Philadelphians to petition Congress, but denouncing slavery as "a cancer of immense magnitude, that would some time destroy the body politic." The petition was "couched in as decent and respectful terms as was possible." Some had poured scorn on the petitioners' lack of education. Admittedly most were illiterate and had had to "sign" with an X. Did that mean they were any less entitled to seek redress from Congress? "A great reason why they could not write was their being brought up in early life in slavery."[8] In the end, Thacher was the only congressman who voted in favor of considering the petition. In just three years the mood of the House had changed. In 1797 more than thirty representatives had spoken up for the right of people of color to at least be heard. By 1800 that number had dwindled to one.[9]

Since Congress was still meeting in Philadelphia in January 1800, and would continue to do so until its removal to Washington, D.C., in November, it was relatively easy for the city's African-American community to get word of its deliberations. One of those who followed the debate on the petition with intense interest was James Forten. In the aftermath of the debate he wrote a heartfelt letter of thanks to Congressman Thacher. In later years his letter would take on a life of its own. White Quaker Susanna Emlen secured a copy for her father in England and told him something of its remarkable author. Daniel Coker, an African-American religious leader and teacher in Baltimore, praised the initial petition in his *Dialogue between a Virginian and an African Minister*, and expressed his approval of Forten's letter, adding Forten's name to his "List of . . . the Descendants of the African race, Who Have Given Proof of Talents."[10] It is easy to see why Emlen and Coker responded as they did, for James Forten's letter was both eloquent and very much to the point.

He began with an expression of his sense of mingled gratitude and dejection—gratitude to Thacher as a courageous and fair-minded individual, and dejection that so few in Congress shared his views.

> When the hand of Sorrow presses heavy on us, and the generality of mankind turns unpityingly from our complaints[,] if one appears who feels for and commiserates our situation, endeavours all in his power to alleviate our condition, our bosoms swell with gratitude and our tongues instinctively pronounce our thanks.

James Forten voiced his own feelings, but he also wrote on behalf of the petitioners, and the wider community for which they spoke. Significantly, he used "We" when he referred to "Africans and descendants of that unhappy race." He might have to look to his great-grandfather to establish the link with Africa, but it was there, and it was no less real after three generations in America. Not for a moment was Forten rejecting his identity as an American, a citizen of the republic he had fought for. Rather, he was acknowledging himself to be a more complex individual, an American man of color, a descendant of Africa who was also an American.

The plea to Congress for action had been made on behalf of the nation's slaves. "Seven hundred thousand of the human race were concerned in our petition." As for those like himself who had their legal freedom, "we knew not but ere long we might be reduced to Slavery." However, unlike their brothers and sisters in the Caribbean, who had turned to violence to loose the shackles of slavery and racial oppression, the Philadelphians believed it was "only" by the actions of the "general government" that "we can . . . be relieved from our deplorable state."[11]

Forten was painfully aware of the horrific images the two words "St. Domingo" aroused in the minds of most whites. Eighteen months earlier, white Philadelphians had been thrown into paroxysms of fear by rumors that hundreds of "French Negroes" were sailing up and down the Delaware. There were reports that a rebellion was about to break out on the vessels quarantined near Fort Mifflin. Someone claimed to have seen a "sloop of war manned only with negroes." Supposedly the sloop had sent out a boat, which had "been seen the whole day plying around all the other vessels which have negroes on board. . . . There is now in those vessels between 250 and 300 negroes, well armed, trained to war, and saying they will land. They know no laws and count their lives for nothing." What had spawned the report was nothing more than the arrival of two shiploads of white refugees from Saint Domingue, along with fifty-five unarmed slaves, all of them firmly under the control of their masters.[12] Even so, terrified whites could not get out of their minds the image of bands of armed black men rampaging through the city, intent on looting, raping, and killing. Forten was anxious to make it clear to Thacher and his colleagues in Congress that the free men of color of Philadelphia were seeking redress not at the point of a sword or a bayonet but by a calm, reasoned, and respectful approach to the "general government."

Answering the charges of intellectual inferiority that so many members of Congress had leveled against the petitioners, Forten spoke not only for himself but for those who lacked his early advantages. He had had an education. They had not. Did that make them less entitled to air their complaints?

> Though our faces are black, yet we are men, and though many among us cannot write because our rulers have thought proper to keep us in ignorant [*sic*], yet we all have the feelings and the passions of men, are as anxious to

enjoy the birthright of the human race, as those who, from our ignorance, draw an argument aganest [*sic*] our petition.

Indeed, one of the strong points of the petition was that it "ha[d] in view the diffusion of knowledge among the African race, by unfettering their thoughts and giving full scope to the energy of their minds."[13]

Forten applauded Thacher's readiness to concede that "by principles of natural law our thraldom is unjust." Empathizing as the New Englander did with the aspirations of the black Philadelphians, he could surely appreciate their sorrow. "Judge what must be our feelings to find our Selves treated as a species of property, and levelled with the Brute creation, and think how anxious we must be to raise ourselves from this degrading state." With the rejection of their petition, "A deep gloom now envelopes us," relieved only by the knowledge that "there is one who will use all his endeavours to free the Slave from Captivity . . . and preserve the Free Black in the full enjoyment of his rights."[14]

THE PRESSURE TO end slavery continued. Just a matter of weeks after Congress rejected their petition, black Philadelphians approached the state legislature. On January 28, 1800, the Pennsylvania House received a document "from a number of free blacks in the city of Philadelphia, stating their willingness to be taxed for the purpose of emancipating the slaves within this commonwealth."[15] The house was intrigued by the offer. It would cost white taxpayers nothing, and compensated emancipation was something slave owners were likely to welcome. Members quickly drafted and passed a bill that would have resulted in the freeing of all the remaining slaves in the state. However, the bill failed in the Senate and, somewhat surprisingly, met with a decided negative from the Pennsylvania Abolition Society. PAS members spoke out against it because it implicitly recognized the legality of slavery, rewarded slave owners, and imposed a discriminatory tax. They contended that holding an individual in bondage violated the state constitution and they were engaged in an effort to get slavery in Pennsylvania declared unlawful in the courts. Passing a bill to free slaves by paying off slaveholders would undermine the PAS's efforts.[16] In this instance black abolitionists clashed with white abolitionists not about their shared goal but about the best means of achieving it. The result of their disagreement was that men and women not covered by the Gradual Abolition Act of 1780 remained in bondage until they died, were manumitted, or managed to secure their freedom through self-purchase or escape. Not until 1847 would the state of Pennsylavnia outlaw slavery completely and liberate all those still being held as slaves.

There is nothing to indicate how far, if at all, James Forten was involved in this contentious approach to the state legislature, or in a petition Philadelphia's free people of color submitted to President Thomas Jefferson in 1801.[17] However, that he was vitally concerned about the persistence of slavery, and the whole issue of justice and fair treatment for the African-American community, is beyond question. In his letter to Thacher, Forten had emphasized the essential equality of all Americans and the need for a sweeping but peaceful reordering of society. In 1801 he took his argument several steps further in a statement to the members of the PAS.

Through the 1790s the members of the PAS had been reaching out to Philadelphia's free people of color, trying to secure for them and their children employment, education, and protection from oppression. Admittedly, the white abolitionists might differ with members of the black community on certain issues, as they had, for instance, over the initiative to end slavery in Pennsylvania. However, they were more supportive of the interests of people of color than the vast majority of white Philadelphians. The PAS made practical efforts to improve the lives of black citizens. Its Committee on Education collaborated with a committee of the Free African Society to investigate the situation of black families in the city and its adjoining districts. Members visited individual households, spoke to community groups, and regularly issued circulars replete with well-intentioned (if paternalistic) advice. During the 1790s James Forten was not apparently active in working with the PAS in its various undertakings. He left that to his seniors, men such as William Wilshire, Cyrus Bustill, Caesar Cranchell, Absalom Jones, and Abraham Inglis.[18] However, by the early 1800s that would change, and the PAS would become very much aware that James Forten was a man whose opinions carried weight among the black citizens of Philadelphia.

In 1801 the PAS prepared yet another address "which we have believed it our duty to lay before the people of colour. . . . [I]t was read to them . . . at their several places of worship, and also at three societies which they have formed with the benevolent design of assisting each others' families, in times of sickness and misfortune."[19] One of those three societies was the Friendly Society of St. Thomas, and on behalf of the members its president, James Forten, expressed to the PAS their "gratitude . . . for the numerous benefits which you have conferred on such of [our] brethren as have fallen under your Notice, and for the unceasing anxiety which you manifest for the temporal and eternal happiness of the African Race." However, "Precious and delightful as liberty is, it cannot alone give happiness but may rather . . . be considered as the means by which we may attain it, by unfettering and ennobling our minds and raising us to the knowledge of what we are, and for what we were intended."[20] The PAS address had emphasized the need for religion, and Forten and the other men in the Friendly Society echoed that. "Without Religion to guide our Actions and controul the passions, liberty might have been to us a source of evil," and he thanked the members of the PAS for doing what they could to encourage it.

Even to the poor Slave Religion affords the greatest comforts; harassed by the cruelty of a Master, he pours out his Sorrows before his Creator, and is consoled by the belief that tho' his pilgrimage thro' this life is painful indeed, yet he will arrive at last at that place, where the Colour of a Man is immaterial, and where the Slave and the Master are alike.

Forten spoke of free people like himself as being "Attached to our race by the Tie of Sympathy." They believed sincerely that the good conduct of the individual had a direct impact on the well-being of the entire community. "The dark ignorance under which many of our brethren labour, is to us a Source of regret, and a strong desire exists to remove it, for while it does exist we can hardly hope to remove the prejudices against us, or to raise the African race to the rank of Man in the Creation."[21]

Of course, Forten may have been tailoring his message for the white abolitionists and telling them what they wanted to hear. On the other hand, there is ample evidence that combating "dark ignorance" was one of his major goals. In a sense, it was his only goal. Dispel ignorance and the nation would indeed live up to the principles enshrined in the Declaration of Independence. That goal of rooting out ignorance explained Forten's devotion to Freemasonry, with its pursuit of spiritual enlightenment. It explained his determination to see African-American children given the benefits of education. And it explained his desire to reach out to hostile whites. Once let light break in upon *their* "dark ignorance" and the result would be not only the abolition of slavery but the creation of a society from which prejudice and injustice had been banished forever.

Enlightenment took many forms, and James Forten was prepared to cooperate with anyone who saw as he did and shared his aspirations. He was intrigued, for instance, in 1801 when Philadelphia printer William W. Woodward brought around a subscription paper. Woodward proposed the publication in two volumes of an antislavery novel translated from the French, the Marquis de Bois-Robert's *The Negro Equalled by Few Europeans*, and selected poems by the African-born poet Phillis Wheatley (c. 1753–84). There was nothing unusual in soliciting advance orders. Publishers routinely did so in order to ensure a work would sell before they risked too much capital. However, in a radical departure from established practice, Woodward approached black Philadelphians as well as whites. James Forten willingly handed over the price of a copy of the new work, as did a number of other people of color. Here was the perfect answer to those congressmen who considered black people to be simple-minded because of their lack of formal education. Let their willingness to support intellectual endeavors stand alongside the work of the African prodigy Phillis Wheatley and the French nobleman's denunciations of slavery and racial prejudice. Of the almost 400 individuals who subscribed to the publication, at least twenty-two were black. There may in fact have been more, but the evidence in the censuses and directories is insufficient to identify them by race. Heading the list were ministers Richard Allen and Absalom Jones. Forten's name was there, as were the names of fellow artisans and shopkeepers. Men such as William Gray, Thomas Mount, Cyrus Porter, Joseph Randolph, Peter Richmond, and Henry Stewart were certainly not rich, but they had a dollar or two to spare for a worthy cause. Among the white subscribers were a number of people Forten would have known, including a neighbor on Shippen Street, Captain John Patton, and merchant John Soullier, from whom Forten bought his home on Lombard Street.[22]

The Negro Equalled by Few Europeans told of the enslavement of the noble African youth Itanoko, the kindness of the young Frenchman Ferdinand, Itanoko's eventual rescue, and the series of events that reunited him with his beloved Amelia, daughter of the virtuous Frenchman Dumont and Dumont's Senegalese wife. Great literature it was not, but Forten, Allen, Jones, and white antislavery sympathizers must surely have warmed to its sweeping indictment of slavery and the slave trade. As for Wheatley's poems, they were fairly well known, but, thanks to Woodward, they now reached a new audience.[23]

Another publishing initiative a few years later proved to James Forten that one's allies might be drawn from the enemies of one's enemy. "Ally" was not necessarily synonymous with "friend." Irishman Thomas Branagan shared James Forten's goal of enlightening Philadelphians with regard to slavery and racism, but how he achieved that goal probably caused Forten some heart-searching. Branagan was a slave trader and plantation overseer turned itinerant preacher and critic of slavery.[24] However, much of his criticism flowed from his anger at the impact slavery had on poor whites. In 1804, in his *Preliminary Essay on the Oppression of the Exiled Sons of Africa*, a project Forten's friend Richard Allen helped fund, he announced, "A New Work, Entitled, Avenia; or A Tragical Poem on the Slavery and Commerce of the Human Species, Particularly the African; In six books, with explanatory notes on each book." He planned to leave subscription papers for "The friends of liberty and humanity, who wish to facilitate . . . the publication of the said poem" with Allen, Absalom Jones, James Forten, and Jacob Knows, a white man who ran a shoe store on Market Street.[25]

How aware was James Forten of the full range of Branagan's views? Some were Forten's own. As Branagan wrote in the afterword to *Avenia:* "[W]ith what ideas of justice can such persons . . . take the reigns [*sic*] of government . . . who rob their African brethren of their lives and liberties, because forsooth they are black?"[26] Other sections might have made Forten wince. Branagan estimated there were 15,000 black people living in Philadelphia, and that was something he found deeply disturbing.

> The encouragement of slavery in the southern states, is of infinite injury to the poor white people in the northern states. . . . While thousands of Africans are monthly imported into South Carolina, hundreds abscond and seek an asylum in the northern states, where they are on an equality with the whites.[27]

Forten might have argued that he did not see too much wrong with the equality Branagan alleged existed in the North, although he could have pointed out it was far less complete than the Irishman imagined.

In 1805, the year that saw the publication of *Avenia*, the prolific Branagan also wrote *Serious Remonstrances, Addressed to the Citizens of the Northern States, and Their Representatives*. In this work he advocated settling black people, by force if necessary, in the Western territories recently acquired from France in the Louisiana Purchase. Blacks and whites must live apart, he insisted. Any whites who chose to settle in the projected colony must consent to be ruled by black people.[28] Of northern free people of color he wrote:

> Can they forget the injuries their ancestors met with from Americans. . . .
> [C]an they help feeling an involuntary disgust to their tyrants, their children,
> their color and their country?. . . [I]f a certain family used my father and his
> family . . . as the christians do the exiled Africans, could I forget it?[29]

Forten might respond that "exiled African" though he was in one sense, he considered himself an American and America his country. If he could accept the notion of African Americans being "strangers in a strange land" as merely a point of philosophical difference, he was probably less sanguine about some of Branagan's other statements. The Irishman created a nightmare scenario of "the slaves in Delaware" rising up to "subjugate their tyrants" and marching on Philadelphia, where they would link up with the "fifteen or twenty thousand blacks and mulattoes" who lived there. Interracial sex, coerced or consensual, was part of the nightmare. With migration and interbreeding, Philadelphia would be half-black "in the course of a few years."[30]

Branagan insisted it would not work to give black people equal rights and let them live among the whites. Who would want a black president or senator? Who would welcome a black marriage partner for their son or daughter? Violence must ensue, "for as sure as Africans are exalted to a participation of the privileges of citizens . . . so sure the tragical scene acted in Hispaniola will be re[en]acted in America."[31] Branagan hastened to add that some of his best friends were black, but he wasn't sure how far he could trust them! "All the Blacks are by no means included in my animadversions; there are many of them . . . (some of which I know myself) who are men of information and respectability, but I must add, men who are naturally aspiring to gain an ascendancy over their fellows, something like his negro majesty, the emperor Dessalines" of Haiti.[32] This, then, was how Branagan saw James Forten—as too clever and ambitious for his own good and the good of his white neighbors—a Jean Jacques Dessalines in the making.

THOMAS BRANAGAN WAS not alone among white Philadelphians in being tormented by the horrors of "St. Domingo" and judging every ambitious and articulate person of color to be another Emperor Dessalines. Ironically, Branagan was more disposed than most whites to view with sympathy the plight of black men and women. Few of his neighbors could get the images of black rebellion out of their heads, and in the summer of 1804 it seemed their worst fears were about to come true.

Just after the annual Independence Day celebrations, the Philadelphia newspaper the *Freemen's Journal* carried a disturbing account of racial unrest in Southwark and on the fringes of Philadelphia proper. Bands of young black men, "armed with bludgeons, &c.," did battle with the constables on the evening of July 4. The next night the sheriff came out with a posse and made arrests. There were also reports of two black men wandering around with cutlasses and clubs.[33] An anonymous correspondent to the same newspaper told an even more alarming tale. According to him, on the night of July 4 a group of black youths collected on Small Street, "formed themselves into a company, and appointed a captain, lieutenant and ensign," although at this point he conceded they were unarmed. On Small Street they mugged "a poor inoffensive old man." On Fifth Street they robbed "A young gentleman," and when a female resident tried to intervene, "they declared they would despatch her also." They then carried out another assault and a home invasion. By this point the assailants numbered a hundred and were armed. The next night their ranks swelled to between one and two hundred, and they proceeded through the streets, "damning the whites, and saying they would shew them *St. Domingo.*" "A Subscriber" did not explain how he had been able to follow this armed mob from street to street for two nights without himself being molested. Unrest there may have been, but perhaps not on the scale he alleged. Whether a cold and calculating troublemaker or simply the victim of his own overactive imagination, "A Subscriber" seized the opportunity to issue a wake-up call. "[A] considerable number of strange black people have been noticed loitering about. . . . Should there not be an enquiry made?"[34]

There were plenty of whites throughout Philadelphia and its neighboring counties who thought as "A Subscriber" did. In December 1804 residents of Delaware and Chester Counties pushed for action by the Pennsylvania legislature. They wanted a tax imposed on all free people of color for the support of any who became public charges. That particular initiative failed, but others would follow.[35] Philadelphians were just as energetic as their fellow Pennsylvanians in demanding restrictions. Again and again they petitioned for curbs on black migration into the state, the harsh punishment of black vagrants, and lengthy prison terms for black lawbreakers. The image of African Americans as an indolent and criminally minded subset of the general population was growing.

James Forten and others of the black "better sort" responded in various ways to this increasing unease on the part of white citizens. They promoted education, urged tough punishments for *any* lawbreakers, regardless of race, and endeavored to prove that there were many African Americans, themselves included, who prized respectability and good order. The same year as the July Fourth unrest, Forten and other members of his church achieved their long-cherished goal of opening a school. With the help of Bishop White, St. Thomas's Church was able to get funding from the Associates of Dr. Bray in London for the school.[36] The vestry appointed a board of trustees, whose duty it was "to visit the school once in every month, to examine the scholars, note the progress made," and inform the vestry of any improvements that they deemed necessary in the operation of the school. James Forten was on that first board of trustees, as were old friends such as John Bowers, William Gray, Peter Richmond, and Robert Douglass.[37]

In 1809 the members of St. Thomas's established the Society for the Suppression of Vice and Immorality. It was endorsed by a number of prominent whites as a worthy initiative. They praised those in the black community "who, in respect to intellect and moral improvement, rank high among their fellow citizens" and welcomed the creation of "a society, the express object of which, is to ameliorate the condition of their brethren . . . by the suppression of vice and the communication of moral and religious instruction."[38] Needless to say, James Forten was involved in the work of the society.

Try as they might, though, Forten and the men of his stamp, eminently respectable middle-class men of color, could not stem the rising tide of racial hostility. White Philadelphians were growing increasingly resentful of the presence of *any* black people in their midst, and they were not shy about making their feelings known. Violence against their persons and their institutions, especially their churches, was a tragic fact of life for Philadelphian's African-American residents. The kind of "spree" William Otter described participating in sometime in 1807—an invasion of a black church in the Northern Liberties and an assault on worshippers as they tried to escape the mayhem—was all too common.[39] A foreign visitor to the city in 1809 was shocked at the "liberties taken in the public streets, where boys of ten or twelve . . . seem to think, that they are privileged in insulting this unfortunate class of our fellow-beings almost indiscriminately." During a recent snowstorm, "the poor negroes could not stir out, without being pelted with Snow Balls by these thoughtless creatures, whilst more matured, and therefore, less excusable manhood seemed to encourage the sport."[40]

A host of factors came together to make Philadelphia a far less welcoming place for people of color in the 1800s than it had been in the 1790s. Economic uncertainty plagued many of the city's residents. The impact of Jefferson's embargo on a city that lived by overseas trade was nothing short of devastating. Thrown out of work, or fearful that they soon would be, whites took out their frustrations on those they were accustomed to look upon as "legitimate" targets. Images of "St. Domingo" coupled with news of servile insurrections closer to home—Gabriel Prosser's planned uprising in Virginia, rumblings in Maryland, anything that seemed to suggest black people were taking matters into their own hands and asserting their rights to freedom and equality—fed racial tensions in Philadelphia. Exacerbating an already volatile situation was the fact that Philadelphia was a city under pressure. White immigrants were flooding in, as were black people from the Upper South. The window of opportunity that had enabled many hundreds of slaves to gain their freedom in the 1790s had been slammed shut. Manumissions were tightly restricted. Those lucky enough to gain their freedom in Virginia and North Carolina were given an ultimatum—leave the state within a set period of time or face reenslavement. Elsewhere in the Upper South the law did not drive out the newly freed, but lack of economic opportunities and the fear of kidnappers did.[41] Wave upon wave of black Southerners fled north to Philadelphia, the first city they came to after crossing the Mason-Dixon line. Some thrived in this new setting, but many did not. Poverty-stricken and in a far more desperate situation than the black migrants of the 1790s, these men and women were more likely to seek relief at the almshouse, beg in the streets, and fall foul of the officers of the law.[42] For a goodly number of these new arrivals the city's taverns, brothels, and gambling dens had more appeal than the institutions patronized by James Forten and other "respectable" people of color.[43] Of course, there was nothing surprising in that. Plenty of Philadelphia natives, white as well as black, preferred grogshops and whorehouses to churches and mutual improvement societies. However, the notion soon gained currency that black people, especially those from the South, were addicted to "vice." White citizens insisted that something had to be done. Their city was being swamped by a horde of lawless, disorderly, and unproductive black paupers. They demanded action from the authorities to curb the influx of black migrants, and for good measure they included in those demands restrictions on the freedom of long-term black residents.

DESPITE THE GROWING racial antagonism in the city, James Forten found reason to be hopeful. The African-American community was not without friends. The members of the Pennsylvania Abolition Society were still working to bring an end to slavery and to see that free people of color were protected in the enjoyment of their rights. During the 1800s Forten developed close ties with a number of the most dedicated individuals in the PAS. He also found allies in unexpected places. One of those allies was a young white Southern patrician, James Gillespie Birney. After graduating from Princeton, Birney came to Philadelphia in 1810 to study law with United States District Attorney Alexander J. Dallas. He ran in the fashionable circles of the city during his four years there, but he also made friends with Forten and white abolitionist Abraham L. Pennock. The existence of slavery had long since begun to gnaw at Birney. He had lived with the institution in Kentucky, he had pondered over it at Princeton, and his continued doubts about its legitimacy were fed by Forten and Pennock. Two decades later Birney would emerge as a leading critic of the slave system.[44]

By 1807 James Forten believed he saw signs that the federal government was becoming less intransigent on the issue of slavery. At long last it was poised to act to end the overseas slave trade. A bill outlawing the trade passed both the House and the Senate and was signed into law by President Jefferson. As of January 1, 1808, no more slaves would be imported into the United States. Given that Britain had announced a similar ban, this did indeed look like the beginning of the end for the institution of slavery. Let the trade in slaves come to an end, Forten and his allies reasoned, and the total abolition of chattel slavery could not be far behind. A major battle in the war had been won. Complete victory must surely be in sight. It did not occur to the likes of Forten that some of the delegates from the Upper South supported the ban because it would mean they and their constituents could get better prices for their excess slaves when they sold them to the cotton planters of the Lower South. Limiting the supply of slaves by ending importation from Africa and the West Indies made sound economic sense.

Unaware of any hidden agenda at work, black Philadelphians, in common with members of the African-American communities in Boston, New York, and other towns and cities throughout the North, believed that the end of the slave trade was truly something worth celebrating. James Forten and representatives of Philadelphia's black churches and mutual benefit societies began planning a day of thanksgiving. On May 10, 1807, Forten was one of a number of "Africans and their descendants" who got together to decide how best to mark the New Year and what they confidently predicted would be a new beginning. Absalom Jones, Richard Allen, Belfast Burton, and James Forten (the only one of the four not born into slavery) were chosen "to draft suitable resolutions for the occasion, and to correspond with other religious societies in the Union." They resolved "That our gratitude is due to our ALMIGHTY FATHER, for having influenced the minds of men to condemn a trade, which ought never to have commenced." They vowed that "on each return of the day on which the prohibition . . . commences, we will endeavour to evince the gratitude we feel, by acts of benevolence and brotherly regard . . . and by public prayer and thanksgiving." A committee was chosen to organize celebrations at St. Thomas's African Episcopal Church, Mother Bethel, and "the Anabaptist meeting." Forten, Jones, Allen, and Burton were joined on that committee by other prominent men in the community.[45]

Nothing short of a catastrophe could have kept James Forten away from St. Thomas's Church on January 1, 1808. An announcement of the day's schedule of events appeared in the city's leading newspaper, *Poulson's American Daily Advertiser*, complete with favorable editorial comment—an encouraging sign that African Americans were not without white well-wishers.[46] Absalom Jones began his sermon, appropriately enough, with a verse from Exodus. Exhorting his hearers to be grateful to God and to their friends among the whites, he ended with the injunction: "Let us constantly *remember the rock whence we were hewn, and the pit whence we were digged.* . . . [I]t becomes us . . . to acknowledge, that an African slave, ready to perish, was our father or our grandfather."[47]

James Forten probably helped organize the January 1 observances in following years, and he undoubtedly spent a good part of each New Year's Day in church giving thanks for the ending of the slave trade. On January 1, 1812, the orator was his close friend, the young African-American printer Russell Parrott.

On January 1, 1813, members of various benevolent societies processed to St. Thomas's Church. The announcement in the newspaper noted that "His honor the Mayor . . . having been informed of the . . . intended arrangement, has given it his cordial approbation." Forten was not a member of any of the societies listed in the announcement, but he was probably present at the church that day.[48] In 1814 and 1816 Russell Parrott was again the speaker, and Forten was almost certainly in the audience on both occasions to encourage his friend. In 1818 one of the sponsoring groups for the January 1 celebration was the Friendly Society of St. Thomas, the organization Forten had once presided over. There was another procession to St. Thomas's the following year.[49] On two occasions, in 1823 and 1830, the orators were sons of a man James Forten held in the highest esteem. Like their father, John Gloucester, Sr., Jeremiah and John Jr. were both Presbyterian ministers. Like their father, both had been born into slavery. Listening to these two eloquent and erudite young men, Forten could feel something akin to paternal pride, for he was one of those who had helped John Sr. raise the money to buy his sons out of slavery.[50]

The January 1 orations were invariably well worth listening to, and the annual observances showcased the talents of African-American preachers, but as the years passed, and the end of the slave trade was not followed by the complete abolition of slavery, Forten's enthusiasm, like that of other black Philadelphians, may have started to wane.[51]

BESET BY OCCASIONAL bouts of despair about the likelihood that slavery and racism would ever be eradicated, and that a more just society could be achieved, James Forten took solace in his strong religious faith, turning again and again to his church and to his much-loved minister. The links between Forten and Absalom Jones endured until the older man's death. Jones offered his friend and parishioner advice on a host of issues, and comfort during various crises. He received James Forten into the church when he presented himself as a candidate for adult baptism.[52] He joined him in marriage to his first wife, Martha, and counseled him when she died. He officiated at Forten's wedding to Charlotte Vandine and christened most of their children. He was there when James and Charlotte lost their young daughter, and when James's mother died. In a very real sense Absalom Jones was a surrogate father to James Forten and St. Thomas's his spiritual home. All that is not to imply that Forten was a devout but largely silent member of the congregation, or that he confined himself to helping oversee the church school and giving advice on financial issues. Many times in his long life James Forten plunged into the turbulent waters of vestry politics. Whenever church historian Rev. William Douglass made a discreet reference to a "tumult" or a "disagreement among the congregation" in his *Annals of St. Thomas*, a little digging soon reveals the redoubtable Mr. Forten weighing in on one side or the other.

Of course, not all of James Forten's dealings in church matters were contentious. Sometimes he was simply bringing his business expertise to bear on a particular problem. That was the case with the lottery. At least until the 1830s, organizing a lottery was considered a perfectly respectable way of raising funds.[53] St. Thomas's needed money for basic maintenance, and white Episcopalians agreed to help run a lottery for the church. An approach was made to the Pennsylvania legislature, and in 1804 it approved "An Act to raise by way of Lottery, a sum not exceeding eight thousand Dollars, for . . . the African Episcopal Church of St. Thomas." The proceeds were to be used "for the purposes of discharging the debts" of the church and enabling the congregation to finish work on the church building. Seven white Episcopalians were named commissioners.[54]

Things got off to a shaky start when five of the commissioners declined to act. Absalom Jones and the members of the vestry, who included Forten, decided they must take the initiative. They petitioned the legislature to name replacement commissioners, and the lottery finally got under way.[55] By September 1807 the commissioners announced they had "engaged the Wheels, now occupied by the Commissioners of the Bustleton and Smithfield Turnpike Lottery." They had already sold "A large number of Tickets." Drawings began in November. The lottery was eventually wound up in 1810, although it is unlikely that the proceeds were sufficient to discharge all the church's debts.[56]

The business of the lottery was straightforward enough. A problem had arisen and it needed to be addressed as quickly and efficiently as possible. Accustomed to dealing with a wide range of financial and legal matters, James Forten took a hand. Sorting out the tangle over commissioners for the lottery simply meant talking to the right people and filing the necessary paperwork. However, other issues were less easily resolved.

During the first decade of the nineteenth century St. Thomas's was thriving. Many more black churchgoers were attracted to Methodism, but St. Thomas's had well over 500 communicants and, as Absalom Jones proudly noted, "a great many more . . . constantly attend worship."[57] Still, Jones was not getting any younger, and ministering effectively to this many people was no easy task. There was also the question of succession. What would happen when Jones died or when his failing health forced him into retirement? Some members of St. Thomas's took steps to provide him with an assistant, and that prompted what William Douglass referred to delicately as "the noise of an angry tumult."

According to Douglass, a certain faction (he named no names) "open[ed] a communication" with one Alexander Cook Summers in Jamaica.[58] Summers arrived in Philadelphia in 1809 and an arrangement was made (by whom is not clear) for him to officiate at St. Thomas's free of charge from time to time. Convinced he would eventually be offered a full-time paid position at the church, he moved his family to Philadelphia. Douglass's account has it that Summers presented the letter of invitation he had received to the vestry. They "expressed their indignant surprise at the course which had been thus pursued" and appointed a committee to wait on Bishop White "for his counsel and advice, in relation to what they conceived to be a wicked attempt to create a division in the church." The bishop proposed an interview between Summers and the vestry, but Summers angrily refused to attend. At that point, according to Douglass, some members of St. Thomas's who supported Summers withdrew and began meeting for worship in a room on Zane Street.[59]

In fact, things were less straightforward than that. Summers's supporters included some very influential men—Robert Douglass, Richard Farrell, James Forten, Robert Gordon, Thomas Morgan, George Vandine, John Williams, and Shandy Yard. They were a tight-knit little group. Forten had frequently served on the vestry, and he, Gordon, and Douglass were trustees of the church's day school. Yard was one of James Forten's closest friends, and Vandine a relative by marriage. The fact that the principal document in the case is in James Forten's very distinctive handwriting suggests he was the spokesman for this little clique.[60] Yet, powerful though Forten and his friends might have been, on this occasion they overreached themselves. Their influence was not strong enough to ensure acceptance of Summers by the rest of the members of St. Thomas's.

In an effort to garner support, Forten's faction appealed to Bishop White and Dr. Benjamin Rush to mediate.[61] They also drew up a circular setting forth their version of events. They wished to ease the life of "our venerable aged Pastor" by hiring an assistant, and they asked people to pledge to pay so much per quarter into a fund "for the Maintenance of another Coloured Minister." It is clear from the tone of the circular that Forten's group envisaged an appeal to white well-wishers. The fund would be managed by a person chosen by a committee and approved of by the bishop. They wanted their assistant minister placed on the same footing as the assistant ministers in the white churches. The only proviso was that "the minister and vestry of the said church be willing and agreeable for the execution of the aforesaid plan, and give satisfactory proofs to the bishop, and two other gentlemen nominated by us, that they will admit and receive the assistance of the newly proposed minister, on honourable and equitable terms."

They explained that Summers "was by the invitation of our present minister and the apparent warm approbation of the vestry for three months last year, constantly employed as an officiating minister . . . gratuitously . . . to the satisfaction of all parties." The minister, vestry, and congregation had pressed him to settle in Philadelphia. He came, at considerable expense to himself, "confiding in the honour and integrity of the officers and rulers of the African Church." He has "done nothing to forfeit that universal good opinion entertained for him . . . by all ranks of the African Church." They felt that he could not "be passed over with neglect, without an indelible stain upon African probity, piety, and sincerity."[62]

At this distance in time it is not easy to see what the appeal of Summers was. He was obviously younger than Jones. He may also have been better edu-cated. Rebuffed by the majority of church members, Summers spent several years teaching school in Philadelphia. Perhaps Forten and his friends hoped that Summers, as Jones's eventual successor, would need no dispensation from the bishop in the matter of classical languages, and that that would entitle St. Thomas's to representation in the convention. Perhaps they had gotten wind of another candidate and they wanted to get "their" man in first. Certainly it was a bold power-play on their part to go outside the congregation to Bishop White and to old friends such as Benjamin Rush. Maneuver as he might, Forten could not get the appointment for Summers. However, it would not be the last time he would make a bid to get the candidate of his choice into the pulpit of St. Thomas's.

IN THE SUMMER of 1812 the United States lurched and stumbled into a second war with Britain. Like most Northern men of business, especially those in the maritime trades, James Forten was probably less than enthusiastic about the war. He may even have shared in the grim predictions of disaster. As the Revo-lutionary War had done decades before, the War of 1812 would test Forten's patriotism and his sense of himself as an American. However, it would do so in very different ways from that earlier conflict, when he had shared a sense of comradeship with his fellow prisoners on the *Jersey* and had felt optimistic about the war's outcome. In the course of the War of 1812 he would find his commu-nity reviled and its members rejected as unworthy of full citizenship—until disaster loomed.

This second war with Britain began badly for the United States. It would not be marked by many American victories, but Forten, ever the patriot, joined in celebrating those victories that were achieved. On August 19, 1812, some 750 miles out in the Atlantic, Isaac Hull's *Constitution* bested the Royal Navy frigate *Guerrière*.[63] When the news of this triumph over British sea power reached Philadelphia, the citizens were ecstatic, and none more so than James Forten, who gave $10 to a subscription to buy pieces of silver plate for Hull and his first lieutenant. It was an acknowledgment of victory, and it was also a cel-ebration of belonging. Forten was sharing in "the Glory acquired for our Coun-try."[64] His buoyant mood would be short-lived, though.

It was galling to realize in the months that followed that there was a per-ception on the part of some whites that African Americans had to be coerced and cajoled into taking part in the war effort. In January 1813, for example, "A Volunteer," writing in the *Democratic Press*, suggested black Philadelphians would make ideal cannon fodder. They contributed nothing "to the mainte-nance or support of government." There were too many of them anyway, and they "could be better spared than any other class of the population."[65] Offen-sive though such statements were, the question of whether black citizens would or should serve in the military would not really arise until the British actually threatened the city.

"A Volunteer's" sentiments about free people of color were shared by many white citizens, who were becoming increasingly frustrated at the failure of the Pennsylvania legislature to take action to ban black migration into the state and keep a tight rein on long-term black residents. Almost a decade had passed since the first call for tougher laws back in 1804. Petitions had been submitted. Laws had been drafted, but none had made their way to the governor's desk. By 1813 members of the legislature were being deluged with calls for something, *anything*, to be done about the numbers of black people in the state. Politicians took note of the clamor. After all, it came from voters.

On January 18, 1813, the house appointed a committee to consider closing Pennsylvania's borders to black migrants.[66] Plenty of whites liked what they heard and urged lawmakers to go further. On February 23 Jacob Mitchell presented to the house a petition from "sundry" Philadelphians stating that, while almost 10,000 free people of color appeared in the census, "there are about 4000 runaway Negroes" living in the city and its districts "who are not on record." Black people in general were "becoming nuisances" and the petitioners "pray[ed] that provision may be made by law to oblige them all to be registered[,] authorising the sale for a term of Years of those who shall be convicted of Crimes . . . and also that a tax may be levied upon them for the support of their own poor."[67] A couple of weeks later, Mr. Sergeant presented two petitions "from the mayor and aldermen and others, citizens of the city of Philadelphia" asking for the registration of all black people in the city, for a special tax on them, and "that in cases of conviction for offenses, they may be obliged to serve until the persons interested may be indemnified."[68]

The officers of the Pennsylvania Abolition Society learned of the proposed restrictions and submitted a petition of their own asking that the legislature not pass a law that would "violate humanity[,] justice and the establish'd principles of the Constitution of the United States."[69] The African-American community also reacted. On March 20 "Mr. Sergeant presented a remonstrance from sundry free people of color in the city and county of Philadelphia."[70] And one of those free people of color set everything else aside to compose his own defense of his community.

The authorship of *Letters from a Man of Colour* was an open secret. When John Brown Russwurm and Samuel E. Cornish reprinted the *Letters* in consecutive numbers of their newspaper, *Freedom's Journal*, in 1828, they prefaced them with the observation that they were "from the pen of one of our most intelligent and respectable citizens of Colour in the U. States." They added: "[W]e are anxious they should circulate far and near, and be perused by friend and foe." On the copy of *Freedom's Journal* at the New York Public Library in which the first of those *Letters* appeared, someone obligingly wrote "James Forten."[71]

James Forten's *Letters from a Man of Colour* is a bold and persuasive appeal to justice and common sense. He described his reflections as "the simple dictates of nature . . . the impulse of a mind formed . . . for feeling." He might insist that his letters "are not written in the gorgeous style of a scholar, nor dressed in . . . literary perfection," but his pamphlet is obviously the work of an educated man.[72] Forten stated his argument with a clarity few could gainsay, throwing back at white patriots their own much-vaunted sentiments.

Even the most cursory reading of *Letters from a Man of Colour* reveals that James Forten was not merely literate but very well read. He prefaced his appeal with four lines of verse from the work of the English Whig poet and essayist Joseph Addison on the beauty of liberty. Over the years Addison's words became part of the lingua franca of republican freedom, trotted out at various times of protest and celebration. Forten might have seen them reprinted in any one of a number of places or he might actually have owned a copy of Addison's works.[73]

Addison was far better known for his 1713 play, *Cato*, than for his poetry, and that suggests yet more about James Forten's forays into literature. We know from his writings that the image of Cato was one that resonated with him. He occasionally used "Cato" as a pen name.[74] For him "Cato" was not one of those classical names, like Caesar and Pompey, that slave owners found it humorous to foist on their unfortunate bondsmen. He identified himself with Cato the Roman patriot (95–46 B.C.), the implacable defender of liberty. He took the name back to its Roman roots, at least as they were represented in the writings of Addison and other Whigs, such as poet and playwright James Thomson, and Trenchard and Gordon, the authors of *Cato's Letters*.[75]

Like others of the Revolutionary generation, Forten had come of age, both in years and in intellectual development, reading the works of the great Whig theorists. What the Whigs had to say on the subject of Cato and liberty struck a chord with many literate Americans in the 1770s and beyond. For Forten, a black reader, the central theme was not so much (or not simply) liberty from British tyranny, but liberty from racial oppression.

Forten read about Cato in the writings of the Whigs and he probably saw Addison's *Cato* performed in Philadelphia. While Forten strenuously opposed "vice" and "immorality," he was not the dour killjoy some might think him. According to one of his contemporaries, he was a habitué of the old theater in Southwark until it closed in 1817. Although rather old-fashioned by the time of its demise, it still boasted a first-rate company. Apparently James Forten could often be seen of an evening occupying the front bench in the gallery and watching such perennial favorites of the eighteenth- and early nineteenth-century theatergoer as *Hamlet*, *Julius Caesar*, *Venice Preserved*, *She Stoops to Conquer*—and Addison's *Cato*.[76]

Cato, although seldom performed today, was extremely popular in the eighteenth century. George Washington mentioned it in his correspondence. Another admirer was Benjamin Franklin.[77] It also had certain elements likely to appeal to James Forten. There was Cato himself, who chose death rather than the loss of his precious liberty, and there was Cato's disciple, the Numidian prince, Juba, who outshone many of the Roman characters in the play in terms of selflessness and moral purity, proving himself, in effect, Cato's intellectual heir. Here, in this African champion of liberty, was a potent image, indeed, for James Forten.[78]

Trying to determine what Forten read and when and where he read it necessarily involves a great deal of guesswork. Sadly, his library has long since been scattered, although all the indications are that he and his family were voracious readers. As for his theatergoing experiences, he never commented on them directly, and after the Southwark Theatre closed, he probably found it far from pleasant to attend the Chestnut or Walnut Theatres and be relegated to the third tier, where all black patrons, regardless of wealth and refinement, were accommodated. Even if he had to give up attending the theater, rather than expose himself and his family to humiliation, he was obviously a man steeped in the prose, poetry, and drama of his time. The meanings he extracted from works of literature were not always those the writers intended, but they mattered to him and spoke to his situation. In 1813, when he needed an introduction to his *Letters from a Man of Colour*, he delved into his collection of books, or perhaps simply into his capacious memory, and found Addison's lines on liberty.

If Forten had immersed himself in the works of Addison and the British Whigs, he was equally familiar with the writings of the Founding Fathers. He knew what they meant, even if others had chosen to put a different gloss upon them with the passage of time. In his *Letters from a Man of Colour* he demanded a return to the purity of the texts. "We hold this truth to be self-evident, that GOD created all men equal, and is one of the most prominent features in the Declaration of Independence and in that glorious fabrick of collected wisdom, our noble Constitution." He went on to stress the universality of "this truth." "This idea embraces the Indian and the European, the Savage and the Saint . . . the white Man and the African, and whatever measures are adopted subversive of this inestimable privilege, are in direct violation of the letter and spirit of our Constitution."[79]

The bill to which James Forten so strenuously objected had failed in the Pennsylvania Senate but was to be held over to the next session. His was a preemptive strike to ensure it died. He hoped by the next session that "the white men, whom we should look upon as our protectors," would have become convinced of the injustice of the proposed legislation.[80] Pennsylvania had a glorious name to uphold. "This is almost the only state in the Union wherein the African race have justly boasted of rational liberty and the protection of the laws." Forten appealed to the "descendants of the immortal Penn" to continue their humane treatment of their black neighbors, and assured them that if they did so, "the blessing of the African will for ever be around you."[81]

He wrote of his concern for "the honour and dignity of our native state" if the bill became law.

> [T]he advocates of slavery, the traders in human blood, will smile contemptu-ously at the once boasted moderation and humanity of Pennsylvania! What, that place, whose institutions for the prevention of Slavery, are the admira-tion of surrounding states and of Europe, become . . . the oppressor of the free and innocent![82]

Then he advanced an argument particularly close to his heart, that of merit and respectability. "Many of us are men of property . . . but should this become a law, our property is jeopardized, since the same power which can expose to sale an unfortunate fellow creature, can wrest from him those estates, which years of honest industry have accumulated." He was no apologist for the lawbreaker. Criminals, black or white, deserved punishment. But the regrettable fact that "there are a number of worthless men belonging to our colour" should not blind lawmakers to the merits of the African-American community as a whole.[83] Surely, he argued, African Americans had earned the right to equal treatment before the law. "Many of our ancestors were brought here more than one hun-dred years ago; many of our fathers, many of ourselves, have fought and bled for the Independence of our country. . . . [L]et the motto of our Legislature be: 'The Law knows no distinction.'"[84]

Forten's pamphlet, so obviously written from the heart, set forth with ad-mirable clarity his sense of his community's situation. They were "Africans," bound by common ancestry to their "countrymen" who suffered in slavery else-where in the hemisphere. But they also shared with their white "countrymen" in the Revolutionary heritage because they had helped create it. As for equal-ity, for Forten that meant giving every man, regardless of race and condition, an equal chance of success, and letting "character" determine the result. Some would fall by the wayside, while others—and can one doubt Forten had himself in mind?—would make the best of their opportunities.

Forten set the Revolutionary generation against their heirs and found the latter sadly wanting. He praised "Those patriotick citizens, who, after resting from the toils of an arduous war, which achieved our Independence," framed a state constitution that declared: "All men are born equally free and indepen-dent, and have certain inherent and indefensible rights, among which are those of enjoying life and liberty." This was the body of laws under which people of color and whites had been privileged to live. Now it seemed that lawmakers were denying the basic humanity of black people. "[W]hy are we not to be considered as men? Has the GOD who made the white man and the black, left any record declaring us a separate species?"[85]

He wrote of his belief that the framers of the state constitution had been fair-minded men who had intended black people to be their equals under the law, "for just emerging from unjust and cruel mancipation, their souls were too much affected by their own deprivations to commence the reign of terrour [*sic*] over others." They had been eminently just and liberal in their views. "They knew we were deeper skinned than they were, but they acknowledged us as men, and found that many an honest heart beat beneath a dusky bosom. They felt that they had no more authority to enslave us, than England had to tyrannize over them."[86]

While James Forten was marshaling his arguments and getting his pamphlet ready for the printer, Dr. Benjamin Rush, the man he considered one of the finest exemplars of that Revolutionary generation, died. It is hard to imagine that Forten did not tear himself away from his desk for an hour or so to stand in the street with his head bowed as Rush's coffin was carried past. He may even have attended the funeral service at Christ Church. Returning to the task in hand, Forten inserted into his text a brief tribute to Rush. He contended that Rush and his like had been true friends of freedom, zealous defenders of independence in every sense of the word. "Sacred be the ashes, and deathless be the memory of those heroes who are dead; and revered be the persons and the characters of those who still exist." These men had been simply incapable of depriving an individual of equal treatment under the law because of the color of his skin.[87]

Moving on to specifics, James Forten hoped to demonstrate that the bill before the legislature was riddled with "evils . . . fatal to the rights of freemen, and . . . characteristick of European despotism." If a black family received a visit from a friend from another state, they must report that individual's presence to the Register within twenty-four hours or pay a hefty fine.[88] And how would black people be expected to show that they had complied with the law? Must they wear a collar? And must they register their children within twenty-four hours of their birth? "Yes, ye rulers of the black man's destiny, reflect on this; our *Children* must be registered." He demanded to know "What have the people of Colour been guilty of" that they should be subjected to such treatment. "O miserable race, born to the same hopes, created with the same feeling, and destined for the same goal, you are reduced by your fellow creatures below the brute."[89]

One of the worst features of the proposed law, according to Forten, was that it would give sanction to those individuals who already considered African Americans "a different species . . . little above the brute creation."[90] Drawing very probably on personal observation, he sketched a scenario in which the Constable could all too easily transform the business of law enforcement into sport. He could single out some luckless man of color in the street and demand to see his certificate. If the man fled, the Constable could "raise the boys in hue and cry against" him.[91] The unfortunate man would be chased down, hustled away in chains, imprisoned until an "owner" appeared, and if none appeared—because he was a free man and had none—he would be sold for seven years. Contemplating this, Forten could not restrain himself. "My God, what a situation is his. Search the legends of tyranny and find no precedent."[92]

Forten ended his appeal to white lawmakers with an admission that his "feelings are acute." He had not "intend[ed] either accusation or insult to any one." If his eloquence was insufficient to produce the desired effect, he wrote, "I trust the eloquence of nature will succeed, and that the law-givers of this happy Commonwealth will yet remain the Blacks' friend[s], and the advocates of Freemen."93

If James Forten hoped his pamphlet would change the hearts and minds of his fellow citizens, he was sadly disappointed. The legislative package failed, largely because it was unworkable, but the clamor for restrictions continued. In early 1814 the Pennsylvania House received yet another petition from the white inhabitants of Philadelphia County demanding action.94 However, in a matter of months voters and lawmakers would have a crisis of truly alarming proportions to cope with, one that would drive every other consideration into the background.

THE STRUGGLE AGAINST Britain had gone badly. There had been victories, but too few to turn the tide of war in America's favor. And even victories could prove costly. Shortages of men and materiel offset most of the gains America's forces achieved. By the late summer of 1814 Britain had extricated herself from the conflict with Napoleon in Europe and was free to concentrate her troops, many of them battle-hardened veterans from Wellington's Peninsular campaign, against the Americans. A tempting target, psychologically if not militarily, was Washington, D.C. On August 24 the capital of the United States fell to a well-planned British assault. By nightfall fires were burning across the city.95

On the morning of August 26 James Forten probably left his sail loft to attend a mass meeting in the statehouse yard to respond to the capture of Washington and fears of an attack on Philadelphia. An appeal had gone out to all "citizens" to come together "to make arrangements for combining with effect the services of all the citizens in defence of a cause that is common to all without distinction."96 At that August 26 meeting a Committee of Defense was organized. Four men were chosen from each ward and district, "whose duty it shall be to apply to each able-bodied inhabitant" in their respective neighborhoods "to promote and encourage the immediate formation of volunteer companies, and that every exertion be made to provide arms and accoutrements."97

The city's first line of defense was to be a huge earthwork along the Schuylkill. Because no troops could be spared for this massive construction project, the work must be done by civilian volunteers. Various appeals were made. Irish and Scots immigrants were urged to prove their devotion to their adopted nation by giving a day's labor on the defenses. Quakers had it pointed out to them that this was *defensive* work, and therefore in keeping with their peace testimony. Masters of vessels were requested to release their crews for service.98 And it was at this point that the city fathers remembered the African-American community.

In the late 1830s "Captain" Jonathan Tudas was eager to tell anyone who would listen how he had single-handedly mobilized the black community. Supposedly he had approached the United States Engineer and offered the services of "the black pioneers."[99] James Forten did not dignify Tudas's claim with a counter-claim. Tudas was someone Forten knew all too well. He had been expelled from St. Thomas's, and from virtually every other black church in the city, for various misdeeds. Discord and open scandal followed him wherever he went.[100] The likelihood that the city fathers had approached him was very remote. The account James Forten's friend, poet and abolitionist John Greenleaf Whittier, gave in the *National Era* in the 1840s was probably closer to the truth. "On the capture of Washington . . . it was judged expedient to fortify . . . the principal towns and cities exposed to similar attacks. The Vigilance Committee . . . waited upon . . . James Forten, Bishop Allen, and Absalom Jones, soliciting the aid of the people of color in erecting suitable defenses."[101]

James Forten was itching to contribute to the war effort. He was prepared to have his apprentices and journeymen do defense work, even though it would cut into his profits. On September 8 the Committee of Defense noted the receipt of "A letter from James Forten offering to *make*, gratuitously, canvas covers, or bags, for the use of the volunteers." The letter was referred to the Committee of Supplies.[102] Now Forten had the chance to mobilize every able-bodied man in the African-American community. The Committee of Defense had come to him, Allen, and Jones. He had the military experience the two ministers lacked. It fell to him and his trusted friend, Russell Parrott, to rally Philadelphia's men of color to the common defense.

Aided by the black ministers—after all, the best way to reach people was from the pulpit on a Sunday—Forten and Parrott collected the names of those men willing to labor on the fortifications. On September 19 Parrott put a notice in *Poulson's American Daily Advertiser* telling the black volunteers the Committee of Defense had set September 21 as the day for them to work. They were to meet at sunrise, at South Sixth Street, between Walnut and Prune, with a day's food. He appealed to "Those Gentlemen that have men of colour in their employment" to kindly "suffer them to join their brethren in this laudable undertaking."[103] The response from the African-American community was overwhelming. On the appointed day "2,500 colored men assembled in the State House yard, and from thence marched to Gray's ferry, where they labored without intermission. Their labors were so faithful and efficient, that a vote of thanks was tendered them by the Committee." African Americans, in common with various white groups, actually gave a second day of labor.[104] As for James Forten, his son-in-law recalled that he had done his fair share. He had marched "with twenty of his journeymen" to the assembly point and had labored alongside "his persecuted and oppressed brethren."[105]

James Forten gave to the war effort in every way he could. He obviously would have fought if called upon to do so. However, that was something the authorities could not countenance, despite the pressures on them. On August 30, the Sub-Committee of Defense rejected the suggestion of one Louis M. Merlin, a French-Canadian craftsman and a neighbor of Forten's on Lombard Street.[106] Merlin urged the committee "to have organized a legion of people of color, to be

called the Black Legion, and to be commanded by white officers." The committee responded that it was "improper" to create such a regiment "when there is so
short a supply of weapons and accoutrements for our white citizens."[107] Some
whites recognized that their black neighbors were anxious to take an expanded
role in the conflict. For instance, in a letter to *Poulson's*, "A Citizen" offered "A
Hint to the People of Colour:" The "Great Body" of white men were preparing
to march, and "it would be highly honourable if all the free people of colour were
to form themselves into parties . . . to take tour of duty to work at the Batteries."
He added: "Indeed I have no doubt they would cheerfully give their aid, even in
actual service, were they furnished with the means."[108]

There may, in fact, have been a black military unit formed, but getting at
the truth of the matter and James Forten's role (if any) is not easy. On December 14, 1814, the Pennsylvania Senate, hard-pressed for troops, appointed a
committee to consider the expediency of raising black infantry regiments.[109]
Years later, in 1855, a number of black citizens, among them William Forten,
the sailmaker's youngest son, petitioned the state legislature for redress of grievances, offering as proof of their loyalty their fathers' service during the War of
1812. They noted that men of color had helped build the fortifications along
the Schuylkill, and that "A battalion of colored troops was at the same time
organized in the city, under an officer of the United States army; and they were
on the point of marching to the frontier when peace was proclaimed."[110] In
their monumental history of Philadelphia, Scharf and Westcott stated, "During the summer and autumn [of 1814] . . . there was a brigade of blacks recruited . . . in Philadelphia, but by whom does not seem to be now known."
However, they insisted that elderly people in the city distinctly remembered
having seen armed black men drilling and preparing to meet the British in
battle if an attack on Philadelphia ever materialized.[111]

EAGER THOUGH HE was to prove his patriotism in any way open to him, James
Forten longed for peace. That longing was shared by many of his fellow citizens. When peace finally came, it was greeted with an outpouring of joy. On
February 15, 1815, Forten wrote his old friend Paul Cuffe in Massachusetts
with the news the two men had been waiting for.

> It has pleased the Almighty disposer of all things, to once more bless this late
> distracted country with Peace. . . . [I]t is out of the power of man to describe
> the great joy that was mannifested by all classes of Society in this City[. I]ndeed
> the peopul for some time appeared to be all most frantic, for the interference
> of Divine Providence in staying the sorde of the destroying Angel.[112]

The restoration of peace between the United States and Great Britain would
pave the way for the revival of an undertaking dear to the hearts of Cuffe and
Forten. For Paul Cuffe it would see a dream move closer to realization. For
James Forten it would prove an exercise in frustration. *His* dream would turn
into something more akin to a nightmare.

8

THE AFRICAN ENTERPRISE

THE RESTORATION OF peace between the United States and Great Britain was welcome news to James Forten, and it was news he knew would be equally pleasing to his old friend, New England merchant and shipowner Captain Paul Cuffe. Forten and Cuffe both relied on international trade for their livelihood and they recognized that war was bad for business. Both were deeply religious men who preferred peace to war for moral and spiritual reasons. And both rejoiced at the ending of the war because it meant they could at long last revive a project that had come to mean a great deal to them. What neither James Forten nor Paul Cuffe could know was that in two short years they would be separated by a widening ideological gulf and that the scheme they both embraced with such enthusiasm in 1815 would, by 1817, cause great trepidation within the Northern free black community.

LONG BEFORE PAUL CUFFE spoke to him about it, James Forten was well aware of the existence of the British colony of Sierra Leone. Even if he had heard nothing about plans to establish an African colony during his time in England in 1784–85, he learned about it soon after his return. William Thornton, a British abolitionist who inherited a West Indian sugar plantation and scores of slaves, resolved to free them and send them to a place where they could start over. Intrigued by talk in London of creating a "homeland" on the West African coast for Britain's black poor, he thought of extending the scheme to his slaves, and ultimately to all the descendants of Africa, free or enslaved, throughout the British empire—and to those in regions that had until recently been part of the empire.[1]

Thornton came to the United States in 1786 eager to preach to anyone who would listen about the merits of the scheme. After a friendly reception from people of color in New England, he took his message to Philadelphia. In his address "To the Black Inhabitants of Pennsylvania, assembled at one of their stated meetings in Philadelphia" in 1787 he observed:

> It is in contemplation by the English to make a free settlement of Blacks on the Coast of Africa. . . . They are desirous of knowing if any of the Blacks of this country be willing to return to that Region which their fathers originally possessed, and finding many in Boston, Providence and Rhode Island very anxious of embarking for Africa, wish also to be informed if any of the Blacks in Pennsylvania are inclined to settle there.[2]

The members of Philadelphia's Free African Society, men James Forten would have known well even if he was not among their number, mulled it over, and even corresponded with organizations such as Newport's African Union Society, but their verdict was that emigration to Africa was not for them.[3] They were doing well enough in America.

The Sierra Leone project went ahead without the support of the Philadelphians. The colony absorbed some, but by no means all, of the African-American men who had fought for Britain during the Revolutionary War. It became home to hundreds of Jamaican maroons, and when Britain outlawed the overseas slave trade, it was the place where Royal Navy vessels took "recaptured" Africans (people rescued from illegal slavers). The colony had its early troubles. Corruption and inefficiency on the part of the Sierra Leone Company translated into suffering and death for many of the early settlers. Finally, in 1807, the British government took over the colony. The Sierra Leone Company was disbanded and a group of abolitionists, churchmen, and philanthropists came together in London to form the African Institution. Eschewing the profit motive, they insisted their goal was to redress the wrongs done to the peoples of Africa. They would "civilize" them, spread the Christian faith, and promote trade in commodities other than human beings. Such talk interested prominent Quaker reformers on both sides of the Atlantic, and it was the Quaker link that drew Friend Paul Cuffe into the scheme. In time Cuffe would involve James Forten in the Sierra Leone project.

SUPERFICIALLY AT LEAST, James Forten and Paul Cuffe had a great deal in common. Both were free men of color who made good livings from their involvement in the maritime trades. Both had gone to sea as youths, Cuffe as a whaler and merchant sailor, Forten as a privateer. Both had been imprisoned by the British during the Revolutionary War. Both had felt the sting of American racism, but both had done well financially. Forten had left the sea for the sail loft. Cuffe had remained a seafarer. Eventually, through a combination of hard work and good luck, he had graduated from humble mariner to master of a fleet of some half dozen vessels.[4]

White Americans who heard about Cuffe and Forten or read of their exploits often made the mistake of thinking of them as virtually identical. However, there were significant differences between them, and those differences shaped their personalities and their responses to the world around them. Paul Cuffe, some seven years James Forten's senior, had been born on Cuttyhunk, one of the Elizabeth Islands in Buzzard's Bay off the southern coast of Massachusetts. He was the son of an African man and a Native American woman.[5] The link with Africa was far more direct for him than it was for Forten. Cuffe could recall listening to his father reminisce about his early life in West Africa. James Forten, born and raised in a major urban center, not on an isolated New England farm, had a childhood very different from Cuffe's. As for his sense of "belonging," his Africa had no definite location. That his great-grandfather was an African he knew, but pinpointing a precise place on the African continent and a people from whom he could trace his descent was impossible. An "African" he might be, but his Africa was not Cuffe's Africa.

If James Forten's identity was complex, Paul Cuffe's was even more so. Sometimes he would refer to himself as an African, sometimes an Indian, and sometimes a "mustee," the child of an African and an Indian.[6] Never did he turn his back on his mother's people. His wife, Alice Pequit, was a Native American. His sister, Mary, married a Native American, Michael Wainer, Paul's partner in many of his business ventures. Like Cuffe, James Forten married a woman of Indian ancestry, but Charlotte Vandine's forebears also included Africans and Europeans, and her ties to a Lenni Lenape past in the Delaware Valley were very different to the links Alice Pequit, Michael Wainer, and Ruth Moses, Cuffe's mother, had to the native peoples of southern New England.

Added to these differences of upbringing, ancestry, and racial connectedness were those of religion. Paul Cuffe was increasingly drawn toward the spiritual quietism of the Society of Friends. In practical terms that meant most of his religious contacts were with whites, because the doctrine of the Inner Light had made little headway among African Americans, and Quakers did not actively proselytize. James Forten was an Episcopalian. True, he readily associated with white Episcopalians, but he and his family belonged to a black church, and the life of that church meant a great deal to him.

Despite their differences, a close friendship developed between the two men. There were many occasions over the years on which they could have met. Cuffe was in Philadelphia as early as 1793 to sell a cargo of whale oil and bone, and purchase "iron . . . for bolts and other work suitable for a schooner of 60 or 70 tons."[7] Perhaps he took the opportunity to inquire about sails. Even if he intended to get his new vessel fitted out back home in Westport, Massachusetts, he may well have heard of the young black man who was proving such a success as foreman of Robert Bridges's sail loft. He would certainly have heard of Forten by the time he took over the loft in 1798.

Paul Cuffe made Philadelphia a regular port of call and usually combined philanthropy with business. As the stronghold of American Quakerism, as a major commercial center, and as a city that was home to growing numbers of free people of color, Philadelphia had obvious attractions. He was back many times over the years. In 1808 he met with Pennsylvania Abolition Society president James Pemberton, a fellow Quaker. In 1809 he paid an "agreeable visit" to white Friends John James and Alexander Wilson. On that trip he enrolled his son, Paul Jr., "in a high school in Williams' [Willings] Alley . . . taught by a Friend."[8] Perhaps young Paul occasionally visited with the Fortens during his time at school in Philadelphia.

James Forten did various errands for Cuffe. When Cuffe was having trouble with a wayward relative, Forten intervened. Sailor John Marsten, who was married to Cuffe's niece, had left home for Philadelphia and Cuffe was not sure he intended to return. Could Forten track him down and talk some sense into him? The wily Marsten was one of the few individuals who got the better of James Forten, even managing to persuade the sailmaker to loan him some money, which (needless to say) he neglected to pay back.[9]

Forten watched over Cuffe's business interests in the city. He helped unmask an imposter who was passing himself off as Cuffe's son.[10] He also dealt with the matter of the *Alpha*, a 268-ton vessel of which Cuffe and John James were joint owners. In 1814 John James was in serious financial difficulties. Cuffe had promised to pay various craftsmen for their work on the *Alpha*. However, he had not done so and now they were clamoring for their money and, so Forten feared, getting ready to sue. "[S]uch a step in this City w[h]ere your cradet and carracter stands so very high, would be of infenit and ereparable hurte." Forten had financial reasons, as well as personal ones, for being interested in the tangled affairs of the *Alpha*. He had worked on her sails and his bill had not been paid.[11]

When the *Alpha* or any of Paul Cuffe's other vessels were in port, James Forten did running repairs. He had regular business dealings not only with Cuffe but with Cuffe's nephew, Paul Wainer, who was part owner of the sloop *Resolution*.[12] Forten worked on the *Resolution*, the *Alpha*, and various vessels owned by Cuffe and his relatives.[13] The friendship between Forten and Cuffe may also have advanced Forten's business in another way, for Cuffe had many contacts with white Quakers, quite a few of whom were shipowners. If they did not know Forten, a recommendation from Cuffe might have helped generate orders, because the close-knit community of Friends tended to trust one another's judgment in commercial matters as well as spiritual ones. Ultimately, it was that same Quaker network that prompted Cuffe to consider prospects for trade and philanthropy far beyond the shores of America. And where Paul Cuffe went, James Forten would follow, at least for a time.

IN DECEMBER 1807 Paul Cuffe made one of his regular business trips to Philadelphia. While he was in town he heard from James Pemberton and other white abolitionists about the African Institution and the colony of Sierra

Leone.[14] Perhaps on that same visit Cuffe discussed with James Forten the possibility of trading ventures with the African colony. The New Englander was certainly interested. Possibly Forten shared that interest. Neither was averse to making money, and if worldly profits could be combined with serving a good cause, so much the better.

Intrigued though Cuffe was by the prospects for trade in Sierra Leone, his plans for a voyage to the colony had to be put on hold until tensions between the United States and Britain cooled and the economic warfare each side had been engaging in came to an end. However, the months of waiting were not wasted. Philanthropists on both sides of the Atlantic, Quakers and non-Quakers, had been writing to one another about Cuffe, and several of them had contacted him directly. James Forten's name also surfaced in their correspondence. He was identified not merely as a friend of Cuffe's but as an enterprising man of business in his own right and someone of proven integrity who might also be able to help advance the interests of the African colony.[15]

By the fall of 1810 international tensions had calmed sufficiently for Paul Cuffe to begin planning his voyage. He sailed into Philadelphia aboard the *Traveller* on December 4. Though he was preoccupied with supervising the loading of his cargo and overseeing last-minute repairs to his ship, he made sure he found time to consult with Friends about his African enterprise.[16] Quite possibly he also discussed it with James Forten and other men of influence within the African-American community.

Paul Cuffe sailed for Sierra Leone on December 27, arriving in the capital of Freetown on March 1 of the following year. The voyage had been a grueling one for him and his crew, but he lost no time making contact with Governor Columbine, the highest-ranking British official in the colony; the colonists themselves; and various local rulers. He pinned his hopes on winning trading concessions from the British, for he was well aware that, without the necessary license to trade, his vessel and its cargo could be seized. Cultivating good relationships with the colonists was also essential, and he was able to convince a number of them to form the Friendly Society of Sierra Leone. Under his direction, they drew up a petition to Governor Columbine and to Parliament asking for help for any "foreign Brethren" who came to the colony to promote farming, trade, and whaling.[17] Satisfied he had done all he could on this trip, Cuffe set sail for England.

In England Cuffe met with the leaders of the African Institution. While he was not able to get firm commitments on every matter relating to his African venture, he felt sufficiently encouraged to return to the colony before heading back to the United States. At this point his plans embraced the promotion of trade and "civilization" through the agency of a few judiciously selected emigrants who would cooperate with well-established settlers. He had no thought as yet of a wholesale resettlement scheme.[18]

Cuffe arrived back in the United States in April 1812 unaware of just how badly relations between the United States and Britain had soured during his absence. As yet a state of war did not exist between the two nations, but it seemed imminent. Going ashore in Westport to see his family, Cuffe returned to the *Traveller* to find that a revenue cutter had seized the vessel on the grounds that he had been trading illegally with the enemy. His friends urged him to take his case to the president, reasoning that a personal approach might not only get the charges against him dropped but might win him a powerful ally— and a powerful ally he would surely need if he was to have further dealings with the British at a time of rapidly escalating tensions. Armed with letters from prominent New England merchants and political figures, Cuffe set off to see President James Madison. He secured the release of his vessel and her cargo, and wrung from Madison a promise of future assistance.[19]

On the trip to Washington, Cuffe had had no time to stop off to see old friends such as James Forten. On the way back he had more leisure. He spent a day or two in Baltimore, where he met with white foes of slavery and with leaders of the African-American community, among them teacher and minister Daniel Coker. In Philadelphia he called on a number of Quaker acquaintances. He also noted in his journal that while he was in Philadelphia he "Met with the people of Color." He was greatly encouraged by their response to his description of the Sierra Leone scheme. "I believe there was something opperating that good will come out of [it] toward Africa. . . . It was proposed that there should be a society gathered for the purpose of aiding[,] assisting and communicating with the Sierra Leone Friendly Society, as well as with the [A]frican Institution in London." The evening after the meeting, Cuffe, James Forten, and Rev. Absalom Jones called upon Dr. Benjamin Rush and talked over prospects in Sierra Leone with the aging abolitionist.[20]

From Philadelphia, Cuffe moved on to New York, where he consulted with prominent people of color such as Peter Williams, Jr., and William Hamilton and with white sympathizers. On his return to Westport he wrote Quaker reformer William Allen, one of his staunchest supporters in Britain and a leading member of the African Institution, describing the steps he had taken:

> I have visited Baltimore, Philadelphia and New York. . . . Called the people of Couller to gether and find great Satisfaction. It . . . was advised that Each of these places Should out of the first Corectors [characters] of the people of Coulour form a Soci[e]ty to Communycate with Each other . . . [and] Correspond with the African Institution and with the Friendly Society at Sierra Leone.[21]

Cuffe's letter crossed in the mail with a letter from Allen and fellow abolitionist Thomas Clarkson. Writing on behalf of the African Institution, they outlined what the organization was prepared to do for Cuffe. He would receive land in Sierra Leone to use as he chose. "If you choose to establish all your family, and to close your days there . . . so much the better." They promised to help any settlers he took to the colony, but they emphasized that they preferred quality over quantity. He should begin by transporting no more than eighteen persons, all of whom must be legally free and willing to place themselves under British rule. A few at least should be "persons of some property" with the resources to hire local laborers and "recaptured" Africans.[22] Cuffe passed on their instructions to James Forten. He would rely on Forten for practical advice as he pushed ahead with his plans and for help to recruit suitable colonists.

THE OUTBREAK OF war between the United States and Britain in the summer of 1812 inevitably meant delay and frustration for Cuffe and his growing number of supporters. Eventually, he and they decided it was worth putting his case to Congress on the grounds that it was a philanthropic undertaking. Hopefully, lawmakers would see it in that light and exempt him from the ban on trade with Britain and her colonies. His petition was duly presented to Congress on January 7, 1814.[23]

Regardless of its ultimate fate, Cuffe felt his petition had given the cause some much-needed publicity. "I have Be[e]n Made acquainted with many wellwishers . . . w[h]ich I should have Been [a] Stranger to had not it Been for the memorial being made publick."[24] It was just as well he could take a philosophical view of things, for he soon received bad news. The Senate had drafted a bill permitting him to trade with Sierra Leone, but the House had rejected it.[25]

Cuffe refused to be downcast. One reason for his optimism was that the various auxiliaries of the African Institution seemed to be flickering into life at long last. He described the Philadelphia group, headed by James Forten, as "a small soci[e]ty of good caractors" whose function was to correspond with the African Institution in London and vouch for the worthiness of potential emigrants.[26] In August he wrote a friend that he had just heard from Forten "that the Institution was Compleatly form[e]d." The New Yorkers had done little since his 1812 visit, but a further visit in 1814 had had a good effect. They had shown themselves "Verry zealous for the good Caus of Africa and Conecluded to form them Selves into a Society for the Same Purpose of that in Philadelphia."[27]

Thanks to news reports about his petition to Congress, various people contacted Cuffe to ask for information about Sierra Leone or to share with him their own plans. One such individual was white evangelical minister Samuel J. Mills. Early in 1814 Mills wrote Cuffe about his idea of founding a colony for people of color somewhere in America. Cuffe endorsed the idea, although with reservations. "My plan is to take to Africa some Sober Stedy peopel of Colour in order to incourage Sobriety and industry and to interduce cultervation and Coomersce."[28] An American colony was something he was not necessarily opposed to, but his thoughts and energies were centered at this point on Sierra Leone and on a very small-scale resettlement program.

And what of James Forten? Even though the war had put a temporary halt to their plans, he and Cuffe were still in touch with one another. In the summer of 1814, for instance, Forten wrote to tell Cuffe of the death of his young daughter. Cuffe, a loving parent himself, wrote back to offer what comfort he could, adding: "I much recommend thy free n [frequent?] wrightings, and am always Glad to find a faithful heart to take up for the Ingered part of mankind."[29]

The year 1815 would prove a momentous one for the African enterprise, but it began on an anxious note for Cuffe. Nearly a month into the New Year he had not heard from Forten and he was worried. Cuffe wanted to get his reaction to an idea he had been mulling over. Why didn't "a number of peopel of Colour . . . lay down a Sum of money . . . So as to Come into Common Stock and Build a Vessell of a bout 200 tons for an african trader"? It would enable them "to keep up & open an intercourse between the united States, africa &c which I Conceive Could be done with profit and mutual advantage."[30]

Forten's reply was well worth waiting for. He had just heard that the Senate had ratified the Treaty of Ghent, ending the war with Britain. Trade was picking up, and "there has been a grate deman[d] for Vessels." He added: "I approve very highly of your propesition of Building a Ship for the African traid by the men of Colour, so as to come in common stock."[31] It goes without saying that Forten knew who would be making the sails for the new ship. It was common practice for sailmakers and others in the maritime trades to become part owners of vessels, sharing in the returns from successful voyages and ensuring commissions for the various repairs that needed doing. If James Forten acquired a few shares in the "African trader" Cuffe was talking about building, he would just be following the lead of his white competitors. The difference was that his investment would be in a black-owned and operated ship, and the profits would go to black men in the United States and Africa.

Cuffe was overjoyed at the news of peace and began making plans to sail to Sierra Leone in the fall. He asked Forten to speak to the other members of his group in Philadelphia to "obtain the names of all those who may wish to go . . . and furnish me with . . . certificates of their Character."[32] Forten reported back that he and his friends were delighted to learn that Cuffe was making plans for a voyage to Africa and he promised that they would find him some recruits.

On the economic front, however, things were less rosy. The *Alpha*, which had become a source of contention between Cuffe and co-owner John James, had still not been sold: "indee[d] all mercantile business seemes to be at a stand." Why didn't Cuffe use the *Alpha* for a voyage to New Orleans? Forten had heard merchants there were desperate to get their cotton to Europe. Cuffe could take a cargo to Liverpool, which would give him a chance to talk to the directors of the African Institution in London about their support for his voyage in the fall.[33]

Paul Cuffe had other plans for the *Alpha*. If she was unlikely to fetch a good price, "had not thee and the African society better buy her in for an African transport?" There were other possibilities. "[I]f you think her too costly for such accommodation, and you wished to join in an adventure in the whale fisheryes . . . I think she might be imploy'd to good advantage." As for the African scheme, about ten or fourteen families from Boston were ready to go with him to Sierra Leone, and he was receiving more letters of inquiry every day.[34]

Encouraged by what they had learned from Cuffe, Forten and Russell Parrott, the young printer who collaborated with him through the 1810s in so many of his undertakings, set to work. They located two couples who wanted to go to Sierra Leone, Antoine and Elizabeth Servance and Samuel and Barbery Wilson. For both of the men this was a chance to return home. Born in Senegal, Servance had been enslaved and sold to the French on Saint Domingue. A resourceful individual, he had seized his moment during the upheavals of the 1790s and stowed away on a ship bound for Philadelphia. There he had found work and done fairly well, but the desire to go back to Africa had never died.[35] Wilson, a "Congo man," had achieved some fame in Philadelphia as a healer, but he, too, longed to return home.[36] Inured to the climate, and familiar with the various crops that could be grown in the region, these were precisely the kinds of colonists Paul Cuffe and the African Institution wanted.

Cuffe arrived in Philadelphia in the summer and met the four would-be emigrants. He admired Servance's spirit of perseverance. As he explained to William Allen, Servance intended to become a merchant. He could "write a good intilenagle hand[,] read well & [is] pretty well vers[ed] in arithmetic." A fiercely independent man, Servance considered himself no one's inferior. "I have heard him say . . . whether the black man had not 2 Ey[e]s & 2 Ears & white men had no more &c Could he not sea with his ey[e]s he[a]r with his ears &c." Wilson, "an industrious man" and "a professor of the Methodist [faith]," planned to farm.[37]

The $200 passage money paid by the Wilsons exhausted their meager savings.[38] Servance was more fortunate. He owned a house and lot in Philadelphia's Northern Liberties, which he transferred to Absalom Jones for a nominal sum to pay for his and his wife's passage.[39] Because the property was appraised at well over $400, Cuffe accepted it as collateral and advanced Servance a considerable sum to purchase trade goods. However, collecting on that security proved difficult. Numerous times over the next couple of years James Forten, Absalom Jones, and white merchant Samuel R. Fisher got together to discuss how best to dispose of Servance's real estate, which was rapidly being swallowed up in ground rents.[40]

On September 20, 1815, with the departure of Cuffe and the settlers just weeks away, Forten and Parrott inserted a notice in *Poulson's American Daily Advertiser* apprising the public of the Sierra Leone venture. Paul Cuffe wanted to go to Africa "for the purpose of aiding in the civilization and improvement of the inhabitants of that country, and also to promote the desirable object to take with him a few sober industrious families." They drew attention to the existence of the Philadelphia African Institution, and noted the recruitment of four "persons of good moral character."[41]

In early October Forten reported to Cuffe that he was receiving various inquiries about the African venture. People were asking whether the African Institution would pay for their passage, and the members of the Philadelphia organization needed to know what to tell them. Servance and Wilson had incurred considerable expenses. Would those expenses be refunded? What about the half-dozen other families who wanted to go? And would the African Institution "bare the expences of those who may have a desire to return . . . [if] the climit . . . did not agree with them"?[42] Cuffe thought the African Institution might pay some expenses, but they should not count on it. There were other things Forten and his friends should be attending to besides fielding questions about who would pay for what. For one, Cuffe was concerned about the lack of communication between the Philadelphia organization and the societies in London and Sierra Leone.[43] Actually, Forten and Parrott needed no prodding. They were already working on a letter to the officers of the African Institution. They wrote of their "well grounded hope . . . [that] you would be pleased to hear of the exertions we are making towards eradicating the prejudices and uncharitable-like feelings of such as are not with us." So far they had confined themselves to selecting suitable emigrants—"persons of good report, united with a knowledge of the cultivation of produce familiar to the African climate, or those useful branches of the mechanic arts, as would render them serviceable." Under "the articles of our Association" they could do more, but they held back in deference to the parent organization. Deftly hidden toward the end of the letter was the meat of it. "It would afford us much satisfaction if we could know what privilege your Government would be disposed to grant to such as may hereafter emigrate . . . [and] if any exemptions would be made in favour of this Institution, provided it should embark in any commercial enterprise for the purpose of civilizing Africa."[44] Whatever else Forten and Parrott had in mind, they obviously hoped to turn a profit from the African enterprise.

Meanwhile, Paul Cuffe had heard again from Samuel J. Mills. The young minister wrote that more and more white people in America were turning their attention to Africa and the plight of her scattered children.[45] Two more letters a few months later described plans to educate African-American men at the Presbyterian College at Parsippany, New Jersey, to work in African missions.[46] Cuffe welcomed anything that would prove to a doubting public the intellectual capacity of men of color. He also mentioned that he had read reports that slaveholders were alarmed by signs of growing restlessness among their slaves. Frankly, he told Mills, it was their own fault, but if the only stumbling block to emancipation was the want of somewhere to resettle ex-slaves, then hopefully progress would soon be made.[47] Although Cuffe was not yet advocating a mass exodus, he was moving in that direction.

The Traveller set sail from Westport in early December 1815. On board were thirty-eight emigrants (including the four Forten and Parrott had recruited), seven crew members, and Cuffe himself. The crossing was a rough one. The *Traveller* battled gales and mountainous seas, but she and her passengers arrived safely in Freetown in the spring of 1816. Almost as stormy as the Atlantic were Cuffe's negotiations with colonial officials. His license from the British government had not arrived, and only the letters he had secured from prominent individuals in Britain convinced the governor to let him unload and sell his cargo. He ended the voyage decidedly out of pocket. Something would have to be done before he could contemplate another trip to Sierra Leone. Still, he hoped for the best.[48]

Once Cuffe returned home, he put his friends to work to recruit more settlers. To James Forten he wrote: "I wish Thee To make particular inquiry of The Constitution and cost of a rice Mill and A man who understands errecting and managing a sawmill . . . a watch repairer I think would meet with encouragements." He did not expect to make another voyage to Africa that year, "as it is necessary that I should have some further Understanding with the British Goverment before I go again." In what may have been an allusion to the plan he was mulling over for a larger settlement of liberated slaves in Africa, he observed: "I think it is time som[e] steps were Taken to prevent insurrections without using voilance."[49] As he had said to Rev. Mills, slave owners could free themselves from their fears of servile rebellion only by manumitting their human property. If the sticking point was their reluctance to live alongside men and women who had once been their slaves, then something must be done to address the issue, possibly the founding of a separate settlement.

In Philadelphia Forten did his best on Cuffe's behalf. He tried but failed to find someone who understood rice mills, nor could he find anyone to operate a saw mill, but he promised to keep looking. In a postscript he noted: "I red the reporte of your Voyage . . . which gave greate sattisfaction to the whole congregation [of St. Thomas's], the same was don[e] in Richard Allens Church."[50]

James Forten may have been indulging in some wishful thinking when he wrote of "greate satisfaction" prevailing in Philadelphia with regard to the African enterprise. Trouble of some sort was brewing. John James advised Cuffe that "There has been some *prejudices* spread among the people of Colour respecting thy views of going to Sierra Leone, that I think highly necessary to be removed."[51] Cuffe passed on the information to Peter Williams, secretary of the New York African Institution.[52] Whatever was causing uneasiness on the part of at least some of the Philadelphians was soon reasoned away by their brethren in New York, and Cuffe congratulated Williams on having "Got the Institution in Philadelphia . . . to wear the yoak of Christian Benevolence."[53] However, the Philadelphians' misgivings soon resurfaced.

IN EARLY DECEMBER 1816, from his lodgings in the nation's capital, Rev. Robert Finley, a young Presbyterian minister from Basking Ridge, New Jersey, sent a letter to Paul Cuffe. He had never met the New England merchant, but he had heard a great deal about him and hoped to interest him in a scheme he had been devising. For some time Finley had been searching for a way to aid people of color in the United States, "particularly . . . those who are . . . free." He described how he and others were distressed by their "unhappy situation" and feared that situation might become even worse. "Most thinking persons" were pinning their hopes on emigration. They "indulge a hope that could the more virtuous and industrious . . . free people of color be removed to the coast of Africa with their own consent, to carry with them their arts, their industry and above all their knowledge of Christianity . . . great and lasting benefits would arise to the people who might remove thither and to *Africa itself.*" Would Cuffe join in promoting such a worthy undertaking?[54]

Cuffe wrote back to say he hoped Finley and his friends would be "guided by wisdom's best means." He sent information about Sierra Leone, but he cautioned that if very many people were prepared to emigrate, another site would have to be found, since the British would probably not welcome an influx of Americans into their colony. Perhaps there should be two colonies, one "on the course [coast] of Africa, and another in the united States."[55]

Cuffe knew little of Finley, other than that he seemed genuinely concerned about the plight of black people. Had he read the short pamphlet Finley was working on, he might have been less encouraging and more apprehensive about what this zealous young clergyman had in mind. In his *Thoughts on the Colonization of Free Blacks,* Finley argued that slavery must be abolished because of its "injurious effect on the morals and habits of [the] country."[56] However, while he recommended the passage of laws making it easier to manumit slaves, he urged that freedom be made contingent on colonization.[57] He was deeply concerned about racial "intermixture," and that was one reason why he insisted the colony be located in Africa. Obviously a strong case could be made for selecting a site in the interior of North America, but the lower cost "would be . . . counterbalanced, by having in our vicinity an independent settlement of people who were once our slaves."[58]

Finley's motive in traveling to Washington was to interest other like-minded men in his project. Anything as wide-ranging as founding a colony would require the support of the federal government and the backing of key political figures, as early as possible. Finley was well connected to begin with. His brother-in-law, Elias B. Caldwell, was Clerk of the Supreme Court. One of Caldwell's closest friends was influential lawyer Francis Scott Key. Through Caldwell and Key, Finley was able to recruit the likes of Speaker of the House Henry Clay, war hero and up-and-coming politician Andrew Jackson, and Bushrod Washington, the late president's nephew. Other recruits to what would become known as the American Colonization Society included John Randolph of Roanoke, future presidential candidate William H. Crawford of Georgia, New Hampshire's Daniel Webster, and Richard Rush, former Attorney-General of Pennsylvania and James Forten's one-time lawyer.[59]

Samuel J. Mills had not been included on Finley's guest list, but he had heard what was being planned and had hastened to Washington in time to take part in a preliminary meeting on December 21 chaired by Henry Clay. Paul Cuffe learned of the meeting in a letter from Mills and wrote back to say how pleased he was to learn of the earnest commitment of the gentlemen in Washington. He thought the area to the south of Sierra Leone looked good for a small settlement, "but were their a willingness for a Pritty general Removal" he suggested a colony in the region of the Cape of Good Hope. He noted that auxiliaries of the African Institution had been formed in New York and Philadelphia, gave Mills the names of James Forten and Peter Williams, and expressed his wish that "these Instertutions . . . be brought as much into action as would be best, by that means the Colour[e]d Peoppelation of these large Cities Would be more awakened then from . . . a stranger."[60]

Meanwhile, back in Washington, the American Colonization Society had officially come into being. Its list of officers was impressive. Finley and Caldwell had interested many of the nation's most prominent men in their cause. While the motivation of some might have been the evangelizing of Africa, for the majority it was most definitely the conviction that black people, especially those not held in bondage, must be separated from white people. Still, the society's constitution spoke of colonizing free people of color "with their consent." As for the issue of eradicating slavery, organizers argued that that was something best left vague. After all, a significant number of them were slaveholders.[61]

There was considerable press coverage of the birth of the American Colonization Society, not all of it favorable.[62] Philadelphians got their first inkling of what was being discussed in the nation's capital on December 30 when a report from a Washington paper, the *Federal Republican*, was reprinted in *Poulson's American Daily Advertiser*. The Washington editor extolled the merits of colonization and even saw in it justification for the horrors of slavery. He envisaged ex-slaves emigrating to Africa to "become in the hands of Divine Providence, the instrument[s] of introducing amongst [their] savage brethren, the blessings of civilization."[63]

A few days later, *Poulson's* carried an account of Henry Clay's speech on colonization. The House Speaker had made much of the concern he and other benevolent whites had long felt for the plight of free people of color. They were "[d]esirous of promoting the prosperity and happiness of our country," and that evidently entailed the wholesale deportation of black people—at least those who were legally free. There was no mention of ending slavery, and no acknowledgment that "our country" embraced both black and white Americans.[64]

News stories about the American Colonization Society appeared regularly in the Philadelphia press over the next week or so. *Poulson's* published the ACS's constitution and a list of the prominent politicians who held office in the organization. On January 10 the editor of *Poulson's* noted the first signs of alarm among free people of color. A group of black men in Georgetown had met to declare their unwavering opposition to an African colony, although they were willing to consider a settlement on the Missouri River.[65] A few days later, *Poulson's* reprinted a letter from the *New-York Courier*. Written in a parody of black dialect and signed "Sambo," it was plainly the work of a white man. However, amid the crude racist humor there was a serious message. White Americans had taken Africans as slaves, used and abused them, and could not simply send their descendants "back" to a continent many had never seen because they no longer wanted them around. "Sambo" hit the nail on the head when he declared: "Ah Mr. Clay. I guess you pretty cunnin feller. I guess you want to get rid of color people—and you dont care much w[h]ere he go, if he only go away." "Sambo" suggested facetiously that black people form a society to send Clay back to the land of *his* ancestors.[66]

The press coverage, coupled with rumors, had a chilling affect. By the middle of January many black Philadelphians were in a state of panic. They were convinced nothing less was being contemplated than their forced removal to Africa. As for James Forten, he saw no cause for panic. Nevertheless, as a man of influence within the community, he could not simply ignore a matter that he heard being spoken of everywhere—at church, in the street, and probably in his own sail loft.

On January 8, 1817, Paul Cuffe wrote Forten to update him on the latest developments. "I have lately Resev'd a letter from a Gentleman in the City of Washington, Anouncing to me the concerne that rests at the seat of Government, for the well fare of the People of Colour. They Mention to me whether I will join them, in going to . . . Africa to seek a Place where the People of colour Might be Colonized." He had written back telling them about "the African institutions in Philadelphia, Newyork &c in order that a Correspondence might be open'd with them."[67]

What Cuffe did not know, and what Forten's reply glossed over, was that a crisis was developing in Philadelphia. Forten did admit to Cuffe that "the People of Colour here was very much fritened." He also told his friend that there had been a meeting on the subject of colonization at Mother Bethel Church.[68] What he neglected to mention was that he and Russell Parrott, the two most active members of the Philadelphia African Institution, had taken charge of that meeting and had helped write a series of resolutions condemning colonization. Getting a sense of the precise sequence of events in Philadelphia is not easy, and Forten's letter to Cuffe complicates matters rather than clarifying them. Fortunately, his is not the only account we have. Clearly, a great deal was happening. The stories in the press about the American Colonization Society, and the rumors that were floating around about the discussions in Washington, had stirred up strong emotions among Philadelphia's men and women of color. Somewhere in the middle of all this were James Forten and his friends from the Philadelphia auxiliary of the African Institution, trying to assess how best to respond to the deep-seated fears of their community.

There is nothing to indicate who called the meeting at Mother Bethel, which apparently took place in the second or third week of January. Perhaps it was James Forten and his allies who organized it, in the mistaken belief that they could calm people's fears, or perhaps it was simply something that grew out of the determination of scores of black Philadelphians that they must present a united front in the face of what they perceived as a grave threat to themselves and their entire community. If the attendance at the meeting reflected the depth of their concern, they were very worried indeed. Forten estimated that 3000 people crowded into Mother Bethel. The church was filled to overflowing. Forten was also obliged to tell Cuffe that the mood of the meeting was decidedly hostile toward colonization and that "there was not one sole that was in favour of going to Africa."[69]

At this point James Forten obviously thought the rest of the black population was overreacting. He was confident that no one planned to round them up and ship them off to Africa or anywhere else against their will. He believed, a few unfortunate statements notwithstanding, that the founders of the ACS were well-intentioned individuals, and he hoped Philadelphia's people of color would come to see that once their fears subsided. As he told Cuffe,

> [I]t apperes to me that if the Father of all mercies, is in this interesting subject (for it apperes that they all think that sum thing must and aut to be don but do not know w[h]ere nor how to begin) the way will be made strate and cleare. . . . [M]y opinion is that they will never become a people untell they com[e] out from amongst the white people, but as the majority is decidely against me I am determend to remain silent, except as to my opinion which I freely give when asked.[70]

Although his letter to Cuffe might suggest otherwise, James Forten had been anything but a silent observer at the Mother Bethel meeting. He seems to have reasoned that if his community wanted to go on record as being opposed to deportation, he could support that. And certainly the resolutions he and Russell Parrott helped draw up at the meeting were clear enough on that point. They wrote: "WHEREAS our ancestors (not of choice) were the first successful cultivators of America, we . . . feel ourselves entitled to participate in the blessings of her luxuriant soil, which their blood and sweat manured."[71] They viewed "with deep abhorrence the unmerited stigma attempted to be cast upon the reputation of the free People of Colour" by the likes of Henry Clay "'that they are a dangerous and useless part of the community.'"[72] They went on to express their sense of affinity with the slaves: "[W]e never will separate ourselves voluntarily from the slave population of this country; they are our brethren by the ties of consanguinity, of suffering, and of wrongs; and we feel that there is more virtue in suffering privations with them, than fancied advantages for a season."[73] In essence there was nothing here that represented a radical departure from Forten's earlier views. He had never favored forced resettlement. In all of his dealings with Cuffe and the African Institution in London he had only ever had in mind voluntary emigration. He had always spoken of the moral obligations of free people of color to work for the freedom of the enslaved. And he had never ignored offensive remarks of the kind that Henry Clay was now making.

The Bethel meeting had closed with the appointment of a committee to consult with Philadelphia congressman Joseph Hopkinson and plans to call a general meeting. The members of that committee were Forten; Parrott; ministers Absalom Jones, Richard Allen, and John Gloucester; barber Robert Douglass; oysterman Francis Perkins; grocer Robert Gordon; painter and glazier James Johnson; teacher Quamoney Clarkson; and fruit dealer Randall Shepherd.[74] At least some, and quite possibly all, of these men were officers of the Philadelphia branch of the African Institution. Apart from Forten and Parrott, Jones and Allen were in fairly regular correspondence with Cuffe, and Gordon and Douglass were mentioned in his letters. As for the rest of the committee members, Gloucester, Johnson, Clarkson, and the others were among the most influential and most prosperous in their community. It would not be surprising if they were involved in Cuffe's plans and active in the Philadelphia branch of the African Institution. Now here they were, with Forten and Parrott, not so much attacking the whole notion of a colony, as making sure it was the right kind of colony, founded on the right principles, and with the best interests of people of color in mind.

Several days after the meeting at Mother Bethel there was another meeting, this one with Rev. Robert Finley.[75] Unfortunately, the only account of how the meeting was arranged and what exactly was discussed is a third-hand one. According to a biographer of Finley, Isaac V. Brown, the young minister was traveling back from Washington to his home in New Jersey when he passed through Philadelphia and met John Gloucester. Like Finley, Gloucester was a Presbyterian minister. He was also a good friend of Samuel J. Mills, and it was probably through Mills that Gloucester and Finley had heard of one another.[76] According to Brown, Finley learned from Gloucester "that there was considerable perturbation in the minds of the people of color, produced by the proceedings at Washington." A meeting had been called—the meeting at Mother Bethel—"and a committee . . . appointed . . . to take this subject into consideration." Finley asked for an interview with the committee, and Gloucester arranged it. Finley found the members of the committee "considerably alarmed at the proposed plan of colonization, and strongly prejudiced against it." He spent the better part of an hour talking with them, and "At length they declared themselves fully satisfied . . . that the designs of the gentlemen who proposed and advocated the scheme were benevolent and good, and that the thing in itself was desirable for them."[77]

As to where exactly the colony should be located, there were different opinions. "[S]ome thought they should have a part of our back and uncultivated lands . . . others thought Africa would be the most suitable place." Brown's informant identified two men who were particularly vocal in favor of Africa.[78] James Forten

> was animated on the subject. He said their people would become a great nation: he pointed to Hayti, and declared it as his opinion that their people could not always be detained in their present bondage; he remarked upon the peculiarly oppressive situation of his people in our land—observing that neither riches nor education could put them on a level with the whites, and the more wealthy and the better informed any of them became, the more wretched they were made; for they felt their degradation more acutely.

He insisted Africa was the best place for a colony. "He observed to those present, that should they settle anywhere in the vicinity of the whites, their condition must become before many years as bad as it now is."[79] After detailing Richard Allen's equally enthusiastic response, Brown's anonymous informant observed: "The committee of whom I speak were of the most respectable class of blacks. So far as I recollect, this is the substance of what Dr. Finley told me."[80]

Disentangling truth from fiction (or at least wishful thinking) is no easy matter. Would Forten have spoken of America as the white people's country and not his own? It seems unlikely, but then what is one to make of his comment to Cuffe that "they will never become a people untell they com[e] out from amongst the white people"? Yet even here, why use "they" if he meant "we"? Forten's statements to Cuffe and to Finley (assuming the account in Brown's biography accurately reflected what he did say) suggest he may well have been trying to work out for himself what he saw as the future of black people—and how he saw his own future.

Forten had heard talk of schemes to colonize people of African descent many times before. Sometimes it came from proven friends, such as Quaker abolitionist John Parrish, who had called on Congress in 1806 to set aside homesteads for free blacks in the "western wilderness," and James Pemberton's niece, Ann Mifflin, who wanted to see "Returning Societies" created to help men and women of color relocate to West Africa.[81] Forten's sometime ally, the Irish-born evangelist Thomas Branagan, attacked slavery but felt blacks and whites must live apart for their mutual well-being.[82] And then there were the children of the diaspora themselves, like the black New Englanders back in Forten's youth, who had demanded a place apart from white people, where they could live "under their own vine and fig tree."[83] In the 1830s James Forten would insist that separating black Americans from white Americans was "as impossible as to bale out the Delaware with a bucket," but perhaps in 1817 he was wavering, not yet sure in his own mind whether voluntary colonization was a good thing, at least for some in the black community, or an unmitigated evil.[84]

As for Paul Cuffe, he had made up his mind. On February 28 he wrote John James that "the African Institution in phelidelphia Seems to be Alarm[e]d

. . . but my desire to th[em?] are to be quiet and trust in god."[85] To Forten he expressed his pleasure that the Philadelphia African Institution was still active. "[A]ltho they seemed to be [a] littel alermed at the movement of being colonized in a free State don't be uneasy but be quiet and trust in god, who hath done all things well." He had been asked repeatedly for his views, "but it is quite useless to give thee my opinion on the Subject, when work speaks louder than words."[86]

Through the spring of 1817 and into the summer James Forten remained a supporter of the African enterprise. On April 14 he contacted Cuffe on behalf of Thomas Ash, "a Merchant I work for, and a very greate friend of mine," who wanted information about commercial opportunities in West Africa. Forten himself was eager to know "whether you have had any late information from Africa."[87]

He had to wait several months for a reply, and when it came it was not in Cuffe's hand. Too sick to hold a pen, Cuffe had had to dictate his letter to a family member.[88] Forten lost no time writing back. He and his family were concerned to learn their friend was so ill, but he had some news he was sure would cheer Cuffe. "[W]e have . . . in our City an African Prince, the grandson of King Surker from the co[a]st, about 50 leag[u]es to the south of Sierra Leone." The child, "a smart promising lad," had been "sent . . . to Havanna and from their to the Abolition Society for his education." Forten was hopeful the kindness shown the boy would draw King Sherker closer to the friends of abolition in Philadelphia and that that would "result in something advantage[ou]s to the community."[89]

The arrival of King Sherker's grandson in Philadelphia was a peculiar episode, and one that showed the strength of James Forten's reputation as a man of wealth, influence, and probity. In Havana to pick up a cargo of sugar and coffee, Philadelphia captain Charles Perry had happened to meet merchant Alonso Munoz. Munoz had explained that he was facing an embarrassing dilemma. King Sherker, an important slave-trading contact of his in West Africa, had entrusted his grandson to him with instructions to have him educated, but Munoz could not find a suitable school for the child in Cuba. Still, he wanted to keep the king's goodwill. What could he do? Perry presumably told Munoz about Forten, for Munoz alluded in the letter he wrote Forten to "your respectability [which is] already well known here" and to the information he had received from an unnamed "friend" about the black sailmaker's involvement in the antislavery movement. He begged Forten to seek out a school in Philadelphia for the young prince.[90] Then he dispatched his letter, the child, and various trade goods to Forten in care of Captain Perry.

On July 12 Perry's brig, the *John Bergwin*, anchored at the quarantine hospital in Philadelphia. After clearing the health inspection, dealing with the Inspector of Customs, and giving orders for his cargo to be sent to his warehouse, Perry made his way to Forten's sail loft.[91] An understandably startled

Forten looked up from his work to find Perry, a familiar enough figure on the wharves, with an African boy of about eight or nine in tow. What, Perry asked, should he do with the sacks of coffee Munoz had sent over from Havana to pay for the lad's schooling?

Forten took the prince into his home and sought an interview with the members of the Pennsylvania Abolition Society. He handed over Munoz's letter, which explained that Sherker wanted his grandson "teached the english language[,] writing & calculating." The king was a wealthy man. He had sent trade goods to cover the boy's first six months of schooling, and Munoz felt sure he would send more.[92]

The officers of the PAS listened to Forten, read Munoz's letter, and eventually agreed to step in. After a few days with the Fortens, the prince, christened "George Sherker," was sent to live with Grace and Robert Douglass, and enrolled in the PAS school.[93] Many years later Forten would discover to his chagrin that, despite the good treatment "George" received at the hands of Philadelphia's abolitionists, King Sherker did not abandon the slave trade.[94] However, in 1817 he was very optimistic that the king might be persuaded not only to give up selling slaves but to help the fledgling colony in Africa. And Forten remained convinced there *must be* a colony. Referring to 300 slaves left in the care of the PAS under the terms of the will of a Virginia slave owner, he observed: "I hope and pray that the time is not far distant when there will be an Asylum for those poor Soles to take their rest."[95] Increasingly, though, Forten was coming to question whether the American Colonization Society was the appropriate organization to oversee an African colony. He was not yet prepared to reject all ideas of resettlement, either in Africa or closer to home, in the Western territories of America, but the fears so many of his neighbors were continually expressing about the true intentions of the ACS leadership, particularly the likes of Henry Clay, were beginning to make him rethink his support for the society.

ALTHOUGH JAMES FORTEN and many others in the black community probably thought of the ACS as a powerful organization on account of the friends it had in high places, it actually met with less success than its illustrious founders had hoped. After its inaugural meeting, its officers had sent a request to Congress for help to establish a colony. Congress had referred their request to the Committee on the Slave Trade. Alarmed at the expense of founding an African settlement, and in some cases worried about the constitutionality of the United States becoming a colonizing power, the members of the committee had suggested the ACS simply cooperate with the British and send any emigrants it could round up to Sierra Leone.[96]

Refusing to give up, the men in the inner circle of the ACS decided to send someone over to West Africa to investigate and report back on the best site for an American-sponsored colony. But paying the expenses of even one agent would cost money, and so the ACS undertook a series of fund-raising initiatives. In the summer of 1817 the push began to create an auxiliary in Philadelphia. A meeting to discuss the ACS's agenda was held at City Hall on August 6.[97]

Apparently no people of color were present at the meeting. This was an effort on the part of the ACS leadership to gain the support of wealthy and influential whites. However, black Philadelphians could follow in the press the various accounts of what had been said. Elias B. Caldwell had insisted that colonization would bring about the abolition of slavery "at no distant time," but not everyone in his audience had been convinced by his eloquence.[98] An individual who signed himself "Do Justly—Love Mercy" wrote to *Poulson's American Daily Advertiser* suggesting that before any more time or money was spent on the scheme, the friends of colonization should catechize "Southern Gentleman" and demand to know, "Are you prepared solemnly and formally to resolve, that the Slavery of your fellow creatures, is hateful in the sight of Heaven and Good Men?"[99] "P" reported that when the resolution to form an auxiliary was brought forward, "a great number of people, altho' certainly a minority, left the room."[100]

Despite the misgivings of some of those at the August 6 meeting, an ACS auxiliary was formed.[101] If some white Philadelphians were uneasy, many of their African-American neighbors were truly alarmed—and James Forten was now among their number. On August 10 he chaired a protest meeting at the schoolhouse in Green's Court. Together he and Russell Parrott drew up an *Address to the humane and benevolent Inhabitants of the city and county of Philadelphia*—precisely the kinds of people the ACS was trying to enlist. They began with an acknowledgment of past favors. Philadelphia's men and women of color had been emancipated, "many . . . by your aid." They were striving to prove themselves good citizens. It was with "sorrowing regret" that they had seen the colonization plan develop "under the auspices . . . of gentlemen . . . who . . . are amongst the wisest, the best, and the most benevolent . . . in this great nation." Accepting, at least for the purposes of this address, that the champions of colonization wished them well, they took the opportunity to "humbly and respectfully urge" that they did not wish to be colonized, at least not as the ACS wanted to colonize them, "nor will it be required by any circumstances, in our present or future condition, as long as we shall be permitted to share the protection of the excellent laws, and just government which we now enjoy."[102]

To those who argued that colonization would help end slavery, they answered that progress was already being made. "Every year, many of us have restored to us by the gradual, but certain march of the cause of abolition— Parents, from whom we have been long separated—Wives and children whom we had left in servitude—and Brothers, in blood as well as in early sufferings from whom we had been long parted."[103] They painted a grim picture of what would happen if forced colonization occurred. Planters would deport "Those among their bondmen, who feel that they should be free, by rights which all mankind have from God and from nature," while "the tame and submissive will be retained, and subjected to increased rigour." Slaveholders would pay scant attention to family ties, and the horrors of the middle passage would be repeated. "Parents will be torn from their children—husbands from their wives—brothers from brothers—and all the heart-rending agonies which were endured by our forefathers . . . will be . . . renewed."[104]

Despite his growing antagonism toward the ACS, James Forten had been careful not to denounce "all plans of colonization." Even as late as August, he had not apparently given up on the Sierra Leone scheme. If the ACS was a organization of duplicitous individuals intent on propping up the institution of slavery by forcibly removing free men and women of color, the same could not be said of the African Institution. But his only real link to the African Institution was Paul Cuffe, and Cuffe was ominously silent. As week after week passed without a word from Cuffe, Forten grew increasingly apprehensive. He knew Cuffe had been in poor health. Around the middle of September a letter came from Rhoda Cuffe, Paul's daughter. It contained the news Forten feared.[105] Paul Cuffe was dead.

Cuffe died on September 7, 1817. Other deaths followed in rapid succession. Robert Finley accepted the presidency of the University of Georgia, only to succumb to malaria soon after arriving to take up his duties in the fall of 1817.[106] Samuel J. Mills had rushed to Paul Cuffe's bedside when he learned how sick he was, and thereafter pushed ahead with plans for a colony. Authorized by the ACS to visit the West African coast and survey possible sites for a settlement, he and a friend, college professor Ebenezer Burgess, left Philadelphia for London in November 1817. From London they traveled to the Sierra Leone region, where they made contact with settlers, and generally left a good impression with local rulers. On their way back, Mills, whose health was never particularly good, fell sick with a fever. He died on June 16, 1818, at age thirty-six and was buried at sea.[107]

Despite the deaths of Finley and Mills, the American Colonization Society survived. However, it made few converts among Philadelphia's free people of color or among free blacks elsewhere in the North. The officers of the ACS might reject as "unfounded" and "sanctioned by no declaration or acts of this Society" rumors that free people were "to be constrained to migrate," but it was too late.[108] The damage had been done. One of those who could not be convinced to endorse the ACS was James Forten. While at first he had insisted that the society was composed of good men who had the best interests of free people of color at heart and he had stood out against a groundswell of hostile opinion within the African-American community, he had come to share the views of the majority of black Philadelphians. The ACS was a pernicious organization and they would have nothing to do with it. From the autumn of 1817 until his death a quarter of a century later, Forten helped lead the charge against the ACS.

JAMES FORTEN'S WAR against the ACS—and that was truly what his campaign amounted to—began with the meeting at the schoolhouse in Green's Court on August 10, 1817, and intensified with Paul Cuffe's passing. The pressure from ACS supporters only strengthened his resolve and heightened his contempt for their organization. Nothing, it seemed, was beneath them.

In June 1818 Forten's sensibilities were deeply wounded when he read in a Philadelphia newspaper a series of fictitious dialogues extolling the merits of colonization. Set in "the courts of heaven," the dialogues consisted of an interchange of opinions among William Penn, Paul Cuffe, and Absalom Jones. The spirit of Cuffe explained what he had tried to accomplish during his years on earth. Penn thought it a wonderful scheme but Jones was less enthusiastic. In the anonymous author's grand design Jones played the role of devil's advocate. Why, he demanded to know, must people of color emigrate at all? If they must go, could they not make their new home on America's Western frontier? Eventually, though, he was won over to the cause of colonization.[109] The dialogues could not have come at a worse psychological moment for James Forten. He was still mourning Paul Cuffe. Absalom Jones had also died and Forten was grieving his loss. To see the memories of his dearest friends used in this way to serve a cause he was now convinced was deeply injurious to his—and their—community must have been repugnant in the extreme.

James Forten was eager to share his views on the ACS with any benevolent white person who might be targeted by the organization so they would not be deceived, as he had been. The assembling of the American Convention for Promoting the Abolition of Slavery in Philadelphia in December 1818 provided him with an ideal opportunity for spreading the word. On behalf of the convention, its president, Richard Peters, Jr., Forten's lawyer and friend, invited him to explain to the delegates why he and other people of color had such a negative opinion of the ACS. Forten jumped at the chance. He gave the convention "a general account of the condition of the people of colour in Philadelphia," presumably emphasizing that they were striving to be good citizens and had no wish to leave the city they considered their home. The delegates thanked him and noted the strength of black opposition to colonization. They reprinted the *Address to the humane and benevolent Inhabitants of the city and county of Philadelphia* as part of their proceedings, and Forten must have been gratified to see that the sense of the majority was decidedly against the ACS.[110] These representatives from the Pennsylvania Abolition Society and its sister organizations were precisely the kinds of people the ACS was hoping to win over with its talk of "one day" bringing about the abolition of slavery.

With James Forten now leading the charge, African Americans in Philadelphia continued their attacks on the ACS. On November 16, 1819, Forten and Russell Parrott presided over a "very numerous" meeting called to respond to an address made by the ACS to the people of color in New York and Philadelphia who might consider becoming colonists. Forten and Parrott insisted that the Philadelphians had already explicitly stated their opposition, and nothing had occurred to change their minds. If anything, the insistence of the ACS leadership that the society did not intend to interfere with slavery only intensified their hatred of the organization. While "a few obscure and dissatisfied strangers among us" might delude themselves and dream of becoming "presidents, governors and principals, in Africa," the Philadelphians wanted the ACS to be in no doubt that "there is but one sentiment among the respectable inhabitants of color . . . which is, that it meets their unanimous and decided disapprobation."[111]

The pressure continued. A few weeks later the *Union United States Gazette* printed a letter from someone who signed himself "A Man of Color." While there is no definitive proof that the letter was Forten's work, there is strong circumstantial evidence to suggest it was. The pen name was one he often used. And when an anonymous writer, "Paul," took "A Man of Color" to task, Russell Parrott, Forten's trusted ally, sprang to his defense.[112]

The communication started out with an unambiguous statement on a subject dear to James Forten's heart: liberty. "There appears to us, by the history of every age and nation, nothing more sacred . . . than Liberty; a right which God has bestowed on all." The colonization scheme was bound up with the question of liberty. "We have . . . coolly and deliberately investigated the projected plan . . . and we are of opinion, that it is calculated to perpetuate Slavery in this Land of Liberty." The black community, or at least the "respectable" part of it, was implacably opposed to colonization. There was an unmistakable note of frustration in the letter. "It is evident that some, who have very lately appeared among us, have given their sanction to the proposed colony; and this, perhaps, gave rise to a recent solicitation made us by the present Agent: but we do assure the Public, that our resolution, to concur with nothing that has yet been offered us, is not, in the slightest degree, altered." The "scientific gentlemen" who put forward the idea of a colony had not yet decided whether it was to be located in Africa or in the wilds of North America. Frankly, neither was acceptable. Africa was a land inhabited "by those who have little to designate that they belong to the human species, and infested with reptiles of the most savage nature." An American colony was no more attractive. "[W]e may readily suppose that it would be in some cold region where the brute creation can scarcely live."

Alluding to the growing crisis over the extension of slavery into Missouri and the rest of the territory acquired from France in the Louisiana Purchase, "A Man of Color" acknowledged the urgency of the matter. Colonization was nothing less than a vast conspiracy to enslave those people of color who had won their freedom, and render the bondage of the enslaved perpetual. The situation was critical. It was imperative that "every true spirited descendant of Africa . . . be upon his . . . guard against any measure that may be the means of ensnaring him into . . . slavery."[113] While the logic of Forten's argument is not always clear—how exactly would agreeing to go to Africa lead to the extension of slavery into the Western territories?—the letter attests to his sense of alarm.

Over the next few years James Forten and other opponents of colonization had good reason to be apprehensive, for, despite serious financial problems, the ACS did not simply fade away. Back in the spring of 1819 Congress had passed a piece of legislation entitled "An Act in addition to the acts prohibiting the Slave Trade." Under the provisions of that new law, sponsored by Virginia's Charles Fenton Mercer, a staunch supporter of the ACS, the president of the United States was authorized to use the navy to patrol the Atlantic to prevent Americans from participating in the slave trade. He also had the power "to appoint a proper person or persons, residing upon the coast of Africa" to receive any Africans the navy rescued from illegal slavers. The sum of $100,000 was appropriated for enforcement.[114] Mercer and other ACS stalwarts insisted that using the $100,000 to found a colony was the best way to enforce the law. President Monroe, who personally favored colonization, mulled over whether he had the authority to establish a colony, but his Secretary of State, John Quincy Adams, convinced him such a move would be unconstitutional.[115]

The friends of colonization took another tack. The president might not be empowered to establish a colony, but he could send a warship to West Africa with the necessary supplies and civilian "workers" to set up a naval station. And an agent from the ACS, a private, nongovernmental entity, could go along to buy land. Monroe was won over. In early 1820, eighty-six black men, women, and children left for Africa from New York on the *Elizabeth*, escorted by the warship *Cyane*.[116] Their destination was Sierra Leone, but the ACS had no intention of collaborating with the British. They would stop off in the colony only long enough to decide on a permanent place of settlement somewhere else along the West African coast.

The expedition almost ended in disaster. Negotiations with African rulers went nowhere. All of them were understandably wary of these newcomers. As for the well-being of the emigrants, none of the ACS enthusiasts back in the United States had given much thought to the impact of African diseases or the African climate. They were "Africans" and surely that conferred upon them total immunity from malaria and the like. Those assumptions were soon proven tragically wrong. Not only did all three of the white officials who had gone out on the *Elizabeth* die of "fever," but so did dozens of the settlers. Control of the grief-stricken and demoralized survivors fell to Daniel Coker, Paul Cuffe's ally from Baltimore, who had been persuaded to throw in his lot with the ACS. Appalled by what he had experienced, Coker eventually chose to settle with his family in Sierra Leone.[117]

Despite the dreadful losses among the emigrants on the *Elizabeth*, further expeditions were despatched, and inevitably there were more deaths. Vastly exceeding his orders, Lieutenant Robert Field Stockton of the United States Navy entered into the bargaining for land for the colony. Putting a loaded pistol to the head of King Peter, who controlled the Cape Mesurado region to the south of Sierra Leone, Stockton forced him to agree to the terms the Americans offered him and his people. The American colony, soon to be christened Liberia, was born at the point of a gun.[118]

Needless to say, Lieutenant Stockton's high-handed action produced a legacy of distrust and hostility. By the end of 1822 the settlers were fighting for their lives against a coalition of forces from various local peoples. So much for the vision of the exiled children of Africa returning to civilize and christianize the continent of their ancestors! Scores of Africans were killed or injured by gun- and cannon-fire as the newcomers defended themselves. It was, to say the least, an inauspicious beginning. Although a truce was eventually worked out, it was an uneasy one. As for relations between the emigrants, white officials, and the parent organization, there were constant complaints of indolence, insubordination, high-handedness, and broken promises.[119]

Whether or not he knew of the circumstances under which Liberia came into being, James Forten was determined not to support it in any way. He was well placed to receive graphic accounts of the suffering of the settlers. Some of them were old neighbors, and others had family and friends living in Philadelphia. Terra Hall, fifty-five years old, freeborn, and a hat-maker by trade, had gone out on the *Elizabeth*. He returned home in 1822 with news of his Philadelphia shipmates. Laborer Thomas Spencer had died in the clash with King Peter's people. Blacksmith Wilson Carey had cut his losses and moved to Sierra Leone with his brother and his children. His wife, Elizabeth, had died of fever. Hairdresser John Augustine and his entire family had succumbed to malaria. The litany of death and disillusionment went on and on.[120]

Like James Forten, most black Philadelphians rejected the blandishments of the ACS, but they knew the colonizationists had made converts. The ACS reported in 1822 that "One hundred black persons in the City of Philadelphia have expressed their desire to remove to Africa."[121] Even if that was an exaggeration—and economic hard times, combined with pervasive racism, made Liberia look more appealing to some people of color than an uncertain future in the City of Brotherly Love—James Forten learned firsthand in 1823 how powerful the allure of Africa could be for someone he thought he knew so well.

Back in 1815 or 1816 Forten would have been most encouraging had any member of his work force announced a wish to go to Africa. His pointed questions to Paul Cuffe about the extent of "Sail Makers buisness" in Sierra Leone probably had to do with plans to establish a favorite apprentice, and in time perhaps a son, as overseer of a sail loft in the colony.[122] By 1823 he was appalled that anyone connected with him should think about leaving for Africa. Yet that was precisely what Francis Devany was doing.

Devany had been born a slave in Charleston, South Carolina, in 1797. Somehow he had acquired his freedom and had relocated to Philadelphia when he was in his teens. After at least one voyage as a sailor, he had apprenticed himself to Forten to become a sailmaker. In 1823 Devany announced his decision to embark for Liberia with his wife and their two children. Financially, Devany did well in the colony. He got his start thanks to the Colonial Agent, who put him in charge of a small coasting vessel. He soon accumulated enough money to set himself up as a trader in the Liberian capital of Monrovia, named in honor of ACS well-wisher President Monroe. In less than six years, by his own estimate, Delany was worth between $15,000 and $20,000.[123]

Eager to play him off against his former employer, the ACS published Devany's glowing accounts of life in Liberia. "We are all going on with some elegant improvements to our farms. . . . Monrovia now looks like many little towns in America, with nice stone or frame buildings . . . and . . . is as happy a little community as any . . . you will find of its size in America." Devany neglected to mention that within months of the family's arrival, his wife and children had died.[124]

The pressure on James Forten to follow the lead of his erstwhile apprentice never let up. Callers at his home or his place of business generally found him courteous but firm. He would listen to their arguments and then respond with arguments of his own. He understood that not every white person who advocated colonization was a defender of slavery. Some of them, he conceded, were noble-hearted and truly selfless. They wanted to help the enslaved and improve the situation of free people of color. How sad that such earnest souls had been deceived by the ACS. The likes of Quaker merchant Elliott Cresson, and young Gerald Ralston, son of Philadelphia businessman and philanthropist Robert Ralston, could always be sure of a polite reception when they called on James Forten, but they could not get him to share their enthusiasm for Liberia.

Only occasionally did Forten let his irritation show through. Evidently he did so one day toward the end of 1824 when Mr. Cowles, a young white New Englander, showed up on his doorstep on his way to Washington for the ACS annual meeting. Cowles had come, as others had before him, in the hope of convincing James Forten of the error of his ways. He left 92 Lombard Street an hour or so later after a most distressing experience. He found in Forten an implacable foe, and a rather more militant one than he had bargained for. "Mr. F." spoke of divine retribution for the sins of slavery and racial oppression.

> [H]e said repeatedly, that reasoning from the righteousness of God and from the manifest tendency of events he was brought to the conclusion that the time was approaching and to judge from his manner, was already at the door when the 250,000,000 who had for centuries been the oppressors of the remaining 600,000,000 of the human race would find the tables turned upon them and would expiate by their own sufferings those which they had inflicted on others.

Cowles was thoroughly upset and found such "doctrines highly repugnant to [his] feelings."[125]

If James Forten would not back the ACS, an old ally, Richard Allen, was wavering. As senior bishop of the rapidly growing African Methodist Episcopal denomination, perhaps he had visions of establishing mission stations in Liberia with the help of the ACS. In any event, it was Allen who tipped off ACS officer William B. Davidson in February 1827 about a worrying new development. "[A] man of Colour named Cornish has recently arrived here from N[ew] York and was exerting himself to oppose the Colonization plan." He intended to do this by establishing a newspaper "with a view of detering . . . people from emigrating and giving to the public mind an impression unfavorable to our cause." Allen had learned that Forten was backing Cornish's efforts. Davidson confessed he was disturbed by Allen's news.

> The ideas of Cornish & Forten are that the people of Colour . . . are by birth entitled to all the rights of freemen and ought to be admitted . . . to a participation of all the enjoyment of Citizenship . . . and that Africa is a land of destruction where the Sword will cut off the few wretched beings whom the climate spares.[126]

The alliance between James Forten and clergyman-turned-newspaper-editor Samuel Cornish is an interesting one. Forten had known Cornish for more than a decade. A freeborn native of Delaware, Cornish had come to Philadelphia around 1815 to train for the ministry with Forten's friend John Gloucester. Cornish often preached at First African Presbyterian when Gloucester was ill. After serving as an itinerant preacher, Cornish made his home in New York.[127] His brother, James, worked in Forten's sail loft.

Back in 1824, before he came to Philadelphia to call on Forten, Mr. Cowles had stopped off in New York to discuss colonization with Cornish. Cowles conceded that Cornish had expressed himself with "more rational and manly feeling than I was exactly prepared for." The black preacher pointed out that Africans and their descendants had endured "toils and hardships . . . to make this country what it is." It was their home and he "thought they had therefore a good right to enjoy it." There were, Cornish admitted, some ACS supporters who "would pluck out their eyes" if it would help the black community, but they were in the minority. "Such were the feelings of . . . contempt with which [most] regarded the blacks that they could not rest so long as the possibility remained of their . . . mingling with them in the various scenes of life."[128] Cornish's views remained unchanged three years later when he sat down to discuss tactics with James Forten.

The newspaper Cornish was in Philadelphia to promote was *Freedom's Journal*. He represented a group of prominent black New Yorkers who felt the time had come for people of color to sponsor a press to defend their interests. The group included men such as William Hamilton and Peter Williams, whom Forten knew personally or by repute. At the founding meeting Cornish was invited to become senior editor, a post he accepted for six months. John B.

Russwurm, one of the first men of color in the United States to gain a college degree, was appointed as junior editor.[129] Fund-raising efforts on behalf of the paper began in a number of communities. James Forten was pleased to contribute, knowing *Freedom's Journal* would give him a powerful weapon in his crusade against the colonization society.

Around the publication of the first issue of *Freedom's Journal*, Forten was following with deep interest a debate in the Philadelphia press. The exchange was prompted by a bill in the Pennsylvania legislature to appropriate $2,000 "to be expended by the Am^n Col^n Soc. in removing to Liberia such free persons of colour . . . as may be willing to emigrate."[130] On March 21 "P" observed that Henry Clay, in an address to the annual meeting of the ACS, had insisted the organization's focus was not on ending slavery but on relocating free people.[131]

"P" was quickly taken to task by "A Member of the Colonization Society," who insisted he had misrepresented the views of both Clay and the ACS.[132] Forten was soon drawn into the debate. Writing to *Freedom's Journal* as "A Man of Colour," he observed: "Mr. Clay particularly informs us, that it is to have nothing to do with the delicate question of Slavery," and pointed out that converts to the cause of colonization "do not penetrate the real views of the Colonization Society, who have carefully disguised their intentions; which have since the formation of the society been aimed at the liberty of the free people."[133]

Under the same pen name, Forten wrote again a few months later. He had come across an article in the Princeton *Patriot* in which the author had made not-so-subtle threats against *Freedom's Journal* for printing Forten's letter. The New Jersey writer hoped the sentiments were not those of the editors of *Freedom's Journal*, and warned that if they continued publishing letters critical of colonization, "the Journal will lose all its patrons among the friends of colonization." Forten responded that "respectable and industrious" black citizens had every reason to distrust a society "which . . . allows a member . . . publicly to declare that its object is to get rid of the free people of colour."[134]

DESPITE HIS VERY public opposition, the ACS leadership continued its efforts to win James Forten over. Had he chosen a different path, there is every reason to believe he could have ended his days as the first president of Liberia. Or if he had not lived long enough, that honor might well have gone to one of his sons. The influence he enjoyed in Philadelphia, home to one of the largest and most sophisticated communities of free people of color in the nation, coupled with his obvious success in business, made him someone the ACS desperately wanted to recruit. James Forten's son-in-law, Robert Purvis, referred to a "clique of clerical wolves who besieged [Forten] in terms of flattery, assuring him that he would become the Lord's [*sic*] Mansfield of their 'Heaven born republic.'" Purvis was never anything other than an implacable foe of colonization, but there is evidence to support his contention that Forten was offered every kind of inducement to get him to emigrate to Liberia, or at least mute his criticism.[135]

In December 1827 Elliott Cresson gave ACS secretary Ralph R. Gurley some advice about Forten. Cresson had made "frequent endeavours to convert" him, "so far, at least, as to induce him to establish a trading line between Ph[iladelphi]a & Liberia." Convinced "blacks are sometimes more accessible thro' the channel of *flattery* than any other," Cresson thought flattery might do the trick in this case. "Forten is a man of both *wealth* and *respectability*, & if our colonial agent would open a correspondence with him as *such*, pointing out the great commercial advantages which would result from a line of packets respectably conducted & supported by a moderate capital it would perhaps effect the object." Cresson considered Forten's conversion of vital importance. "His coming into the measure would do great good in our City. His opinion has great weight with our coloured population."[136] Back in 1815, when Paul Cuffe had suggested it, Forten had been very interested in part ownership of a vessel in the West African trade, but not now, and not in partnership with a society he loathed and feared.

Still, the ACS made one important convert. When Samuel Cornish resigned from the editorship of *Freedom's Journal* at the end of six months, citing his poor health and his wish to move his family into the countryside, John B. Russwurm took it over. Well read, articulate, and full of energy, he soon became dejected. *Freedom's Journal* was teetering on the verge of bankruptcy, and Russwurm was never sure from week to week whether he would be paid for his editorial duties. Promises from the ACS that his prospects would be brighter in Liberia and that he would be appointed editor of the colony's newspaper, the *Liberia Herald*, worked a transformation in his attitude with regard to colonization. James Forten, Samuel Cornish, and many other Northern free people of color were appalled when they read the February 14, 1829, issue of *Freedom's Journal*. Russwurm publicly and unequivocally renounced his opposition to the American Colonization Society and declared his intention to give up his editorship and emigrate to Liberia.[137]

The sense of betrayal was immense. As Russwurm described it to ACS secretary Ralph R. Gurley in May 1829, a "violent persecution" had "been raging against" him in Philadelphia. Nevertheless, he remained optimistic. "The cause is gaining ground in the minds of many who are ashamed to acknowledge it; and the day I believe is not far distant, when all our people who would be an accession to the colony, will be as anxious to locate themselves there, as foreigners now are of emigrating to America."[138]

Apart from Russwurm's defection—and that was serious enough—there were other reasons for James Forten to worry. In 1829 the Pennsylvania legislature passed a resolution endorsing the ACS. The state's senators and congressmen were urged to do all they could to support it at the national level.[139] Even old friends were jumping on the ACS bandwagon. Richard Peters, who back in 1818 had given Forten the chance to explain to white abolitionists how the black community felt about the ACS, took an active part in a procolonization meeting in Philadelphia in December 1829, praising the ACS for "its influence in the Southern States, by which a number of those who were born in slavery have been emancipated." Peters and his friends pledged to collect funds for the society only "on condition that they be applied exclusively to the . . . transportation, and . . . support, of slaves, who being willing to join the Colony, can be liberated only with a view to their emigration," but that was no consolation to James Forten.[140] As far as he was concerned, any endorsement of the ACS was a mistake. Peters and other white abolitionists were well intentioned. Forten knew they genuinely believed that by supporting the ACS they were helping to free the slaves of the South. That was why the ACS was so dangerous. It appealed not only to the avowed enemies of black Americans but to many of their staunchest friends. The ACS was deceiving them as it had once deceived him.

In spite of the support for colonization that was being shown in many quarters, James Forten refused to abandon the struggle. Bleak though things looked by the end of the 1820s, the next decade would bring him powerful new allies in his battle against the ACS—as well as a crop of new enemies. During the 1830s "colonization" would become the rallying cry of any white person opposed to the presence of free people of color anywhere in the United States.

9

THE LIMITS OF BROTHERHOOD

WAGING WAR AGAINST the American Colonization Society demanded a great deal of James Forten's time and attention after 1817. When he was not supervising his work force or overseeing his growing family, he was often to be found chairing a protest meeting or penning yet another letter to the press denouncing the ACS. However, although he did battle against the champions of colonization with all the energy he could muster, there were other causes that demanded his attention, other battles that needed to be fought.

The late 1810s and 1820s in Philadelphia brought economic and social upheavals. The City of Brotherly Love was a city under pressure, and as James Forten knew only too well, brotherly love could all too easily disappear when men and women were faced with crises that impacted on their everyday lives and undermined their sense of well-being. In the Panic of 1819 scores of businesses failed, hundreds of citizens were jailed for debt, and many more found themselves out of work, forced to turn to friends, neighbors, the network of private charities, or the almshouse for relief. Recovery eventually came, but the wait was a long one, too long for some. There were outbreaks of epidemic disease—typhoid in 1818 and the dreaded yellow fever in 1820. Even in so-called healthy years, tuberculosis, typhus, pneumonia, workplace accidents, intemperance, and the like took their customary toll. Few of Philadelphia's working people, black or white, earned enough to be able to set anything aside for the proverbial rainy day. When families suffered the loss of a breadwinner they were plunged into poverty virtually overnight.[1]

Adding to the uncertainty of life in the city was the rapid pace of population growth. In 1810 the total population of Philadelphia County was just under 92,000. By 1820 it was almost 113,000, and by 1830 it had rocketed to almost 189,000.[2] Inevitably there were problems as Philadelphia felt the strain of a burgeoning population at a time of economic stagnation. Migrants, black and white, continued to flock to the city and its adjoining districts in a desperate search for better opportunities—a search that often ended in frustration and bitter disappointment. Philadelphia was also the destination for thousands of immigrants, most from Ireland and the majority possessing little in the way of resources to help them gain an economic foothold in the city. Since its founding, Philadelphia had absorbed wave after wave of newcomers from Europe. However, the upsurge in the 1810s and 1820s was all the more noticeable because it came after a sharp decline in immigration in the early years of the century. The end of the Napoleonic Wars and the relative safety of the sea lanes brought tens of thousands of foreigners to American shores. As James Forten knew from what he saw and heard in the streets of his native city, significant numbers of those newcomers made for Philadelphia.

White Philadelphians, and not a few of their black neighbors, displayed their antipathy toward the immigrants, especially the Irish, in innumerable ways. As a group they were blamed for everything from lawlessness to outbreaks of epidemic disease. But if there was one segment of the population more than any other that whites deemed unwanted and "expendable," it was people of color.

James Forten had heard the same arguments before. He was to hear them voiced again and again in the 1810s and 1820s with renewed ferocity. Blacks, so it was alleged, took jobs away from white people. They were too assertive and did not know "their place." There was a sense among so many whites that it was acceptable to find fault with black people. They were a surplus population, unwelcome in the city, and legitimate targets for everything from racist name-calling to open violence. White Philadelphians were convinced the city—*their* city—was being overrun by hordes of lawless and lazy ex-slaves, who contributed nothing to the general well-being. They were also sure there were more black people in Philadelphia than ever appeared in the census. That some African Americans had good reason to avoid the census-taker was doubtless true, because an encounter with any white official could spell disaster for an escaped slave. In fact, though, the African-American population was about to enter a period of decline. Though it grew numerically—just over 9,500 in 1810, slightly over 12,000 in 1820, and over 15,500 a decade later—the white population was increasing much more rapidly. The percentage of people of color rose only slightly between 1810 and 1820 and decreased over the next ten years.[3] As for charges of pervasive poverty and criminality, the economic marginalization of Philadelphia's black citizens meant growing numbers were indeed to be found in the almshouse and the penitentiary.[4] That most members of the African-American community were industrious and law-abiding was a reality many whites preferred to ignore. Still, perceptions mattered more than numbers, and plenty of white residents were convinced Philadelphia would be better off if it could somehow get rid of people of color.

It was not just the pressure of population growth and economic instability that led to a rising tide of racial antagonism. Amid the crisis over the Missouri Compromise some of Philadelphia's white "better sort" were beginning to recognize the explosive potential of slavery. Scarcely had the question of the extension of slavery into the territories been settled when word reached Philadelphia of the Denmark Vesey conspiracy in Charleston, South Carolina. The image of African Americans, free and enslaved, conspiring to overthrow the slave system and assert their rights terrified Southern whites, but there were many in the North who found that image almost as disturbing. Coupled with anxieties over slavery was the broader philosophical question of the inclusiveness of the American republic. Could it embrace people of color as well as whites? Did black people have any future in America? As James Forten realized only too well, plenty of whites who had never contributed a cent to the American Colonization Society were coming to see the expulsion of black Americans as a solution to all of society's ills.

But if the African-American community was an increasingly embattled community, it was also a community riven with internal conflicts. The values espoused by the likes of James Forten were not necessarily shared by all of Philadelphia's free people of color. When he spoke of the threat posed by the ACS he spoke for the overwhelming majority of the city's African-American residents, but on other issues he spoke for one segment of black Philadelphia. Convinced though he was that he was acting in the best interests of every member of his community, he knew he had his critics. Doubtless he was able to take comfort from the certainty that he would get them to see sense in time. Still, on more than one occasion he had to acknowledge that they did not value his opinions or share his goals. But then he was a leader, and being a leader often exacted a high price.

Through the late 1810s and 1820s James Forten would grapple with everything from racial violence to the rights of free people of color to congregate in the streets, from the provision of public education for African-American children to the choice of a minister for his church. His battles would be fought in the press and in the vestry, in meeting after meeting, on street corners, on the wharves and in the warehouses along the Delaware, and in innumerable conversations with his neighbors, black and white. In the 1810s and 1820s he would become embroiled in a host of issues, and in more than one initiative that seemed to run counter to everything he had ever said or supported.

AT FIRST GLANCE nothing is more surprising than James Forten's enthusiastic advocacy of emigration to Haiti. The man who was such an outspoken and relentless critic of the ACS not only was willing to countenance mass emigration to Haiti but was ready to do everything in his power to promote it. On closer consideration, though, the Haitian scheme does not represent simply a momentary aberration. Through the 1810s and well into the 1820s James Forten had no objection to any person of color trying to better his situation by leaving the country. The problem he had with the ACS was not that its leading men advocated emigration but that they insisted people of color *must* leave because they had no place in America. Forten begged to differ. Nevertheless, he had been very careful to explain back in 1817 that he did not oppose all emigration plans. After all, he had helped Paul Cuffe find recruits for Sierra Leone. Might there not be another place of settlement outside the control of the hated ACS that was equally acceptable? James Forten's thoughts began to turn to the Caribbean.

The image of an independent republic governed by black men had obviously intrigued him for years. As he told ACS founder Robert Finley when they met in 1817, Haiti gave him the proof he needed that the descendants of Africa "could not always be detained in their present bondage." Its very existence inspired him to hope that the children of the diaspora "would become a great nation."[5] He read a great deal about Haiti. He talked with people who had been there—sailors, merchants, and individuals such as John Appo and Antoine Servance, who had lived there. He had ample opportunity to satisfy his curiosity, for there was a great deal of contact between Philadelphia and Haiti. Although their city was home to one of the largest concentrations of Saint Dominguan refugees anywhere in the country, and although they had heard stories of atrocities perpetrated against French slave owners by their former slaves, Philadelphia merchants had no qualms about doing business with the new masters of France's erstwhile colony. No sooner had Haitian independence been declared on New Year's Day 1804 than there were complaints from France that Philadelphians were trading with Haiti's new head of state, Jean-Jacques Dessalines, fitting out vessels for him, helping him get arms, and recruiting skilled workers for him. The Philadelphians would doubtless have replied that when one was in trade, prejudices and ideological differences took a backseat to profit.[6] After Dessalines was assassinated in 1806, there was a brief period of chaos and Haiti split into two separate entities. Needless to say, Philadelphia merchants traded with both regions.

James Forten was not the only free person of color to be intrigued by the potential of Haiti. Haiti was the subject of innumerable addresses and sermons. Again and again African-American orators linked the abolition of slavery and the securing of full civil rights in the United States to the success of Haiti. And some at least were prepared to go further than talking. In the summer of 1818, for instance, the "black and colored men of the city of New York" approached President Jean-Pierre Boyer to inquire whether they would be welcome to settle in his part of Haiti. The reply from his secretary-general, Joseph-Balthasar Inginac, was very positive. He promised them land bounties and assisted passages, and added his hope that "a great number" of those he termed "our unhappy fellow countrymen" would decide to "come and console themselves beneath the protection of our laws."[7]

If the New Yorkers were interested in Boyer's southern region of Haiti, Philadelphians were more inclined to consider the northern region controlled by Henri Christophe. As much as anything, that preference had to do with the arrival in their city of a man who knew Christophe and was in some respects his emissary. In the fall of 1818 Philadelphia's African-American community welcomed into its midst a gentleman "of pure African blood [and] . . . of highly polished manners."[8] Born into freedom in Connecticut, the son of a West African woman and an African-American Revolutionary War veteran, Prince Saunders had managed to acquire an education that the likes of James Forten, himself a literate and well-read individual, could not help but envy. After attending a school in Vermont, teaching for a time in Connecticut, and then enrolling in Moor's Charity School at Dartmouth College, Saunders was recommended in 1808 by the president of Dartmouth for the post of teacher of the African School in Boston.[9] He rose rapidly to a position of influence within Boston's black community, becoming secretary of the African Masonic Lodge and founding an interracial cultural organization, the Belles Lettres Society. He also collaborated with Paul Cuffe to arouse interest in the Sierra Leone scheme in Boston and was reportedly engaged to one of Cuffe's daughters.[10]

In 1815 Saunders and Thomas Paul, a close friend and the leader of Boston's black Baptists, sailed to England on business for the African Masonic Lodge. While in London, Saunders was introduced to the abolitionists Thomas Clarkson and William Wilberforce.[11] To the two Englishmen, both of them fervent admirers of Henri Christophe, Saunders seemed an ideal ally. They wanted to open negotiations with Christophe on everything from furthering abolition in the Americas to spreading the Anglican faith, but they needed a reliable intermediary. Prince Saunders was the very man they had been looking for. He was well educated, he shared their commitment to antislavery and reform, and he was a man of color. Sent off to Haiti by Clarkson and Wilberforce in 1816, Saunders was warmly welcomed by Christophe, who promptly sent him back to London to recruit teachers for the schools he was planning to establish throughout his kingdom. On this second visit to the British capital Prince Saunders was lionized by British aristocrats, some of whom took his first name for a royal title. He played the role of African royalty to the hilt, but he also took the time to consult with his antislavery friends and to publish his *Haytian Papers*, in which he praised Haiti and its enlightened ruler. He was back in Haiti by year's end, but he had a falling-out with Christophe soon after his return. The king considered the publication of the *Haytian Papers* a breach of trust, because Saunders had acted without his permission. Reportedly, Christophe was also angry about the expenses Saunders had racked up in London, expenses Christophe was now being asked to cover. Dismissed as a royal advisor, Saunders returned to the United States. He published a second edition of his *Haytian Papers* in Boston in 1818 and then made his way to Philadelphia.[12]

One of the first to extend the hand of friendship to Prince Saunders in Philadelphia was James Forten. In a sense, the New Englander was not a stranger. Forten had heard about him from Paul Cuffe. It was almost certainly Forten who invited Saunders to address the newly established Augustine Society and brought him to the attention of other prominent individuals in the city's African-American community.

Shortly before Saunders arrived in Philadelphia, James Forten and a dozen or so other influential men of color had come together to form the Augustine Education Society. Their goal was to improve the prospects of African-American children in the city by founding a school for them. Casting around for a name for their organization, they hit upon one that seemed highly appropriate. They could not ask for a better patron than St. Augustine of Hippo (354–430), arguably the greatest of the Church Fathers. A son of Africa (he had been born in Rome's North African provinces), a teacher, and a man of great learning, he had defended the Christian faith in a time of trial. In the minds of Forten and his friends, St. Augustine united piety, intellectual endeavor, and "African" achievements. And when it came to finding a suitable speaker to inaugurate their lecture series, they looked to a descendant of Africa who was devoted to both learning and religion.

On September 30, vice-president James Forten formally introduced Prince Saunders to the Augustine Society. Members were treated to such a memorable speech from their guest that they begged for a copy for publication. After praising the pursuit of education and making mention of various luminaries of ancient Greece and Rome, Saunders shifted his focus to the present day, specifically, to Henri Christophe's Haiti. There "the gardens of the Academy are thronged with youth, whose ardour to reap its fairest flowers, would even vie with that evinced by the hazardous enterprize of the intrepid Jason of antiquity, when he cast the watchful Dragon, and seized . . . the Golden Fleece."[13] It is hardly surprising that the speech Saunders gave that evening should have generated great enthusiasm among an audience already predisposed to think well of Haiti and the Haitian people.

Saunders went from strength to strength, aided by the friendship and support of James Forten. It was Forten who secured him introductions within the African-American community and among his white antislavery friends. At the end of 1818 Saunders appeared before the American Convention for Promoting the Abolition of Slavery, the same august body whose president, Richard Peters, had invited Forten to explain to the delegates why he opposed African colonization. Saunders held forth on the wealth of Haiti and its tremendous potential. If a peace treaty could be negotiated between the heads of state of the northern and southern parts of Haiti, "there are many hundred of . . . free people in the New England and middle states who would be glad to repair there immediately to settle." He appealed to the abolitionists to take on the role of peacemakers, assuring them that British abolitionists would applaud their efforts and work with them in such a laudable endeavor.[14]

From Saunders James Forten imbibed a very positive notion of Haiti and its ruler. He may well have heard Saunders talk of Thomas Clarkson's hopes that the whole island of Hispaniola could be united. Clarkson envisaged a peaceful agreement between the two halves of Haiti. He also hoped the United States would purchase Spain's claims to the eastern part of Hispaniola and give the land to Christophe for him to colonize American people of color. Certainly, well-placed white friends in Philadelphia such as Roberts Vaux and Richard Peters were aware of this plan.[15]

Through 1819 and into 1820 Thomas Clarkson worked to persuade Christophe to pardon Saunders for his past indiscretions. Emphasizing his belief that the United States would buy and transfer to him Spain's territories on Hispaniola as a refuge for African Americans, the English abolitionist urged Christophe to begin working on a resettlement scheme without delay. That required an intermediary, and the best available was Prince Saunders.[16] Christophe saw the sense of this and relented. After the better part of two years in Philadelphia, during which time James Forten had tried unsuccessfully to secure for him the appointment as minister at St. Thomas's African Episcopal Church, Saunders was summoned back to Haiti to receive his orders. He returned to Haiti in the autumn of 1820, but things quickly fell apart. Christophe was facing a mutiny among his troops, some of whom were conspiring with Jean-Pierre Boyer. News that Christophe had suffered a crippling stroke strengthened the opposition forces. It would only be a matter of time before his reign came to an end. Christophe held his kingdom together as well as he could and tried to conduct business as usual. Saunders was to have an audience with him on October 5 and sail for Philadelphia the following day to set the emigration scheme in motion. The two did have some preliminary discussions, but the intensifying crisis, and then Christophe's suicide, prevented anything further. Saunders found himself trapped in Haiti.[17] In the ensuing chaos that brought Boyer to power, he barely escaped with his life. Eventually he managed to get back to Philadelphia, where Forten and his other friends doubtless rallied to his aid.

In June 1821 Saunders wrote Thomas Clarkson from Philadelphia: "I was the bearer of letters from some of the most respectable people of colour in this City . . . upon the subject of their immigrating to [Haiti]. . . . They vested me with full authority to make every arrangement for them and . . . instructed me to act . . . as their representative in Hayti."[18] Was James Forten the writer of one of those letters? Had Henri Christophe listened as Saunders talked about his Philadelphia friend, who had done so well in business and exerted so much influence within the African-American community? Perhaps Forten had flirted, however briefly, with the notion of emigration. But if he had not, some of his closest friends had. Almost two years later, Prince Saunders had not given up hope of leading a massive exodus. As late as 1823 he was still writing to Clarkson about Haitian emigration.[19] In fact, the Haitian scheme was about to be revived, but not under his auspices.

Loring D. Dewey, the ACS agent in New York City, was finding it difficult to convince either black or white New Yorkers of the merits of Liberian emigration. It wasn't that they were opposed to emigration; it was rather that they did not think Liberia was the best place for a settlement. "Among the Coloured People" Dewey detected "a preference for Hayti over Africa." As for the whites he spoke with, they refused to pledge any money at all to support the ACS, but they did promise their "ready aid to promote emigration to Hayti." Dewey concluded it was worth investigating further. In March 1824, entirely on his own initiative, he composed a detailed letter of inquiry to Haiti's head of state asking whether he would support emigration and what, if anything, his government would be prepared to do for the settlers.[20]

Dewey's letter of inquiry came at a crucial time for Jean-Pierre Boyer. He was desperate to get recognition from the United States for Haiti or, failing that, a promise of neutrality in the event that France mounted any kind of offensive to try to retake her lost colony. Every one of his approaches had been rebuffed. Like the majority of Southern politicians, President James Monroe was distinctly uneasy about recognizing a nation that had come into being as the result of a successful slave uprising.[21] However, the letter from Dewey gave Boyer and Secretary-General Inginac reason to hope. Convinced Dewey was writing on behalf of the ACS and with the full knowledge of its powerful backers in Washington, among them Monroe, Boyer lost no time replying. He promised a warm reception to anyone who chose to settle in Haiti. He was delighted to have the opportunity to collaborate with the noble-hearted gentlemen of the ACS in promoting emigration to his island. The only suggestion of Dewey's he could not agree to was that the ACS should establish a semiautonomous colony in Haiti. He assured Dewey there would be no need for that. The settlers would be granted Haitian citizenship "as soon as they put their feet on the soil of Hayti."[22]

On the surface at least, Boyer's invitation was very attractive. Emigrants who came to work "unimproved" land would get free passage, provisions for several months, and three acres of land apiece, "together with as many more acres as the government may judge them entitled to, as a reward for their *sobriety, industry,* and *economy*." Sharecroppers or tenant farmers were also welcome. They would have to repay the cost of their passage after six months, but once they had met their obligations to their Haitian landlords they would be free to buy land and work for themselves. As for "Mechanics, Traders, Clerks, or School Masters," they could come as well, but they must also repay the cost of their passage in six months. Boyer envisaged the emigration of 6,000 people in the first year.[23] Armed with his instructions and authorized to charter vessels in American ports, Boyer's emissary, Jonathas Granville, was dispatched to Philadelphia to set things in motion.

Many years later, Dewey would insist that the decision to start the emigration program in Philadelphia had been unwise. The Quakers were firmly in control there and they considered "that every measure concerning the blacks which did not originate from them was mistaken." They tried to take over the scheme, and when that did not work they sabotaged it.[24] With hindsight, it might have been better to begin work in New York, but in the summer of 1824 prospects looked very bright indeed in Philadelphia. Granville won over Nicholas Biddle, president of the Bank of the United States, merchant prince Stephen Girard, and publisher Mathew Carey. The Marquis de Lafayette, in the city on his triumphal tour of the United States, called on Granville and promised to help him, as did his wealthy young protégée, Scottish reformer Frances Wright.[25]

What his new friends did not know was how deeply Jonathas Granville hated the United States. Nothing in his previous experience had prepared him for what he encountered there. Educated in Paris, he had been a junior officer in Napoleon's army and had seen service in the Emperor's campaigns in France, Germany, and Austria. Elegant and refined, he was accustomed to mixing with men of his social class, without distinctions of race. An accomplished musician and poet, a skilled swordsman, an experienced diplomat and civil servant, he found all that counted for nothing in the United States. He was a man of color and no more.[26] Although his white acquaintances described him as most assuredly a "gentleman," he was seldom treated as such. In fact, he was openly insulted on more than one occasion. Again and again he begged Boyer to recall him and entrust the work of recruiting emigrants to Dewey.[27] Boyer turned down his requests. Distasteful though his situation was, he had a mission and he must see it through to the end.

Resigned to a sojourn of several months in "this abominable country" and aware of the far-reaching implications of his task, Granville set to work. He had already made contact with prominent whites. Now he must exercise his charm and eloquence on the free people of color. He carefully hid from the likes of James Forten what he really thought of them. Only in his letters to Boyer could he be candid. He had met "brothers who could appear with advantage in the most distinguished society . . . [and] do honor to our country." It shocked him to see them "accorded less respect than the poor white man who cleans their boots," but it shocked him even more to see that "they are as accustomed to this state of things as we are to the sun." As for the black poor, he shrank from associating with them. "Whenever I am with them I feel their debasement reflects on me."[28] He simply did not understand the lives American people of color lived or the things that concerned them. He was particularly frustrated by their quibbling about religious freedom.

> The Quaker wants to know if he will be obliged to join the national guard, the Protestant asks if we could pass a law preventing . . . reviews of the national guard from taking place on a Sunday, and the Methodist asks if a man can be deprived of the freedom to preach God's law. Unfortunately, it is among this last class of lunatics that most of our people are to be found.[29]

Wisely, Granville kept his opinions to himself. So adept was he in disguising his irritation with the "lunatic" Methodists that the key figure in promoting the Haitian project in Philadelphia was none other than Bishop Richard Allen of the African Methodist Episcopal Church. Allen began corresponding with President Boyer and Secretary-General Inginac. He even sent over to Haiti one of his sons, who stayed with Inginac and was very favorably impressed.[30] Allen clearly had visions of planting AME mission stations in Haiti. He eventually licensed two men to preach to the settlers and presumably to any Haitians who cared to come to their meetings for worship.[31] He also started recruiting emigrants.

James Forten may well have been invited to the meeting Richard Allen called at his house on Spruce Street on June 29 to discuss the Haitian plan. Allen drew together "a number of People of Color, from the different Churches." There was "considerable discussion," but eventually it was agreed to appoint a committee "to take into consideration the propriety of calling a public meeting." The committee met and organized a meeting at Mother Bethel for the evening of July 6.[32]

If Forten was not present at the preliminary discussions, he surely attended the Bethel meeting. After all, Haitian emigration had become a topic of general conversation in the black community. The Bethel meeting also harked back to the rallies against African colonization Forten had chaired in the late 1810s. However, this meeting was firmly under Richard Allen's control. It was well attended. Those present heard secretary Francis Webb read the correspondence between Dewey and Boyer, Boyer's instructions to Granville, and a letter from Thomas Paul, Prince Saunders's friend, who had visited to Haiti. After that, it was resolved that "the emigration to . . . Hayti will be more advantageous to us than to the Colony in Africa." A twenty-person committee was appointed "to devise . . . such measures as shall . . . be deemed most expedient for the promotion of the above object." By the time the committee met at Mother Bethel three days later a note of caution had crept into the proceedings. It was decided to wait to do anything further "until Citizen Granville returns"—he had gone to New York—"or until we get further information to act upon."[33]

Within weeks the Philadelphians felt they did indeed have enough information to proceed. Possibly the fact that the hated American Colonization Society had disowned Dewey and denounced the Haitian plan as a threat to its African colony made it seem attractive.[34] If the ACS disapproved, perhaps the scheme had something to commend it. On August 13, eighteen "weighty men" in the African-American community came together to form the Haytien Emigration Society of Philadelphia. The president was Richard Allen, and serving on the Board of Managers was none other than James Forten.[35]

The society quickly set about its work. "An office to receive applications, and to aid the emigrants to embark, was immediately opened."[36] The managers undertook to inspect every ship before it left and make certain the passengers had all they needed for the voyage. Forten and his colleagues also put together a pamphlet explaining in detail the terms under which people could settle in Haiti. As leading members of the black community, they threw their weight behind the scheme. They knew "from bitter experience" how limited the opportunities for people of color were in the United States. They insisted: "We are your brethren in colour and degradation; and it gives us a peculiar delight to assist a brother to leave a country, where it is but too certain the coloured man can never enjoy his rights."[37] They dismissed reports that some of those who had already made their way to Haiti were unhappy and wanted to return home. "We would remind our brethren, that as we have long been the victims of oppression . . . we ought to put little confidence in evil reports, which are circulated by people inimical to our welfare." They discounted rumors of an imminent French invasion of Haiti, but contended that even if the rumors were well founded, that "should not deter our going." Haiti was "the very sun of our hopes" and American people of color had a duty to fight to defend the one and only black republic in the New World.[38]

Jonathas Granville had obviously won over the Philadelphians. He met with a similar degree of success when he took his message to New York. The Haitian project proved "very popular" with New Yorkers in general and won the resounding approval of "the most respectable part" of the city's black population. Two of James Forten's friends, Samuel Cornish and Peter Williams, Jr., were especially supportive, and Williams actually embarked on a fact-finding mission to Haiti.[39] Eventually, with the help of people of color and his various white supporters, Granville spread the word about Haitian resettlement as far south as Baltimore, as far north as Boston, and as far west as Indiana.[40]

Determining just how many people took up President Boyer's invitation is not easy. Inginac spoke of 6,000 whose passages had been paid for by his government. Other sources put the total exodus at between 8,000 and 13,000.[41] As for how many of the total were Philadelphians, here one is on even shakier ground. In August 1824 Richard Allen wrote Boyer to inform him that hundreds of "respectable and hard-working" people of color in Philadelphia were ready to leave.[42] The first ship, the *Charlotte Corday*, sailed on August 23 with about thirty families on board. When Jonathas Granville and Loring D. Dewey left Philadelphia on the brig *Four Sons* just before Christmas, "a large number of emigrants" left with them. By the spring of 1825 a total of twenty vessels had left and two more were making ready to sail.[43] Of course, it is possible that not all those who left from Philadelphia were Philadelphians. The port may have been the point of embarkation for people from Maryland, Delaware, and New Jersey.

And what was James Forten's response to all of this activity? It was very positive. Not only did he agree to serve as one of the managers of the Haytien Emigration Society but he gave the scheme his heartfelt endorsement. When young Mr. Cowles called on him toward the end of 1824 to solicit his support for the American Colonization Society, he found Forten implacably opposed to African emigration, but very favorably inclined toward Haiti. "He thinks he sees in the great men of Hayti the deliverers and the avengers of his race. He sees in San Dom[ingo] . . . a refuge either already provided or soon to be set open for those who wish to fly." But Forten himself had no intention of going anywhere. Cowles noted: "[H]e seems to have a stern satisfaction in being w[h]ere he is and as he is."[44]

James Forten knew many of those who had opted to seek a new home in Haiti. There was ex-slave Belfast Burton, a man of considerable influence in the community and a much-respected healer. Burton wrote back to let his old friends know he was well pleased with his new situation.[45] Oysterman John Summersett, one of the managers of the Haytien Emigration Society and a friend of Forten's from the Augustine Education Society, also opted to emigrate. He reported that the Haitians had received him and his companions "more like brothers than strangers." In his opinion, "no African of candid or industrious habits can deny this being the happy land of African liberty."[46]

Two of Forten's apprentices left, one for Cap-Haïtien and the other for Port au Prince. Both did well and neither was inclined to return to Philadelphia.[47] Other men of color skilled in the maritime trades decided to take up President Boyer's invitation. In fact, Boyer had instructed Granville to do everything he could to make emigration especially attractive to them. He had plans to establish a dockyard at Samaná, in what is now the Dominican Republic, and he needed artisans who could operate it. Granville was to send to Samaná

> forty artizans of African blood, such as carpenters, wood-sawyers, blacksmiths, caulkers, rope-makers, sail-makers, &c., who would be capable of working in a timber-yard, at small vessels for cruising on the coasts of the country, which vessels will be bought from them by [the] Government.

Granville reported back that he had been able to find all forty in Philadelphia.[48] His success must have denuded the wharves, at least temporarily, of skilled black craftsmen—and provided James Forten with a host of correspondents who could keep him apprised of conditions in Haiti.[49]

There was also a family connection, for among the emigrants was Charlotte Forten's younger brother, Charles Vandine. Although he may have learned the sailmaker's trade in his brother-in-law's loft and worked for him over the years, he also signed on from time to time as a sailor. In fact, twenty-four-year-old Charles had just returned from a voyage to Liverpool on the *Algonquin* in the autumn of 1824 when he made his decision to go to Haiti. He had been entered on the *Algonquin's* crew list as a dark-complexioned white man, but Vandine had no intention of trying to "pass." However whites saw him, he regarded himself as a man of color, and Haiti as a land that offered him more than he could ever hope to find in the United States. When Loring D. Dewey met Charles Vandine in Cap-Haïtien in February 1825, Vandine "informed

[him] . . . that his situation was far better than it could have been at this time in America."[50] Vandine eventually left Cap-Haïtien for Port au Prince, and it was there that he raised a family, including a daughter whom he named for his sister back in Philadelphia.[51]

In time President Boyer rethought his generous invitation. He alleged that emigrants and ships' captains were conspiring to defraud his government. People were arriving with no intention of staying, getting their passages paid for, splitting the money with the captain of their ship, and heading straight back to the United States. To put a stop to that, Boyer ended the system of assisted passages.[52] He also discovered that the Americans were less tractable than he had supposed. Many of them were abandoning the countryside for the towns. Boyer and his advisers had envisaged them working as farmers or farm laborers, not swelling the ranks of the urban unemployed. More to the point, Boyer had learned that Dewey had been disowned by the ACS. He no longer had any influential white friends who might help Haiti gain the recognition of the United States. The emigration scheme had been a waste of time and money, at least as far as Boyer's long-range goals were concerned.

If Boyer was disappointed, so were some of the settlers. To begin with, Haiti was hardly the prosperous land of liberty they had heard described. Decades of warfare had taken their toll. Plantations had been neglected, many towns were in ruins, and the infrastructure (such as it was) left much to be desired. As for the promise of equality and brotherhood, the Americans soon discovered that to be welcomed into the upper echelons of Haitian society it was necessary to have money and education. It also helped to be light-skinned. Boyer and the rest of the Haitian elite were of European as well as African ancestry. They scorned the masses of darker-skinned Haitians and seldom admitted to their ranks anyone who could not claim at least a few white forebears. The Haitians might have broken the shackles of slavery, but they had not been able to create a society in which equality of opportunity prevailed.[53]

Something of the plight of the American settlers was captured by the nineteenth-century Haitian writer Beaubrun Ardouin. He described how they found themselves in the midst of "a people whose language they could not understand . . . and on whose faces they saw mocking smiles, in spite of all the good will they pledged them."[54] As for participating in the political process, they were soon disabused of that notion. A British observer, Charles Mackenzie, admittedly no friend of the Haitians, recounted how the Americans had tried to run one of their number in a local election. On polling day they "proceeded in a body" to the polling place. Once there, "they were entered in at one door and civilly handed out of the opposite one, without having been allowed a solitary vote."[55] Relegated to the masses of the rural poor and despised as "foreigners" when they had hoped to be received as brothers and sisters, several thousand gave up in disgust and headed back to the United States. They returned to a setting that, for all its evils, was at least familiar.

Although he might not continue to advocate mass emigration to Haiti, James Forten maintained an active interest in Haitian affairs for the remainder of his life and got news of developments in Haiti through his network of acquaintances. Robert Douglass, Jr., the son of his old friends Grace and Robert Douglass, went to Haiti in the 1830s. He spent a year and a half traveling across the island, painting, meeting people, and sight-seeing. His reports to friends and family back home were very enthusiastic.[56] There were reports from the craftsmen who had gone to Samaná—men Forten knew from the shipyards, the rigging lofts, the rope walks, and the sail lofts along the Delaware. There were his two apprentices. There was his wife's brother. Perhaps Forten even heard occasionally from Prince Saunders, who returned to Haiti and ended his days in Port au Prince.[57]

Haiti had a significance for James Forten that nothing could efface. The reality of life on Haiti might not be all he had been led to believe, but the image of an independent republic created out of a massive uprising against slavery and governed by men of African descent had a powerful hold on his imagination. By the late 1820s Forten was convinced America's free people of color must stay in the land of their birth, whatever the personal costs, but to denounce Haiti and all that it stood for was another matter entirely. Haiti might not be the land of African brotherhood he had once hoped it would be, but it lived on in his consciousness as proof "that his people would become a great nation." And if "African brotherhood" was a slippery and elusive concept when it came to unifying African Americans and Haitians, James Forten knew it could be just as elusive much closer to home.

EVERY SUNDAY, COME rain or shine, James and Charlotte Forten marshaled the members of their extended family and set off to walk the half-dozen blocks from their home on Third and Lombard to St. Thomas's African Episcopal Church on Fifth and Adelphi. Pausing outside the church for a few moments to greet friends and acquaintances from across the city, they eventually made their way inside and took their places in the family pew close to the pulpit. Surrounded by their children, their servants, half a dozen of James's apprentices, and the occasional visitor, they settled down to await the solemn procession to the altar of minister and acolytes and the call to worship. St. Thomas's was where the Fortens belonged. It was where James and Charlotte had received adult baptism and where they had been married. Most of their children had been christened there. In time Charlotte and three of her daughters, Margaretta, Harriet, and Sarah, would be confirmed there.[58] Another daughter, little Charlotte, lay buried in the churchyard, close to her paternal grandmother. As for James Forten, he was a trustee of the church school and a founding member of the African Friendly Society of St. Thomas.[59] For the Fortens, and for many of their friends, St. Thomas's was more than just the place where they gathered on Sunday mornings. In a very real sense it was a vital center, a place of faith, of

rejoicing, and of remembrance. It would continue to be so for James and Charlotte Forten and their children for decades to come.

After his defeat in the matter of an assistant minister back in 1810, James
Forten had apparently never considered selling his pew, withdrawing from St.
Thomas's, and going off to join Bishop Allen at Mother Bethel or his good friend
John Gloucester at First African Presbyterian. Although he and his band of supporters had been outmaneuvered in their bid to foist Alexander Cook Summers
on the congregation, Forten remained steadfast in his commitment to St.
Thomas's. Others had drifted away. Robert Douglass had transferred his allegiance to First African Presbyterian in the wake of the Summers affair. Two
members of the group had died. Shandy Yard had left Philadelphia.[60] One or
two of the others had abandoned St. Thomas's—but not James Forten. St.
Thomas's was his church and he refused to let this one setback drive him away. If
erstwhile friends looked coldly upon him for a while and criticized him as high-
handed and interfering, so be it. For several years he was denied a place on the
vestry—or perhaps he chose to remain aloof. However, on Easter Monday 1817
his name appeared once more on the list of candidates for the vestry and he
returned to his former position of influence in church affairs.[61] Either the unfortunate matter of Summers had receded into the background, or his fellow church
members had concluded it was unwise and short-sighted to overlook the talents
of one of the wealthiest and best-connected men in the congregation.

As they had done back before the Summers episode, Forten's colleagues
on the vestry valued his ability to take care of business. That was evident in the
assignments they gave him. In August 1817 he helped settle the books of
churchwarden Joseph Randolph. When it became painfully obvious Randolph
had played fast and loose with church funds, Forten took a hand in the distasteful task of suing him.[62] In September he was on a committee "to attend the
Sale of the Estate of . . . John M[ades] Elliott," a longtime member of St.
Thomas's who had remembered the church in his will, "and also to attend the
Recorders Office and therein make necessary inquiries Most advantageous to
the Church."[63] That same month Forten was one of several vestrymen appointed "to draw up ways and Means of giting in the Monies due St. Thomas's
Church." They conducted "a full & deliberate investigation" and concluded
that the church was in a "Critical Situation." They urged the summoning of all
the members to a meeting so they could "lay a Statement of the whole Debts &
Credits before them." The following January, Forten addressed the congregation on the extent of the crisis. He also helped draft a report on the need for
prompt payment of pew rents. Those more than a year delinquent would be
given six months to pay, after which time their pews would be sold. It eventually became necessary to adopt even more stringent measures. Not only would
there be a late fee but delinquents would also find themselves barred from
voting in church elections.[64] Of course, parting church members from their
money did not necessarily make one popular, but it was something that had to

be done for the good of the congregation. In matters of business James Forten had been obliged to take people to court before now. He would not shrink from doing his duty by his church. He would enforce the rules without fear or favor.

James Forten was fully aware that the church needed men of wealth and probity to support it. People must meet their obligations, and he led by example, willing to pledge his own money and his reputation to help St. Thomas's. In May 1819 a committee of the vestry was appointed to wait on him in the matter of a bond for treasurer William Thomas.[65] The following year, when his old friend Joseph Cassey was chosen to serve as Treasurer, Forten pledged himself in the amount of $1,000 to guarantee Cassey's faithful performance of his office.[66]

Still unresolved in all of this, though, was the question of a suitable successor for Absalom Jones. The congregation voted at various times to provide him with assistants of one kind or another. On February 7, 1818, for example, James Forten was directed to inform oysterman and longtime church member Cato Collins that he had been selected to become a lay reader.[67] But what would happen when Rev. Jones died or became too feeble to carry out his duties?

On Friday, February 13, 1818, James Forten received an urgent summons to an emergency meeting of the vestry. Absalom Jones had succumbed to typhus earlier that day.[68] Forten closed his sail loft on the following Monday afternoon and took his place in the solemn procession from the parsonage on Powell Street to St. Thomas's Church. Absalom Jones's funeral was attended by "a considerable number of the Clergy, and other respectable white inhabitants, and by an immense concourse of people of colour." The service was conducted by Bishop William White, the man who had ordained Jones to the priesthood.[69]

The church got by for several months with the help of lay readers and sympathetic white clergy while the search began for a new minister. By year's end there was agreement. On December 16, James Forten was one of five vestrymen appointed "to Wait upon . . . Mr. Prince Saunders . . . to ascertain from him Whether he will . . . Serve the Congregation of St. Thomas's Church as a Reader or Minister." The eloquent and erudite Saunders, known to some in the community by repute long before he came to Philadelphia, had won over not just Forten but the majority of the members of St. Thomas's. He accepted the invitation, promising to serve the congregation to the best of his ability. Presumably he envisaged a brief stint as lay reader, after which he would move rapidly to deacon and then receive ordination into the priesthood. Forten and the other members of the committee reported that they had scrutinized his credentials and they were authorized by the vestry "to lay them before the Congregation."[70]

Despite the optimism of Saunders and his supporters, things moved slowly. Not until the following June was it reported that a committee composed of vestrymen and members of the congregation had been formed to call him to be a lay reader. There had been a meeting on May 23 at which one vestryman reported "he saw [a] great disposition . . . highly favourable" to Saunders, "and had it not been for two persons who interrupted them a Committee would have been appointed."[71] Who voiced opposition and why is unclear. What is clear is that one of Saunders's most vocal supporters was James Forten.

More trouble lay ahead for Saunders when he inadvertently violated one of St. Thomas's traditions. On October 20, 1819, the vestry reported: "A Note Came . . . this Evening from Mr. Prince Saunders appologizing . . . [for] the empropriety of . . . introducing the Music in to St. Thomas Church on the 12th inst." His apology was accepted, although there is nothing to indicate the precise nature of his offense. Did he incorporate into the service music many considered secular and "ungodly"? Did he have parts of the liturgy sung that had previously been spoken, and thus lay himself open to the charge of having "high church" or even "Papist" leanings? Whatever he did, he weathered that particular storm and on May 13, 1820, authorization was finally given "to lay Prince Saunders, before the Congregation . . . to see whether or not they would Elect Him as their Minister."[72]

The vestry went ahead and consulted lawyer Richard Peters, Jr. about the procedure for choosing a minister, but then further trouble arose. On July 13 the vestry reported the receipt of a letter from Bishop White "to Say that thear was a Certain Charge brought against Prince Saunders While he was in H[a]yti." Someone had informed the bishop of Henri Christophe's allegations that Saunders had exceeded his authority and had defrauded the Haitian government. "[U]nder the present existing Circumstance"—the chaotic state of affairs on Haiti—"there has been nothing as yet to Clearly Substantiate Said Charge, nor has Mr. Saunders himself been able to give that general Satisfaction necessary to Clear up the Charge." Reportedly the charge, which was of a "serious nature," had been in circulation for twelve months. There was "Considerable discussion" among the vestrymen. Things had reached an impasse when, quite unexpectedly, "Mr. James Forten presented Several Letters to the Vestry[;] one of them was purported to have been from Mr. Clarkson of London." Nothing in the vestry minutes explains precisely what the letters were or how they had come into Forten's hands. Perhaps they were character references Saunders did not feel it appropriate to present on his own behalf, or perhaps the well-connected Forten had been in touch with white abolitionists in Britain. They did Saunders no good, anyway. They were "severally Read but nothing in either of Said Letters was Sufficient to Remove" the charges "from the minds of the present Vestry."[73] Saunders left for Haiti several weeks later and the search for a successor to Absalom Jones began anew.

After Saunders disappeared from the scene, two rival candidates took his place. One very obviously had the support of James Forten, for he was none other than Forten's close friend and collaborator, Russell Parrott. Parrott, "a regular communicant, and a very talented young man," got the approval of the vestry on January 28, 1822. However, the vote was split and it was only with the chairman using his casting vote that Parrott and his supporters prevailed. The following month Bishop White licensed him as a lay reader. "But this selection failed to give the general satisfaction to the congregation desired," and at their April 20 meeting the vestry released him from any obligations.[74] Even while Parrott's nomination was before the vestry, a large faction of the congregation was agitating for the appointment of another man.

Parrott's rival was Jacob Oson, a man almost thirty years his senior. A casual reference to Oson's having "spent the hot season in some of the most unhealthy of the West Indies islands" suggests he may have been a native of the Caribbean, but he was living in New Haven, Connecticut, by 1805.[75] Although not as well-read as Parrott, Oson was a man of no mean accomplishments, as evidenced by his 1817 oration, *A Search for Truth; or, An Inquiry for the Origin of the African Nation*, which he delivered to receptive audiences in a number of communities. He operated a school in New Haven, studied theology under Rev. Harry Croswell at New Haven's Trinity Church, and, so Croswell reported, had for many years desired ordination.[76] Croswell was impressed with Oson's piety and his intellectual abilities and recommended him for the Philadelphia appointment. He was invited to Philadelphia and interviewed, and on October 23, 1821, the "male part of the congregation of St. Thomas' Church" met "for the purpose of considering the propriety of calling Mr. Jacob Oson to the ministry." Letters of recommendation were read, among them one from Bishop White, and it was "on motion Resolved that Mr. Jacob Oson be taken for a candidate for . . . holy orders and handed over to the ordaining committee."[77]

Even though Parrott seemed willing to bow out gracefully, things did not go smoothly for Oson. On December 29, 1821, his supporters met at the home of hatter Tobias Barclay to draft a petition to Bishop White. "[A]ccording to the Resolve of the Congregation," the members of "the Committee" had been to see Jackson Kemper, the white minister who had oversight of St. Thomas's, and raised the matter of Oson's appointment. They were disturbed about the question of the appointment "not being layd before the . . . ordaining Committee as the Congregation Expected." Kemper had told them "that it was for want of one more Signer to his Credentials."[78] Could Bishop White help them?

They explained to the bishop that trouble had arisen at St. Thomas's after the death of "their beloved Pastor," Absalom Jones. Since his passing, they had "been without the advantage of a regular Minister," and "the Congregation has . . . suffered a decline." They feared that "unless some Minister be established . . . the members will become scattered even more wide than at present." They were ready to defer to the bishop on the matter of "the qualifications or fitness of a person for their Pastor," but they drew his attention to Oson, "a descendant of the African race." They praised his integrity, his zeal "in the Cause of his Heavenly Master," and his "labours for the Welfare of the immortal Souls of his fellowmen." There had been criticism of his "want of a Classical or sufficient education," but "with all diffidence and humility," they contended that, "being themselves generally illiterate it is their opinion with unwearied zeal and steadfast Faith and Piety his knowledge of the world's learning will be equal to expound . . . the plain truths of the Gospel."[79] This was a less-than-subtle swipe at Prince Saunders, Russell Parrott, and the church members such as Forten who had supported them. In a tussle between piety and learning, Oson's friends backed piety. Forten would doubtless have answered that he required of his minister piety *and* learning. Indeed, could a man who took as one of his heroes that paragon of holiness and intellectual endeavor St. Augustine be content with anything less?

In all, eighty-eight male members of St. Thomas's signed the petition to Bishop White. Some were laborers, others were porters or sailors. A few were more prosperous. Moses Anderson was a sailmaker, while John Bowers was a clothier, James Johnson a cabinet-maker, Matthew Black a brassfounder, John Jematrice a hairdresser, and Plin Clover a blacksmith.[80] Generally, though, they had less education than Forten and his friends. Over one third signed with an X, and many who signed their names did so in a manner that suggests they were barely literate. Few could match Forten's orthographical flourishes.

It is revealing to see who did not sign. Absent were the names of prominent members of the church such as John P. Burr, Solomon Clarkson, James Cornish, Robert C. Gordon, and (not surprisingly) Russell Parrott and James Forten. If Forten and his friends were uneasy about Oson's educational background, they were supported by Jackson Kemper. He was reluctant to proceed because of a letter he had received from Connecticut Bishop Thomas C. Brownell stating that Oson "does not possess sufficient talents and information for the Society in Philadelphia."[81] Rev. Croswell rallied to the defense of his friend, endorsing him once more and sending along a testimonial from the leading men of New Haven as regards the excellence of his character. It did no good. On February 14, 1822, Croswell noted the receipt of "a long letter and documents" from Kemper, "giving the reasons why Jacob Oson ought not to be settled over the African Church—that is, his want of education." Croswell wrote yet again to Kemper, but to no avail. Oson did not get the appointment.[82]

With Oson gone, James Forten could have mounted a new offensive to get Russell Parrott into the pulpit, but he must have known it would be useless. Parrott's health was failing. Forten had lost too many friends to tuberculosis not to know what Parrott's rattling cough, his shortness of breath, and his thin face and frame meant. When Russell Parrott died at age thirty-three on September 3, 1824, Forten mourned him as he would have done a son or a younger brother. The two had worked tirelessly on so many issues, from promoting Paul Cuffe's emigration plans to battling the American Colonization Society, from rallying black men to the common defense during the War of 1812 to promoting schools for African-American children. Forten was probably the unnamed "colored man" who penned the tribute to Parrott that appeared in

Poulson's American Daily Advertiser. The writer eulogized Parrott as a man who had "possessed all those traits of character, which render an object estimable in the eye of wisdom and goodness." Talented and selfless, he had devoted himself to the well-being of his community, "and had it pleased Heaven to spare his life, he would . . . have entered upon the functions of the Gospel ministry." James Forten undoubtedly did everything in his power to help Sarah Parrott and her two children.[83] With Russell Parrott's passing had died, at least for the time being, Forten's best hope of seeing a learned and pious man of color occupy the pulpit at St. Thomas's.

Things went from bad to worse. No suitable candidates for the ministry stepped forward. The whole business of the Oson appointment was rehashed and there were recriminations on both sides. Helping to keep things in a state of turmoil was someone James Forten knew only too well. "Captain" Jonathan Tudas, who claimed the credit for having mobilized the African-American "pioneers" back in 1814, relished causing trouble. Tumults and quarrels seemed to follow him wherever he went. Rather unwisely, Tudas made trouble at Mother Bethel in 1823, and the supporters of Bishop Allen, whom he had had the temerity to malign, went after him. Tudas, they declared, was a menace to good order. When he had belonged to St. Thomas's he had, with "the help of others managed to keep the church in confusion for years," requiring the intervention of the state supreme court.[84] The precise nature of the trouble he caused is not clear, and the surviving Pennsylvania Supreme Court records contain no mention of a case involving St. Thomas's, but there *was* a great deal of acrimony, and someone like Tudas could well have helped things along.

Racial perceptions may have combined with intellectual attainments and the machinations of "Captain" Tudas to keep the congregation of St. Thomas's in a state of turmoil. In a letter written some six and a half years after the dispute over Oson, Bishop White observed: "There are Fueds among them [black Episcopalians]; & it has been said, that one cause is a Jealousy entertained by the Blacks, against some of the mixed Breed, who have received a better Education, & are accused of taking too much on themselves on that Account."[85] While blacks and mulattoes may have aligned themselves against one another at St. Thomas's, in the final analysis ancestry and phenotype seem to have been less important than sharp differences over the nature of worship and the desirability of an educated ministry. Evidently, one faction was opting for emotionalism and another for a more restrained form of piety in keeping with mainstream Episcopal practice. Those fundamental disagreements about faith and practice were not easily resolved, and they would beset other churches besides St. Thomas's.[86]

Despite the factionalism that threatened at times to destroy the church, James Forten continued to be involved in its communal life. When the Sons of St. Thomas was incorporated in 1829, his name appeared on the list of members. True, the society was for men between the ages of twenty-one and forty-five, and Forten was in his early sixties, but ex-sailor Anthony Cain, the vice-president (and one of the signers of the Oson petition), was a year or two older than Forten. The society was founded to do more than help its members and their families in times of need. It was to "more effectually unite in the bonds of peace and brotherly communion its members, [and] assist in the extension of the cause of religion and morality and good feeling among our color."[87] Those were goals Forten had long espoused, but "good feeling" and "brotherly communion" were difficult to achieve after all the wrangling. Forten's name was noticeably absent from the roster of vestrymen for a decade after the Oson dispute.[88]

With no suitable African-American candidate for ordination presenting himself after the departure of Jacob Oson and the death of Russell Parrott, Bishop White had no alternative but to name a white clergyman to take charge of St. Thomas's, at least on a temporary basis. In 1827 a South Carolinian, Peter Van Pelt, began conducting services at the church. He was obliged to report that the absence of a minister had taken a heavy toll on membership. From 400 or 500 the number of communicants had dwindled to sixty-five.[89] Van Pelt's tenure saw a marked improvement. Some erstwhile members returned and the church attracted some new members. Van Pelt was reportedly well liked by the congregation, and he left in 1830 not because of any unrest at the church—his parishioners sincerely regretted his departure—but to take up the post of secretary of the Domestic and Foreign Missionary Society.[90]

In 1831 the church was put under the care of another white man, Jacob M. Douglass. Like Van Pelt, he established a good rapport with the congregation. He began a weekly evening lecture series and showed a degree of sensitivity to the concerns of church members. In 1834, for instance, he reported he had "not made the collections recommended by the convention, as the major part of the congregation . . . are far from being wealthy, and . . . they esteem it their duty to contribute primarily to the support of their own poor."[91]

Well liked and sympathetic though Van Pelt and his successor were, they were no substitute for a fully qualified African-American incumbent, and James Forten never abandoned hope of getting the right candidate. At long last his faith was rewarded. In 1833 the members of St. Thomas found the man they were looking for. Born free in Baltimore in 1805, William Douglass was "of unmixed [African] blood." Educated by black emigrationist Daniel Coker, and proficient in Greek, Latin, and Hebrew, he was the equal of any white seminary graduate. He was also well connected socially, having married the daughter of one of Baltimore's wealthiest men of color, Hezekiah Grice.[92] Douglass was a minister in the African Methodist Episcopal church when he came to Philadelphia in 1833 to attend the annual black national convention. He attracted the attention of two of St. Thomas's most prominent members, James Needham and Robert C. Gordon. They got together with John Bowers, John L. Hart, and James Forten to ask Douglass to abandon his AME congregation in Baltimore and seek ordination as an Episcopal priest. Douglass readily agreed, moved his family to Philadelphia, and embarked on a year-long study of the Episcopal liturgy.[93]

Here, at long last, was a worthy successor to Absalom Jones, a man who rivaled Saunders and Parrott in learning. James Forten did everything in his power to advance Douglass's candidacy. And now that he was back on the vestry after a decade-long absence, he was in an excellent position to do so. On November 18, 1835, he and his fellow vestrymen reported to "the Standing Committee of the Diocese of Pennsylvania" that they had been acquainted with Douglass for seventeen months, during which time he "hath lived piously, soberly and honestly; and hath not . . . written, taught, or held any thing contrary to the doctrine or discipline of the Protestant Episcopal church."[94] In 1835 Bishop Henry Onderdonk, assistant bishop of the diocese, reported that William Douglass, deacon, had taken charge of St. Thomas's. He ordained him to the priesthood on February 14, 1836, observing: "I take the opportunity of recording my very favourable estimation of his highly respectable intellect, and most amiable qualities. . . . He ministers to a congregation at unity in itself, much attached to him."[95]

At long last James Forten had the candidate of his choice in the pulpit of St. Thomas's. William Douglass prized learning and was a model of decorum. St. Thomas's was a byword for refinement and dignity, its minister a truly learned man, well able to take part in theological debates with his white peers. In 1839 an English visitor to Philadelphia, George Combe, attended Sunday service at St. Thomas's and was impressed: "The church was commodious and comfortable, and the congregation respectable in their appearance." Combe judged the sermon equal to that he would hear in a white church and he found "the whole demeanour of the congregation . . . becoming and devout."[96] It was an inescapable fact, though, that during the lengthy struggle over the choice of a minister many of the men and women who had once occupied the pews at St. Thomas's with James and Charlotte Forten had forsaken the church for other congregations. St. Thomas's was well on its way to becoming the bastion of genteel piety that W. E. B. DuBois knew in the waning years of the nineteenth century when he wrote his classic study, *The Philadelphia Negro*.[97] As William Douglass conceded in his history of the church, "It is not the boast of St. Thomas, that the mass of our people has . . . been won to her standard. Yet it cannot be . . . denied, that she has exerted a powerful influence for good." His church, he was proud to say, had as its hallmarks "taste, order and intelligence."[98]

LONG BEFORE THE troubles that beset his church, James Forten had learned the hard lesson that one could not please everyone all the time. Doing for his community what he sincerely felt needed to be done sometimes earned him harsh criticism. As a man of influence, he had to make decisions that he knew full well would anger and alienate certain individuals. He might even be forced to do what he felt instinctively was expedient, even if it violated his most cherished principles. With racial tensions rising in Philadelphia in the aftermath of the War of 1812, he had tough choices to make, but he never shrank from making them.

In the summer of 1818 a group of young African-American men got together for what they considered an eminently worthy purpose. They proposed to form a black fire company to be known as the African Fire Association. Fire companies existed in neighborhoods all across Philadelphia and were generally seen as worthwhile institutions in a city that lacked a professional fire-fighting force. Young white men gathered during evenings to practice extinguishing fires, keep their fire engines, ropes, hoses, and ladders in a state of readiness, and basically show themselves to be public-spirited and courageous citizens. Why, asked Derrick Johnson, Joseph Allen, and their friends, should well-conducted young men of color not emulate their white neighbors? Believing that Philadelphians, irrespective of race, would support such a selfless undertaking, the would-be firefighters began soliciting subscriptions to buy equipment.[99]

They were in for a rude awakening. Furious at what they regarded as an open assertion of equality on the part of the African-American community, the white fire companies called an emergency meeting and resolved that

> The formation of fire-engine and hose companies by persons of color will be productive of serious injury to the peace and safety of citizens in times of fire, and it is earnestly recommended to the citizens of Philadelphia to give them no support . . . as there are as many, if not more, companies already existing than are necessary at fires or are properly supported.

The first protest meeting was held on July 9. A committee was appointed to meet with authorities and a further meeting was called for July 13.[100] A slew of angry letters was sent to the press, and Mayor Wharton was forced publicly to deny allegations that he had encouraged the black firefighters.[101]

No further action was necessary on the part of the white community. James Forten and a few of the other "weighty men" in the black community acted quickly to defuse a situation they believed could all too easily lead to violence. Forten convened a meeting at the home of George Jones, Absalom Jones's nephew, on July 17, to express regret at the actions of "a few young men of colour." Although their plan to form a fire company "may have emanated from a pure and laudable desire to be of effective service," it was clearly unwise and was likely to prove detrimental to "the happiness" of the black community as a whole. In fact, as soon as they had become aware of the plan, "we made every effort to repress" it. Now, in the hope of forestalling violence, they asked the publishers of the various city newspapers to print their proceedings.[102]

Opposed by the white community and by their own elders, Johnson, Allen, and the other members of the African Fire Association had to give way. Despite their understandable frustration at the "erroneous construction put upon our late undertaking," they knew better than to try to face down the likes of James Forten.[103] Forten could breathe a sigh of relief at having dealt with this particular crisis, but it would not be long before others arose and he and the other "weighty men" in the African-American community needed to take decisive action to avert racial violence.

THE WINTER OF 1821 was an especially hard one. The Delaware was frozen over for weeks, trade literally came to a standstill, and people were thrown out of work. By the spring the almshouse was bursting at the seams.[104] Some Philadelphians threw themselves on the mercy of city authorities and begged for relief. Others set about relieving their wants by preying on their neighbors. Of course, street crime, whatever the race of the perpetrator, was hardly a new phenomenon in Philadelphia, but in late 1821 and early 1822 newspapers were having a field day reporting on black criminality. The city was gripped by panic. That there were black lawbreakers was obvious. That there were plenty of white lawbreakers was something the newspapers chose to ignore.[105]

Not unexpectedly, certain elements in the white community responded to the reports of a black crime wave with demands for swift and rigorous action. On February 16, 1822, "the young men of the City of Philadelphia" organized a meeting. Seven from each ward were chosen "as a committee of superintendance . . . to adopt such measures as they may deem expedient to suppress the alarming nightly depredations" of their black neighbors. Three were deputed to meet with the mayor to discuss tactics for suppressing black street crime.[106]

James Forten and other influential members of the African-American community were alarmed by newspaper reports of street crimes perpetrated (or allegedly perpetrated) by blacks. They knew they must act quickly or face the prospect of gangs of white men meting out their own brand of "justice." Bishop Allen took the initiative, chairing a meeting at Mother Bethel just days after the white meeting, "for the purpose of devising measures to assist the municipal authorities in suppressing the alarming excess of crime." A committee, comprising of Allen, James Forten, Robert Douglass, and other highly respectable men of color, was chosen to write a report.[107]

Their report mixed shame with reproach, class pride with calls for action. They were "Deeply impressed with sorrow for the recent depredations . . . and burdened with shame that they should have been traced to that unfortunate portion of society to which we belong." As men of color they were painfully aware that they existed "as aliens in our native country, in all respects, but in devotion to its interests." They feared the consequences of the crime wave to themselves and their community. "As men who have happiness, privileges, and reputation involved . . . we call upon the humanity of the public, not to withdraw their confidence . . . not to leave to ignominy and misery all that is honest and respectable among us." It was the same plea Allen and Jones had made back in 1793 after the yellow fever epidemic, and the same plea "A Man of Colour" had made in 1813. Their white neighbors should judge them as they themselves would wish to be judged—not as an undifferentiated mass of humanity, but as individuals, some slothful and criminally inclined, but most honest and hard-working.

Still, crime must not go unpunished, and Allen and Forten and the others were determined "to impede the march of depravity." They proposed the establishment of their own Committee of Vigilance to cooperate with the mayor and the police to suppress crime and curb the proliferation of "tippling-houses, gaming-houses, petty pawn-brokers, dance and eating-houses" where law-breakers of both races congregated.[108] Their message was clear. African Americans had no monopoly on crime and whites none on virtue. Let the law-abiding citizens band together, regardless of race, and wage war on crime.

Ironically, and quite unexpectedly, the alleged crime wave brought one fairly positive result. Back in 1818, Philadelphia had begun a public school system, to which African-Americans children were not admitted, although their parents paid taxes. Not coincidentally, it was in 1818 that James Forten and others organized the Augustine Education Society. Angered and distressed at "the formidable barriers that prejudices, powerful as they are unjust, have reared to impede our progress," they resolved that black children would have access to "all the useful and scientific branches of education," even if they had to found their own school.[109] In 1822 reformer Roberts Vaux, a champion of education, an abolitionist, and an acquaintance of Forten's, used the white public's concern over street crime to suggest that educated people of color were less prone to criminal behavior. Pressured by Vaux and the Pennsylvania Abolition Society, the city opened the first tax-supported school for black children in the old Presbyterian meeting-house on St. Mary Street.[110]

Optimistic though Forten and others in the African-American community were to begin with, the experiment did not live up to their expectations. The schools were strictly segregated, and the facilities in the African-American schools woefully deficient. Much was left to be desired regarding the quality of instruction, although there were notable exceptions. Two white teachers, James M. Bird and Maria C. Hutton, who had charge of the black public school closest to Forten's home, were highly regarded by African-American parents and praised for their devotion to their students. But even the most dedicated of teachers was limited as to what he or she could achieve in an old, overcrowded building.[111] James Forten's vision of black and white children studying side by side in the same classroom and growing up in an environment where race was irrelevant was far off indeed.

JAMES FORTEN HAD every reason to be disheartened as the years went by. Nothing, it seemed, could stem the tide of racism. In the furors over the African Fire Association and the black "crime wave," he and his allies had intervened to prevent racial violence, but they were only delaying the inevitable. Assaults by whites on their black neighbors were certainly not new. Back in 1813, in his *Letters from a Man of Colour*, Forten had taken to task drunken whites who defiled the July Fourth celebrations by driving him and other black veterans from the streets. Alcohol-induced brawling and name-calling was one thing, but organized violence was quite another, and Forten had only to look around him to realize that the Philadelphia of the 1820s was both more violent and more racially polarized than the city of his youth. Worse, white violence attracted little comment in the press, while black violence invariably raised a firestorm of protest.

In September 1824, at the very time James Forten and his friends were recruiting emigrants to go to Haiti, Philadelphia newspapers were full of reports of a "serious riot." On September 7 a black man was brought before Judge Levy on a charge that he was a runaway slave. Levy ordered him remanded in jail. En route to the Arch Street jail, the officers encountered an estimated "one hundred and fifty blacks, armed with bludgeons, who attempted a rescue." In the melee "the officers held on to their prisoner, but retreated." The mayor's court adjourned abruptly, so the magistrates, constables, and all the officers of the court could assist the sheriff's officers.[112] No wonder Haiti looked attractive to people of color who saw one of their own seized in the street for preferring liberty to enslavement and those who came to his aid arrested!

Another violent outburst perpetrated by whites just a year later brought a very different response. One Sunday in November 1825 a group of young men smoking cigars tried to enter Mother Bethel. Richard Allen's congregation never turned away white visitors, but the men were asked to extinguish their cigars before coming in to attend the service. Angry that Allen and his congregation should presume to dictate to them how they should behave, they found some way of surreptitiously putting a mixture of salt and cayenne pepper in one of the stoves in the church. Acrid smoke filled the nostrils of the worshippers. Panic ensued, and in the stampede one woman was killed and another church member severely injured.[113] Evidently no arrests were made and little, if anything, was done to track down the perpetrators.

James Forten could be in no doubt that his city was becoming a more dangerous place for men and women of color. In the mid-1820s the African-American community was rocked by news that a kidnapping ring was operating in its midst and preying on its children. Of course, abduction under cover of the 1793 Fugitive Slave Law had long been a risk any black citizen ran. No less a person than Richard Allen had been taken up as an alleged runaway on one occasion, although in his case his prominence saved him. Mariners venturing into Southern ports had also been targeted. But this time Philadelphia was the base of operations for a well-organized gang that spirited away black children and youths, ferried them to Delaware, and from there shipped them to points south. James Forten's children were not especially vulnerable, because they were not likely to be lured to some secluded spot by the offer of an hour's casual employment or a hot meal. Still, Forten and other well-to-do people of color were not deaf to the pleas of poorer parents desperate to find out what had happened to their children. They played a crucial role in alerting the mayor and the Pennsylvania Abolition Society to what was going on and in trying to bring the kidnappers to justice.[114] For anyone who needed reminding, the kidnapping scandal of the mid-1820s was yet another eloquent argument as to why free people of color must work to bring about the complete abolition of slavery. As long as slavery existed in any state in the Union, all black people were potentially valuable commodities.

THE RISING TIDE of intolerance he saw all about him could not help but make James Forten feel anxious about the future. What kind of world would his children inherit? He had put his faith in the Revolutionary ideals of liberty, equality, and brotherhood, and yet so much had happened to make him question those ideals. The vast majority of black Pennsylvanians were legally free, but the laws of the state that had made them free had not mandated equality of opportunity. And even when the law did not appear to take note of race, so many of Forten's white neighbors did. Why could they not see black citizens as they were—some well-to-do, some "middling," and all too many poor but respectable? Must everything a person of color did or said be viewed in a negative light? Were they to be denied a right to live and prosper in the nation they had been born in, the nation many of them had fought to create and defend?

Especially galling was the realization that respectability and virtue counted for nothing in the case of a man or woman of color. If, for instance, James Forten saw Edward Clay's cartoons of "Life in Philadelphia"—and he could hardly escape seeing them, for they were immensely popular—then he must have been repulsed, for the people Clay was parodying were the likes of Forten and the members of his circle. Clay's targets were men and women of color who, in his opinion, got above themselves. They paraded in fashionable clothes, held musical evenings, carried visiting cards, and aspired to a level of gentility he and his audience considered appropriate only for whites. James Forten never sought to "act white." He simply sought respect for himself, his family, and his community. Alas, he was to find that respect harder and harder to obtain with each year that passed.

What seemed on the surface a fairly trivial matter, the purchase of an organ by the members of St. Thomas's Church, brought a surprising degree of anger and frustration. By nature James Forten was not an irascible or vindictive man, but this particular episode touched a nerve. The question was a contentious one to begin with. Some members of the church disapproved of the whole idea of musical accompaniment, but Forten and his allies had prevailed. An organ was bought and installed, and none other than Forten's young ward, Ann Appo, was appointed organist. Then came the press comment. A writer for the *United States Gazette* noted that "An Organ has recently been purchased by the Vestry of St. Thomas' Church. A Colored woman . . . acts as Organist." It requires no great amount of guesswork to identify the individual who in April 1828 wrote to *Freedom's Journal* under the name "Respect." To begin with, the congregation, and not the vestry, had bought the organ. "As to the disrespectful manner in which the Organist is introduced . . . I will merely ask if it had been any other Episcopal church in this city, would he have written 'a white woman, a member of the Congregation, acts as Organist.'"[115] Did the organist's race matter, and why must a refined and accomplished African-American female be referred to as a "woman" rather than a "lady"?

Too many of Forten's contemporaries insisted that men and women of color, whatever their degree of refinement, could not and never should aspire to be "ladies" and "gentlemen." John Fanning Watson, for instance, bitterly lamented the passing of "the old days" when black Philadelphians "knew their place."

> In the olden time, dressy blacks and dandy *colour'd* beaux and belles, as we now see them issuing from their proper churches, were quite unknown. Their aspirings and little vanities have been rapidly growing. . . . Once they submitted to the appellation of servants, blacks, or negroes, but now they require to be called coloured people, and among themselves, their common call of salutation is—gentlemen and ladies. Twenty to thirty years ago, they were much humbler.[116]

To that James Forten could have replied that twenty to thirty years earlier people of color, especially the "better sort," had more white friends than they appeared to have now.

THE 1820S ENDED on an ominous note for James Forten. He saw his community under attack and he also saw it voiceless. On November 29, 1829, "a riot between blacks and whites arising out of some personal cause of quarrel in which others than the original disputants became involved took place." There is nothing to indicate that Forten's family members or any of his properties were attacked, but this was a sign of things to come. Over the next decade there would be more race riots. In every one of them whites would be the aggressors and blacks the victims.[117]

And who was there to speak up for people of color? In the face of such open hostility James Forten was well aware of the need of the African-American community for a press of its own. *Freedom's Journal* had died in the spring of 1829 with the defection of its editor to the American Colonization Society. In New York, Forten's ally, Samuel Cornish, was gamely trying to keep alive a successor, the *Rights of All*. To do so he needed subscribers in other communities besides his own. In Philadelphia Forten eagerly came to his aid. At a meeting at the Wesley Church on Lombard Street in October 1829 he was one of twenty-one "gentlemen" appointed to a committee to secure subscribers for the newspaper, which was praised as "the principle vehicle through which our rights are impartially asserted."[118] But the paper failed within a matter of weeks, its demise an ominous sign of how isolated and how vulnerable the African-American community was.

On one level, of course, James Forten knew Philadelphia's 15,500 people of color were not entirely friendless. They were linked by ties of kinship and friendship to black communities, large and small, across the country. They shared news, heard of one another's concerns, and tried to relieve one another's wants. In the decade to come James Forten and others would struggle to find ways to unite African Americans in a nationwide effort to secure freedom and equality. The 1830s would also see a host of white friends commit themselves to the antislavery cause and to the struggle for equal rights for people of color. But if he found reason to hope, James Forten would also find cause for deep anxiety during this decade. He and his community would witness an all-out assault on their freedom, their rights, and their sense of themselves as Americans. The threat would come not just from gangs of unruly whites intent on driving black people out of Philadelphia, but also from the forces of law and order, as legislators sought to reduce them to a position of powerlessness. Against this onslaught James Forten would use every tactic he could think of to assert his own rights and those of every man and woman of color, not just in Philadelphia but throughout the nation.

10

NEW FRIENDS OF FREEDOM

A S THE 1820S drew to a close, there was no respite in James Forten's war against the forces of colonization. It was obviously disheartening to him to see how many well-meaning individuals in Philadelphia's white community had been won over by the American Colonization Society's propaganda. Forten's lawyer, Richard Peters, had given the ACS his grudging support. Bishop William White, his denomination's spiritual leader in Pennsylvania, had endorsed it. Even the likes of abolitionist Roberts Vaux had been convinced. What Vaux found so repugnant in 1820 he had come to see as a necessary if regrettable "solution" to America's racial problems by 1830.[1] White churches in Philadelphia and in many other towns and cities throughout the North often dedicated their July Fourth collections to the cause or held special concerts of prayer, with donations going to advance the work of the ACS. Benevolent female Friends in Philadelphia sponsored two black women to teach at a school in Liberia, and there were similar initiatives elsewhere among other well-intentioned whites.[2] It was all very depressing to Forten and other free people of color, who were sure the ACS aimed at nothing less than their expulsion from America.

The pressure on James Forten to change his stance on colonization was unrelenting. The most influential supporter of the ACS in Philadelphia, Elliott Cresson, often called at 92 Lombard Street. As a wealthy Philadelphia gentleman whose family had been in trade in the city for several generations, he knew Forten quite well. Sometimes he brought with him other champions of colonization, such as ACS secretary Ralph R. Gurley. Forten received them with his customary politeness, but he did not change his mind, and they had to resort to publicizing the success his one-time apprentice, Francis Devany, had achieved in Liberia.

In 1830 Devany made a visit home to Philadelphia "partly on acc[oun]t of his health and partly on business." He stayed with friends just a few blocks from the Forten home.³ It is quite likely that at some point during his stay he ran across his erstwhile employer. Devany left Philadelphia for Washington, where the ACS had arranged for him to testify before a congressional committee on life in Liberia. Not surprisingly, he spoke in glowing terms of the colony and its prospects. "Being asked how much he considered himself . . . worth, he replied that he computed his property at $20,000."⁴ He had amassed far less than Forten, but he had done well and the ACS made much of his rags-to-riches story. Devany remained a thorn in James Forten's side until his death from tuberculosis in 1833 at age thirty-five.⁵

Everywhere James Forten looked he seemed to see the forces of the ACS at work, using every means at their disposal to "persuade" free men and women of color to emigrate, while saying precious little about promoting the abolition of slavery. In 1829, when the authorities in Cincinnati moved to enforce Ohio's long-neglected Black Codes, Forten was not alone in interpreting this as a manifestation of the spirit of colonization. Overnight, blacks in Cincinnati were faced with the stark alternative of posting a hefty cash bond to guarantee their "good behavior" or leaving the city. For good measure, white citizens followed up the actions of the authorities with some "persuasion" of their own, rampaging through black neighborhoods and attacking black-owned homes and businesses.⁶

If this was a tactic to get African-American residents to agree to go to Liberia, it did not succeed. Some took their chances and stayed in Cincinnati, hoping that their failure to comply with the law would be overlooked and that city officials given the task of enforcement would grow lax after the initial crackdown. Others, though, decided that they must leave, but chose as their new home Canada, not Liberia. The Wilberforce settlement in Canada West, named for the British champion of abolition William Wilberforce, attracted most of the exiles.⁷ If the leaders of the ACS were disappointed that Liberia did not gain hundreds of new settlers as a result of developments in Cincinnati, plenty of whites in that city were happy enough about the way things had worked out. As James Forten would soon learn, significant numbers of white Philadelphians felt the same way about their African-American neighbors. They did not care whether black people went to Liberia, Canada, or Haiti. They just wanted to be rid of them. Even if the ACS gained few recruits, Forten insisted that the society was ultimately responsible for the rising tide of racial hatred in the nation as a whole.

THE OHIO CRISIS was a crucial factor in convincing men of influence in African-American communities across the North and the Upper South of the need for concerted action. Somewhat surprisingly, James Forten took no part in the "undignified scramble for leadership" that preceded the first black national convention, which was ostensibly called to coordinate relief for the Ohio refugees.[8] He was as concerned as anyone about the plight of the refugees but he knew more was at work. In large part this was a tussle between black leaders in New York and those in Philadelphia to assert their right to speak for all people of African descent everywhere in America. The redoubtable Bishop Richard Allen, Forten's sometime friend and sometime adversary, knew the New Yorkers had issued circulars calling for a national assembly. Like Forten, he had probably received one, for the New York–based Wilberforce Colony Society had sent copies to "influential persons of color" in various cities. However, Allen was not about to let the New Yorkers dictate policy. He issued his own call for a convention to be held in Philadelphia.[9]

When the delegates met at Mother Bethel on September 15, 1830, Allen was firmly in control, while Forten was conspicuous by his absence.[10] Accounts of the convention written decades later assumed Forten was there. Martin R. Delany listed him as having been among the stalwarts of the convention movement, while an article in the *Anglo-African Magazine* in 1859 named "the merchant prince" as one of the "giants" of the 1830 meeting.[11] The fact remains that Forten was *not* there. He took no part as Allen set about creating a parent body, headquartered in Philadelphia, to oversee virtually every matter of importance to free people of color.[12]

Quite possibly James Forten was worried about the strong endorsement of Canadian emigration he knew would come from the convention. He was right to be concerned. Although the delegates expressed regret over the circumstances that had made it necessary for Ohio's black citizens to emigrate, they spoke of resettlement not as a response to oppression but as a chance for industrious and ambitious men and women "from our large cities" to make a new start for themselves.[13] Forten may well have feared that this signaled a resurgence of Bishop Allen's support for African colonization. After all, if Canada was a land of opportunity, might not Liberia be viewed in the same light? Only three years before, Allen had gone behind Forten's back to warn ACS supporters in Philadelphia about the anticolonization newspaper he and Samuel Cornish were trying to start. Allen had eventually issued a statement rejecting colonization, but it would be understandable if Forten suspected that the bishop and some of his allies were wavering in 1830. And as the head of the rapidly growing AME Church, Allen was someone whose opinion carried a great deal of weight in the African-American community. As the convention drew to a close and as he reflected on the situation of people of color in his own city and across the nation, James Forten had good reason to feel apprehensive.

OVER THE YEARS Forten had never refused to work with whites who shared his commitment to the elimination of slavery and its twin evil, the prejudice of caste, but by 1830 he was saddened to see how many of his old abolitionist

friends had grown lukewarm. The Pennsylvania Abolition Society was struggling gamely on, sponsoring schools, defending alleged runaways picked up on
the streets of Philadelphia by slave catchers, and trying to assist black Pennsylvanians illegally held in bondage in the South. However, the PAS had had to weather
a wave of defections in the wake of the Missouri crisis. Missouri's admission to
the Union as a slave state and the prospect of the balance between the slave states
and the free states being upset generated fierce partisan debate inside and outside
Congress in 1819 and 1820. The Missouri Compromise took a great deal of the
heat out of the rhetoric, but slavery had moved to center stage and it would not
soon disappear. Awakened to the volatile nature of the slavery question, dozens
of members had resigned from the PAS or become inactive, comforting themselves with the hope that slavery would die of its own accord in a generation or
two or—just as bad in Forten's mind—trusting to the vague promises of the ACS
that it could solve all of America's racial problems.[14] James Forten still had his
circle of white antislavery friends, most of them Quakers. Thomas Shipley, Joseph Parrish, Isaac T. Hopper, and the tireless antislavery editor Benjamin Lundy
all enjoyed his affection and his trust. James and Lucretia Mott were frequent
visitors to 92 Lombard and through them Forten and his family came to know
Sarah and Angelina Grimké, the sisters who had chosen exile from their native
South Carolina and separation from their slave-holding kin rather than continue
to lead lives of privilege based on the exploitation of slave labor. Still, in 1830
organized antislavery seemed very weak when compared with the power and
wealth ranged against it. And, of course, so many of those whites who considered
themselves abolitionists seemed reluctant to address the larger dimensions of
race in America. If Forten was occasionally frustrated and downcast, he had good
reason to be, but he was about to find a young ally who would inject new life into
the antislavery movement.

Superficially at least, James Forten had little in common with William Lloyd
Garrison. Forten was a black Philadelphian, a veteran of the Revolution. Garrison was a white New Englander four decades his junior, who had only heard
his elders talk of the Revolution. James Forten had been a leading figure in
Philadelphia's African-American community for over thirty years. Garrison
conceded that he had grown up in Newburyport, Massachusetts, oblivious to
the existence of the town's tiny African-American population and certainly
unaware of the needs and concerns of black Newburyporters. Not until he
moved to Boston had he encountered many people of color, let alone spoken
with any as friends and equals. And yet, despite all the differences in their backgrounds, James Forten and William Lloyd Garrison were drawn together as
friends and collaborators.[15]

What created a bond between the two men was a passionate commitment
to antislavery and an equally passionate hatred of the American Colonization
Society. They were also united by an intense faith in something that Forten
termed "the spirit of the times," an invisible but no less potent force that he

and Garrison, in common with many other reform-minded individuals in the era of the religious revival known as the Second Great Awakening, believed was sweeping the globe. They were sure that a great change was coming and that, sooner or later, all vestiges of oppression would be swept away on a flood tide of benevolence and brotherly love. The only question was how long they would have to wait before that day of jubilee arrived.

His friendship with Garrison was something that mattered profoundly to James Forten and cheered the last decade of his life. It was hard for Forten not to warm to a white man who confessed: "I never rise to address a colored audience, without feeling ashamed . . . of being identified with a race of men who have done you so much injustice." Here was an individual who had decided to dedicate his life to the cause so dear to Forten's heart and who was prepared to do more than mouth platitudes.[16]

When Garrison met James Forten he was feeling his way, burning with a desire to help rid America of the sin of racial oppression and trying to reach out to form not just alliances born of expediency but friendships based on mutual respect. Forten responded with his characteristic warmth and generosity. When Garrison paid him and his family a visit, Forten let him know how much they had enjoyed his company: "[S]uch meetings are cheering, they are as green spots in the journey of life."[17] He raised funds for Garrison, channeled information to him, and shared with him his hopes and fears for the future. On his deathbed James Forten would speak of his love and admiration for Garrison, and Garrison would affectionately remember the black sailmaker as someone who had helped confirm him in his mission and stood by him in his many trials.

William Lloyd Garrison was a less-than-successful printer and newspaper editor when he first met James Forten. Like Forten, he had known dire poverty in his early years, and like Forten, he had struggled against heavy odds to master a skilled trade. He had served his apprenticeship with a printer in his native Newburyport and then branched out on his own, editing a series of short-lived journals before discovering his life's work.[18]

His growing conviction that slavery was a sin that had to be eradicated without delay eventually led him into a partnership with Forten's old friend Benjamin Lundy. In fact, it was his meeting with Lundy when the Quaker editor made a trip to Boston in 1828 that converted Garrison to antislavery. It was his own reading and his deep reflections that convinced him that the kind of gradual approach to abolition championed by Lundy and many other white opponents of slavery was inherently sinful. As for colonization, although Garrison accepted an invitation to speak at an ACS fund-raiser in Boston on July 4, 1829, he was no convert to the cause. Like Lundy, he initially regarded it as an expedient, a necessary evil that might relieve the sufferings of some of those in bondage. His July Fourth speech dealt more with the horrors of slavery and racial prejudice than with the blessings of life in Liberia.[19] As his friendship with James Forten and others in the free black community grew and deepened, so did the intensity of his opposition to colonization.

In 1829 Garrison joined Lundy in Baltimore as coeditor of the *Genius of Universal Emancipation*, a paper James Forten subscribed to and the entire Forten family read. By then the young New Englander had become convinced that neither gradual abolition nor colonization was morally acceptable. He soon ran into trouble when he used the *Genius* to assail a New England shipowner who was in business with a Baltimore slave trader in the interstate transportation of slaves. Convicted of malicious libel despite the best efforts of his lawyer, and unable to pay the fine, Garrison languished in jail for a month and a half until the New York merchant and philanthropist Arthur Tappan paid the fine for him. Garrison emerged from jail more resolute than ever. He would begin his own antislavery paper and it would be more militant in tone than the *Genius*. But he would need backers.[20]

Exactly when and how Garrison met James Forten is not clear. The two may have been introduced by Robert Purvis, the young man who was courting Forten's daughter Harriet. Years later Purvis recalled that Garrison had come to visit him on his release from jail and had "unfolded to [him] his plans."[21] However, there may have been no need for an intermediary. Garrison was in Philadelphia in the late summer of 1830 to deliver a series of lectures at the Franklin Institute "to audiences consisting largely of Quakers and Negroes."[22] It is possible that James Forten attended one or more of those lectures and that a friendship was formed between him and Garrison before the younger man left to make his way back to Boston, where he planned to launch his new paper, the *Liberator*.

James Forten was one of the people Garrison wrote to when he began raising money for the new venture. His initial letter to Forten has not survived but Forten's reply has. Forten wrote on December 31, 1830, just as the first issue of the *Liberator* was about to roll off the press, to let the young editor know he would help in any way he could. *Freedom's Journal* was dead, doomed after John B. Russwurm's defection to the ACS, but this new initiative gave Forten reason to hope, despite all the setbacks the cause of abolition had encountered over the years. "[M]ay the 'Liberator' be the means of exposing, more and more, the odious system of Slavery, and of raising up friends to the oppressed and degraded People of Colour." His fellow citizens *must* see the error of their ways, and the *Liberator* would serve as a much-needed wake-up call. "Whilst . . . the spirit of Freedom is marching with rapid Strides, and causing Tyrants to tremble; may America awake from the apathy in which she has long slumbered. She must, sooner or later, fall in with the irresistible current." He sent Garrison the names and addresses of twenty-seven subscribers he had found for him in Philadelphia and a banker's draft for $54 as an advance payment for their subscriptions, money Garrison described years later as "most timely aid." Garrison published an extract from Forten's letter in the second number of the *Liberator* to refute notions of black intellectual inferiority, adding: "We are acquainted with the writer, and very proud . . . of his friendship."[23]

A few weeks later Garrison printed part of another letter "from the intelligent and highly respectable gentleman alluded to in our second number." He also expressed the hope that "our Philadelphia friend will occupy our columns as often as possible."[24] James Forten was eager to take up that invitation. The *Liberator* gave him what he had lacked since the demise of *Freedom's Journal:* a public voice.

In his second letter Forten congratulated Garrison on the success of the *Liberator* and especially on its firm stand against colonization. He pointed to the irony that "one, like myself, whose family has resided in . . . Pennsylvania ever since the great lawgiver, William Penn, came last to this state from England; and who fought for the independence of my country" was constantly being told "that Africa is my country, by some . . . whose birth-place is unknown." The man who had toyed briefly with the notion of racial separation back in 1817 now did not hesitate to declare: "To separate the blacks from the whites is as impossible as to bale out the Delaware with a bucket." He added: "When I look at this globe, containing eight or nine hundred millions of inhabitants, and see that they differ in color from the frozen to the temperate and torrid zones . . . I am astonished that any man should be so prejudiced against his fellow-man."[25]

Week after week, through the medium of the *Liberator*, James Forten, writing under his pen name of "A Colored Philadelphian," reached out to an audience of reform-minded white men and women to share with them his thoughts on the situation of people of color in America. He was also able to communicate with the thousands of African Americans who subscribed to the paper, managed to borrow a copy, or, if they could not read it themselves, had it read to them by their friends. So widespread was its influence that one did not have to be literate to have heard of the *Liberator* and know what it contained.

Eager to make contact with the African-American community, Garrison gladly published the letters and poems that his black readers sent him, and one of his most faithful correspondents was James Forten. If he wanted a forceful denunciation of slavery, a brief essay on the iniquity of prejudice, or a searing indictment of the ACS, he was sure to find what he was looking for in one or another of James Forten's communications.

On February 12, 1831, for instance, Garrison published an extract of a letter Forten had sent him a week or so earlier in which the Philadelphian dwelt on the many disabilities under which people of color labored. "That we are not treated as freemen, in any part of the United States, is certain. This usage . . . is in direct opposition to the Constitution; which positively declares, that all men are born equal, and endowed with certain inalienable rights." Prejudice kept blacks trapped in the lowliest occupations, and even then they were often passed over in favor of white immigrants.

> If a man of color has children, it is almost impossible for him to get a trade for
> them. . . . Even among laborers there is a distinction. During the late snow

storm thousands of persons were employed in cleaning the gutters, levelling the drifts, &c. Among the whole number, there was not a man of color to be seen, when hundreds of them were going about the streets with shovels in their hands, looking for work.[26]

James Forten knew of what he wrote. After his father's death, his earnings from humble chores such as shoveling snow had helped keep him and his mother and sister fed and housed. Now another generation of African Americans was unable to find even that kind of employment.[27]

Forten used Garrison's paper to pose a direct challenge to "our pretended white friends" who were so keen to send him and every other free person of color to Africa. ACS supporters insisted they were promoting colonization because, Forten wrote, "they desire to make a people of us." That assertion angered him and prompted him to issue a challenge to "those guardian angels of the people of color [to] tell me how it is that we, who were born in the same city or state with themselves, can live any longer in Africa than they?" Let the friends of colonization spend their time and money at home, educating people of color, setting aside farming land for them, and "secur[ing] to them all the rights and immunities of freemen." Then "it would soon be found . . . that they made as good citizens as the whites."[28]

An avid reader of the Philadelphia daily paper *Poulson's American Daily Advertiser*, Forten spotted an item about a New Jersey woman who had given $1,000 to the ACS. He passed it on to Garrison with a few choice comments of his own. What a pity that "this highly generous and benevolent lady" had given her money to such a cause "when objects of much greater importance could be obtained by offering a Premium to Master Mechanics . . . to take Colored Children as Apprentices." He used the occasion to tell advocates of colonization, "We ask not . . . their aid, in assisting us to emigrate. . . . [W]e are contented in the land that gave us birth." Though black men had fought and died for America's freedom, "all this appears to be forgotten now—and the descendants of these Men . . . are . . . to be removed to a distant and inhospitable Country, while the Emigrants from every other Country, are permitted to seek an asylum here from oppression."[29]

He commented on other matters as well. He had read a very angry editorial in the *Pennsylvania Inquirer* on the efforts of Garrison and some of his antislavery friends in Boston to repeal the Massachusetts law that banned interracial marriages. "The Editor says, the passage of such a Bill in this Country, and with the enlightened views which characterise the times, is to him a Mystery; but from the tenor of his remarks, he at least has not kept pace with the advancement of which he speaks."[30]

On another occasion Garrison sought opinions on what people of color wished to be called, and Forten enlightened him. A white correspondent to the *Liberator* had contended that "Negro" and "colored" were inappropriate, while "African" was clearly not right, because people of color had been born in the

United States. He had suggested "Afric-American." Garrison thought the term respectful but he wanted to hear what "our *colored* readers" thought. Forten informed him that "Afric-American" was a title "generally disliked . . . by all I have heard express an opinion on the subject."[31] As Garrison struggled to learn about the hopes and fears of men and women of color and understand how they viewed the world around them, Forten offered his new ally the benefit of his wisdom.

DESPITE THEIR VERY different backgrounds, James Forten and William Lloyd Garrison spoke the same language, a language infused with a potent mix of biblical imagery and the spirit of progress. In a speech he gave to black audiences in a number of cities from Boston to Philadelphia in 1831, Garrison boldly declared: "The signs of the times . . . show forth great and glorious . . . changes in the condition of the oppressed. . . . [T]he wave of revolution is dashing to pieces ancient and mighty empires—the hearts of tyrants are beginning to fail them for fear."[32] Forten's speeches and letters contain many of the same phrases and convey an equally powerful sense of the divine hand in human affairs. This is not to imply that, at least in regard to the nature of reform, Forten influenced Garrison's world view or vice versa. It was rather the case that two intensely religious and reflective men read the same passages from the Scriptures, thought deeply about the same issues, and reached the same conclusions.

The appearance of the *Liberator* inspired Forten to believe that change was imminent. After receiving the first two issues, he penned a letter to Garrison containing an optimistic prophesy. "The year 1831 seems to be big with great events. Mankind are becoming more enlightened, and all tyrants, and the tyrants of this country, must tremble." A few weeks later he wrote again. "I will only say . . . that the time is not far distant, when the prophecy which says, 'Ethiopia shall stretch forth her hands unto God,' will be fulfilled."[33]

Later that same year Forten told Garrison about a speech he had just read that "filled [him] with admiration." It was John Quincy Adams's July Fourth oration. It is obvious why Forten thought so highly of Adams's speech. The former president spoke with his customary eloquence about his notion of the legacy of the American Revolution. "Its burning brands have floated on the wings of the wind back to Europe . . . spreading . . . light . . . throughout the regions inhabited by civilized man." This mirrored Forten's own vision of what the Revolution had achieved and might still achieve, if only some of its "burning brands" could be wafted back to America's shores. For him, at least, the American Revolution was a revolution that was as yet incomplete.[34]

In the *Liberator* of August 20, 1831, Garrison published an especially forceful letter from Forten under the caption "Men Must Be Free." Forten had written it in response to a report about a rash of mysterious fires in Fayetteville, North Carolina.[35] He believed the fires were "a visitation from God" for the sins of the slaveholders. He had heard from a Fayetteville native of the savage beating inflicted on a free black man who had dared to joke about the fires. Was it not disgusting, Forten asked, that such a thing could happen "in this boasted land of liberty . . . but which, I am sorry to say, is the worst place for colored persons in the known world?"[36]

All of Forten's favorite themes were contained in the letter: the immortal spirit of liberty, the rejection of colonization, and devotion to a sacred cause. There were also unmistakable echoes of David Walker's *Appeal to the Coloured Citizens of the World*. Forten certainly knew of that controversial work. He had probably read it from cover to cover when it had appeared back in 1829. He might even have met Walker, for the young black North Carolinian evidently spent time in Philadelphia before deciding to make his home in Boston.[37] Although James Forten might have found in the young exile a kindred spirit, he hardly needed Walker to instruct him in the importance of winning the struggle for liberty. Now he wrote Garrison:

> When we . . . hear of almost every nation fighting for its liberty, is it to be expected that the African race will continue always in the degraded state they are now? No. The time is fast approaching when the words "Fight for liberty, or die in the attempt," will be sounded in every African ear . . . and when he will throw off his fetters, and flock to the banner . . . with the following words inscribed upon it—"Liberty or Death."[38]

That time was approaching more rapidly than James Forten could have imagined. His letter appeared in the *Liberator* on August 20, 1831. On the night of August 21, in Southampton County, Virginia, scores of slaves rose up against their masters, with every intention of winning their liberty or dying in the attempt.

In the wake of Nat Turner's bloody rampage in Virginia, James Forten sent an anxious letter to Garrison. He feared for his young friend's safety. Southern whites were panting for vengeance, insisting that Turner and his followers had been inspired to rebel after getting their hands on copies of the *Liberator* and David Walker's *Appeal*. It shocked Forten to the core that "they should still close their eyes, and seek to find the cause from without, when all the materials are so plentiful within." There was nothing that Southern whites could do to Walker, who had died of consumption the previous year, but Garrison was still very much alive.[39] A number of Southern lawmakers had placed a bounty on him, resolved at all costs to kill both the *Liberator* and its editor. Forten was not blind to the danger, "for they [the slaveholders] certainly seem to have the will, if not the power to stop the thunderings of the Liberator; which sounds so loudly in their ears, the cause of the oppressed." Though they had failed to heed the lessons of "the late tragedy," he still hoped that something good would come out of so much suffering and that people would awaken to the true cause of the rebellion. "Indeed, we live in stir[r]ing times, and every day brings news of some fresh effort for liberty, either at home or abroad—onward, onward, is indeed the watchword."[40]

WILLIAM LLOYD GARRISON was never a wealthy man. He lived frugally and did his best to increase the *Liberator*'s circulation, but financial disaster repeatedly threatened over the years. Many of his subscribers, especially those in the various African-American communities of the North, were people of modest means. Subscriptions went unpaid or had to be canceled when financial disaster struck. People often shared their copies of the paper with friends or within an organization. That was all well and good when it came to getting the word out, but it boded ill for the financial well-being of the *Liberator*.[41] When a crisis loomed, Garrison was forced to beg for help, and one of those who repeatedly came to his rescue was James Forten. If not as rich as the likes of Arthur Tappan and the New York real estate magnate Gerrit Smith, he was just as generous with the resources at his command. He never turned down a plea for money from Garrison.

In the summer of 1832, Garrison wrote Robert Purvis and his wife, Harriet Forten, to thank them for their kindness on his recent trip to Philadelphia. His letter also contained a not-so-subtle request for money. He wanted to let his partner, Isaac Knapp, run the *Liberator* for a while so he could "travel through the free States, for the purpose of vindicating the rights of the free people of color, and forming anti-slavery societies." He had talked over his plan with Arthur Tappan and Rev. Peter Williams in New York, and both had approved. Williams had promised to raise $100 for him and Garrison thought Tappan would contribute a similar amount.[42] He obviously felt confident that Purvis and his father-in-law would be as generous as the New Yorkers.

A few weeks later Garrison was forced to ask more directly for help. If he could not raise sufficient funds to pay his debts he would have no alternative but to suspend publication of the *Liberator*. Desperate, he printed up a circular and sent it to some of his richer subscribers. He admitted afterward to Robert Purvis: "It was with much delicacy of feeling . . . that we addressed our Circular to some of our Philadelphia friends, conscious of how much they had done to give stability to the Liberator." Once more they came through for him. He singled out for grateful mention "our friends . . . Forten and yourself."[43] James Forten helped him with his short-term cash-flow problems and extended substantial loans—a total of $450 in four installments between May and December of 1832—to enable him to keep the paper afloat. A far more experienced man of business than Garrison, and a great deal more organized in his commercial dealings, Forten also offered some sound advice about the best ways to market the *Liberator* in Philadelphia.[44]

Over the years James Forten gave generously to various initiatives promoted by Garrison and his allies. At the 1831 meeting of the black national convention in Philadelphia, Garrison, Arthur Tappan, and white evangelical preacher Simeon S. Jocelyn were given the floor to explain in detail their scheme for a black manual labor college to be established in New Haven, Connecticut. They reasoned that the town's "friendly, pious, generous and humane" residents would welcome another institution of educational excellence that might one day rival Yale University. Young men of color from across the United States and the West Indies would flock to the new college to learn farming and various skilled trades while at the same time acquiring a sound classical education. The plan had much to commend it. The college's graduates would be able to become self-supporting and would be examples of black intellectual ability. What was produced on the college's farm and in its workshops would be sold, which would help to keep costs low and enable students from poor families to attend the college.[45]

The delegates to the national convention heartily approved of the plan. Forten's old ally from the war against the ACS, Samuel Cornish, was appointed general agent to collect the $20,000 needed to build the college, and Arthur Tappan (who pledged $1000) was named treasurer. Provisional committees were set up in communities from Albany to Washington to raise funds. The Philadelphia committee consisted of five very successful African-American businessmen: Joseph Cassey, Robert Douglass, Sr., Richard Howell, Robert Purvis, and James Forten.[46]

It is easy to see why Forten lent his name to the undertaking. Not only had it been put forward by three white reformers he held in high regard, but it offered young African-American men precisely the kinds of opportunities he had been trying to provide over the years in his sail loft. Without the chance to learn skilled trades, people of color would continue to be at the bottom of the economic heap. Though he had pleaded again and again with whites to "establish good schools for our children as well as theirs, give them trades, and encourage them after they have become masters of their business," the white community as a whole had not responded.[47] Now it was up to black people themselves and those whites who truly wished them well to take action. The college must be built and it must succeed.

On September 5, 1831, Forten and the other members of the Philadelphia committee issued an address to their "benevolent" fellow citizens. Because the United States was an "enlightened" nation, they thought the plan for the manual labor college needed little by way of justification, "Believing that all who know the difficult admission of our youths into seminaries of learning . . . all who know the efficient influence of education in cultivating the heart and restraining the passions . . . will lend us their patronage." The project even had the endorsement of two venerable white churchmen of Forten's acquaintance, Bishop William White and Bishop Henry Onderdonk.[48]

The humanity and generosity of white Philadelphians were never put to the test. When the mayor and aldermen of New Haven learned of the plan to locate the college in their midst they organized a meeting to thwart it. Simeon S. Jocelyn, a New Haven native, fought valiantly for the college, using every argument he could think of, from civic pride to economic self-interest.[49] However, given his connections with Garrison and other antislavery radicals, and the timing—barely a month after Nat Turner's rebellion—he found few willing to listen to him.

James Forten was shocked when he read the published proceedings of the New Haven meeting. He wrote Garrison of his deep disappointment that "in that large assemblage, but one friend was to be found to stand up in our behalf; none were willing to bring odium on themselves, by taking the part of the oppressed of their own country."[50] The uproar in New Haven did not dampen Forten's enthusiasm for the idea of a manual labor college. When one was opened in upstate New York that accepted students regardless of race, he enrolled his youngest son there. And when Garrison told him of an educational initiative for young women of color, Forten willingly lent his name to it.

In 1832 white Quaker teacher Prudence Crandall provoked the wrath of her community in Canterbury, Connecticut, when she admitted the daughter of a local black farmer to her previously all-white school. The angry reaction of Canterbury's white residents prompted her to consider transforming her school into one exclusively for African-American students. She traveled to Boston to consult Garrison, who encouraged her and supplied her with introductions to various antislavery friends, among them James Forten.[51] In the spring of 1833 the *Liberator* announced that Forten would act as one of the referees for Crandall's school for "Young Ladies and little misses of color." He had no daughter of his own he could send to her school. Harriet was married, Margaretta and Sarah were too old, and Mary's health was too delicate for her parents to think of letting her leave home. But he could at least lend the young teacher his name and the weight it carried in the African-American community.[52]

Forten's name might have induced other black parents to entrust their daughters to Prudence Crandall, but it could not save her school. In the ensuing months, outrage followed outrage in Canterbury. White townspeople smashed the school's windows, polluted its well, and constantly harassed Crandall and her pupils. Crandall was eventually imprisoned for breaking a newly enacted law forbidding the education of black people from other states in Connecticut. In the summer of 1834 Forten and his family finally had the chance to meet Crandall when she came to Philadelphia to explore the prospects for opening a school for African-American pupils there. White antislavery activists Lucretia Mott and Esther Moore, both of them friends of the Fortens, were delighted. They went with Crandall to call on "our most reputable colored people, and engaged a sufficient number to warrant her beginning here," but opposition from more conservative white abolitionists in the city obliged her to give up the idea.[53]

IN THE FACE of intense opposition, James Forten, William Lloyd Garrison, and the growing numbers of antislavery radicals pressed on for change. In 1833 Forten heartily endorsed Garrison's plan to go to Britain to raise funds and to denounce the ACS. It had not escaped his attention that Elliott Cresson was touring Britain, telling antislavery sympathizers there that Liberia was the salvation of people of color. Something must be done to stop him winning new allies an ocean away. Forten let it be known that he and his friends in Philadelphia were prepared to help in any way they could.

Garrison's allies in Boston took Forten up on his pledge. In March 1833 the New England Anti-Slavery Society authorized Forten and affluent barber and moneylender Joseph Cassey to solicit funds in Philadelphia to help defray the expenses of Garrison's trip.[54] A couple of weeks later, Forten presided at a fund-raising meeting at the First African Presbyterian Church. The hundreds of black citizens who attended adopted a series of resolutions applauding the decision of the New England Anti-Slavery Society to send Garrison to Britain to speak "the truth in relation to American Slavery and its ally, the American Colonization Society." They then proceeded to take up a collection and appoint a committee to "prepare an address, expressive of our sentiments of gratitude to the philanthropists in Great Britain" for the efforts they had made toward the abolition of slavery throughout the British Empire.[55]

Forten and the members of his extended family gave generously to support Garrison's mission. They also did their best to ensure their friend's physical safety. Just before his departure, he was in Philadelphia when a warning came that he was about to be served with writs for libel in relation to the Prudence Crandall case, a ploy to detain him until he could be taken to the South to be "dealt with" by angry slaveholders.[56] His friends urged him to leave the country as soon as possible, and he shuttled between Philadelphia and New York trying desperately to find a berth on a vessel. At one point, when Garrison's enemies seemed to be closing in, Forten's son-in-law, with his carriage and team of fast horses, came to his aid. More than once Robert Purvis had driven fugitives to safety one step ahead of the slave catchers, but this was his first rescue of a white fugitive. He bundled Garrison and his luggage into the carriage and set off at breakneck speed for Trenton, New Jersey. Alas, Garrison still arrived in New York too late to secure a berth and ended up spending several days in hiding before he could set sail for Liverpool.[57]

James Forten and his family aided Garrison with everything at their disposal—money, hospitality, introductions to their friends, and their own deep affection. They also aided him with information. James Forten had a seemingly inexhaustible fund of information, all of it negative, on Liberia and the ACS. As he observed to Garrison, as one of Philadelphia's leading sailmakers, he was exceptionally well placed to know what was going on. "I am well acquainted with all the Masters of Vessels, belonging to this Port, that have been to the Coast of Africa."[58]

In the fall of 1831, Forten summarized for Garrison the contents of a letter he had just received from an unnamed "old friend" in Liberia that recounted the tragic story of the Mars family, a huge clan that had emigrated from Ohio. The friend stated that thirty-one members had died, although John B.

Russwurm, in his capacity as editor of the *Liberia Herald*, claimed that only two had succumbed.[59] Determined to undermine colonization efforts in Philadelphia, Forten, signing himself "F," copied the information and also sent it to *Poulson's American Daily Advertiser*. *Poulson's* had printed Russwurm's rosy descriptions of life in Liberia. Forten insisted, "it is right to hear both sides."[60]

ACS supporters challenged Forten on his facts, and he did admit he might have made one or two errors, but he managed to sort out the details when another friend from Liberia visited Philadelphia a few weeks later. The new arrival reported that the Mars family was from Virginia, not Ohio, and observed that Forten's informant had mistaken the name of the ship they had sailed on. However, there was no mistake when it came to their grim fate. All but two had died.[61]

James Forten had an exceptional intelligence-gathering system in Liberia and it took the ACS quite some time to figure out who was at the heart of it. By the summer of 1833 Russwurm confessed to ACS secretary Ralph R. Gurley: "I am afraid we have some of Garrison's spies in our colony." He need not have looked any further than his own business partner to find the chief spy. For months Joseph R. Dailey had been reporting on conditions in Liberia to Robert Purvis.[62] Purvis promptly handed over the letters to his father-in-law and Forten passed them on to Garrison, who selected excerpts for inclusion in the *Liberator*.

Joseph R. Dailey was someone James Forten and his extended family had known and liked for many years, and he was implicitly trusted by them. Admittedly, he had voluntarily emigrated to Liberia, something Forten felt no sensible person of color should do, but he was making amends by exposing the true state of affairs in the colony. Originally from Richmond, Virginia, Dailey had at some point relocated to Philadelphia and become a sailor. There were various ways in which Forten could have met him. Because Dailey was an Episcopalian, he probably worshipped at St. Thomas's African Episcopal Church with Forten and his family.[63] Perhaps Forten hired Dailey from time to time, as he did other sailors, to do some of the simpler sewing tasks in his sail loft. Dailey also boarded at 193 Cedar Street, just a couple of blocks from the Forten home.[64]

Eventually, Dailey moved to New York, where he found work in a merchant's countinghouse. It was there that he got his grounding in business and met John B. Russwurm. At some point in the late 1820s he began making inquiries about Liberia.[65] Emigrating in 1830 or early 1831, he became Russwurm's business partner. Although enthusiastic about Liberia to begin with, he soon changed his tune.

Dailey's accounts of life in Liberia were devastating. To begin with, he loathed the colonial agent, Dr. Joseph Mechlin, and painted him in the most unflattering terms. Dailey seethed: "Is it not murderous that a man should come 3 Thousand Miles to be free & then have his liberty abridged by another whose moral & intellectual qualifications are insignificant in the extreme?"

When he was not boiling with rage at Mechlin's villainy, he was reporting to his Philadelphia friends on the suffering and misery that pervaded the colony. "The Charleston people are dying daily." Rev. Gibbons had lost his daughter, Mr. Smith's wife was dead, and so on.[66]

Letter after letter hammered home the same message. "The withering hand of death has blasted the sanguine hopes" of so many "hardy pilgrims." Liberia was a "pestiferous Golgotha."[67] The much-vaunted Russwurm was beset by "apathy & listlessness." Dailey was gleeful about the downfall of "His Majesty the Monarch of Liberia," as he called Mechlin. According to Dailey, the ACS leadership had finally found out about his sexual liaisons with some of the female settlers and had recalled him.[68]

Dailey's letters were highly effective, but James Forten had ample proof even closer at hand of the unhealthfulness of Liberia. In 1831 the ACS acquired a schooner, the *Margaret Mercer*, and hired as her captain William Abels, someone Forten knew from the Philadelphia coasting trade. Abels commanded "a *colored crew* . . . all exceedingly well behaved—good-looking men."[69] The cook, Delaware native Robert Ayres, was a longtime resident of Philadelphia who lived with his brother, George, at 46 Lombard. Like the Fortens, both men were members of St. Thomas's Church.[70] Over the next few years Captain Abels and Robert Ayres made several voyages to Liberia. Then tragedy struck. "African fever" carried off virtually the entire crew, including Ayres and his black shipmates. Only Captain Abels made it back to Philadelphia alive.[71] Needless to say, the fate of the crew of the *Margaret Mercer* was something James Forten built into his ongoing argument about the deceptions the ACS was practicing on unsuspecting black people and benevolent whites. The ACS and its supporters had argued that their African descent made black Americans immune to African diseases. The deaths of Ayres and his shipmates proved otherwise.

Despite James Forten's best efforts, the ACS continued to find some people of color willing to emigrate and otherwise well-intentioned whites prepared to donate money to help speed them on their way. Philadelphia was a center of ACS activity in the 1830s and the site of a number of fund-raising events. For instance, on the evening of June 24, 1833, local supporters of the ACS held a great colonization meeting at the Musical Fund Hall. The accounts he read of that meeting must have distressed Forten, for men he knew and respected had taken an active part. Merchant and shipowner Thomas P. Cope presided, and Bishop William White opened the assembly with prayer. ACS secretary Ralph R. Gurley spoke, as did Robert S. Finley, the son of ACS founder Rev. Robert Finley, who insisted that the society's Southern supporters were benevolent people. James Forten was probably among the "colored gentlemen" who called on Gurley and Finley the next morning to let them know exactly what Philadelphia's people of color thought of their organization.[72]

A few weeks later Forten and his allies had another chance to make their views known. On July 10 they arranged a meeting at Benezet Hall at which members of the black community could question three returning emigrants, Messrs. Whittington, Price, and Gibbons. The three men told of mistreatment of the native peoples of Liberia by both settlers and ACS officials. They told of drunkenness and all manner of immoral behavior. They also told of sickness and death among the emigrants. All three had lost family members.[73] If anyone doubted their stories of suffering, they needed only to look at Price. He would later complain to ACS supporters that he had been used by the society's foes. "[T]wo gentlemen who have assumed the right of ruling over all the colored people of this country" had called on him shortly after his arrival in Philadelphia. He was tired and unwell after the voyage from Liberia and he had asked for some time to rest, but they had dragged him off to speak at their meeting that very day.[74] The gentlemen, one of whom was almost certainly James Forten, knew Price's gaunt and haggard appearance would speak more loudly than any words about the unhealthfulness of life in Liberia.

As JAMES FORTEN and William Lloyd Garrison were well aware, there was no shortage of literature on the merits of colonization. The ACS had its own newspaper, the *African Repository*. Each year its officers issued carefully worded reports describing the progress they had made and highlighting anything positive they could find to say about Liberia. And various supporters of the society were producing a steady stream of books and pamphlets stressing the blessings colonization was conferring on free people of color, who, so they insisted, could never truly be happy in America. In the summer of 1831, for instance, Philadelphia printer Mathew Carey published a work entitled *Letters on the Colonization Society*. It proved popular and went into several editions. Carey was the same man who had slandered the black nurses back in the yellow fever epidemic of 1793. The intervening decades had done nothing to change his views about black people. The new pamphlet contained a less-than-subtle swipe at James Forten and others of the black "better sort." Carey contended: "No merit, no services, no talents, can ever elevate the great mass of them [black people] to a level with the whites."[75] The message was clear. Black people could never succeed in America. Emigration was their only hope.

Carey's work and others like it prompted Garrison to begin putting together a rebuttal. To do so he needed detailed information about the operations of the ACS, for which he naturally turned to James Forten. Eager to help, Forten sent Garrison his copy of the latest annual report of the ACS.[76] When Garrison dashed off another request to his Philadelphia friend for material in the spring of 1832, Forten searched his files and sent whatever he could find that he thought might be of use. He urged Garrison on, writing to him that the pamphlet he was working on was all the more important at a time "when the Society is making so many converts, and its influence extending like a torrent, carr[y]ing with it not only a host of avowed enemies . . . but I am afraid some real friends, who are deceived by its specious pretences."[77]

When *Thoughts on African Colonization: or, An Impartial Exhibition of the Doctrines, Principles and Purposes of the American Colonization Society, together with the Resolutions, Addresses and Remonstrances of the Free People of Color* appeared, Forten was delighted. It not only exposed the duplicity of the ACS but also made abundantly clear how the majority of the free black community in the North and Upper South viewed colonization. No one who read Garrison's pamphlet could remain under the impression that the very people the ACS proposed to send to Africa actually wanted to go. James Forten fervently hoped it would expose "the utter inefficiency of the Society to remedy the evils of Slavery for [he] believe[d] that it is with this view that many give it their zealous support."[78]

Word of a crisis in Philadelphia soon reached Ralph R. Gurley at the ACS headquarters in Washington. "[T]he city now *floods* with [Garrison's] late *huge* pamphlet against us. . . . [T]he whole *colored* population are aroused to madness, and our *enemies* are *with* them."[79] Gurley and his allies had cause to be apprehensive. After reading in *Thoughts on African Colonization* how vehemently James Forten and others in the African-American community opposed the ACS, Arthur Tappan, who had given the organization thousands of dollars, began to rethink his generous support. Now he began to ask himself whether his money was being spent in a way that would truly benefit free people of color and bring about the end of slavery, as ACS agents had assured him it would. "[H]e visited Philadelphia, and had interviews with Mr. JAMES FORTEN, and other intelligent and influential men of color." As a result of what he saw and heard, he cut his ties to the ACS.[80] Forten was delighted. *Thoughts on African Colonization* had achieved one important victory, and he looked forward to more.

But *Thoughts on African Colonization* had done more than win over Arthur Tappan; it had gained a great deal of publicity for James Forten's stance on colonization. How Forten crafted and then drew upon "the spirit of 1817" is an object lesson in myth-making. According to his account, as related by Garrison, Philadelphia's people of color, led by none other than himself, had divined the truth about the ACS from the very beginning. They had always known that the agenda of the new society was one that would undermine their rights and threaten their liberty while doing nothing to alleviate the plight of the slaves. Forten had made sure that among the documents he had sent to Garrison were the resolutions of the two protest meetings he had chaired back in 1817. It was not apparent when they were reprinted that between the January meeting and the August meeting he had moved from support of the ACS to all-out opposition.[81]

After reading in Garrison's pamphlet the accounts of the protest meetings, white reformers often asked Forten to tell them more. He was eager to oblige and seized every opportunity to publicize his version of the events of 1817. Unwittingly, ACS secretary Ralph R. Gurley gave him yet another chance to get the word out. In a debate in Philadelphia in 1835 with British abolitionist George Thompson, a friend of the Fortens', Gurley professed his ignorance of the January 1817 meeting. Forten confessed himself "not a little surprised" that Gurley should have been unaware of it. Presumably he had not read that section of *Thoughts on African Colonization*. "But if his memory is not very treacherous, he ought to have known the circumstance, for I related it to him myself in a conversation which I had with him at my home one evening."[82] Forten described the January 1817 meeting as "the largest meeting of colored people ever convened in Philadelphia, I will say 3000, though I might safely add 500 more." No one, he insisted, could have been in any doubt about the mood of the meeting. "[W]hen the question was put in the affirmative, you might have heard a pin drop. . . . But when in the negative, one *long*, loud, aye, TREMENDOUS NO . . . seemed as if it would bring down the walls of the building." He could not help pointing out that "even then, at the very onset, when the monster came in a guise to deceive some of our firmest friends . . . we penetrated through its thickly laid covering, and beheld it . . . as the scourge, which in after years was to . . . force us into involuntary exile."[83] He said not a word about his initial enthusiasm for the colonization scheme.

With Russell Parrott, Absalom Jones, John Gloucester, and the other members of the Philadelphia African Institution dead and buried, there was no one to challenge James Forten's version of events. Thanks, in large measure, to his own efforts and to William Lloyd Garrison's publicity machine, Forten would be remembered as one of the earliest opponents of the ACS. Penning a tribute to him in 1842, white abolitionist Henry C. Wright insisted "it was JAMES FORTEN, who first warned the colored people against that specious scheme of injustice and oppression, the American Colonization Society."[84] As Robert Purvis saw it, his venerated and venerable father-in-law had led the charge against the ACS. He was never deceived by "the enemies of freedom," and he saw through "every device which the scheme of colonization could invent . . . to blind and mislead him." According to Purvis, it was James Forten who convened the celebrated meeting at Mother Bethel, and "Thus, owing to [his] timely efforts and zeal . . . was the main head of this Hydra crushed."[85]

GARRISON'S ANTISLAVERY CAMPAIGN enabled James Forten to spread his message about the pernicious nature of racial prejudice in America. It also gained for him a host of white allies and involved him and his family in a cause that, at least superficially, transcended lines of race. Despite all his long years of cooperation with the Pennsylvania Abolition Society, James Forten had never been invited to join the society. Forten never stopped working with the men in the PAS and he maintained close friendships with a number of them. For him it was not a case of shunning one group of white abolitionists in favor of another. But when the chance arose to join forces with Garrison and the white radicals, he embraced the opportunity to do so.

Garrison and his associates in New England were quick to realize the importance of giving radical antislavery a degree of permanence through antislavery societies. On July 28, 1832, James Forten wrote Garrison to let him know how pleased he was to learn of the formation of the New England Anti-Slavery Society, a sign "that the public are awakening to a right feeling on the momentous question of Slavery, and the condition of the Free People of Color."[86] Antislavery societies began springing up in a number of communities in New England and the Middle Atlantic states, and by the fall of 1833 Garrison and others in the movement determined it was time to form a national society. The city where they decided to meet to establish the American Anti-Slavery Society was Philadelphia. That decision gave James Forten and his family ringside seats at what was truly a momentous event.

In early December 1833, two ACS heavyweights, Robert S. Finley and Professor Wright, were scheduled to lecture in Philadelphia, but they found themselves effectively upstaged by the abolitionists. Ralph R. Gurley, in town for a visit, was taken aback. "They have worked silently, for it was only this morning that I heard they were assembling."[87] He had just heard of it, but ample notice had been given to the friends of the antislavery cause.

The sixty-two delegates convened at the Adelphi Building on Fifth and Walnut Streets on December 4. In terms of age they were a relatively young group and few of them were wealthy. Three were men of color: James G. Barbadoes, one of Garrison's most zealous coworkers in Boston; well-to-do Philadelphia barber and dentist James McCrummill; and Robert Purvis.[88] James Forten could surely have had a place among the founders had he wanted it, but for reasons of his own he stepped back and let Purvis assume this role. Perhaps he felt that it was time for the younger generation to move to the forefront. Although he was not among the delegates, Forten was almost certainly among the scores of spectators at the Adelphi.[89] And during the course of the convention many delegates and well-wishers took the time to visit him and his family.[90]

James Forten surely approved of the American Anti-Slavery Society's Declaration of Sentiments, for it explicitly linked the abolitionists to the "band of patriots" who had sought freedom from British tyranny in 1776. Like them, the abolitionists would go to war to achieve their goals, but they pledged to fight only with moral force and "the power of love."

Garrison, Purvis, and the other delegates rejected any notion of gradual abolition, demanding that "the slaves ought instantly to be set free." Much as they admired the actions of the British Parliament in providing for compensated abolition throughout the British Empire, they declared their opposition to paying slaveholders to do what was morally right. If anyone deserved payment it was the millions of bondsmen and women who had labored in intolerable conditions to enrich those the delegates condemned as "man-stealers." They denounced as "delusive, cruel and dangerous" any emigration scheme, even if its defenders insisted it would help bring about the end of slavery.[91] As he listened to the proceedings, James Forten could feel very pleased, indeed. His message had come through loud and clear.

It would be overstating the case to say that the formation of the American Anti-Slavery Society energized the Forten family when it came to the question of abolition. James Forten had been fighting to end slavery for a generation before William Lloyd Garrison and most of his allies were born. What the founding of the AAS did was to provide James Forten, his wife, his children, and his friends in the African-American community with a national structure within which to operate.

James Forten was chosen over and over again, for most of the rest of his life, to be an officer of the AAS, although it is uncertain whether he traveled to New York City for the annual meetings. Nor was Forten the only member of his extended family to hold office in the AAS. In 1834 he was elected a vice-president and Robert Purvis a manager. The following year both were named as managers.[92] In 1836 the Forten family was represented by Robert B. Forten, who attended as a delegate from the Philadelphia Young Men's Anti-Slavery Society, and Robert Purvis, who proposed a resolution welcoming emancipation in the British West Indies. Once more Purvis and James Forten were elected managers.[93] In 1837 Robert Forten stayed home, but Robert Purvis attended. Once more he and James Forten were chosen as managers. In 1838 Purvis made the journey to New York with his brother-in-law, James Forten, Jr., where he and his father-in-law were reelected as managers.[94]

At the local level James Forten helped establish the Philadelphia Anti-Slavery Society and served on its Board of Managers.[95] Most of the men in the society were in their forties and fifties, but the younger abolitionists in Philadelphia were determined not to leave the fight to their elders. In 1835 James Forten, Jr., Robert B. Forten, Robert Purvis, and a number of other young men of color had joined with several dozen white abolitionists to form the Young Men's Anti-Slavery Society of Philadelphia.[96] Young and old alike saw the need for a radical antislavery organization at the state level. In the fall of 1836 James Forten, his two eldest sons, and his son-in-law put their names to a circular addressed to the Friends of Immediate Emancipation in the State of Pennsylvania calling for the formation of a state affiliate of the AAS.[97] So committed to the cause was Forten that, early in 1837, when he was seventy years old, he made the grueling hundred-mile journey to Harrisburg to attend the inaugural meeting of the Pennsylvania State Anti-Slavery Society in his capacity as a "Citizen of Philadelphia." Robert Purvis accompanied with him as a delegate from the Young Men's Anti-Slavery Society of Philadelphia.[98] The following year, when the convention met at the ill-fated Pennsylvania Hall in Philadelphia, Forten attended as a delegate from the Anti-Slavery Society of the City and County of Philadelphia.[99]

The Forten women were not prepared to be left out. The men who organized the AAS aimed at racial inclusiveness, but women, irrespective of race, were not admitted to membership, at least not yet. Garrison and the other men in the abolitionist movement urged them to form their own societies. The Philadelphia antislavery women and many of their sisters throughout the North heeded that call. In December 1833, within days of the formation of the AAS, James Forten's wife, three of his daughters, and a future daughter-in-law helped found the interracial Philadelphia Female Anti-Slavery Society. At the very first meeting Margaretta Forten was appointed to the committee charged with drawing up a constitution. Over the years the Fortens held various offices in the society, and they would eventually serve as delegates to the national conventions of antislavery women.[100]

From the AAS on down to the local groups, all of these new societies were explicitly interracial in their composition. In practice, though, they varied with regard to the policy-making roles black members were allowed to play. Neither James Forten nor any other man of color could be truly said to be a policy-maker in the AAS in the 1830s. While Forten and Robert Purvis held the titles of managers, the AAS had well over a hundred members on its Board of Managers. The role of men of color in the national organization was largely symbolic. Real power lay in the hands of a small inner circle, all of whom were white.[101] Forten's power was probably greater in the state organization than in the national one, and greater still in the city-wide society, since these groups were smaller and more intimate than the national one. Ironically, Charlotte Vandine Forten and her daughters were much more influential in the Philadelphia Female Anti-Slavery Society, but then the very idea of women, black or white, organizing and taking a public stance on any issue was a novelty. At least in the 1830s, Philadelphia's female abolitionists seem to have been more successful at erasing, or at least minimizing, the lines of race than their male counterparts.

DURING THE 1830s and into the 1840s abolition was at the core of the Forten family's social life. They attended meetings of antislavery organizations. They helped fund the *Liberator* and the other abolitionist journals that sprang up across the North. They raised money for the antislavery cause and they found various ways to assist fugitives from the South. They also entertained abolitionists. William Lloyd Garrison visited regularly and was universally beloved. Lucretia Mott wrote of spending an evening with him at James Forten's and being "highly interested in the conversation."[102] In their letters to friends in Philadelphia, Sarah and Angelina Grimké often asked to be remembered to the Fortens.[103] When they needed information about anything related to the antislavery cause, from the fate of the black men who had fought in the Revolutionary War to the impact of racism, they felt comfortable approaching the Fortens.[104] Others involved in the antislavery movement begged to be introduced. George Thompson, who had met Robert Purvis in London, wrote to let Purvis know he would be passing through Philadelphia on a visit and asked to meet James Forten, about whom he had heard so much.[105] Purvis willingly complied with his request. Garrison's brother-in-law, Henry Benson, wrote to his brother about a most enjoyable evening he had spent with Thompson and Garrison at the Forten home.[106] It was during another lively evening at 92 Lombard Street that George Thompson met Angelina Grimké.[107] By the mid-1830s James Forten and his family had indeed become antislavery celebrities, and any abolitionist who came to Philadelphia was eager to visit them.

Not all their interactions with their white coworkers were as congenial as the friendly exchanges described above. James Forten confessed that he and his family were sometimes offended by insensitive remarks or by actions that they regarded as invasions of their privacy.[108] But if he and they recognized that the new antislavery radicalism had not entirely erased the lines of race, they obviously still welcomed the energized abolitionist campaign. They were reassured by the knowledge that they and the rest of the African-American community were not fighting a lonely battle. If their relationships with their white coworkers were not all they might have wished for, they knew that those relationships were warmer and far closer than the relationships they enjoyed with the majority of their white neighbors.

11

"ABOLITION PROPERTY"

I T IS DIFFICULT not to conclude that James Forten was being somewhat disingenuous when he wrote to William Lloyd Garrison on March 21, 1831, that the *Liberator* "has roused up a Spirit in our Young People, that had been slumbering for years." Although it might have been true that some members of Philadelphia's small but influential African-American elite had rejected the notion that they were connected in any way with the nation's slave population, that was unlikely to have been the case with James Forten's children. They had grown up hearing their father and his friends speak of the injustice of human bondage, and of the role people like themselves, men and women linked by "consanguinity[,] . . . suffering, and . . . wrongs" with those still held in bondage, must play in eradicating slavery. Perhaps Forten was being more frank with Garrison when he assured him that "we shall produce writers able to vindicate our cause."[1] He looked to his children and to Robert Purvis to use their talents and their education to the task.

James Forten's children came of age as radical abolitionism was gaining more and more white adherents. They shared in the work of antislavery—writing, speaking, serving on antislavery committees, and helping found radical antislavery societies. They forged friendships with white proponents of "Garrisonian" abolition. They traveled to antislavery conventions. They studied at interracial schools founded on abolitionist principles. They also made contact with others like themselves—educated and affluent young men and women of color committed to a less-than-popular cause. Their very presence served that cause, helping white antislavery advocates disprove notions of black intellectual inferiority. Of course, being on display, "a credit to one's race," or, in the words of Robert Purvis, "abolition property," was not always a comfortable feeling, but they accepted it with as much grace as they could. Whatever disappointments and setbacks he would have to face in the tumultuous decade of the 1830s, James Forten would have the pleasure of seeing his children and his much-loved son-in-law emerge as articulate champions of the cause he had struggled to advance for so many years.

It was hard not to take an interest in antislavery if one lived under James Forten's roof. There was ample reading matter at hand, for Forten subscribed to a host of antislavery publications, and friends from as far away as Britain and Liberia sent him items they thought might be of interest. Adding to the intellectually stimulating atmosphere at 92 Lombard Street was the constant stream of callers—African Americans of all social classes, some from Philadelphia and others from further afield, white abolitionists; churchmen; reformers of one sort or another; writers; editors; the occasional politician; and dozens of visitors from all over the United States and Britain referred to Forten by his network of acquaintances.

One literally never knew whom one might run into in the Forten home. James Forten liked company. He "was extremely hospitable to strangers, who were invariably interested in his agreeable conversation and polished manners."[2] Members of the Pennsylvania legislature called on him at his sail loft, "and one or more of them visited his family, and joined their company at the tea-table."[3] There they met not only the renowned businessman and reformer but his wife, who was by all accounts a gracious hostess, and his talented children.

After a visit to Philadelphia in the summer of 1832, Garrison observed to an acquaintance:

> I wish you had been with me . . . to see what I saw, to hear what I heard. . . .
> There are colored men and women, young men and young ladies, in that city,
> who have few superiors in refinement, in moral worth, and in all that makes
> the human character worthy of admiration and praise.[4]

During his sojourn he had been the guest of James Forten's daughter and son-in-law, and had spent several evenings at 92 Lombard Street with other members of the Forten family. As he confessed some months later, he might be known to many black Philadelphians by reputation, but, as yet, he had "associated with scarcely a dozen of their number"—and most of that dozen were members of James Forten's family or friends of his.[5]

ON SEPTEMBER 3, 1831, Robert Purvis, the young man James Forten had come to look upon as a son, truly became a member of the family when he married Harriet Davy Forten. The wedding was a private ceremony at the Forten home, and it was apparently a very stylish affair. There was a last-minute crisis when a death in the family of Jacob M. Douglass, the white minister serving St.

Thomas's, prevented him from officiating. However, it was a sign of Forten's standing that no less a person than Bishop Henry Onderdonk, the assistant bishop of the diocese, offered to take Douglass's place.[6] Though private, the event still attracted the attention of white Philadelphians as well as African Americans. There was gossip in the business community that Forten had used his money to buy Harriet "a whiter species" of husband, for the light-skinned Purvis was often taken for a white man, but if there was any "sacrifice of . . . fortune" it was not on Forten's side.[7] Robert Purvis, in addition to identifying as a man of color, and being an ardent abolitionist, was rather wealthier than his father-in-law.

At some point in the 1820s, Robert Purvis had made a crucial decision about his life. Thanks to the generous legacies he had received from his father and elder brother, he was a very wealthy man. His money had bought him an excellent education. Even more important than his wealth and refinement was his appearance. He looked white. He went wherever he chose in the North. His money and his striking good looks made him an attractive marriage prospect. Ambitious mothers and their daughters took notice of him. He told white abolitionist Samuel J. May he "had traveled much in stage-coaches, and stopped days and weeks at Saratoga and other fashionable summer resorts, and mingled, without question, among the beaux and belles."[8] He could have chosen to be white. Some of his father's friends advised it. He saw little of his African-American mother. He need only dwell upon his English ancestry, stay out of South Carolina, where his family connections were known, and rely on his money and his light skin to do the rest. Perhaps he should do as his father had wished and move to Britain. Robert rejected all the well-meant advice. He chose to be a man of color. He began speaking out against slavery, identifying himself as one "bound with those in chains." And he began courting Harriet Forten.

Robert had all the qualities James and Charlotte Forten could wish for in a son-in-law. The fact that he was shaping up to be a good man of business was an added bonus. One might argue that, with all the successful entrepreneurs in his background, from his grandfather to his uncles to his parents, Robert could not be other than a talented and resourceful businessman, were it not for the fact that his brother, Joseph, would prove hopelessly inept when it came to money matters.

For the first few months of their married life Robert and Harriet lived at 92 Lombard, and then Robert bought a two-story house for them on Lombard and Ninth.[9] The new house was clearly intended to become their family home, but Robert soon began buying other pieces of real estate for investment. Most of his purchases in Philadelphia were in New Market Ward, near various properties his father-in-law owned. His partner in a number of these ventures was James Forten's old friend Joseph Cassey.[10] The two bought property in the city and also invested in real estate in Bucks County. At one point the Purvises and the Casseys shared a home in Bucks County, the "Grove."[11]

As Cassey spread his interests to New Jersey, so did Purvis.[12] When his son-in-law's interests in banking, railroad stock, and the like were coupled with his real estate investments, almost all of which were managed in such a way that they yielded a handsome profit, James Forten could feel very secure about Harriet's financial future. Toward the end of 1832 Harriet and Robert presented James and Charlotte with their first grandchild, a boy, whom they named William, after Robert's father and older brother.[13]

Robert and Harriet became increasingly involved in the work of antislavery, she through her membership of the Philadelphia Female Anti-Slavery Society and he through a number of organizations, including the American Anti-Slavery Society. They wrote, raised funds for the abolitionist cause, and willingly broke the law by sheltering runaways in their home. Robert also emerged as a forceful antislavery orator.

In 1834 Robert decided to make a trip to Britain to advance the antislavery cause and to try to settle his father's estate.[14] According to Garrison, he was also hoping "to benefit his health, which [was] precarious."[15] The first step was to secure a passport. He submitted an application, and a "special passport" was issued stating that he was "a free person of colour born in the United States" and requesting simply that he be given "all lawful Aid and Protection."[16] It was far less than the full passport given a white American and smacked strongly of the "free papers" given a person of color in the slave South or, even worse, the pass issued to a slave going about an errand.

As soon as he received this "special passport" Purvis called upon James Forten's old friend, Quaker philanthropist Roberts Vaux, to express his "regret & dissatisfaction" that he had been denied the title of "*citizen of the United States.*" He pointed out that seamen's protections acknowledged citizenship, even if the bearers were men of color. He was also worried that anything less than a full passport would be inadequate if he extended his travels to mainland Europe. Vaux promised to help. He wrote the Secretary of State, explaining that Purvis's father had been "a Merchant of great respectability," that Purvis had inherited a handsome estate, that "he lives as a Gentleman," and that he had received a college education. As for the vexed question of race, "his African descent . . . is scarcely perceptible . . . his hair is straight, & many Southern complexions are as dark, in which not a drop of negro blood imparts the tinge."[17] The full passport was duly issued, and Vaux had the pleasure of taking it to 92 Lombard while the Fortens and the Purvises were entertaining some abolitionist friends to tea. The passport arrived in the nick of time, because Purvis was booked to sail from New York in a few days.[18] He had originally booked passage on a vessel out of Philadelphia, but one of the owners had begged him to cancel after another passenger, Bernard Carter, a wealthy and well-connected white Southerner, "hearing that a colored man was to be one of the number, had declared that he would not go out on the same vessel with a negro."[19]

Purvis's trip to Britain was a great success. Garrison's letters of introduction to leading British reformers meant he was overwhelmed with offers of hospitality.[20] He did his share of sight-seeing, and, as he told Garrison, he made use of every opportunity to publicize the antislavery cause. He described, for instance, how an abolitionist acquaintance had taken him to the House of Commons and presented him to the great Irish patriot Daniel O'Connell. Purvis's friend introduced him to O'Connell simply as "an American gentleman." The Irishman, taking Purvis for a white American, declined to shake hands. However,

> when he understood that I was not only identified with the Abolitionists, but with the proscribed and oppressed colored class in the United States, he grasped my hand, and warmly shaking it, remarked—*"Sir, I never will take the hand of an American . . . without first knowing his principles in reference to American Slavery, and its ally, the American Colonization Society."*

Purvis was delighted to be able to report back to his American friends on the enlightened views of O'Connell and on the kind and sympathetic treatment he received from so many of the people he met in Britain. If he ever felt uncomfortable at being, in a sense, put on display as a "representative" man of color, he never mentioned it. In fact, he seems to have relished being regarded as "Abolition property" and concluded "that there is a very *'particular* price' set upon such property . . . when the color of the building happens to fall below the inconstant and wavering shade of white, to the more substantial black or brown."[21] In short, the role of spokesman for black America was one he accepted gladly.

Leaving England, Purvis traveled to Scotland, where he met some of his cousins and spoke at a meeting of the Glasgow Emancipation Society. He also helped open a correspondence between the Ladies' Anti-Slavery Society of Glasgow and the Philadelphia Female Anti-Slavery Society.[22] Then it was time to arrange his passage home.

Coincidentally, he found himself booked on the same vessel as Bernard Carter, the well-to-do white Southerner whose anger at having to sail with a black man as a fellow passenger had forced Purvis to change his travel plans. Carter failed to recognize Purvis as a man of color, and in fact sought out the elegant and obviously wealthy young man at every opportunity. Others followed Carter's lead, and Purvis became a universal favorite. On the last night of the voyage he arranged a surprise.

> A parting dinner had been given by the captain, at which Mr. Purvis distinguished himself in a speech for which he . . . received many compliments. After the dinner he informed the steward that he was a colored man, and directed him to make public the disclosure. . . . It was at first disbelieved. . . . Mr. Purvis confirmed the statement, and . . . it produced much excitement, gravity, discomfiture, and merriment, as the whole force of the situation was realized.[23]

Purvis did not suffer as a result of the disclosure. He finished the voyage without being turned out of his cabin and sent to steerage or being ostracized by his fellow passengers, with the exception of Carter and his entourage.

Harriet did not accompany her husband on his trip to Britain. With young William to care for, and pregnant with her second child, she remained at home.[24] During the months Purvis was visiting with British abolitionists and speaking at various venues in England and Scotland, she was attending meetings of the Philadelphia Female Anti-Slavery Society with her mother and sisters. Her antislavery work became an extension of her husband's, and her role—which she happily accepted—was that of wife, mother, and hostess to a stream of reformers who knew of Robert's work and were attracted by his eloquence. Her younger sister, Sarah Louisa, on the other hand, emerges from her writings as a feisty young woman, opinionated, sometimes outspoken, and most definitely someone who wanted to be "out in the world." She had her doubts about the attractions of the married state and did not marry until she was in her mid-twenties, by which time she had achieved some degree of celebrity as an antislavery poet.

Perhaps it was the appearance of the *Liberator* that prompted sixteen-year-old Sarah to begin writing, or perhaps she was already writing and Garrison's newspaper offered her the chance to get her poetry into print. She certainly lost no time sending her work to Garrison. She mailed "The Grave of the Slave" to him after reading the very first issue of the *Liberator*. Garrison had said he was anxious to publish poems, especially those written by women, and most especially those written by women of color. She was happy to oblige, although she preferred to keep her identity a secret. She signed her work "Ada." Garrison published "The Grave of the Slave" in the *Liberator* of January 22, 1831. In the poem Sarah wrote of death as a release from suffering for the slave.

> Poor slave! shall we sorrow that death was thy friend,
> The last, and the kindest, that heaven could send?
> The grave to the weary is welcomed and blest;
> And death, to the captive, is freedom and rest.[25]

The poem was later set to music by her father's friend, composer Francis Johnson.[26]

The following week, still unaware of the identity of "Ada," Garrison published "The Slave Girl's Address to Her Mother." On this occasion "Ada" struck a more militant note, one she would return to in her prose writing. The nation, she insisted, was risking divine retribution for countenancing the sin of slavery.

> Oh! ye who boast of Freedom's sacred claims,
> Do ye not blush to see our galling chains;
> To hear that sounding word—"that all are free"—
> When thousands groan in hopeless slavery?
> . . No more, no more! Oh God, this cannot be;

Thou to thy children's aid wilt surely flee:
In thine own time deliverance thou wilt give,
And bid us rise from slavery, and live.[27]

A few weeks later the *Liberator* published "Past Joys," in which "Ada" reflected on her own life and that of the slave. A free person like herself might
feel sorrow at leaving home and family, but the slave, "Poor Afric's son," knew
a far deeper grief.

The mother, wife, or child he loved,
    He ne'er shall see again;
To him they're lost—ay, dead indeed:
    What for him doth remain?[28]

Garrison soon found out who "Ada" was. James Forten wrote him: "I have
discovered by accident that these pieces were written by one of my Daughters."[29] With her identity now an open secret—Garrison did not print her
name, but he gave his readers enough background information to put a name
to "Ada"—Sarah continued to send her poems to the *Liberator*. Occasionally
she tapped a sentimental vein for her inspiration. "The Farewell," written in
the summer of 1832, when she was eighteen, is a poem of poignant regret to a
young man about to enter "the gay and busy world" whom she fears will be
attracted to others.

Another's lips will charm thee then,
    Another's voice will praise;
Thou wilt forget we e'er have met
    In past and happy days . . .

It is, of course, tempting to conclude that this poem resulted from an unhappy
love affair, and to try to guess the name of the man with whom Sarah enjoyed
"friendship's early dream."[30]

Sarah also tried her hand at prose. On March 14, 1831, she penned a piece
entitled "The Abuse of Liberty" and signed it "Magawisca," a fanciful Indian
name and perhaps a nod to her own complex racial heritage.[31] She began by
noting that the United States "offers to every white man the right to enjoy life,
liberty, and happiness." But "those who cannot show a fair exterior, no matter
what be the noble qualities of their mind, are to be robbed of the rights with
which they were endowed by an all-wise and merciful Creator, who, in his
great wisdom, cast a sable hue over some of the 'lords of creation.'" She ended
with a solemn warning:

[C]an you think he, that Great Spirit, who created all men free and equal—
He, who made the sun to shine on the black man as well as the white, will
always allow you to rest tranquil on your downy couches?—No,—he is just,
and his anger will not always slumber.[32]

By the time "Prayer" appeared in the *Liberator*, its editor had learned that "Ada" and "Magawisca" were one and the same. In this poem "Ada" wrote of prayer as a "sacred right," a communion with God that "none are denied."

> Man bends the heart and bows the knee,
> And knows in prayer that he is free.[33]

Unless one reads her other poems, one might assume "Ada" was telling slaves to put their faith in God and look for relief in the hereafter, but James Forten's daughter was no apologist for the slave system. Her poem, "The Slave," is worth quoting at length, partly for its literary merit, but more importantly for what it reveals about the lessons her father had taught her. The child of a Revolutionary War veteran, she had grown up hearing about the role of black men in that conflict, about the professions of love of freedom made by black and white alike, and about the waning of that libertarian fervor.

> Our sires who once in freedom's cause,
>   Their boasted freedom sought and won,
> For deeds of glory gained applause,
>   When patriot feelings led them on.
> And can their sons now speak with pride,
> Of rights for which they bled and died,—
> . . . Oh, surely they have quite forgot,
> That bondage once had been their lot;
> The sweets of freedom now they know,
> They care not for the captive's wo[e].
> The poor wronged slave can bear no part
> In feelings dearest to his heart;
> He cannot speak on freedom's side,
> Nor dare he own a freeman's pride . . .
> . . . And sad and hard his lot must be,
> To know that he can ne'er be free;
> . . . And will not justice soon arise,
> And plead the cause of the despised?
> For oh! my country, must it be,
> That they will find a foe in thee?[34]

Many months later she returned to the theme of the nation's failure to live up to its revolutionary heritage. Yes, she admitted, there were lands benighted by "heathenism darkness," but missionaries and reformers had work to do at home. She begged:

> Speak not of "my country," unless she shall be,
> In truth, the bright home of the "brave and the free!"[35]

Sarah Forten's work appeared in journals other than the *Liberator*. In March 1836 the editor of the *Philanthropist* received a poem, signed "Sarah Louisa," passed on to him by a friend. The anonymous friend noted that the poem, "A Prayer," was the work of "a colored female residing in Philadelphia." The writer went on: "I ought to have said *young lady*, even at the risk of exciting a *sneer* in certain doughfaces[,] for her whole deportment bears testimony to the fact that she is such." Her talents were brought forward to vindicate the intellectual equality of all persons of color. "We have here another proof of the folly of the assertion which ignorance and prejudice united, have attempted to palm upon the world; viz;—that the colored race are incapable of intellectual and moral elevation."[36] Likewise, when the *Lowell Observer* republished a number of Sarah's poems from the *Liberator* in the early weeks of 1833, the editor's fulsome praise pointed to them as examples of black artistry and intelligence. "We have inserted several interesting pieces . . . by a young lady of color. They are interesting because they evince intellect, which, by many, is supposed not to belong to that much injured class."[37]

Sarah continued writing. She tackled a wide range of subjects, including "A Mother's Grief" and in her 1833 poem "Life," the mutability of human existence and the inevitability of suffering.[38] But most of her poems dealt with the iniquities of slavery. Some were inspired by a few lines read somewhere, or a story she had conjured up. "The Slave Girl's Farewell" had its origin in a tale, read or imagined, of "A young girl . . . living with her mother in one of the West Indian islands, quite unconscious of her being a slave. Her master, on leaving the Island . . . cruelly separated the girl from her parent forever."[39] Others were inspired by her regard for various abolitionists. With the departure of Garrison for England in 1833, Sarah wrote a poem to the *Hibernia*, the "gallant bark" carrying "to old Britain's shores" the "Champion of the slave."

> He goes to raise the standard high,
> And freedom's flag unfurl,
> And to proclaim the rallying cry
> Of freedom to the world.[40]

The birth of the AAS in Philadelphia in December 1833 brought forth a veritable flood of verse from the Forten household. Margaretta wrote a poem, which was published in the *Emancipator*, and Sarah penned "The Separation" for the *Liberator*. She had followed the doings of the convention avidly and was deeply moved by the coming together of abolitionists, black and white, from across the nation. The departure of "that little band" of old and new friends after the convention left her both joyful and sad.

> Their works shall live when other deeds,
> Which ask a nation's fame,
> Have sunk beneath Time's whelming wave,
> Unhonored and unnamed.[41]

Sarah Forten's most famous poem, written just days after "The Separation," would feature in the proceedings of another equally significant antislavery convention. In spite of its title, "An Appeal to Woman" was a powerful challenge, rather than a gentle appeal, to white women to acknowledge their sisterhood with those "'whose skin may differ'" from their own. Eloquent and so clearly written from the heart, it distinguished Sarah as a poet of no mean ability. In essence, it was a response to a poem, "Kneeling Slave," written by a white Quaker, Elizabeth Margaret Chandler, who died in 1834 at the age of twenty-seven. Chandler's poem read:

> She is thy sister! shall her cry,
> Uncared for, and unheeded, pass thee by?
> Wilt thou weep to see her sink so low,
> And seek to raise her from her place of woe?
> Or has thy heart grown selfish in its bliss,
> That thou shouldst view unmoved a fate like this?[42]

Sarah Forten read and admired Chandler's work.[43] She may well have met Chandler, who lived in Philadelphia from 1814 to 1830.

In "An Appeal to Woman" Sarah went several steps beyond the Quaker poet. Her appeal was not against slavery alone, but against its companion, prejudice. Published first in the *Lowell Observer*, it was spotted by Garrison and reprinted in the *Liberator* in 1834. Three years later the first stanza would grace the *Appeal to the Women of the Nominally Free States*, a pamphlet published by the officers of the first antislavery convention of American women. They could hardly have found anything more appropriate.

> Oh, woman, woman, in thy brightest hour
> Of conscious worth, of pride, of conscious power,
> Oh, nobly dare to act a Christian's part,
> That well befits a lovely woman's heart!
> Dare to be good, as thou canst dare be great;
> Despise the taunts of envy, scorn and hate;
> Our "skins may differ," but from thee we claim
> A sister's privilege, in a sister's name.[44]

When it appeared in the *Liberator* the poem brought poetic responses from other antislavery advocates. Sarah had obviously touched a nerve.[45]

Her contact with abolitionists and reformers, black and white, energized Sarah and broadened her horizons. Her friendship with Elizabeth Whittier, sister of the antislavery poet John Greenleaf Whittier, was one both women valued. For Sarah there was the confidence that some friendships could bridge the racial divide. For the sickly and introspective Elizabeth, who preserved Sarah's letters, there was the pleasure of writing to someone who shared her dedication to abolition and her enjoyment of reading. In October 1835 she wrote in her journal: "[T]his morning I finished a letter to Sarah L[ouisa] F[orten]. Oh! I know I should love that girl—[I] wonder if I shall ever see her."[46]

In the fall of 1835, when she learned of her friend's latest bout of illness, Sarah had no hesitation in offering her the hospitality of the Forten home, and no reason to believe that hospitality would be rejected because of the source from whence it came. "[W]hy cannot you make us a long visit?. . . . [N]o one in the world would be more proud than myself to take you by the hand and welcome you to our happy family circle."[47] Through Elizabeth she came to know other white female abolitionists. When Elizabeth's neighbor, Harriet Minot, added a friendly postscript to one of Elizabeth's letters, Sarah was delighted to make the acquaintance of "'A Sister Abolitionist.'"[48] When Elizabeth's friends visited Philadelphia, Sarah enjoyed socializing with them. One was Miss Morse of Boston, "a clever pleasant young woman" whom Sarah found, in the many months the New Englander stayed in Philadelphia, to be "free from predjudice and possessed of a pure and noble mind."[49]

Her involvement in the antislavery movement gave Sarah a sense of purpose, a feeling of being dedicated to a noble cause. Reading her letters, one glimpses a young woman caught up in a whirl of activities, a vital member of a household where such activities were deemed praiseworthy and encouraged.

Sarah was not shy about doling out criticism when she felt it was warranted. Deeply though she admired Garrison, for instance, she could not always approve of his conduct. After the editor was almost killed by an angry mob in Boston in October 1835, Sarah, her brother James, and her friend and future sister-in-law Mary Wood joined an interracial group of "citizens, friendly to the Abolition of Slavery" who met to deplore the violence displayed to Garrison and to testify to their deep regard for him.[50] However, Sarah confessed to Elizabeth that she was

> grieved to the very soul he should have left the city. . . . I hope your Brother will write to him entreating his immediate return—as the enemies of our cause will have room to accuse him of cowardice—I woman as I am—would never yield an inch in the prosecution of what I considered my duty.[51]

Sarah greatly admired the Grimké sisters. In the fall of 1836 she wrote to Elizabeth of her eagerness to get hold of a copy of Angelina Grimké's *Appeal to the Christian Women of the South*. She had heard that it was "an admirable work . . . full of holy zeal—powerful reasoning—and affectionate remonstrance."[52] A few weeks later she and her mother, as officers of the Philadelphia Female Anti-Slavery Society, had the pleasant duty of signing a Certificate of Recommendation for Angelina as she embarked on a lecture tour.[53]

Sarah felt comfortable enough the following year to respond to a letter from Angelina Grimké asking about the impact of prejudice upon her and her family. Sensing that Grimké truly wanted to understand what so many white abolitionists found it more comfortable to ignore, Sarah spent some time composing a letter that was both tactful and honest. She wrote of her own commitment to antislavery and the energizing effect it had had on one "who has untill very lately lived and acted more for herself than for the good of others. I confess that I am wholly indebted to the Abolition cause for arousing me from apathy and indifference, shedding light into a mind which has been too long wrapt in selfish darkness."[54]

As for racial prejudice, she conceded: "I am peculiarly sensitive on this point, and consequently seek to avoid as much as possible mingling with those who exist under its influence." She acknowledged feelings of "discontent and mortification" at seeing "many . . . preferred before me, who by education, birth, or worldly circumstances were no better than myself, THEIR sole claim to notice depending on the superior advantage of being *White*." However, she was striving to "bear and forbear."

She expressed her own strong mind as to race relations. By this point she was less willing than her father to accept that the whites of the Revolutionary generation had been benevolent and that their sons had betrayed them. She believed "there has always existed the same amount of predjudice in the minds of Americans towards the descendants of Africa; it wanted only the spirit of colonization to call it into action." Given the restrictions black men and women faced when they made any move to improve themselves, especially when it came to education, "I only marvel," she wrote, "that they are in possession of any knowledge at all."

She did not overlook the possibility that even white abolitionists might carry the "dark mantle" of racism. "I recollect the words of one of the best and least predjudiced men in the Abolition ranks. Ah said he, 'I can recall the time when in walking with a colored brother, the darker the night, the better Abolitionist was I.'" However, she was willing to forgive some manifestations of prejudice on the part of those whites who professed their hatred of slavery. They made "great sacrifices to public sentiment" when they linked themselves to such an unpopular cause. "Many, very many[,] are anxious to take up the cross, but how few are strong enough to bear it." In time, she believed, they would come to realize that slavery and prejudice were two sides of the same coin.[55]

Finally, Sarah expressed to Grimké her understanding that her experience as a black American was tempered by her family's privileged position. "[W]e have to thank a kind Providence for placing us in a situation that has hitherto prevented us from falling under the weight of this evil; we feel it but in a slight degree compared with many others." The Fortens could look inward for entertainment and companionship. "[W]e never travel far from home and seldom go into public places unless quite sure that admission is free to all; therefore we meet with none of these mortifications which might otherwise ensue."[56]

If Angelina Grimké responded directly to Sarah, her letter has not survived. However, Sarah's honest and direct answer to the white abolitionist's queries about the nature of racism no doubt helped Grimké understand its impact at the personal level.

DESPITE HER EARLIER misgivings about what she described as "the thrall" of marriage, Sarah Forten did eventually marry. On January 8, 1838, in a civil ceremony in Burlington County, New Jersey, she wed her brother-in-law, Joseph Purvis. The circumstances surrounding the marriage are curious, to say the least. James and Charlotte Forten announced it in the *Public Ledger* five days after it had taken place.[57] Why was the wedding of Sarah and Joseph not a repetition of the elegant nuptials they had arranged for Harriet and Robert? James Forten was still a very rich man and could have given Sarah all the trappings Harriet had had. It is possible that James and Charlotte did not know about the wedding until they were presented with a fait accompli. Did the couple elope? Did Sarah think she might be pregnant?

On the surface, Sarah and Joseph had little in common. He certainly did not share her antislavery fervor. His interest in abolition seems to have been confined to taking out a subscription to the *Liberator*.[58] Nor is there any evidence he was much given to literary pursuits. Still, he had money. Sarah had known him for many years. And at almost twenty-four she was dangerously close to becoming an old maid. Perhaps she accepted Joseph's proposal of marriage because she did not anticipate receiving any other offers.

Joseph was by no means unwelcome as a son-in-law. In terms of wealth, he could certainly provide for a wife and a family. Like his brother, he had been using his inheritance to make investments in real estate. His holdings were mainly in Bucks County. In 1835, for instance, he laid out over $13,500 for a house and a 205-acre farm in Bensalem Township. He continued his investments after his marriage, buying two more farms and renting them out.[59] However, he did not have Robert's flair for business. Late in 1838, when Sarah gave birth to her first child, their marriage seemed happy enough, but problems would soon surface. She and Joseph had moved to Bensalem and away from her friends and family. She resigned from the Philadelphia Female Anti-Slavery Society because she lived too far away to attend meetings. She stopped writing, too preoccupied with raising children—she would have eight in twelve years—and running a farm, a task for which she was totally unprepared. For Sarah the "thrall" of marriage and family was far heavier than it was for Harriet.

JAMES AND CHARLOTTE Forten's eldest daughter, Margaretta, did not marry. Eventually, after her father's death, she became a teacher. Like Sarah, Margaretta wrote poetry when she was a young woman. If not of the same quality as that produced by Sarah, it was sincere and obviously struck a chord with her fellow abolitionists. Like Sarah, she was overjoyed at the assembling of so many abolitionists in her native city in 1833. To the delegates to the inaugural meeting of the AAS she wrote:

> Ye blessed few! who now have stood the storm,
> Of persecution, in its direful form;
> Unmov'd have faced the foe in stern array,
> Clad in bold armor for the dread affray;
> Your banner floats—its motto may be read,

"DOWN WITH OPPRESSION! FREEDOM IN ITS STEAD!"
Who are the great and good in this fair land?
Ye who are foremost in this holy band;
Ye blessed few! may God's protecting arm,
O'er ye be spread, to shelter ye from harm . . .

She sent her poem to the editor of the *Emancipator* and he published it.[60] She wrote for her friends, contributing poems to the albums of Amy Matilda Cassey; Gerrit Smith's daughter, Elizabeth; and her future sister-in-law, Mary Virginia Wood. She was also an artist. For Amy Cassey's album she painted a vase of flowers to accompany one poem and another floral contribution for the poem "Forget-Me-Not."[61]

Like her younger brothers and sisters, Margaretta was well-educated and took pride in her intellectual accomplishments. However, like them, she soon discovered that to be black and "refined" could be most uncomfortable. One could not exhibit one's abilities without exciting comment from white abolitionists, and even the firmest of friends could prove insensitive.

James Forten tried to explain that situation to antislavery editor Nathaniel P. Rogers, writing of his and his family's "surprise" (he might have said "sorrow") "that our friends should wonder at our being just like other people."[62] Forten's rebuke followed comments Rogers had made in his paper, *The Herald of Freedom*, about him and his eldest daughter. In the fall of 1838 Forten sent Rogers five dollars, observing that he had been receiving the *Herald* for a year and had had no bill. He thought highly of the paper. "God grant its trumpet voice may penetrate the remotest corners of guilty America, and arouse her from that supineness which threatens to involve her in ruin—that she may see the error of her ways, and be constrained to follow the glorious example of Great Britain, and proclaim universal liberty to the enslaved." He wished Rogers well and promised "future remittances."[63]

A simple thank-you would have sufficed, but Rogers saw fit to print the letter, with accompanying comments that the Forten family found offensive in the extreme. To begin with, Rogers wanted readers to know how well James Forten could write. He assured "our generous minded pro-slavery sneerers" that "JAMES FORTEN OF PHILADELPHIA is a 'NIGGER.'" He then went on to praise the Forten family and remark upon their accomplishments. He could not resist publishing the following "anecdote" because it was "too good to be lost." Mr. Robert J. Breckinridge of the ACS had been taking tea with the Fortens.

[A]t tea [Breckinridge] disputed him [James Forten] on some point of Haitian politics. To sustain his position, Mr. F. called on his daughter for a document he had received from a correspondent at St. Domingo. It was produced and handed to Mr. B. It was in French, and Mr. B. not being acquainted with that language, Mr. F. directed his daughter to read it to him. She did. Mr. Breckinridge expressed surprise at her acquaintance with the French—but going into a Colonization meeting in the city after tea, he argued the *natural incapacity* and *inferiority* of the colored people as a reason why they should be sent to Africa.[64]

The *Herald's* account of the episode soon appeared in the *Liberator*, although without the accompanying racial epithets.

Rogers hoped Forten would "pardon us . . . for the remarks we make," but on this occasion James Forten felt a reproof, albeit a mild one, was called for. He tried to explain to the *Herald's* editor how he and his family felt about their every utterance, their every move, being commented upon. Their privacy was constantly being violated, and they heartily disliked the "well meant, though injudicious, and sometimes really impolite notice which is taken, if any of us happen to do, or say any thing like other people." After all, "if we have the same opportunity's of education, and improvement, what is there to prevent our being just like others, who have these advantages?" He recalled a visit to his home a few evenings before by a white abolitionist. In the course of the visit, he "requested my Daughter to open the Piano, adding that he had never heard a colored Lady play." Forten observed: "he would not, I dare say, for the world have said this, had he thought it would have wounded her feelings, or that it conveyed to her mind, the appearance of rudeness." He added: "I might mention many little incidents like this. . . . You will not think these remarks as applying only to me, and mine, but to my brethren generally." As for "hateful" names, it was bad enough when they came from avowed enemies. It was even more "grating to our feelings" when they came from friends.[65] This was hardly the first time the Fortens' privacy had been invaded and their sensibilities wounded by their white allies in the antislavery movement, and it would not be the last.

Although they resented intrusions into their private lives even by their white abolitionist friends, James Forten and his family generally kept their feelings of irritation to themselves. Now and again, though, as in Forten's letter to Rogers, that irritation showed through. On another occasion Sarah Forten complained to Elizabeth Whittier about the actions of an "officious person" who had "little regard for our feelings." What had irked Sarah was the fact that someone had seen fit to copy a poem from her sister Harriet's album and send it to Garrison, who promptly printed it in the *Liberator*, assuming that the Fortens knew all about it. The poem was very complimentary and it was written by a sincere friend, Elizabeth's own brother, but the point was that it was private and not intended to be read by all and sundry.[66]

John Greenleaf Whittier's poem, "To the Daughters of James Forten," represented the poet's personal rejection of prejudice. The "vain and proud" might refuse to claim the Forten women as sisters, but he hoped he had risen above such baseness. He was ready to offer them "A *brother's* blessing with a *brother's* prayer."

> And what, my sisters, though upon your brows
> The deeper coloring of your kindred glows,

Shall I less love the workmanship of Him
Before whose wisdom all our own is dim?
Shall my heart learn to graduate its thrill?
Beat for the white, and for the black be still?
Let the thought perish: —while that heart can feel
The blessed memory of your grateful zeal—
While it can prize the excellence of mind,
The chaste demeanour and the taste refined,—
Still are ye all my sisters—meet to share
A *brother's* blessing and a *brother's* prayer.[67]

Harriet, Sarah, and the rest of the family were proud of the tribute. They showed the album to visitors, and many read the poem. However, the poem was private in the sense that it had been written for them alone. They were appalled when they saw it in print in the *Liberator*. They knew Whittier, a modest and self-effacing individual, had not sent it to Garrison, and they realized, to their annoyance, that someone had violated their privacy, doubtless under the mistaken impression that they would not mind. Sarah was angry and so, evidently, were other members of the family. In time, though, she and her siblings would learn to develop a protective shell to cope with episodes such as this and try to accept that their talents, and the public notice they attracted, did, in some sense, advance the antislavery cause.

BY THE EARLY 1830s James Forten, Jr., and his younger brother, Robert, were proving that they, like their sisters, had made good use of the education their father had given them. They were articulate, well read, and obviously dedicated to abolition. James Forten took great pride in them and was pleased to have their talents recognized, provided that the recognition was of the kind he and they considered appropriate.

For Garrison's information, Forten wrote him in March 1831 to identify the writer "F," whose work Garrison had just published in the *Liberator*, as his nineteen-year-old son, James Jr.[68] In his letter, "F" had described his pleasure in reading the *Liberator*. "It is a work, which has excited within us feelings that have been too long slumbering. Its columns most unquestionably convince us that the spirit of liberty is awakened." He called on the "false friends of freedom" to heed "the glorious and republican actions of our illustrious father Lafayette," who was evidently one of his heroes.

Behold him struggling against the strong arm of oppression, and devoting his whole life to the cause of liberty; and boldly denouncing . . . the heinous crime of slavery! Our hearts are filled with unspeakable gratitude to this warm and true-hearted republican.

For those like himself "who enjoy some of the blessings of freedom," the "star of emancipation . . . has shone feebly . . . for its real brilliancy is obscured by the dark cloud of slavery." He feared for the future of a nation that rejoiced over "the downfall of tyranny in foreign nations" while permitting human bondage at home. "The time cannot be far distant, when Justice, armed more powerful than human aid can afford, will break the bonds of oppression, and wield the sceptre of liberty and independence throughout the nation."[69] Clearly, James Jr. had imbibed his father's teachings.

By the time he was in his early twenties, James Forten, Jr., was much in demand as an antislavery speaker. On April 14, 1836, he gave an address to the Philadelphia Female Anti-Slavery Society. In some respects it was standard fare, beginning with a sense of the speaker's unworthiness and warm praise of the organization to which he was speaking. He condemned "the dangerous doctrine of gradualism" and urged the women to press for immediate and radical change, though they must anticipate opposition.[70] He recognized that they were in the midst of a "desperate struggle" between *"freedom and despotism— light and darkness,"* but he urged them to fight by making abolition "the topic of your conversation amidst your acquaintances, in every family circle, and in the shades of private life."[71]

In his speech James Forten displayed his learning as he fit slavery into his knowledge of natural God-given human rights—"the right to the produce of our own labour, to our limbs, life, liberty and property." He reminded his audience that those rights were not secure in Philadelphia, where a person could all too easily be apprehended as an alleged fugitive. "If our property be destroyed by a cowardly and ruffian mob, our persons maltreated and our limbs broken, the hand of charity is scarcely extended to the sufferer."[72] Black people were denied equal access to places of education and worship, yet "there is nothing that our enemies can bring against us but the colour of our skin."[73]

Opening the topic of his speech from the local to the national level, he pointed to the recently enacted Gag Rule, which forbade the consideration of antislavery petitions by Congress, and argued that the South was perverting the entire political process to advance its own interests. Worse, the North seemed to be knuckling under to demands that antislavery societies be forcibly disbanded and antislavery sentiments silenced. "Freemen are, in one sense, threatened with slavery; the chains are shaken in their faces, and yet they appear unwilling to resist them." He spoke as he did because of his deep love for his country, and his fears for her future.[74] "[H]onesty . . . has fled from the South, long ago; sincerity has fallen asleep there; pity has hidden herself; justice cannot find the way; help is not at home; charity lies dangerously ill; benevolence is under arrest; faith is nearly extinguished; truth has long since been buried, and conscience is nailed on the wall." He ended by reminding the antislavery women that their sisters in Britain had been in the vanguard of abolition.[75] Would they be content to do less than the British women? He appealed to his audience as women and as Americans. They must struggle onward, regardless of the barriers raised against them. They must face down their critics and do what they instinctively knew to be right, for they had a vital role to play in bringing about the ultimate victory of the abolitionist crusade. Forten's words were very well received, and the members of the society requested a copy of his speech for publication. Individuals such as Sarah Douglass, who cited a line from the address in a poem, were deeply touched by it.[76]

James Forten, Jr., shared his antislavery zeal and his craving for intellectual improvement with his friend James McCune Smith. The same age as Forten, Smith was anxious to train as a physician, but unable to gain admission to any medical school in the United States on account of his race. In 1832 Smith went to Scotland to earn his M.D.[77] The Philadelphian and the expatriate corresponded regularly. From those letters one gets a sense of James Jr.'s dedication to abolition and his admiration of his fellow antislavery activists.

Through Smith, Forten was able to feel part of the international community of antislavery activists. If the struggle in the United States seemed at times to be a losing one, Forten could reflect that gains were being made elsewhere. The British had finally outlawed slavery. America must surely do so before many more years elapsed. Smith had sent over from Scotland a medal commemorating the abolition of slavery throughout the British Empire. Forten considered British emancipation an act "that gives to monarchical Britain the preeminence over our boasted republic." Independence Day celebrations in the United States left him unmoved, or at least moved him only to painful reflections. "[W]hile our orators are pouring forth their praises upon the virtue and liberty of America," men and women were still held in bondage in the South.

In his letters to Smith, Forten described the level of opposition abolitionists were encountering—opposition he attributed to the very success they had already achieved. There had been anti-abolition meetings in Philadelphia, as well as mob attacks on black citizens and on white antislavery activists. Still, he had faith that their cause would prevail. He was particularly gratified to learn from Smith that, before he died, "the brave and generous *Lafayette*" had joined the Glasgow Emancipation Society, and he was warm in his praise of British abolitionist George Thompson, who "has come among us bearing the armour of *justice, love and truth*."[78]

A talented and obviously ambitious young man, Forten may have envied Smith his chance to get a university education and to experience life in a country where, by Smith's account and the account of his own brother-in-law, Robert Purvis, prejudice against people of color was far less pervasive than what he experienced every day in his native Philadelphia. If he did not have the educational opportunities his friend enjoyed in Scotland, James Jr. recognized that his father's wealth had still secured for him advantages few other young men of color had had. He felt an obligation to use his privileged position to help others less fortunate than himself. He became one of the charter members of the Library Company of Colored Persons, an organization he and his colleagues hoped would "add something to the general char[ac]ter of our people for the improvement of our intellectual faculties."[79] He spoke and occasionally sang (he reportedly had a fine singing voice) at antislavery rallies and at various community events. Like his siblings, he wrote poetry, and just occasionally he permitted himself to put his literary and artistic talents to use for purposes other than antislavery and moral uplift. He may have used those talents to pay court to a family friend, Martina Dickerson, whose album contains a number of examples of his work, including an ornate title page he drew for it.[80] But whatever feelings he may have had for Martina, he eventually married a New Yorker, Jane M. Vogelsang. Perhaps it was through his friendship with Smith, originally from New York, that he met his future wife, or perhaps he met her when he was in New York in 1838 for the annual meeting of the AAS.[81]

James and Charlotte were probably very pleased with their eldest son's choice of a wife. Jane Vogelsang came from a socially prominent African-American family. Her father, Peter, had emigrated to the United States from the West Indies, most likely St. Croix, and had been involved for several decades in a variety of causes, from abolition to moral reform and civil rights. He was also a successful and well-connected businessman, the "manager of the steamers on the Albany line."[82] Jane's older brother, Peter Jr., a friend of James McCune Smith's, was following in his father's footsteps.[83] Nothing is known of her mother, Maria Miller, but she may have been related to William Miller, Robert Purvis's stepfather. Through the Vogelsangs, ties were established between the Fortens and yet another prominent black family in New York City. Jane's brother married into the De Grasse family, who were active in abolition and the battle for legal and political equality.[84] An accomplished young woman whose education matched that the Fortens had given their own daughters, Jane would not feel out of place at 92 Lombard Street. The wedding of James Jr. and Jane M. Vogelsang took place on January 13, 1839, in New York City.[85] Within a year James and Charlotte had another grandson, James Vogelsang Forten.

ROBERT BRIDGES FORTEN, arguably the most gifted of Forten's sons, made his debut as a public speaker on November 7, 1834, when he addressed the members of the Philadelphia Female Anti-Slavery Society. His speech began with the usual admission of the speaker's lack of ability, coupled with the insistence that it was "a duty devolving on all those who have had even the least advantages of an education to employ the same, to the well-being of their fellow mortals."

> [T]o the real philanthropist, it is a source of unspeakable gratification to know, that in almost every city and town throughout the free . . . States, Anti-Slavery Societies are seen rearing their heads above the prejudices, that so meanly debase the character of the American people. . . . Those sounds we hear breaking upon our ears, are the chains of millions vibrating to the shouts of liberty and independence.

He had special words of encouragement for his female audience. In the great cause "we find woman in all her intellectual power, taking an active part in the

general melioration of mankind." Of women, he said: "Their acts spring instinctively from the heart, by nature ardent, by inheritance generous. . . . Their
smiles will check the iron rod of the tyrant, and melt the savage despot into
mercy."[86] It was the role of women to educate the next generation so that "not
one child can be found to pollute the shores of republican America, with the
footsteps of prejudice." He urged American women to emulate the women
antislavery activists of "the mother country" who were, in large part, responsible for Britain severing "the iron chain, in all her provinces."[87]

He ended by speaking of his own situation as a free man of color:

> I am "a man more sinned against than sinning." My color alone stands a par-
> tition-wall between me and my elevation—color, the effect of a cause known
> only to the great Giver of all gifts. . . . Prejudice in color must be admitted, by
> every candid person, to be one of the greatest evils that can take possession of
> the human breast . . . I call upon you . . . to resist the monster.[88]

Robert's first appearance as an antislavery speaker earned him warm praise
from Philadelphia's female abolitionists. Over the years he would address other
antislavery organizations, emphasizing again and again the need for immediate
action to end slavery and banish forever the evil influence of racial prejudice.
He spoke out on issues besides slavery and racism. Temperance was a cause
that concerned him, as it did his father.[89] He also worked to advance education
for men and women, black and white. As far as he was concerned, any reform
that made America a more enlightened and more virtuous nation was worth
promoting.

Robert Forten emerges from his speeches and writings as an articulate,
sensitive young man, a zealous abolitionist who craved the companionship of
others who thought as he did. Like his elder brother, he was active in the Young
Men's Anti-Slavery Society of Philadelphia.[90] He also found a friend in Daniel
Alexander Payne, who arrived in Philadelphia in 1835 on his way to the Lutheran
Theological Seminary in Gettysburg. A native of Charleston, South Carolina,
the teacher and future AME bishop was introduced to fellow Charlestonian
Robert Purvis, and through him he met the Fortens. He called James Sr. "venerable," and he was impressed by his children, "equally divided as regards sex,
and all talented." But it was Forten's second son whom he most admired. Robert was "a polished orator, a more than ordinary mathematician, and . . . gifted
with a poetical vein." He constructed a nine-foot-long telescope, ground and
set his own lenses, and had it accepted for exhibition by the Franklin Institute.
He also contributed a poem for Payne's album on the glories of ancient Rome.[91]

A romantic young man, as well as an articulate one, Robert soon formed a
deep attachment to one of his sisters' friends, Mary Virginia Wood. It was an
attachment that was as strong on her side as it was on his. He courted her with
poetry, and in the course of a few months Charlotte and James Forten married
off another of their children.

The Fortens knew Mary Wood and her sister almost as well as they knew the Purvises. Mary and Annie Wood had arrived in Philadelphia in the early 1830s from the small town of Hertford, off the Ablemarle Sound, in Perquimans County, North Carolina. Mary was in her late teens and Annie just a toddler.[92] Despite the difference in their ages, and the gossip that may have given rise to, they were not mother and daughter. All the available records describe them as sisters. They arrived apparently without their parents or any other family members. There is nothing to indicate how and with whom they lived in Philadelphia, but whatever arrangements Mary made or had made for her were judged eminently suitable by her peers. Charlotte and James Forten would hardly have allowed their daughters to associate with one whose reputation was in any way tarnished, and they certainly would not have approved of their son's growing attachment to her.

While the background of Mary and Annie Wood is not easy to trace, one fact is abundantly clear. They had wealthy friends. Money had been spent on Mary's education. She was genteel, accomplished, and an ardent supporter of abolition. There were no black Woods in Hertford, but various white men by the name of Wood were prominent members of the community in the early decades of the nineteenth century. On Front Street alone there was a John Wood, sometime clerk of the county, a John S. Wood, and a Captain James Wood. As one historian of Perquimans County commented: "This family has from time immemorial stood high in the community, & has sent out into the world many fine representative people."[93] Quite possibly two of those "fine representative people" were Mary and Annie.

In certain essentials, the story of Mary and Annie Wood resembled that of Robert and Joseph Purvis. They were probably the daughters of a well-to-do white man and a free woman of color or one of his "chattels personal." Perhaps their father had been forced to send them north out of a concern for his reputation. Perhaps he wanted to give them opportunities they could never have in North Carolina. Or perhaps he was anxious about their physical safety. A near neighbor of Mary's, and a young woman close to her in age, remembered the terror that swept the black community of Edenton, North Carolina, in the aftermath of Nat Turner's rebellion. Harriet Jacobs recalled how a white "search party" turned her home upside down in an effort to find incriminating "evidence."[94] Once the panic subsided, the white citizens calmed down, but they could not dismiss the fear that every slave was another Nat Turner and every free person of color another David Walker. Laws were passed restricting the lives of free and slave alike. Free blacks, especially those with education, were viewed with great suspicion.[95] Maybe this was what had driven the Wood sisters out of North Carolina.

Mary Wood soon became a great friend of the Forten children. Almost all of them contributed to her album. The sickly and serious-minded Mary Isabella wrote a rather charming piece on the purpose of an album, the pages of which might contain everything from "risible trifles" to "mementoes of esteem."[96] James Jr. wrote a verse "On Time." "T. B.," perhaps Thomas Butler, Jr., or Thomas J. Bowers, both of whom were members of the Fortens' social circle, contributed an acrostic, "The Dream," the first letter of each line spelling out the name "Mary Wood." Another admirer paid a graceful tribute with a play on Mary's middle name, Virginia. The state of Virginia, this writer declared, was blighted by "The tale which Slav'ry tells." But the young woman who was called Virginia was "A Dian in the gleaming west . . . Of Southron girls amongst the best." One who signed himself "Southron"—perhaps North Carolinian Frederick A. Hinton, perhaps Georgian Joseph Willson, both of them friends of the Fortens—wished for Mary a peaceful and prosperous life, and expressed the hope that she would choose a husband, since 1836 was a leap year and tradition decreed that in a leap year a woman could propose to the man of her choice.

Mary had no need to take advantage of leap year. She had no lack of suitors and happily accepted a proposal of marriage from the most persistent of them. Soon after he met her, Robert Forten had set about courting Mary in the appropriate genteel fashion, writing poem after poem for her album, each suitably decorous and chaste, and yet expressing friendship, regard, and a deepening affection.

Mary and Robert were married at St. Thomas's Church on October 18, 1836. The evening service was conducted by the church's new minister, Rev. William Douglass. The couple's first child, Charlotte, was born on August 17, 1837, in her grandparents' home.[97] The following year Robert and Mary left 92 Lombard and acquired a home of their own, renting 12 Jefferson Row from Robert Purvis before buying it outright in 1839. (Even though it was a family deal, Purvis made a profit of $300.)[98] Their second child, a son, was born on May 15, 1839. They named him Gerrit Smith Forten in honor of the New York abolitionist and reformer.[99]

IN TIME JAMES and Charlotte Forten's youngest son, William, would make his mark as an abolitionist and a crusader for civil rights, but in the 1830s, while his older siblings were distinguishing themselves in the antislavery cause, William was only in his early teens, too young to take an active role in very many endeavors. Still, James Forten had plans for him. In 1835, when William left the Pennsylvania Abolition Society's Clarkson School, he was dispatched to Oneida Institute in Whitesboro, New York, in the heart of the "burned-over district." Oneida was truly a product of the Second Great Awakening. It had been founded in 1827 by George Washington Gale, the man who converted evangelist Charles Grandison Finney. It had produced antislavery radical Theodore Dwight Weld and was a hotbed of abolitionist fervor. True, there had been a schism in 1832 between the gradualists and the immediatists, between the advocates of African colonization and their opponents, but the men of Weld's (and Forten's) stamp had won out. Gale had retired, ostensibly for reasons of health, and the institute was now directed by Beriah Green, who was committed to "immediate, unconditional, and uncompensated emancipation." James Forten probably met Green, a close friend of Gerrit Smith's, at the founding of the AAS.[100]

Oneida was run on the manual labor system, with students working at a wide range of skilled trades while they secured a classical education. It was strictly interracial by the time William Forten arrived. One student recalled encountering there

> a motley company of emancipator's boys from Cuba; mulattoes; a Spanish student; an Indian named Kunkapot; black men who had served as sailors, or as city hackmen, also the purest Africans escaped from slavery; sons of American radicals, Bible students scanning Hebrew verse with ease . . . enthusiasts, plowboys and printers; also real students of elegant tastes, captured by the genius of President Green.[101]

William was twelve or thirteen when he was sent to Oneida. The trustees had approved the admission of young men of color only the year before, and Green had been eagerly spreading the word. William began his studies in the "juvenile" or preparatory department. In time he might graduate to the upper division, which required students to be at least fifteen, "to be able to furnish proof of a good intellectual and moral character, to be of sound health, and demonstrate competence to teach a common or elementary school and recite the Greek grammar."[102] William's classmates included several young black men who would go on to play prominent roles in the antislavery movement, among them Henry Highland Garnet, Amos Gerry Beman, Alexander Crummell, and Amos N. Freeman.[103]

William was still at Oneida in 1836, but he had left by 1837. Perhaps he was homesick. Perhaps he was not sufficiently well prepared for the rigorous course of study. Regardless, his father's enthusiasm for the school endured. In Oneida's "crisis year" of 1839, when it seemed the institute might close for lack of funds, James Forten and Robert Purvis pledged to buy the right to ten years' free tuition and room rent for poor but deserving black students.[104]

THE FORTEN CHILDREN inherited a great deal from their father: their staunch support of abolition, their love of learning, and their eloquence. But their mother was also an important influence on their lives. If Charlotte Vandine Forten features in visitors' descriptions of the household at 92 Lombard it is as a kind and attentive hostess, as James Forten's faithful and conscientious spouse, as the mother of a group of talented young men and women, but seldom as a force in her own right. Admittedly, bearing nine children and raising eight, superintending a large household, regulating apprentices and servants, dealing with a host of callers, and being prepared to entertain all and sundry left little time for anything else. However, she did have interests beyond her immediate family circle. She was a zealous member of her church. She was active in the Philadelphia Female Anti-

Slavery Society. She had her own friends, both African-American women, such as Grace Douglass, Amy Cassey, and Hetty Burr, and white women, such as Hannah M. Blayney, sister of Willis H. Blayney, high constable of Philadelphia.[105] She also wrote poetry. As "CF" she contributed a poem, "The Mother's Joy," to the album of family friend Mary Ann Dickerson in 1834. It is the closest we get to a personal comment from James Forten's wife.

> Thine is a happy lot sweet boy:
> Oh! that mine were the same,
>   Like thee, to be my Mother's joy,
> Like thee, to lisp her name.
>   My mother's spirit, long has fled
> This world of woe and pain;
>   But I do hope, although she's dead,
> To meet with her again.[106]

IN THE 1830s the Forten household was alive with antislavery activity. Few abolitionists who visited the city missed the chance to introduce themselves to James Forten and his family. They dined at 92 Lombard, took tea, or simply came to call. What they saw and heard fascinated them. Forten himself was an imposing figure. Six feet tall, he literally towered over most of his guests.[107] Witty and well informed about a host of issues, he was well worth listening to, and the story of his life enthralled visitor after visitor. Charlotte, gracious and kindly, was a thoughtful hostess, attuned to the needs of her guests, and a "personality" in her own right. But James and Charlotte were increasingly willing to step back and make their children the focus of attention. They had done their best, giving them the finest education they could. How their children used that education, and how they displayed through their myriad activities the lessons their parents had taught them about the duties that came with the privileges they enjoyed, would help shape the course of organized antislavery and reform in Philadelphia and beyond. Gradually the younger generation of Fortens came to accept that they were "abolition property." Freeborn, well educated and affluent they might be, but their parents had never intended that they should use their many advantages to separate themselves from the less fortunate members of the African-American community. Their feelings might be bruised by insensitive remarks from white abolition allies. They might feel uncomfortable at being, in a sense, put on display as exemplars of black intellectual equality. But they knew and understood the millions in bondage in the South endured far worse than wounded feelings. If they were "abolition property," so be it. The antislavery cause was their cause and it was one they would never abandon.

12

TIME OF TRIAL

W HAT EVEN THE most zealous of white abolitionists were inclined to overlook was that freedom from slavery was not synonymous with full citizenship. A black man or woman need not wear a slave's shackles to be "unfree." Every day of their lives free people of color grappled with the reality of discrimination. In most states of the Union the law relegated them to a situation of quasifreedom. They lived in a particular state, but they did not "belong" to it in the same way that their white neighbors did. Their presence was tolerated, nothing more. And as the racial violence that beset so many communities in the 1830s and 1840s made abundantly clear, it was not at all certain that their presence would continue to be tolerated.

James Forten was a perennial manager of the American Anti-Slavery Society. His sons and his son-in-law were officers in that same organization. His wife and daughters helped found the Philadelphia Female Anti-Slavery Society, one of the first women's abolition societies in the nation. The Fortens and the Purvises regularly entertained the likes of William Lloyd Garrison, Samuel J. May, James and Lucretia Mott, George Thompson, and the Grimké sisters, the white leaders of radical antislavery. They helped sustain antislavery journals, spoke and wrote in support of abolition, and enjoyed an extensive correspondence with abolitionists on both sides of the Atlantic. Although they were among the luminaries of the movement, when all was said and done, they lived lives that were severely restricted by law and custom. In the 1830s and early 1840s those restrictions would press ever more tightly upon them. While battling alongside their white allies for freedom for the slaves of the South, they were also fighting a war much closer to home. Their white friends knew something of their struggles and would often wish them godspeed, but those struggles were frequently swallowed up in the larger battle to put an end to the South's "peculiar institution."

That his future and the future of his children, his grandchildren, and his entire community were inextricably linked to the persistence of chattel slavery south of the Mason-Dixon line James Forten knew only too well. Remove slavery, he reasoned, and the prejudice of caste would die with it. But in the last decade of his life he was constantly reminded that so many whites in his home state, a state that had long since taken steps to outlaw slavery, cared little about the continued existence of slavery beyond the borders of Pennsylvania. What they resented was the notion of black people becoming their equals, asserting their rights to "do what the white man can do, and go where the white man can go." Again and again James Forten the abolitionist would have to face up to a stark reality. In his native city, the city where he had risen from humble apprentice to successful man of business, the city he had willingly defended in times of crisis, his own freedom was far from secure.

James Forten was no stranger to the depths of white racism. He had witnessed mob violence before. He had read in the press and heard on the streets attacks on black people as lazy, ignorant, and lawless parasites. Despite his optimism about the liberalizing "spirit of the times," he anticipated more battles before the glorious millennium. As he soon discovered, the battles of the 1830s would be fiercer and bloodier than anything he had previously experienced.

ON NOVEMBER 23, 1831, a number of young white men got together at Upton's Tavern in Dock Street, not far from Forten's sail loft, to discuss a matter of the utmost urgency. They were certain Nat Turner and his rebel band had not acted alone. Virginia's bondsmen, they were convinced, had been incited to violence by Northern free people of color, who had flooded the South with "incendiary publications . . . and are . . . even now, secretly feeding the firebrand which has been hurled amid the peaceful habitations of our southern brethren."

Much as they sympathized with their "southern friends," these young white workingmen were unhappy about moves in the South and certain states in the Midwest to require all free black residents to post a bond to ensure their "good behavior" or leave. It was bad enough that a host of these "dishonest and abandoned" wretches had found their way to Canada. If another war with Britain broke out, the British military authorities north of the border could deploy these black expatriates, all of them "burning with hatred and revenge," against the United States. More troubling still was the knowledge that some of the outcasts from the South and the Midwest had taken refuge in Pennsylvania. The young men at Upton's Tavern demanded that the Pennsylvania legislature pass a law forcing these unwelcome newcomers to go elsewhere, and they urged that lawmakers also take steps to expel those blacks already living in the state. It was common knowledge that most would gladly emigrate if the means could be found to speed them on their way, "and the meagre minority . . . now averse to it, could easily be convinced." Frankly, they did not much care where their black neighbors went, "provided it has no connexion with this hemisphere."[1]

These young white workingmen soon proved that they had influential friends in Harrisburg. Or perhaps it is more accurate to say they were just giving voice to concerns that were shared by other whites, some of them in positions of power in state government. Whatever the truth of the matter, on December 17, 1831, less than a month after the meeting at Upton's Tavern, legislators were alerted to the "danger" facing Pennsylvania. According to Mr. Vansant of Philadelphia County,

> Virginia and Maryland are about to pass . . . penal enactments, for the purpose of expelling their free black population . . . whereby the adjoining states without some counteracting provision . . . must be overrun by an influx of ignorant, indolent and depraved population.

He urged swift action. A bill was speedily drafted and on December 19, Franklin B. Davis, another Philadelphia lawmaker, moved for a second reading.[2]

The provisions of House Bill 446 were truly draconian. Any person of color entering Pennsylvania would have twenty days to post a $500 bond or be arrested and forcibly removed from the state. Newcomers and long-term residents must register in the county where they lived and could not move from county to county at will. Employers of unregistered people of color would be fined, with a share of the fine going to whoever had tipped off the authorities. Special censuses would be taken so the law could be enforced. The bill also proposed the repeal of the state's fugitive slave law in favor of the much harsher federal law.[3] The message was clear: African Americans from other states could expect a chilly reception in Pennsylvania, and those already in the state were there under sufferance.

Appalled by the Upton's Tavern meeting and by what they had heard about House Bill 446, James Forten, Robert Purvis, and William Whipper, a recent arrival from Columbia, Pennsylvania, who was making a name for himself as both a businessman and a community activist, organized a meeting of their own on January 4.[4] The message they and the rest of the black community had for their white neighbors was that the charges against them were "illiberal and unfounded" and leveled by "a few *officious* young men" who most certainly did not belong to the "respectable part of our citizens."[5]

Led by Forten, Purvis, and Whipper, Philadelphia's people of color launched their own public relations initiative. They were proud of their state and appreciative of its "*mild* and benevolent laws." Pennsylvania was hardly in danger of being overrun by thousands of African-American migrants, but the state's "mighty fame" as a haven of liberty for men and women of "all nations, kindred and tongues" had naturally attracted blacks as well as whites eager to settle in a place where they could feel secure in their freedom. They expressed shock and sadness at allegations that black Philadelphians had "figur[ed] in the *Southampton tragedy*." They denied accusations that "our reading of [David] Walker's pamphlet and our support [of] the Liberator have been the . . . cause, of this much to be lamented circumstance." They urged their critics to subscribe to Garrison's *Liberator* and judge for themselves whether it incited slaves to violence. As for the story floating around in the city that a white woman living close to the scene of the Virginia slave uprising had confessed to being "an agent for a gang of black desperadoes in Philadelphia," it was utterly without foundation.[6]

James Forten knew he must do more than simply hold a meeting to set the record straight. He cast his mind back to a similar crisis almost twenty years before, the crisis that had inspired him to write his *Letters from a Man of Colour*. It was not enough just to take to task the Upton's Tavern "gentry." The African-American community must reach lawmakers and convince them that restrictive legislation was both unfair and unnecessary. It might be too late once a new law was on the books.

After their meeting disbanded, Forten, Purvis, and Whipper set to work to draw up a suitably respectful statement on behalf of themselves and the rest of Philadelphia's African-American community. They then prevailed on Jesse R. Burden, a legislator from Philadelphia, to present it to the state senate. No abolitionist, Burden thought the statement at least deserved to be read, as it was written by "men who merited . . . regard and respect." Others beside Burden took note of it. Samuel Breck observed that its principal author was "a black *gentleman* . . . maugre [in spite of] his black face."[7]

The three petitioners put their case clearly. Why, they asked, "at a moment when all mankind seem to be struggling for freedom," did the great state of Pennsylvania contemplate such an oppressive law? During the Revolutionary era the white citizens of many states, Pennsylvania foremost among them, had recoiled at the notion of imposing slavery on others while rejecting it for themselves. Pennsylvania had taken steps to abolish slavery, "and from that time her avowed policy has been . . . to preserve unimpaired the freedom of all men, whatever might be the shade of complexion with which it may have pleased the *Almighty* to distinguish them." What had happened to change things?[8]

Demands to toughen the fugitive slave law were, the three men insisted, truly shocking. Pennsylvanians had proven themselves more devoted to liberty than the federal government, stipulating that an alleged runaway must have a hearing before a judge, and not before a common magistrate, who was vested only with the power to rule on matters where less than a hundred dollars was involved. Was liberty worth less? they wanted to know. With their thoughts on the panic that had gripped so many whites nationwide in the wake of the Nat Turner rebellion, they urged lawmakers not to take any hasty action at "this time of excitement, when the minds of men are less qualified for impartial legislation than in calmer periods."9

To strengthen their case they offered evidence that the African-American population of Philadelphia was not burdensome. Black people took care of their own poor *and* paid taxes to support white paupers. "Many of us, by our . . . industry, have acquired a little property, and have become freeholders." They had established churches, Sunday schools, literary and tract societies, and temperance organizations. The more than fifty African-American beneficial societies in Philadelphia not only safeguarded their members against poverty but laid down strict rules of conduct. Despite the refusal of the vast majority of white craftsmen to take on young black men as apprentices, "there are between four and five hundred people of colour in the city and suburbs, who follow mechanical trades." Overall, "we think . . . we will not suffer by a comparison with our white neighbours."10

The facts and figures the three men had compiled were given considerable publicity. Writing in *Hazard's Register,* one white Philadelphian observed that he had "long known that the People of Color . . . are a very improving people." He recommended his fellow citizens read the data about the black population and ponder them, and he added that James Forten, whom he credited with putting the report together, was "well known to his fellow citizens for his . . . industry, talents and probity."11 Several years later, "Benezet," an anonymous Quaker, asked "our estimable citizen James Forten" for information on the African-American community that he could publish in the Quaker journal *The Friend.* Forten gave him a copy of the 1832 report.12

The legislature adjourned for the summer in 1832 without taking action on House Bill 446, but lawmakers voted to hold it over until the next session.13 Pennsylvania's black citizens had won a reprieve, but for how long? Over the following months there were further protests and more memorials, each posing the same question Forten, Purvis and Whipper had asked. What had free people of color done to deserve such treatment? They had always thought that they were citizens, "and . . . that within this Commonwealth, they could do what the white man can do, and go where the white man can go." They were not the innovators; they were just defending the status quo. "The colored population merely ask to be left as they are."14

HOUSE BILL 446 was eventually lost in committee, but black Philadelphians, James Forten among them, were soon forced to confront an unpalatable truth. They were not "to be left as [they] are." The legislature was flooded with petitions, by far the largest number of them from Philadelphia, demanding strict curbs on black migration into Pennsylvania and urging support for the American Colonization Society in the hope of encouraging black people already resident in the state to depart for Liberia.15 While some white citizens pursued constitutional methods of dealing with what they saw as a serious problem, others preferred to operate outside the law. During the 1830s and into the 1840s violence or the threat of it surfaced in Philadelphia with distressing regularity.

On July 4, 1832, the *Julius Pringle* docked at one of the wharves along the Delaware. On board were ninety-two black men, women, and children. Freed from slavery by North Carolina Quakers, they were bound for Liberia when their ship was obliged to make an unscheduled stop in Philadelphia for some essential repairs. Within minutes the waterfront was alive with rumors. These people had come to stay. They were allies of Nat Turner. There were hundreds of them, all armed to the teeth. A mob soon gathered—some elements in it doubtless fired up with liquor since it was Independence Day—and the ship was forced to sail downriver to Chester.[16]

Nor did emotions cool with the change of seasons. On October 10 there was a fight between blacks and whites in Moyamensing, one of Philadelphia's unincorporated suburbs, where cheaper housing and lower rents had encouraged many African Americans to make their homes. In this confrontation one black person was killed and ten people, all of them black, were arrested. However, because the unrest came in the midst of a major outbreak of election violence, the press took little notice of it.[17] Nevertheless, it was an ugly episode that demonstrated how rapidly relations between blacks and whites in and around Philadelphia were deteriorating. It could be only a matter of time before an incident like this escalated into a full-blown race riot.

In July 1834, Forten's old friend Benjamin Lundy noted in his newspaper, the *Genius of Universal Emancipation*, rumors "about certain arrangements now making, to get up a MOB in this city . . . similar to that which has so recently been excited . . . in New York."[18] Philadelphia was simmering in what had been a very hot and humid spell when one of James Forten's younger sons, probably Thomas, was set upon in the street on the evening of August 9. He had been sent on an errand and was returning home when he was attacked "by a gang of fifty or sixty young men in blue jackets and trowsers, and low-crowned straw hats." He took at least one blow to the head before escaping. A white neighbor followed the assailants "out of regard for the lad's father" and heard them agree to meet again in the same spot two nights later. The neighbor told Forten, who contacted the mayor, John Swift. Two nights later the police were waiting and made several arrests.[19] The kind of random attack that Thomas Forten had suffered was hardly unusual, but tensions were building in the city, and this apparently isolated act of violence proved the prelude to an explosion of racial violence that would last for three successive nights.

The riot began the day after Mayor Swift and his men had arrested some of those responsible for the assault on Thomas Forten. The flash point was the Flying Horses, a carousel on South Street above Seventh. It was popular with both blacks and whites, and that occasioned "difficulties." Rumors began circulating that some whites had been insulted at the carousel by a bunch of blacks and that a number of black youths known to frequent the Flying Horses had attacked the headquarters of a white fire company. The rumors did their work. On the night of August 12, "a detachment of boys and very young men" converged on the Flying Horses "and stimulated a quarrel," in the course of which they completely demolished the carousel and the building that housed it.[20]

Proceeding to neighborhoods where they knew many black people lived—St. Mary Street in the city, and Bedford and Baker Streets in Moyamensing—they started attacking homes, barging in and destroying anything they could get their hands on.[21] Whites put lights in their windows and their homes were spared. Any black person unlucky enough to meet the rioters in the street was beaten. The authorities in Moyamensing seemed powerless to stop them, but in the city itself Mayor Swift and his police managed to rout them.[22]

The unrest was far from ended, though. In the course of the next two nights the mob wreaked havoc on the southern fringes of the city and in adjoining Moyamensing and Southwark, the areas with the highest concentrations of black residents. Swift did what he could. He summoned the posse comitatus and swore in as deputies men he considered reliable. He also mobilized a troop of cavalry and several companies of volunteer infantrymen. His intervention saved more than a few black lives. For instance, on the evening of August 13, word spread that Benezet Hall, a black-owned meeting hall on Seventh near Lombard, "was filled with several hundred armed negroes." The mob rushed to the building, found it shuttered, and milled around outside baying for blood, but they were kept from entering it by Swift and his forces. After all the rioters had gone home, Swift went inside and found "several frightened negroes." But the mayor and his men could not be everywhere at once. While they were busy at Benezet Hall, lawbreakers had a field day elsewhere, attacking black churches and meetinghouses, invading black-owned homes, and generally terrorizing the African-American community.[23]

Inevitably, there were casualties. The *Pennsylvanian* reported that one elderly black man had been killed and a number of people seriously injured. The rioters even abused the dead. In one house a corpse awaiting burial was thrown out of its coffin and in another "a dead infant was . . . cast on the floor, the mother being at the same time barbarously treated."[24]

Many black residents of Moyamensing and Southwark fled across the Delaware "and formed a sort of bivouac in the fields." Others took refuge with friends in the city proper, reasoning that Swift and his men were more effective than the authorities in the outlying districts. The editor of the *Pennsylvanian* sympathized with them. "Their little property is totally lost, and many were driven from their dwellings . . . almost without a rag of clothing."[25] But it was not just the poorer members of the black community who suffered, judging by the destruction. The *Philadelphia Inquirer* reported that thirty-seven houses had been destroyed, "some of them substantial brick tenements," and that property wrecked or looted included "feather beds, mahogany sideboards, tables, looking glasses, China ware, [and] chairs."[26]

James Forten had a harrowing time. Not only was one of his sons attacked, but he himself received death threats. He reported them to Swift and the sheriff, both of whom undertook to guarantee his safety. They made good on their promise. "His house was guarded by a horse patrol, who continued in their rounds to pass it at short intervals."[27] His apprentices also rallied to his defense. "[T]hrowing aside [his] Quaker principles," young Ezra Johnson "armed himself with all the ardor of his revolutionary sire, to protect . . . the family and property of his master."[28] Forten told an English visitor, Edward Abdy, that he received an additional offer of help from an unlikely quarter. "An Irishman, of the name of Hogan, behaved most nobly. . . . Having heard that Mr. Forten's house was likely to be attacked, he offered his services to defend it. 'Whoever,' said he, 'would enter at this door, must pass over my dead body.'"[29]

It was probably James Forten's opposition to the American Colonization Society, as much as his wealth and social status, that caused him to be singled out. Elsewhere in his account of the disturbances, Abdy mentioned that "One of the sufferers, a man of wealth and great respectability, was told afterwards . . . that he would not have been molested, if he had not, by refusing to go to Liberia, prevented others from leaving the country."[30]

During the course of the riot a number of whites were arrested, but there were few public condemnations of the violence. Although a committee of inquiry was convened, its conclusions gave little comfort to black residents. The committee basically blamed them for the trouble, isolating as causes white fears over job competition, the aggressive tactics some blacks used to rescue fugitive slaves from the officers of the law, and the noisy services at certain black churches.[31] No wonder that when British novelist Harriet Martineau spent Christmas Day of 1834 with the Fortens she found the usually optimistic James Forten "depressed . . . at the condition & prospects of his race."[32] The riot, coupled with the silent acquiescence of so many "respectable" white citizens, had taken a toll on him.

THE FOLLOWING SUMMER another riot shattered the uneasy calm. The populace was already stirred up by the case of alleged runaway slave Mary Gilmore. The defense had made much of the fact that she was reputed to be white, and she was able to secure her freedom. Hot on the heels of the Gilmore case came the murderous attack on his master by a deranged black servant.[33]

Once word of the attack got out, a crowd composed largely of "the very lowest classes . . . apprentices and half grown boys" gathered in the neighborhood of Sixth and Seventh, and Lombard and South Streets, precisely the area in which the bulk of James Forten's rental property was located.[34] There were isolated assaults that night, but the real trouble broke out the following night. Mayor Swift responded with his characteristic energy, establishing a police presence "in the southern section of the city, in the vicinity of the scenes of former disturbances." However, he had no jurisdiction outside city limits. The mob was left to rampage in Southwark unopposed. They spared black women and the elderly of both sexes, but any young man of color they chanced upon was beaten unmercifully. In the Shippen Street neighborhood, where James Forten had owned his first home and where he still held several pieces of real estate, numerous houses were broken into and ransacked.[35]

The destruction was greatest on Red Row, a collection of shacks near Eighth and Shippen inhabited exclusively by poor blacks. One dwelling was set on fire and the rioters watched gleefully as the flames spread. When the firemen arrived to douse the fire the mob told them to leave. Gentle persuasion failed, so the rioters resorted to cutting the firefighters' hoses and pelting them with stones. Finally, amid fears the fire would burn out of control, "respectable" whites took a hand. As the editor of the *Philadelphia Gazette* observed: "It was a contest of honest . . . citizens anxious to . . . save the city from conflagration, against a band of midnight brawlers."[36]

The trouble continued elsewhere. Some black residents nailed their doors shut, but the rioters tore down the flimsy barricades. A few copied the tactics of their white neighbors and placed candles in their windows, hoping the rioters would assume they were white, too. In fact, the mob did attack some white homes, either by mistake "or because the inmates were companions of colored people." As they had done the year before, many black families fled with what they could carry.[37]

Individually or in small groups, some African Americans tried to fight back. One unnamed black citizen armed himself with an axe and prepared to meet force with force. Only the timely arrival of the city constable saved him from being lynched.[38] On the second night of unrest a rumor started up "that a three story brick house in St. Mary street was garrisoned by armed blacks, who were resolved . . . to sell their lives dearly." The challenge was irresistible. The mob headed off to St. Mary Street, but the mayor had forestalled them. It was just as well that he had, for the rumor proved well founded.

> [A] body of coloured men . . . armed with knives, bludgeons and pistols, had sought refuge in the house. . . . They had taken the sashes of the upper windows out—had provided themselves with a large pile of stones, and were prepared to resist to the death any attempt to dislodge them.

The editor of the *Philadelphia Inquirer* insisted they were local residents who merely sought shelter from the rioters and not blacks seeking a violent confrontation. The city solicitor and the Recorder intervened, persuading the defenders to leave by the rear of the building while the mayor and the police held back their would-be attackers.[39]

In the aftermath of the riot, William Lloyd Garrison received a description of it from an unnamed black correspondent in Philadelphia, possibly James Forten or his son-in-law. Although the writer praised the conduct of some whites, notably the fire fighters, he was infuriated by much of the commentary

in the press, "which contents itself with recommending to the colored population, meekness and propriety of conduct, keeping in doors, &c. . . . [W]e look
in vain for a . . . vindication of our rights, as a deeply injured and unoffending
people."[40]

THE FORTENS COULD not insulate themselves from the waves of lawlessness
that were sweeping across Philadelphia. In addition to the assault on James
Forten's son and threats against Forten himself in 1834, in 1835 some of Forten's
real estate in Southwark and the city proper had most likely sustained damage.
Two years later, on a peaceful Sunday afternoon in the early summer of 1837,
the residents of 92 Lombard Street were relaxing after a morning spent at church,
and perhaps preparing to return to St. Thomas's for an evening service, when
they heard the ominous sounds of raised voices and smashing glass. On Fifth
and Lombard, just yards from their front door, a crowd was gathering. A short
while earlier, a number of young whites had been engaged in an altercation
with a group of black men. There had been some stone-throwing and then a
pistol shot rang out from a house where an African-American man lived. Apparently the shot was an accident. The man had been cleaning his gun when it
went off, wounding him in the hand. However, the whites scattered, spreading
reports that a white boy had been shot. A mob collected and besieged the home
of the shooter, but quick action on the part of the mayor prevented further
unrest. Although the trouble was soon suppressed, it was likely to break out
again. Abolitionist Lewis C. Gunn observed that the area of Fifth and Lombard
was a favorite haunt of white apprentices, where, safe from the eyes of their
masters, they could indulge in all sorts of mischief.[41]

Year after year the violence continued, often sparked by the most trivial of
causes—an exchange of words, a "disrespectful" look, a rumor that the black
people in one or another neighborhood were getting above themselves in some
way and needed to be taught a salutary lesson about deference to whites.[42]
Sometimes the violence escalated into a full-blown race riot. Sometimes it ended
with a few arrests and some property damage. All too often the perpetrators
escaped punishment. Philadelphia's black residents could only pray for a cessa-
tion of the violence and prepare themselves for the next outbreak. But as de-
moralizing as the continued outbreaks of rioting were, black Philadelphians,
and in fact black people across the entire state of Pennsylvania, were about to
suffer another assault, arguably a far more serious one. That assault would come
not from a band of "midnight brawlers" but from the very men charged with
making the law.

BACK IN 1822, when Philadelphia was a somewhat more tranquil city than it
was in the 1830s, Samuel Breck was out walking one day when he was "ac-
costed" by "A Negro man named Fortune . . . offering his hand to me." Breck
was surprised, but, "knowing [James Forten's] respectability," he stopped and
shook hands. Forten politely informed Breck that Breck was in his debt.

[H]e told me that at my late election to Congress, he had taken 15 white men to vote for me. In my sail loft (he said) I have 30 persons at work . . . and among them are 22 journeymen—15 of whom are white . . . All the white men went to the poles and voted for you.

As he walked away, Breck pondered the peculiar status of men of color in Pennsylvania. He believed they could vote if they were tax-payers, but at least in the eastern half of the state, "owing to custom, prejudice or design, they never presume to approach the hustings."[43]

So much for Breck's interpretation of the exchange, but what did James Forten make of it? It is easy to see why he wanted to support Breck with whatever influence he had at his disposal. Breck was a well-connected man of business and he opposed slavery. Only the year before, he had introduced into the Pennsylvania Senate a bill to emancipate the state's remaining slaves.[44] Sympathetic though Forten knew Breck to be, he did not use the chance meeting to remonstrate with him about his exclusion from the polls. Whether or not he considered himself entitled to vote at this point was immaterial. As an employer of white men in an era when the privacy of the voting booth was unknown, James Forten *did* take part in the political process, albeit indirectly. He paid his workers and considered himself justified in telling them how to vote and accompanying them to the polling-place to make sure they obeyed his orders. If we are to believe what he told Breck—and there is no reason not to—he enjoyed not one vote but fifteen.

But could Forten vote and did he believe himself to have the right to do so? The question has no easy answer, for it hinged on the interpretation of a single word. The Pennsylvania constitution of 1790 enfranchised "every freeman, of the age of twenty-one years, having resided in the State two years next before the election, and within that time paid a State or county tax, which shall have been assessed at least six months before the election."[45] Was a "freeman" the same as a "free man," a man who was not a slave? Some contended that any man, regardless of race, who was legally free and met the other requirements was a qualified voter. Others answered that "freeman" was a term that could only be applied to whites and that no man of color, however "free" and however prosperous, could vote in Pennsylvania.

Divining the true intent of the framers of the 1790 constitution was not easy. Many years after the convention, when most of the participants were dead, a friend of Forten's, white abolitionist Joseph Parrish, contacted one of the few survivors, former United States Secretary of the Treasury Albert Gallatin. Gallatin admitted his memory of some long-ago events was rather hazy. Nevertheless, "I have a lively recollection that . . . the proposition pending before the Convention limited the right of suffrage to 'free white citizens &c.' and that the word 'white' was struck out on my motion." Gallatin had not been upholding the rights of black men, although he conceded that had been the result of his motion. He had been afraid the wording might be construed as disqualifying darker-skinned Europeans like himself. He referred Parrish to the printed proceedings of the convention, but they contained no mention of that particular debate.[46]

So who was qualified to vote in Pennsylvania? Uncertainty prevailed for decades. In 1796 a petition was sent to the state senate from Huntingdon County to require masters to educate their black servants because "many were poorly fitted to exercise citizenship to which they had been admitted." In 1807, when lawmakers were considering legislation to limit the rights of free people of color, a move was made to exempt those black men who were "legal voters." Obviously at some times and in some localities African Americans were considered "freemen," and some, at least, came to the polls. In 1826 a perplexed Governor Schulze asked, "Is the term freeman so construed in one district as totally to exclude, and in another freely to admit persons of color to exercise the right of suffrage?"[47] The answer was "yes."

In rural counties with few black residents, it hardly mattered if a handful voted. They were unlikely to determine the outcome of an election. But in Philadelphia County, the county with by far the largest concentration of African Americans in the state, hundreds of them freeholders and hence taxpayers, white citizens argued they had good cause to feel apprehensive.[48]

Whatever the 1790 constitution said, the tyranny of the majority ruled. Foreign visitors were made very much aware of the power of "custom" in relation to black men and the franchise. In 1831, the French travelers Alexis de Tocqueville and Gustave de Beaumont asked a Philadelphia acquaintance if black men could vote. He replied they had the legal right to do so, but "The law with us is nothing if it is not supported by public opinion . . . and the magistrates don't feel strong enough to enforce the laws favourable" to blacks. In 1834, Edward Abdy observed that black people in Pennsylvania had the right to vote, "but they seldom or never make use of it in Philadelphia." A year later, fellow Englishman Andrew Bell noted that there was "no positive law to prevent their taking part in elections; and knowing this, I asked a Philadelphian why they did not come to the poll[s]? His answer was significant, 'Just let them try!'"[49]

How did James Forten and other affluent men of color in Philadelphia view the whole matter of the franchise? Their few public statements suggest that, at least until 1837, they saw voting rights as rights better left untested. Back in 1813, in his *Letters from a Man of Colour*, Forten had insisted: "We wish not to legislate, for our means of information . . . are . . . so circumscribed, that we must consider ourselves incompetent to the task; but let us, in legislation, be considered as men."[50] Of course, legislating was not necessarily the same as voting. Forten could have been sensible of his right to vote while denying any wish to run for public office, but there is no evidence that he ever turned up at the polls to cast his vote on election day. He did not raise the matter of the franchise in the statement he and Whipper and Purvis submitted to the state legislature in 1832, nor did the other African-American men who presented their own petitions and memorials. Indeed, "the People of Colour of the County of Philadelphia" contended they did not expect or even want a broad declaration of their rights, especially the right to vote. "These slumbering privileges need not be awakened now."[51] Confident of his control over the political loyalty of his white employees or fearful that a bold assertion of his "slumbering privileges" would provoke violence, James Forten apparently found it prudent to avoid the whole question. So, evidently, did the vast majority of well-to-do black men in Philadelphia, the very men who would have to lead the charge if their rights were to be recognized.

Some observers began to warn that "slumbering privileges" had an unpleasant way of disappearing. In 1831 an unnamed white Philadelphian wrote to the *Liberator* to urge the city's men of color to act. They had apparently accepted the "illegal means" used to keep them from the polls, but the writer insisted that it was time for them to respond. Let them "hold themselves in readiness for the ensuing elections" and demand their rights.[52] One man did rise to the challenge. The fiery ex-slave Junius C. Morel tried to galvanize the community on the issue of the franchise. He organized the "Political Association." "Funds were collected, eminent counsel consulted, and matters . . . made ready to assert our claim." However, as he later recalled, "a vain temerity on the part of some, and a suicidal apathy on the part of others, prostrated my designs."[53]

If black Philadelphians such as James Forten were understandably cautious, given the growing propensity for violence on the part of their white neighbors, men of color elsewhere in the state *were* prepared to take a stand. That is hardly surprising, in view of the fact that some of them had been accustomed to vote. In Luzerne County in 1835, for instance, William Fogg presented himself at the polls on election day, only to be turned away. He brought suit and the County Court of Common Pleas upheld his rights as a "freeman" and a taxpayer. The verdict was appealed to the Pennsylvania Supreme Court.[54] Others besides Mr. Fogg would insist on their rights over the next few years.

As for the opposition forces, they, too, were gathering. The year before Fogg's initial suit, Chambersburg lawyer John F. Denny, an avowed supporter of the American Colonization Society, had no hesitation in declaring: "That the coloured man is clothed with the political rights and privileges of the white man, is an opinion, that . . . never *generally prevailed* in Pennsylvania. He has always been viewed as a *quasi* freeman only." While black men voting was "a prevailing custom" in some counties, "custom" could not legitimize a practice that was "destitute of all legal foundation."[55]

In 1837, when white Pennsylvanians decided to revise the state's constitution, it was not with a view to barring black men from voting. It was to bring Pennsylvania into line with many of her sister states by abolishing property qualifications for the franchise. However, at least some of the delegates who gathered in Harrisburg on May 2, 1837, for the first session of the so-called Reform Convention recognized that not imposing a ban on black voting would enfranchise virtually every man of color in Pennsylvania. Instead of worrying about a few hundred black voters, they would have to worry about tens of thousands.

The first sign of trouble came on May 12 when John B. Sterigere of Montgomery County proposed restricting the franchise to white men. In fact, Sterigere composed and submitted an entire constitution for consideration. Buried in the mass of verbiage was the racial limitation. He was ruled out of order and the delegates moved on to other business, but Sterigere was an obstinate man and refused to give up without a fight.[56] As the convention progressed, he emerged as one of the most vociferous opponents of voting rights, and indeed any substantial civil rights, for people of color.

Various members of the African-American community soon realized they had cause to worry. In Philadelphia in early June Frederick A. Hinton, a prosperous barber who served on the vestry at St. Thomas's with James Forten, called a meeting to discuss reports he had received from Harrisburg about a legal assault on black rights. He suggested the drafting of "a respectful memorial to be accompanied with an exhibit of the moral, social and religious institutions and improvement" of Philadelphia's people of color. His suggestion was approved, and he and Presbyterian minister Charles W. Gardner were appointed to present the memorial.[57] Forten may or may not have been at the meeting, but the approach, a respectful statement supported by facts and figures, was one that surely had his endorsement.

The reports from Harrisburg proved well founded. On June 23 Benjamin Martin of Philadelphia moved to limit the franchise on the basis of race and, ironically, he used the example of James Forten to prove his point. The size and relative affluence of his city's black population, Martin declared, posed a serious problem. If no restrictions were written into the new constitution, "There are some . . . wards . . . [where] they will be able, not only to carry the wards, but to distribute all the offices, independent of the wards." In Martin's opinion, no man of color, not even James Forten, a "black gentleman" who "has accumulated property [and] obtained a respectable standing," should ever be permitted to vote. A racial restriction must be written into the new constitution or else Pennsylvania would be faced with a prospect Martin found almost too horrific to contemplate. The dregs of the Southern free black population, "a refuse population, ignorant, indolent, and fit to be instruments of evil," would move to Pennsylvania to have the chance to vote, debasing the already deplorable condition of the resident blacks. Lacking the intellectual ability to make a sensible choice at election time, newcomers and native-born would fall prey to the wiles of "some master of intrigue."[58]

African Americans had their defenders. On July 8, when a move was made to reject unread a petition from Pittsburgh's people of color, Thaddeus Stevens of Adams County moved that it should be read because he considered black people worthy of consideration as human beings.[59] Charles Brown of Philadelphia County agreed regarding the petition, but was fearful about the larger question of the franchise. "It would be the destruction of this people . . . if you attempted to give them political equality . . . and if you give them that equality, you must guarantee it. . . . We must . . . contemplate man with his prejudices and passions, and move with . . . caution."[60]

The convention adjourned on July 14 and did not reassemble until October 17. A great deal happened during the recess. In its July term the Pennsylvania Supreme Court ruled in the case of *Fogg v. Hobbs* that the 1790 constitution excluded all men of color from the franchise.[61] In the October election in Bucks County, between thirty and forty black men presented themselves at the polls and their votes were accepted. The election was decided by a slim margin and the result promptly challenged in the courts.[62] Meanwhile, John B. Sterigere spent the summer traveling the state and alerting whites to the fact that men of color were voting in some counties.[63] He stirred up a veritable hornets' nest.

On November 16 Sterigere presented a petition from citizens of Bucks County "praying that a constitutional provision may be made, prohibiting negroes from the right of suffrage." There was some discussion about whether the petition should be printed, enraging John Cummin of Juniata. The memorial from Pittsburgh's blacks had been printed. Surely, he thundered, a petition from white men deserved the same treatment.[64]

By the end of November the Reform Convention had relocated to the Musical Fund Hall on Second and Locust in Philadelphia, and that made it far easier for James Forten and other black Philadelphians to follow its deliberations. Events were also taking place outside the convention. The decision of Judge Fox on the black voters in Bucks County was handed down in December. Fox found that black men were not and had never been citizens.[65]

The debate raged on among the delegates at the Reform Convention through the end of 1837 and into the New Year. On January 17, Benjamin Martin made a formal motion to the convention to introduce the word "white" before "freemen" as a qualification for the franchise. He reasoned that voting would lead to an equality which was unnatural and contrary to the law of God. It would mean the elevation of the black man and an inevitably debasement of the white man.[66] The redoubtable Mr. Sterigere was determined to have his say. On this occasion he professed concern for people of color. "[I]f you permit a negro to vote, you . . . subject him to insult and injury." However, he was obviously more concerned about whites than about blacks, deeming it "an insult to the white man to . . . ask him to go to the polls . . . with negroes."[67]

William P. Maclay of Mifflin County made the point, reiterated by James Forten and others in their numerous petitions, that depriving men of color of one right would lead to the loss of others, "until we make slaves of them." William Meredith of Philadelphia was unmoved. It was enough that they were free. Why give them any more rights? Still, he was for letting the courts settle the matter. Alternatively, the convention could opt for New York State's solution and permit black men who owned, freehold, a certain amount of property to vote. That would show "people were willing to bestow the right of suffrage on those who are worthy to exercise it."[68]

Debate continued over the next few days. Although professing himself to be no champion of "amalgamation," James Merrill of Union County spoke in defense of the propertied class in the black community. "If a coloured man has lived among us until he has acquired a right of soil, ought he not to be admitted to the polls?"[69] This argument was endorsed by Walter Forward of Allegheny County. "Give the black man his rights, and you . . . make him a contented, and perhaps a useful citizen; but, take away from him those rights . . . and his bosom will rankle with hate." He shocked many by saying that he found it in no way repugnant to sit next to a man of color in a legislative assembly.[70]

On January 20, when the vote on racial restrictions was to be taken, the order was given to clear all black spectators from the gallery, in the words of the *National Enquirer*, "to prevent them from witnessing the tyrannical proceedings of their . . . would-be 'lords and masters.'" Hustled out by the sergeant at arms were John P. Burr, Thomas Butler, James Forten, Jr., and "another highly respectable . . . colored man." The four "made no resistance to the . . . outrage, though physical force was brutally applied in their ejectment."[71]

After the expulsions the debate became even more acrimonious. A petition from members of Philadelphia's white mercantile community was presented. In a tortured argument its authors contended: "If they [black men] have the right of suffrage by the constitution, as it now stands, their not having been permitted during the long lapse of half a century, the exercise of it . . . is . . . conclusive proof . . . they ought not to have it."[72] John M. Scott of Philadelphia proposed amending Martin's resolution to permit the legislature to enfranchise black men twenty years after the adoption of the new constitution. Other delegates pointed to the prejudices people of color already had to contend with. Depriving them of the right to vote could only make them more vulnerable. Mercer County's James Montgomery noted the past service of men of color. "[I]t strikes me that it would be a poor way to pay them for fighting the battles of their country, to deprive them of their votes."[73]

Amid a growing hubbub, for the time was late and delegates were growing weary, Walter Forward made an impassioned plea for justice.

> What . . . was the situation . . . of the coloured people at this time? Why, we found mobs gathering about their houses—insulting the inmates, and sometimes knocking down their houses. . . . And, good God, for this you are to take away the rights of those black men! Instead of bringing the ruffian aggressors to condign punishment, you are about to deprive the black man of an invaluable right! This is your apology—your reason![74]

The delegates were no more inclined to listen to him than they were to Joseph Hopkinson, who offered what he considered conclusive evidence that black men had been recognized as voters by a judicial decision soon after the ratification of the 1790 constitution. Most delegates did not care about a decades-old case. They were concerned about the here and now. The question was called and the amendment to insert the word "white" into the constitution passed by a vote of 77 to 45.[75]

The next day was the Sabbath. It requires no great powers of imagination to guess what the ministers in Philadelphia's sixteen African-American churches preached about at Sunday services. When the delegates reconvened on the Monday several of them tried to salvage something for the state's black "freemen." James Dunlop of Franklin County proposed that "persons of this commonwealth, now citizens thereof . . . who may be excluded by the term 'white,' shall be entitled to the rights of suffrage," provided they had resided in the electoral district for three years, owned property worth at least $200, and paid tax on it.[76] The amendment was rejected. In fact, the debate gave another delegate the chance to take a swipe at "the yellow man—Fortune—who, by-the-by, had the *mis*-fortune to possess the wrong colour," but who had "large real estate, and . . . money in abundance." James Merrill then tried to make it a matter of education and intelligence.[77] He too was unsuccessful.

THE DELEGATES FINISHED their work on February 22 and departed for home. It was now up to the voters—the white voters—to decide in the fall election whether to ratify their handiwork. James Forten and the rest of the African-American community were left to assess their options. They concluded that the only course left to them was to appeal directly to the electorate. The white reformers in the Pennsylvania Abolition Society reached the same conclusion. They adopted Forten's approach of presenting the facts and letting them speak for themselves. With the help of Rev. Charles W. Gardner, they conducted an ambitious census of the people of color in the city and districts of Philadelphia, intending to prove that they were hard-working and by and large virtuous members of society. Their findings were summarized in two pamphlets which they distributed to anyone in a position to influence the outcome of the vote.[78]

Members of James Forten's extended family and some of his longtime allies in the black community engaged in their own effort to plead their case. At a large meeting at St. Paul's Lutheran Church held soon after the Reform Convention disbanded, a seven-man committee was given the task of preparing a statement to white voters. Chaired by Robert Purvis, the committee included among its members Robert Bridges Forten.[79]

The authors of *The Appeal of Forty Thousand* (the number of black men across the state who would be disfranchised under the new constitution) begged their "fellow citizens" to give them a fair hearing, cautioning, "When you have taken from an individual his right to vote, you have made the government, in regard to him, a mere despotism; and you have taken a step towards making it a despotism to all." Surely, they reasoned, black people were "already sufficiently the objects of prejudice." Why make their condition worse?[80] They asked the same question they and others in their community had asked so many times. What had they done to deserve such treatment? They pointed to the heroism of African Americans during the Revolutionary War and the War of 1812, and their selfless devotion during the yellow fever epidemic. While they did not single out James Forten, they referred to men of color who had endured "the horrors of the Jersey Prison Ship" for the liberty of their country.[81]

At a subsequent meeting chaired by an old ally of James Forten's, barber and fellow vestryman John P. Burr, *The Appeal of Forty Thousand* was read and approved. James Forten, Jr., served as secretary, along with longtime Forten employee James Cornish. James Forten, Sr., also attended and spoke in support of *The Appeal*. The meeting believed the hand of the ACS to be at work in this latest move to deprive people of color of their cherished rights, and they appointed five men, Forten among them, "to draw up a remonstrance against the Colonization Society." Collections were to be taken up at the various black churches to pay for a massive printing of *The Appeal*, and those authorized to raise funds included Robert Purvis and Robert B. Forten.[82]

It is possible James Forten did more than just endorse the printing of *The Appeal* and dip into his pocket to help pay for it. The English writer Frederick Marryat was in Philadelphia at some point between the spring of 1837 and the fall of 1838, and he recalled that during that time

> a curious case was decided. A coloured man, by the name of James Fortin, who was, I believe, a sailmaker . . . but at all events a person not only of the highest respectability, but said to be worth 150,000 dollars, appealed, because he was not permitted to vote . . . and claimed his rights as a citizen. The case was tried, and the verdict, a very lengthy one, was given . . . against him. I have not that verdict in my possession; but I have the opinion of the Supreme Court in one which was given against him before.

He added: "It is a remarkable feature in the tyranny and injustice of this case, that although James Forten was not considered white enough . . . to *vote* as a citizen, he has always been white enough to be *taxed* as one."[83]

A search of Pennsylvania Supreme Court reports for the period 1820–41 has failed to uncover any details of a case in which Forten sued for his rights as a "freeman." Maybe Marryat mistook *The Appeal of Forty Thousand* for a court action. Perhaps he heard his Philadelphia acquaintances talk about the rich black sailmaker as an exceptional individual whose name had surfaced several times at the Reform Convention. He could even have obtained a copy of the verdict in the case of *Fogg v. Hobbs* and mistaken "Fogg" for "Forten." The uncertainty of the timing of Marryat's visit makes it impossible to determine whether Forten brought suit (if he did) in 1837 as a preemptive strike, or later, after the Convention had done its work.

Just possibly James Forten saw trouble coming even before the Reform Convention met and sued to establish his rights, and by implication the rights

of every black "freeman." Quaker abolitionist Thomas Earle, who had succeeded Richard Peters, Jr., as James Forten's lawyer in the mid-1830s, had
been chosen as one of the delegates to the Reform Convention. Earle probably
had a shrewd sense of what might happen at the convention. He could have
alerted James Forten, who was his good friend as well as his client, and advised
him to take action. Maybe it was in the context of a lawsuit that Forten sought
out his old friend Daniel Brewton and asked for Brewton's help to prove that
he was indeed a worthy citizen who deserved to vote. On March 15, 1837,
Brewton went with Forten to one of Philadelphia's aldermen and swore out a
statement that Forten "participated in the Revolution . . . and was a *prisoner* on
board of the Prison ship 'Old Jersey' . . . with me."[84] Unfortunately, there is no
conclusive proof that James Forten did anything about his voting rights, other
than lend his support to *The Appeal of Forty Thousand*, but Marryat's recollections and Brewton's testimony raise the tantalizing possibility that he did.

In the weeks leading up to the fall election there were numerous editorials
about the new constitution. Much was said and written about the question of
the black vote. The African-American community had a few friends. An unnamed white Quaker, possibly Thomas Earle, made a forceful argument based
on precedent and the nature of hearsay.[85] More compelling, though, at least
for the average white voter, were pleas to disfranchise black men for the good
of the state. The *Pennsylvanian* even went so far as to publish an alarming (and
completely unfounded) report that a black voter in York County had come
close to being elected to Congress.[86] Not surprisingly, on October 9 whites
went to the polls and ratified the constitution by a huge majority.

British Quaker Joseph John Gurney was in Philadelphia at the time and
was aghast at the sheer size of the majority. As for the impact on Philadelphia's
people of color, "This . . . act of degradation was received . . . with deep sorrow.
. . . I was told, that a white boy was observed seizing the marbles of a coloured
boy in one of the streets, with the words, *'You have no rights now.'* The latter
submitted in silence."[87] According to African-American journalist Mary Ann
Shadd Cary, who heard the story from her father, when the constitution was
ratified, "the Purvis', the Forten's, the Gordon's and the Cassey's hung crape
from their doors, emblematic of departed liberty."[88]

WELL MIGHT THE Fortens and their friends mourn for "departed liberty." The
same year that witnessed the loss of black voting rights also saw the destruction
of Philadelphia's "temple of freedom," Pennsylvania Hall, which James Forten
and his extended family had helped finance. When it was burned to the ground
not by a mob of young thugs but by the city's "gentlemen of property and
standing," and when there was strong circumstantial evidence that the authorities had allowed this to happen, they could only conclude that they had indeed
lost their "check upon oppression."[89]

For several years before they had begun raising funds to build Pennsylvania Hall, various groups of reformers in Philadelphia had been grappling with

the problem of where they could hold their meetings. Many places had refused to host anything that could be considered even mildly controversial. Mobs tended to form at the slightest provocation, and the managers of meeting halls and the vestrymen of the city's various churches had no wish to see their windows smashed or worse. Faced with constant rebuffs, temperance activists, antislavery crusaders, the advocates of "free labor," and a host of others had come together to build their own meeting hall.

The project had been financed by the sale of 2,000 shares at $20 apiece. Although most shareholders had been white, a significant number of well-to-do black citizens had subscribed as well. It is not clear whether the Fortens and the Purvises had owned shares, although they probably had, since Sarah Forten had been one of the fund-raisers for the Philadelphia Female Anti-Slavery Society.[90]

Shareholders had been pleased with the new building. Located in the heart of the city on Sixth between Race and Cherry, Pennsylvania Hall had been a handsome two-story structure, with stores, a lecture room, committee rooms on the lower floor, and a large assembly room on the upper floor. Although most of the money to build Pennsylvania Hall had come from individuals and organizations distinctly antislavery in their sympathies, the managers insisted the hall would not be for the exclusive use of abolitionists. It could be hired "for *any purpose not of an immoral character*."[91]

Pennsylvania Hall was to be opened amid much fanfare in May 1838. Antislavery poet John Greenleaf Whittier, an old friend of the Fortens', had written a poem for the occasion. Although he was not scheduled to speak, William Lloyd Garrison had traveled down from Boston. With him had come Maria Weston Chapman, one of the founders of the Boston Female Anti-Slavery Society; the promising young antislavery orator Abby Kelley; and other female abolitionists from New England, who were to attend the second annual convention of female abolitionists to be held at Pennsylvania Hall.

Many of the Fortens' friends had converged on Philadelphia for the grand opening of Pennsylvania Hall. Some, at least, had found the time to dine or take tea at 92 Lombard Street. The Fortens and the Purvises took a lively interest in all that went on in and around the hall. Harriet Purvis and her sisters had intended to take part in the women's antislavery convention. There was to be a meeting of the eastern branch of the Pennsylvania Anti-Slavery Society, of which James Forten, his son-in-law, and his two eldest sons were officers. They had probably planned to attend some of the lectures as well. Philadelphia reformer Arnold Buffum was to speak on temperance and New England activist Charles C. Burleigh had undertaken to discuss "the wrongs of the Indians," a topic that might well have appealed to the Fortens, given Charlotte Vandine Forten's ties to the region's Native American peoples. There were also to be speeches about free labor, a cause both Harriet and Robert Purvis were interested in.[92]

While the Fortens and the Purvises were socializing and planning which events to attend, many in Philadelphia's white community were looking on in horror, convinced "amalgamation" had come to their city. There were stories of white women parading arm in arm with black men and white men escorting black women into Pennsylvania Hall. Someone spotted the wife and sister of one of the city's leading black businessmen walking near the hall with their cousin, who was somewhat darker that they were, "and the mob raised the shout that a black man was walking with two 'pretty white girls.'" Harriet Purvis was seen being helped from a carriage by her husband, who was taken for a white man.[93]

Another story going around was that a white woman who had just wed a black man was to give an antislavery address. This grew out of garbled reports of the wedding of antislavery orators Angelina Grimké and Theodore Dwight Weld, which took place on May 14. Both bride and groom were white, but a black minister officiated and a number of African Americans attended both the ceremony and the "free labor" reception.[94] Placards began appearing around the city condemning all abolitionists as traitors and Pennsylvania Hall as a haven of everything that was ungodly and immoral. All right-thinking citizens were urged to band together to root out this evil in their midst.[95]

There was no lack of response. On May 15 several windows were broken and the crowd milling around outside the hall jeered and shouted while the reform societies met. On the evening of May 16, when Angelina Grimké was scheduled to give an address, the crowd was even more agitated. The event proved highly controversial, because Grimké had already been taken to task by New England ministers for stepping out of her "appropriate" female role and speaking before a "promiscuous" company of men and women. Philadelphians were no more liberal than New Englanders on that point. Rumors about the race of her husband, and the indisputable fact that her audience was mixed in terms of race as well as gender, heightened the mob's fury. Stones crashed against the shuttered windows as Grimké spoke.[96]

The following morning the antislavery women continued their convention, but in the evening they adjourned at the request of Mayor Swift, who expressed fears for their safety and for the maintenance of public order. Swift made a show of receiving the keys of the hall from the managers. He then locked the doors, assured the angry crowd outside that there would be no more meetings that evening, wished them all goodnight, and retired to his home. As soon as he was out of sight, someone forced open the doors. Dozens of enraged "gentlemen" poured in and ransacked the hall before turning on the gas jets. Within minutes Pennsylvania Hall was ablaze. When the fire fighters turned up they played their hoses on nearby buildings and completely ignored the hall. Within a few hours the "temple of liberty" was a smouldering ruin.[97] Sidney George Fisher, himself a Philadelphia gentleman, recorded in his diary that it was "a mob of well-dressed persons" who destroyed the hall, with "the police scarcely interfering." He also observed that "many respectable persons, tho' they do not defend these outrages, blame them faintly."[98]

Up to this point those African Americans who had attracted the attention of the rioters had done so less because of their race than because of their association with an extremely unpopular cause. There were even expressions of sympathy for the black rank and file who were not actively involved in antislavery.[99] Of course, this was little consolation to James Forten and his family.

Over the next two nights, when very "ungentlemanly" mobs of poor whites attacked a number of black homes as well as the Shelter for Colored Orphans and the First African Presbyterian Church, they were dealt with fairly efficiently by the city authorities.[100] That fact, along with Mayor Swift's prompt action a couple of weeks later to forestall another episode of racial violence, lent credence to reports that he had deliberately stood back and allowed the "gentlemen" to burn down Pennsylvania Hall. Swift was known to take a very dim view of the abolitionists and to regard Pennsylvania Hall as a blot upon the landscape. He could generally be counted on to try to curb the excesses of the mobs of poor white workingmen and apprentices who spread terror into the city's residential neighborhoods, but he preferred to look the other way when "respectable" Philadelphians destroyed a building the very existence of which he and they found deeply offensive.[101]

The Pennsylvania Hall episode heightened existing racial tensions in Philadelphia and opened wide growing divisions among the ranks of white abolitionists, a development James Forten could not but deplore. The antislavery women continued their convention after the destruction of their meeting place, adopting a resolution proposed by Angelina Grimké that they make common cause with people of color "by appearing with them in our streets . . . by visiting them at their homes and encouraging them to visit us, receiving them as we do our fellow white citizens."[102] An understandably anxious Joseph Parrish urged Lucretia Mott to expunge the resolution from the minutes, which she refused to do. Parrish then "called some of the respectable portion of the colored people together . . . and advised them not to accept such intercourse . . . and to issue a disclaimer of any such wish."[103] If James Forten was embroiled in this potentially explosive issue he left no record of it. However, Parrish was an old and much-respected friend, and the meeting was held at the home of another good friend, Robert Douglass. It would have been surprising if Forten had not at least been aware of it. He and his family were being faced with an agonizing dilemma. Should they abide by their conviction that race was supremely unimportant, or should they try to keep the peace by backing down and withdrawing into their own immediate circle?

IN THE FACE of so much anger from his white neighbors, James Forten resolutely refused to abandon the struggle. He still hoped to change both their hearts and their minds. The way to do this, he fervently believed, was through a wide-ranging reform of the nation's basic moral standards. An enlightened, a moral, a truly *reformed* citizenry, he reasoned, would find injustice of any kind totally unacceptable.

In the last years of his life James Forten embarked on yet another battle. His goal this time was nothing less than to transform America. It was, to say the least, an ambitious undertaking. It would be ridiculed, and it would expose the deep fissures within the African-American community, but it was a battle he would not, indeed, could not, shrink from, whatever the toll it took upon him. It might cost him some of his personal prestige and it might lose him several of his dearest friends. No matter. He was supremely confident that the final victory would be worth the inevitable casualties.

Somewhat surprisingly, at least on the face of it, James Forten opted to use the black national convention movement to pursue his agenda. He had taken no part in the first convention in 1830, leaving Richard Allen to preside unchallenged. Another convention was scheduled to meet in Philadelphia in 1831. Forten took a passing interest because it was at this convention that William Lloyd Garrison, Arthur Tappan, and Simeon S. Jocelyn put forward the idea of a black manual labor college. However, Forten was less than complimentary about the way the convention's officers went about their business. Meticulous in his own affairs, he could not abide inefficiency in others.[104]

The 1832 convention brought to Philadelphia Ralph R. Gurley and Robert J. Breckinridge, two of the most vocal champions of the American Colonization Society. They spoke to the delegates, but they made no converts, and Gurley fared badly in a debate with Garrison. They also called at 92 Lombard Street to take tea with James Forten and heard him talk in no uncertain terms about his contempt for their organization and their colony.[105]

The following year Forten was once more watching from the sidelines, but the delegates to the black national convention did have a role for him to play. Frederick A. Hinton observed that the ACS had recently elected as vice-presidents the Marquis de Lafayette and "several of our distinguished citizens." The honorary vice-presidents in some cases did not know of their election and in others were ignorant of the true nature of the ACS. Hinton moved that Rev. Peter Williams of New York and "our worthy and highly esteemed fellow-citizen" James Forten write to Lafayette and the others "for the purpose of explaining to them, the views and wishes of the people of colour."[106]

The 1834 convention met in New York City. Forten did not attend, but several of his close associates did, including his young friend William Whipper. The issue of moral reform dominated the proceedings. After lengthy discussions, delegates voted that the convention should "organize itself into a National Society for the general improvement of the free people of colour."[107] Precisely what that meant remained to be seen.

The 1835 convention met in Philadelphia. It was at this convention that James Forten finally moved from the periphery to the very center. On the evening of the second day, two of the delegates brought up the issue of a national organization dedicated to reforming the whole of American society. The initiative did not meet with unanimous approval. After what the minutes discreetly referred to as "a warm and animated discussion," the majority eventually voted to form "a National Moral Reform Society." Few of the delegates envisaged that the new organization would replace their annual meetings. Actually, that was precisely what James Forten, Robert Purvis, the indefatigable William Whipper, and an appreciable number of their friends intended. Incorporated into the minutes of the convention was the new society's bold statement of principles, accompanied by an "Address to the American People" setting forth the organization's aims and objectives. Heading the list of officers was James Forten as President.[108] At the age of sixty-nine, as resolute and as determined as he had ever been, he prepared to embark on a crusade to reform the nation.

The force behind what was to be known as the American Moral Reform Society was the irrepressible William Whipper. Only thirty-one in 1835, he had attended every meeting of the black national convention movement. On one level an astute and successful businessman, on another a visionary, he was a difficult man to debate. He was eloquent and he was unstoppable. When he was not speaking about his vision of America, he was writing about it. Convinced of the rightness of his cause, he would never back down.[109]

Looking at Whipper's relationship with Forten it is easy to jump to the conclusion that Whipper wore down the older man by the sheer force of his enthusiasm and persuaded him, albeit with a certain degree of reluctance, to lend his name to the new organization. That was not, in fact, what happened. If less energetic than the youthful Whipper, James Forten nevertheless gave the American Moral Reform Society his whole-hearted support. Whipper, a friend of several years' standing, an ally in the petitioning effort back in 1832, was someone Forten trusted. He also warmed to Whipper because he recognized that they had the same goals in mind.

It was Whipper who issued the call to the 1836 AMRS convention, summoning to Philadelphia "every *American,*" without regard to race, who was committed to the great principles of "EDUCATION, TEMPERANCE, ECONOMY, and UNIVERSAL LIBERTY." Forten, Whipper, and the other officers of the society followed up with specific invitations to reformers such as Gerrit Smith.[110]

The delegates convened on August 8, 1836, at Wesley Church, about four blocks from James Forten's home. The largest group was (not surprisingly) from Philadelphia and the next largest from Baltimore. Peeved that their brothers in Philadelphia had wrested control of the black national convention movement from them, no New Yorkers attended. This intercity squabbling was to be one of the things that poisoned the atmosphere over the next few years.[111]

The Philadelphians pushed ahead, regardless. Following an opening prayer, President James Forten "rose and delivered a very eloquent address, on . . . Moral Reform. He depicted in a lucid manner, the contrast between the situation of the colored people in 1780, and that of the present time, introducing some very interesting incidents in illustration of the subject."[112] Unlike the vast majority of delegates, he had witnessed Pennsylvania's transformation from a slave state. The Gradual Abolition Act of 1780 was real to him in a way it was not for most of his audience. This was his chance to reflect on what had been, what was, and what could come to pass if they kept their hearts and minds focused on "reform."

As things moved on, there were speeches from white well-wishers and resolutions praising education, temperance, and thrift. William Whipper spoke up on a number of issues, including, as the proprietor of a free labor store, the need to shun the products of slave labor. James Forten, Jr., emerged as a presence in his own right, proposing and seconding motions and giving an "animated and eloquent speech" on education. Robert Purvis spoke movingly on the horrors of slavery. He also outlined an ambitious plan to raise a thousand dollars to carry on the work of the society, begin a monthly periodical, and establish a manual labor school.

James Forten presided throughout with his customary politeness and his regard for good order. As the proceedings drew to a close, John C. Bowers proposed a resolution that was unanimously adopted: "That the thanks of this Meeting be tendered to James Forten, Sr. for the able and efficient manner in which he has presided over the deliberations of this body and for the great interest evinced by him."[113]

Obviously a great deal went on behind the scenes after the convention adjourned. The 1837 meeting was scheduled for August, but a call went out for delegates at the very beginning of the year. In the long-winded "call," William Whipper outlined a sweeping program encompassing everything from establishing a press to petitioning for the abolition of slavery in the District of Columbia.[114] In a further call a few months later, AMRS officers asked delegates to bring information on "the number of the colored population in your place; how many paupers and criminals . . . how many Churches, Clergymen, Schools and Teachers, Bible Classes, Literary Societies, Lyceums and Debating, Mutual Relief, Moral Reform and Temperance Societies . . . also the amount of Real Estate, owned by them, the number of Mechanics, Merchants, and any other information that you may deem of importance."[115] Here, once more, was James Forten's favorite tactic of trying to educate white people about the honesty, the integrity, the general worthiness of their black neighbors.

The printed proceedings of the 1837 convention began with the society's declaration of sentiments, a document Forten was surely in agreement with. The AMRS officers deplored "the depressed condition of the coloured population," spoke of their glorious lineage as "the offspring of a parentage, that once, for their excellence of attainment in the arts, literature and science, stood before the world unrivalled," and condemned the institution of slavery which had brought them so low. They boasted that their revolution was not intended to be a violent one aimed at personal aggrandizement but a moral one in which the goals were freedom and justice and the only weapon "divine justice."[116]

Things got under way on the morning of August 14. As he had done the previous year, James Forten gave the opening speech. This was followed by recommendations from various delegates embracing the encouragement of education, the founding of a manual labor school "in some suitable place," and the desirability of practicing peace, economy, and "moral, upright and correct deportment."[117] James Forten, Jr., once more took an active role, praising New Yorker Samuel Cornish's new paper, the *Colored American*, and giving a speech on education lasting over an hour.[118]

Although the carefully edited minutes tried to gloss over disagreements, the convention was far from harmonious. The trouble came when the committee appointed to draw up an agenda made its report. Frederick A. Hinton gave his version of events in a letter to the *Colored American*. The committee's first resolution read, "that we recommend to the free people of color the establishment of schools . . . wherever it might be practicable and safe." Hinton explained that the reference to "free people of color" had been included only "inasmuch as our enslaved brethren exist, geographically speaking, beyond our sphere of action."

William Whipper, Robert Purvis, and several others had immediately protested against the use of "free people of color" and any other phrase that designated people according to race. Hinton concluded that they did so because they were ashamed of their African ancestry. The committee's resolution about the establishing of schools was voted down and Hinton alleged that dirty tricks had been used to defeat it. According to him, a large majority of the delegates were inclined to favor it, but Whipper, Purvis, and the members of their clique had managed to get the vote delayed until such time as they had the upper hand. The venerable president also did his part, using his casting vote to kill the resolution.[119]

Samuel Cornish did his best to widen the breach. His first editorial about the convention had been very enthusiastic. He had written of "a redeeming spirit in the land."[120] After the first day's sessions he wrote coeditor Philip A. Bell back in New York: "We deem it a privilege to be here. . . . Something good must and will grow out of this Convention."[121] However, praise rapidly turned to condemnation. In a subsequent editorial Cornish told his readers: "The colored citizens of Philadelphia . . . are visionary in the extreme." The AMRS was "scattering its feeble efforts to the winds." James Forten was indeed a "venerable" individual, but he could not keep the excitable delegates in check. "A man of delicate [and] sensitive feelings is disqualified to govern a Society made up of such elements as comprise the 'Moral Reform' Association." Whipper, Purvis, and others Cornish declined to name were "vague, wild, indefinite and confused in their views." There must be a clear, practical and agreed-upon agenda. "To conclude, the President of the Society, whom we *most highly esteem* . . . will excuse us in saying, were we in his place, we would resign. His sensibilities are *too keen* and his feelings *too excitable*, to govern the MODERN ELEMENTS."[122]

What had gone wrong? Why had such a noble and high-minded undertaking turned sour? The fundamental problem was a deep philosophical divide over the question of race. Whereas Hinton, Cornish, and others jumped to the conclusion that Forten, Whipper, Purvis, and their circle were ashamed of being black, they in fact aimed at the creation of a society in which race was simply irrelevant. They were striving to create a national mindset in which skin color and ancestry no longer determined an individual's status in society. This was what had moved Whipper at the 1835 national convention to urge "our people to abandon the use of the word 'colored' when . . . speaking or writing concerning themselves." This was what prompted James Forten in 1839 to try to explain to a white abolitionist how he and others felt about "the well meant, though injudicious, and sometimes really impolite notice which is taken, if any of us happen to do, or say any thing like other people."[123] Neither Forten nor Whipper was ashamed of being black. They were striving for nothing less than a new understanding of what it meant to be an American. Their vision of a new, reformed America was one in which race was not the measure of all things. Alas, they were soon to discover they were swimming against the tide. Whites were not prepared to abandon race as a definition of status, and blacks were not about to change their sense of self-identity. *They* might have reached a new level of understanding, but they had few converts.

The basically pacific William Whipper soon joined battle with Samuel Cornish, leaping to the defense of himself, his friends, the AMRS, and its esteemed president. "[T]he President of the Convention will consider it a poor compliment to his declining years, if after having been the hero of seventy winters, he shall now be considered to possess 'sensibilities too *keen*, and feelings too *excitable*, to preside over the Moral Reform Society.'"[124] Cornish was unmoved. He observed that he had received fourteen letters on the subject of the AMRS convention but he had no intention of publishing them and allowing them to monopolize his newspaper. He shrank from causing further disunity in a population that needed desperately to sink its differences and work for the good of the whole.[125]

Despite Cornish's good intentions, the matter refused to die. Over the ensuing weeks more pieces were published and others besides Whipper and Hinton were drawn into the fray.[126] A particularly vociferous critic was Junius C. Morel. Having alienated himself from a number of his old friends in Philadelphia, he launched an all-out assault on the AMRS from his new home town of Harrisburg. Moral reform, he claimed, was the work of the churches and not of such individuals "as brother Cornish justly terms 'the modern elements.'" He called for the money raised to finance "this unsound *experiment*" to be given to the American Anti-Slavery Society.[127]

Despite the growing chorus of criticism, James Forten and his circle pressed on, issuing a call to another meeting in 1838. They refused to abandon their principles. In fact, they made it as explicit as they could that they wanted to gather together all reform-minded people, without regard to race or creed. Arbitrary divisions had produced a "moral *miasma*" which had for too long poisoned the nation. America, they insisted, was founded on liberty and equality, and they would not depart from those principles.[128]

On the morning of August 14, 1838, James Forten, two weeks short of his seventy-second birthday, mounted the speaker's platform at the Second African Presbyterian Church to declare the third convention of the American Moral Reform Society in session. He followed with "some brief and appropriate remarks on the subject of Moral Reform, together with a touching appeal to the young men present." James Forten, Jr., as recording secretary, then read the constitution and declaration of sentiments.[129]

It goes without saying that William Whipper was on hand, offering resolutions on everything from the evils of strong drink to the abandonment of racially separate churches.[130] Unmistakable signs of dissension arose when it came to the report of the business committee, which urged that no new initiatives be pursued when so much was pending from the previous year.[131]

Despite criticism about the organization's agenda (or lack thereof), even its foes had to admit that James Forten did his best to keep things under control. Samuel Cornish, eager to mend fences with one of his oldest friends, observed: "The President . . . discharged his duty with a great deal of impartiality, and notwithstanding . . . the tendency of all debates to depart from the subject, the greatest order and decorum was preserved."[132]

Soon after the convention disbanded, James Forten and the AMRS leadership made their first foray into newspaper publishing. They announced their intention to issue a journal "to disseminate the principles" of their organization. Referring (although not by name) to Cornish's *Colored American*, they declared that without a press of their own their "objects have been grossly misunderstood." Their journal, sixteen pages and issued monthly, cost a dollar for a year's subscription. It would be called the *National Reformer*, and its principle editor would be that tireless crusader for moral reform, William Whipper. Samuel Cornish graciously welcomed the appearance of the new journal.[133]

One of the first items of business for the *National Reformer*'s editorial board was to decide how best to handle a letter the AMRS had received from William Watkins, one of the most prominent members of Baltimore's large free community of color, just before the 1838 convention. Watkins did not attend and sent a long letter explaining why he was breaking his ties to the organization. Amidst allegations that they had deliberately not read it at the convention, the leaders of the AMRS "cheerfully" printed Watkins's letter, which by then had already appeared in the *Colored American*.[134] They prefaced it with a lengthy commentary on precisely what they meant by downplaying the word "colored." "[W]e have too long witnessed the baneful effects of distinctions founded in hatred and prejudice, to advocate the insertion of either the word '*white*' or 'colored' as landmarks . . . for the promotion of religion, morality, or civil government."[135]

Watkins's letter was very much to the point. He found the term 'colored' positively "endearing." He asked: "Are you afraid . . . the *use* of the word will *remind* the white people . . . that one-sixth portion of their fellow-countrymen may, by certain physical peculiarities, be distinguished from themselves?" He had no taste for philosophical debates about the divisive nature of race. As far as he was concerned, black people were the most in need of help. It was on them that the AMRS must focus its energies. If white Americans could be made to abandon their prejudices so much the better, but in the short term the African-American community must look inward and address the concerns of its own members.[136]

As 1838 DREW to a close, James Forten reflected on what had truly been for him a time of trial. He had lost the right to vote, in common with every other black "freeman" in the state. It had been made abundantly clear to him that he was no longer a citizen. Pennsylvania Hall was a burned-out shell, its ruins a stark reminder that few whites in his native city had any use for abolitionist "fanatics." As for his notion of creating a society in which race was not the measure of a person's worth, some of his oldest friends, people he believed thought as he did, had told him in no uncertain terms they considered him a dreamer. Had his long career as a community leader come to an end? Was it time to retire from the struggle and spend his remaining years focusing inward on his family and preparing to pass his business on to his children? No. He would not back down. Foolish? Perhaps he was. Visionary? Certainly. But his battle to reform the nation was not a battle he was prepared to walk quietly away from. He would see it through to the end.

13

DEATH OF A PATRIARCH

I N THE LAST few years of his life James Forten confronted a series of crises that tested his religious faith, his confidence in the power of reform to regenerate America, and his hopes for his community. He faced personal tragedies and business difficulties. He fought unsuccessfully against legal assaults on the rights of men and women of color, and he agonized over bitter divisions among old allies. He saw his long-cherished beliefs assailed, and even occasionally found himself the target of veiled criticism from within the African-American community. Through it all he struggled for a sense of inner calm, reconciling himself to those things he could not change, offering advice even when he feared it would not be heeded, and accepting debilitating illness and death with a dignity that drew admiration from friend and foe alike.

AS JAMES FORTEN'S long life drew to a close, he and his community were spared the intense violence they had endured earlier in what had been a tumultuous decade. Did that mean whites had become less hostile to the presence of people of color in "their" city? Hardly. Black people and black-owned buildings continued to be regarded as legitimate targets by angry or frustrated whites. However, not every localized incident escalated into a full-blown riot. By and large, racial violence was tolerated by the authorities as part of the fabric of urban life. The lawless elements in the city and its districts could feel reasonably confident that they could go about their business without fear of prosecution. In 1840, for instance, the presidential election was marred by sporadic outbreaks of looting and destruction. On the evening of October 30 "the *mobites*" attacked Mother Bethel "and broke out most all of the front windows." Not until they attacked a white-run tavern did the mayor intervene. As one black writer observed: "*King Alcohol* was too sacred . . . to be treated with impunity."[1] It was pure chance that there was no massive explosion of rage on that occasion, or on others. The potential for it remained. James Forten would not see another race riot on the scale of 1834 or 1838, but his family and his community would within months of his passing. If Forten entertained the hope that racial hostility was waning in Philadelphia, he was sadly mistaken.

Violence seemed to peak at times of economic upheaval, and Philadelphia was mired in a recession during the last years of Forten's life. It was a crisis that reached out to involve him, as it did virtually everyone in business. The Panic of 1837 was rooted in Andrew Jackson's war against the Philadelphia-based Second Bank of the United States. Bank president Nicholas Biddle had responded to Jackson's veto of the bank's new charter and his withdrawal of federal funds by calling in loans and precipitating a drastic tightening of credit throughout the Union, as a way for Biddle to show both the power of the bank and the need for sound fiscal policy. The strategy backfired, and the consequences were truly alarming.

Other factors were at work besides the personal and ideological conflict between Jackson and Biddle. The extent of foreign investment in American businesses put the nation's economy at risk. A political crisis in France or the failure of a major banking house in London could compromise American financial stability. Far-reaching changes were also taking place in America's economic and social structure. The end result of all this was the Panic of 1837, which lasted into the early 1840s. The first business failures spawned others, and the slide into recession was soon unstoppable. New York banks suspended specie payment on May 10, 1837, with banks in other Northern cities following suit the next day. Not until James Forten was dead and buried would the Philadelphia banks begin functioning as they had done before the panic.[2] Biddle's bank struggled on until 1841, when it failed and the once-powerful bank president went bankrupt. At the local level all of this translated into a tidal wave of bankruptcies and unemployment.

Inevitably, this instability impacted upon James Forten's business interests. With so many sectors of the economy in trouble, those who made their living building and fitting out vessels could hardly expect to be immune. Shipyards laid off workers.[3] Plans for new vessels were abandoned. Shipowners thought twice about which repairs were essential and which could wait until the end of another sailing season. Vessels still entered and left port, but both departures and arrivals declined, and Forten, like a host of other craftsmen involved in the maritime trades, suffered.

Then there was the credit crunch and the desperate shortage of "sound money." Forten continued making loans and buying up notes as he had done for decades, but the risks were now much greater than at any time since the

Panic of 1819. In common with every other member of the business community, Forten had to worry about how much a paper debt was actually worth. The rate by which a note was discounted might vary by several percentage points within a day or two, and that could spell ruin even for the most cautious investor.[4] Businesses that seemed sound failed overnight, and hitherto prosperous merchants defaulted on their debts. Those who had loaned them money and accepted their notes were left with nothing more than a bunch of worthless paper.

Writing a decade after Forten's death, African-American journalist Martin R. Delany described both the sailmaker's grace under pressure and the scale of his losses.

> On the failure of an extensive house, T & Co. . . . Mr. Forten lost . . . nine thousand dollars. Being himself in good circumstances . . . hearing of the failure of old constant patrons, he called at the house. . . . Mr. T., on his entering the warehouse door, came forward [and], taking him by the hand observed, "Ah! Mr. Forten, it is useless to call on us—we are gone—we can do nothing!" at which Mr. Forten remarked, "Sir, I hope you think better of me than to suppose me capable of calling on a friend to torture him in adversity! I came, sir, to express my regret at your misfortune, and if possible, to cheer you by words of encouragement. If your liabilities were all in my hands, you should never be under the necessity of closing business."[5]

It is a touching vignette, but it owes more to Delany's powers of imagination than to verifiable facts. Forten could no more weather such a loss than anyone else in the business community, and if he did come to call on "old constant patrons," it was not simply for social reasons. Gracious James Forten might be; naïve he most definitely was not when it came to matters of business.

James Forten had long since taken James Jr. and Robert into the business. By 1837 the firm that had been James Forten & Co. was listed in the city directories as James Forten & Sons. Gradually, Forten transferred more and more of the daily business of the loft to his sons. They signed receipts, collected money due the firm, paid the workmen, dealt with suppliers, and sought out new orders. However, what should have been a smooth transition as James Forten headed into semiretirement was not. The younger Fortens were entering the business world at a most unpropitious time. The economic crisis was a fact of life any businessman had to deal with, but they were also encountering a hardening of attitudes with respect to race. The white "gentlemen of the pave" who James Jr. and Robert had to interact with were a very different lot from those their father had known in the 1790s and 1800s. A foreign visitor to Philadelphia at the time of Forten's funeral related his findings about Forten and the city's business community.

> I was rejoicing that his colour had proved no impediment to his rising in the world, and that he had been allowed so much fair play as to succeed in overtopping the majority of his white competitors, when I learnt, on further in-

quiry, that, after giving an excellent education to his children, he had been made unhappy, by finding they must continue . . . to belong to an inferior caste. . . . [N]ot long before his death, he had been especially mortified, because two of his sons had been refused a hearing at a public meeting where they wished to speak on some subject connected with trade.[6]

It was galling for James Forten to feel that prejudice within the business community, instead of decreasing with the passage of time, was growing in intensity. He knew he had succeeded against the odds. He had worked hard for his success, but he always acknowledged the help he had received—from Robert Bridges, from Willing and Francis, from William Deas and Patrick Hayes, from a host of white merchants and captains who had given him commissions and been ready to do business with him. Their successors, he had good reason to fear, were men of a very different stamp, and that boded ill for his sons.

Looking back on a lifetime of battles lost and won, how confident could James Forten feel about matters other than business? Had he, for instance, managed to hammer home his message about the pernicious nature of the American Colonization Society? On one level he could feel fairly sure that he had. Few in the African-American community in the North openly supported the ACS, and many of its critics spoke of the example Forten had set them. In their 1840 pamphlet, *The Colonization Scheme Considered*, Forten's old ally, Samuel Cornish, and Theodore S. Wright saw an unbroken link between the great protest meetings of 1817 and the most recent denunciations of colonization. Describing "the largest meeting ever yet held of the colored people of the free States" in 1817, presided over by James Forten, they noted that at that meeting "there was not a single voice . . . which was not raised for decisive, thorough condemnation" of colonization.[7] The sentiment of the black men and women of the North in 1817 remained their sentiment in 1840.

White friends in the antislavery movement spoke of James Forten's stand again colonization, and some, Gerrit Smith and Arthur Tappan among them, confessed to having been won over from support of the ACS after talking with Forten or reading his eloquent and carefully reasoned attacks on the society. He had shown them, they declared, that the ACS was most definitely *not* committed to the eradication of slavery. They even wrote poetry about Forten's intransigence on the issue of colonization.

> James Forten, right well
> I love to hear tell
> Of *thy* aid in our much boasted war;
> And mark with what scorn,
> Does thy noble heart spurn
> The friends of Liberia's shore,
> James Forten!
> The friends of Liberia's shore.[8]

Closer to home, black Philadelphians held protest meetings whenever the ACS reared its head. For instance, there was a great anticolonization rally at St. Paul's Lutheran Church on January 7, 1839. Robert Purvis and others came together to respond to a suggestion that vessels be built to operate between the United States and Liberia, "and that said vessels . . . be manned and navigated by colored men, who are to become owners of the same." If the ACS really wanted to do something to promote black economic advancement, they insisted, it should turn over to the black community half the sum it proposed to spend on the ships.[9] Echoing Forten's response in the 1820s to similar offers of profit and prestige in return for backing colonization, this new generation stuck to Forten's principles.

Despite the poetry, despite the protests, James Forten had reason to feel uneasy. The ACS had been weakened, but not destroyed. The colonization of free black people as far away from the United States as it was possible to ship them was the rallying cry of so many whites, from Southern slaveholders to Northern rioters. Only a minority of them belonged to the ACS, but they shared the society's goals. And a new emigration scheme being discussed in the black community seemed to be bolstering the belief of white proponents that colonization was feasible and might even be acceptable to some African Americans.

With the abolition of slavery throughout the British Empire, planters on various West Indian islands were desperately short of manpower and willing to offer generous terms to anyone prepared to labor in their fields. The planters of Trinidad, encouraged by one of their number, American-born William H. Burnley, began a concerted campaign to win over free people of color in the United States. They extolled the wonders of their island, held out the prospect of immigrants quickly graduating from laborers to landowners, and appointed agents in various cities up and down the Eastern seaboard to recruit settlers. On December 4, 1839, the *Archer* left Philadelphia with a party of emigrants bound for a new life on Trinidad. The zealous promoter of the emigration scheme in Philadelphia was none other than Frederick Augustus Hinton, a friend of Forten's sons, a fellow vestryman of Forten's at St. Thomas's, and a man he had known and worked with for over a decade.[10]

Throughout 1839 and into 1840 the Trinidad scheme provoked many heated exchanges among black Philadelphians as its merits and flaws were debated.[11] Was it, perhaps, with Forten that ACS officer Benjamin Coates spoke a couple of weeks before the *Archer* sailed from Philadelphia full of Trinidad-bound emigrants? Coates wrote to a fellow ACS member: "[O]ne of the influential men (colored) told me the other day when [I] ask[ed] him how he reconciled it [the Trinidad scheme] in those who opposed colonization in Africa . . . 'I cannot Sir[.] I agree with you it is very inconsistent.'"[12]

Ultimately the Trinidad scheme failed. Too few people went. Some of those who did go returned home or moved to other British colonies in the Caribbean. The planters on Trinidad complained that many of the settlers they did get were far less tractable than they had supposed. However, the very fact that the scheme had found any black supporters was profoundly disturbing to James Forten. It raised the specter of a new and perhaps ultimately successful emigration initiative. For more than two decades he had been preaching the message that the free people of color must never abandon their brothers and sisters in bondage, however attractive the inducements for doing so. Would a new generation give up the struggle to stay in America at all costs, and look instead to the Caribbean, to Canada, or to Africa? Forten could not be sure of the answer.

Other matters were equally troubling. In the face of legal oppression and mob actions, African Americans seemed unable to agree on an effective course of action. Much of the controversy swirled around the very organization Forten headed, the American Moral Reform Society. By 1839 he was less active in the AMRS than he had been a few years earlier when it was founded, but even if he was now only the figurehead and the organization's real leaders were his son-in-law and William Whipper, Forten still believed in its platform. Visionary it might be, but he insisted, as did his younger colleagues, that America needed to be reformed from the bottom up. Convinced Americans would eliminate slavery and racism only when they had tackled a whole host of moral evils, from alcoholism to the denial of rights to women, he feared for the cause of reform and for the nation. It hurt him to find himself preaching to a handful of the converted. It hurt to have old friends attack him as hopelessly out of touch with the real needs of African Americans and advise him to disband the AMRS. However, he refused to abandon his principles. As long as he was physically able, he spoke in favor of a sweeping moral reformation, wrote about the need for one, and gave generously to a variety of organizations he hoped would bring one about.

Despite the savaging it had received from its critics after the conventions of 1837 and 1838, the AMRS struggled on gamely. In April 1839, John P. Burr, chairman of the board of managers, issued a call to "brethren without respect to creed or color" to assemble in August for the organization's third annual meeting.[13] The convention met as planned. The AMRS's newspaper, the *National Reformer*, noted, "The venerable President, JAMES FORTEN, though in feeble health and laden with years, presided throughout, with that dignity and urbanity so peculiarly characteristic" of him.[14]

Though Forten might have presided, the real power now lay with the younger generation, William Whipper, Robert Purvis, and Daniel Alexander Payne, now a rising star in the AME Church. In essence this was a statewide rather than a national undertaking. The avowed enemies of the AMRS in the African-American community stayed away, and, to the chagrin of Whipper, so did most white reformers. As he observed in an editorial in the *National Reformer*, "A stranger coming in to view the meeting would say at once, that it was a colored convention, while our principles forbid us making such a distinction." However, in a break with tradition, women were present as delegates. The male members declared that "what is morally right for man to do, is morally right for woman," and invited their wives, sisters, and daughters to share with them the task of "carrying out the great principles of moral reform."[15]

Despite this innovation, the proceedings covered familiar territory. Delegates praised William Lloyd Garrison, extolled the benefits of education, condemned the ACS, and urged all true patriots, irrespective of race, to join an antislavery society. A great deal of time was taken up with censuring the editor of the *Public Ledger* for carrying notices for runaway slaves.[16] The convention disbanded with an agreement to meet the following August.

After December 1839 the AMRS was essentially voiceless. Facing heavy financial losses, the *National Reformer* was obliged to suspend publication. Although its editor assured readers that the suspension would be temporary, the *National Reformer* never reappeared.[17] The AMRS would now have to rely on other newspapers, some of them decidedly hostile, to announce its meetings and publicize its work.

Despite growing opposition, the AMRS refused to abandon its struggle and went ahead with plans for another meeting. On June 28, 1840, a call went out to "all the Anti-Slavery Societies throughout the land, and all the Churches—Temperance, Education and Moral Reform Societies among the colored people to send delegates," as well as "the friends of our improvement in *this country*." Eschewing the "demon of caste," the board of managers announced they would admit all well-wishers, regardless of race.[18] According to the *Colored American*, attendance was poor. There were "But four boroughs out of the city represented by five delegates," and no delegates from further afield.[19] The *Liberator* and the *National Anti-Slavery Standard* carried more extensive reports of the four-day convention. Once more, delegates put their faith in moral reform, whose "principles are alike applicable to the people of every nation. . . . It embraces both sexes and every complexion; and fills illimitable space with its power." They praised the actions of the American representatives at the World's Anti-Slavery Convention in London for refusing to take their seats when they learned women were excluded. There was a stern denunciation of "ministers of the Gospel who refuse to speak against the evil of slavery." Perhaps Forten the temperance crusader was responsible for the final resolution:

> Resolved, That the taverns and porter houses kept by our people, are the most fruitful sources for corrupting the morals of our young men, and bringing them to untimely graves,—therefore, every person that will keep open these highways to ruin, ought to be entirely discountenanced by every Christian, every parent, and every lover of his country.[20]

Forten's commitment to temperance was of long standing. Everything he saw and read convinced him that drinking was both harmful and immoral. Moreover, the spread of temperance within the black community would "take out of the mouths of the enemies of liberty their objections to the colored man's liberty." As for his own habits, it was his boast that "he never once tasted ardent spirits, as a drink."[21]

The AMRS delegates met in August 1840 amid a rising chorus of calls for a truly national convention. The calls came from many quarters. From Harrisburg, Junius C. Morel urged a revival of the convention movement. There was so much to be discussed—West Indian emigration, factionalism within the antislavery movement, temperance, education, the support of the black press. He appealed for unity and begged each of the communities formerly represented in national conventions to send delegates. Philadelphia would be represented by "the Patriarchal Bowers, and Forten," and among the younger men by Hinton, Burr, Purvis, Whipper, and others.[22] In fact, a so-called National Reform Convention was scheduled to meet in New Haven in September 1840, but there was precious little agreement on an agenda. Some black Philadelphians had endorsed the initial call, among them Whipper and Purvis. Presumably they were attracted by its name. However, when they realized only black men were to be admitted as delegates, they very publicly withdrew their support. Their principles, they declared, forbade them to countenance racial exclusion.[23]

Through the spring and summer of 1841 the wrangling about a convention continued. In Pennsylvania there were demands for a statewide meeting, as well as a national convention. The small but very vocal African-American community in Pittsburgh proposed a meeting in Harrisburg for the late summer, urging that black Pennsylvanians must unite if they were to regain the right to vote. Would Philadelphians join their brothers in the western part of the state?[24] Some Philadelphians seemed very willing to do so. Others were far less supportive. Two individuals made their opposition very clear, apparently in letters to the convention committee in Pittsburgh. Lewis Woodson identified them as William Whipper (who objected on philosophical grounds) and an individual "distinguished alike for his age, his wealth, and his private virtues"—almost certainly James Forten—who objected to the expense involved. A less respectful commentator referred to the pair as "the patriarch of Philadelphia and the youthful sage of Columbia."[25]

The AMRS convention of August 1841 was held shortly before the state convention. The AMRS delegates roundly condemned it, insisting that the whole idea was ill-conceived. They did recognize the need for some truly national meeting "for the purpose of disseminating our principles, and devising means for the elevation of the 'colored population,'" but they wanted to be in charge of the agenda.[26] It was a supremacy they were unlikely to achieve.

On August 23, shortly after the AMRS convention disbanded, a host of black Philadelphians, among them some of James Forten's oldest friends, met to elect delegates to the state convention. One speaker after another made the point that the AMRS members were "not in number equal to one in a thousand of the colored citizens of Philadelphia," and that in condemning racially exclusive meetings they spoke for a tiny minority.[27] In the end, not a single delegate from Philadelphia attended the convention, although the minutes noted that a

letter had been received from "a great meeting of the City and County of Philadelphia" endorsing the convention, and it was agreed to add to the roll the
names of the twenty delegates who had been chosen.[28]

Philadelphians might not have sent a single delegate to the state convention, but a committee appointed at the August 23 meeting began exerting pressure for a national convention. Many of their goals were ones shared by
Forten—reaching agreement on remaining in the United States, devoting their
resources and energies to promoting "education, temperance and economy,"
and securing the full rights of citizenship. How he reacted to their proposal to
approach the federal government "for a grant of public land, to be open for all
who may settle upon it for agricultural or other purposes" is another matter.[29]

Wrangling over ends and means was not confined to black reformers. James
Forten was painfully aware of deep rifts in the predominantly white antislavery
movement by 1839. Writing to Joshua Leavitt to decline an invitation to the
upcoming National Anti-Slavery Convention in Albany, New York, he professed his hope that if only "the time and talent now unhappily wasted, in an
unprofitable controversy among brethren . . . [be] turned against the common
enemy slavery and its attendant evils, how much good might now be seen in
the holy cause, which we all profess to have so deeply at heart."[30] In fact, the
1839 meeting would prove very rancorous, with heated debates over the role of
women in the antislavery movement, the alleged anticlericalism of Garrison
and his allies, and a whole host of issues. By 1840 organized antislavery had
split into two opposing camps—a dismal prospect, indeed, for those such as
Forten, who insisted that abolitionists must combine their efforts if they were
to have any chance of helping the slaves achieve their freedom. However, Forten
continued to side with the so-called Garrisonians, even as old friends were
drawn to a radically different approach. In the fall of 1839 he and Robert Purvis
were chosen as delegates from the Philadelphia City Anti-Slavery Society to
the Pennsylvania Anti-Slavery Society, both of them "Garrisonian" organizations.[31] Forten would probably have said that both were societies that advocated principles of liberty and equality he had espoused when his beloved friend
Garrison was in his cradle. If critics insisted they were "Garrisonian," so be it.

IT SADDENED FORTEN to differ with friends in the African-American leadership
in his own city and elsewhere over their agendas. It saddened him to see white
friends such as Garrison and Gerrit Smith trading insults when both were committed to ending slavery. However, in the last years of his life there were matters closer to home that saddened him far more deeply than ideological
disagreements. The Forten family endured a devastating double tragedy in 1840.
On May 11, just a few days short of his first birthday, little Gerrit Smith Forten,
Robert and Mary's son, died of "cerebral irritation." For James and Charlotte
the child's death brought back painful memories of the loss of their young
daughter, Charlotte, so many years before. They attended their grandson's
funeral at St. Thomas's Church on the afternoon following his death, offered

what comfort they could to his bereaved parents, and steeled themselves for another loss.[32] Mary Virginia, their much loved daughter-in-law, was deathly ill with consumption.

Robert tried to prepare himself. In reply to a letter of condolence from Gerrit Smith on the death of his young namesake, Robert wrote:

> [T]here are few who need more of christian fortitude than I, for my afflictions seem to multiply upon me. The severe illness of my affectionate wife tells me that the same hand which has removed my child must very soon lead her to the enjoyment of that eternal peace which passeth all understanding.[33]

Mary succumbed to tuberculosis less than two months later. Her death devastated the entire Forten family. Her "sweet disposition . . . intelligent mind . . . [and] clear judgement" had made her a universal favorite long before Robert began courting her. According to Daniel Alexander Payne, who assumed the role of Mary's spiritual adviser, she became ill around the beginning of 1840. The early symptoms of tuberculosis were unmistakable, and Mary set about preparing her soul for judgment. She read the Bible with greater fervor than before and felt deeply the "sins and pollutions of her heart." The night before her son died she became "justified in faith" and found "peace with God." Contented with what she felt must be, she gave herself up to reading, prayer, and conversation about spiritual matters. On July 8, with Robert's relatives gathered around her bed, she declared: "It would be a glorious sight to behold an entire family in Heaven." She had words of comfort for her young sister, Annie. To James Forten, the man who had become a second father to her, she said, "I hope, my dear father, to meet you in Heaven, I wish all the family to be there, every member." She said farewell to her little daughter, Charlotte, and told her weeping husband not to mourn because she was so ready to die. Friends and family gathered around her bed, fanning her in the summer heat, until her death.[34] For James Forten there was yet another funeral, and the task of trying to comfort a heartbroken son, left alone to care for his three-year-old daughter. The house on Jefferson Row contained too many bitter memories, so Robert sold it and moved back to 92 Lombard Street, where his mother and eldest sister helped bring up young Charlotte.[35]

Friendship and intellectual endeavor gave Robert some measure of comfort. Daniel Alexander Payne had opened a "Male and Female Seminary" for African-American children.[36] Robert craved activity and the school offered it. Payne advertised that he had recruited "Mr. ROBERT FORTEN to deliver lectures on Astronomy, and give the pupils telescopic views of the heavens, whenever a class can be formed." At Payne's request Robert even wrote a "Morning Song" for the children to sing at the start of each day's classes.[37] He also continued to work with his brother-in-law on the Vigilance Committee, assisting the hundreds of desperate runaway slaves who showed up in Philadelphia each year, many of them with their masters or professional slave catchers in hot pursuit.[38] James and Charlotte probably hoped that their son would find solace in teaching and in working to help others and anticipated that, once a decent interval had passed, he would marry again. After all, he was barely twenty-seven.

The loss of their grandson and daughter-in-law, and the agony their son was going through, obviously touched James and Charlotte Forten deeply, for they were fond parents. There was also their perennial anxiety over their youngest daughter. Mary Isabella, never robust, seemed to be growing worse rather than better. Her lungs were affected, and hope of a permanent recovery was fading. The Fortens, like so many of their contemporaries, were painfully aware of the nature of consumption, even if they could only speculate about its cause. The disease might kill quickly, as it did in the case of Robert's wife, or it might take many years to weaken its victims before it finally claimed them. It might even go into remission, leading the sufferers and their friends to hope for a spontaneous cure. However, it generally recurred, sapping the strength of the afflicted still further and rendering them ever weaker. That seemed to be the course the disease was taking with Mary Isabella. All her parents could do was to pray for her recovery and prepare themselves for her death. It never occurred to them that, in tending to her, sitting with her, spending so much of their time with her, they were exposing themselves and the other members of the household to infection.

But if there was sorrow for James and Charlotte, there was also joy. By 1840 Harriet and Robert Purvis had presented them with three grandsons, Robert Jr., William, and Joseph, and a granddaughter, Harriet (known affectionately as Hattie). Robert's daughter, little Charlotte, was a great favorite. Sarah and Joseph had two children, Joseph and James. And James Jr. and Jane had produced an heir, James Vogelsang Forten. Margaretta remained unmarried, but she had already distinguished herself as a community activist, taking a leading role in the female antislavery movement. William, although only in his mid-teens, was obviously bright and able. Thomas might not be as intellectually gifted as his siblings, but he was learning the sailmaker's craft and would always have a job working for his brothers.

With his sons in control of the family business, James Forten moved toward retirement and settled into the role of elder statesman. Recognition came from many quarters. In the summer of 1841 the young men of the Demosthenian Institute, an African-American literary society, began publishing a newspaper, the *Demosthenian Shield*. The feature article each week was "Sketches of Eminent Colored Men in Philadelphia." The first number carried an account of the career of "the venerable patriot, James Forten."[39] British novelist Harriet Martineau, who had visited the Fortens in 1834 while on her tour of the United States, sent James Forten a copy of her new novel, *The Hour and the Man*, based on the life of Haitian hero Toussaint L'Ouverture.[40] The English Quaker Joseph Sturge, an acquaintance of John Greenleaf Whittier's, came to town in the spring of 1841, carrying with him letters of introduction to the leading abolitionists in Philadelphia. He recalled:

Among others, I had the pleasure of seeing JAMES FORTEN, an aged and opulent man of colour, whose long career has been marked by the display of capacity and energy of no common kind. The history of his life is interesting and instructive, affording a practical demonstration of the absurdity, as well as injustice, of that prejudice which would stamp the mark of intellectual inferiority on his complexion and race.[41]

Despite his advancing age, James Forten remained devoted to the antislavery cause. He served that cause in so many ways, not least as a conduit of information. Friends on both sides of the Atlantic sent him press clippings they thought would interest him, which he often passed on to the various antislavery editors he knew. For instance, he sent the editor of the *Pennsylvania Freeman* an account from the *London Chronicle* of the presentation of a fine piece of silver plate to the Marquis of Sligo on behalf of "the negroes of Jamaica" for "his unremitting efforts to alleviate their sufferings and to redress their wrongs" during his tenure as governor of the island. The item was picked up from the *Freeman* by the editors of the *Colored American* and reached an even wider audience.[42]

Despite his deteriorating health, James Forten continued to serve the cause. In May 1841, when the eastern branch of the Pennsylvania Anti-Slavery Society was meeting in Philadelphia, he and his two eldest sons attended a fundraiser for the Vigilance Committee. In what was probably one of his last public appearances, he shared the platform with old friends from the antislavery movement, Garrison, Charles C. Burleigh, and Nathaniel P. Rogers. He also took paternal pride in listening to his sons. Robert "delivered a brief address of the finest declamatory style," while James Jr. "sang the 'Pilgrim Fathers' . . . in a manner that would have won a foreign singer at our theatres or concerts, no small applause."[43]

Even after James Forten could no longer speak in public, he still wrote. A letter he sent Garrison in September 1841 was published in the *Liberator* with a flowery preface. Readers were asked to note that the letter was written "almost in *copper-plate style*." As for its writer,

> Among the colored citizens of the republic, there is not one who is held in higher estimation than the venerable JAMES FORTEN . . . not merely because . . . he has risen to affluence, but . . . on account of his gentlemanly qualities, shining virtues and intellectual and moral characteristics.

Garrison also drew attention to Forten's service in the Revolutionary War, and the fact that an "Ungrateful country" had chosen to ignore it. Forten sent his friend an account of his indifferent health, but the old enthusiasm for their shared commitment was still there. "It gives me great pleasure, in reading it from week to week, to hear of the successful progress of our cause; and I never lay down the Liberator without feeling my faith in its final, and I trust speedy triumph, renewed and invigorated." He added: "Although unable to participate actively in anti-slavery labors, my interest in it is undiminished, and as ardent as ever."[44]

Forten was never lacking in gratitude to those white friends who had stood by his community in times of crisis and who continued to work for an end to racial oppression. Philadelphia lawyer David Paul Brown was one such friend. Forten knew Brown had "nobly defended" the rights of people of color at the Reform Convention, and over the years, in his capacity as a lawyer, he had frequently represented black kidnap victims and alleged fugitive slaves gratis. Assuming his health permitted, Forten was probably in attendance at Mother Bethel on February 11, 1841, when his son-in-law presented two silver pitchers to Brown as a testimony of the community's appreciation for his many efforts on their behalf. Forten had almost certainly contributed toward their purchase. The pitchers were engraved with a familiar figure—a kneeling slave with hands raised to breast in supplication.[45]

Zealous abolitionists that they were, James Forten and his family followed with avid interest the fate of the *Amistad* captives, but one did not have to be an antislavery sympathizer to be transfixed by the story of the *Amistad*. From the day in August 1839 when a United States revenue cutter brought the Cuban slaver and her human cargo into New London, Connecticut, Americans were fascinated. As the story unraveled, they took sides. Joseph Cinqué and the other Africans on board who had risen up and killed their oppressors were either heroes or villains. Those such as James Forten and Robert Purvis, who saw them as courageous freedom-fighters, urged that they be set free by the American courts. After all, they had been illegally seized in Africa and sold as slaves by citizens of a nation, Spain, that had outlawed participation in the overseas slave trade. Cinqué and the others had escaped from their shackles as they were being shipped from Havana along the Cuban coast to the plantations of Puerto Príncipe. Admittedly, they had killed several people on the *Amistad*, but they had done so in defense of their liberty. All they had ever wanted was to return to their homeland. The machinations of the surviving crew members—men they had spared to take them back to Africa—had resulted in their interception off Long Island by the *Washington*. For those who were active in the antislavery cause, and for many other sympathetic observers, the case was clear. The *Amistad* captives should be freed from the Connecticut jail where they were being held and repatriated. If anyone deserved punishment, it was those who had sought to deprive them of their freedom in defiance of law and natural justice.

On the other side were those who argued that murders had been committed and the murderers must be punished. There were also legal and diplomatic implications. The status of the captives was unclear. Perhaps they were in fact slaves under Spanish law. Was an American court prepared to confiscate "property" from the legitimate owners? More to the point, what would the impact be on America's slaves if Cinqué and the others were allowed to go free?

The *Amistad* case became a cause célèbre for the antislavery forces as it worked its way through the American court system. Not until March 1841 did the United States Supreme Court hand down its judgment that the *Amistad* captives were entitled to their freedom. Eventually some of them, including Cinqué, returned home, thanks, in large part, to the efforts of their abolitionist allies.[46]

The Fortens and the Purvises followed every twist and turn in the *Amistad* case. Robert Purvis even commissioned a portrait of Cinqué by New Haven artist Nathaniel Jocelyn, brother of the abolitionist Simeon S. Jocelyn. He then had prints of the painting made in Philadelphia by engraver John Sartain and donated them to the American Anti-Slavery Society to be sold at a dollar apiece to benefit the organization.[47]

In a curious twist of fate, the *Amistad* captives brought back to James Forten a half-forgotten episode, the arrival of the young African prince, "George Sherker," on his doorstep in the summer of 1817. The boy's care and education had raised hopes that, through the kindness extended to the child, his grandfather, King Sherker, the ruler of the Gallinas, could be weaned away from the slave trade. However, when Cinqué told his story, it became painfully obvious that the king was still trading in human beings. Kidnapped by his own people because of an outstanding debt, Cinqué had been traded to "King Sharks, who reigned in the Gallinas area."[48] So much for Forten's optimism.

Other matters beside the struggle to end slavery demanded James Forten's attention. In the summer of 1840 he did battle with the Philadelphia Board of Education when it proposed to close the Lombard Street School, the only public high school for black students in the city. Forten could afford to educate his children privately, but he spoke up for the many hundreds of African-American parents who could not. The Lombard Street School had been having difficulties since the 1833 transfer of James M. Bird, the white teacher who was much respected by black parents and by the African-American community as a whole. The rapid teacher turnover after Bird's departure contributed to a sharp decline in enrollments. That, in turn, prompted the controllers to consider closing the school.[49] On behalf of the community, James Forten met with the directors on June 30 to try to dissuade them and to promise that he and his friends would do everything in their power to increase student numbers.[50] The following day the Pennsylvania Abolition Society's Committee to Improve the Condition of the African Race and "a few of our coloured friends," including Forten, conferred. The "coloured people's Committee" seemed, in the minds of the white abolitionists, "fully sensible of the importance and necessity of their doing everything in their power to induce the Directors to continue the Lombard Street Schools for Coloured Children." Satisfied that Forten and other black leaders would make good on their pledge "to take prompt and decisive action," the white committee determined there was nothing more for it to do.[51] The controllers agreed to reappoint Bird, and the PAS hoped that would correct some of the problems. Fearing their own Clarkson School was drawing students away from the Lombard Street School, the PAS closed it and transferred ownership to the board of controllers, who promptly reopened it as a school for whites.[52] How Forten felt about that is not clear. His sons had been educated at the Clarkson School. His victory in getting Bird reappointed and the Lombard Street School kept open would prove a hollow one indeed if the Clarkson School had been sacrificed in the process.

JAMES FORTEN HAD enjoyed good health most of his life. His letters contain only occasional mentions of minor complaints, but early in 1841, in his seventy-fifth year, he became seriously ill. When Garrison visited him in the spring he was still ailing. By the end of August he was worse. He wrote Garrison that there had been occasional respites, but "the complaint is now renewed, and I am at present suffering from a more than usually severe attack of it."[53]

Whatever the nature of Forten's illness, the humid summer in Philadelphia can hardly have helped. He experienced increased difficulty breathing. However, the obvious diagnosis, that he had contracted tuberculosis from his daughter and his daughter-in-law, does not fit the symptoms. His condition seemed more like asthma than anything else. In fact, his minister, William Douglass, referred to it as an "asthmatic complaint." The breathing difficulties were accompanied by edema, the accumulation of fluid in the extremities and eventually in the lungs and around the heart. For years Forten had been inhaling filaments from the canvas he worked with. He had been using twine and cordage treated with all manner of chemical concoctions to preserve it from the elements. Perhaps the prolonged exposure to a variety of allergens had finally caught up with him. On the other hand, the edema and breathlessness might well have been symptoms of congestive heart failure. Without detailed case notes from his physician, it is impossible retrospectively to make a definite diagnosis. Whatever the cause of his illness, Forten accepted his growing weakness with patience and resignation. He had lived a long life. His family was well provided for. He refused to complain. If his illness proved a mortal one, so be it.

By November, Forten was confined to his home.[54] He knew it was time to put his business affairs in order. He had made his will five years earlier and saw no reason to change it. Charlotte was to receive all his household goods, one third of his real estate, and one third of his personal property. His sister was guaranteed the lifetime use of the house he had bought for her, and his executors were ordered to keep it in good repair and pay the taxes on it. The minister, church wardens, and vestry of St. Thomas's were to receive $100 "towards the purchase of a Burial Ground for said Church." Another $100 went to the Philadelphia Anti-Slavery Society. Everything else was to be divided equally among his eight surviving children and their heirs. Sensible of the legal situation with respect to married women's property, he stipulated that his daughters should retain the absolute right to their inheritance, "and so that the same shall not be liable to the Debts or engagements of any Husbands they . . . may marry . . . previous to their marrying I do enjoin on my said Daughters to execute such formal settlements as may be deemed requisite to carry my wishes . . . into effect." Charlotte, James Jr., and Robert were to carry on the sail loft "for their joint account." He appointed as executors Charlotte, Margaretta, and Robert Purvis. Charlotte would be the guardian of their minor children unless and until she remarried.[55]

Although James Forten did not alter his will during his final illness, there was one outstanding matter to be attended to. On January 4, 1842, his lawyer was summoned to his bedside to draw up a deed relating to the family home. In return for a token payment of $1, James and Charlotte made over the house and lot to James Jr. and Robert Purvis. They could let it and give the rental payments to Charlotte, or allow her to occupy it. Should she remarry, her new husband would have no control over the property. On her death it would be divided among the Fortens' surviving children or their heirs. Fully aware of the urgency of the matter, Forten had the deed recorded without delay.[56]

Ill though he was, he "still saw those who called to see him, and told his family to admit all, for he seemed to wish to give the parting hand to all his fellow citizens and friends." Stephen H. Gloucester came to visit his old benefactor, and Forten "spoke of the satisfaction it gave him to think that he had done any thing in helping to free [Gloucester's] family." He remembered John Gloucester with fondness and encouraged Stephen and his younger brother, James, to follow in their father's footsteps. Gloucester observed: "There are many, like myself, who owe much to him for their freedom."[57]

Another visitor was Forten's lifelong friend Daniel Brewton. Now the steward of the Philadelphia Lazaretto, the quarantine hospital on Tinicum Island, Brewton had never forgotten Forten's selfless act on the *Jersey* sixty years before. The two had shared so much; they had grown old amid the same sights, sounds, and smells—the creaking of ships' timbers, the smell of pitch and tar, the feel of canvas and cordage. They spoke the same language of the sea and of ships. It was an emotional farewell, which left Brewton in tears.[58]

Daniel Alexander Payne recalled that he often spoke with Forten in those last weeks about the state of his soul. "The first time that I asked him if he felt prepared to die, he said, 'I am ready to leave this world when my Creator calls me.'"[59] Forten told his minister and friend, William Douglass, "that he was perfectly satisfied with the Lord's dealings toward him. 'The Lord's goodness and mercy have followed me all my days; and the same kind hand is still over me. What he does is right.'" On February 28, when he was bedridden and struggling for breath, he again gave Douglass testimony of his faith: "'I am a dying man; and I wish to inform you, that . . . I have the comfortable hope, when this tabernacle falls, of entering into that house not made with hands.'" The following evening he bid farewell to his family. He told his two eldest sons to take care of their mother, and then he turned to the man who had been another son to him. To Robert Purvis he said (according to Payne): "I love you so much that I could take you in my bosom, and carry you with me to heaven." He charged Purvis never to forget the plight of the "perishing slaves." A few hours later, when a friend, most likely William Douglass, inquired about the state of Forten's soul, the old man replied: "'Happy! happy! happy! . . . I feel peace that passeth all understanding. Lord, let thy kingdom come, thy will be done on earth as it is in heaven.'"[60] During his last two or three days he was unable to speak, but he "showed signs of rationality . . . almost to the last." He died at nine o'clock on the morning of Friday, March 4.[61]

James Forten's funeral took place at St. Thomas's Church two days later. The procession was truly remarkable. J. Miller McKim, a white friend from the Pennsylvania Anti-Slavery Society, described it in a letter to the *National Anti-Slavery Standard*.

> The vast concourse of people, of all classes and complexions, numbering from three to five thousand, that followed his remains to the grave, bore testimony to the estimation in which he was universally held. Our wealthiest and most influential citizens joined in the procession; and complexional distinctions and prejudices seemed . . . forgotten, in the desire to pay the last tribute of respect to the memory of departed worth.[62]

Abolitionist Henry C. Wright's report of the funeral echoed McKim's:

> At his funeral, I could but exclaim . . . HE HAS TRIUMPHED! He gained a victory over a nation arrayed against him: for, around his dead body, *complexion* was forgotten. Many of our most beloved and respected citizens were present, to testify their respect for the deceased, and their sympathy for his afflicted family.[63]

Those who walked behind Forten's coffin included "many merchants, shippers, and sea-captains, who had known and respected him for years." Lucretia Mott described it as "a real amalgamation funeral."[64]

That sense of the passing of a unique individual who had, however briefly, bridged the racial divide was evident not only among his fellow abolitionists but also among the public more generally. The *United States Gazette* described his funeral as "one of the largest . . . seen in Philadelphia for a great length of time." White mourners "followed [Forten] to his grave as a token of their regard for the excellency of his character. He had won the respect of men of all persuasions, and all shades of complexion, and they bore testimony to the unvarying probity of his conduct in all his various relations in life."[65] The *Public Ledger* was more muted in its praise. Describing the funeral procession, the editor wrote: "Such a general sinking of respect to color as the speckled line presented, probably was never before witnessed in this city," although he was careful to note that blacks and whites walked separately. "[W]e did not see the different colors coupled."[66]

St. Thomas's Church was filled to capacity for the funeral. In his eulogy William Douglass pointed out that Forten had lived to see one, and another, and another, of his old associates . . . fall before the resistless arm of death. With few remaining, who could sympathize with him in the recollections of his youthful days, he stood in our midst like an old stately tree among young saplings, spared by the woodsman, as a relic of former times.

Family and friends were not unprepared for his death. "The old oak that has braved the fury of a thousand storms, we naturally expect to see fall by its own weight at last, and give place to the young branches nourished at its side."

Douglass recalled Forten's deep concern about temperance. The last time Forten had been well enough to attend church, this had been the subject of their discussion. "'O, Mr. Douglass, only look at the rising generation; look at the young men that are coming up:—what will become of them, if they be not duly impressed with the importance of this subject? Sir, this subject cannot be too frequently brought before them.'"

In the seven years Douglass had served at St. Thomas's he had come to know Forten very well. The older man had befriended him and confided in him. The two had served on many committees together. Douglass had been greatly impressed by Forten's demeanor. He was

> frequently called to preside in public meetings, and in very few instances . . . was he ever known to fail, as he took the chair, to set before the audience, the importance of preserving harmony. . . . And should any disorder occur . . . none could appear to be more pained . . . than he, nor be more ready to restore things to their equitable and quiet state again. . . . If matters were conducted in that orderly and regular manner, that would justify him at the close, in congratulating them on the harmony and unanimity that prevailed, he would always do it, with manifestations of the greatest delight.

While many self-made men were "mean and parsimonious," that could not be said of James Forten.

> His heart and hand were ever open to supply the needy; and to every species of distress, he was ever ready to give relief. Nor was his generosity regulated by any complexional distinctions. He stopped not to inquire to what nation they belonged, in whose behalf an appeal was made; it was always enough for him to know, that the appeal was made in behalf of *suffering humanity*. Hence, all those societies whose operations tend to the benefit of man, such as literary, temperance, anti-slavery, bible, tract, and missionary societies, *all* found in him a liberal patron.

Douglass conceded that if "he manifested a deeper interest" in the first three, "it was doubtless owing to the great concern that he always evinced for the elevation and improvement of that unfortunate class, with which he was particularly identified." Education and temperance would not only benefit black men and women by improving the quality of their lives, but would "stop the mouths of the enemies of freedom."[67]

Tributes flowed in from many quarters. On March 10 the Philadelphia Female Anti-Slavery Society noted the passing of Forten, one of their most generous supporters, and of longtime member (and Forten family friend) Grace Douglass, and resolved to pursue the work "to which they devoted their energies" with renewed diligence.[68] The editor of the *Peoples' Press* dwelt on Forten's consistency of character. So many people lost with the passing years the "enthusiasm and high principles" of their youth. Not Forten. "Had James Forten of sixteen been introduced to James Forten of seventy-six, the two would not only have recognized each other, but would have rushed to a mutual and cordial embrace."[69]

From Boston Garrison wrote in praise of his "venerable friend." He observed:

> He was a man of rare qualities, and worthy to be held in veneration to the end of time. He was remarkable for his virtues, his self respect, his catholic temper, his christian urbanity. An example like his is of inestimable value . . . in the mighty struggle now taking place between liberty and slavery—reason and prejudice.[70]

The *Herald of Freedom* noted Forten's passing, although evidently editor Nathaniel P. Rogers had not taken to heart Forten's strictures about continually harping on race, for he observed: "We venerate [Forten] infinitely the more for his disqualifying race." Rogers also commented on the attitude of Philadelphia's whites with regard to Forten. "It would have seemed a sort of sacrilege to despise him, and they made him an exception to his race."[71] The *North American* observed: "His strict integrity and great amenity of manners made him many warm friends among our best citizens." Incidentally, the newspaper gave him the title of "citizen" which the law denied him, although the editor did preface it with the word "coloured."[72] Even the *African Repository* printed a brief memorial.

> We see announced in the papers the death of JAMES FORTEN of Philadelphia. He was much respected, and justly so, not only by his colored brethren, but by the population generally of that city. . . . He was in error . . . on the subject of African Colonization, but we believe him to have been an upright and virtuous man.[73]

There was a whole series of memorial meetings. The first was held the day after the funeral at the First African Presbyterian Church. Philadelphians attended "without distinction of complexion." African-American businessman Stephen Smith presided, and the meeting chose seven men to prepare memorial resolutions to be sent to the press and to the Forten family. James Forten was eulogized as an "honorable patriarch," an example of industry, of "filial and fraternal affection" for his care of his widowed mother and sister, and "one of the brightest ornaments" of society. "[N]otwithstanding the most discouraging and crushing obstacles [which] beset his path, he rose to be a man of extensive intelligence, unusual benevolence . . . exalted virtue, and great respectability."[74]

On the evening of March 30, at Mother Bethel, Robert Purvis delivered a memorial address on the life of his father-in-law. Noting that about half of the 3,000 to 4,000 mourners at Forten's funeral were white, Purvis observed: "[T]here is a resistless power, which a virtuous man can wield in his death, to the overthrow of feelings the most foul, unnatural, and detestable. Prejudice, soul-crushing, man-despising, God-hating prejudice, was victimized on the 6th of March, 1842."[75] Even in death James Forten continued to serve the antislavery cause. Copies of Purvis's address were offered for sale at the Anti-Slavery Office in Philadelphia, with the proceeds going to advance the work of abolition.[76]

On April 17, in the Second African Presbyterian Church, Stephen H. Gloucester delivered his tribute. According to Gloucester, Forten was well known for both his hospitality and his many gifts to charity. "The oppressed man, the mariner, the soldier, the Indian, all found in him a friend."[77] As Gloucester acknowledged, James Forten had been a true and most liberal friend to himself and his family.

After the eulogies had been given and the memorial addresses printed and circulated, his fellow citizens continued to speak and write about James Forten's personality, his achievements in business, and his dedication to the causes he believed in—at least for a while. In 1845 an anonymous writer, identified only as a member of the Philadelphia bar, observed that Forten "died much lamented." He went on to point to him as "A singular instance of a colored man rising to fortune and respect by sheer industry and correct deportment." Another writer, an unnamed "merchant of Philadelphia," also singled out Forten's "correct deportment," as well as his "integrity and genuine politeness." One can only speculate about the impact on James Forten's sense of self of the need to maintain "correct deportment" at all times and in all facets of his life. However, it would undoubtedly have pleased him to read the lawyer's final verdict upon him: "He was an honest man."[78]

14

LEGACY

J AMES FORTEN CAST a long shadow. His legacy was a complex one that both burdened and blessed his heirs. There was the constant pressure to live up to his example. Abolitionists, black and white, expected a continued commitment from the family. Many in the African-American community looked to the Forten clan for leadership and guidance. And then there was the question of continued success in business. James Forten had been a self-made man. His sons, who had received far better educations and many more material advantages than he, could surely improve on their inheritance. Those who traded with the firm of James Forten and Sons expected it. In so many ways the Forten name weighed heavily on James Forten's heirs, overwhelming some of them as it energized and inspired others to carry on his work.

EVEN AS THEY buried James Forten, made graceful replies to the letters of condolence that poured in, and tried to adjust to life without his redoubtable presence, the Fortens knew they must soon part with another family member. James Forten's last months had been saddened by the realization that his youngest daughter would not long survive him. In failing health for many years, Mary Isabella died of consumption on July 16, 1842, at age twenty-seven. Eulogized as a young woman of "finished mental culture" and deep religious faith who "moved in the circle of her acquaintances, admired and beloved," she was buried beside her father in St. Thomas's churchyard.[1]

Business matters took no account of personal tragedies. As they struggled to reconcile themselves to the loss of two family members in less than six months, the Fortens had to settle James Forten's estate. That was no easy matter. The appraisers, his sometime foreman, Charles Anthony, and a neighbor, sailor Robert Archibald, valued his estate at $67,108. His real estate amounted to almost $20,000—not including the Lombard Street home which he had transferred to Robert Jr. and Robert Purvis shortly before his death. There were tools and goods in the sail loft worth almost $500, cash amounting to over $1,700, furniture worth $1,100, clothing and a handsome watch valued at $150, and almost $3,500 in stocks. However, as was the case with most "gentlemen of the pave," Forten had loaned out a substantial amount of his capital, and these were bad times for calling in debts. Bonds and mortgages amounted to $1,028. There was $4,337 in discounted notes judged "Doubtful." In book debts $4,105 was judged "good" and a staggering $31,779, almost half the value of the estate, "Doubtful."[2]

The Fortens were looking at a crisis in the making, but that was not immediately obvious. Many of the charges on the estate were modest enough. To begin with, there were medical bills and funeral expenses for James and Mary—payments to physicians George Lingen and William E. Horner, to Mrs. Ash (probably a layer out of the dead), to undertaker William H. Moore, and to the sexton at St. Thomas's. The family commissioned elaborate headstones for James and his daughter. Stonecutter Thomas Farley was paid a total of $385 for his work.

There were tradesmen's bills, most under $50, to white tailors Jacob Reed and William B. Taylor, to African-American shoemaker John Lucas, to white shoemaker Ezekiel J. Young, to dentist Jacob Huckle, to dry-goods merchants Albertson and Roberts, and to cabinetmaker Charles Frisby. There was the pew rent at St. Thomas's. There were the expenses of keeping the sail loft running. On April 2, Forten's executors paid out $134 for journeymen's wages for the previous month. There were small payments to various merchants, most of them neighbors—$7 to Benjamin E. Bunker of 78 South Wharves; $5 to hardware dealer Robert Lesley; $45 to brothers Hall W. and J. C. Mercer, of 21 South Wharves; over $60 to ship's carpenter Richard Wilson; $2.75 to tinsmith Edmund Yates; $18 to hardware merchants Isaac B. Baxter and Son; $4.30 to tinmen Trough and Lehman. There were the expenses incurred by any landlord—a ground rent on one of the Forten properties, and the water tax on all of them, small sums paid to house painter David Bevan, and to carpenters Edward and John Venning (fellow members of St. Thomas's), costs of cleaning the house on Ninth Street, repairs, a padlock, new glass. There may have been a dispute over Abigail Dunbar's tenancy of the house her brother had left her. In May 1842 Forten's executors paid a lawyer for an "Opinion in regard to [the] House in Washington Court."

Forten's executors, his widow, his eldest daughter, and his favorite son-in-law, set about realizing what they could. They sold his shares in the Farmers' and Mechanics' Bank, the Southwark Bank, the Philadelphia Exchange, the

Atlantic Insurance Company, and the Mount Carbon Railroad Company.[3] They completed a real estate sale of the Bridges's home, 259 South Front Street, begun before his death. The would-be purchaser was merchant Jonathan F. Ohl, who had been Forten's neighbor and business acquaintance for two decades. Ohl's warehouse was at 104 South Wharves, near the Forten sail loft. As the owner or part owner of at least five vessels, he had probably ordered sails from Forten and Sons or had repairs done in their loft. Forten had promised to sell Ohl the Front Street property for $5,500, with the full amount to be paid in a year. Forten's executors petitioned the Orphans' Court for permission to close the deal. Pending completion of the sale, Ohl lived in the house and paid rent, which was applied to the purchase price.[4]

There were regular rental payments from others besides Ohl. Forten had owned a number of properties that he let. African-American renters included carpenter John Venning, who leased a house on Barley; laborer Ashmead Hall, who rented 2 Washington Court, next to Abigail Dunbar's home, at $4 per month; and grocer William Banton, who rented a house on Second and Shippen. As for his white tenants, dry-goods merchant Alfred P. Fassitt leased 245 Pine for a modest $7 per month. "Tailoress" Mary Cooper rented 67 George. Maria Bancroft rented one of Forten's properties on Front Street. A physician, Heber Chase, rented 111 South Ninth, at $37.50 per quarter. When he moved out, Forten's executors let the premises to Lucy Grosvenor as a boardinghouse at a higher rent. "Gentleman" James Veacock rented Forten's old home, 50 Shippen, for $30 per quarter. When he left, it was leased to a Polish shoemaker, Charles Alter. Another tenant was tavern-keeper Conrad Schild. James Forten might not have approved of the consumption of liquor, but he knew the worth of a tenant who paid his rent on time.[5]

The rents came in regularly, and there were other credits to the Forten estate. In the summer of 1843 the County of Philadelphia paid $125 in damages, compensation, perhaps, for losses sustained during the rioting of the previous August. (The county had awarded the congregation of Second African Presbyterian damages for the destruction of their church in the riot.) The sale of Forten's personal effects and clothing netted $650. But the estate would be badly encumbered unless and until a score or more of debtors paid what they owed.

Most of Forten's loans had been to shipowners and merchants who were neighbors and men he had known for many years. Jonathan Latour, an importer of "salad, or sweet oil," lived next to the old Bridges home on South Front. He had been a shipowner since the War of 1812. He repaid $124.[6] Elderly merchant and shipowner John Welsh, a neighbor from South Wharves, paid back almost $300.[7] Welsh's neighbors, Isaac Lloyd and his son, were indebted to Forten for almost $230. Lloyd, in his seventies and, like Forten, a native of Pennsylvania, had most likely known the sailmaker for years. Francis Gurney Smith, consul for the republic of Texas, who lived not far from the Fortens on Lombard Street, paid back almost $60. Then there were the influential Copes, Henry and Alfred, large-scale shipowners who ran a packet service between Philadelphia and Liverpool. They paid back almost $1,000. Stephen Baldwin paid over $300. John Graham, master of the brig *Cuba*, paid more than $850. Captain John Martin paid over $120, but that was not all he owed. French merchant Jonathan B. Bernadou, in business at 89 South Wharves, and, like Lloyd and Forten, an older "gentleman of the pave," paid up. Then there were payments from younger men busy establishing themselves in business. One such was Joseph P. Vogels, a shipbuilder, lumber merchant, and partowner of the barque *Clarion*. He lived at 47 Lombard. There was commission merchant Robert Huddle, of 40 Lombard, who owned the brig *Colombian*. He repaid over $200 in installments. Owners of the brig *Braganza* and businessmen on South Front, George and John Diehl paid the estate over $320.[8] Altogether, Forten's executors recouped about $3,000, most of the "good" book debts.

Forten had borrowed as well as loaned, obviously on the assumption he would be able to pay his creditors when the various loans he had made were repaid. That was slow in happening, and almost immediately his notes came due. In March 1842 his executors paid a note in favor of David Brooks and Co. for $608. There were many more—over $220 to commission merchant William Craig, of Craig and Sargant, of 9 North Wharves, and almost $550 to Robert McGregor and John Caldwell. The firm of James Forten and Sons was indebted to commission merchants and shipowners Dexter Stone and Samuel Grant of South Wharves for almost $1,000. There were some other significant payments, again mostly to neighbors and business associates of long standing. And the loans did not dry up once James Forten was dead. The biggest debt of all, over $1,700, was to Peck and Co., merchants, of 19 South Wharves. It had been negotiated by Robert and James Jr. and may have been a vain attempt to consolidate some of the debts of James Forten and Sons. Robert even tried to shore up the firm with his private money. In January 1844 his father's estate paid his note of $500.

The facts were inescapable. James Forten's business empire was in serious financial trouble by the time he died. He may have lost touch with market conditions as his health deteriorated. He may have been too trusting. An English visitor who asked about him was told that he "lost a great part of his riches by lending money with more generosity than prudence."[9] But this was a difficult business climate in which to be successful. Many firms failed in the Panic of 1837. In 1842 economic recovery was a long way off. Forten's contemporary, diarist Sidney George Fisher, wrote of a city where

> The streets seemed deserted, the largest houses are shut up and to rent, there is no business, there is no money, no confidence and little hope, property is sold every day by the sheriff at a fourth of the estimated value of a few years ago, nobody can pay debts, the miseries of poverty are felt by both rich and poor.[10]

Like so many of its counterparts, the firm of James Forten and Sons was the victim of forces beyond its control.

Over the years James Forten had made regular appearances in the District Court and the Court of Common Pleas to recover sums of money due him. Now his sons found themselves in court confessing they could not meet their obligations. The first unmistakable sign that the firm of J. and R. B. Forten was in trouble came in the District Court's December 1843 term, when Robert Purvis sued his brothers-in-law for debts of over $1,800. They lost the case and were obliged to pay not only the amount due, but interest and legal costs as well.[11] Worse was to follow. In March 1844 merchant James Maull, Jr., of 89 South Front Street, sued to recover more than $400 due him. This was a debt of some months' standing: the previous June the Forten estate had paid him interest on his note. Forten and Maull's father were old rivals. For years James Maull, Sr., had operated a sail loft on Spruce Street Wharf. The younger Maull knew the Fortens were in trouble. He either could not afford to extend more credit or was disinclined to do so. The Forten brothers did not trouble to file an affidavit of defense. They knew they could not pay.[12]

The Maull lawsuit signaled the start of an onslaught by the Fortens' creditors. The firm of Mecke, Plate and Co. had a substantial debt to recover. An initial payment of over $200 had been made by his executors just weeks after Forten's death, and another payment of over $300 a few months later. The partners in the firm, merchants George H. Mecke, Christopher H. Plate, and John Leppien, had their premises at 54 South Front, a couple of blocks from the Forten loft; Forten and his sons were well known to them in the way of business. They knew that the firm was in trouble and that they must move quickly if they hoped to recover any of their money. Again James and Robert Forten did not attempt to defend the action.[13]

Robert Purvis's second suit, commenced on March 13, 1844, the day he received his first judgment against his wife's brothers, reveals even more about the contours of the creditor-debtor network on the Philadelphia waterfront. The Fortens owed Purvis money, but they were, in turn, owed various sums. Purvis sued them and their creditors. There were plenty of them. There were two young Frenchmen, Pierre Louis and Edmond Laguerenne, who operated an import business at 59 Front Street, and were neighbors of J. and R. B. Forten and of Mecke, Plate and Co. Captain Rinier Skaats lived a few blocks away at 273 South Front. Captain John Martin, of 222 South Front, owed substantial sums to the Forten estate, as did merchant Charles I. Tully of 101 South Front. John Devereux was in business at 79 South Wharves, just along from the Forten sail loft. William S. Smith was next door to Tully at 80 South Wharves. And then there were those from slightly further afield—J. C. Benedict, a retailer of iron chests, who did business at 83 Dock Street; cordwainer John McDermott from Fourth and Barker; and Adam Southern, who sold crockery at 248 South Second. The Laguerennes, Devereux, and Martin had made partial repayment.[14] Forten and his sons had extended loans, as they had always done, to men they knew and trusted, but the economy had turned sour, too many of their creditors had failed to pay up, and the firm could not meet its obligations.

Robert Purvis won his second case against his in-laws and more judgments followed. James Forten, Jr., promptly decamped to New York, leaving his brother to answer as best he could. His departure occurred between March 2, 1844, when he acknowledged service of a writ in the case of *Mecke, Plate and Co. v. James and Robert Forten*, and April 20, when the sheriff reported that he could not find James to serve him with a writ in another case.

The writs kept coming in with dreadful regularity, as did the resulting judgments against the now "late" firm of J. and R. B. Forten. In a case that dragged on for many months due to Robert Forten's attempt at self-defense, Ramon de la Sierra received an award in his favor of a staggering $833. Another old neighbor, coppersmith Francis Harley, Sr., of 78 South Front, recovered almost $500. Merchant Joseph W. Ham, of 43 South Wharves, won a judgment in the amount of $582.[15] Then there was grocer William Harbeson, a former neighbor of Robert Forten's when he and his first wife lived on Jefferson Row. In a case that Robert tried to contest, Harbeson was awarded $863. The grocer was less successful when he brought suit against Robert Purvis, probably on the grounds that Purvis was one of the executors of the Forten estate. Purvis emerged victorious with a judgment against Harbeson.[16] William W. Smith tried the same tactic of suing the Fortens and Purvis. Once more Purvis defended himself with vigor and with first-rate legal counsel.[17] He had no intention of sharing in the financial disaster overtaking the Forten family.

The Fortens responded as best they could to the crisis, struggling to recover money due them. Charlotte and the other executors sued Captain Peter Anderson for over $1,600 in March 1845 in what may have been a disputed real estate transaction.[18] They also disposed of property. On February 5, 1844, with Purvis's second action pending, they sold the house and lot at 111 South Ninth Street for $3,000, less than Forten had paid for it back in 1812.[19] Another sale followed four days after the judgment, on February 14, 1844. An old acquaintance, conveyancer Benjamin G. Mitchell, bought a house and lot on Lombard, between Tenth and Eleventh, and a lot on Barley, near Eleventh, for $2,850. He may well have been helping a family he knew and respected. One week later he traded both properties to Joseph Purvis for exactly what he had paid for them.[20]

The financial nightmare dragged on for a decade. Finally, in January 1853, Robert Purvis returned to court to sue the already bankrupt Robert and the absent James. This time he was out to recover $8,000. He was awarded the full amount with damages. The only assets the Forten brothers had left were their shares in the real estate inherited from their father. After Mary Isabella's death, the shares had been redistributed and they now held two-sevenths. As a result of Purvis's legal victory, the Fortens had to endure the humiliation of seeing two shares of their real estate put up for public auction. Needless to say, it was Purvis who bought the shares and kept the estate intact. And it was by no means a negligible estate. There was the house and lot on Shippen that Robert Bridges had bought on behalf of his young foreman back in 1792; the house, lot, and buildings on George Street that Forten had acquired in 1803; the house on Ninth and Lombard bought from Richard Peters, Jr., in 1812; two houses and lots between Sixth and Seventh, and Pine and Lombard; and the family home at 92 Lombard.[21] After the sheriff's auction further sales were necessary. In January 1854 the property on Ninth and Lombard was sold for $1,300 and the payment of a yearly rent. On the same day the properties on George Street and Shippen Street were sold for $2,400.[22]

The Fortens sold the sail loft for what they could get to two former employees in 1844 or 1845. It was an ideal marriage of experience and capital. George Bolivar, a wealthy young African-American migrant from North Carolina, teamed up with Charles Anthony, a Pennsylvania native who had worked his way up from apprentice to foreman under James Forten, just as Forten had done under Robert Bridges.[23]

Had the firm of J. and R. B. Forten remained solvent a few years longer, there might have been a recovery. The change from sail to steam, sometimes cited as the reason for the firm's demise, was a long time coming, and steam vessels carried auxiliary sails for many years. The 1850s saw the heyday of the clipper ships. Clippers carried vast amounts of canvas, sometimes so much they became unwieldy, and captains pushed their ships hard. The result was plenty of work for sailmakers, with frequent repairs and orders for new suits of sails. During the Civil War there were military contracts. Soldiers needed tents, and, as it had done in the past, the government turned to civilian sailmakers to supply them.[24] If they could have dragged themselves out of the financial quagmire, the Fortens would have prospered in the 1850s and 1860s. But the crash came too soon. They were not reduced to poverty overnight, but the decline in their fortunes was obvious to everyone in the business community.

AFTER HIS DECAMPMENT to New York City in the spring of 1844, James Forten, Jr.'s movements are difficult to trace. That was doubtless intentional, for he did not relish the prospect of being hounded by his creditors. James was fortunate that his wife was in a position to help support the family. A well-educated woman and a native New Yorker with many friends among that city's African-American elite, Jane Vogelsang Forten found work as a teacher. By 1849 she headed the "female department" of New York Colored School, No. 2.[25] The school's superintendent was family friend Charles L. Reason, and, when he left to take an appointment at Central College in upstate New York, the Fortens sent their son, James, there to complete his education.

Central College was a unique experiment, committed from its founding to "equal rights and Christian reform." Financed by Gerrit Smith and the American Baptist Free Mission Society, Central admitted "all persons, of both sexes, of good moral character." The choice of an isolated location had been deliberate: free from the corrupting influences of urban life, students would be more receptive to the "Moral influences, Republican habits, and Christian example, associated with Manual Labor." In the classroom they received an academic education. In Central's workshops and on its 150-acre farm they learned mechanical skills and husbandry. Central was also a training ground for reformers. Daily classes in "Extemporaneous Speaking" were intended to fit the likes of young Forten to take their place on the speaker's platform and discourse eloquently on the rights of women and the wrongs of the slaves.[26]

James may still have been at Central when his mother fell ill. Jane Forten died of tuberculosis on July 16, 1852, at age thirty-three.[27] In 1858 young James's cousin, Charlotte, described a meeting with Mr. Vogelsang, Jane's brother. The meeting, a very amicable one, brought back fond memories of "dear Aunt J[ane]." A few weeks later there was a visit from James. Charlotte had not seen her cousin for some time, and observed in her journal: "How greatly he is changed. I should not have known him!"[28]

James Vogelsang Forten and his father eventually went their separate ways, although there may have been a brief reunion during the Civil War. James V. Forten, who gave his occupation as "farmer," enlisted in the United States Navy in New York on June 27, 1863. He was posted to the *Saratoga*, where he served in the only capacity available to him as a man of color—officers' steward. He went on to serve on the *Vermont* and was discharged at the Brooklyn Navy Yard on July 1, 1865.[29] His father enlisted in the Navy at Baltimore in September 1864 and was discharged three years later. Aged forty-nine at the time of his enlistment, he gave his occupation as "mariner." In all those years since he had last featured in the Forten family correspondence, he had apparently been at sea, using the skills learned in his father's sail loft. In 1865 he was assigned to the *Tuscarora*, as was a twenty-five-year-old sailor named "James D. Forten."[30] Was the younger man his son? He was the same age as James V. Forten, but he listed his trade as "carpenter" and his place of birth as Salem County, New Jersey. However, James V. Forten eventually settled in New Jersey. Quite possibly James D. and James V. Forten were one and the same.

As for James Forten, Jr., after his discharge from the Navy he disappeared from the records. Family letters do not mention him. He does not feature in the pages of Charlotte Forten's journal. An extensive search of United States and Canadian censuses has failed to find him. The only trace of him is in a deed disposing of some family property. James Forten, Jr., reportedly died some time before his sister Margaretta, and she died early in 1875. According to the deed, James V. Forten was his only child.[31]

James Vogelsang Forten moved to New Jersey, married, and fathered twelve children, only five of whom survived him. In the decades after the Civil War he sank inexorably into poverty. He tried, without success, to get a pension for his wartime service, but was rejected as "not disabled for manual labor to a pensionable degree." In 1886 he was working as a gardener in Haddonfield. In 1900 he and his son, James E. Forten, were living in Centre Township, Camden County, New Jersey, and working as coachmen. James Vogelsang Forten died in that town on May 27, 1907.[32]

UNLIKE HIS ELDER brother, Robert Bridges Forten left an impressive paper trail. Life was not easy for James Forten's second son in the early 1840s, following the double tragedy of the loss of his wife and infant son. Then came the deaths of his father and sister, the family's financial crisis, and what amounted to betrayal by his brother. James's flight to New York left Robert to endure the ignominy of bankruptcy alone.

Robert struggled to make a home for himself and his daughter. He left 92 Lombard and rented a house on nearby Powell, where he had friends. There was clothes dealer William Chew and his family—his wife Hetty, who mothered little Charlotte and was fondly remembered by her, daughter Emily, the Chews' married son, John, and his wife and children. Another neighbor was Frederick A. Hinton. Hinton's daughter, Ada, offered companionship to Charlotte, while Hinton sympathized with Robert in his grief, for he knew what it was to lose a young wife and beloved children.[33] And one constant in Robert's life was the friendship of Robert and Harriet Purvis. Even when Purvis was suing to recover money from the family firm, he took pains to show Robert he trusted him as an individual.[34] It was through Purvis that Robert met his second wife, Mary Hanscome.

WHEN THOMAS HANSCOME arrived in Philadelphia from South Carolina in 1845, there were excellent reasons why Robert Purvis should befriend him and equally compelling reasons why he should shun him. Both were Charlestonians, both the sons of women of color by wealthy white men, and both had been left handsome fortunes by their fathers. But there the similarities ended, for Hanscome was a slave owner and Purvis an outspoken foe of slavery. Purvis may have assumed Hanscome was moving North because he loathed slavery. In fact, what Hanscome was turning his back on was his unenviable position as a free man of color in a slave society.

The story of the complex web of relationships that linked the Fortens and the Purvises with the Hanscomes and their kinfolk began in Charleston around 1810. As William Purvis and Harriet Judah welcomed the arrival of their second son, Robert, Thomas Hanscome, a planter in St. James and Goose Creek Parish, some fifteen miles outside the city, embarked on a liaison with Nancy Randall. If she was a slave, Hanscome freed her before the birth of their first child. All six of their children were born free. Thomas Hanscome died in 1831, leaving an estate worth over $330,000. His will contained numerous bequests to friends, to his church, to Charleston's Orphan House, and to the College of Charleston. William Purvis bequeathed almost everything he owned to his "beloved friend" and their sons. Hanscome dealt less generously with his mistress and their children, but his death left them richer than most Charlestonians, irrespective of race. Nancy received $15,000 in stocks, the contents of the house on Charleston's Tradd Street she had shared with Hanscome, the use during her lifetime of another home on Greenhill Street, and the services of thirteen slaves and their offspring. Her children, Joseph, Thomas, James, Louisa, Elizabeth, and Mary, got the proceeds arising from the sale of the Tradd Street house, and one slave apiece. A $150,000 trust fund was also established for them.[35]

One by one, the Hanscomes allied themselves with Charleston's aristocracy of color. In 1833 Louisa married cotton gin maker William P. Dacosta. Six years later Elizabeth married John George Garden, the son of a mulatto planter from St. Paul's Parish. In 1841 Thomas married Mary Sophia Inglis, the daughter of slave-owning barber Thomas Inglis. In 1843 Mary wed John Lee, Jr., the son of tailor John Lee and Eliza Lee, a pastry cook and hotelier who enjoyed the patronage of well-to-do whites. James's first wife, Serena Elizabeth Walker, came from a family much like his own. Her father, John Walker, was a rich white Charlestonian of Scottish descent, and her mother, Ann Jones, had been Walker's slave.[36]

Who, then, was the Mary Hanscome who came to Pennsylvania with Thomas Hanscome and his family in 1845? She was not his sister. In 1845 that Mary Hanscome was the wife of John Lee, Jr., and the mother of a year-old son.[37] The woman Robert Forten married was the widow of Thomas's brother, Joseph.

Joseph was the eldest child of Thomas Hanscome and Nancy Randall. In 1833 he turned twenty-one and came into his share of his father's estate. He used his inheritance to buy the 600-acre Woodland Plantation, in St. James and Goose Creek Parish. No record of his marriage has been found, but it probably took place soon after the purchase of Woodland. His wife's name was Mary. Like Joseph, she was a free person of color and a native of South Carolina. The couple had one child, a daughter, who died in infancy. Then Joseph fell ill. His will, written on his deathbed, directed his executors to sell everything he owned. Nancy Randall was to receive $2000, and the residue was to be invested for his widow. The interest was hers for her lifetime, but on her death the principal would go to Joseph's brother, Thomas. Joseph died on August 4, 1838, and early the following year Woodland was auctioned off, together with fifteen slaves. After the payment of Joseph's debts and the bequest to his mother, there was still a respectable sum left to be invested for Mary.[38] She chose not to live alone but to make her home with her in-laws.

To Joseph Hanscome, his mother, his siblings, and the families into which they married, slaves were as acceptable a form of wealth as any other. Nancy Randall made legal arrangements regarding her slaves to ensure herself a comfortable old age. Thomas bought slaves from his in-laws. James fought another man in court over the ownership of slave property and traded in slaves with his sister, Louisa Dacosta. As Thomas prepared to move North, he entrusted his slaves to his brother-in-law, John G. Garden. He would live in Pennsylvania, where slavery was illegal, but he would continue to enjoy the profits his slaves produced. As for Mary, she owned no slaves when she married Robert Forten, but she was a woman of means, thanks to her first husband's slave investments.[39]

Thomas Hanscome, his wife, their two young daughters, and his brother's widow stayed in Philadelphia while they determined their next move. It was probably then that the Purvises met them and introduced them to Harriet's brother. In August 1845 Thomas bought a farm in Warminster, Bucks County, whose mortgage Robert Forten witnessed. Soon the tie between Forten and the Hanscomes grew closer than a business relationship. On November 6, at Neshaminy Presbyterian Church in Bucks County, Robert Forten married Mary Hanscome.[40]

Robert had found a stepmother for Charlotte, and a wife and companion to fill the void left by Mary Virginia's death. The fact that his bride had money was a welcome bonus. Mary Hanscome, in her late twenties and financially independent, surely welcomed the chance to have her own establishment again after more than six years of living with Thomas and his wife. Inevitably, she had been obliged to cede to the much younger Mary Sophia the role of mistress of the household. However fond the women were of one another, Mary could hardly have relished a life that was, in essence, that of a maiden aunt. Robert Forten, a widower with one child and a respected family name, was a good match. But in her eagerness to remarry she could not overlook his financial plight. Two days before the wedding the couple executed a settlement under the terms of which Mary's property rights were vested in her future mother-in-law in trust for any children she (Mary) might bear. This was a wise precaution. Without a settlement stipulating that Robert had no control over his wife's property, his creditors could seize virtually everything she brought to the marriage.[41]

Mary put her money to good use, buying a modest estate in Warminster, close to the Hanscomes. In 1850 the Fortens were working a forty-acre farm, with land, livestock, crops, and machinery worth $4,000. Their household comprised themselves, their two sons, Wendell Phillips and Edmund Quincy, Robert's daughter, his brother, Thomas, and a white maidservant.[42]

Even in his rural retreat—a retreat paid for, whether he realized it or not, with the proceeds of slave labor—Robert could not turn his back on the antislavery cause. He deplored the proslavery stance of the American churches, regretting that so many abolitionists remained in fellowship with them. True reformers must shun "marble hearted atheism" and espouse "that code of moral laws ushered into the world at the birth of Christ . . . which condemns all sin and demands immediate repentance." The missionary efforts of the established churches drew forth bitter condemnation. They overlooked "the heathen of our own country—who pass by the poor slave . . . on their way to emancipate the heathen of foreign lands."[43]

He continued to take the orthodox Garrisonian line. In 1849, for instance, he was shocked when Frederick Douglass claimed the Constitution was not a proslavery document. Forten pointed to the provision that individuals "bound to service or labor" in one state could not gain their freedom through flight to another state. The Supreme Court had ruled that the Constitution defended slavery, but even "had the . . . Court decided . . . it was more anti-slavery than the Declaration of Sentiment[s] of the Anti-Slavery Society . . . [he would] not . . . swear to support it, so long as [that] clause . . . remains in it."44

After the Compromise of 1850, Forten and Douglass sank their ideological differences and joined other "colored men, who have long made the best interests of their race . . . their study" for a convention in New York. Delegates agreed "the one great evil . . . suffered by the free colored people [is] . . . the want of money."

> Any man who has learned a useful trade . . . and has the talent for conducting it on his own account, ought so to conduct it, because all the . . . profits would . . . be his, and he would . . . have a fair opportunity of assisting his brethren by employing them . . . [I]f he has not the means of setting up . . . on his own account, then . . . he ought to be furnished with the means.

The delegates recommended "a fund . . . be established . . . for the purpose of loaning . . . money to colored men of integrity." Alas, the American League of Colored Laborers was stifled at birth by the very evil it was intended to combat—lack of funds.45

Robert knew all about the problems arising from lack of funds. Perhaps he and Mary were inefficient farmers, or perhaps the needs of their family outstripped the income generated by the farm. Whatever the case, by the mid-1850s they were beset by financial difficulties. They eventually determined to try their luck elsewhere. Mary sold the farm in the spring of 1854 at a decent profit, so there was capital for a new start.46 But where? Robert contemplated New England. He and his sister, Harriet, traveled to Salem, Massachusetts, to visit Robert's daughter, who was in school there. They also went to Providence, New Bedford, and Boston. During their visit Boston was thrown into turmoil by the arrest of fugitive slave Anthony Burns. Robert took a keen interest in Burns's fate and did all he could to assist local abolitionists to secure the man's release. He left still undecided about where to make his new home. However, as his daughter feared, the outcome of the Burns trial—Burns was returned to slavery—determined him against New England.47 Eventually Robert and Mary resolved to leave the United States for Canada.

The Hanscomes had preceded them. In 1853 Thomas and Mary Sophia had sold up and moved to Toronto.48 Several years earlier, Thomas's sister, Elizabeth Garden, had settled in Pennsylvania with her husband and their children. The Gardens opted to emigrate to Canada with the Hanscomes. Eventually, Mary Sophia's brother, Thomas Inglis, joined the exodus.49

The Hanscomes and the Gardens prospered in Canada, but more was at stake for them than material success. Many Americans of African descent fled to Her Majesty's dominions to evade the slave catchers. What the light-skinned Hanscomes, Gardens, and young Inglis evaded as they crossed the 49th parallel was the burden of race. They "passed." In 1871 John Garden told the census-taker he and his family were Americans of Scottish descent. A decade earlier Thomas Hanscome had reported there were no persons of color in his household.[50]

The Hanscomes and the Gardens settled close to each other in Toronto's St. James Ward. Hanscome became a wood and coal merchant, while Garden worked as a machinist. Hanscome was still in business when he died in the fall of 1894. Mary Sophia outlived him, dying in 1899. Their eldest daughter, Alice, was still living in Toronto in 1926. As for the Gardens, Elizabeth died in 1877 and John in 1880, but several of their children were listed in the city directories through the 1890s.[51]

Robert and Mary Forten may initially have stayed with the Hanscomes in Toronto, but they eventually settled in London, Ontario. Had the Hanscomes and the Gardens found an ardent abolitionist and an unrepentant "man of color" in their midst an embarrassment? Was the decision to make for London the result of a bitter disagreement, or did opportunities there just seem brighter? London, with its community of escaped slaves and its active antislavery society, certainly offered Robert ample scope for his abolitionist endeavors. London's Anglican Church even sponsored a missionary to minister to the fugitives.[52] Sadly, in London Robert could work to further the cause he believed in so passionately, but he could not find profitable employment. The 1856 directory for the city lists him as being without an occupation. In the spring of 1857 he wrote his daughter that he was thinking of moving to Britain. Another letter a few months later in answer to her appeal for funds revealed the extent of his difficulties. Charlotte observed: "It is as I thought. He is *utterly unable* to assist me."[53]

In 1858 or early 1859 the Fortens took passage for England. They made their new home in London's Kentish Town at 10 Alma Street. Kentish Town was not a slum in the 1850s, but neither was it the capital's most fashionable neighborhood. Although the Fortens did not become rich in England, they did better financially than they had in Canada. It took a while for Robert to find work, but he was eventually hired as a "commercial agent" for Houghton Lucas and Co., "an extensive stationery house" in the City.[54] He lost no time involving himself in antislavery activities. In 1859 he joined the London Emancipation Committee, which also numbered among its members Sarah Parker Remond, the sister of young Charlotte Forten's host in Salem, Charles Lenox Remond.[55] But just when Robert could feel he was again in a position to support his family and be of service in the abolitionist struggle, tragedy struck. On June 13, 1860, his thirteen-year-old son, Wendell Phillips Forten, died after a three-week battle with typhus.[56] It was an appalling loss. Robert and Mary had journeyed thousands of miles to make a new life for themselves and their children. Now one of their sons was dead.

The Fortens and their surviving son stayed in London through the early 1860s.[57] Robert followed events in the United States as best he could from

3000 miles away. As the Civil War entered its third year, he decided he could watch from the sidelines no longer. His old friend, Daniel Alexander Payne, recounted how Robert returned from England upon learning that President Lincoln had authorized the recruiting of black troops. He "made proper arrangements for his family" in England, but informed none of his relatives in America of his decision. Payne allowed himself literary license in describing the encounter between Forten and "his venerable mother" at "the old homestead."

> She . . . asked: "Robert, what brought you here?" His reply was substantially these words: "When now on the eve of the triumph of freedom how could I, or any other colored man in whose bosom a love of country, race, and liberty dwells, remain in a foreign land? I am come to help break the bonds of the slave and aid in the triumph of liberty."[58]

Robert turned to poetry, as he had before, to express his emotions. The *Liberator* published his "song," "The Negro of America," composed in his mother's home, or perhaps even on the ship bringing him back from England.

> Come, rally round the stars and stripes,
>   Now emblems of our hope;
> And stand ye forth as men of fate,
>   'Gainst whom no foe can cope.
> Though traitor rule, with crimson hand,
>   Our Union's pride hath slain,
> The negro's arm shall be the charm
>   That gives it life again.[59]

Friends advised him against enlisting. His race would preclude a commission, and he would be in the ranks with men thirty years his junior. He would not listen. On March 2, 1864, he was mustered into Company A of the 43rd Regiment, United States Colored Troops, to serve for three years or the duration.[60] He was just a few months short of his fifty-first birthday.

He enlisted as a private but was rapidly promoted to sergeant major and sent to report to Colonel Bowman, who was recruiting black soldiers in Maryland. Forten's powers of persuasion won many to the Union standard. His speeches, each "full of logic and . . . eloquence . . . in a great measure contributed to the . . . success which . . . attended Bowman's efforts." Bowman was impressed, speaking of Forten not just as a good soldier but as "a gentleman."[61] However, "the great exertions he . . . made and the exposure to which he was highly unused, began to tell upon his health." Ordered back to Philadelphia's Camp William Penn, he caught a cold while drilling his men in the rain. He struggled on regardless, until he became so sick he was obliged to ask for a few days' leave. He made his way back to Lombard Street, and a doctor was sent for immediately. It was too late. On April 25 he succumbed to typhoid.[62]

Robert's funeral two days later was widely reported. It was, after all, "Novel and interesting" to have "Military . . . honors . . . paid, for the first time in this city, to the remains of a colored man." Philadelphia's abolitionists turned out in force. Lucretia Mott and J. Miller McKim eulogized Robert at the family home. Then, with an escort of sixteen soldiers, his coffin was taken on the short journey to St. Thomas's. He was laid to rest "in the family vault in view of curious and wondering thousands," and three volleys were fired over his grave.[63]

Tributes flooded in. On May 30 "a resolution was agreed to by the Supervisory Committee for the Recruitment of Colored . . . Troops . . . expressive of their high appreciation of his character and of the services he . . . rendered to his country." And in the House of Representatives Congressman William D. Kelley paid homage to his companion from childhood days.[64] All this, however, did not spare his widow a two-year battle to get the soldier's pension due her.

Her husband's death left Mary virtually penniless. The legacy from her first husband had long since gone. The war wiped out whatever remained of her South Carolina investments. On May 3, 1865, she presented herself at the United States Consulate in London and filed her claim for a pension.[65] Everything should have been straightforward, but it was not. Her application was initially rejected because she had given Robert's regiment as the Pennsylvania 43rd. William Forten cleared that up, establishing that his brother had actually served with the 43rd Regiment, United States Colored Troops. There were other complications. The Commissioner of Pensions needed proof that Robert had been "free from any physical disability when enlisted." His army record said nothing about the cause of his death. He had, after all, died at home, and not in a military hospital under the care of an army doctor. His family in Philadelphia got an affidavit from the physician who attended him, stating that he had died of typhoid contracted in camp.[66]

Mary haunted the London Consulate, completing yet more forms, but by the fall of 1866 she still had not been awarded a pension. Back in Philadelphia, Margaretta Forten decided to take a hand and wrote the Commissioner of Pensions. Her brother's widow wanted to return to the United States, but without a pension she lacked the means to do so. Robert had moved to England "chiefly on account of his children, that they might not feel the depressing influences of prejudice." But when the call came for men of color to serve in the Union forces it "at once aroused all the feelings of his patriotism . . . [H]e saw as he fondly thought . . . the dawning of a brighter day on the destinies of his race." She continued: "[W]e have tried hard to furnish all the required testimony, months and almost years have elapsed & as soon as one difficulty is . . . answered, another has been . . . started." The pension was "but a small pittance, from a great country to the widow of one of her humblest, though devoted defenders." Finally, on January 9, 1867, Mary was awarded $8 per month, with arrears from the day of Robert's death.[67]

That was not the end of her troubles. In 1872 she was still in Kentish Town, in lodgings on Healy Street, probably a reflection of her worsening financial plight. Confusion over yet more paperwork had resulted in a delay in her receiving the pension. After more frantic letter-writing she finally got the money due her and returned to the United States to live with Robert's family.[68] She may have died soon after her return. There are no entries in the pension file later than the spring of 1876, and she does not appear as a member of the Forten household in the 1880 census. The records do not indicate whether Edmund came back to the United States with his mother or whether he made his home in England. A deed disposing of family property indicates only that he died unmarried and without issue sometime between 1875 and 1886.[69]

As for Mary's stepdaughter, Charlotte, her story is too well known to need retelling here in much detail. In 1853, when she was sixteen, Robert sent her to Salem, Massachusetts, to be educated in that city's integrated schools.[70] She boarded with the Remonds, members of Salem's African-American elite. Antislavery orator Charles Lenox Remond had married an old friend from Philadelphia, Amy Cassey, widow of Robert Purvis's sometime business partner Joseph Cassey. It was while Charlotte was living with the Remonds that she began keeping a journal. During her years in New England she met and was befriended by many prominent abolitionists, among them William Wells Brown, Maria Weston Chapman, Lydia Maria Child, William Lloyd Garrison, William Cooper Nell, Wendell Phillips, Sarah Parker Remond, and John Greenleaf Whittier.

Charlotte entered into correspondence with some of the great personalities of her day. From English novelist Harriet Martineau she received a kind letter in response to a letter of her own. The poem she wrote to the "Noble and Honored Sumner" some months after his near-fatal beating "as a very slight expression of the deep gratitude and admiration with which you are regarded by a youthful member of that oppressed class which the white American finds guilty of a skin not colored like his own" marked the start of a lengthy friendship.[71]

Wendell Phillips, who knew of her father's move to Canada and deplored it as the loss of a much-needed antislavery advocate, praised her for her "decision to stay and share the fight," adding: "You owe this to the noble name you bear."[72] Although she would not confess it until many years later, at this point in her life Charlotte would willingly have emulated her father. "[W]hen the suffering seemed too keen to bear, I thought of this country only as a hateful prison-house, from which I would gladly have [fled] had not duty bound me here."[73] But there was always "duty." Charlotte was intensely aware of just how much she owed to her "noble name." She venerated her grandfather, of whom she had only vague memories. She read his letters and delighted in talking with those who had known him. It troubled her deeply that there was so much dissension among his children. Perhaps with her mind on her Uncle James's defection, she wrote: "Would that some of his [James Sr.'s] family resembled [him], I grieve to say they *do not*; far, far from it."[74]

When Charlotte completed her schooling at Higginson Grammar School in 1855, she enrolled in the Salem Normal School. After several unsuccessful attempts to find a post as a governess, she was hired by Salem's Board of Education to teach at Epes Grammar School, making her the first African American in Salem's history to teach in a predominantly white school.[75] What cut short her career was not racial antagonism but poor health. Always delicate and prone to the "lung fever" that had killed her mother, she was forced to resign and return to Philadelphia in 1858. There she taught her Aunt Harriet's children and assisted her Aunt Margaretta in her school. She resumed her teaching post in Salem in 1859, only to resign again a few months later because of illness. By 1861 she was once more in Philadelphia teaching at Margaretta Forten's school.[76]

In 1862, as determined as ever to live up to her family's "noble name," she battled skeptical white officials to secure a place as a teacher to the freedmen in the newly liberated Sea Islands of South Carolina. She had to contend with the climate, her poor health, and the suspicions of many of the freedmen, who did not know quite what to make of her. She recorded her impressions of life on the Sea Islands in letters to her old friend, the poet John Greenleaf Whittier, and it was Whittier who persuaded her to send the letters to the *Atlantic Monthly*.[77]

Never physically strong, Charlotte contracted a severe case of smallpox early in 1864.[78] Just as she was recovering, she received the news of her father's death. Illness and grief completely incapacitated her, and her friends insisted she return home to recuperate. Once she had recovered sufficiently, she cast around for something to do, some way to be of service. Well educated and deeply committed to reform, but with limited means and impaired health, her opportunities were severely restricted. Whittier tried to get her a place in a Massachusetts sanitarium in the hope she might recover her health. She was, he insisted, "a young lady of exquisite refinement, quiet culture and lady like and engaging manners." However, the director of the sanitarium feared for his livelihood if he admitted a woman of color.[79]

At war's end Charlotte moved to Boston to become secretary of the Teachers' Committee of the New England branch of the Freedmen's Aid Society. For years she had written poetry and prose, some of which had been published. Now she tried her hand at translating. In 1869 Scribner's published her translation from the French of *Madame Thérèse; or, The Volunteers of '92*, a popular novel by Emile Erckman and Alexandre Chatrian. In 1870, back in Philadelphia living with her grandmother, aunt, and two bachelor uncles, she reported her occupation to the census-taker as "Authoress."[80] When her health permitted, she taught school with her aunt, but she was obviously eager to do more. She contemplated going to England to lecture on the plight of the freedmen, but when she approached influential Irish abolitionist Richard Webb, he advised her not to attempt the trip unless she could fund it herself. He and American reformer Edmund Quincy cautioned: "The abolition of slavery has put an end to the prejudice in favor of color in England and black people must make their way like white ones."[81] Whittier, Ralph Waldo Emerson, and Thomas Wentworth Higginson tried to get her a position at the Boston Public Library. As Whittier told Charles Sumner, whose help he enlisted, she was "a fine scholar, reads and speaks German and French." She applied but did not get the appointment.[82]

In 1871 Charlotte moved to Charleston, South Carolina, to teach at the Shaw Memorial School. Her cousin, Henry Purvis, Harriet and Robert's son, had married into a Charleston family, so Charlotte had a network of acquaintances to make her feel welcome in a strange city. As she confessed to Charles Sumner, she was often deeply disturbed by what she saw in the place she called "this chief city of rebeldom, where the idea of *equality* is as repugnant as in the most despotic government of the earth." She described seeing "in a shop window on the principal street here, two pictures—one of Stonewall Jackson & the other of Beauregard. Under the former were the words 'His People leaned on him, & he on God," and under the latter "*Sans peur et sans reproche.*" To an old, trusted friend like Sumner she could reveal her deepest feelings. "I think only those who have suffered deeply from the cruel cruel prejudice in this country can know how it *embitters* as well as depresses, how it gradually weakens & undermines ones faith in human nature."[83]

A year later she took a teaching appointment in Washington, D.C., and moved in with another cousin, Charles Purvis, and his wife. In 1873 she became a clerk at the Treasury Department.[84] Five years later, on December 9, 1878, at age forty-one, she married Francis J. Grimké, a Presbyterian minister twelve years her junior, and the nephew of reformers Sarah and Angelina Grimké.[85]

While the Grimké sisters had left South Carolina and thrown themselves into the antislavery struggle, their slave-owning brothers had stayed behind. After the death of his wife, Henry Grimké had taken as his concubine his slave, Nancy Weston. Nancy was always given to understand she and the three sons Grimké had fathered would be treated as free persons and provided for, but when Henry died, she and her children sank into poverty. Eventually Grimké's white son tried to put Francis and his elder brother, Archibald, to work in his household. Both proved recalcitrant. After a beating, Francis fled. Tracked down and sold, he remained a slave until 1865.

At war's end Francis and Archibald enrolled in a school in Charleston run by New England abolitionists. Their teachers soon recognized their intellectual potential and arranged for them to go North to further their education. A lucky chance brought them into contact with their aunts, who had been unaware of their existence. They acknowledged the young men and scrimped and saved to help pay for their schooling. The brothers studied at Lincoln University, and then Francis entered the law school at Howard. After a year he determined on the ministry instead and transferred to Princeton Theological Seminary.[86] Charles Purvis was teaching at Howard when Grimké was a student there and may have introduced the young man to his cousin, but there had, in fact, been an earlier meeting. On his arrival in Boston back in 1865, en route to a school in nearby Stoneham to prepare for college, a teenaged Francis had met Charlotte, then in her late twenties, at the office of the Freedmen's Aid Society.[87]

Her old friend Whittier thought Charlotte's match eminently suitable. Grimké was "well spoken of" and he would find in Charlotte "a cultivated, graceful woman who is at least his intellectual equal."[88] Whittier proved right in his prediction that the two would be happy together. Their one abiding sorrow was the death of their only child, Theodora, in 1880. Most of their married life was spent in Washington, where Francis was the pastor of the Fifteenth Street Presbyterian Church. Always in frail health and bedridden for the last year of her life, Charlotte Forten Grimké died on July 22, 1914.[89]

JAMES FORTEN'S ELDEST child, Margaretta, proved one of the enduring sources of strength in the family. Her assistance in the matter of a pension for her sister-in-law was typical of her character. She found out whom to contact, marshaled her facts, and set forth the matter succinctly and coherently. Several years later she came to the rescue of her sister Sarah, devising a solution to her financial problems and laying it before the appropriate authorities. James Forten had made an excellent choice when he appointed Margaretta one of his executors.

Margaretta put her education to good use. In 1850 she opened a private school where she taught "branches similar to those taught in Grammar Schools." Most of her students were day pupils, but some boarded in the Forten family home. There were parents eager to entrust their daughters to her, for her family name was a respectable one and her own reputation unassailable. When wealthy Charlestonian William Ellison, Jr., sent his daughters, Elizabeth and Henrietta, to Margaretta on the eve of the Civil War, he was sending them to someone he felt he knew. The mulatto Ellisons were friends of the Lees and the Inglises. Mary Lee and Thomas Hanscome, Mary Inglis's husband, were the siblings of Joseph Hanscome, who was Mary Forten's first husband, and so on. The network linking wealthy free people of color in one city to those in another had its uses.[90]

She might take school fees from a slave owner such as Ellison, but Margaretta Forten would have no truck with slavery. (Perhaps she envisaged converting Ellison's daughters to abolitionism.) For more than four decades she and her sister Harriet were stalwarts of the Philadelphia Female Anti-Slavery Society, attending meetings, circulating petitions, collecting money to aid fugitives, and helping organize the society's annual fair.[91] As Margaretta had assisted at the birth of the organization in 1833, so she was present at its dissolution. On March 24, 1870, she moved the adoption of the resolution that adjourned it once and for all. With the passage of the Fifteenth Amendment she considered that "The object for which this Association was organized is accomplished."[92]

As housekeeper to her mother and brothers, as the beloved aunt to a score of nieces and nephews, as a promoter of "good works" within the African-American community, as a respected teacher, as a shrewd woman of business, Margaretta Forten made her presence felt in innumerable ways.[93] She was mourned by many when she died of pneumonia on January 14, 1875, at age sixty-eight in the home where she had been born. She was buried at Lebanon Cemetery. Some years later her brother, William, had her remains moved to the cemetery of the Church of St. James the Less.[94]

THE YEAR JAMES Forten died was an especially stressful one for Harriet and her husband. They lost the man who had, in a sense, been father to them both. Robert Purvis, fatherless since the age of sixteen, had revered Forten and been treated by the older man as a much-loved son. Harriet and Robert were also close to Mary Isabella. In fact, it was Robert who wrote the fond tribute that appeared in the *National Anti-Slavery Standard*. Soon after Mary's death there were the first indications that the firm of J and R. B. Forten was teetering on the edge of insolvency. Robert Purvis, as James Forten's executor, tried to bail out the firm, and then faced the unenviable prospect of having to sue his brothers-in-law. On top of everything else came a harrowing episode of racial violence that struck at the heart of Robert and Harriet's faith in the ultimate triumph of reform.[95]

The Purvises, like James Forten, were dedicated to the cause of temperance. Alcohol, they insisted, brought a whole train of evils—disease, poverty, crime, and violence. Remove the demon alcohol, and society would be immeasurably better. Persuade black men and women not to drink, and improve not only the quality of their lives but demonstrate their moral worth, and, indeed, their moral superiority, over their white detractors. In the spring and summer of 1842 Robert Purvis and his friends were busily organizing a great August 1 temperance march, a joint celebration of the anniversary of emancipation in the British Empire and freedom from the "bondage" of strong drink. The reason why the peaceful parade degenerated into a bloody race riot depended on who was telling the story. The black marchers passed too close to an Irish neighborhood, and rocks began to fly. Job competition and racial antipathy may have prompted the initial assault, but there were rumors that liquor sellers were behind the trouble. The temperance crusade was proving too effective. It was eating into their profits and had to be stopped.[96]

In the two days of rioting that followed the August 1 outbreak, black churches were attacked, black homes burned, and black people set upon in the street. The riot was especially traumatic for Robert and Harriet Purvis. Learning that their house had been marked for attack, the fundamentally peaceful Robert rushed Harriet and the children out of the city and sat for hours on the staircase, a rifle across his knees, protecting his family's home. A mob besieged the house, waiting for him to emerge. A week later, when the rioting had finally subsided, white abolitionist Henry C. Wright wrote to him. He was about to leave for England and wanted statements from Purvis, James Forten, Jr., and other "educated and enlightened" African Americans to show to British reformers. Purvis's reply indicates how deeply the whole episode had shaken him. "I am sick—miserably sick—Every thing around me is as dark as the grave . . . nothing redeeming, nothing hopeful, despair black as the face of Death hangs over us—And the bloody Will, is in the heart of the community to destroy us."[97] He and Harriet began preparing to move out of the city.

In 1843 they purchased a "Mansion" and 104 acres of land in Byberry township, some twelve miles outside Philadelphia.[98] This remained the family home for over thirty years. Robert enjoyed the role of gentleman farmer. He derived the major part of his income from his investments in real estate and stocks. However, he and Harriet worked to make their farm thrive. Their main emphasis was on cereal production and dairying, but they also sold meat and fresh fruit to the Philadelphia market. Harriet was as interested in farming as Robert and was, according to her niece, a very good judge of horses.[99] The Purvises were especially interested in animal husbandry and selective breeding, and they had the money with which to experiment. They entered their livestock in area shows and won many prizes, but Robert's participation was not always welcomed by his neighbors. In 1846 there was a move to expel him from the Bensalem Horse Company, a local association of livestock breeders, on the basis of race. A few years later, after winning a string of prizes for his poultry at the Agricultural Fair, he was told that black people could no longer show their birds.[100]

In their Byberry home Harriet and Robert entertained abolitionists and reformers from all over the country and abroad. Harriet was a gracious hostess. A cultured woman, she enjoyed music and art. Well read and refined, she took pleasure in discussing with her fellow members of the Gilbert Lyceum the poetry of Byron and the novels of the Brontës, and she could argue for argument's sake over the authorship of Shakespeare's plays.[101] One visitor, Sallie Holley, described her as "very lady-like in manners and conversation [with] something of the ease and blandness of a southern lady."[102]

Harriet entertained Holley, the Garrisons, the Motts, Elizabeth Cady Stanton, Susan B. Anthony, and many other reformers. She also fed and housed guests whose presence she was careful to keep secret. As they had done in their Philadelphia home, she and Robert had a special room constructed at Byberry to accommodate runaway slaves waiting to move on to the next safe house. Robert kept a meticulous record of those they aided, "until the trepidation of his family after the passage of the Fugitive Slave Bill . . . forced him to destroy it."[103]

The Purvises were radical abolitionists who insisted they could not compromise on principles, even if it cost them old friends. In 1848 they broke with the church Harriet had attended all of her life and Robert the better part of his. They sold their pew at St. Thomas's, donated the proceeds to the abolitionist cause, and withdrew from the church, which they considered "pro-slavery in its position."[104] A few years later there was a rancorous and very public quarrel with Frederick Douglass, based perhaps as much on personality differences as on ideology. The fiery ex-slave assailed Purvis's father for having amassed "*blood-stained riches*" from the labor of slaves. Purvis was outraged, insisting that his father had "made his money . . . by honest mercantile pursuits" and had raised his sons to work for abolition and racial justice.[105]

The Purvises were essentially partners in the work of antislavery. If the concerns of her household and her family kept Harriet closer to home than Robert, that did not mean she saw her role as a limited one. She was a dedicated and hard-working member of the Philadelphia Female Anti-Slavery Society. When Robert was president of the eastern branch of the Pennsylvania Anti-Slavery Society from 1845 to 1850, she served as his secretary.[106] Her efforts complemented his. They were a team.

There were times, though, when the struggle seemed overwhelming. In the early 1850s Harriet and Robert considered emigrating. Sarah Pugh, a white friend from the Philadelphia Female Anti-Slavery Society, reported that Harriet had told her: "[I]f you had staid longer in Eng[land] . . . you might perhaps have seen us over there—for ourselves we might endure to the end—as we have suffered so long—but for our children it is a question whether we ought not to seek another home."[107] There was plenty to make them think long and hard about their future and the future of their children in the United States. Harriet and Robert had learned long ago that wealth could not shield an individual from racism. In some respects it made it more galling and more oppressive. In 1847 and again in 1853 they did battle with the local school board. The Purvises paid the second highest school tax in Byberry, only to find their children barred from the local schools and forced to attend a "miserable shanty" of a school some distance away. Robert refused to pay the school tax.[108] Nor were the Purvises and their children welcome to seek enlightenment elsewhere. At the same time that Harriet and Robert were fighting the authorities in Byberry in 1853, their son, Robert Jr., Sarah Parker Remond, and "Miss Wood," probably Annie Wood, the sister of Mary Virginia Wood Forten, were the victims of an "outrage" at the Franklin Institute. Young Purvis's "own color [was] too light for suspicion," but the eagle-eyed door-keeper spotted Sarah Remond and insisted they leave immediately. Robert came home very "excited," and told his father what had happened. Robert Sr. demanded to know "why didn't you die, rather than submit to this insult?" The Purvises sued unsuccessfully in the aldermen's court over the expulsion.[109]

Harriet and Robert Purvis were drawn increasingly to the radical wing of the abolitionist movement. In the summer of 1856 they identified themselves as "Disunion Abolitionists." Robert even characterized the assault on his friend Charles Sumner as "timely" because it would put "backbone" into the North.[110] In 1857, in the aftermath of the Dred Scott decision, which he vigorously protested, Purvis and other Pennsylvanians, black and white, called upon "their fellow citizens of the free States" to meet in a convention "to consider the . . . expediency of a Separation between the Free and Slave States."[111] In a speech in 1860 he insisted he took pleasure in his disfranchisement, since it freed him from the guilt he must otherwise share in. He confessed himself disgusted with both major parties for, in effect, countenancing slavery.[112]

When the war finally came, the Purvises threw their energies behind the Union effort. Harriet continued working with the Philadelphia Female Anti-Slavery Society to organize fairs and raise funds to assist the freedmen and women.[113] Robert worked at recruiting black troops. In September 1863, as "Aid-de-camp to Major Stearns in the recruiting service," he presented a flag to the sixth regiment of United States Colored Infantry at Camp William Penn on behalf of the African-American citizens of Philadelphia.[114] However, although he applauded the decision to allow black men to enlist, he worried that the government would not "secure the right kind of men" as officers. He wanted commissions for black men.[115]

After the war a degree of disillusionment soon set in. On September 13, 1866, Harriet told her friends in the Female Anti-Slavery Society about a talk she had attended the night before.

> The Speaker, Judge Pitkin, of Louisiana, said that the nation had more to fear from the conservatism of the North than anything else; even the Radicals were not ready to go as far as the Union men of the South, who knew from actual experience that negro suffrage and negro equality could alone save the Union. He was loudly applauded. Mrs. Purvis said she felt . . . how useless was all this applause when she could not . . . take a seat in the [street]cars. . . . She thought there was very little desire on the part of Philadelphians that the colored people should ride in the cars: even the Committee who had the matter in charge had done nothing for fear of injuring the Republican party.

Getting the Philadelphia streetcars desegregated became one of her goals. True, she had a carriage at her disposal, but that was hardly the point. Her tired feet were no more the issue than were Rosa Parks's almost a century later. What mattered was principle. After all, what had been won in four years of bloody fighting if these very tangible vestiges of inequality were allowed to remain?[116]

Harriet and Robert Purvis had many contacts with Radical Republicans in and out of Congress. A particular friend, and someone whose advice they valued, was Wendell Phillips. In the fall of 1867 Robert was sounded out by one George B. Halsted about taking General O. O. Howard's place as head of the Freedmen's Bureau. Halsted intimated that Howard was to be removed and insisted it was "a matter of duty, for a 'colored' man to take his place."[117] Convinced Andrew Johnson was trying to destroy the Freedmen's Bureau and use prominent African Americans like Purvis "to confuse & divide the loyal sentiment," Phillips advised against acceptance. Purvis investigated and discovered Halsted was actually Johnson's private secretary and not the selfless liberal he had pretended to be.[118] Halsted had approached other black leaders, including Frederick Douglass, and they had turned him down.

In all their campaigning for "equal rights" Harriet and Robert had never envisaged "rights" as rights for men alone. They had long championed the women's suffrage movement. Their commitment to a broad agenda of reform intensified with the securing of Emancipation. Robert became a vice-president of the American Equal Rights League. He spoke at the New York City convention in May 1867, sharing the platform with, among others, Elizabeth Cady Stanton, Frederick Douglass, Charles Lenox Remond, Sojourner Truth, and Lucretia Mott.[119] When the movement split, Purvis remained with the suffragists, declaring "he would rather his son should never be enfranchised, unless his daughter could be also, that, as she bore the double curse of sex and color, on every principle of justice she should first be protected."[120] In fact, at the Washington, D.C., convention of the National Woman's Suffrage Convention in January 1869, Purvis rebuked his son, Charles, "for his narrow position" in arguing that black men must get the vote at once, and that women, black and white, could wait.[121]

The Fifteenth Amendment was eventually ratified, without the enfranchising of women. The Purvises rejoiced about what had been achieved and hoped for more to come. On April 26, 1870, Robert Purvis stood on the same platform as Frederick Douglass (with whom he had eventually made his peace) and promising young orator Octavius V. Catto, to lead the celebration of the passage of the amendment.[122] Eighteen months later Catto was dead, gunned down in the street, on election day, October 10, 1871. The occasion brought appalling violence, as many white Philadelphians showed what they thought of the idea of black men voting. As for the police, when they deigned to interfere at all it was on the side of the rioters.[123]

As Reconstruction drew to a close, Robert Purvis was one African-American leader who rethought his party loyalty. Initially a loyal Republican, he became disenchanted when it seemed that party leaders were taking the black vote for granted and offering precious little in return. In the lead-up to the 1871 election in Philadelphia he had denounced as cynical and self-serving a faction in the local Democratic Party that was intent on "cajoling and deceiving the colored man into their net." They had hit upon the idea of naming a new school for black children at Sixth and Lombard the James Forten School. "If . . . the spirit of James Fortin could have arisen . . . he would have denounced both Messrs. Fox [the mayor] and Cassidy as enemies of his race . . . and . . . scorned the words that fell from their polluted lips."[124]

Three years later Purvis was no longer such a good "party" man. In the 1874 mayoral race he lost a great deal of his influence by urging black voters to vote not along party lines but according to who would do most for them. The Republicans won, and this enhanced the prestige of Purvis's brother-in-law, William Forten, who told black voters that the Republicans were their best

friends.[125] Purvis's flirtation with the Democrats—or at least his recommendation that African-American voters look closely at a candidate's credentials and
not his party affiliation—brought vicious attacks. Black Philadelphian and Republican Party loyalist M. A. S. Carr, for example, went so far as to charge that
the light-skinned Purvis was turning his back on his race. "Purvis claims . . . to
be other than colored though I knew his mother[,] a tight headed negro lady
and a dear good woman."[126] It is hardly likely Harriet Judah Miller would have
recognized herself from Carr's description!

In the mid-1870s the hurly-burly of politics took a back seat to concerns
very close to home. Robert was very worried about his wife's health—and with
good cause. Harriet had nursed two sons with tuberculosis and buried both of
them. Now she, too, had consumption. She died, aged sixty-five, on June 11,
1875. She was buried at the Friends' Fair Hill Burial Ground, on Germantown
and Cambria Streets in Philadelphia.[127] Two years later the Purvises' youngest
child, Georgianna, succumbed to the same disease.[128]

A grief-stricken and desperately lonely Robert remarried in a Quaker ceremony in Bristol, Bucks County, on March 5, 1878. His second wife, Tacie
Townsend, was a white abolitionist seventeen years his junior. Her father had
been a neighbor of the Purvises in Byberry, and the two families had known
each other for years. Tacie had been a great favorite with the Purvis children
and a close friend of Charlotte Forten's.[129] The Purvis and Forten families
responded well to the marriage. Robert and Harriet's son, Charles, had married a white woman, and Tacie was a family friend of impeccable reformist
credentials. However, there may have been opposition from Charles's brother,
Henry. Certainly there was an estrangement between father and son.

Robert Purvis outlived most of his colleagues from the abolitionist era. In
1880, writing to John Greenleaf Whittier, he observed that they and one other
individual were the only survivors of the illustrious group that had met in 1833
to establish the American Anti-Slavery Society.[130] However, advancing age did
not silence the old reformer, nor did concerns about losing popularity. He was
as ready as ever to speak out. In the early 1880s he joined the patrician Committee of One Hundred, a predominantly white organization, whose members
wanted clean government and were prepared to cross party lines to get it. Their
campaign ended in a dismal failure and "business as usual" prevailed at both the
city and state level.[131] At the Pennsylvania Abolition Society's celebration of
the twenty-fifth Anniversary of Freedom in 1889, Robert Purvis departed radically from the script, denouncing the Republican head of Philadelphia's Department of Public Works for his treatment of black job applicants.[132] But Purvis
was never an unquestioning adherent of the Democrats. In 1884 he endorsed
the Greenback–Labor Party, believing neither of the major parties really cared
about racial equality.[133]

His eightieth birthday found Robert active, mentally alert, full of reminiscences about antislavery days and yet keenly interested in contemporary events,

and still very much a figure in reform circles. He was as ready as he had ever been to attack a new wave of colonizationists, to do battle with those who contended men and women of color were somehow "lesser" Americans, to pour scorn on politicians from any party who preached one thing and did another.[134] He was very much involved in the campaign for women's suffrage, even if he was no longer able to attend conventions. Tacie shared his commitment, as Harriet had done. Robert's role was recognized. At the convention of the National American Woman Suffrage Association of 1899, the year after his death, Elizabeth Cady Stanton led the delegates in a tribute to him. His widow continued to support the movement.[135]

Robert Purvis suffered a stroke at the end of March 1898, and died three weeks later at his Philadelphia home on Mount Vernon Street. He was eighty-seven years old. After a funeral service at the Spring Garden Unitarian Church attended by prominent politicians and reformers, he was buried beside Harriet at Fair Hill.[136] His will revealed that even after raising and educating eight children, generously supporting a host of reform causes, and maintaining himself as a "gentleman," he was still a very wealthy man.[137] After Robert's death Tacie moved to Kennett Township in Chester County to live with relatives. She died there on October 5, 1900.[138]

BY ALL ACCOUNTS, Harriet and Robert Purvis's marriage had been a happy one. Friends from childhood, they loved and respected one another. Their goals were the same. They were partners in the crusade to reform the nation. But they had their sorrows, and those sorrows ran very deep. They lost three of their eight children. Dedication to a cause, the ending of slavery, the achieving of racial equality, women's rights, may have been, in some sense, a way of coping with personal grief.

Soon after it opened, the Purvises sent two of their sons, Robert and Joseph, to study at Central College with James Forten, Jr.'s son. Well away from major cities, the environment should have been a healthy one. It was not. In the spring of 1851 a "faint Indian mist" rolled over the area, bringing with it an epidemic of "brain fever," or meningitis. Many of the students were infected. Most recovered, but not Joseph. He died on May 8 and was buried in the little graveyard on the hillside overlooking the school. He was fourteen years old.[139]

Joseph may have been a rather delicate youth. His cousin Charlotte, herself no stranger to illness, spoke of him as having "devoted himself to study beyond his strength." His death devastated his family and friends. One of his teachers, William G. Allen, described him as "Generous, high-minded, and . . . energetic." He had shown great promise as an antislavery advocate. A former student wrote:

> I wanted him to live . . . because he was so bright a star; and . . . because the light which this star emitted, was calculated to enlighten . . . the world. His

was a noble purpose. He was bound to rid this country of its wickedness, its oppression, its deep-seated and devilish prejudice. . . . His race needed him; his country needed him.[140]

Six years later, Harriet and Robert lost their eldest son, William, to consumption.[141] Then William's younger brother, Robert, began to display the same symptoms.

Robert Purvis, Jr., whom his cousin Charlotte loved for his "mischievous" ways and "careless gayety,"[142] was emerging as a committed and articulate champion of the same causes espoused by the rest of the family—antislavery, reform, and steadfast opposition to colonization. He had also inherited his father's sound business sense and carved out a career for himself as a commission merchant. By 1860, in partnership with a white friend, Joshua Peirce, he had amassed some $4,500. This had not been achieved without some difficulty. He had applied to a white businessman of impeccable abolitionist credentials for a position and been turned down, an experience also suffered by his friend, Joseph C. Cassey, the son of Robert Purvis's old business partner.[143]

Racism also blighted his emotional life. Flirtatious Ellen Wright, Lucretia Mott's niece and a fellow member of the Junior Anti-Slavery Society, enjoyed playing the field, but her fondness for Robert's company was sufficient to worry some members of her family. He would walk her home after meetings, and they shared nicknames—she was "Little Dorrit" and he was "child," a fact that amused her because he was seven years her senior. Ellen was quite frank in her journal: "Robert has African blood in his veins, which in this country is considered a disgrace (God help us!) his features [are] entirely European. . . . Robert hasn't asked me to marry him! Probably hasn't thought of anything so serious—I enjoy him very much, & should grieve to refuse to be his wife—but I never could be."[144]

Any thoughts Robert might have had of marriage were soon overwhelmed by anxiety about his health. In December 1858 Ellen paid a visit to the Purvises. Robert spoke to her of his fears of "Consumption — of which he has such a dread and expects to die." She observed the following February: "Robt. looks very thin, & has [a] sore throat & other blighting indications. . . . [T]his dread expectation of consumption sits like the nightmare upon him."[145] Robert's worst fears were realized. He died on March 19, 1862, at the age of twenty-eight. His mother was prostrate with grief. He had shown such promise and been so universally popular. He had indeed been "all his fond parents could desire." It seemed especially cruel that he should have survived the meningitis outbreak at Central College that had claimed Joseph, only to succumb to tuberculosis. He was buried in the Friends' Burial Ground at Byberry.[146]

The Purvises' elder daughter, Harriet, or Hattie, rivaled her brother Robert in her commitment to reform. Lively and witty, she was a great favorite with her cousin Charlotte. Anxious to give her a good education, her parents sent her to Eagleswood, an interracial school in New Jersey operated by the Grimké sisters and Angelina's husband, Theodore Dwight Weld. There one of her classmates was Ellen Wright. A close friendship developed between Hattie and her "Lovely Ellen." Presumably Hattie introduced Ellen to her brother. Hattie and Ellen exchanged news about mutual acquaintances and about their flirtations. Hattie was under no illusions about the racial injustices she and her family encountered every day. In 1856, at age seventeen, she wrote Ellen: "I have been teaching my little brothers and sisters . . . for there is no school here for them to go [to], except a *Public School*, and there they are made to sit by their selves, because their faces are not as white as the rest of the scholars. Oh! . . . how it makes my blood boil."

Like her cousin Charlotte, Hattie had a great sense of the need to accomplish things. "Oh! this is such a busy world . . . I am almost discouraged some times: how the days do steal on us, and steal from us."[147] She never married. For many years she was the resident daughter in her parents' Byberry home. Active with her mother and aunt in the Female Anti-Slavery Society in the 1850s and 1860s, in later years she played an equally enthusiastic role in the Pennsylvania Woman Suffrage Association and the National American Woman Suffrage Association. In 1899 she and her niece, Alice, her brother Charles's daughter, crossed the Atlantic with Susan B. Anthony to attend the International Council of Women in London.[148] Her father had provided generously for her in his will. She had a home of her own, an income from investments, and the means to pursue an agenda of social reform. She was especially close to her niece. When Alice moved to Boston to practice medicine, aunt and niece moved in together. They lived on Mount Auburn Terrace, on Winthrop Street in Watertown. Harriet died in Worcester, Massachusetts, on April 4, 1904, while on a visit to friends. She was sixty-four. A shrewd businesswoman who had invested wisely, Hattie's estate was valued at $26,000. Apart from bequests to a couple of friends, she left everything to the members of her extended family.[149]

ROBERT AND HARRIET'S fifth child, Charles Burleigh Purvis, never knew his grandfather. He was born on April 14, 1842, just a few weeks after James Forten's death.[150] He attended Oberlin College and then Wooster Medical College (later the Medical College of the Western Reserve). Graduating in March 1865, he was commissioned in the United States Army as acting assistant surgeon with the rank of first lieutenant. He almost lost his life during those last weeks of the war. He contracted typhoid while working with the freedmen in Washington, D.C. However, he made a speedy recovery and in 1867 was appointed assistant surgeon to the Freedmen's Hospital in Washington. Two years later he became Professor of Materia Medica and Medical Jurisprudence at Howard University. From 1873 until his retirement more than three decades later, he held the chair of obstetrics and diseases of women and children at Howard.[151]

Charles had his moments in the limelight and his low points. In 1869 he and another black physician were denied membership of the Medical Society of the District of Columbia. Scarcely a decade later he was the first doctor on the scene when President Garfield was shot. The aid he gave to the dying president brought him advancement. Garfield's successor, Chester Arthur, appointed Purvis surgeon-in-chief of the Freedmen's Hospital.[152] He was ousted from that position in 1893. He had been outspoken in his criticism of certain aspects of the hospital's administration, but, more to the point, he was a staunch Republican when the Democrats came to power.[153] There were black physicians who were Democrats, and they had to be rewarded. A campaign of slander and innuendo about his allegedly "upper class" ways and his rejection of his racial background was countered by warm praise from many in the community, who spoke of his dedication and hard work. However, it was not enough. Party affiliation was what mattered.

Charles knew all about political in-fighting and its consequences. He had been censured by some black Washingtonians in 1883 when he ran for school trustee. An editorial in the *People's Advocate* alleged Purvis "aspires to represent the colored school interest" but "sends his children to a white school."[154] Like his close friend and perennial ally, Frederick Douglass, he endured criticism for his marriage to a white woman. But if he knew the perils and pitfalls of power, he also knew what it meant to wield influence. He was no stranger to the halls of Congress—or at least to the committee rooms on Capitol Hill. Over the years, in his capacity as surgeon-in-chief of the Freedmen's Hospital, he gave testimony on everything from transportation of meat and livestock to civil service efficiency to charities and reformatories. Even after his dismissal, he represented the hospital in House and Senate hearings about the annual appropriation for the District.[155]

Charles Purvis married twice. On April 13, 1871, he wed Ann Hathaway, a white woman from Eastport, Maine. The couple moved into a home at 1118 Thirteenth Street, and it was there that their two children were born — Alice on February 17, 1872, and Robert on August 9, 1873.[156] Ann Purvis died on June 15, 1898. One of Charles's most treasured possessions was a miniature of her, which he wore on his watch chain and eventually bequeathed to Alice.[157] After Ann's death he remained in their Washington home, alone except for two servants. Eventually he married again. Like his first wife, his second was a white New Englander. Jennie C. Butman was from Manchester, New Hampshire. The couple were married in Philadelphia by Unitarian minister and family friend Frederic A. Hinckley on March 9, 1901.[158]

Meanwhile, Charles's daughter Alice had qualified as a physician and had made her home in the Boston suburb of Watertown with her aunt. In 1904, when she was thirty-two, she married Frederick H. Robie, a forty-year-old white bookkeeper.[159] Charles decided to retire from Howard, sell his home in Washington, and move to Boston to be near Alice. He passed the Massachusetts State Board examinations and was able to practice in that state. His home at 109 Gainsborough Street was also his surgery. He continued to practice for a year or two before retiring completely. He maintained his ties with Howard, serving as a trustee from 1908 to 1926. Charles B. Purvis died on January 30, 1929, in Los Angeles, where he and his wife usually spent the winter months.[160] He died a very wealthy man. He made generous provision for Jennie, for Alice and her two sons, and for Robert (who had trained as a dentist) and his sons. He also left $100 apiece to the children of his brothers, Henry and Granville.[161]

IN THE YEARS immediately after the Civil War, Charles's brother Henry was among that band of educated young African Americans from the North who made their way south and entered politics. Barely twenty-two years old, Oberlin-educated Henry was elected to the South Carolina House of Representatives as a delegate from Lexington County in 1868. From the state house he went on to serve for five years, from 1872 to 1877, as adjutant-general of the state militia.[162] He married a Charlestonian, Ella Zenobia Barre, the daughter of a French wine merchant and his mulatto "housekeeper," and made a life for himself in the city of his father's birth.[163] That life was, at best, precarious. Black carpetbaggers were loathed by the defeated Confederates on account of their race, their educational attainments, their "gentility," and their espousal of Radical Republican politics. Purvis knew of friends who had been murdered. He himself had been threatened. But he persisted. South Carolina was his home and he was not about to leave. Back in Philadelphia Harriet Purvis told friends she lived in constant fear for Henry's safety—and with good reason.[164]

Why then did Robert Purvis disinherit his son? Surely he admired the courage and steadfastness Henry displayed. And yet, when he wrote his will in 1887, he named all his surviving children except Henry as executors. Then he added a codicil awarding Henry's share of his estate to Ella. She would get regular payments from his executors until the eldest of Henry's children turned twenty-one, at which point they would divide amongst themselves the legacy that would have been their father's. The breach widened. In 1894 Robert revoked the first codicil and added another. His executors were not to pay a cent to Henry's family until Henry was dead.[165]

What had caused the rift? Perhaps there had been bitter words over Robert's second marriage. Or perhaps the trouble stemmed from what Robert saw as a sellout. Certainly, the evidence points to Henry having made his peace with the Democrats as South Carolina was "redeemed." Making peace proved profitable. Henry was variously inspector of customs for the port of Charleston, bailiff in the federal court in Charleston, and a clerk in the office of the United States marshal.[166] The price of compromise had been worth the sacrifice of ideals. Perhaps that was what his father could not forgive.

Even though he managed to get a series of patronage jobs, Henry needed his share of his father's estate. Without it, he and his family were on the edge of genteel poverty by 1900. Henry and Ella had seven children, five of whom survived infancy. They also took in a nephew of Ella's, Clarence Ferrette (the census-taker wrote "Farrell").[167] They struggled to give their children a decent education and send them into the world able to support themselves. One son, Charles, became a skilled craftsman, while another, Robert, worked as a book-keeper, and then as a shoemaker. Augustus followed in the footsteps of his Uncle Charles. After briefly attending Wesleyan University in Connecticut, he moved on to the University of Michigan, where he received his B.A. in 1909 and his M.D. in 1911. As late as 1940 he was listed in the "Colored Depart-ment" of the Charleston city directory as a physician.[168] Both of Henry's daugh-ters attended Howard University. In 1910 Marie received a certificate from the Academy, presumably the preparatory department. She may have died young. She was not mentioned in her Uncle Charles's will, although he left legacies to her siblings. As for Louisa, she received a diploma from Howard's Commercial College in 1911 and another from its Teachers' College in 1913. She returned to Charleston, where she married a Mr. Bell. Henry Purvis died on September 28, 1907, and then, belatedly, his children received their share of their grandfather's estate.[169]

HARRIET AND ROBERT'S youngest son, Granville Sharp Purvis, born in 1846, did well financially. He attended Oberlin for several years and then continued his studies at Howard, graduating as a doctor of pharmacy. By the time he was in his mid-twenties he had settled in Detroit.[170] He set up in business at 991 Jefferson Avenue, lived for a time above the store, and then bought the adjoin-ing premises and made his home there. Like his father and grandfather, he knew the wisdom of diversifying his interests. In 1885 he entered into partner-ship with one Peter J. Spieles. The two ran the Wolverine Nickel Works, where they undertook "Gold, Silver, Nickel, Copper, Brass and Bronze Plating . . . [and] Polishing in all its branches." They also supplied fancy metal numbers for doors. The pharmacy generated a good income, and Granville made other investments as well. He eventually moved farther away from his business pre-mises and bought a home on Pingree Avenue. By the turn of the century he had carved out a niche for himself in Detroit's African-American upper class. His name last appeared in the city directory in 1906.[171]

A bachelor at least as late as the 1900 census, he married on April 21 of that year. Race complicated his emotional life. His bride was more than twenty years his junior, and she was white. Michigan law forbade interracial marriages, and there was no way Granville could attempt to "pass," even if he had been inclined to do so. A family friend observed that Robert and Harriet Purvis's five eldest children were light-skinned and had European features, but the three youngest, Granville, Henry, and Georgianna, were "much darker." There was one way around the impasse. Granville and his fiancée, Elizabeth M. Gleason, went to Philadelphia and took out a marriage license. She listed her address as 1118 Thirteenth Street in Washington, D.C., the home of widower Charles Purvis. The marriage ceremony was conducted by Frederic A. Hinckley, the same man who had officiated at Robert Purvis's funeral.[172] Granville and Elizabeth had one child, a daughter, Marion, who was born in Detroit in 1903 or 1904.[173]

Several years after Marion's birth, Granville retired from business and moved with her and Elizabeth to England. In 1908 the *Oberlin Alumni Register* reported that Granville was living in the fashionable resort town of Bournemouth. In fact, he had settled in nearby Christchurch, buying a house he christened "Byberry" in memory of his childhood home. It was there that he died, at age sixty-six, on August 29, 1911, of tuberculosis.[174] Elizabeth and Marion stayed on in England for some years, and Marion received her early education there. Eventually, in 1920, they returned to the United States and made their home in Los Angeles, the city where Charles and Jennie Purvis wintered.[175]

SARAH FORTEN PURVIS's life seemed placid enough in 1842. Her happiness was clouded by the deaths of a much-loved father and sister. Still, she was married with three children and her family was prospering. The Purvises lived on Eddington Farm, the estate in Bensalem, Bucks County, Joseph had bought in 1835.[176] They were supported by the income from the farm and from various rental properties. Periodically during the 1840s Joseph sold off parts of his estate, sometimes at a loss, sometimes at a profit. He also dabbled in real estate in Philadelphia with a modest degree of success.[177] Martin R. Delany described him as "an amateur stock farmer."

> Every animal on [his] farm is of the very best breed—Godolphin horses, Durham cattle, Leicestershire sheep, Berkshire swine, even English bull-terrier dogs. . . . Mr. Purvis supplies a great many farmers with choice breeds of cattle, and it is said that he spends ten thousand dollars annually, in the improvement of his stocks.

Certainly the Agricultural Census of 1850 reveals a very successful farming enterprise—a farm valued at $30,000, with substantial investments in machinery and livestock. Brother Robert's farm was modest by comparison.[178]

On the surface, family finances looked good, but they may not have been. In 1844 Joseph mortgaged Eddington Farm and another tract of land.[179] He eventually sold the farm at a profit in 1853 perhaps because, quite simply, his family (he and Sarah now had eight children) needed a larger home. The Purvises used the proceeds of the sale to purchase another farm in Bensalem, "Fairview," and additional land in Bensalem and nearby Bristol. At the same time Joseph mortgaged other parts of his estate.[180] Then he embarked on a series of complex real estate transactions in Bucks, Philadelphia, and distant Elk Counties. Did he and Sarah think they could gamble successfully on the property market, or were the various deals brought about by dire financial necessity?[181] One fact is abundantly clear. Joseph was not the most methodical of businessmen. On January 17, 1857, he died suddenly.[182] He had made no will. All his children were minors. Sarah was left to care for them and settle an estate that was far more muddled than her father's had been. She renounced her right to serve as administrator, and the Bucks County Orphans' Court appointed lawyer Anthony Swain to act in her stead. The court also named guardians for the Purvis children. Joseph and William selected as their guardian a neighbor, Jesse G. Webster. Webster also became the guardian of James, who was judged to be mentally incompetent. Guardianship of the younger children went to Margaretta Forten.[183]

Swain set to work to settle the estate. He completed the real estate deals begun by Joseph before his death. Then there were his debts to be cleared, his workers paid, and his children provided for. It was soon obvious that more land would have to be sold. Purvis's assets minus his real estate amounted to under $3,000, but he owed over $7,000—to neighbors, to various people he had done business with, to his farmhands and servants, and to his brother. He was also delinquent on his state, county, and school taxes.[184] With Sarah's consent and the permission of the Orphans' Courts in Bucks and Philadelphia Counties, Swain began auctioning off extraneous tracts in a bid to keep the family farm intact. Despite his evident anxiety to do well by Sarah and her children, he was trying to get good prices for land in the midst of the Panic of 1857. Eventually he was obliged to ask the courts' permission to mortgage Fairview.[185]

The older Sarah Purvis was not the equal of feisty, energetic young Sarah Forten. Burdened with financial woes, and eight children, one of them, in the words of the Orphans' Court, "a Lunatic," she simply could not cope. Charlotte Forten visited her aunt in 1858 and reported: "As usual a scene of confusion and disorder greeted me." She could not help reflecting how differently everything was managed by Aunt Harriet at Byberry.[186]

The Purvises of Fairview survived the vicissitudes of the Civil War thanks to the business acumen of Margaretta Forten. In 1863 she persuaded Sarah to return to court. The sisters proposed to borrow enough money to pay off the liens against the estate and improve the farming land. The land itself would be the security. With the wartime boom in food prices, the farm would generate enough income to repay the loan.[187]

With or without Margaretta's knowledge, Sarah also approached some of her old antislavery friends for help. She secured a loan from Theodore Dwight Weld. He was not a rich man, and he was in serious difficulties when Sarah neglected to repay the loan. In the fall of 1869 he wrote to remind her of the debt. Her story was a pathetic one. "[W]e have had many losses with our Farming operations and many debts to meet, so that there never seemed a time when I could make a settlement—but I have it in mind — and have not forgotten it." When the farm was sold she would pay Weld what she owed him.[188]

There was no sale at that point. In 1869 Margaretta was back in court seeking permission to mortgage the property again. Fairview "was in a dilapidated condition." She wanted authorization to borrow $1,200 to cover essential repairs and pledge the farm as security. The court consented.[189]

The strategy worked, but it would only delay, and not prevent the breakup of the estate. As the Purvis children came of age, the farm had to be subdivided. Two of Sarah's sons died—Alfred on April 27, 1865, at nineteen, and the "Lunatic" James on February 18, 1870, at twenty-nine.[190] Their shares went to their siblings. Emily married John Quincy Allen, a "colored" teacher from Philadelphia, on August 12, 1869. Eventually they moved to Albany, New York. In 1871 Emily and John laid claim to her share of the estate, and that necessitated a sale.[191]

Emily's older sister, Sarah, married into the influential Boseman family of Troy, New York. William S. Boseman was the youngest child of Benjamin Boseman, a steward on a Hudson River steamboat, and Annaretta Boseman. William's older brother, physician Benjamin Jr., was a political ally of Sarah's cousin, Henry, in South Carolina. William was a law student at Howard University and Sarah a teacher in the Washington, D.C., public schools when they met.[192] The couple decided to make a new life for themselves in Kansas, and they persuaded Sarah's youngest brother, Alexander, to accompany them. In 1873, from Neosha Falls, Woodson County, Kansas, Sarah and Alexander filed for their shares of their father's estate. To satisfy their claims there was another sale. Sarah Purvis and two of her children, William and Annie, managed to raise the cash to buy out Sarah and Alexander.[193]

On September 9, 1873, Joseph Purvis, Jr., sold his claim to his mother and two siblings for $100. Financially, this was the family's last gasp. On April 24, 1875, Sarah, William, and Annie declared bankruptcy and their remaining property was sold for the benefit of their creditors.[194] Several months earlier Margaretta Forten had died. Now Sarah returned to her childhood home to take her place as daughter-in-residence and housekeeper for her mother and brothers. Sarah, William, and Annie spent the rest of their lives in Philadelphia. Had it not been for Charlotte Vandine Forten's income from her rental properties and the fact that James Forten had left his family the Lombard Street home, Sarah would have been homeless and destitute. As it was, brother William's purchase of a family plot in the cemetery of St. James the Less in the days of his affluence spared her the final indignity of being buried in a pauper's grave. Sarah Forten Purvis died at the family home on October 30, 1884.[195]

After Sarah's death, Annie and William moved out of their grandmother's home and into lodgings. William worked at a series of jobs, most of them fairly low-paying. He was variously listed in the censuses and directories as an unemployed farmer, a canvasser, and a paper bag manufacturer. However, he had inherited James Forten's mechanical skills, and eventually he became a reasonably successful inventor. While his sister kept house for him at 3045 Fontaine Street, in Philadelphia's Thirty-Second Ward, he worked on various inventions and improvements. Around 1901 he formed the Union Electric Construction Company, and did well enough to maintain an office in the Philadelphia Bourse. He had at least a dozen patents relating to the manufacturing of paper bags—prosaic enough items, but vital to the economy. There were other patents, including three "on electric railroads, one on a fountain-pen, another on a magnetic car-balancing device, and still another for a cutter of roll-holders." Self-taught (he never received a college education, unlike his brother Alexander, who spent two years at Oberlin), William simply looked around him and applied his talents to solving everyday engineering problems. William Purvis died in 1914 and Annie Purvis in 1917. They were buried beside their mother.[196]

Sarah and Joseph Purvis's eldest son, Joseph Jr., was the family member no one talked about. He had proven a trial to his parents and an embarrassment to his siblings. Perhaps, as the eldest child of affluent parents, he had been spoiled. Neighbor George S. Buck recalled that when Joseph was young, "his people were very well off and there was no necessity of his working." Brother William bore that out, stating that their mother "was in very comfortable circumstances and could afford to keep us from working . . . and educate us." Joseph may have been rather wild when he was in his teens. A white neighbor recalled that he went on "sprees" and "got to living fast" before he went into the army. Possibly the neighbor, John S. Paul, was jealous of the Purvises, and not above kicking a man when he was down. In 1884 he recalled that Joseph's family was "wealthy when his father was alive [and] the whole family was brought up in luxury [and] did not know much about work."[197]

Joseph put the blame for his misfortunes—his poor health, his addiction to alcohol, his inability to hold down a job — to his army service. He had rushed to enlist when the call had gone out for black volunteers, and on March 16, 1864 he was mustered in as a private in Company B, 43rd Regiment, United States Colored Troops. The situation at Camp William Penn was far from ideal. The barracks was full of white soldiers, and the black recruits were sent to sleep outside in tents. They had no groundsheets. The best they could do was to put straw between themselves and the bare ground. It rained heavily and snowed. Samuel Draper, who had worked for Joseph's uncle, was in the same tent with him and had some sympathy for him. "Purvis wasn't used to anything of that kind[,] always being used to a good home and it very quick give him the rheumatism." Col. Wagner, he recalled, took pity on him, excused him from drilling and standing guard, and put him in charge of the horses. On a march from Annapolis to Alexandria Joseph literally fell by the wayside and was transported to the Freedmen's Hospital in Washington, where he was discharged as unfit on July 15, 1864. He returned home, worked on the farm when he was able, and gradually recovered his health. In March 1865 he reenlisted, and was discharged in October of that year.[198]

Once back in civilian life, he took to drinking again. He became a drifter, selling subscriptions to books and newspapers, and driving a carriage for a white family. He also "peddled medicines and doctored among the colored people." In 1886 his family charitably described him as a "farmer." In 1904, when he was boarding with an African-American family in Chester County, he called himself a "medicine vendor."

Over the decades he got a pension, had it disallowed, petitioned to have it restored, and then to have it increased. Disabled by rheumatism and suffering from related heart ailments, he took what work he could get. His claims that his war service had incapacitated him were always complicated by the testimony of friend and foe alike that he drank whenever he had any money. He died in the Chester County Poorhouse on September 19, 1906.[199]

LIKE HIS OLDER brothers, James Forten's youngest child, William Deas Forten, had been trained as a sailmaker. Over the years he often listed himself in the directories and in the censuses as a sailmaker.[200] However, there is little evidence that he ever spent much time in the Forten loft cutting and sewing canvas. William was set on emulating his father, not as a master sailmaker but as a community leader and reformer.

William Forten emerged in the early 1850s as one of the leading members of the newly revived Vigilance Committee. In the fall of 1851 he was appointed to a Special Vigilance Committee. The Fugitive Slave Law had just been passed, and black Philadelphians wanted to make sure they were prepared to challenge it if and when the need arose. They did not have long to wait. With the wave of arrests that followed the killing of slave owner Edward Gorsuch by runaway slaves and their allies in the Christiana Riot, Forten and his colleagues sprang into action. They appealed for funds from "the friends of Freedom" to hire legal counsel for the alleged "traitors" and offer relief to their families. Donations poured in from as far away as Chicago, Sacramento, and San Francisco. As for the committee members, they visited the prisoners regularly in the Moyamensing jail to bring them food, clothing, and other essentials.[201] The Christiana crisis marked William Forten's emergence as a community leader.

The young Philadelphian was proud of his illustrious father and probably alive to the influence that James Forten's reputation gave him. In 1855 William, his elder brother, Robert, and five other black men petitioned the state legislature for the franchise in the name of "the Colored Citizens of Philadelphia." Advancing the service of African-American men during the Revolutionary War as a reason why people of color should be counted as citizens, they observed: "The late James Forten . . . well known as a colored man of wealth, intelligence, and philanthropy, enlisted in the American navy under Captain Decatur, of the Royal Louis, was taken prisoner . . . and . . . confined on board the horrible Jersey prison ship."[202]

When the Civil War came, William threw himself behind the Union cause with a fervor his father would have admired. He sought out allies such as Charles Sumner and began a correspondence with him, requesting reports about Confederate atrocities and sending him news of what he feared was a resurgence of procolonization sentiment.[203] On July 6, 1863 he attended a massive recruiting rally, joining old friends such as John P. Burr, Alfred S. Cassey, Stephen Smith, William Whipper, and the Cattos, father and son, in issuing a call: "Men of Color, to Arms! . . . Fail Now and Our Race is Doomed on this the soil of our birth."[204] His older brother answered that call. His death shook William profoundly. Robert, he wrote Sumner, "came from the enjoyment of liberty[,] equality & citizenship in England to do battle for their recognition in this his own native land." Nor was he alone. "The black-man, disowned—dishonored—disgraced and dehumanized[,] trampled in the dust . . . now lifts his head and proudly walks into the front ranks of certain death unprotected[,] unregarded; in order that the Country may have a Constitution."[205]

In the last months of the war black Pennsylvanians organized an equal rights convention in Harrisburg. William Forten attended as a delegate from the Ladies' Union Association of Philadelphia, a group dedicated to caring for sick and wounded black soldiers.[206] He soon became a major figure in the Equal Rights League, an organization with strong Republican ties dedicated to the enfranchisement of African-American men. Founded in Syracuse in 1864, it spread quickly. By 1866 there were fifty-one local branches in Pennsylvania alone. In August 1865, at the Pennsylvania State Equal Rights League meeting in Harrisburg, Forten was elected to the advisory committee.[207]

His involvement in public life continued. Early in 1866 he and two other black Philadelphians petitioned Congress on behalf of the Pennsylvania Equal Rights League for full civil rights. He was an honorary member of the National Convention of Colored Soldiers and Sailors that met in Philadelphia in January 1867.[208] His reputation grew, and he was much in demand as a speaker. As he wrote Congressman Leonard Myers early in 1868, he had many engagements and an extensive correspondence. If the Radical Republican Myers would get him copies of his speeches and those of like-minded House members, he would "send them just where the doubting are to be found and where Copperheads may *be influenced*." It galled Forten that he still could not vote, but, even "though *disfranchised* and disowned, I am still a living vital Acting Man, undetered by the base Actions of false friends or the hatred of open foes of freedom's Cause."[209] Later that same year, at the meeting of the State Equal Rights League, he issued a stern warning to Southern black voters. They must side with the Republicans, or see all progress to civil and social equality halted.

William Forten took a keen interest in the debate surrounding the drafting of the Fifteenth Amendment and did not shrink from criticizing proven friends. When Congressman George S. Boutwell of Massachusetts, a leading Radical, moved to insert wording that the franchise could not be withheld on the grounds of race, color, or previous condition of servitude, Forten begged Sumner to use his influence to have the wording changed.

We cannot have this thrust to endless days in our faces that we are a *Race of Slaves*—We want no reference to Race or Color, or . . . previous condition, engrafted on the great National Charter. . . . Let the Constitution of the U.S. contain nothing so . . . Antirepublican in character as *Race*[,] *Color or Previous Condition*. There must be no *Color* known to *Americans* but the National one.[210]

He tried his own hand at drafting an amendment that would enfranchise every male citizen of twenty-one or more, for every election, "unless guilty of [a] crime for which he has been duly convicted by impartial law."

William's admiration for Sumner deepened. In the spring of 1871 he asked the senator for a copy of his recent speech on the annexation of Santo Domingo, a speech "for which every American and especially those who have so long been outraged should consider himself to you sir, deeply indebted."[211] A few months later he wrote to thank Sumner for forwarding a copy of one speech and to ask for a copy of another. As corresponding secretary of the Pennsylvania Equal Rights League he thought Sumner's Supplementary bill should "reach the remote Counties and stir the people to action."[212]

Like his father before him, Forten became an informal adviser to many in Philadelphia's African-American community. People consulted him about their problems, asked him to intercede with various officials, and sought his advice on a myriad of concerns. This role made him painfully aware of ambiguities in the law. In March 1870, for instance, he helped a black alien seeking naturalization complete the necessary paperwork. However, the district court judges, all good Republicans, rejected the application because the law said only white men could be naturalized. Forten wrote to Sumner to point out that political expediency, as well as justice, demanded that the law be changed. "[T]here are a large number of Colored Men who have been driven to the 'Canadas,' and adjacent Islands to us, who now . . . have returned to aid in voting the Country's enemies and Slavery's supporters out of . . . power." He begged Sumner to find a way of striking down "this barrier disqualifying so many men, whose votes will all be needed."[213]

In 1872 Forten and other newly enfranchised African-American leaders in the state, among them William Howard Day (like Forten a sailmaker's son), John Mercer Langston, and William Nesbit, formed the Union Central Republican Club to mobilize the black vote and ensure the election of Republicans at all levels, confident that they would champion legislation favorable to the black community. Forten was one of the authors of a pamphlet distributed to black voters by the Republican Congressional Committee. *Grant or Greeley— Which?* consisted of excerpts from letters, speeches, and editorials "by colored men and their best friends," all trying to show that Grant was truly committed to racial equality. Forten was in distinguished company. The other contributors included Frederick Douglass, William Lloyd Garrison, John Mercer Langston, Wendell Phillips, and House Speaker James G. Blaine. Later that same year Forten succeeded in his bid to become one of Pennsylvania's presidential electors.[214]

William Forten's résumé over the next few years was essentially that of a politician and political organizer. In 1874 he was on a committee of the State Equal Rights League that called for a national convention in Washington to push for passage of the Civil Rights bill. That same year he traveled extensively in Pennsylvania's mining regions, rallying the faithful to the Republican cause. In 1876 he was chosen as an alternate to the Republican Party convention, but declined to serve because he feared it would cost the party votes.[215] As election fever heated up in 1877, a man matching the description of Frank Kelly, the alleged assassin of Forten's friend Octavius V. Catto, was arrested in Chicago. Forten was a member of the Republican committee that traveled to Chicago to identify him. Kelly was returned to Philadelphia, put on trial, and acquitted in what many regarded as a gross miscarriage of justice.[216]

Increasing visibility had its drawbacks. William Forten had his critics within the African-American community. In early 1877, there was a Convention of Colored Voters at Philadelphia's Liberty Hall. Many of those who attended condemned Forten for not showing up and for not using his influence with white politicians in Philadelphia to get more appointments for black men. George Cornelius said "that he had no doubt but that Mr. Forten had done great things for the colored race, but any one who lived in the Fifth Ward knew that it was very hard for a colored man to obtain that gentleman's influence." However, Guy Barton reminded the audience that "Forten and his father before him had done more than any others to help the colored man."[217]

As some, like his brother-in-law, abandoned the Republicans in disgust and frustration, William remained loyal, but loyalty was increasingly difficult. He and his associates insisted adherence to the GOP must be a prerequisite for membership in the Equal Rights League. This resulted in yet more defections. Some of his erstwhile allies met in Pittsburgh in the summer of 1878 to form the People's League, pledging to work for the "intellectual, industrial, mechanical, and social improvement" of all African Americans, whatever their party affiliation. He tried to effect a reconciliation but was forced to concede that Republicans had often broken their promises to black voters.[218]

The black vote remained an important factor in Philadelphia politics until 1884. The candidate for mayor that year was the incumbent, Democrat Samuel King. During his first term the situation of black Philadelphians changed markedly for the better. Substantial numbers of African-American citizens were prepared to vote for him over his Republican challenger—but not Forten. Through the Equal Rights League he and his allies urged loyalty to the Republicans. The Republicans won and thereafter felt confident enough to ignore the possibility of a black defection. Demographics also helped, as Italian and Jewish immigrants were recruited into the party. African Americans no longer counted, and nothing needed to be done by way of favors to keep them in line.[219] Forten and his friends had outlived their usefulness.

With his own and his brother's means severely restricted after their mother's death, William reluctantly decided they must move out of the family home. In the spring of 1888, Robert Purvis, James Forten's last surviving trustee, made the property over to Thomas and William. They mortgaged it and eventually sold it to a couple of white speculators, who would convert it into a tenement house. The Forten brothers moved into lodgings at 1218 West Tucker Street in North Philadelphia.[220]

On April 6, 1898, at age seventy-five, William entered the Stephen Smith Home for Aged and Infirm Colored Persons. It can hardly have been a congenial setting for the aging politician, but he had little choice. According to Frances Ella Still, the daughter of his old ally William Still, "Mr. Forten was without funds and the family had died out."[221] In almost every way Forten was an atypical resident of the home. The average "inmate" was female, Southern-born, and with little formal education. Still, he made the best of his situation, grateful perhaps to have a roof over his head and three meals per day. The last of James and Charlotte Forten's nine children, he died at age eighty-six on March 8, 1909.[222]

Many years earlier, when William had been a force to reckon with in Philadelphia politics and when he had been courted by the city's white power brokers, he had bought a family plot in the cemetery of the prestigious Episcopal church of St. James the Less. He was eventually buried there, close to the Wannamakers and other Philadelphians who had known both wealth and power. There was no money for a tombstone. Today, four of James Forten's children and two of his grandchildren lie in a plot designated only by a numbered marker.[223]

THOMAS FRANCIS WILLING Forten is the most enigmatic of James Forten's children. He took no part in any of the reform causes that claimed the attention of the rest of his family. He never signed a petition, joined a society, or lent his name to anything. He was evidently less intellectually gifted than his siblings. He may even have suffered from some mental impairment. But he was not without intelligence. At various times his niece, Charlotte, mentioned him reading aloud to the family from works such as Rowan Hinton Helper's *The Impending Crisis in the South* and a tome on British art.[224] Quite simply, for whatever reason, Thomas was the family ne'er-do-well, boarded out with and provided for by whomever had the means and the inclination to assist him.

In the 1840s and 1850s Thomas made the rounds of his Bucks County relatives—Sarah and Joseph Purvis and Robert and Mary Forten. In 1844 he was described in a deed as a farmer from Bucks County. In 1850 he was a member of brother Robert's household in Warminster. Four years later, still a Bucks County resident, he was variously listed as a farmer and a gentleman.[225] He may have been living in Bucks County long after Robert's departure for Canada. In 1860

Sarah Purvis's neighbor, Rhoads Wright, reported that he employed one Thomas "Fortune," a Pennsylvania-born mulatto, as a farmhand.[226]

At some point in the 1860s Thomas returned to Philadelphia. By 1870, the brother of a rising star in Pennsylvania's Republican Party, he had secured an appointment as a United States Marshal. A decade later he was on the staff of the Inspector of Customs. He continued working in the Customs Office until 1886, by which time William's ability to get patronage jobs had ebbed away. In the early 1890s Thomas found work as a butcher.[227] He died on February 12, 1897, at age sixty-nine and was buried in the cemetery of St. James the Less beside his sisters, Margaretta and Sarah.[228]

As FOR JAMES Forten's widow, she endured the sorrow of burying all five of her daughters, two of her sons, and nine of her grandchildren.[229] She saw the decline of the family fortunes, the bankruptcies of three of her children, and the ignominious flight of her eldest son just one step ahead of his creditors. Small wonder that her namesake, Robert's daughter Charlotte, wrote of her grandmother having endured much "sorrow and fatigue."[230]

Charlotte Vandine Forten remained active in the antislavery movement she had supported for so many years, and she did what she could to help her children and ensure herself a modicum of comfort in her old age.[231] Her world had never been bounded by the nursery, the kitchen, and the drawing room. The wife of a successful businessman, she had learned the value of real estate. During her long widowhood she used her dower money to purchase ground rents.[232] Apparently, she was able to recoup some of the family's financial losses, especially as the economy recovered from the impact of the Panic of 1837. In 1850 her real estate holdings were put at $65,000. Twenty years later she was still worth $15,000. In the last years of her life she took steps to provide for the two sons who lived with her, making over to them for a nominal sum most of her rents.[233]

In old age, Charlotte Vandine Forten was a dignified lady. One family member recalled "Grandmother Forten" as representing "a picture for any book, sitting beside a white marble table in her spacious living room always sewing or knitting, a black lace cap . . . covering her glistening white curls." Robert Purvis described her at ninety-five as being "in the enjoyment of excellent health, & unimpaired mental faculties."[234] She died in December 1884, just days short of her hundredth birthday, in the home where she had lived for almost eighty years. She was buried at Lebanon Cemetery. Eventually, when St. Thomas's churchyard was sold in 1887, the remains of Charlotte's husband, her son Robert, daughters Charlotte and Mary, and three of her grandsons were moved to Lebanon.[235]

AND WHAT OF the other members of James Forten's extended family? Abigail Dunbar outlived her brother by more than three years. She died of "mortification" (gangrene) on September 18, 1846, at age eighty-three and was buried at St. Thomas's.[236] Of the fate of three of her four children, almost nothing is known. Margaret Dunbar Lewis may have stayed in Philadelphia. The Board of Health records note the death of an African-American woman by the name of Margaret Lewis on February 27, 1852. She was sixty-four, about the age Abigail's daughter would have been, but the name was common enough.[237] One of Abigail's granddaughters, another Abigail, married Richard Nugent, a laborer from Washington, D.C., and settled with him and their daughter in San Francisco.[238]

Abigail's youngest child, James Forten Dunbar, found a home in the United States Navy. From 1846 to 1865 he was almost constantly at sea. He turned up at ports up and down the Atlantic seaboard. On October 28, 1846, at age forty-seven, he enlisted on the *Stromboli* in Boston. Two years later he was on the famed USS *Constitution*. He enlisted in New York and then in Norfolk, Virginia. There was no hope of a commission, but he was seldom turned down for "general service." He was a skilled sailmaker, but he was prepared to ship out as a cook if necessary.[239]

A series of personal tragedies made shore life less and less appealing. His wife, Mary, died. In 1844 he lost his daughter, Abby, and four years later, while he was at sea, news reached him that his son, James, was dead.[240] The navy became his home and his shipmates a substitute family. He was still in the service when the Civil War broke out. Back in Philadelphia, perhaps on a visit to his Forten relatives, he enlisted on April 26, 1861, for three years. He reenlisted several more times during the course of the war. He was rejected at least once, presumably on account of his age.[241] On January 31, 1865, he reportedly deserted from the USS *Princeton*.[242]

In his old age James Forten Dunbar returned to the city of his birth. There was no mistaking who or what he was. He most likely walked with the rolling gait of a sailor, and his arms were heavily tattooed, with a ship, a mermaid, a man and a woman, and a family group—perhaps a visual reminder of his lost wife and children.[243] At some point after the war he was admitted to the United States Naval Asylum in Philadelphia as a "beneficiary." His politically well-connected cousin, William Forten, had probably come to his aid. In the asylum James had food, clothing, lodging, an allowance, tobacco, medical care, and accommodation. Although the monthly musters described his character and habits as "very good," there had been some early difficulties. He had been admitted once and been found by the officers of the asylum to be "very troublesome and bad." He had been expelled or had left, but was readmitted "on condition" on August 3, 1867. This time he had to conform to the rules of the asylum, for he had nowhere else to go. He died there on November 26, 1870. The official who recorded his passing composed the following piece of doggerel:

There is a motto 'All things must have an end'—
And this old sailor opposite whose name these lines are penned
Has paid the debt of nature—
This, as by his record verified, was no common lot
Though after years of service
Thrust in the earth to be forgot.[244]

James Forten Dunbar's fate could have been his uncle's, had not circumstances elevated one from sailor to successful businessman, and kept the other in the station of ordinary seaman.

HARRIET JUDAH MILLER, the mother of Robert and Joseph Purvis, seemed set to rival Charlotte Vandine Forten and Abigail Dunbar in longevity. The Millers left New York for Philadelphia in the early 1840s, when William was appointed minister of Wesley Methodist Church. He died on December 6, 1845, after a lengthy illness. In his will he left Harriet the contents of their Philadelphia home. Under the terms of a deed of trust executed back in 1832, the house was hers. Miller had bought it for her with the money her eldest son had left her. He held title to the property during his lifetime, after which it was to pass to her and then to Robert and Joseph.[245] Harriet Miller did not remarry. In her old age she remembered her Charleston kinfolk and sent for a widowed niece, Sarah Judah Vickers, to live with her. In 1860 the census-taker found the two women living in modest comfort in Harriet's home at 618 North Seven Street in Philadelphia's Thirteenth Ward. Harriet's will, made shortly after her husband's death, left her estate to her sons and their children. In 1868 she added a codicil leaving Sarah Vickers $500.[246]

In the fall of 1869, Harriet Miller decided to travel to Charleston to see her sister, Mary. Given her age—she was eighty-five—and the unsettled state of affairs in the South, it was an ambitious undertaking, but she refused to be deterred. She had probably not seen Mary in the half-century since she left South Carolina and moved north with William Purvis and their sons. Harriet reached Charleston safely, but on her way back to Philadelphia she suffered a massive stroke. She was brought back to her home, where she died on December 10.[247]

ANNIE WOOD, THE sister of Mary Wood Forten, Robert's first wife, married one John Webb, a reasonably well-to-do native of Pennsylvania, in the 1850s. The couple settled briefly in New Jersey before moving to Philadelphia. By 1870 John was dead and Annie and her children moved in with her widowed sister-in-law, Elizabeth Iredell. The last mention of Annie is in the 1885 city directory. Listed as Ann Webb, widow of John, she was living at 110 Gothic Street in Philadelphia's Fifth Ward.[248]

Shortly after James Forten's death, a young niece of Charlotte Vandine Forten's turned up in Philadelphia. Named for her aunt, she was the daughter of Charles Vandine, Charlotte's brother, who had gone to Haiti many years before and become a successful merchant. She taught school for a while before marrying into one of Philadelphia's prosperous African-American families and moving to Cincinnati with her new husband.[249]

AND WHAT OF James Forten's legacy? Through the 1840s both black and white abolitionists praised him for his efforts in support of the cause. As a champion of civil rights he was celebrated by the likes of Frederick Douglass and Martin R. Delany, and by a host of lesser-known orators and writers. He was held up as a paragon of virtue and achievement—a rich black man who had used his wealth to help others less fortunate than himself, a courageous fighter for American independence who had deserved better of the country he had helped create. The image of James Forten was repeatedly appealed to by black Pennsylvanians. Those who had known him best saw to that. In 1848, at the Pennsylvania State Convention in Harrisburg, a committee that included Robert Purvis and William Whipper took note of Benjamin Martin's speech a decade earlier at the infamous Reform Convention. He had contended that he knew only one man of color who had truly benefited from religion and education and had carved for himself a niche in society. And yet nothing would spare this exemplary individual. James Forten, along with the rest of the African-American community, "must be *immolated*, not on account of his *condition*, but mark ye! it is his *complexion*." They ended with a paeon of praise to Forten. "JAMES FORTEN, though dead, his example still lives in the memory and affections of those who knew him. If we imitate his virtues, our influence will dissolve mountains of prejudice."[250]

However, as the years passed, the memory of James Forten's life and accomplishments began to fade. He was remembered by some. Crusading black journalist Mary Ann Shadd Cary, on a return visit to Philadelphia from Canada in 1857, wrote of how "James Forten fresh from the Revolution, gave earnest of his hatred of Slavery and love of liberty." On the eve of the Civil War the *Christian Recorder* called upon black Pennsylvanians to "show by our actions, that we are worthy sons of noble sires. Let the proud historic deeds of James Forten . . . animate us to place on record an enduring claim, to the affectionate regard, justice and humanity of the people of Pennsylvania."[251]

As the leaders of the antislavery movement passed away, and tributes were published, mention was often made of James Forten's role in the struggle. In 1882, for instance, two of Garrison's sons embarked on a massive four-volume biography of their father and applied to Robert Purvis for a portrait of Forten. He answered that there was one in the possession of his mother-in-law, but: "In my judgment, I believe, you can paint with your pen, a more satisfactory likeness, of that excellent man, than any you may get from the very poor one Mrs. F. has."[252]

Community historian William Carl Bolivar, writing in the *Philadelphia Tribune* as "Pencil Pusher," did his best to keep before the public at the turn of the century the achievements of the men and women of Forten's generation. In general, however, new names and new causes had come to the fore. In the age of Booker T. Washington and W. E. B. DuBois, no one paid much attention to James Forten.

Within two generations of his death, James Forten had been relegated to a historical footnote. His business had disappeared. His home had been sold. His children and grandchildren were dead or scattered about the country. Some of those descendants were mired in poverty. A few had "passed" into the white population. And even more effective in virtually erasing his legacy were changes in the social and political climate of the United States and of his native city. As William Forten found out in the 1880s, neither major party had any need to court the black vote. It was a basic assumption of white politicians in both parties that black voters would vote Republican. Men such as William Forten were thrust aside, and with them went their families' history of activism and influence. The brief obituary the *Public Ledger* printed when William Forten died in 1909 did not even get his father's name right.[253] As for the antislavery movement, that was "old news," a battle won. Some names were remembered, but not many, as new causes demanded the attention of reformers. In 1949, when Ray Allen Billington published a brief article on James Forten, he entitled it "Forgotten Abolitionist."[254] I hope this book has shown that James Forten was far more than an abolitionist, and that he and his legacy have been for too long forgotten.

ABBREVIATIONS

Organizations

AAS	American Anti-Slavery Society
ACS	American Colonization Society
AMRS	American Moral Reform Society
PAS	Pennsylvania Abolition Society
WPA	Works Projects Administration

Archives and Document Collections

APS	American Philosophical Society, Philadelphia
BAP	Black Abolitionist Papers
BCC	Bucks County Courthouse, Doylestown, Pennsylvania
BPL	Boston Public Library
CCL	Charleston County Library, South Carolina
CNA	Canadian National Archives, Ottawa, Ontario
FRC	Family Research Centre, London, England
HSP	Historical Society of Pennsylvania
LCP	Library Company of Philadelphia
MSA	Massachusetts State Archives, Boston
Nat Arch.	National Archives, Washington, D.C.
NBFPL	New Bedford Free Public Library
NEHGS	New England Historic Genealogical Society, Boston
ODHSL	Old Dartmouth Historical Society Library
PA Arch.	Pennsylvania Archives
PCA	Philadelphia City Archives

PRO   Public Record Office, London
PSA   Pennsylvania State Archives, Harrisburg
SCSA   South Carolina State Archives, Columbia, South Carolina
USC   University of South Carolina

Newspapers and Periodicals

AfRep   *African Repository*
ASA   *Anti-Slavery Advocate*
ASB   *Anti-Slavery Bugle*
ASR   *Anti-Slavery Record*
CA   *Colored American*
CR   *Christian Recorder*
Eman   *Emancipator*
FDP   *Frederick Douglass' Paper*
FJ   *Freedom's Journal*
GUE   *Genius of Universal Emancipation*
HR   *Hazard's Register*
Lib   *Liberator*
NASS   *National Anti-Slavery Standard*
NECAUL   *National Enquirer and Constitutional Advocate of Universal Liberty*
NR   *National Reformer*
NS   *North Star*
PAppeal   *Pacific Appeal*
PA Gaz   *Pennsylvania Gazette*
PF   *Pennsylvania Freeman*
PL   *Public Ledger*
Poulson   *Poulson's American Daily Advertise*
ProvFree   *Provincial Freeman*
VF   *Voice of the Fugitive*
WAA   *Weekly Anglo-African*

NOTES

Introduction

1. James Forten died on the morning of March 4, 1842. His funeral was held on the afternoon of March 6.

2. Lyell, *Travels in North America*, 207.

Chapter 1: "Born in His Majesty's Dominions"

1. Gloucester, *Discourse*, 18.

2. Abdy, *Journal of a Residence and Tour*, vol. 3, p. 129; May, *Some Recollections*, 287.

3. Nash and Soderlund, *Freedom by Degrees*, 12.

4. Nash, *Forging Freedom*, 8.

5. Turner, "Slavery in Pennsylvania," 143; Nash and Soderlund, *Freedom by Degrees*, 15.

6. Isaac Norris to Jonathan Dickinson, 1703; quoted in Turner, "Slavery in Pennsylvania," 143.

7. Friends were required to take their slaves to their Sunday meetings, but throughout the colonial period there was no move to grant either free or enslaved blacks full membership in the Society of Friends. Nash and Soderlund, *Freedom by Degrees*, 29.

8. Turner, "Slavery in Pennsylvania," 144. On the early foes of slavery, see Nash and Soderlund, *Freedom by Degrees*, 43–45.

9. Hazard, comp., "Minutes of the Provincial Council of Pennsylvania," in Wax, "Africans on the Delaware," 45.

10. Complaints about "tumultuous gatherings" of slaves in Philadelphia surfaced again and again over the years. See Turner, "Slavery in Pennsylvania," 145–46.

11. The 1726 "Act for the Better Regulating of Negroes in this Province" stipulated that children of mixed racial parentage were to be bound out until age thirty-one. It is not clear how such children were treated before 1726. Nash, *Forging Freedom,* 35.

12. Watson, *Annals of Philadelphia,* 479.

13. May, *Some Recollections,* 287.

14. Quoted in Soderlund, "Black Women in Colonial Pennsylvania," 62.

15. Ibid., 51.

16. On the legal restrictions on free blacks as a result of the 1726 law, see Brouwer, "The Negro as a Slave and a Free Black," 148–49, 154, 158.

17. May, *Some Recollections,* 287.

18. Gloucester, *Discourse,* 19.

19. *Poulson,* May 31, 1806.

20. On sex ratios in the city's black population, see Nash and Soderlund, *Freedom by Degrees,* 23–24.

21. Abdy, *Journal of a Residence and Tour,* vol. 3, p. 130. Lydia Maria Child "borrowed" from Abdy when she wrote *The Freedmen's Book,* but when she said of Forten that "as far as he could trace, they [his ancestors] had never been slaves" (101), she was misquoting Abdy. Forten told Abdy when the Englishman visited Philadelphia in 1834 that, so far as he was aware, no member of his family was a slave *then.*

22. In 1804, when James Forten and various relatives sought adult baptism at St. Thomas's African Episcopal Church, among the group was an eighty-two-year-old woman whose name was given as "Margarett Waymouth." If this reference is to Margaret Fortune, it is not clear why she would have been baptized by her maiden name, unless she and Thomas were never legally married. St. Thomas's African Episcopal Church, Philadelphia, Parish Register. I thank the minister, vestry, and members of St. Thomas's Church for giving me access to the register.

23. Gloucester, *Discourse,* 18.

24. Lambert Cadwalader to Thomas Fortune, August 25, 1770, Cadwalader Collection, HSP.

25. St. Paul's Church, Philadelphia, Baptisms, 1782–1828, Marriages, 1759–1829, Burials, 1790–1852, p. 292, HSP.

26. Quoted in Nash, *Forging Freedom,* 19.

27. Gough, *Christ Church,* 68–70.

28. Van Horne, ed., *Religious Philanthropy,* 21.

29. Horsmanden, *The New-York Conspiracy,* 81, 87, 98–100, 163, 178, 218–19, 252, 258, 262, 268, 277, 289, 310–14, 325; Davis, *"A Rumor of Revolt,"* 79, 81–82, 83, 84, 88, 90, 96, 130, 157, 187, 190; Hodges, ed., *Black Loyalist Directory,* 16, 48, 54, 77, 78, 127, 129, 137, 155. See also Hoff, "Frans Abramse Van Salee," 66.

30. Quoted in Burnston, "Babies in the Well," 170.

31. Effective Supply Tax (1780), 193; Supply Tax (1782), 346. (Old Swedes) Gloria Dei—Marriages, 1795–1816, p. 1960, HSP. The name Primus Fortune was not uncommon. A thirty-year-old man by that name, formerly the slave of Isaac Warner of Philadelphia, left America with the British in 1783. Hodges, ed., *Black Loyalist Directory,* 127.

32. U.S. Census, 1810: Moyamensing, 130, and New Market Ward, 279; 1820: Southwark, 111, and North Mulberry, 123; Philadelphia directory, 1803; Abajian, comp., *Blacks in Selected Newspapers, Censuses, and Other Sources: A Supplement,* 364.

33. U.S. Census, 1790: Philadelphia, 229; 1800: Philadelphia, 419.

34. U.S. Census, 1820: Philadelphia, Locust Ward, 60; Minutes of the African Lodge, Philadelphia, 1797–1800, Library of the Grand Lodge of Massachusetts.

35. "Record of Servants and Apprentices," 225.

36. *PA Gaz*, January 8, 1767; Philadelphia County Deeds, A.W.M., Book 48, 57, PCA.

37. *PA Gaz*, December 15 and 22, 1757; February 23, 1758; July 14, 1768; September 6, 1770; May 25 and November 16, 1774; Philadelphia County Wills, Book Q, 443, no. 361 (1784); PCA.

38. Only two other black women in colonial Philadelphia left wills. Soderlund, "Black Women in Colonial Pennsylvania," 65–66.

39. Philadelphia County Wills, Will Book O, 258, no. 196 (1768).

40. On the relationship between Cadwalader and Stevenson, see Philadelphia County Wills, Will Book W, 188, no. 111 (1791).

41. Bruns, "Benezet and the Negro," 111; Hornick, "Anthony Benezet," 373, 376–77.

42. Nash and Soderlund, *Freedom by Degrees*, 89.

43. Cleary, "'She Will Be in the Shop,'" 194–95.

44. Newman, "Black Women," 276–89. If she did operate some kind of unlicensed drinking establishment, she never fell foul of the law. Her name does not appear among the list of those indicted between 1720 and 1768 for running an illegal tavern. Manges, "Women Shopkeepers," 79, 80.

45. *PA Gaz*, October 3, 1751.

46. Crane, ed., *Drinker Diary*, vol. 1, pp. 63, 204 (entries for June 24, 1760, and October 7, 1774); Berlin, *Many Thousands Gone*, 62. There is no record of the burial of Ann Elizabeth Fortune, or any black or mulatto woman, in the register of Christ Church in August 1768. (At this point, burials at St. Paul's were recorded in the Christ Church register.) Because Ann Elizabeth made her will on August 10 and it was probated on August 20, she obviously died in the interval.

47. Jensen, *Maritime Commerce of Colonial Philadelphia*, 96.

48. Goldenberg, *Shipbuilding in Colonial America*, 50–51.

49. *PA Gaz*, August 16, 1770; see also July 6, 1785.

50. Gloucester, *Discourse*, 18.

51. For an indication of the range of Edward Bridges's business activities, see *PA Gaz*, December 28, 1739; September 11, November 13 and 27, 1740; January 1, March 12, and July 9, 1741.

52. Clark, *Inscriptions at Christ Church*, 526.

53. *PA Gaz*, October 8, 1741; February 3, 1747; June 13, 1754; Roach, ed., "Taxables in Philadelphia," 40; Ruschenberger, *Sketch of the Life of Dr. Robert Bridges*, 4.

54. Robert Bridges—Account and Receipt, July 2, 1767, Pennsylvania Misc. Papers, Penn and Baltimore, Penn Family Papers, 1756–68, HSP.

55. Proprietary Tax, 1769, p. 179, Provincial Tax Assessment Ledgers: 17th and 18th Penny Provincial Tax, City and County of Philadelphia, 1774, p. 37, PCA; Christ Church, Marriages, 1709–1800, p. 4350, HSP.

56. Nash, "Slaves and Slaveowners," 243–44, 247, 249, 250–51.

57. Nash and Soderlund, *Freedom by Degrees*, 16; Berlin, *Many Thousands Gone*, 182–83.

58. Briggs, "Sails and Sailmakers," 10.

59. Horsley, *Tools of the Maritime Trades*, 158–59. On the encounters sailmaker's apprentice Stephen Allen and his workmates had with the press gang in New York, see Gilje and Rock, eds., *Keepers of the Revolution*, 29. On African and African-American seafarers in the colonial era, see Bolster, *Black Jacks*, chaps. 1–2.

60. Mead, *Bent Sails*, 3.

61. Ibid. See also Steel, *Art of Sail-Making*, 19.

62. Horsley, *Tools of the Maritime Trades*, 159.

63. Kipping, *Elementary Treatise*, iii–iv.

64. Steel, *Art of Sail-Making*, 5; Brewington, "Sailmaker's Gear," 279–80; Horsley, *Tools of the Maritime Trades*, 170, 172.

65. Brewington, "Sailmaker's Gear," 282; Marino, *The Sailmaker's Apprentice*, 4.

66. Horsley, *Tools of the Maritime Trades*, 159, 175; Brewington, "Sailmaker's Gear," 291–92.

67. Horsley, *Tools of the Maritime Trades*, 175, 177.

68. Brewington, "Sailmaker's Gear," 283–85, 286.

69. Lambert Cadwalader to Thomas Fortune, August 25, 1770, Cadwalader Collection, HSP.

70. Salinger and Wetherell, "Wealth and Renting," 829.

71. Proprietary Tax, 1769, p. 190. Although the transcription says "Holloway," there was no one by the name of Israel Holloway listed in the *Pennsylvania Gazette* for the entire eighteenth century. Israel Hallowell, however, was a well-to-do carpenter and probably a relative of Thomas Hallowell, who appraised the estate of Thomas Fortune's sister. On Cannon, see 17th and 18th Penny Provincial Tax, 1774, 14.

72. *PA Gaz*, September 22, 1768; October 5, 1769; June 14, 1770; September 1, 1773; Rosswurm, *Arms, Country and Class*, 89, 102, 104, 107–8, 260–61; Philadelphia County Wills, Will Book S, 70, no. 21 (1782).

73. Purvis, *Remarks*, 4.

74. Gloucester, *Discourse*, 19. Gloucester apparently got the story from Thomas Clarkson's *History of the Abolition of the Slave-Trade*, vol. 1, p. 461.

75 Hornick, "Anthony Benezet," 155.

76. *Brief Sketch of the Schools for Black People*, 16.

77. Ibid., 7–8.

78. Hornick, "Anthony Benezet," 130.

79. Benezet, *Pennsylvania Spelling-Book*, 95–100, 115.

80. Hornick, "Anthony Benezet," 408–9. "Minutes of the Committee's appointed by the Three Monthly Meetings of Friends of Philadelphia to the Oversight and care of the School for Educating Africans and their descendants Commencing the 28th of the 5th Month 1770," Friends' Historical Library, Swarthmore.

81. Purvis, *Remarks*, 4; Gloucester, *Discourse*, 19.

82. *Marshal Diary*, in Cumming and Rankin, *The Fate of a Nation*, 32.

Chapter 2: In the Service of His Country

1. Bruns, "Benezet and the Negro," 104, 106–7; Nash, *Race and Revolution*, 11; Zilversmit, *The First Emancipation*, 94–97; Wood, "Liberty Is Sweet," 161, 162.

2. *Pennsylvania Journal*, September 13, 1775, in Clark, "The Sea Captains' Club," 49–50.

3. Jackson, *With the British*, 275; Tinkcom, "The Revolutionary City," 128, 134.

4. For one particular standoff between a black man and a white "gentlewoman" near Christ Church, see *Pennsylvania Evening Post*, December 14, 1775, in Wood, "Liberty Is Sweet," 170.

5. Purvis, *Remarks*, 11.

6. *NS*, March 10, 1848; also *Lib*, March 11, 1842.

7. Deborah Norris to Sally Wistar, January 27, 1777, in Nicholson, "Sober Frugality and Siren Luxury," 126.

8. Tinkcom, "The Revolutionary City," 129.

9. Tilley, *The British Navy*, 111–13; Jackson, *The Pennsylvania Navy*, 100; Tinkcom, "The Revolutionary City," 127.

10. Mishoff, "Business in Philadelphia," 165.

11. Ibid., 166.

12. Cumming and Rankin, *The Fate of a Nation*, 174.

13. Jackson, *With the British*, 16; Captain John Montresor, quoted by Mishoff, "Business in Philadelphia," 165.

14. Clark, "James Josiah," 458–59; Tilley, *The British Navy*, 113.

15. Tilley, *The British Navy*, 114–15; Clark, "James Josiah," 459–60.

16. James Forten to William Lloyd Garrison, February 23, 1831, BPL.

17. Tinkcom, "The Revolutionary City," 140.

18. Quarles, *The Negro in the American Revolution*, 135.

19. Mishoff, "Business in Philadelphia," 174–76.

20. Jackson, *With the British*, 20, 173; Brown, *The Good Americans*, 85.

21. Jackson, *With the British*, 89, 91–92; Mishoff, "Business in Philadelphia," 68–69.

22. Mishoff, "Business in Philadelphia," 147–49, 151, 176–77.

23. Cumming and Rankin, *The Fate of a Nation*, 208.

24. Tilley, *The British Navy*, 139–40; Brown, *The Good Americans*, 233–34.

25. Jackson, *With the British*, 261.

26. Ibid., 266–67.

27. Jackson, *The Pennsylvania Navy*, 13.

28. Library of Congress, *Naval Records*, 217 (*Active*), 254 (*Comet*), 325 (*Hannah and Sally*), 390 (*Mercury*), 409 (*Page*), 438 (*Retaliation*). He also bonded three vessels, the *Speedwell, George*, and *Industry*. Ibid., 317, 351, 460. See also Mathew Irwin and Robert Bridges to the Supreme Executive Council, August 25, 1778, and Bridges to Joseph Reed, May 7, 1777, Records of Pennsylvania's Revolutionary Governments, 1775–1790, PSA.

29. Tinkcom, "The Revolutionary City," 146–47. On the "Fort Wilson" riot, see Rosswurm, *Arms, Country and Class*, 205–27.

30. For the text of the law, see Bruns, ed., *Am I Not a Man and a Brother*, 446–50. On the various arguments for and against its passage, see Zilversmit, *The First Emancipation*, 124–37, and Nash, *Forging Freedom*, 60–64.

31. Forten may have had his doubts the following year when some legislators tried to undermine the abolition law. On the campaign against abolition and the black response to it, see Kaplan and Kaplan, *The Black Presence*, 30–31.

32. Jackson, *The Pennsylvania Navy*, 13, 416n.

33. Schroeder, "Stephen Decatur," 199–200; McManemin, *Captains of the Privateers*, 303–5; Clark, "That Mischievous *Holker*," 40–44, 46–47.

34. Library of Congress, *Naval Records*, 449; "List of Prizes taken by his Majestys Ships in North America under the Command of Rear Admiral Graves, between the 20 Aug. and 31 Octr. 1781," in Chadwick, ed., *Graves Papers*, 154–55.

35. McManemin, *Captains of the Privateers*, 305–6; Clark, "That Mischievous Holker," 44.

36. Purvis, *Remarks*, 4.

37. "Letters of Marque, 1778–82," 638.

38. The ditty bag might well be a proof of the sailmaker's skill, showing in its construction all the stitches and types of rope work he had mastered. See Marino, *The Sailmaker's Apprentice*, 2.

39. *National Era*, July 22, 1847.

40. McManemin, *Captains of the Privateers*, 306, 307.

41. Purvis, *Remarks*, 5; Gloucester, *Discourse*, 20.

42. Colledge, *Ships of the Royal Navy*, 21. Colledge confuses matters by stating that the *Active* was captured in 1780. However, the Graves correspondence and the Philadelphia newspapers report that she was taken in 1781.

43. *The Freeman's Journal*, August 22, 1781; *Pennsylvania Evening Post, and Public Advertiser*, August 24, 1781; *Pennsylvania Packet*, August 23, 1781; Chadwick, ed., *Graves Papers*, lxvii.

44. *Pennsylvania Packet*, August 28, 1781; *Pennsylvania Evening Post, and Public Advertiser*, August 24, 1781.

45. Purvis, *Remarks*, 5.

46. Larrabee, *Decision at the Chesapeake*, 177. On the various delays and the general confusion among British naval and military leaders over French plans, see ibid., 179. Hood did send a duplicate of the dispatch he had entrusted to Delanoe. Graves received it on August 28. Chadwick, ed., *Graves Papers*, lxvii.

47. James Forten to William Lloyd Garrison, February 23, 1831; BPL.

48. Purvis, *Remarks*, 5. Forten stated that three ships intercepted the *Royal Louis*— the *Amphion*, *La Nymphe*, and the *Pomona*. There was a Royal Navy vessel called the *Pomona*, a sixth-rate ship of the line. Colledge, *Ships of the Royal Navy*, 269. However, the logs of the *Amphion* and *La Nymphe* are quite explicit. There was no third vessel in the convoy. According to the *Pomona*'s log, in early October she was off the Turks and Caicos. *Pomona*, Master's Log, ADM 52/2459, PRO.

49. Biddle, ed., *Autobiography of Charles Biddle*, 152–53.

50. Colledge, *Ships of the Royal Navy*, 31, 246; introduction to *The Narrative of John Blatchford*, 104.

51. *Amphion*, Master's Log, October 1, 1781, ADM 52/2133, PRO.

52. *La Nymphe*, Captain's Log, October 8, 1781, ADM 51/638, PRO. According to the sea calendar at this period, the day began at noon, not midnight. It was at noon that the master and the captain took their sights, plotted their position, and began the day's entry in their respective logs. It was also at noon that the cycle of watches began. Thus, something that happened aboard ship at 2 p.m. on October 2 happened on October 1 by shore reckoning. To avoid confusion, I have used shore reckoning in the text, but in the notes I have kept the date of the entry as it appears in the log. On shipboard time-keeping, see Rodger, *The Wooden World*, 39.

53. *La Nymphe*, Master's Log, ADM 52/2427; *La Nymphe*, Captain's Log; *Amphion*, Master's Log, entries for October 8, 1781.

54. Crisp, ed., *Visitation of England and Wales*, vol. 16, p. 100; Syrett and DiNardo, eds., *Commissioned Sea Officers*, 26; introduction to *The Narrative of John Blatchford*, 105, 107–8; Miller, *Sea of Glory*, 302–3; James, *The British Navy in Adversity*, 287.

55. *La Nymphe*, Master's Log, October 8, 1781.

56. *Amphion*, Master's Log and Captain's Log (ADM 51/39, part 1), October 9, 1781. As master, Morris was responsible for matters of navigation. Bazely, as captain, determined how and when to give battle.

57. *Amphion*, Master's Log and Captain's Log, October 8–9, 1781.

58. Morris estimated there were 180 men on board the privateer, but Bazely's log and the official entry in the Graves Papers record 188. "List of Prizes," in Chadwick, ed., *Graves Papers*, 154–55.

59. *Amphion*, Captain's Log, October 9, 1781; Library of Congress, *Naval Records*, 395, 425; "List of Prizes," in Chadwick, ed., *Graves Papers*, 154–55; *La Nymphe*, Captain's Log, October 8–9, 1781.

60. *La Nymphe*, Master's Log, and *Amphion*, Captain's Log, October 9, 1781.

61. *Amphion*, Captain's Log and Master's Log, October 10, 1781.

62. Purvis, *Remarks*, 5.

63. Morrice, *The Young Midshipman's Instructor*, 1, 3–4, 6–7.

64. John Bazely, Jr., had enlisted in 1780 as a midshipman on the *Apollo*, a vessel commanded by his father, and when Captain Bazely was given command of the *Amphion*, he managed to have him transferred. Henry was at sea for the first time. As a "captain's servant" or "king's letter boy," he was training to be a midshipman. Muster of the *Amphion*, ADM 36/9561, PRO. On the role of the captain's servant, see Lavery, *The Arming and Fitting of English Ships of War*, 161; Proctor, "Michael Fitton," 206; and Rodger, *The Wooden World*, 27–28, 266–67.

65. Purvis, *Remarks*, 5, 6. Apparently Forten gave reformer Edward S. Abdy a slightly different version of events. Abdy, *Journal of a Residence and Tour*, vol. 3, p. 130.

66. Other vessels taken by the *Amphion* and *La Nymphe*, acting alone or in concert, included the ten-gun brig *Rambler*, out of Philadelphia "on a cruise"; the *Favorite*, a privateer out of New London; and the *Lively Buckskin*, a merchantman en route to Baltimore from Cap François in Saint Domingue. "List of Prizes," in Chadwick, ed., *Graves Papers*, 154–55; *La Nymphe*, Master's Log, October 12–13, 1781.

67. *Amphion*, Captain's Log, October 12, 1781. *La Nymphe* discharged her prisoners in New York on October 16. *La Nymphe*, Master's Log and Captain's Log, October 16, 1781. The *Royal Louis* attracted the attention of British naval authorities in New York. They thought her "remarkably well built" and a valuable addition to the Royal Navy. Admiral Thomas Digby to Philip Stephens, October 17, 1781; ADM 1/490, 34, PRO. I am grateful to researcher W. M. P. Dunne for this information. For a brief description of the *Royal Louis*, renamed the *Albacore*, see Colledge, *Ships of the Royal Navy*, 26.

68. *Amphion*, Captain's Log and Master's Log, October 14, 1781.

69. Ibid., October 15–16, 1781. The *Juno* was owned by a consortium headed by Blair McClenahan. Robert Bridges helped pay her bond. Library of Congress, *Naval Records*, 363; "List of Prizes," in Chadwick, ed., *Graves Papers*, 154–55.

70. *Amphion*, Master's Log, October 18–19, 1781.

71. Ibid., October 20–21, 1781.

72. *Amphion*, Captain's Log, October 23, 1781; *Amphion*, Master's Log, October 22–23, 1781.

73. Muster of the *Jersey*, September 1781–May 1782, ADM 36/9579, PRO. Forten was incorrectly listed as a member of the crew of the *Juno*. He was practically the last prisoner transferred from the *Amphion*. Evidently, Bazely kept him behind after the other men from the *Royal Louis* were handed over in the hope that he would change his mind and agree to go to England.

74. Gloucester, *Discourse*, 21–22; Purvis, *Remarks*, 6.

75. John Bazely, Jr., eventually became Vice Admiral of the Blue. Henry retired as a captain. Crisp, *Visitation of England and Wales*, vol. 16, p. 92, and vol. 17, p. 124; Syrett and DiNardo, eds., *Commissioned Sea Officers*, 26.

76. Purvis, *Remarks*, 6–7; Gloucester, *Discourse*, 22; Abdy, *Journal of a Residence and Tour*, vol. 3, p. 131. Forten's fears of being enslaved may have been baseless, for the *Jersey*'s muster indicates Bazely handed over all his prisoners, black and white.

77. Bowman, *Captive Americans*, 51–56. The Forton Prison was often called the Fortune or Forten Prison in captives' memoirs. Ibid., 63n, and Kaminkow and Kaminkow, comps., *Mariners of the American Revolution*, 215.

78. Colledge, *Ships of the Royal Navy*, 185; Lavery, *The Ship of the Line*, vol. 1, p. 171; Fox, *Adventures of Ebenezer Fox*, 96–97; Bowman, *Captive Americans*, 43.

79. Dandridge, *American Prisoners*, 237; Bowman, *Captive Americans*, 43.

80. Fox, *Adventures of Ebenezer Fox*, 99; Dring, *Recollections*, 13; Bowman, *Captive Americans*, 97.

81. Dring, *Recollections*, 24; Dandridge, *American Prisoners*, 259.

82. Dring, *Recollections*, 27, 39, 42.

83. Fox, *Adventures of Ebenezer Fox*, 101.

84. Ibid., 101, 193; Bowman, *Captive Americans*, 18, 46–47; "The Destructive Operation of Foul Air, Tainted Provisions, Bad Water, and Personal Filthiness upon Human Constitutions," in the Appendix to the *Narrative of John Blatchford*, 117–21.

85. Dandridge, *American Prisoners*, 341; Fox, *Adventures of Ebenezer Fox*, 106; Dring, *Recollections*, 31–35.

86. Dring, *Recollections*, 45–47, 72–73; Bowman, *Captive Americans*, 47.

87. Dring, *Recollections*, 25, 37; Fox, *Adventures of Ebenezer Fox*, 109–10.

88. During Forten's incarceration, the *Jersey*'s commanding officer was Lieutenant Sporne. Banks, *David Sproat*, 49.

89. Dring, *Recollections*, 129, 145; Fox, *Adventures of Ebenezer Fox*, 134–35, 142, 144, 147–49.

90. Bowman, *American Captives*, 20, 48–49.

91. Purvis, *Remarks*, 7–8.

92. Estimates of the number of captives on board the *Jersey* at the time of Forten's imprisonment range from 500 to 1200. British War Office records list a total of 8000 persons as having been held on the *Jersey* during the war. American sources, many of them admittedly highly polemical, put the total much higher. Banks, *David Sproat*, 19; Dandridge, *American Prisoners*, 247; Bowman, *Captive Americans*, 60.

93. Bowman, *Captive Americans*, 44; Dring, *Recollections*, 51–54.

94. Bowman, *Captive Americans*, 20, 48–49.

95. Fox, *Adventures of Ebenezer Fox*, 111. On estimates of the number of deaths, see Dandridge, *American Prisoners*, 252; Dring, *Recollections*, 104.

96. Dandridge, *American Prisoners*, 238–39.

97. Bowman, *Captive Americans*, 5, 113–14. On the legal status of prisoners, see Knight, "Prisoner Exchange and Parole," 201–22.

98. Introduction to Dring, *Recollections*, vi.

99. Fox, *Adventures of Ebenezer Fox*, 133; Banks, *David Sproat*, 6, 8.

100. David Sproat to Major MacKenzie, May 10, 1783, in Banks, *David Sproat*, 102. Introduction to Dring, *Recollections*, viii.

101. *PA Gaz*, October 24, 1781; Purvis, *Remarks*, 7.

102. Purvis, *Remarks*, 8.

103. Abdy, *Journal of a Residence and Tour*, vol. 3, p. 132; *NS*, March 10, 1848.

104. Dring, *Recollections*, 43.

105. Purvis, *Remarks*, 11.

106. Forten, *Letters from a Man of Colour*, 7.

Chapter 3: Mr. Bridges's Apprentice

1. A search of the available records has failed to reveal much about William Dunbar's background. In 1780 one Dunbar, a mariner, was living in Walnut Ward. He owned property valued at £1200 and paid an assessment of £4 4s. The individual's first name is not listed, and there is no indication as to his race. "Effective Supply Tax, City of Philadelphia, 1780," 202.

2. St. Paul's Church, Philadelphia, Baptisms, 1782–1828; Marriages, 1759–1829; Burials, 1790–1852, p. 292, HSP.

3. Purvis, *Remarks*, 8.

4. On Truxtun and the *Commerce* during the Revolution, see McManemin, *Captains of the Privateers*, 353. The *Commerce* had been built in Philadelphia in 1782. *Lloyd's Register . . . 1784*.

5. Lloyd's of London described the *Commerce* as a "constant trader" and rated her A1, the highest designation in terms of seaworthiness. *Lloyd's Register . . . 1784*. It is worth noting that Truxtun was a slave owner. During the Revolutionary War he used some of his prize money to purchase Hannah Cole as a domestic. However, he eventually turned against the institution of slavery. In 1795, expressing his regret "that any man can make use of the term [Slave], in these United States," he set about freeing Hannah and her daughter. Truxtun to Thomas Harrison, September 18, 1795, Loose Corr., PAS MSS, HSP.

6. On Truxtun's early career, see Ferguson, *Truxtun of the Constellation*, 1–50.

7. Truxtun, *Remarks, Instructions, and Examples*, xvii–xviii.

8. *Pennsylvania Packet*, April 22, 1784.

9. Crane, ed., *Drinker Diary*, vol. 1, pp. 421–22, entry for April 24, 1784.

10. Albion, *Square-Riggers on Schedule*, 7–9. I thank Professor W. Jeffrey Bolster of the University of New Hampshire for his perspective on possible routes.

11. Albion, *Square-Riggers on Schedule*, 9.

12. The *Commerce* reached Dover on May 26 or 27, and Gravesend on May 28. Given her relatively deep draft—fourteen feet when fully laden—she may have anchored at Tilbury, rather than in the Pool of London. *New Lloyd's List*, May 28 and June 1, 1784.

13. Marshall, *Dr. Johnson's London*, 54–57.

14. The *Commerce* sailed from Gravesend on July 6, and was forced to ride at anchor off the Downs until the wind changed. (It was common for ships trying to enter

the English Channel to wait in the shelter of the Downs for a favorable wind.) She eventually sailed from Deal on July 12, arriving in Philadelphia on September 15. *New Lloyd's List*, July 9 and 16, 1784. *London Chronicle*, July 13–15, 1784; *Pennsylvania Packet*, September 16, 1784; Williamson, *The English Channel*, 30–31.

15. Banbury, *Shipbuilders of the Thames and Medway*, 18, 22, 111–14, 116, 123, 133, 135, 142, 144, 148.

16. Davis, *The Rise of the English Shipping Industry*, esp. 62–64, 66–68, 70–71, 78.

17. Marshall, *Dr. Johnson's London*, 220–46.

18. Ibid., 33–34.

19. Dabydeen, *Hogarth's Blacks*, 39.

20. On the social and legal implications of the Sommersett case, see Bauer, "Law, Slavery, and Sommersett's Case," 121–69; Shyllon, *Black People in Britain*, 24–25; Walvin, *Black and White*, 47–48; Linebaugh, *The London Hanged*, 134–37.

21. Walvin, *Black and White*, 52, 61; Edwards and Walvin, *Black Personalities*, 20–21; Scobie, *Black Britannia*, 13, 23, 24; Dabydeen, *Hogarth's Blacks*, 12–39; Linebaugh, *The London Hanged*, 341, 349, 351, 353. On the annoyance of one high-class Londoner at the presence of "Men of colour in the rank of gentlemen . . . and tawny children playing in the squares," see Edwards, "Black Personalities in Georgian England," 41. For a survey of black society in England's capital at the time of Forten's sojourn, see Gerzina, *Black London*.

22. *The Orthodox Churchman's Magazine* (1802), in Shyllon, *Black Britannia*, 29.

23. Quoted in Edwards and Walvin, *Black Personalities*, 45.

24. Quoted in Walvin, *Black and White*, 48.

25. Brown and Senior, *Victorious in Defeat*, 173.

26. Quoted in Edwards and Walvin, *Black Personalities*, 25.

27. Walvin, *Black and White*, 58. On the plight of the black Loyalists in Britain, see Hodges, ed., *Black Loyalist Directory*, xxviii.

28. Hodges, ed., *Black Loyalist Directory*, 227–38; Norton, "The Fate of Some Black Loyalists," 405.

29. Brown, *The Good Americans*, 188.

30. Brown, "Negroes and the American Revolution," 561.

31. Norton, "The Fate of Some Black Loyalists," 404.

32. Ibid., 418, 422.

33. Ibid., 407.

34. Ibid., 410; on the early trials and tribulations of the colony, see 408–16, 418–26.

35. Brown and Senior, *Victorious in Defeat*, 173–74. On Sierra Leone and the black Loyalists, see Hodges, ed., *Black Loyalist Directory*, xxix–xxxix, 227–62.

36. Purvis, *Remarks*, 9.

37. Hornick, "Anthony Benezet," 430–31, 435.

38. Walvin, *England, Slaves and Freedom*, 97.

39. Ibid., 99–100.

40. Fowler, *Jack Tars and Commodores*, 8.

41. On Margaret Dunbar's approximate date of birth, see (Old Swedes) Gloria Dei—Marriages, 1795–1816, p. 2133, HSP. On Nicholas's date of birth, see Seamen's Protection Certificates for the Port of Philadelphia (1810), Nat Arch.

42. Crane, ed., *Drinker Diary*, vol. 1, p. 422, entries for May 4–5, 1784.

43. Purvis, *Remarks*, 9. Forten began his apprenticeship rather later than most craftsmen. Stephen Allen, a white youth a couple of years younger than Forten, became an apprentice in a New York sail loft when he was twelve. Gilje and Rock, eds., *Keepers of the Revolution*, 27.

44. Christ Church, Baptisms, 1769–94, pp. 719, 775, 814, 924, 963, 1105, 1157, 1258, HSP. Three more children had died in infancy. Christ Church, Burials, 1709–85, pp. 3188, 3192, 3360.

45. "Warranties of Land in the County of Northumberland," 64, 70. On the scope of Bridges's business activities and his understanding of the economy, see Brown, "A Philadelphia Merchant," 400, and Schultz, ed., "Small Producer Thought," 124–32.

46. In fact, although he was listed in the directories and tax lists as a sailmaker until his death, he had already begun to style himself "Robert Bridges, merchant" as early as 1779. Philadelphia County Deeds, D, Book 13, pp. 111, 113; Book 36, p. 252, PCA.

47. Purvis, *Remarks*, 9. See also Gloucester, *Discourse*, 22–23.

48. Purvis, *Remarks*, 9.

49. Marino, *The Sailmaker's Apprentice*, 467; Bezanson et al., *Prices and Inflation*, 290, 292, 295. On colonial efforts to produce high-quality sailcloth, see Crosby, *America, Russia, Hemp*, 22, and Hall, "Sailcloth for American Vessels," 130–35. On Bridges as a tentmaker, see Jonathan Ladd Howell to Charles Biddle, July 29, 1776, Records of Pennsylvania's Revolutionary Governments, 1775–90, PSA.

50. Crosby, *America, Russia, Hemp*, 20–21, 23–24, 30.

51. Kipping, *Elementary Treatise*, 39.

52. Most of the books on sail-making produced during Forten's lifetime and in the two decades after his death were highly derivative. The basic source was David Steel's *The Elements and Practice of Rigging and Seamanship* (London, 1794). The two-volume work was eventually broken down into a number of smaller volumes and the section on sail-making published separately as *The Art of Sail-Making* (London, 1809). It sold well on both sides of the Atlantic and went into numerous editions. The anonymous author of *The Elements and Practice of Rigging* (London, 1821) just reprinted Steel's 1809 work, with the addition of new tables for gores, lengths of boltrope, and the like calculated "according to the present practice in his Majesty's dock-yards, and in the merchant-service." (ibid., iv). When United States Navy Sailmaker Ware Branson, Jr., wrote his *Art of Sailmaking* around 1858, he turned immediately to Steel, incorporating the bulk of Steel's work into his own, adding patterns for one or two newer types of sails and a few words about sail-making for steam vessels. Branson, *Art of Sailmaking*.

53. It was customary for a vessel's sails to be made and replaced in her home port. Her owner or his agents could alert the sailmaker, have the canvas ready, and tell him what new sails would be needed. Hall, "Sailmaking in Connecticut," 80.

54. Marino points out in *The Sailmaker's Apprentice* (215) that it did not work to measure an old sail that needed replacing. If it had been in use long enough to need replacing, it had stretched.

55. It was thought advisable to take diagonal measurements because a sail could well be pulled out of "true" when bent to the yard. Thus, a sailmaker who simply took the length and the breadth of a sail risked making a new sail that bore little resemblance to the old one. As Ware Branson observed in his *Art of Sailmaking* (76): "Many ridiculous mistakes are made by persons who imagine that they have all the necessary

dimensions in the four sides, never thinking that it may be put out of shape by increasing or decreasing the distances of the opposite corners." See also Marino, *Sailmaker's Apprentice*, 132.

56. Horsley, *Tools of the Maritime Trades*, 162.

57. Steel, *Art of Sail-Making*, 18, 19.

58. Brewington, "Sailmaker's Gear," 291. The cutting out of a sail was a complicated task. New York sailmaker Stephen Allen noted that "it is therefore the last business taught an apprentice." See Gilje and Rock, eds., *Keepers of the Revolution*, 31.

59. Brewington, "Sailmaker's Gear," 294.

60. Hall, "Sailmaking in Connecticut," 34, 87.

61. Kipping, *Elementary Treatise*, 135.

62. Ibid., and Horsley, *Tools of the Maritime Trades*, 164.

63. Kipping, *Elementary Treatise*, 41.

64. Ibid., 156–57.

65. Marino, *The Sailmaker's Apprentice*, 12; Horsley, *Tools of the Maritime Trades*, 164.

66. Kipping, *Elementary Treatise*, 113.

67. Horsley, *Tools of the Maritime Trades*, 164.

68. Kipping, *Elementary Treatise*, 46.

69. Ibid., 67, 70. Hall, "Sailmaking in Connecticut," 8.

70. Horsley, *Tools of the Maritime Trades*, 181.

71. Kipping, *Elementary Treatise*, 77.

72. Steel, *Art of Sail-Making*, 136; Kipping, *Elementary Treatise*, 77–78.

73. Kipping, *Elementary Treatise*, 90.

74. MacGregor, *Merchant Sailing Ships, 1775–1815*, 7.

75. Cowan, *Essay on the Construction of Sails*, 3, 6.

76. Cooper, ed., *Personal Recollections*, 9; Child, *The Freedmen's Book*, 103.

77. Kipping, *Elementary Treatise*, 165.

78. There is no mention of James Forten, Robert Bridges, or Willing and Francis in any of the following: *Letter from the Secretary of State, Accompanied With a List of the Names of Persons to Whom Patents Have Been Issued; A List of Patents Granted by the United States from 1790 to 1820*, and *Early Unnumbered U.S. Patents, 1790–1836*.

79. Philadelphia County Deeds, T.H. Book 179, pp. 244, 248.

80. County Tax Duplicates, 1793: Southwark West, 289, 1794: 169; Tax of 1798 (microfilm); County Tax Assessment Ledger, Southwark West, 1799: 7, 1801: 48, 1802: 46, 1803: 48; City Tax Duplicates, 1795: 292, 1798: 299, 1800: 107, PCA. The property was subject to a ground rent, but Forten eventually extinguished it.

81. "A List of the Taxable Inhabitants residing within the County of Philadelphia, taken agreeably to an Act of the General Assembly, intitled 'An Act to provide for the enumeration of the taxable inhabitants, and Slaves, within this Commonwealth,' passed the 7th day of March 1800," County Records, film 2937, PSA; Davies, *Some Account of the City of Philadelphia*, 17.

82. Klepp and Smith, "Marriage and Death: The Records of Gloria Dei Church," 184.

83. In New London, sailmaker John Kingsbury Pimer (1807–84) was a renter for the whole of his career. Accession Notes and Catalogue Description, Pimer Papers, Blunt–White Library. There is little information on the renting of lofts in Philadelphia in Forten's time. (See *PA Gaz*, October 25, 1764.) It is not clear what the standard

practice was. Possibly some sailmakers rented their lofts while others bought them outright.

84. Gloucester, *Discourse*, 23.

85. *NASS*, March 10, 1842. Like other artisans, Forten needed to borrow to pay wages and purchase supplies while he waited for payment from his customers. His initial difficulties securing credit may have had less to do with his race and lack of family connections than with the relatively inflexible nature of the banking system in Philadelphia by the late 1790s. See Wright, "Artisans, Banks, Credit," 218–19, 233, 234.

86. Gloucester, *Discourse*, 23.

87. *North American*, March 5, 1842.

88. Thomas Willing's autobiographical writings cited by Slaski, "Thomas Willing," 252. On Willing's career, see ibid., 235–52, and Wright, "Thomas Willing," 525–60.

89. Christ Church, Burials, 1785–1900, p. 3577; *Poulson*, January 20, 1800; *True American Commercial Advertiser*, January 21, 1800; Philadelphia County Wills, Will Book Y, 281, no. 24 (1800).

Chapter 4: "A Gentleman of the Pave"

1. Stevenson, ed., *Journals of Charlotte Forten Grimké*, 298 (entry for April 4, 1858).

2. Notation on reverse of James Forten to Samuel Breck, July 22, 1828, Breck Papers, HSP.

3. James Forten to Paul Cuffe, February 15, 1815, Cuffe Papers, NBFPL.

4. Clement, *Welfare and the Poor*, 36; Singleton, *Letters from the South and West*, 6; Baker, *Review of the Relative Commercial Progress*, 70.

5. Quoted in Gilje and Rock, eds., *Keepers of the Revolution*, 127.

6. Adams, "Wage Rates in Philadelphia," 23.

7. Dillwyn Letters, I, quoted in Rasmussen, "Capital on the Delaware," 41.

8. Adams, "Wage Rates in Philadelphia," 25–26.

9. Hutchins, *American Maritime Industries*, 175–76; Adams, "Wage Rates in Philadelphia," 50–51.

10. Salvucci, "Philadelphia and Havana," 44–46, 49.

11. Goldstein, *Philadelphia and the China Trade*, 34, 54, 62.

12. Rasmussen, "Capital on the Delaware," 186–87.

13. Oliver, "Travel by Water," 293–95; see also 302–3.

14. Adams, "Wage Rates in Philadelphia," 27.

15. *Diary of William Dunlap*, 370.

16. *The Monthly Repository of Theology and General Literature* 2, no. 18 (June 1807): 338.

17. Ritter, *Philadelphia and Her Merchants*, 145.

18. Crosby, *America, Russia, Hemp*, 125–26, 210.

19. Adams, "Wage Rates in Philadelphia," 194, 208.

20. Hickey, *The War of 1812*, 227.

21. Quoted in ibid., 228.

22. Schultz, *Republic of Labor*, 196, 197; Blackson, "Pennsylvania Banks," 339; Hickey, *The War of 1812*, 224–25.

23. James Forten to Paul Cuffe, January 5, 1815, Cuffe Papers. Cuffe employed Forten as an intermediary to help his business partner. He sent Forten a draft on a

New York house in the amount of $50 and instructed him: "[S]hould thee think it . . . advisable to hand this money to John or family without letting them Know what hand it comes . . . from do so." Cuffe to Forten, January 29, 1815, Cuffe MSS, ODHSL. John James's business recovered briefly, but he was declared bankrupt in 1819. Moak, comp., *Insolvency Petitions*, 60.

24. Clement, "The Philadelphia Welfare Crisis," 150, 151.

25. Mintz, *Moralists and Modernizers*, 82.

26. Adams, "Wage Rates in Philadelphia," 194.

27. *Niles' Register*, January 16, 1830.

28. Hutchins, *American Maritime Industries*, 183; Schulz, *Republic of Labor*, 196; Adams, "Wage Rates in Philadelphia," 33.

29. *Niles' Register*, March 24, 1827, and June 21, 1828.

30. Tooker, *Nathan Trotter*, 83–84.

31. Albion, "New York Port," 71–74, 76.

32. Geffen, "Violence in Philadelphia," 395; Wilson, *Stephen Girard*, 317–8.

33. *ASR*, December 1835.

34. *NS*, March 10, 1848.

35. Sarah Forten to Angelina Grimké, April 15, 1837, in Barnes and Dumond, eds., *Weld and Grimké Letters*, vol. 1, p. 381.

36. Charters of Incorporation, Book 4, p. 186, PSA.

37. Ritter, *Philadelphia and Her Merchants*, 22.

38. Ibid., 23.

39. *NASS*, March 10, 1842.

40. Purvis, *Remarks*, 11. Although Purvis supplies months and years for four of the rescues, a search of Philadelphia newspapers has not revealed anything about the circumstances.

41. Abdy, *Journal of a Residence and Tour*, vol. 3, pp. 131–32.

42. On the particular dangers faced by black sailors, see Bolster, *Black Jacks*, 149, 184, 185, 200–201, 202.

43. James Forten to Paul Cuffe, March 4, 1817, Cuffe Papers.

44. William Wright to James Fortune, October 12, 1822, Loose Corr., Incoming, 1820–49, PAS MSS; Philadelphia Crew Lists, 1822, p. 24. Wright's protection indicates that he was born in Philadelphia in 1787 and was literate. Seaman's Protection Certificates, Port of Philadelphia (1808), Nat Arch. Gaul's intentions with regard to Wright are unclear, but he was short of funds. Less than a year after this episode he filed for bankruptcy. Moak, comp., *Insolvency Petitions*, 44.

45. Wainwright, "Diary of Samuel Breck, 1814–1822," 505.

46. St. Paul's Church, Philadelphia. Baptisms, 1782–1828; Marriages, 1759–1829; Burials, 1790–1852, p. 303, HSP. The younger Anthony spent some time at sea. Seamen's Protection Certificates, Port of Philadelphia (1808), Nat Arch.

47. *Elevator*, July 25, 1875.

48. *PAppeal*, October 1, 1870.

49. Ibid., August 8, 1874.

50. *Elevator*, January 24, 1868, and August 8, 1874.

51. PAS, *Register of the Trades of the Colored People*. Philadelphia Crew Lists, 1841, p. 45.

52. PAS census, 1838, PAS MSS.

53. State Tax Assessment Ledger, New Market Ward, 1842: 107, 1843: 110, PCA.

54. On the efforts of master craftsmen elsewhere in the North to curb drinking among their workers during this period, see Johnson, *A Shopkeeper's Millennium*, 55–61.

55. Moak, comp., *Guardians of the Poor*, 21, 23. On Jones's subsequent career, see Abajian, comp., *Blacks in Selected Newspapers, Censuses, and Other Sources*, vol. 2, p. 391.

56. King, "Sailmakers and Ship Chandlers," 226. See also the papers of New London sailmaker John Kingsbury Pimer at Mystic Seaport's Blunt–White Library.

57. Purvis, *Remarks*, 10.

58. *New York Tribune* in *Lib*, May 13, 1864.

59. Philadelphia directory, 1819; Philadelphia Board of Health Records; Ritter, *Philadelphia and Her Merchants*, 198.

60. Ship Disbursements, 1797–1800, 1801–7, 1808–15, 1819–23, Stephen Girard Papers (microfilm), APS.

61. Ruschenberger, *Sketch of the Life of Dr. Robert Bridges*, 4.

62. Ship Registers of the Port of Philadelphia, Pa., 83, 139, Blunt–White Library; *True American Commercial Advertiser*, December 22, 1808.

63. Christ Church: Marriages, 1800–1900, p. 4726; Ship Registers of the Port of Philadelphia, 76; Vessel Registers, 1803–4, Independence Seaport Museum, Philadelphia.

64. Ritter, *Philadelphia and Her Merchants*, 49–51.

65. Fowler, *Jack Tars and Commodores*, 186; Ritter, *Philadelphia and Her Merchants*, 195.

66. "Charles Ware, Sailmaker," 267.

67. Tappan, *Life of Arthur Tappan*, 161.

68. "Charles Ware, Sailmaker," 267.

69. Ship *Tontine* bills, Barry–Hayes Papers, Box 10, Independence Seaport Museum. The *Tontine* cleared Philadelphia for Nice on March 6, 1822. Philadelphia Crew Lists, 1822, pp. 44–45.

70. Brig *Emma* bills, Barry–Hayes Papers, Box 8.

71. Ibid.

72. Ibid.

73. Ibid.

74. Ibid.

75. Hutchins, *American Maritime Industries*, 210–11.

76. MacGregor, *Merchant Sailing Ships, 1815–1850*, 141–42.

77. *NASS*, March 10, 1842.

78. "Poulson's Scrapbook of Philadelphia History," vol. 4, p. 16, LCP.

79. Abdy, *Journal of a Residence and Tour*, vol. 3, p. 132.

80. Crosby, *America, Russia, Hemp*, 24.

81. For an overview of the problems involved in getting a reliable supply of sail duck, see Hall, "Sailcloth for American Vessels," 130–45.

82. Garitee, *The Republic's Private Navy*, 119.

83. Ibid., 118–19.

84. Baughman, *The Mallorys of Mystic*, 16.

85. *Relf's Gazette*, February 11, 1822.

86. *Niles' Register*, December 15, 1823, and May 8, 1824.

87. Ibid., February 4, 1826.

88. Hutchins, *American Maritime Industries*, 124; Crosby, *America, Russia, Hemp*, 26n.

89. *GUE* 12 (May 1831): 6; Philadelphia Female Anti-Slavery Society, Minute Book, 1839–44, HSP. On the commitment to Free Produce, see also Brown, "Cradle of Feminism," 146–47.

90. Tooker, *Nathan Trotter*, 4.

91. Purvis, *Remarks*, 17. See also Gloucester, *Discourse*, 25.

92. On other African-American moneylenders and "note-shavers," see Walker, *History of Black Business*, 88.

93. St. Thomas's African Episcopal Church, Philadelphia, Vestry Minutes, 1813–21; I thank the minister, vestry, and members of St. Thomas's Church for giving me access to this source. Philadelphia County Wills, Will Book 6, p. 560, no. 23 (1818), PCA.

94. Philadelphia County Wills, Will Book 3, p. 20, no. 107 (1809); *True American Commercial Advertiser*, October 3, 1809; Philadelphia directories, 1805 and 1806. Maris lived at 263 South Front and Bridges at 261. The 1805 directory lists a firm of merchants, Sloan and Bridges, at 198 South Water.

95. Wainwright, ed., "Diary of Samuel Breck, 1827–1833," 243.

96. James Forten to Samuel Breck, July 22, 1828, Breck Papers, HSP. On Marckley's service in the Pennsylvania Senate, see Philadelphia directory, 1820. It is unlikely Breck attended very quickly to the matter of the loan. On July 25 his only child died of typhus.

97. *James Forten and Charlotte His Wife v. Henry Powers*, Common Pleas: Appearance Docket, March to December, 1810, p. 175, PCA.

98. Martin, *Martin's Bench and Bar*, 301, 308. Richard Peters, Sr. (1744–1828), was the nephew of Anglican cleric Rev. Richard Peters. The younger Peters was born in 1779 and died in 1848. For an indication of the prominence of Richard Peters, Jr., in antislavery circles, see Thomas Clarkson to Roberts Vaux, January 31, 1820, Vaux Papers, HSP. There was a double link between the Peters and Willing families. A sister of Richard Peters, Jr., was married to one of Thomas Willing's sons.

99. *James Forten v. Jacob Vanderslice*, District Court: Appearance Docket, March to September 1812, p. 427; March 1814 to September 1814, p. 357; Execution Docket, June 1814; December 1814; September 1816, unpaginated; Philadelphia directories, 1810–11; Philadelphia Board of Health Records.

100. *James Forten v. Jonathan Jenks*, District Court: Appearance Docket, March to September, 1814, p. 376; Execution Docket, September 1818, unpaginated; Philadelphia directories, 1805, 1813, 1817–18.

101. Philadelphia County Deeds, I.C. Book 32, p. 455; Sheriff's Deeds, Book D, 177. Duffield left Philadelphia for Washington, D.C., where he died in 1821 at age forty. *Relf's Gazette*, November 24, 1821. Emily and Robert Murdock died within weeks of one another in 1817. *Poulson*, November 12 and December 18, 1817.

102. *James Forten v. Miles H. Hughes*, District Court: Appearance Docket, September 1814 to September 1815, 637; Philadelphia directory, 1818.

103. *James Forten v. George L. Seckel*, District Court: Execution Docket, September 1816, unpaginated; Philadelphia directory, 1817. Seckel's business affairs went from bad to worse. He was insolvent by the fall of 1820. Moak, comp., *Insolvency Petitions*, 97.

104. *James Forten v. Francis Hearis, Chester Barley, Paul S. Brown, William Tabele*, District Court: Appearance Docket, December 1819 to March 1820, p. 545.

105. *James Forten v. John R. Mullin*, District Court: Appearance Docket, December 1819 to March 1820, p. 545; Philadelphia directories, 1816 and 1818.

106. *James Forten v. Henry Witmer*, District Court: Appearance Docket, March 1820 to March 1821, p. 336; Philadelphia directory, 1821. Witmer was either unlucky or improvident. He was declared insolvent in 1829. Moak, comp., *Insolvency Petitions*, 59.

107. *James Forten v. Edward Tilghman*, District Court: Appearance Docket, March 1820 to March 1821, p. 626; Execution Docket, September 1821, unpaginated; Philadelphia directories, 1816, 1820. Moak, comp., *Insolvency Petitions*, 109.

108. *James Forten v. Thomas Ellis*, District Court: Appearance Docket, March to September 1821, p. 136; Philadelphia directory, 1820. This was the same property Forten had sold some years before to Joseph Kenton. Kenton had sold it to Ellis, subject to the payment of a ground rent to Forten. Now Forten regained possession of the property. Philadelphia County Deeds R.L.L. Book 19, p. 236.

109. *James Forten v. Thomas Hope and William McPherson*, Common Pleas: Appearance Docket, September 1820 to June 1822, p. 153; Philadelphia directory, 1819.

110. *James Forten v. J. and H. Brady*, Common Pleas: Appearance Docket, September 1822 to March 1824, p. 335; Philadelphia directory, 1825.

111. Ship Registers of the Port of Philadelphia, 11, 80–81, 178, 186.

112. *James Forten v. Joseph Beylle, Joseph Severlinge and Andrew Curcier*, District Court: Appearance Docket, December 1825 to March 1826, p. 211; Philadelphia directories, 1817, 1825. On Beylle's business activities, see *Relf's Gazette*, February 11, 1822. Philadelphia County Wills, Will Book 10, p. 446, no. 170 (1832).

113. *James Forten v. Thomas Reily*, District Court: Appearance Docket, June to September 1824, p. 47; Philadelphia directory, 1823.

114. *James Forten v. William R. Boyer*, District Court: Appearance Docket, June to December 1826, p. 293; Philadelphia directory, 1825.

115. *James Forten v. Joseph Head*, District Court: Appearance Docket, June to September 1826, p. 77; Wainwright, ed., "Diary of Samuel Breck, 1827–1833," 227.

116. *James Forten v. Andrew Hodge and William L. Hodge*, December Term 1823; Pennsylvania Supreme Court, Appearance Docket, December Term 1817–December Term 1823, p. 477, PSA. On Andrew Hodge, see Ritter, *Philadelphia and Her Merchants*, 84.

117. *Anna Diamond Excrs. &c to the Estate of John Diamond deceased v. James Forten*, Common Pleas: Appearance Docket, March 1832 to December 1833, p. 130; Philadelphia directory, 1825, 1829.

118. See also *James Forten v. Francis H. Nicolle & Edward Thompson*, District Court: Appearance Docket, December 1825 to March 1826, p. 301; *James Forten v. John Hughes who suro. William Sammers*, District Court: Appearance Docket, December 1824 to March 1825, p. 200. Thompson and Hughes both eventually declared bankruptcy. Moak, comp., *Insolvency Petitions*, 58, 108.

119. *James Forten v. Elias Wolohon*, Common Pleas: Execution Docket, March 1831 to September 1835, p. 160.

120. Philadelphia County Deeds, I.C. Book 18, p. 418. On the steps that went into building a home, see Rilling, "Building Philadelphia," chap. 1.

121. Philadelphia County Deeds, I.C. Book 15, p. 397; Mortgages E.F. Book 10, p. 532. Eventually a small piece of land at the tail end of Forten's property came on the market and he bought that. Philadelphia County Deeds, I.C. Book 15, p. 395.

122. Philadelphia County Deeds, I.C. Book 15, p. 393.

123. Rilling, "Building Philadelphia," 34.

124. Philadelphia County Deeds, I.C. Book 19, p. 62.

125. Ibid., I.C. Book 19, pp. 491, 486, 500, and R.L.L. Book 18, p. 92.

126. Ibid., Book 26, p. 192.

127. Ibid., 196.

128. Ibid., I.W. Book 7, p. 70.

129. There is no record of this deed. However, a summary of it is included in Philadelphia County Deeds, Book A2, p. 526. The sellers were James and Elizabeth Williams and the sale took place on December 12, 1816.

130. Philadelphia County Deeds, T.H. Book 179, p. 244. It was a sensible move on Forten's part to seek confirmation of his rights at this time. Cornelia Bridges Patton, Harriet Bridges Davy, Robert Bridges, Jr., and Edward Bridges had all died intestate. The claims of Cornelia and Harriet had passed to their children. As for Emily Bridges Murdock, she and her husband had signed over their real estate interests to John Duffield. On the complex nature of the Bridges estate, see Sheriff's Deeds, Book B, 64; PCA.

131. Sheriff's Deeds, Book C, 122; Philadelphia County Deeds, I.H. Book 4, p. 408; A.M. Book 22, p. 413.

132. Philadelphia County Deeds, M.R. Book 19, p. 655. One of the witnesses to the deed was James Forten's eleven-year-old daughter, Margaretta. Apparently she was already being given some insight into her father's affairs.

133. Philadelphia County Deeds, G.W.R. Book 4, p. 49.

134. Ibid., Book 37, p. 182.

135. Philadelphia County Mortgages, G.W.R. Book 8, p. 533; Book 11, pp. 153–55; Book 12, p. 624; Book 15, pp. 718–19, PCA. Philadelphia County Deeds, A.M. Book 46, p. 86. Mary certainly needed the money. With the deaths of her siblings, she found herself raising various orphaned nieces and nephews. U.S. Census, 1820: Philadelphia, New Market, 257, 1830: 202. When she died in 1841, she was worth only $500. Administration file no. 342, Book P, 185. Christ Church, Burials, 1785–1900, p. 3840.

136. Philadelphia County Deeds, A.M. Book 45, p. 242.

137. Ibid., G.W.R. Book 4, p. 49; Book 5, p. 643; Mortgages G.W.R. Book 12, p. 625. On the relationship between mortgager and mortgagee, see Rilling, "Building Philadelphia," 54.

138. Philadelphia County Deeds, A.M. Book 22, p. 407.

139. County Tax Assessment Ledger, Southwark West, 1810: 103, and County Tax Duplicates, 1810: 351, 1814: 347. U.S. Census, 1810, Southwark, 116; Philadelphia directory, 1814.

140. County Tax Duplicates, Southwark West, 1816: 217, 1817: 190, 1819: 114; Philadelphia directory, 1816–19. Interestingly, Erwin is listed as white in the city directories and as black in the 1820 census. U.S. Census, 1820: Southwark, 70. For the tenants at the time of Forten's death, see Philadelphia County Wills, Will Book 15, p. 445, no. 87 (1842).

141. Philadelphia directory, 1831.

142. U.S. Census, 1820: Southwark, 104; County Tax Duplicates, Southwark West, 1817: 173, 1818: 156, 1819: 99–100, 1822: 104; Philadelphia directory, 1817, 1822. The Yorks were longtime residents of Southwark. They were living there when the 1790 census was taken.

143. County Tax Duplicates, Cedar, 1814, p. 91; Philadelphia directory, 1814. Washington Court ran north from 205 Lombard.

144. Samuel Porter was not an uncommon name. Forten's tenant may have been the same man who was listed as heading a household of five people of color in Moyamensing in 1820. County Tax Duplicates, Cedar, 1817, p. 187. U.S. Census, Moyamensing, 1820: 166, Locust, 1820: 59; Philadelphia directories, 1814, 1817. Cordwainer's Alley ran from Seventh to Eighth between Pine and Lombard.

145. County Tax Assessment Ledger, New Market, 1809: 64, 1810: 60; County Tax Duplicate, New Market, 1810: 269.

146. Although it pertains to New York rather than Philadelphia, the discussion of landlord–tenant relationships in Blackmar's *Manhattan for Rent* is very useful. See esp. 236–46.

147. Susanna Emlen to William Dillwyn, December 8, 1809, Dillwyn MSS, HSP. It was the custom for a gentleman's friends to visit him in the late morning for a week after the wedding, drink punch with him, and kiss the bride. See Nicholson, "Sober Frugality and Siren Luxury," 80.

148. Ritter, *Philadelphia and Her Merchants*, 46–47.

149. *NASS*, March 10, 1842.

150. Philadelphia County Wills, Will Book 2, p. 301, no. 56 (1807); Board of Health Records; Ship *George Washington*, in Ships' Papers, Box 8, Barry–Hayes Papers; Crew Lists, 1804: 186, 1807–9: 29; Christ Church, Marriages, 1800–1900, p. 4656.

151. Philadelphia County Wills, Will Book 7, p. 412, no. 179 (1821).

152. Ibid., Will Book 6, p. 623, no. 151 (1818).

153. *Laws of the General Assembly . . . 1828–29*, pp. 201–12. See also Baker, *A Review of the Relative Commercial Progress*, 29. Fisher, "Maritime History of the Reading, 1833–1905," 160–61, 162–63.

154. *North American*, March 5, 1842.

155. "Great Men," in *NS*, March 10, 1848.

156. PAS census, 1838; State Personal Tax Assessment Ledger, New Market Ward, 1832, p. 211.

157. James Forten to William Lloyd Garrison, February 2, 1831; BPL.

158. Forten to Garrison, December 31, 1830, BPL.

159. Forten to Garrison, July 28, 1832, BPL.

Chapter 5: "Our Happy Family Circle"

1. Dunbar's voyages are less easy to reconstruct than those of his sons because the records for this early period are scanty. However, he seems to have been the "William Dunbar" who sailed into Philadelphia on the *Regulatore* from Madeira in May 1802 and made a voyage on the *Dispatch* to New Orleans later that same summer. Passenger Lists, Arrivals in Philadelphia, 1800–1882, Nat Arch, Mid-Atlantic Division, Philadelphia.

2. Philadelphia directories, 1792, 1798, 1799.

3. The closest match was a Quaker family by the name of Beaty living within the area covered by Darby Monthly Meeting in the late 1750s and early 1760s. Records of Darby Monthly Meeting, 1682–1891, HSP. The Philadelphia directory for 1800 does list a Samuel Baetty, a ladies' shoemaker, living at 270 South Third Street. There is no indication whether he was black or white. A free woman of color by the name of Hannah Beattie, perhaps a sister or a widowed sister-in-law, headed a household of four in Pine Ward in 1830. She was a near-neighbor of Forten's nephew, James Forten Dunbar. U.S. Census, 1830: Philadelphia, Pine Ward, 338.

4. *Poulson,* November 14, 1803, June 2, 1804; *True American Commercial Advertiser,* June 2, 1804. A cryptic and somewhat confused entry in St. Thomas's Parish Register records the baptism of Martha Forten on May 22, 1804. Perhaps, in failing health, she had sought baptism in the hope of spiritual salvation, if not physical recovery. St. Thomas's African Episcopal Church, Philadelphia, Parish Register.

5. Gloucester, *Discourse,* 24.

6. *Poulson,* January 29, 1805.

7. Ibid., April 10, 1805.

8. Philadelphia directories, 1818–20, 1824–25. Philadelphia County Wills, Will Book 15, p. 445, no. 87 (1842), PCA.

9. (Old Swedes) Gloria Dei—Marriages, 1795–1816, p. 2133, HSP.

10. On slavery and the status of free people of color in Delaware, see Essah, *A House Divided,* and Williams, *Slavery and Freedom in Delaware,* 185–218, 249.

11. In 1810 Lewis headed a household of six in Cedar Ward. The family's address was 99 Shippen. The following year the family was living at the rear of 86 Gaskill. By 1816 Lewis had left the Forten sail loft and was working in a nearby loft at 110 South Wharves. He and Margaret and their children had moved to lodgings in Pottery Alley, just off Shippen. U.S. Census, 1810: Philadelphia, Cedar Ward, 255, 1820: Philadelphia County, Moyamensing, 166; Philadelphia directories, 1811, 1816, 1817.

12. Philadelphia directories, 1811, 1813, 1814; U.S. Census, 1810: Philadelphia County, Moyamensing, 129. There were other Dunbars in Philadelphia who may have been related to Abigail and William. The 1802 directory listed a David Dunbar, race unknown, as a sailor. Four years later he was an oysterman, an occupation dominated by African Americans. Philadelphia directories, 1802, 1806. In 1820 John Dunbar headed a household of eight free people of color in Southwark. In 1817 George Dunbar, a thirty-two-year-old mulatto born in Philadelphia, secured a seaman's protection certificate. U.S. Census, 1820: Southwark, 125; Seamen's Protection Certificates for the Port of Philadelphia (1817), Nat Arch.

13. Seamen's Protection Certificates, Port of Philadelphia (1810); Philadelphia Crew Lists, 1810, p. 75; 1815, p. 102; 1816, p. 113.

14. William Forten Dunbar's seaman's protection certificate indicates that he was born in 1792. Philadelphia Crew Lists, 1813, p. 37; 1817, pp. 187, 344, HSP. He did eventually marry, although I have been unable to discover the name of his wife. In 1824 he and his family were living with his mother in Washington Court. Philadelphia directory, 1824.

15. Seamen's Protection Certificates, Port of Philadelphia (1810).

16. Philadelphia Crew Lists, 1819, p. 123; 1821, p. 27; 1823, pp. 163, 226; 1825A, p. 122; 1826A, p. 59; 1828, p. 118.

17. Christ Church: Marriages, Confirmations and Communicants, 1800–1900, p. 4787, HSP.

18. Philadelphia directories, 1825, 1829, 1830.

19. U.S. Census, 1830: Philadelphia, Pine Ward, 338; Philadelphia city directory, 1833. Philadelphia Crew Lists, 1838, p. 298. For a more detailed account of Dunbar's career in the United States Navy, see below, pp. 373–74.

20. *Poulson,* December 13, 1805.

21. See undated photograph in Box 40–43, folder 1807, Francis J. Grimké Papers, Moorland–Spingarn Research Center, Howard University.

22. Douglass, *Annals of St. Thomas*, 107–10. Philadelphia County Deeds, D., Book 41, pp. 66, 69, PCA. Philadelphia directories, 1793, 1796, 1802, 1810–11, 1813–14, 1816–20, 1822. U.S. Census, 1790: Philadelphia, 1810: Southwark, 86.

23. Marriages at Gloria Dei, 940.

24. U.S. Census, 1800: Bucks County, Pa., 234; Philadelphia directories, 1793, 1796, 1802–4, 1810–11; Yellow Fever Deaths in Philadelphia, 1793, 1797, 1798, p. 345, HSP. Catherine Vandine died at age forty-three on April 28, 1811, and was buried at St. Thomas's; Philadelphia Board of Health, Cemetery Returns, PCA.

25. Philadelphia directories, 1813–14, 1816–20, 1822; Seamen's Protection Certificates, Port of Philadelphia (1820); Philadelphia Crew Lists, 1821, p. 33; 1824, pp. 36, 284, 286; 1825A, p. 220; U.S. Census, 1810: Philadelphia, Cedar Ward, 249; 1830: Middletown Township, Bucks County, 180.

26. Philadelphia Crew Lists, 1824, pp. 284–86. George Vandine was baptized on the same day as Charlotte and James Forten. St. Thomas's Parish Register.

27. St. Paul's Church, Philadelphia, Baptisms, 1782–1828, Marriages, 1759–1829, Burials, 1790–1852, pp. 56, 60, HSP. In 1850 James H. Vandine, a twenty-two-year-old brickmaker and a native of Pennsylvania, lived in Kensington's Seventh Ward. He was listed as black. Three young Vandines lived near each other in Middletown Township, Bucks County. Garret, a sixteen-year-old mulatto, was working on one farm; Susan, a thirteen-year-old listed as white, was working on another; and Hannah, a ten-year-old black girl, was working on a third. U.S. Census, 1850: Philadelphia County, Kensington, Ward 7, p. 509; Middletown Township, Bucks County, pp. 306, 323, 326.

28. *Poulson*, May 31, 1806. James Forten's mother may have been the "Margarett Waymouth," age eighty-two, baptized with him, his wife, and his brother-in-law at St. Thomas's Church soon after his second marriage. St. Thomas's Parish Register.

29. For instance, in 1801, according to the directory, his immediate neighbors were two white sailors, Stephen Russell (at 48 Shippen) and John Tree (at no. 52). Both would go on to become masters of vessels. (Philadelphia Crew Lists, 1802, p. 8; 1806, p. 249). A year earlier African-American grocer Edward Godfrey had been living at no. 51.

30. St. Thomas's Parish Registers.

31. Ibid. Philadelphia Board of Health, Cemetery Returns for 1813–14, "African folder," PCA. I am grateful to Reg Pitts for sharing with me his research on Charlotte's brief life.

32. St. Thomas's Parish Registers. Christ Church: Baptisms, 1769–1794, p. 1157; *True American Commercial Advertiser*, May 10, 1804; *Poulson*, May 10, 1804; May 18, 1809. The Davys owned the schooner *Sukey and Peggy*, and the ships *Monticello*, *Lewis William*, and *Active*. Ship Registers of the Port of Philadelphia, Blunt–White Library; Vessel Registers, 1803–4, Independence Seaport Museum, Philadelphia; Philadelphia directory, 1805; Philadelphia Board of Health Records, HSP.

33. St. Thomas's Parish Registers.

34. Ibid.

35. Sarah Louisa is not listed in the register of St. Thomas's Church, so her exact birth date cannot be ascertained. Assuming the entries for the other children are correct, she would have come between James and Robert, or between Robert and Mary, in birth order. In either case, Charlotte endured four confinements in a little over four years.

36. The Register of Baptisms for Christ Church gives Mary Isabella's birthdate as April 2, 1816, but this is an error. James Forten wrote his friend Paul Cuffe in April of

1815 to announce her birth. Christ Church: Baptisms, 1794–1819, p. 2061; Forten to Cuffe, April 6, 1815; Cuffe Letters, ODHSL.

37. The Fortens had taken their older children to St. Thomas's to be baptized. However, Absalom Jones died in 1818 and the church was left without a minister. Mary Isabella and Thomas Willing Francis were baptized at Christ Church on July 16, 1819, by Rev. Jackson Kemper. Christ Church: Baptisms, 1794–1819, p. 2061.

38. William Deas first appeared in the Philadelphia directory in 1797. One tragedy after another befell his family over the next decade. He and his wife, Martha, lost a daughter in 1799. Then William died. Martha, eight months pregnant and in failing health, was left to make provisions for the family. She died in 1807. Philadelphia Board of Health Records; Philadelphia directories, 1797–98, 1805; Ship Registers of the Port of Philadelphia, Vessel Registers, 1803–4; Records of the Second Presbyterian Church, Philadelphia—Baptisms, Marriages and Burials, 1745–1823, pp. 213–16, 417, 421, HSP; inscriptions in the burying ground of the Second Presbyterian Church, Philadelphia, 57, HSP; *Poulson*, January 6, 1806; August 7, 1807; April 24, 1824; Philadelphia County Wills, Will Book 2, p. 140, no. 76 (1807); Administrations, Book K, 231, file 7; 406, file 212, PCA.

39. James Forten, *Letters from a Man of Colour*, 6.

40. *Lib*, January 18, 1833.

41. Sarah L. Forten to Elizabeth Whittier, November 9, 1835; George Whittier Pickard Papers, Houghton Library, Harvard.

42. Lapsansky, *Neighborhoods in Transition*, 46–47. Green Tree and Mutual Assurance policy 8898, HSP. See also policy 1917.

43. U.S. Census, 1810: Philadelphia, New Market Ward, 684.

44. U.S. Census, 1820: Philadelphia, New Market Ward, 263; 1830: New Market, 217; 1840: New Market, 165; PAS census, 1838.

45. Indenture Book D, 1795–1835, p. 113, PAS MSS, HSP. Elbert did not stay with Forten after his term of indenture expired. In 1811 he applied for a seaman's protection certificate and became a sailor. Apparently, Forten did not give him any formal schooling. He was illiterate and made his mark on his application. Seamen's Protection Certificates, Port of Philadelphia (1811).

46. Indenture Book D, 1795–1835, p. 98, PAS MSS.

47. In 1838, for instance, all seventeen people in the Forten household were members of St. Thomas's. PAS census, 1838, PAS MSS, HSP.

48. Brown, "William D. Kelley," 316–17. *Congressional Record*, 38th Cong., 1st sess., 1997.

49. Silcox, "Delay and Neglect," 450–51.

50. On the Bustills and the Douglasses, see Bustill–Mossell Family Papers, Box 1, folder 1, Nathan F. Mossell Papers, University of Pennsylvania Archives.

51. *PF*, March 17, 1841. On Chamberlin, see Philadelphia directory, 1830, 1833; U.S. Census, 1830: Spring Garden, 272. In "Politics in a Box," Marie Lindhorst makes a convincing argument (272) that "Elizabeth," whose story "Zillah," alias Sarah Douglass, recounted in the *Liberator* (August 18, 1832), was Sarah's sister. According to "Zillah," Elizabeth's parents enrolled her in a local school. Despite a painful diseased hip, she excelled at her studies and won the praise of her teacher. However, when the white pupils complained to their parents, the teacher asked her to leave. After that she was

taught at home by her mother. She died in 1819, the same year her parents and the Fortens began their own school.

52. Elliott Cresson to R. R. Gurley, August 23, 1828, ACS Incoming Corr., August 5–October 19, 1828, ACS Papers (microfilm), BPL.

53. May, *Some Recollections*, 287–88.

54. Stevenson, ed., *Journals of Charlotte Forten Grimké*, 52 (entry for March 11, 1856); Joshua Coffin to Edwin P. Atlee, April 17, 1834; Alonzo Lewis to Edwin P. Atlee, April 16, 1834; Benjamin Greenleaf to Edwin P. Atlee, April 17, 1834, Board of Education Minute Book, 1830–39; Joshua Coffin to ____, February 12, 1836; Board of Education, Treasurer: Accounts, Bills and Receipts, 1836–37, PAS MSS, HSP. The roll books do not survive for the years when James Jr. and Robert attended the Clarkson School. On their younger brothers, see Accounts [undated], Board of Education; "Statement of Teacher, 1835"; "Teacher's Statement G. [Joshua] Coffin, 1836"; Board of Educated, undated roll book; and Clarkson School Roll Book, 1834–35, PAS MSS.

55. Stevenson, ed., *Journals of Charlotte Forten Grimké*, 208, 233 (entries for April 4 and June 28, 1857).

56. Winch, ed., *The Elite of Our People*, 99.

57. On "George Sherker," see below, pp. 194–95.

58. Major and Saunders, *Black Society*, 18; Philadelphia County Wills, Will Book 6, p. 623, no. 151 (1818), PCA. A light-skinned mulatto, Appo was listed in the 1800 census as white. In 1810 he was black. U.S. Census, 1800: Philadelphia County, 135; 1810: Cedar Ward, 262; Philadelphia Board of Health Records.

59. Southern, *The Music of Black Americans*, 127. *FJ*, December 26, 1828; Philadelphia Board of Health Records.

60. Christ Church: Marriages, 1800–1900, p. 4768. For a brief account of Johnson's career, see Southern, *The Music of Black Americans*, 105–14.

61. *The Purvis Family, 1694–1988*, 231, 235.

62. Moore, *Columbia and Richland County*, 72; Revill, comp., *Some South Carolina Genealogical Records*, 311; Philadelphia County Wills, Will Book 9, p. 5, no. 150 (1826); Burke, *Genealogical and Heraldic History*, 1869.

63. *The Purvis Family, 1694–1988*, 231, 335–37, 350–51.

64. Burridge continued to take an interest in his South Carolina investments. He died at sea on July 22, 1816, on a voyage to Charleston. Charleston County Wills, vol. 33 (1807–18), p. 1239, SCSA; International Genealogical Index (microform), NEHGS; Holcomb, comp., *Marriage and Death Notices*, 303; Holcomb, comp., *South Carolina Naturalizations*, 81, 96; Charleston directories, 1802, 1806, 1807, 1816.

65. Robert Purvis to R. C. Smedley, in Smedley, *History of the Underground Railroad*, 353–54. Baron Judah is a shadowy figure. Purvis probably knew only the brief outlines of his family history passed on by his mother. There was a Jewish community in Charleston dating back to the colonial period, and a significant number of the men who settled in Charleston before 1775 were from Germany. There were several by the last name of Judah, but no mention of a "Baron Judah." Hagy, *This Happy Land*, 7, 12–13, 340–41. The author of an article in the *Anti-Slavery Bugle* (November 3, 1860) gave "Baron" Judah's first name as Daniel, and said he never married Dido but "sustained toward her the practical relation of a kind and faithful husband." Dido and Judah's children were Daniel, Mary, and Harriet. Philadelphia County Wills, Will Book 66, p. 109, no. 639 (1869).

66. *Lib*, September 16, 1853.

67. Smedley, *The Underground Railroad*, 354. *The History of Sandford and Merton* was written by Thomas Day (1748–89), an English admirer of Rousseau. The work achieved the status of a children's classic. It follows the progress of two very different boys, Tommy Merton, the overindulged son of a Jamaican planter, and the virtuous Harry Sandford, a farmer's son. Day's work preaches the virtues of thrift, self-discipline, honest toil, simple living, and kindness to one's fellow creatures. *Sandford and Merton* has a strong antislavery message. One episode recounts the story of a virtuous Arab slave who repaid his liberators for their kindness when *they* were enslaved. In another episode an "honest Negro" saves Tommy from serious injury (the result of the boy's own stupidity) and tells him both about the variety of the human family and the injustices of slavery.

68. Misc. Records, Secretary of State, Bills of Sale, vol. 4S (1818–20), SCSA.

69. Charleston County, Court of Equity, Bill 74 (1836), SCSA.

70. Misc. Records, Secretary of State, Bills of Sale, Book 4F (1811–13), pp. 55, 105, 110.

71. Disentangling fact from fiction regarding Harriet Judah's legal status is not easy. Her son insisted she was freeborn. At the time of her death in 1869, one Philadelphia newspaper printed a story that she had been born a slave and had been purchased by William Purvis. She saved his life when "a band of desperadoes" were plotting to kill him, and in gratitude he freed and married her. Another Philadelphia paper had a slightly different version of events. According to that account, she was born a slave but became free at the age of nineteen. It was as a free woman that she saved the life of William Purvis. Yet another assertion of slave status surfaced in a law case brought against Harriet and her sons by two of William Purvis's nephews. They hoped to avoid repaying a loan their uncle had made to them shortly before his death. They alleged that Harriet was a slave under South Carolina law and that her sons had inherited her unfree status. The entry on Harriet's household in the Pennsylvania Abolition Society's 1856 census further confuses the issue. In 1856 Harriet was living on South Seventh Street with a niece, Sarah Vickers. The census-taker noted that one of the women had been born a slave and the other had been born free in a slave state. Unfortunately, he did not indicate which of the two had been a slave. *Morning Press*, December 14, 1869; *Sunday Dispatch*, November 19, 1869; Charleston County, Court of Equity, Bill 74; *Education and Employment Statistics of the Colored People of Philadelphia*, 1856, PAS MSS, HSP.

72. William Pervis's account, PAS Board of Education; Clarkson School: Tuition Account Book, 1819–22, PAS MSS, HSP.

73. Philadelphia directories, 1820–24.

74. Philadelphia Board of Health Records. *Poulson*, October 4, 1826; *Columbia [South Carolina] Telescope*, October 17, 1826; Records of the Second Presbyterian Church, Philadelphia, 473, HSP. It is not clear where Harriet and her sons were living in 1826. The funeral took place from the home of "Mrs. Hopkins." Susannah Hopkins, a widow, ran a boardinghouse at 75 South Eighth. Philadelphia directories, 1825–26.

75. Philadelphia County Wills, Will Book 9, p. 5, no. 150 (1826). Most of the estate consisted of stocks and promissory notes.

76. Walls, *The AMEZ Church*, 567; U.S. Census, 1800: New York, Ward 6, p. 846; 1810: Ward 6, p. 145; 1820: Ward 6, p. 32.

77. Walls, *The AMEZ Church*, 47, 50, 68, 90–91, 124, 129, 172–73, 567.

78. *FJ*, June 22, 1827, February 1, 1828. Thanks to Harriet's inheritance from her lover and her eldest son, she and Miller enjoyed a very comfortable lifestyle. Thomas Fletcher, the executor of the estates of William Purvis, Sr. and Jr., paid the couple "Sundry Sums of Money . . . at different times." Philadelphia County Deeds, A.M. Book 29, p. 187, and Book 61, p. 337.

79. Margaret Hope Bacon generously shared with me the results of her efforts to identify the school the Purvises attended. The standard works on Robert Purvis state that he went to Amherst College. However, neither his name nor that of his brother appears in the college records. The records of neighboring Amherst Academy do list Joseph as having been enrolled from 1828 to 1830. Unfortunately, the registers for 1824–26, when Robert was probably a student there, have not survived. Daria D'Arienzo, Archivist of Amherst College, to Margaret Hope Bacon, December 21, 1994.

80. Philadelphia County Wills, Will Book 9, p. 189, no. 72 (1828); Philadelphia Board of Health Records; *Poulson*, April 7, 1828; *FJ*, April 11, 1828.

81. Abdy, *Journal of a Residence and Tour*, vol. 3, p. 130.

82. Koelble and Bryson, comps., *Guardians of the Poor*, 125.

83. When Elizabeth, Nicholas and Jane's daughter, married in 1828, both of her parents were listed as "deceased." Gloria Dei—Marriages, 1816–73, p. 2523.

84. Acting Committee, Minute Book, 1822–42, p. 39, PAS MSS. On Morton, see Philadelphia directory, 1820; U.S. Census, 1820: Moyamensing, 165; 1830: Moyamensing, 54; 1850: Philadelphia, North Ward, 277.

85. New Orleans directory, 1823; Robert Layton to James Forten, May 2, 1825; Loose Corr., incoming, 1820–49, PAS MSS.

86. Layton to Forten, May 2, 1825.

87. Watts and Lobdell to Thomas Shipley, November 10, 1825, PAS, American Convention, f. 1 (1797–1825), Corr., Incoming, PAS MSS; New Orleans directory, 1823.

88. Minute Book, vol. 3 (1825–47), p. 60, PAS MSS.

Chapter 6: Brother Forten

1. For indications of the size of Philadelphia's black population in the mid-1780s, see Klepp, "Bills of Mortality," 223, and Nash and Soderlund, *Freedom by Degrees*, 18.

2. Jones, *A Thanksgiving Sermon*, 339–40. James Forten to Hon. George Thatcher, Philadelphia, 1800, Cox, Parrish, Wharton Papers, vol. 14, p. 65, HSP.

3. Wax, "The Demand for Slave Labor," 331–45.

4. For Shandy Yard's background, see (Old Swedes) Gloria Dei—Marriages, 1795–1816, p. 1960, HSP; and his indenture to James Yard in Indenture Book C, PAS MSS, HSP. On Servance, see Paul Cuffe to William Allen, April 1, 1816, Cuffe Papers, NBFPL.

5. Crane, ed., *Drinker Diary*, vol. 2, p. 1327 (entry for August 4, 1800); Committee of Guardians: Indenture Papers for Africans taken from the slave schooner *Prudent* by Captain Maloney of the *Ganges*, and Indenture Papers for Africans taken from the slave schooner *Phoebe* by Captain Maloney of the *Ganges*, in Manumissions, Indentures and Other Legal Papers, PAS MSS.

6. Philadelphia Crew Lists, 1804, p. 242.

7. The *Pennsylvania Gazette* contains numerous advertisements for runaways from vessels arriving from the Caribbean in the late 1780s and 1790s. Interestingly, at least

two of the fugitives were described as skilled sailmakers. Like Forten, they may well have realized they could make good money in a major seaport.

8. On the origins of the Gordons, see Philadelphia County Wills, Will Book 7, p. 129, no. 44 (1820), PCA, *Poulson*, September 12, 1829, and U.S. Census, 1850: Philadelphia, Dock Ward, 279. On Douglass and Cassey, see Winch, ed., *The Elite of Our People*, 162–63.

9. On the numbers of slaves who benefited from manumission and various self-purchase arrangements in the Upper South in the decade or so after the Revolutionary War, see Berlin, *Many Thousands Gone*, 278–81.

10. For an discussion of gradual emancipation in New Jersey, see Hodges, *Slavery and Freedom in the Rural North*, 116–70.

11. On the flight of New York slaves to Philadelphia, see White, *Somewhat More Independent*, 129, 130.

12. For Bowers's New England origins, see Seamen's Protection Certificates, Port of Philadelphia (1809), Nat Arch; for Gardiner's background, see U.S. Census, 1850: Philadelphia, Dock Ward, 503.

13. Douglass, *Annals of St. Thomas*, 119–21; Bustill–Mossell Family Papers, Box 1, folder 1, Nathan F. Mosell Papers, University of Pennsylvania Archives; PAS, Manumission Book A, and PAS, Acting Committee Minutes, 1784–88, p. 74, PAS MSS.

14. Nash and Soderlund, *Freedom by Degrees*, 127.

15. Zilversmit, *The First Emancipation*, 158. The fitting out of slaving vessels in the state also became illegal.

16. The PAS Minute Books for 1787–1800 and 1800–1824 contain numerous references to violations of the Gradual Abolition Act and the mistreatment of apprentices. PAS MSS.

17. Nash and Soderlund, *Freedom by Degrees*, 18.

18. Ibid., 173–82.

19. For an indication of the efforts the PAS did make to supervise indentures, see Minutes of the Committee of Guardians, 1790–1802, and the various PAS Indenture Books, PAS MSS.

20. Nash and Soderlund, *Freedom by Degrees*, 18; Klepp, "Bills of Mortality," 223.

21. Nash, "Forging Freedom," 40, 42.

22. Their wills indicate that at least some African Americans were doing fairly well financially. See, e.g., Philadelphia County Wills, Will Book Y, 186, no. 156 (1799); 304, no. 41 (1800); Will Book 1, 453, no. 12 (1806), all in PCA. The various deed books for Philadelphia County for the period 1785–1800 bear this out. A number of men and women of color accumulated sufficient cash to be able to buy real estate.

23. *Account of the Grand Federal Procession*, 1–18.

24. Wilson, *Stephen Girard*, 142, 149–50.

25. Miller, "The Federal City," 193.

26. Forten, *Letters from a Man of Colour*, 4

27. *Lib*, January 22, 1831.

28. Scott, "The Common Wind," 202–9.

29. Smith, "Andrew Brown," 326.

30. See, e.g., Rowe and Smith, "Prisoners for Trial Docket," 289–319.

31. Nash and Soderlund, *Freedom by Degrees*, 180.

32. Rowe and Smith, "Prisoners for Trial Docket," 306; Paul Cuffe to William Allen, April 1, 1816, Cuffe Papers, NBFPL.

33. Nash, "Reverberations of Haiti," 47, 50.

34. In the fall of 1793 there were reports that the French Commissioners on Saint Domingue had abolished slavery there and that emancipation throughout the rest of France's empire would shortly follow. A group of "citizens of color of Philadelphia" drafted a letter to the National Assembly in Paris praising the move, thanking members for "breaking our chains" with this "immortal decree" and promising to "tell our children of your good deeds." "Les citoyens de couleur de Philadelphia à l'Assemblée Nationale," in Revolutions de Saint-Domingue, vol. 3, no. 13, John Carter Brown Library. It is not clear whether the letter was actually sent. Presumably it was from ex-slaves from Saint Domingue living in Philadelphia, but it is possible members of the free black community had a hand in drafting it. If so, it might indicate considerable sympathy for the French on the part of Philadelphia's free community of color.

35. Brown, *Memoirs of the Rev. Robert Finley*, 101.

36. S. H. Cowles to Leonard Bacon, February 9, 1825, Bacon Family Papers, Box 1, folder 1, Sterling Library, Yale. I am grateful to David Brion Davis for bringing this letter to my attention.

37. *Fair American*, Ships' Papers, Independence Seaport Museum, Philadelphia.

38. Powell, *Bring Out Your Dead*, 18, 46, 65.

39. Ibid., 12–17, 26–27.

40. Ibid., 71–84; Smith, "Andrew Brown," 326–27; Pernick, "Politics, Parties, and Pestilence," 559–86.

41. Powell, *Bring Out Your Dead*, 107–10.

42. Nash, "Reverberations of Haiti," 54.

43. *Minutes of the Proceedings of the Committee . . . 1793*, appendix.

44. Benjamin Rush to Julia Rush, September 17, 1793, in Butterfield, ed., *Letters of Benjamin Rush*, vol. 2, p. 666.

45. Powell, *Bring Out Your Dead*, 234, 265–67. Powell's total is 3,881. *James Robinson's Directory for 1803* (288) puts the death toll at 4,002.

46. Crane, ed., *Drinker Diary*, vol. 1, p. 502.

47. Benjamin Rush to Richard Allen, n.d., MS, Corr. Benjamin Rush, vol. 38, p. 32, HSP.

48. Rush, *Account of the Yellow Fever*, 95–96.

49. Benjamin Rush to Richard Allen, n.d., MS, Corr. Benjamin Rush; Rush, *Account of the Yellow Fever*, 97; Rush to Julia Rush, September 25, 1793, in Butterfield, ed., *Letters of Benjamin Rush*, vol. 2, p. 684. For discussion of the demographic impact of the epidemic on Philadelphia's black population, see Lapsansky, "Abigail, a Negress," 61–78; and Crane, ed., *Drinker Diary*, vol. 1, p. 502n.

50. Jones and Allen, *Narrative of the Proceedings*, 12.

51. Carey, *A Short Account of the Malignant Fever*, 78.

52. Jones and Allen, *Narrative of the Proceedings*, 5–7.

53. Ibid., 7–9.

54. *James Robinson's Directory for 1803*, 288.

55. *PA Gaz*, February 21, 1798. On the 1794 law, see Jable, "Aspects of Moral Reform," 345.

56. *PA Gaz*, February 21, 1798.

57. Ibid.

58. The legislature did grant permission for streets around churches to be chained off during hours of worship. This law remained in effect until 1831. *HR* (February 12, 1831), 111–12.

59. *James Robinson's Directory for 1803*, 288.

60. "Minutes of the Supreme Executive Council of Pennsylvania," 637. For a related initiative four years earlier, see Nash, *Forging Freedom*, 94, and for a similar move in 1790 by the Free African Society, see Douglass, *Annals of St. Thomas*, 34–35.

61. Philadelphia County Wills, Will Book 15, p. 445, no. 87 (1842).

62. On the early history of the society, see Douglass, *Annals of St. Thomas*, 12–49.

63. Allen, *Life Experience and Gospel Labors*, 24–25; Nash, *Forging Freedom*, 109–12; Winch, *Philadelphia's Black Elite*, 9–10.

64. Corner, ed., *Autobiography of Benjamin Rush*, 208. For an indication of who some of the men gathered at Wilshire's home might have been, see *Extract of a Letter from Dr. Benjamin Rush*, 6–7.

65. Benjamin Rush to Jeremy Belknap, June 21, 1792, in Butterfield, ed., *Letters of Benjamin Rush*, vol. 1, pp. 620–21.

66. For Richard Allen's account of the exodus from St. George's, see Allen, *Life Experience and Gospel Labors*, 25. On the timing of the episode, see Sernett, *Black Religion and American Evangelism*, 117; Nash, *Forging Freedom*, 118–19; and Winch, *Philadelphia's Black Elite*, 9.

67. Nash, *Forging Freedom*, 112–13.

68. Benjamin Rush to Julia Rush, August 22, 1793, in Butterfield, ed., *Letters of Benjamin Rush*, vol. 2, 639. For an almost identical account, see Corner, ed., *Autobiography of Benjamin Rush*, 228–29.

69. Hoare, *Memoirs of Granville Sharp*, vol. 1, pp. 254–55.

70. On the various fund-raising efforts on behalf of the church, see Nash, *Forging Freedom*, 116–21.

71. *Dunlap and Claypoole's American Daily Advertiser*, July 21, 1794.

72. James Forten's name is one of almost 300 in the "Register of Members Up to 1794," in Douglass, *Annals of St. Thomas*, 107–10. The names are not arranged alphabetically. If they are in chronological order, then Forten was a relative latecomer. His name appears more than halfway through the list.

73. For Jones's date of birth, see Douglass, *Annals of St. Thomas*, 119. For Gray's approximate age, see Philadelphia Board of Health, Cemetery Returns, PCA.

74. Charters of Incorporation, Book 8, p. 259, PSA.

75. *Act of Incorporation of the African Episcopal Church*, 21–22.

76. Ibid., 22–23.

77. Ibid., 24.

78. Ibid.

79. Douglass, *Annals of St. Thomas*, 105–6. On Allen's unwavering commitment to Methodism, the faith under which he felt he had been "born and awakened," see Allen, *Life Experience and Gospel Labors*, 29.

80. Lammers, "Rev. Absalom Jones," 177–78.

81. "Eleventh Convention," 30, in Protestant Episcopal Church, *Journals of Five Conventions*. For similar dispensations, see "Ninth Convention," 16, and "Tenth Convention," 21.

82. Lammers, "Rev. Absalom Jones," 176n, 177.

83. *Act of Incorporation of the African Episcopal Church*, iv.

84. Douglass, *Annals of St. Thomas*, 106–7.

85. Various members of the congregation left money and property to the church. See Philadelphia County Wills, Will Book Y, 146, no. 18 (1799); 186, no. 156 (1799); Book Y, 306, no. 43 (1800); 414, no. 101 (1799); 607, no. 101 (1801); and 633, no. 2 (1802).

86. *Constitution of the Friendly Society*, 28.

87. Ibid., 29.

88. Crane, ed., *Drinker Diary*, vol. 2, p. 935.

89. Bullock, *Revolutionary Brotherhood*, 137.

90. Ibid., 158–60.

91. Ibid., 158–59; Grimshaw, *Official History*, 72, 73, 77, 78, 79; Wesley, *Prince Hall*, 34–35, 48–49. For a copy of Prince Hall's request to the Grand Lodge of England for a warrant, see Hall to William Moody, March 2, 1784, in Prince Hall, Letters and Sermons (microfilm), Library of the Massachusetts Grand Lodge. I thank the Librarian of the Lodge, Cynthia Alcorn, for giving me access to this material.

92. Prince Hall to the Free African Society, September 16, 1789, in Grimshaw, *Official History*, 110.

93. Douglass, *Annals of St. Thomas*, 31.

94. Davis, *History of Freemasonry*, 70. Mantore is a rather shadowy figure. I have not been able to find any mention of him in the censuses of 1790 and 1800 or in the Philadelphia directories.

95. African Lodge of Philadelphia to African Lodge of Boston, March 2, 1797, in Records of the African Lodge at Boston, Part A, Letters and Sermons (microfilm), Library of the Massachusetts Grand Lodge. Davis included a somewhat different version of the letter in his *History of Freemasonry*, 73–74. For Grimshaw's description of the letter, see *Official History*, 110. On the importance of the Philadelphians being "Ancients" rather than "Moderns," see Bullock, *Revolutionary Brotherhood*, chap. 3.

96. Grimshaw, *Official History*, 90, 110.

97. Davis, *History of Freemasonry*, 75.

98. Prince Hall to Peter Mantore, March 22, 1797, in Records of the African Lodge at Boston, Part A.

99. Grimshaw, *Official History*, 90, 110. According to Grimshaw, the officers Hall installed were Jones (Worshipful Master), Mantore (Senior Warden), William Harding (Junior Warden), Peter Richmond (Secretary), Richard Allen (Treasurer), Forten (Senior Deacon), Richard Parker (Junior Deacon), and Thomas Depee (Tyler, or doorkeeper).

100. Coil and Sherman, eds., *A Documentary Account*, 38–41.

101. Davis, *History of Freemasonry*, 290–91. As Bullock indicates in *Revolutionary Brotherhood* (208), one generally had to be twenty-one to be considered for admission to a lodge. Forten was in England in 1784–85. He did not turn twenty-one until September 2, 1787.

102. Minutes of the African Lodge, Philadelphia, 1797–1800; Library of the Grand Lodge of Massachusetts.

103. Ibid.

104. Ibid.

105. Ibid.

106. Ibid.

107. Ibid.

108. Bullock, *Revolutionary Brotherhood*, 72.

109. Davis, *History of Freemasonry*, 96.

110. For a note of a visit from five white Masons in the fall on October 26, 1799, see Minutes of the African Lodge of Philadelphia. On the Masonic observances for Washington, see *PA Gaz*, February 26, 1800.

111. Minutes of the African Lodge of Philadelphia, 1813–15 (microfilm), Library of the Grand Lodge of Massachusetts.

112. See, e.g., *Poulson*, July 6 and 9, 1818.

Chapter 7: Reflections of "A Man of Colour"

1. For a brief discussion of the Fugitive Slave Law and the abuses committed under it, see Wilson, *Freedom at Risk*, 41, 47–49.

2. Bergman and McCarroll, comps., *The Negro in the Congressional Record, 1789–1801*, 130–34.

3. In the first edition of *The Black Presence in the Era of the Amercan Revolution*, Sidney Kaplan reproduces the signature list that accompanied the petition (fig. 97, p. 238). The list contains seventy-one names. Forten's is not among them. The original petition has apparently been lost or misfiled. A diligent search of House records and petitions by staff at the National Archives has failed to locate it.

4. Bergman and McCarroll, comps., *The Negro in the Congressional Record, 1789–1801*, 241.

5. Ibid., 243, 244.

6. Ibid., 241, 243.

7. Ibid., 131–34.

8. Ibid., 242. The congressman's name was spelled "Thacher," although Forten and many others referred to him as "Thatcher."

9. For the details of the vote, see Bergman and McCarroll, comps., *The Negro in the Congressional Record, 1789–1801*, 248–49.

10. Susannah Emlen to William Dillwyn, December 8, 1809, Dillwyn MSS, HSP. On Dillwyn's role in linking British and American abolitionists, see Thomas, *Rise to Be a People*, 34–35; Coker, *A Dialogue*, 12–14, 43.

11. James Forten to Hon. George Thatcher, 1800, Cox, Parrish, Wharton Papers, Box 11, HSP.

12. United States Office of Naval Records, *Naval Documents Related to the Quasi-War*, vol. 1, pp. 149, 150; Tise, *American Counterrevolution*, 521.

13. James Forten to Hon. George Thatcher.

14. Ibid.

15. *Journal of the Pennsylvania House*, 10 (1799–1800): 172.

16. Nash and Soderlund, *Freedom by Degrees*, 131–34; Zilversmit, *The First Emancipation*, 203–4.

17. "The Petition of the Free Blacks of the City of Philad[a]," ca. 1801, Cox, Parrish, Wharton Papers, vol. 2, p. 3, HSP.

18. On the cooperation between the Pennsylvania Abolition Society and the Free African Society during the 1790s, see Eberly, "The Pennsylvania Abolition Society," 138.

19. PAS Report to the Seventh American Convention for Promoting the Abolition of Slavery, 16–17, PAS MSS, HSP.

20. PAS, General Meeting, Minutes, 1800–1824, p. 26, PAS MSS.

21. Ibid., 27.

22. The breakdown of subscribers is 312 white males, 59 white females, and 22 free men of color. I have assumed a subscriber was white unless I could establish otherwise. A number of those listed as subscribers did not appear in either the 1800 census or the city directories (1799–1802). Several people had the same name, and some names were obviously misspelled by Woodward. It is therefore likely that more than twenty-two African-Americans actually subscribed. One of the African-American subscribers, Henry Stewart, died between the time he signed Woodward's subscription list and the time the work appeared.

23. *The Negro Equalled by Few Europeans.*

24. For an overview of Branagan's remarkable career, see Leary, "Thomas Branagan."

25. "Proposals" in Branagan, *A Preliminary Essay.* On Knows, see Philadelphia directories, 1800, 1804–5, 1807, 1809, 1811, 1813.

26. Branagan, *Avenia,* 314.

27. Ibid.

28. Branagan, *Serious Remonstrances,* 86.

29. Ibid., 43.

30. Ibid., 45, 80.

31. Ibid., 66, 67.

32. Ibid., 71n.

33. *Freemen's Journal and Philadelphia Daily Advertiser,* July 7, 1804.

34. Ibid., July 9, 1804.

35. *Journal of the Pennsylvania House* 15 (1804): 114; Nash, *Forging Freedom,* 180–81.

36. Dr. Bray's Associates, Minute Book II, 208–10, and 235–37, in Pennington, "The Bray Associates," 22–23; Van Horne, ed., *Religious Philanthropy,* 24; *Philadelphia in 1824,* 131, 132.

37. Douglass, *Annals of St. Thomas,* 110–11.

38. Ibid., 113–14; Catto, *Semi-Centenary Discourse,* 51.

39. Stott, ed., *William Otter,* 58–59.

40. *Relf's Gazette,* November 24, 1809.

41. Berlin, *Slaves Without Masters,* chap. 3.

42. Nash, *Forging Freedom,* 157–58, 173–74.

43. White, "The Death of James Johnson," 755.

44. Birney, *James G. Birney,* 14; Fladeland, *James Gillespie Birney,* 12.

45. *Relf's Gazette,* December 30, 1807.

46. *Poulson,* January 1, 1808.

47. Jones, *A Thanksgiving Sermon,* 335–42.

48. Parrott, *An Oration . . . 1812; Poulson,* January 1, 1813.

49. *Poulson,* January 1, 1814; December 29, 1817; December 31, 1818; Parrott, *An Oration . . . 1814;* Parrott, *An Address . . . 1816.*

50. Jeremiah Gloucester, *An Oration . . . 1823,* and John Gloucester, Jr., *A Sermon . . . 1830.* On the Gloucester family, see Apperson, "African Americans on the Tennessee Frontier," 13. On Forten's role in securing their freedom, see Stephen H. Gloucester, *Discourse,* 27.

51. For an overview of January 1st observances and later freedom celebrations, see Gravely, "Dialectic of Double-Consciousness," 302–17.

52. Register of St. Thomas's African Episcopal Church, Philadelphia.

53. On changing attitudes toward lotteries, see Fabian, *Card Sharps*, 1, 113–16.

54. *Acts of the General Assembly, 1803–4*, 61–62.

55. Petition of the Minister, Wardens and Vestry of the African Episcopal Church of St. Thomas to the House of Representatives of the Commonwealth of Pennsylvania; McAllister Papers, Box 20, folder 34, HSP.

56. *Poulson*, September 22, 1807; *Relf's Gazette*, November 26 and December 30, 1807; *Aurora General Advertiser*, February 27, 1808; Records of St. Thomas's Church Lottery, Archives of Christ Church, Philadelphia. I am grateful to the Archivist of Christ Church for giving me access to this material.

57. Absalom Jones to Dorothy Ripley, June 3, 1803, and Richard Allen to Dorothy Ripley, June 24, 1803, in "Some Letters of Allen and Jones," 440–41. The numbers were fairly stable between 1803 and 1813. See PAS, *Present State and Condition*, 40.

58. Douglass, *Annals of St. Thomas*, 115.

59. Ibid., 115–16; *Philadelphia Tribune*, September 26, 1912.

60. "James Fortin about African Church," August 1810, in MS. Corr. Benjamin Rush, vol. 20, p. 107, HSP. Thomas Morgan was a West Indian, as was Summers. Charter Book 2, p. 234, PSA. There were several men of color in the city directory with the name "John Williams." Forten's associate was probably a hairdresser who lived on Spruce above Eighth. He died in 1812 or 1813. Philadelphia directories, 1811, 1813. On Farrell, see U.S. Census, 1810: Philadelphia, Cedar Ward, 257. George Vandine was probably George Sr., Forten's father-in-law, but he could have been George Jr., his brother-in-law.

61. Ulle, "History of St. Thomas' Church," 66.

62. "James Fortin about African Church."

63. Hickey, *The War of 1812*, 93–94.

64. Subscription list, September 3, 1812; subscription lists, 1744–1862, Box 5-C, Sub-List, HSP.

65. *Democratic Press*, January 13, 1813, in Schultz, *Republic of Labor*, 194.

66. *Journal of the Pennsylvania House* 23 (1813–14): 216.

67. Ibid., 417.

68. Ibid., 481.

69. PAS, General Minutes, Minute Book, 1800–1824, p. 181, PAS MSS, HSP.

70. *Journal of the Pennsylvania House* 23 (1813–14): 388–89.

71. *FJ*, February 22 and 29, March 7, 14, and 21, 1828.

72. Forten, *Letters from a Man of Colour*, 9.

73. The lines on liberty were from Addison's poem, *Letter, From Italy, to the Earl of Halifax*. For the use of those lines in freedom celebrations, see, e.g., the account of the July 4 celebration in Alexandria, Virginia, in *PA Gaz*, July 17, 1793. The same lines were included in the appendix to a pamphlet, *America: A Poem*, that was printed in Philadelphia in 1769. Although Forten was a young child when the pamphlet first appeared, copies may well have been in circulation through the 1770s and beyond.

74. On Forten's use of "Cato" as a pseudonym, see Forten to William Lloyd Garrison, February 23, 1831, BPL, and *Lib*, March 12, 1831.

75. On the image of Cato in the eighteenth century, see Ellison, *Cato's Tears*, esp. chaps. 2–3.

76. "Lang Syne Papers for *Poulson's Daily Advertiser*, March 21, 1828," in *Poulson's Scrapbook of Philadelphia History*, vol. 4, p. 16, LCP; Pollock, *The Philadelphia Theatre*, 200.

77. Ellison, *Cato's Tears*, 206, n. 30.

78. Addison, *Cato*. On George Washington's identification with Juba, see Ellison, *Cato's Tears*, 69. For the Virginia slaveholder the identification is less with Juba the African than with Juba the "Roman" or "Romanized" soldier-hero.

79. Forten, *Letters from a Man of Colour*, 1.

80. Ibid.

81. Ibid., 2.

82. Ibid., 7.

83. Ibid.

84. Ibid., 2–3.

85. Ibid., 3–4.

86. Ibid., 4.

87. Ibid.

88. Ibid., 5.

89. Ibid., 6.

90. Ibid., 8.

91. Ibid., 9.

92. Ibid., 10.

93. Ibid., 11.

94. *Journal of the Pennsylvania House* 24 (1814–15): 101.

95. Hickey, *The War of 1812*, 197–99.

96. Clark, "James Josiah," 483.

97. *Poulson*, August 26, 27, and 29, 1814.

98. Ibid., September 19, 1814.

99. For Tudas's version of the events of 1814, see Delany, *Condition, Elevation, Emigration, and Destiny*, 74–75n.

100. For an indication of Jonathan Tudas's eventful career in Philadelphia, see *Sword of Truth*.

101. *National Era*, July 22, 1847.

102. "Minutes of the Committee of Defense," 101, 115.

103. *Poulson*, September 19, 1814.

104. *National Era*, July 22, 1847; Scharf and Westcott, *History of Philadelphia*, vol. 1, pp. 573–74.

105. Purvis, *Remarks*, 11.

106. Scharf and Westcott, *History of Philadelphia*, vol. 1, p. 575. Merlin lived at 192 Lombard. Philadelphia directory, 1813.

107. "Minutes of the Committee of Defense," 47.

108. *Poulson*, September 3, 1814.

109. *Journal of the Pennsylvania Senate* 24 (1814–15): 56.

110. *Memorial to the Senate and House of Representatives of Pennsylvania from the "Colored Citizens,"* 17. In fact, they were copying word for word from Whittier's article in the *National Era*.

111. Scharf and Westcott, *History of Philadelphia*, vol. 1, p. 575.

112. James Forten to Paul Cuffe, February 15, 1815, Cuffe Papers, NBFPL.

Chapter 8: The African Enterprise

1. Nash, *Forging Freedom*, 101.

2. Thornton Papers, in Fox, *The American Colonization Society*, 40.

3. Douglass, *Annals of St. Thomas*, 25–29.

4. Thomas, *Rise to Be a People*, 7.

5. Ibid., 4–5.

6. Ibid., 7, 12.

7. *Memoir of Captain Paul Cuffee*, 8.

8. James Pemberton to Paul Cuffe, June 8, 1808, and John James and Alexander Wilson to William Dillwyn, June 21, 1809, Cuffe Papers, NBFPL; Thomas, *Rise to Be a People*, 36–38; Cuffe, *Narrative*, 3, 4, 7, 12–13.

9. *Vital Records of Westport*, 244; Forten to Cuffe, January 5, 1815, Cuffe Papers.

10. Cuffe to Forten, January 23, 1817, and Forten to Cuffe, January 25, 1817, Cuffe Papers.

11. Forten to Cuffe, January 5, 1815, Cuffe Papers.

12. Cuffe to Forten, January 8, 1817, Forten to Cuffe, January 25, 1817, and Forten to Cuffe, July 25, 1817, Cuffe Papers.

13. *Ship Registers of New Bedford*, 144, 268, 310–11.

14. Thomas, *Rise to Be a People*, 32–36.

15. Ibid., 40–41, 43–45. *The Monthly Repository of Theology and General Literature* 2, no. 18 (June 1807): 338.

16. "Journal," Cuffe Papers.

17. Thomas, *Rise to Be a People*, 49–50, 53–54.

18. Ibid., 57, 59–64.

19. Ibid., 73–74.

20. Log of the *Traveller*, Cuffe Papers.

21. Cuffe to William Allen, June 12, 1812, Cuffe Papers.

22. Thomas Clarkson and William Allen to Paul Cuffe, July 1, 1812, in Harris, *Paul Cuffe*, 175–78.

23. Wiggins, ed., *Captain Cuffe's Logs and Letters*, 252–53.

24. Cuffe to William Allen, March 6, 1814, Cuffe MSS, ODHSL.

25. Laban Wheaton to Cuffe, March 19, 1814, Cuffe Papers.

26. Cuffe to Cato Sawyer, February 17, 1814, Cuffe MSS.

27. Cuffe to Benjamin Tucker, August 6, 1814, Cuffe MSS; Cuffe to Richard Allen, March 8, 1814, Cuffe MSS.

28. Cuffe to Nath. G. M. Senter, March 7, 1814, Cuffe MSS.

29. Cuffe to Forten, September 23, 1814, Cuffe MSS.

30. Cuffe to Forten, January 27, 1815, Cuffe MSS.

31. Forten to Cuffe, February 15, 1815, Cuffe Papers.

32. Cuffe to Forten, March 13, 1815, Cuffe MSS.

33. Forten to Cuffe, April 6, 1815, Cuffe MSS.

34. Cuffe to Forten, March 27, 1815, Cuffe MSS.

35. On Servance's background, see above, p. 134.

36. Philadelphia directory, 1811.

37. Cuffe to William Allen, April 1, 1816, Cuffe Papers.

38. Cuffe to William Allen, December 4, 1815, Cuffe Papers.

39. Philadelphia County Deeds, M.R. Book 15, pp. 13, 15, PCA.

40. Cuffe to Antona Survance, August 14, 1815, and Samuel R. Fisher to Cuffe, June 5, 1817, Cuffe Papers.

41. *Poulson*, September 20, 1815.

42. Forten to Cuffe, October 10, 1815, Cuffe MSS.

43. Cuffe to Forten, November 22, 1815, Cuffe MSS.

44. James Forten and Russell Parrott to the Directors of the African Institution, November 15, 1815, in African Institution, *Tenth Report*, Appendix F, 70–71.

45. Samuel J. Mills to Cuffe, July 10, 1815, Cuffe Papers.

46. On the school, see Spring, *Memoir of Samuel John Mills*, 118.

47. Cuffe to Mills, August 6, 1815, Cuffe Papers.

48. Thomas, *Rise to Be a People*, 100–104.

49. Cuffe to Forten, August 14, 1816, Cuffe Papers.

50. Forten to Cuffe, September 20, 1816, Cuffe MSS.

51. John James to Cuffe, June 7, 1816, Cuffe MSS.

52. Cuffe to Peter Williams, Jr., June 14, 1816, Cuffe Papers.

53. Cuffe to Peter Williams, Jr., n.d., Cuffe Papers.

54. Robert Finley to Cuffe, December 6, 1816, Cuffe Papers.

55. Cuffe to Finley, January 8, 1817, Cuffe Papers.

56. Finley, *Thoughts on Colonization*, 4.

57. Ibid.

58. Ibid., 7.

59. Staudenraus, *The African Colonization Movement*, 16, 24–25.

60. Cuffe to Mills, January 6, 1817, Cuffe Papers.

61. Waldstreicher, *In the Midst of Perpetual Fetes*, 302–3.

62. *New-York Courier*, January 1, 1817. See also *Niles' Register*, December 26, 1816.

63. *Poulson*, December 30, 1816.

64. Ibid., January 2, 1817.

65. Ibid., January 3, 8, 10, 1817.

66. *New-York Courier*, January 13, 1817, in *Poulson*, January 15, 1817.

67. Cuffe to Forten, January 8, 1817, Cuffe Papers.

68. Forten to Cuffe, January 25, 1817, Cuffe Papers.

69. Ibid.

70. Ibid.

71. *Resolutions and Remonstrances*, 3.

72. Ibid., 3–4.

73. Ibid., 4.

74. Ibid.

75. Forten to Cuffe, January 25, 1817, Cuffe Papers.

76. On the tie between Mills and Gloucester, see *PA Free*, October 4, 1838.

77. Brown, *Biography of the Rev. Robert Finley*, 122.

78. In *Memoirs of the Rev. Robert Finley* (101), Brown refers to the two by their initials, J.F. and R.A. In his 1857 work (122), he names them as Richard Allen and "John Foster." "Foster" is clearly Forten.

79. Brown, *Biography of the Rev. Robert Finley*, 123.

80. Ibid., 124.

81. Parrish, *Remarks on the Slavery of the Black People*, 41–44; Thomas, *Rise to Be a People*, 59, 139–40.

82. On Branagan, see above, pp. 159–60.

83. Douglass, *Annals of St. Thomas*, 25–29; Kaplan and Kaplan, *The Black Presence*, 14–15.

84. *Lib.*, January 22, 1831.

85. Cuffe to John James, February 28, 1817, Cuffe Papers.

86. Cuffe to Forten, March 1, 1817, Cuffe Papers.

87. Forten to Cuffe, April 14, 1817, Cuffe Papers.

88. Forten to Cuffe, July 25, 1817, Cuffe Papers.

89. Ibid.

90. Alonso B. Munoz to James Forten, June 24, 1817, in PAS Minutes, 1800–1824, pp. 260–61, PAS MSS, HSP.

91. *Poulson*, July 14, 1817.

92. Alonso B. Munoz to James Forten, June 24, 1817.

93. PAS, General Meeting: Treasurer's Accounts, 1812–40, p. 125, PAS MSS, HSP. See also General Meeting Minutes, 1800–1824, pp. 282–83, 304, 326–27, 345, 437; and ACS, *Seventh Annual Report*, 116. On Sherker's later life, see George Sherker to the PAS, September 23, 1830, PAS, Loose Correspondence, Incoming, 1820–49.

94. See below, p. 325.

95. Forten to Cuffe, July 25, 1817, Cuffe Papers.

96. *United States Gazette*, January 21, 1817; Staudenraus, *African Colonization Movement*, 34.

97. *Poulson*, August 4, 1817.

98. Ibid., August 8, 1817.

99. Ibid., August 12, 1817.

100. Ibid., August 9, 1817.

101. Ibid., August 18, 1817.

102. "Address of the free people of colour," in *Minutes of a Special Meeting of the Fifteenth American Convention*, i–ii.

103. Ibid., ii.

104. Ibid., iii.

105. Rhoda Cuffe to James Forten, September 10, 1817, Cuffe Papers.

106. In his *Biography of the Rev. Robert Finley*, Brown gives November 3, 1817, as the date of his death (207). However, in his entry on Finley in the *American National Biography*, Egerton states that Finley actually died on October 3 (vol. 7, pp. 932–33).

107. Thomas, *Rise to be a People*, 118; Spring, *Memoir of Samuel John Mills*, 144, 237; *Union United States Gazette*, September 30, 1818.

108. ACS Annual Meeting report (1818), 22, ACS Papers (microfilm), BPL.

109. *Union United States Gazette*, June 6 and June 10, 1818. Although reprinted in Brown's *Memoirs of Rev. Robert Finley* (313–45) and generally attributed to Finley (see, e.g., Waldstreicher, *In the Midst of Perpetual Fetes*, 306–7), the dialogues could not have been written by him, since he predeceased Absalom Jones, who died on February 13, 1818 (Sexton's Records, PCA). The dialogues may actually have been written by Finley's brother-in-law, Elias B. Caldwell.

110. *Minutes of the Proceedings of a Special Meeting of the Fifteenth American Convention*, 39, 49, 51, i–iv.

111. *Niles' Register*, November 27, 1819; *Union United States Gazette*, November 18, 1819.

112. Forten kept a copy of Parrott's letter and forwarded it to the editors of *Freedom's Journal* several years after his friend's death. It was reprinted in *FJ*, July 27, 1827.

113. *Union United States Gazette*, December 11, 1819.

114. For the text of the law, see Bergman and McCarroll, comp., *The Negro in the Congressional Record, 1818–1819*, 319–20. Mercer was an ardent supporter of the ACS and, according to one historian of the movement, he, rather than Finley and Caldwell, deserves the credit for founding it. Egerton, "'Its Origin Is Not a Little Curious,'" 463–80.

115. Staudenraus, *African Colonization Movement*, 50–51.

116. Ibid., 56–57.

117. Ibid., 61–62.

118. Ibid., 59–68.

119. Ibid., 88–93.

120. Shick, comp., *Emigrants to Liberia*, 3, 19, 41, 92; Philadelphia directories, 1818–20.

121. ACS, *Fifth Annual Report*, 24.

122. On Cuffe's response to Forten's query see Cuffe to Peter Williams, Jr., June 14, 1816, Cuffe Papers.

123. ACS, *Thirteenth Annual Report*, 40; Seamen's Protection Applications (1815), Port of Philadelphia, Nat Arch; Shick, comp., *Emigrants to Liberia*, 28.

124. *AfRep* (October 1827): 250; Shick, comp., *Emigrants to Liberia*, 28.

125. S. H. Cowles to Leonard Bacon, February 9, 1825, Bacon Family Papers, Box 1, folder 1, Sterling Library, Yale. (I am grateful to Professor David Brion Davis for bringing this letter to my attention.) The signature appears to be "S. H. Cowles," but the handwriting is not easy to decipher, in part because the writer adopted the space-saving device of writing a page, turning the page ninety degrees, and writing across what he had already written.

126. Much the same news was passed on to Gurley by Gerald Ralston. He did not mention Forten, but he did add a few other details. Cornish had called on Ralston's father, on Richard Allen, and on "a number of others friendly to your Society" in hopes of getting support. Ralston Sr. and Allen had sent him away with a flea in his ear, but he "obtained many subscribers among our colored people." William B. Davidson to Gurley, February 6, 1827, and Gerald Ralston to Gurley, February 16, 1827, ACS, Domestic Letters, January 20–March 20, 1827.

127. Pease and Pease, *Bound with Them in Chains*, 141.

128. S. H. Cowles to Leonard Bacon, February 9, 1825.

129. *FJ*, March 16, 1827.

130. William B. Davidson to R. R. Gurley, March 24, 1827, ACS, Corr. Incoming, March 21–June 28, 1827.

131. *Poulson*, March 21, 1827.

132. Ibid., March 24, 26, 28, and 31, 1827.

133. *FJ*, May 18, 1827. A decade later Cornish reprinted the letter in the *Colored American* with the observation: "The following is from the pen of that intelligent, and ever watchful Patriot, James Forten." *CA*, May 13, 1837.

134. *FJ*, June 8, 1827.

135. Purvis, *Remarks*, 14–15. Lord Mansfield had handed down the verdict in the Sommersett case. On the significance of the case for the opponents of slavery, see above, p. 59.

136. Elliott Cresson to R. R. Gurley, January 21, 1828; ACS Corr. Incoming, December 12, 1827–February 9, 1828.

137. *FJ*, February 14, 1829. On Russwurm's career, see *American National Biography*, vol. 19, pp. 117–18.

138. John B. Russwurm to R. R. Gurley, May 7, 1829, ACS Corr. Incoming, April 28–June 26, 1829.

139. Carey, *Letters on the Colonization Society*, 17.

140. *AfRep* (January 1830): 342.

Chapter 9: The Limits of Brotherhood

1. Clement, "The Philadelphia Welfare Crisis," 152.

2. Nash, *Forging Freedom*, 143; *HR*, March 1831, pp. 172–73.

3. Nash, *Forging Freedom*, 143.

4. Ibid., 214.

5. Brown, *Biography of the Rev. Robert Finley*, 123.

6. Logan, *Diplomatic Relations with Haiti*, 173.

7. *Niles' Register*, October 17, 1818; see also July 1, 1820, and *Union United States Gazette*, November 18, 1819.

8. Douglass, *Annals of St. Thomas*, 124.

9. Brown and Rose, comps., *Black Roots in Southeastern Connecticut*, 362; Hodges, "Prince Saunders," in Garraty and Carnes, eds., *American National Biography*, vol. 19, p. 308.

10. Hodges, "Prince Saunders," 308. Saunders's fiancée was presumably either Alice or Rhoda Cuffe. Cuffe's other daughters were already married by the 1810s.

11. Hodges, "Prince Saunders," 308.

12. Griggs and Prator, eds., *Christophe and Clarkson*, 45, 92; Hodges, "Prince Saunders," 308; White, "Prince Saunders," 530.

13. Saunders, *An Address Before the Pennsylvania Augustine Society*, 3–9. The allusion to Jason and the Golden Fleece was very apposite, given that Saunders and at least some of his hearers were Masons. Presumably he also picked up on the name of the organization, for Prince Hall Masons accorded St. Augustine great respect as one who embodied Masonic principles. On Masonic references to the Golden Fleece and St. Augustine, see Wesley, *Prince Hall*, 59, 79, 88.

14. Saunders, *Memoir*, 275, 276–77.

15. Griggs and Prator, eds., *Christophe and Clarkson*, 125; Thomas Clarkson to Roberts Vaux, March 8, 1819, and January 31, 1820; Vaux Papers, HSP. In fact, Paul Cuffe's old friend, merchant John James, arranged for Saunders to meet the Spanish ambassador, Don Luis Onís, in Philadelphia in the fall of 1818. Onís assured Saunders that Madrid would welcome an offer for its claims on Hispaniola. Saunders, *Memoir*, 272–73.

16. Winch, *Philadelphia's Black Elite*, 51.

17. Cole, *Christophe*, 15, 243, 269.

18. Prince Saunders to Thomas Clarkson, July 14, 1821, in Griggs and Prator, eds., *Christophe and Clarkson*, 226.

19. Saunders to Clarkson, May 2, 1823, in ibid., 249. Saunders noted that he had just returned after a six-month sojourn in Haiti and that his visit had left him with a very poor opinion of President Boyer's regime.

20. Dewey, *Correspondence*, 2, 3.

21. Montague, *Haiti and the United States*, 50–52; Logan, *Diplomatic Relations with Haiti*, 207. The United States did not recognize Haiti until 1862.

22. Dewey, *Correspondence*, 8–9, 10, 12. On the matter of Dewey's affiliation with the ACS, see ibid., 8n.

23. Haytien Emigration Society, *Information*, 7–10; Dewey, *Correspondence*, 27.

24. Dewey, *Correspondence*, 17; Dewey to Granville *fils*, May 11, 1865, in *Biographie de Granville*, 239–41.

25. Jonathas Granville to Jean-Pierre Boyer, June 12, 1824, and Granville to Boyer, September 12, 1824, in *Biographie de Granville*, 210 and 229. Granville refers to Carey as Correy, but the context makes it clear he is referring to the Philadelphia printer Mathew Carey. Eckhardt, *Frances Wright*, 81.

26. *Biographie de Granville*, 3–4, 48n., 51–52.

27. *National Intelligencer* in *Niles' Register*, June 26, 1824; Jonathas Granville to Jean-Pierre Boyer, July 21, 1824, in *Biographie de Granville*, 217–18.

28. Granville to Boyer, July 21, 1824, in *Biographie de Granville*, 217.

29. Granville to Boyer, June 26, 1824, in ibid., 214.

30. *GUE*, January, April, June, and August 1825; *United States Gazette*, April 18, 1825.

31. Richard Allen to Jean-Pierre Boyer, August 22, 1824, in *Biographie de Granville*, 225.

32. *Poulson*, July 5, 1824.

33. Ibid., July 13, 1824.

34. On the angry reaction of the ACS leadership to Dewey and the Haitian plan, see *Niles' Register*, July 3, 1824.

35. Haytien Emigration Society, *Information*, 2.

36. Ibid., 3.

37. Ibid., 4.

38. Ibid., 5, 6.

39. *Niles'* Register, July 3, 1824; *United States Gazette*, June 1, 1825.

40. *Biographie de Granville*, 138, 158–62, 170, 220.

41. Miller, *The Search for a Black Nationality*, 81; Hunt, *Remarks on Hayti*, 4.

42. Richard Allen to Jean-Pierre Boyer, August 22, 1824, in *Biographie de Granville*, 224–25.

43. *Niles' Register*, August 28 and December 18, 1824; Haytien Emigration Society, *Information*, 3.

44. S. H. Cowles to Leonard Bacon, February 9, 1825, Bacon Family Papers, Sterling Library, Yale.

45. *GUE*, June 1825. Despite his enthusiasm, Burton did eventually return home. For a brief account of his life, see Winch, ed., *The Elite of Our People*, 134.

46. *United States Gazette*, December 28, 1824, in Jackson, "Origins of Pan-African Nationalism," 116.

47. Hunt, *Remarks on Hayti*, 6.

48. Dewey, *Correspondence*, 25; Granville to Boyer, October 31, 1824, in *Biographie de Granville*, 231.

49. With the division of Hispaniola in 1844, the Samaná settlers found themselves in the Dominican Republic. See *Lib*, November 5, 1847; Ardouin, *Géographie d'Haïti*, 163; Hazard, *Santo Domingo*, 199, 204, 486; Hoetink, "'Americans' in Samaná," 3–22.

50. Philadelphia Crew Lists, 1824, pp. 284–86; *GUE*, March 1825, p. 88. Dewey identified Vandine's brother-in-law as "Mr. J. Foster, of Philadelphia," but the context makes it clear that this was a misprint for "Forten."

51. On Charles Vandine and his family, see *PL*, October 25, 1848. It is not clear whether he married before he left Philadelphia or after he settled in Haiti.

52. *GUE*, August 1825.

53. Montague, *Haiti and the United States*, 11, 13.

54. Ardouin, *Etudes sur l'histoire d'Haiti*, vol. 9, pp. 300–301.

55. Mackenzie, *Notes on Haiti*, 110–11.

56. *CA*, March 3 and June 16, 1838. On the remarkable career of Robert Douglass, Jr., see Winch, ed., *The Elite of Our People*, 127–29.

57. Hodges, "Prince Saunders," 309. Hodges notes that there is nothing in the available Haitian records to support the claims of White ("Prince Saunders," 534–35) and others that Saunders eventually became Boyer's attorney-general.

58. Register of Confirmations by Bishop White 1787 to 1836 inclusive, 148, HSP.

59. Charters of Incorporation, Book 2, p. 28, PSA. The organization was incorporated in 1815.

60. Yard, a sailor, was last heard of in Brazil. Putney, *Black Sailors*, 39.

61. St. Thomas's African Episcopal Church, Vestry Minutes, 1813–21.

62. Ibid.; and *African Church of St. Thomas vs. Joseph Randolph* (March 1820), transcript in Box 33, folder 6, Edward Carey Gardiner Collection, HSP.

63. Vestry Minutes, 1813–21.

64. Ibid., and "Resolutions of the Vestries of St. Thomas's Church, Philadelphia," Archives of the Episcopal Diocese of Pennsylvania at the Presbyterian Historical Society. I thank researcher Earl Johnson for drawing my attention to this document.

65. Vestry Minutes, 1813–21. Thomas, a waiter, lived at 189 South Seventh. Philadelphia directories, 1816–19.

66. Vestry Minutes, 1813–21; Bond and Warrant, Joseph Cassey and James Forten to "The Minister Church Wardens and Vestry Men of the African Episcopal Church of St. Thomas in the City of Philadelphia," Pennsylvania Supreme Court, Eastern District; Judgment Dockets (1817–29), 128; Continuance Docket (July Term 1818 to December Term 1825), 413; DSB Papers (March Term 1822), no. 77; PSA. The actual undertaking is dated June 3, 1820, although the documents were not filed until 1822.

67. Vestry Minutes, 1813–21.

68. Ibid.; and Philadelphia Board of Health, Cemetery Returns; PCA.

69. *Poulson*, February 16 and 19, 1818. On the high esteem in which White held Jones, see his comment in Protestant Episcopal Church, *Journal of the Thirty-Fourth Convention*, 7–8.

70. Vestry Minutes, 1813–21.

71. Ibid.

72. Ibid.

73. Ibid.

74. Ibid.; and Douglass, *Annals of St. Thomas*, 124–25.

75. George Weller to Rev. Edward Bickersteth, June 4, 1827, in C.M.S. Archives, G/AC 20, Misc. Letters, Church Missionary Society, London, in Burkett, "Harry Croswell," 6 (unpublished paper cited with the permission of the author).

76. Burkett, "Harry Croswell," 6.

77. Memorandum, October 23, 1821, in the Episcopal Church Archives, Record Group 50–5, quoted in Burkett, "Harry Croswell," 7.

78. "Extract from the Minutes of St. Thomas's Episcopal Church," Record Group 50–5, Archives of the Episcopal Church, Austin, Texas, courtesy of Randall Burkett.

79. "Petition from members of St. Thomas' African Church, Phila. In favor of Jacob Oson & other testimonials in favor of the same," (1821), Record Group 50–5, Archives of the Episcopal Church. Burkett notes that the original date of the petition, January 21, 1822, was crossed through and December 29, 1821, inserted. Burkett, "Harry Croswell," n. 20.

80. Philadelphia directories, 1818–22.

81. Thomas C. Brownell to Jackson Kemper, March 30, 1821, Jackson Kemper Papers, in Burkett, "Harry Croswell," n. 22.

82. Harry Croswell Diaries, vol. 1, p. 117, entry for February 14, 1822, in Burkett, "Harry Croswell," 9–10. Burkett notes that Oson was eventually ordained in Connecticut in 1828. He planned to go to Liberia as a missionary but died before his departure for Africa.

83. *Poulson*, September 14, 1824. For the record of Parrott's marriage to Sarah Rowland, see *Christ Church, Marriages, 1800–1900*, 4691. On Parrott's standing in the church, see Protestant Episcopal Church, *Journal of the Fortieth Convention*, 12.

84. *Sword of Truth*, 12–13.

85. William White to Edward Bickersteth, June 6, 1827, G/AC 20, Church Missionary Society Archives, London, courtesy of Randall Burkett.

86. A young friend of Forten's would fight a similar battle in the AME Church. See Payne, *Recollections of Seventy Years*, 250–54. White churches were not immune from this kind of conflict. Horton and Horton, *In Hope of Liberty*, 133.

87. Charters of Incorporation, Book 4, p. 352. Forten's last name was misspelled by the clerk in Harrisburg who transcribed the charter. It appears as "Storten" or "Horton." There was no man of color with either last name in Philadelphia in 1829. On Cain, see Philadelphia Crew Lists, 1804, p. 242.

88. St. Thomas's African Episcopal Church, Vestry Minutes, 1821–31.

89. Protestant Episcopal Church, *Journal of the Forty-Fourth Convention*, 16, 20–21, 56.

90. Protestant Episcopal Church, *Journal of the Forty-Fifth Convention*, 40–41; Douglass, *Annals of St. Thomas*, 126–28.

91. Protestant Episcopal Church, *Journal of the Forty-Seventh Convention*, 31.

92. Brown, *The Black Man*, 271–72; Winch, ed., *The Elite of Our People*, 125–26.

93. "Pencil Pusher," in *Philadelphia Tribune*, October 12, 1912.

94. "Recommendation of the Vestry of St. Thomas's Church on behalf of William Douglass," courtesy of Earl Johnson. The original is in the Episcopal Church Archives of the Pennsylvania Diocese.

95. Protestant Episcopal Church, *Journal of the Fifty-First Convention*, 20.

96. Combe, *Notes on the United States*, 62–63.

97. DuBois, *The Philadelphia Negro*, 198–99.

98. Douglass, *Annals of St. Thomas*, 130.

99. Scharf and Westcott, *History of Philadelphia*, vol. 3, p. 1907.

100. Ibid., 1906.

101. *Poulson*, July 9, 10, 14, 16, and 21, 1818.

102. Ibid., July 21, 1818.

103. Ibid., July 23, 1818.

104. Clement, "The Philadelphia Welfare Crisis," 152.

105. For "typical" reports of the crime wave, see *Relf's Gazette*, November 24, 1821; February 11, 14, and 18, 1822; *National Gazette*, October 23, November 24 and 30, 1821.

106. *Relf's Gazette*, February 18, 1822.

107. *Poulson*, March 3, 1822.

108. Ibid.

109. Saunders, *An Address before the Pennsylvania Augustine Society*, 10–12; Nash, *Forging Freedom*, 270.

110. Price, "School Segregation," 123; Silcox, "A Comparative Study," 157–59; Silcox, "Delay and Neglect," 450–51.

111. Silcox, "A Comparative Study," 160–61.

112. *Niles' Register*, September 11, 1824.

113. *Philadelphia Gazette*, November 21, 1825. *Niles' Register* (November 26, 1825) said there were two fatalities.

114. On the depredations of the Cannon-Johnson gang, see Wilson, *Freedom at Risk*, 19–37, and Winch, "Philadelphia and the Other Underground Railroad," 3–25.

115. *FJ*, April 18, 1828.

116. Watson, *Annals of Philadelphia*, 479.

117. Scharf and Westcott, *History of Philadelphia*, vol. 1, p. 624.

118. *Rights of All*, October 16, 1829.

Chapter 10: New Friends of Freedom

1. Zachary, "Social Disorder," 303–4.

2. *AfRep* 7 (April 1831): 45; (October 1831), 245.

3. Joseph Mechlin to R. R. Gurley, March 30, 1830; ACS Incoming Corr., February 12–March 31, 1830; Francis Devany to R. R. Gurley, May 4, in ibid., April 1–June 1, 1830, ACS Papers (microfilm), BPL.

4. ACS, *Thirteenth Annual Report*, 40, 42–43.

5. *AfRep* 10 (May 1834): 90.

6. Baily, "From Cincinnati," 427–40; Wade, "The Negro in Cincinnati," 43–57.

7. On the reception given the refugees in Canada, see Silverman, *Unwelcome Guests*, 27–32.

8. Bell, *Survey of the Negro Convention Movement*, 15.

9. *CA*, October 7, 1837; Bell, "Free Negroes of the North," 448.

10. *Constitution of the American Society of Free Persons of Colour*, ii.

11. Delany, *Condition, Elevation, Emigration, and Destiny*, 16; *Anglo-African Magazine* 1, no. 10 (October 1859): 306–9.

12. *Constitution of the American Society of Free Persons of Colour*, 8.

13. Ibid., 10–11.

14. On the sharp decline in membership, see Eberly, "The Pennsylvania Abolition Society," 51. On the correspondence surrounding the resignation of Forten's lawyer, Richard Peters, Jr., see PAS Minutes, 1800–1824, 341, and Richard Peters, Jr., to the Members of the PAS, April 26, 1821, PAS MSS, HSP.

15. Mayer, *All on Fire*, 3–43.

16. Garrison, *An Address*, 3.

17. James Forten to William Lloyd Garrison, July 28, 1832; BPL.

18. Mayer, *All on Fire*, 3–70.

19. Ibid., 61–67.

20. Ibid., 71–94.

21. Robert Purvis to R. C. Smedley, in Smedley, *History of the Underground Railroad*, 354.

22. Mayer, *All on Fire*, 101; Brown, *The Negro in Pennsylvania History*, 16.

23. James Forten to William Lloyd Garrison, December 31, 1830; BPL; Garrison to Oliver Johnson, March 1, 1874; BPL; *Lib*, January 8, 1831.

24. *Lib*, January 22, 1831.

25. Ibid.

26. Ibid., February 12, 1831.

27. Ibid.

28. Ibid.

29. James Forten to William Lloyd Garrison, February 23, 1831, BPL. Garrison published the letter in the *Liberator* (March 12, 1831) and again in his *Thoughts on African Colonization*, 67–69.

30. Forten to Garrison, March 21, 1831, BPL.

31. *Lib*, July 16, 1831. Forten to Garrison, October 20, 1831, BPL. See also *Lib*, September 24, 1831.

32. Garrison, *An Address*, 4.

33. *Lib*, January 22 and February 12, 1831.

34. Adams, *An Oration*, 12. Identifying the writer as "an intelligent colored gentleman in Philadelphia," Garrison reprinted Forten's letter in the *Liberator* (September 24, 1831).

35. *Lib*, July 16, 1831.

36. Ibid., August 20, 1831.

37. Hinks, ed., *David Walker's Appeal*, xiv–xxv. For evidence that Forten was aware of Walker's pamphlet, see *Remonstrance Against the Meeting at Upton's*, 6.

38. *Lib*, August 20, 1831. For an enthusiastic response to Forten's letter from a white Bostonian who signed himself "Hope," see ibid., September 3, 1831.

39. Hinks, ed., *David Walker's Appeal*, xliv.

40. James Forten to William Lloyd Garrison, October 20, 1831, BPL.

41. For a discussion of subscription patterns, see Jacobs, "Garrison's *Liberator*," 260–62.

42. William Lloyd Garrison to Robert Purvis, June 22, 1832, BPL.

43. Garrison to Purvis, December 10, 1832, BPL.

44. Joseph Cassey to William Lloyd Garrison, February 12, 1833, and James Forten to Garrison, May 6, 1832, BPL.

45. *Minutes and Proceedings of the First Annual Convention of the People of Colour*, 6.

46. Ibid., 7. Howell was eventually replaced by his son-in-law, Frederick Augustus Hinton, a well-to-do barber.

47. *Lib*, March 19, 1831.

48. Ibid., September 24, 1831; *HR*, September 24, 1831; *College for Colored Youth*, 4.

49. *College for Colored Youth*, 5, 8–9.

50. James Forten to William Lloyd Garrison, October 20, 1831; BPL.

51. See Strane, *A Whole-Souled Woman*, for a detailed account of Crandall's career.

52. *Lib*, March 9, 23, and April 6, 1833.

53. Lucretia Mott to J. Miller McKim, September 25, 1834, in Lutz, *Crusade for Freedom*, 43.

54. *Lib*, March 9, 1833.

55. Ibid., April 13, 1833.

56. William Lloyd Garrison to K____, April 17, 1833; BPL.

57. Strane, *A Whole-Souled Woman*, 64–65; Garrison and Garrison, *William Lloyd Garrison*, vol. 1, p. 343.

58. James Forten to William Lloyd Garrison, February 23, 1831, BPL.

59. Forten to Garrison, October 20, 1831, BPL.

60. *Poulson*, October 26, 1831.

61. *Lib*, November 26, 1831. There were many people in Liberia with the last name Mars. There was a family group from Georgia comprising eight people, all free-born—Joseph and Eve Mars, and their six children, ranging in age from one to twelve, who arrived aboard the *Carolinian* on December 4, 1830. The youngest child died almost immediately, and the next eldest and Mrs. Mars a few months later. Then there was a large party of thirty-seven emancipated slaves from Virginia. The first contingent, seven children and four adults, arrived on the *Montgomery* in February 1830. All but one of the children had died by the time the others arrived. The larger party came out on the *Carolinian* in December 1830. They numbered twenty-six. Before the year was out, twenty-two were dead. The remaining four succumbed over the following few months. Shick, comp., *Emigrants to Liberia*, 61–62.

62. John B. Russwurm to R. R. Gurley, August 6, 1833, ACS Incoming Corr., July 16–August 6, 1833.

63. Dailey was ordained a deacon of the Protestant Episcopal Church before he left for Liberia. Joseph R. Dailey to R. R. Gurley, August 9, 1830, ACS Incoming Corr., August 9–31, 1830.

64. Cedar Street was the old name for South Street. Philadelphia directory, 1820, 1821. Dailey had three separate seamen's protections. The first was issued in 1807. He received a new one in 1810 after he claimed the earlier protection "was lost by means of Damage by Salt Water." In 1812 he secured yet another protection after he told the authorities that his 1810 protection had been lost. At least one of these protections found its way into the hands of someone other than Dailey. It was being used by a sailor passing himself off as Dailey while the real Dailey was in Liberia. Seamen's Protection Certificates for the Port of Philadelphia, 1807, 1810, 1812, Nat Arch; Philadelphia Crew Lists, 1812–14, p. 3; 1819, p. 46; 1822, pp. 25, 178; 1826A, pp. 20, 150, 196; 1826B, p. 525; 1830, p. 362; 1833, pp. 134, 248; all in HSP.

65. Joseph R. Dailey to R. R. Gurley, June 30, 1829, ACS Incoming Corr., June 29–July 21, 1829.

66. Dailey to Purvis, April 12, 1833, BPL.

67. Dailey to Purvis, May 21, 1833, BPL.

68. Dailey to Purvis, August 15, 1833, BPL. Mechlin's downfall had more to do with the financial crisis overtaking the ACS in the 1830s than with any sexual indiscretions. Staudenraus, *The African Colonization Movement*, 167, 222.

69. James Bayard to R. R. Gurley, August 25, 1831, ACS Incoming Corr., August 17–September 15, 1831; Robert Blight to Gurley, October 22, 1831, ACS Incoming Corr., September 16–November 4, 1831.

70. Philadelphia directory, 1811; U.S. Census, 1820: New Market, 258; "Petition from members of St. Thomas' African Church, Phila. In favor of Jacob Oson & other testimonials in favor of the same," Record Group 50–5, Archives of the Episcopal Church, Austin, Texas (copy courtesy of Randall Burkett). Ayres had been to Liberia several times before he joined the crew of the *Margaret Mercer*. Philadelphia Crew Lists, 1828, p. 440; 1829, p. 152; 1830, p. 121.

71. Philadelphia Crew Lists, 1831, p. 380; 1835, p. 68.

72. *Eman*, July 13, 1833.

73. Ibid., July 20, 1833.

74. Hodgkin, *An Inquiry*, 33; *AfRep* 9 (September 1833): 203. Price, a freeborn farmer from Maryland, had arrived in Liberia on January 20, 1833, aboard the *Lafayette*. He never returned to Africa after his sojourn in Philadelphia. Shick, comp., *Emigrants to Liberia*, 77.

75. Carey, *Letters on the Colonization Society*, 27.

76. James Forten to William Lloyd Garrison, August 9, 1831, BPL.

77. Forten to Garrison, May 6, 1832, BPL.

78. Forten to Garrison, July 28, 1832, BPL.

79. R. M. Bascom to R. R. Gurley, July 3, 1832, ACS Incoming Corr., May 16–July 3, 1832.

80. Tappan, *Life of Arthur Tappan*, 136–37.

81. Garrison, *Thoughts on African Colonization*, 9–13.

82. *Lib*, August 1, 1835.

83. Ibid.

84. Henry C. Wright to William Lloyd Garrison, March 6, 1842, in *Lib*, March 11, 1842. See also *People's Press*, in *Lib*, April 1, 1842.

85. Purvis, *Remarks*, 14–15.

86. James Forten to William Lloyd Garrison, July 28, 1832, BPL.

87. R. R. Gurley to P. R. Fendall, December 2 and 3, 1833, ACS Incoming Corr., November 21–December 30, 1833.

88. Whittier, "Antislavery Convention," 167.

89. Ibid., 171.

90. For one account of a visit to the Forten home during the convention, see May, *Some Recollections*, 287.

91. *Lib*, December 14, 1833.

92. American Anti-Slavery Society, *First Annual Report*, 15, 32, 36, 38; *Second Annual Report*, 27.

93. American Anti-Slavery Society, *Third Annual Report*, 23, 25, 27.

94. American Anti-Slavery Society, *Fourth Annual Report*, 18, 21; *Fifth Annual Report*, 5, 15.

95. *Lib*, July 30, 1836.

96. *Constitution of the Young Men's Anti-Slavery Society*, 7, 11; Young Men's Anti-Slavery Society of Philadelphia, Committee Reports, 1836–37, HSP.

97. *Lib*, November 5, 1836.

98. *NECAUL*, February 11, 1837; *Proceedings of the Pennsylvania Convention . . . 1837*, 5.

99. *NECAUL*, November 30, 1837.

100. Philadelphia Female Anti-Slavery Society, Minute Books, 1833–38, 1838–39; Board of Managers Minute Books, 1833–36, 1836–39, HSP.

101. For a brief analysis of the power structure of the American Anti-Slavery Society, see Winch, *Philadelphia's Black Elite*, 83.

102. Lucretia Mott to J. Miller McKim, May 8, 1834, in Hallowell, ed., *James and Lucretia Mott*, 119.

103. See, e.g., Sarah Grimké to Sarah M. Douglass, November 23, 1837, in Barnes and Dumond, eds., *Weld and Grimké Letters*, vol. 1, p. 483.

104. Grimké to Douglass, October 22, 1837, in ibid., 470. See also Grimké to Douglass, October 22, 1837, in ibid., 364.

105. George Thompson to Robert Purvis, November 10, 1834, BPL.

106. Henry E. Benson to George Benson, March 27, 1835, BPL.

107. Elizabeth Pease to Angelina Grimké, December 27, 1836, in Barnes and Dumond, eds., *Weld and Grimké Letters*, vol. 1, p. 351.

108. See, e.g., James Forten to Nathaniel P. Rogers, March 29, 1839, Nathaniel P. Rogers Collection, Haverford College.

Chapter 11: "Abolition Property"

1. James Forten to William Lloyd Garrison, March 21, 1831, BPL; *Resolutions and Remonstrances*, 4.

2. *NASS*, March 10, 1842.

3. *NS*, March 10, 1848.

4. William Lloyd Garrison to Ebenezer Dole, June 29, 1832, BPL.

5. Garrison to K____, April 17, 1833, BPL.

6. *Poulson*, September 12 and 16, 1831; *Lib*, September 24, 1831; St. Thomas's African Episcopal Church, Parish Registers. On Harriet's elegant wedding-gown, see Stevenson, ed., *Journals of Charlotte Forten Grimké*, 333 (entry for August 25, 1858).

7. Ritter, *Philadelphia and Her Merchants*, 47.

8. May, *Some Recollections*, 288.

9. Philadelphia County Deeds, A.M. Book 26, 469, PCA.

10. Ibid., A.M., Book 70, pp. 575, 576; S.H.F. Book 26, p. 231; Book 28, p. 58; G.S. Book 6, pp. 721, 723, 725, 726; Book 10, pp. 86, 88; Book 12, p. 405; Book 18, pp. 458, 459; Book 19, p. 114; Book 23, p. 558; Book 24, pp. 275, 491; Book 29, p. 482; Book 42, p. 282.

11. See, e.g., Bucks County Deeds, Book 61, p. 163; Book 63, p. 544, BCC; Stevenson, ed., *Journals of Charlotte Forten Grimké*, 323 (entry for July 7, 1858). As an indication of Robert Purvis's warm regard for the Casseys, see his essay, "Friendship," in "Original and Selected Poetry of Amy Matilda Cassey," LCP.

12. Burlington County, New Jersey Deeds, Book Y³, 546 and Book A⁴, 521 (microfilm), HSP.

13. For the date of William Forten Purvis's birth, see William Lloyd Garrison to Robert Purvis, December 10, 1832, BPL.

14. There was an ugly dispute involving Robert's cousin John, Burridge Purvis's son. He had received a huge loan from William Purvis, Sr., and evidently hoped not to have to repay it. Another Robert Purvis, a cousin of John's, and the son of William's brother, Robert Sr., was also involved. John's siblings in Scotland eventually gave testimony on behalf of Robert and Joseph Purvis after Robert's visit. Charleston District Court of Common Pleas, Judgment Rolls, 1791–1839: 1832, p. 190A; 1836, p. 165A. Charleston County, Court of Equity, Bill no. 74 (1836), SCSA.

15. William Lloyd Garrison to Sir Thomas Fowell Buxton, May 20, 1834; Buxton Papers (microfilm), BPL. See also *ASB*, November 3, 1860.

16. State Department, Index to Special Passports, 1829–87, vol. 1, p. 71, Nat Arch. According to the *Anti-Slavery Bugle* (November 3, 1860), it was Congressman Horace Binney, a friend of Purvis's, who got him the "special passport." Purvis was reluctant to complain directly to Binney, but he did let others know he was less than pleased, and that was when Vaux, a Democrat with contacts in the Jackson administration, intervened.

17. Roberts Vaux to Louis McLean, May 16, 1824, Passports, January 4–December 31, 1834, Nat Arch.

18. Vaux to McLean, May 20, 1834, Passports, January 4–December 31, 1834, Nat Arch; *FDP*, September 15, 1854; Nell, *The Colored Patriots*, 319–20. Three years later James Forten tried unsuccessfully to get a passport for African-American composer and bandleader Francis Johnson. Two factors were at work in Johnson's case. He had no powerful white friends to intercede for him and he was darker-skinned than Purvis. State Department, Index of Passport Applications, 1837 (no. 212), Nat Arch. I am grateful to Charles K. Jones, Johnson's biographer, for this reference.

19. Payne, *Recollections of Seventy Years*, 53; *ASB*, November 3, 1860.

20. William Lloyd Garrison to Robert Purvis, May 20, 1834, BPL.

21. *Lib*, August 23, 1834.

22. Ladies' Anti-Slavery Society of Glasgow to the Philadelphia Female Anti-Slavery Society, September 3, 1834, in PFASS Correspondence, Incoming, 1834–47, HSP.

23. Payne, *Recollections of Seventy Years*, 54. See also the account in the *ASR*, November 1835, Appendix, 151–52.

24. For the approximate date of birth of Harriet and Robert's second child, Robert Jr., see *Lib*, April 4, 1862.

25. "The Grave of the Slave," in ibid., January 22, 1831. The poem was reprinted, along with "The Prayer," under the pen name of "Sarah Louisa," in the *Philanthropist*, March 11, 1836.

26. Jones and Greenwich, comps., *Works of Francis Johnson*, vol. 2, pp. 200–201.

27. *Lib*, January 29, 1831.

28. Ibid., March 19, 1831.

29. James Forten to William Lloyd Garrison, February 23, 1831, BPL.

30. *Lib*, June 30, 1832.

31. In "Poetic Justice," 233–34, Todd Gernes identifies Magawisca as a character in Catherine M. Sedgewick's *Hope Leslie; or Early Times in Massachusetts* (1827).

32. *Lib*, March 26, 1831.

33. Ibid.

34. Ibid, April 16, 1831.

35. Ibid., January 4, 1834.

36. *Philanthropist*, March 11, 1836.

37. *Lowell Observer* in *Lib*, February 23, 1833.

38. *Lib*, July 7, 1832; August 3, 1833.

39. Ibid., June 27, 1835.

40. Ibid., May 25, 1833.

41. Ibid., December 21, 1833.

42. Quoted in Yellin, *Women and Sisters*, 14.

43. Ibid., 15. Sarah copied eight lines of Chandler's poem into the album of Gerrit Smith's daughter. Elizabeth Smith Album, Francis J. Grimké Papers, Moorland-Spingarn Research Center, Howard University.

44. *Lib*, February 1, 1834. See also *An Appeal to the Women of the Nominally Free States*, 1.

45. *Lib*, February 22 and March 1, 1834. Sarah's poem was probably the "very thrilling 'Appeal to American ladies' by a colored female" that inspired a group of white women in Brooklyn, Connecticut, in 1834 to form an antislavery society. Jeffrey, *The Great Silent Army*, 49. Several more poems appeared in various periodicals under the pen name "Ada," but attributing them to Sarah Forten is problematic. To begin with, *this* "Ada" uses the Quaker dating style, "5th month 6" instead of May 6. There are other inconsistencies. They are written from places that, so far as I can determine, Sarah Forten never visited. In "A Farewell to New England" the writer regrets leaving her home in New England. In "The United States Come Last" she refers in a rather muddled fashion to a story that Sarah Forten would have heard many times from the person to whom it actually happened—Robert Purvis's encounter with Daniel O'Connell. Gernes argues convincingly in "Poetic Justice" that the pen name "Ada" was also used by a white New England Quaker, Eliza Earle, and that it was Earle, rather than Forten, who wrote the later "Ada" poems, including the one inspired by Angelina Grimké's *Appeal to the Christian Women of the South* that is most frequently cited as Sarah Forten's work. For the later "Ada" poems, see *NECAUL*, March 22, July 1, 1837; *Lib*, October 29, 1836; June 16, 1837; May 4, 1838; March 29, September 28, 1839; *PF*, August 30, October 3, 1838; *Eman*, November 10, 1836.

46. The dating style makes it difficult to determine the exact date of the letter. See Diary of Elizabeth Whittier (1835–38), typescript, p. 10, Whittier Collection, Haverhill Public Library, Haverhill, Mass. I am grateful to Sally Stephenson, a graduate of the M.A. program in Archival Methods at the University of Massachusetts at Boston, for tracking down the diary.

47. Sarah L. Forten to Elizabeth Whittier, November 9, 1835, George Whittier Pickard Papers, Houghton Library, Harvard.

48. Forten to Harriet Minot, in Forten to Whittier, November 9, 1835, Pickard Papers.

49. Forten to Whittier, November 9, 1835, and September 10, 1836, Pickard Papers.

50. *Lib*, November 28, 1835.

51. Forten to Whittier, November 9, 1835, Pickard Papers.

52. Forten to Whittier, September 10, 1836, Pickard Papers.

53. *NECAUL*, November 19, 1836.

54. Sarah L. Forten to Angelina Grimké, April 15, 1837, in Barnes and Dumond, eds., *Weld and Grimké Letters*, vol. 1, p. 379.

55. Ibid., 380.

56. Ibid., 381.

57. *PL*, January 12, 1838.

58. Joseph Cassey to William Lloyd Garrison, March 23, 1833; BPL.

59. Bucks County Deeds, Book 60, p. 111; Book 64, pp. 130, 354; Mortgages, Book 17, p. 312.

60. *Eman*, January 14, 1834. The poem was signed M. T. F. The author was identified as "the daughter of a highly respected colored gentleman of Philadelphia, with whose history our readers have been made acquainted."

61. Album of Elizabeth Smith, Francis J. Grimké Papers; "Original and Selected Poetry of Amy Matilda Cassey."

62. James Forten to Nathaniel P. Rogers, March 29, 1839, Nathaniel P. Rogers Collection, Treasure Room, Haverford College.

63. *Herald of Freedom*, March 16, 1839.

64. The daughter referred to was almost certainly Margaretta. Only she and Mary were unmarried and living at home at this point. In the 1850s young Charlotte Forten would often write in her journal about discussing French literature with her Aunt Margaretta.

65. James Forten to Nathaniel P. Rogers, March 29, 1839.

66. Sarah L. Forten to Elizabeth Whittier, September 10, 1836, Pickard Papers.

67. *Lib*, September 3, 1836.

68. James Forten to William Lloyd Garrison, March 21, 1831, BPL.

69. *Lib*, March 19, 1831.

70. James Forten, Jr., *An Address*, 4–5.

71. Ibid., 5–6.

72. Ibid., 6–7.

73. Ibid., 7–8.

74. Ibid., 10.

75. Ibid., 10–11, 12, 15–16.

76. *NECAUL*, December 3, 1836. See James Forten, Jr., *An Address*, 8.

77. See Blight, "In Search of Learning," 7–25.

78. James Forten, Jr., to James McCune Smith, September 8, 1835, BPL.

79. Charters of Incorporation, Book 6, p. 54, PSA.

80. Album-Scrapbook of Martina Dickerson, LCP. It was probably James's beautifully drawn map of the United States that a white visitor was shown when he called on James Sr. *NS*, March 10, 1848.

81. American Anti-Slavery Society, *Fifth Annual Report*, 5.

82. Hoff, "Frans Abramse Van Salee," 207–8. On his involvement in antislavery and civil rights, see *Lib*, March 12, 1831; *CA*, July 14 and December 15, 1838. On his business interests, see *FDP*, February 16, 1855. He died in 1844.

83. See *CA*, August 19, 1837; on the connection with Smith, see September 23, 1837.

84. On the Vogelsangs and the De Grasses, see Hoff, "Frans Abramse Van Salee,"

207–9. On the De Grasse family, see U.S. Census, 1820: New York City, Ward 1, 31; 1850: Ward 5, 47–48; and Ripley et al., eds., *Black Abolitionist Papers*, vol. 4, p. 317n. For some years the Vogelsangs were members of the congregation of a predominantly white church in New York, Christ Church. Peter Sr. and Maria were married there on March 28, 1811, and Peter Jr. was baptized there. However, it is not clear whether the family were still attending the church when Jane was born. The records for the period 1819–21 are incomplete. Records of Christ Church, New York City (microfilm), NEHGS.

85. *New York Herald*, January 15, 1839; *New Yorker*, January 19, 1839; *PL*, January 22, 1839.

86. *Lib*, March 7, 1835.

87. Ibid., March 21, 1835.

88. Ibid., March 7, 1835.

89. On a speech he gave on temperance at St. Thomas's African Episcopal Church, see *NECAUL*, February 18, 1837.

90. *Constitution of the Young Men's Anti-Slavery Society*, 7, 11.

91. Payne, *Recollections of Seventy Years*, 51–52.

92. *PL*, October 21, 1836. Mary had been born in 1814 and Annie in 1831. Philadelphia Board of Health Records; U.S. Census, 1860: Philadelphia, Ward 2, p. 296; 1870: Ward 2, dist. 7, p. 345.

93. *Town of Hertford Bi-Centennial*, 31; Winslow, *History of Perquimans County*, 447. The 1820 census of Perquimans County lists 50 free females of color under 14 and 26 between the ages of 14 and 26.

94. Yellin, ed., *Incidents in the Life of a Slave Girl*, 63–67.

95. Morris, "Panic and Reprisal," 52.

96. Mary V. Wood Album, Francis J. Grimké Papers. Distinguishing Mary Isabella's work from that of the other Mary Forten, her sister-in-law, is a matter of comparing handwriting. Mary Isabella wrote "To the Album" in Mary Virginia Wood Forten's album and "Friendship" in Amy Cassey's album. Mary Wood Forten copied Lydia Sigourney's "Difference of Color" into her own album and wrote the poem "Good Wives" for Amy Cassey's album.

97. *PL*, October 21, 1836; *Lib*, November 12, 1836. The directory for 1837 gives Robert Forten's address as 92 Lombard.

98. Philadelphia County Deeds, G.S. Book 4, p. 718.

99. For Gerrit Smith Forten's date of birth, see Philadelphia Board of Health Records.

100. Sernett, *Abolition's Axe*, 32–33, 35, 36–38, 41, 43.

101. Grinnell, *Men and Events of Forty Years*, 30; in Sernett, *Abolition's Axe*, 51.

102. Sernett, *Abolition's Axe*, 41, 54.

103. Other African-American students who attended after Forten were Jermain W. Loguen, William G. Allen, and John V. DeGrasse. Ibid., 52.

104. Warner, "Amos Gerry Beman," 202n; Sernett, *Abolition's Axe*, 53, 58.

105. "Abstracts of Wills Recorded in the Administration Books," 293; and Geffen, "William Henry Furness," 267.

106. "The Mother's Joy," in Album-Scrapbook of Mary Ann Dickerson, LCP.

107. *NS*, March 10, 1842.

Chapter 12: Time of Trial

1. *United States Gazette*, November 30, 1831; *Lib*, December 10, 1831.

2. *Journal of the Pennsylvania House* 56 (1831–32): 48, 58.

3. On the provisions of the proposed legislation, see McCrummill and White, *Memorial*, 11–12.

4. *Remonstrance Against the Meeting at Upton's*, 2. Forten's name does not appear in the printed proceedings, but his subsequent statements make it clear that he chaired it. The pamphlet contains a number of typographical errors. Purvis's name is misspelled and there is a gap where the name of the chairman should be.

5. Ibid., 2, 5. The Upton's "gentry" included a grocer, a hatter, and various other tradesmen. The most vocal, J. Washington Tyson, was not listed in the city directory. Philadelphia directories, 1830–32.

6. Ibid., 6, 7, 8.

7. *Journal of the Pennsylvania Senate* 56 (1831–32): 287; PAS, *Present State and Condition*, 22–23; Diary of Samuel Breck, 1832–33, p. 51, HSP.

8. Forten et al., *To the Honourable the Senate*, 1, 2, 3, 7.

9. Ibid., 4, 6.

10. Ibid., 7, 8.

11. *HR*, June 9, 1832, pp. 361–62.

12. *The Friend* 8, no. 21 (February 28, 1835): 166–67.

13. *Journal of the Pennsylvania House* 56 (1831–32): 58, 710, 979.

14. McCrummill and White, *Memorial*, 2, 7. See also Bowers and Depee, *Memorial*.

15. *Journal of the Pennsylvania House* 57 (1832–33): 23, 27, 87, 91, 100, 109, 127, 136, 144, 150, 158, 186, 261, 372, 428, 645.

16. Opper, "The Mind of the White Participant," 157–58.

17. *Philadelphia Gazette*, October 10, 1832; *United States Gazette*, October 12, 1832.

18. *GUE*, July 1834, 111.

19. Abdy, *Journal of a Residence and Tour*, vol. 3, pp. 319–20. Abdy identified the victim of the mob as one of James Forten's younger sons and simply said he was about fifteen. In August 1834 Thomas was not quite seventeen and William only eleven.

20. On the attack on the fire company, see *Pennsylvanian*, August 20, 1834, in Runcie, "'Hunting the Nigs' in Philadelphia," 191. On the destruction of the Flying Horses, see Scharf and Westcott, *History of Philadelphia*, vol. 1, p. 637; and *Philadelphia Gazette* in *HR*, August 23, 1834, p. 126.

21. While African Americans made up 8.6 percent of the total population of Philadelphia County in 1830, there was considerable variation among the different wards and "liberties." In New Market Ward, where the Fortens lived, blacks accounted for 25 percent of the population. For nearby Cedar Ward the figure was 19 percent, for Locust Ward 24 percent, and for Pine Ward 19 percent. The demographic patterns away from the southern fringes of the city were strikingly different—4.3 percent for High Street Ward, 5.6 percent for Chestnut Ward, and 5 percent for North Mulberry Ward. As for the "liberties," blacks made up 20 percent of the total population in Moyamensing and 10 percent for Southwark West. (The figure for Southwark East was only 2.5 percent). For a ward-by-ward breakdown of the 1830 census, see *HR*, March 1831, pp. 172–73. On the relationship between changing demographics and racial violence, see Lapsansky, "Since They Got Those Separate Churches," 54–78.

22. *Philadelphia Gazette* in *HR*, August 23, 1834.

23. Scharf and Westcott, *History of Philadelphia*, vol. 1, p. 638; *Commercial Intelligencer* in *HR*, August 23, 1834; *Pennsylvanian*, August 15, 1834, in *Niles' Register*, August 23, 1834.

24. *Pennsylvanian*, August 15, 1834, in *Niles' Register*, August 23, 1834.

25. *Pennsylvanian*, August 16, 1834, in ibid.

26. *Philadelphia Inquirer*, undated, in ibid.

27. Abdy, *Journal of a Residence and Tour*, vol. 3, p. 321.

28. *PAppeal*, July 18, 1863.

29. Abdy, *Journal of a Residence and Tour*, vol. 3, p. 321.

30. Ibid., 324.

31. *HR*, September 27, 1834.

32. Harriet Martineau to Charlotte Forten, February 18, 1857, in Cooper, ed., *Personal Recollections*, 39.

33. On the Gilmore case, see *Lib*, August 1, 1835; on the background to the assault on Mr. Stewart by his Ibo servant "Juan," see *HR*, July 18, 1835, and *Niles' Register*, July 18, 1835.

34. Scharf and Westcott, *History of Philadelphia*, vol. 1, p. 641.

35. *Philadelphia Gazette*, July 14, 1835, in *HR*, July 18, 1835.

36. Ibid.

37. *Philadelphia Inquirer*, undated, in ibid.; *Niles' Register*, July 18, 1835.

38. *Philadelphia Gazette*, July 14, 1835, in *HR*, July 18, 1835.

39. *Philadelphia Inquirer*, undated, in *HR*, July 18, 1835.

40. *Lib*, August 1, 1835.

41. *NECAUL*, March 18, 1837.

42. For an illuminating discussion of the interplay between rising black expectations and white notions of deference, see Lapsansky, "Since They Got Those Separate Churches."

43. Wainwright, ed., "Diary of Samuel Breck, 1814–1822," 505. Breck served in Congress from 1823 to 1825.

44. Zachary, "Social Disorder," 301.

45. Purvis et al., *Appeal of Forty Thousand*, 4–5.

46. Albert Gallatin to Joseph Parrish, December 21, 1837; Cox, Parrish, Wharton Papers, vol. 13, p. 81, HSP.

47. *Journal of the Pennsylvania Senate* 7 (1795–96): 43; and 18 (1806–7): 296–97, in Wesley, "Negro Suffrage," 51. On Schulze's query see ibid.

48. On the distribution of African Americans throughout the state, see Luckett, "Protest, Advancement and Identity," 13, 267. Philadelphia had by far the largest concentration.

49. Pierson, ed., *Tocqueville and Beaumont*, 514; Abdy, *Journal of a Residence and Tour*, vol. 3, p. 62; Bell, *Men and Things in America*, 179.

50. Forten, *Letters from a Man of Colour*, 4.

51. McCrummill and White, *Memorial*, 2.

52. *Lib*, March 19, 1831.

53. *CA*, May 3, 1838.

54. *Fogg v. Hobbs*, in *Reports of Cases Argued*, 553.

55. Denny, *An Enquiry*, 21, 23.

56. *Proceedings and Debates*, vol. 1, p. 164.

57. *CA*, June 10, 1837.

58. *Proceedings and Debates*, vol. 3, pp. 82–83, 85.

59. Ibid., 693.

60. Ibid., 696–97.

61. *Fogg v. Hobbs*, in *Reports of Cases Argued*, 553.

62. *Niles' Register*, November 11, 1837.

63. *Proceedings and Debates*, vol. 9, pp. 357–58.

64. Ibid., vol. 5, pp. 414, 416.

65. For the full text of the decision, see *Opinion of the Hon. John Fox*.

66. *Proceedings and Debates*, vol. 9, pp. 320–22.

67. Ibid., 328, 365, 368.

68. Ibid., 333–34. 352.

69. Ibid., vol. 10, pp. 5–6.

70. Ibid., 9–10.

71. *NECAUL*, January 25, 1838; *Pennsylvanian*, January 22, 1838.

72. *Proceedings and Debates*, vol. 10, p. 50.

73. Ibid., 52–59, 70, 74–75, 82.

74. Ibid., 90.

75. Ibid., 97, 106.

76. Ibid., 111.

77. Ibid., 112, 126–27.

78. PAS, *Register of the Trades of the Colored People*, and *Present State and Condition*. For the raw data from which these reports were compiled, see PAS MSS (microfilm), reel 26, HSP.

79. *PF*, March 22, 1838.

80. Purvis et al., *Appeal of Forty Thousand*, 3, 4.

81. Ibid., 12–13.

82. *PF*, March 22, 1838.

83. Marryat, *A Diary in America*, vol. 1, pp. 296–98.

84. Purvis, *Remarks*, 8.

85. *NR*, November 1838, pp. 36–38.

86. *Pennsylvanian*, September 18, 1838.

87. Gurney, *A Visit to North America*, 102.

88. *ProvFree*, August 15, 1857.

89. Purvis et al., *Appeal of Forty Thousand*, 4.

90. *History of Pennsylvania Hall*, 6; Philadelphia Female Anti-Slavery Society, Minute Book, 1833–38, HSP.

91. *History of Pennsylvania Hall*, 3, 6.

92. Ibid., 37, 38, 67, 115, 127.

93. Ibid., 181–82; Sturge, *A Visit to the United States*, 45–47.

94. *History of Pennsylvania Hall*, 168; Mayer, *All on Fire*, 244.

95. *History of Pennsylvania Hall*, 136.

96. Ibid., 123–27.

97. Mayer, *All on Fire*, 245–46; *History of Pennsylvania Hall*, 140.

98. Wainwright, ed., *A Philadelphia Perspective*, 49–50.

99. Manuscript Diary of Augustus Pleasonton, 1838–1844, HSP.

100. Ibid.; *Pennsylvanian*, May 21, 1838, in Brothers, *The United States as They Are*, 364.

101. Scharf and Westcott, *History of Philadelphia*, vol. 1, pp. 654–55.

102. *Proceedings of the Anti-Slavery Convention of American Women . . . 1838*, 8.

103. Lucretia Mott to Edward M. Davis, June 18, 1838, in Hallowell, ed., *James and Lucretia Mott*, 130.

104. *Minutes and Proceedings of the First Annual Convention of the People of Colour*, 4, 5; James Forten to William Lloyd Garrison, August 9, 1831, BPL. The convention movement experienced something of a power vacuum in 1831. Bishop Richard Allen, the driving force behind the 1830 convention, died before the 1831 convention met.

105. *Minutes and Proceedings of the Second Annual Convention of the Free People of Color*, 6, 9, 11; *Lib*, August 1, 1835.

106. *Minutes and Proceedings of the Third Annual Convention of the Free People of Colour*, 26, 30–31. The name was misprinted as "James Foster," but the context makes it clear that Forten was the individual being referred to.

107. *Minutes of the Fourth Annual Convention of the Free People of Colour*, 14–15.

108. *Minutes of the Fifth Annual Convention of the Free People of Colour*, 4–5.

109. For a brief biography of Whipper, see Winch, ed., *The Elite of Our People*, 136–39.

110. *Lib*, July 2, 1836; James Forten et al. to Gerrit Smith, August 15, 1836, BAP microfilm.

111. For a more extensive discussion of the tensions between the two cities and their impact on the convention movement, see Winch, *Philadelphia's Black Elite*, 91–129.

112. *PF*, August 24, 1836.

113. Ibid.

114. Ibid., January 28, 1837.

115. Circular (typed copy), Leon Gardiner Collection, Misc., folder 6, HSP.

116. *Minutes and Proceedings of the First Annual Meeting of the American Moral Reform Society*, 200–201.

117. Ibid., 216, 217–18.

118. *CA*, August 26, 1837.

119. Ibid., September 2, 1837.

120. Ibid., July 29, 1837.

121. Ibid., August 19, 1837.

122. Ibid., August 26, 1837.

123. *Minutes of the Fifth Annual Convention of the Free People of Colour*, 14–15; James Forten to Nathaniel P. Rogers, March 29, 1839, Nathaniel P. Rogers Collection, Haverford College. For illuminating discussions on African-American perceptions of racial difference in antebellum America, see Stewart, "The Emergence of Racial Modernity," 181–236; Price and Stewart, eds., *To Heal the Scourge of Prejudice*; and Bay, *The White Image in the Black Mind*, chap. 1.

124. *CA*, September 9, 1837.

125. Ibid.

126. See, e.g., ibid., September 16, 1837.

127. *NECAUL*, November 2, 1837.

128. *PF*, July 5, 1838.

129. *NR*, September 1838, p. 2.

130. Ibid., 8–9.

131. Ibid., 6.

132. *CA*, August 25, 1838.

133. *PF*, September 13, 1838; CA, December 22, 1838.

134. *CA*, September 15, 1838; for allegations that the letter had been suppressed, see August 25, 1838.

135. *NR*, October 1838, pp. 18, 19.

136. Ibid., 21–23; see also November 1838, pp. 33–34.

Chapter 13: Death of a Patriarch

1. *CA*, November 14, 1840.

2. Tooker, *Nathan Trotter*, 103.

3. Clement, *Welfare and the Poor*, 28.

4. Tooker, *Nathan Trotter*, 148–49.

5. Delany, *Condition, Elevation, Emigration, and Destiny*, 94.

6. Lyell, *Travels in North America*, 207.

7. Cornish and Wright, *The Colonization Scheme Considered*, 4.

8. Jones, *Abolitionrieties*, 11; see also *Lib*, May 22, 1840.

9. *PF*, January 17, 1839.

10. Ibid., December 12, 1839.

11. On the controversy the Trinidad plan stirred up, see ibid., May 7, 1840. For a more extensive discussion, see Winch, *Philadelphia's Black Elite*, 61–66.

12. Benjamin Coates to Samuel Wilkeson, November 27, 1839, ACS Incoming Corr., November 27–December 31, 1839, ACS Papers (microfilm), BPL.

13. *NR*, April 1839, p. 128.

14. Ibid., September 1839, p. 129.

15. Ibid., 129–30, 142.

16. Ibid, 141.

17. Ibid., December 1839, p. 177.

18. *CA*, July 11, 1840; *PF*, July 16, 1840.

19. *CA*, September 5, 1840.

20. *Lib*, October 9, 1840; *NASS*, October 1, 1840.

21. *NASS*, March 17, 1842.

22. *CA*, June 13, 1840.

23. Winch, *Philadelphia's Black Elite*, 122–23.

24. *CA*, March 13, 1841.

25. *CA*, July 3, 1841; on "the patriarch of Philadelphia," see July 17, 1841.

26. *PF*, September 6, 1841. For the call to the state convention, which the AMRS delegates criticized, see *CA*, August 7, 1841.

27. *CA*, September 25, 1841.

28. *Proceedings of the State Convention of the Colored Freemen of Pennsylvania . . . 1841*, 6. The convention was eventually held in Pittsburgh because of opposition from the authorities in Harrisburg.

29. *PF*, December 8, 1841.

30. James Forten to Joshua Leavitt, *Eman*, August 15, 1839.

31. *PF*, October 31, 1839.

32. The Board of Health Records list the date of death as May 11, while the *Public Ledger* (May 12, 1840) gives it as May 10.

33. Robert B. Forten to Gerrit Smith, May 29, 1840, Gerrit Smith Papers (microfilm), Sterling Library, Yale.

34. *CA*, August 29, 1840; Philadelphia Board of Health Records, HSP; *PL*, July 11, 1840.

35. Philadelphia County Deeds, G.S. Book 25, p. 124, PCA.

36. Coan, *Daniel A. Payne*, 55, 58; Simmons, *Men of Mark*, 1082.

37. *CA*, April 3 and 10, 1841.

38. Boromé, "Vigilant Committee," 320–51.

39. *CA*, July 24, 1841.

40. Stevenson, ed., *Journals of Charlotte Forten Grimké*, 218 (entry for May 12, 1857).

41. Sturge, *A Visit to the United States*, 10.

42. *CA*, June 29, 1839.

43. *NASS*, May 13, 1841.

44. *Lib.*, September 17, 1841. Besides the *Liberator*, he continued to subscribe to other abolitionist newspapers. See *NASS*, January 7, 1841.

45. *CA*, February 20, 1841; David Paul Brown Papers, HSP.

46. For a detailed discussion of this complex case, see Jones, *Mutiny on the Amistad*.

47. *NASS*, February 25, 1841.

48. Jones, *Mutiny on the Amistad*, 43.

49. Silcox, "A Comparative Study," 167–68, 170.

50. Silcox, "Delay and Neglect," 455, 457–58; Silcox, "A Comparative Study," 171.

51. Committee to Improve the Condition of the African Race, Minute Book, 1837–53, p. 32, PAS MSS, HSP. The PAS referred to "schools" because a boys' school and a girls' school were housed on separate floors in the same building.

52. Silcox, "A Comparative Study," 77, 172.

53. *Lib*, September 17, 1841.

54. *Demosthenian Shield* in *Lib*, March 18, 1842.

55. Philadelphia County Wills, Will Book 15, p. 445, no. 87 (1842), PCA.

56. Philadelphia County Deeds, G.S. Book 35, p. 621.

57. Gloucester, *Discourse*, 27, 30.

58. Purvis, *Remarks*, 8. Brewton survived Forten by twelve years. Hildeburn, ed., *Inscriptions in St. Peter's Church Yard*, 192.

59. *Demosthenian Shield* in *Lib*, March 18, 1842.

60. Ibid. Because of an apparent misprint, the article says that Forten summoned the family to his bedside on February 21. However, Rev. Douglass insisted it was on February 28, and the later date certainly seems more plausible.

61. *NASS*, May 5, 1842. The cause of death as listed in the Board of Health records is "anasarca." The *Oxford English Dictionary* defines this as "generalized oedema of subcutaneous tissue, with accumulation of fluid in serous cavities." It is also sometimes referred to as dropsy. A notice in one newspaper listed the cause as "dropsy of the head." "Death of James Forten," in "Poulson's Scrapbook of American Biography," vol. 1, p. 203, LCP.

62. *NASS*, March 17, 1842.

63. *Lib*, March 11, 1842.

64. *NASS*, March 10, 1842; Lucretia Mott to Richard and Hannah Webb, March 7, 1842, in Hallowell, ed., *James and Lucretia Mott*, 232.

65. *United States Gazette* in *Lib*, March 18, 1842.

66. *PL* in *Lib*, March 11, 1842.

67. *Lib*, May 5, 1842.

68. Ibid. Grace Douglass died on March 9. *Lib*, March 18 and April 15, 1842.

69. *Peoples' Press* in *Lib*, April 1, 1842.

70. William Lloyd Garrison to Sarah M. Douglass, March 18, 1842, BPL.

71. *Herald of Freedom*, March 18, 1842, in *Lib*, April 8, 1842.

72. *North American*, March 5, 1842.

73. *AfRep* 18 (May 1842): 156.

74. *NASS*, March 24, 1842.

75. Purvis, *Remarks*, 3–4.

76. *PF*, April 1842.

77. Gloucester, *Discourse*, 26.

78. *Wealth and Biography of the Wealthy Citizens*, 10; *Memoirs and Autobiography of Some of the Wealthy Citizens*, 24.

Chapter 14: Legacy

1. Philadelphia Board of Health Records, HSP; *NASS* July 28, 1842; St. Thomas's African Episcopal Church, Philadelphia, Parish Register. Mary Isabella Forten's age is given as twenty-six in the Board of Health Records, but she was actually twenty-seven. She died intestate. See Administration file 300, Book P, 229, PCA. Two family friends, Elizabeth Chew and Ameline Gigon, took the inventory of her estate. Chew was a member of one of Philadelphia's prosperous African-American families. Gigon was a teacher who taught several of the Fortens and the Purvises. Although the census-taker recorded her place of birth as Pennsylvania, she had probably been born in one of the French-speaking cantons of Switzerland. She lived just a few doors away from a Swiss family by the name of Gigon. Gigon was the "Madame G." referred to by Charlotte Forten in her journal. In 1857 Joseph Purvis's executors paid her $20 for tutoring the Purvis children. Stevenson, ed., *Journals of Charlotte Forten Grimké*, 229, 239 (entries for June 15 and July 23, 1857). U.S. Census, 1850: Philadelphia, Moyamensing, Ward 2, p. 299; Joseph Purvis Administration, file no. 10075, Adm. 8, no. 49, BCC.

2. Inventory of the Estate of James Forten; Philadelphia County Wills, Will Book 15, p. 445, no. 87 (1842), PCA. On Anthony, see below. Robert Archibald may have been employed at the sail loft at one time. His connection with the Forten family continued. After Abigail Forten Dunbar's death, he and his family moved into her old home, 1 Washington Court, and paid rent to James Forten's widow. Friends' census (1847), in PAS MSS, HSP.

3. The Farmers' and Mechanics' Bank, established in 1807, merged with the Philadelphia National Bank. The Atlantic Insurance Company, like many other institutions, faced hard times in the early 1840s. In December 1841 lawyer Horace Binney was asked to give an opinion on winding it up. Misc. Legal Papers, case 15, box 30, HSP.

4. Philadelphia County Wills, Will Book 15, p. 445, no. 87 (1842); Philadelphia County Deeds, R.L.L., Book 10, pp. 213–16; Philadelphia Orphans' Court Records, Book 38 (1842–43), 301; Book 39 (1844–45), p. 95, PCA.

5. Philadelphia County Wills, Will Book 15, p. 445, no. 87 (1842); U.S. Census, 1850: various wards; Philadelphia directories, 1840–47.

6. Ritter, *Philadelphia and Her Merchants*, 196, 198. Latour lived in a house that had been owned by Forten's captain from the Revolutionary War, Stephen Decatur, Sr. He sold it to ropemaker Henry Mitchell, and at some point thereafter it was acquired by Culpepper Bridges. James Forten bought the house next door, no. 259, from Mary Bridges in 1833.

7. On Welsh, see ibid., 37, 58–59.

8. Philadelphia directories, 1842–47; U.S. Census, 1850: Philadelphia, various wards; Ship Registers of the Port of Philadelphia; Blunt–White Library; Vessel Registers, 1803–4, Independence Seaport Museum. Diehl had been declared insolvent in 1838. Moak, comp., *Insolvency Petitions*, 34.

9. Lyell, *Travels in North America*, 207. However, there was a general perception that Forten was still very wealthy at the time of his death. One anonymous writer recorded he was "doing a large Business & [was] Comfortably off." Records of Deaths in Philadelphia, 1791 to 1851, County Records, film 2937, PSA. As late as 1845 another fairly knowledgeable observer put the value of his estate at $50,000. *Wealth and Biography of the Wealthy Citizens*, 10.

10. Wainwright, ed., *A Philadelphia Perspective*, 134–35.

11. *Robert Purvis v. James Forten and Robert B. Forten trading &c.*, District Court, Execution Docket, March Term 1844, and Philadelphia County Deeds, R.L.L., Book 24, p. 202, PCA. In a case heard a few months earlier, Forten's executors were able to prove that a certain sum of money owed by his estate had been paid. See *John Magoffin, administrator de bonis non of Henry Patton decd. v. Charlotte Forten, Margaretta Forten & Robert Purvis, Executors of the last will of James Forten decd.* District Court, Appearance Docket, September 1843, p. 131, PCA. The Pattons and the Magoffins were related by marriage to the Bridges family.

12. *James Maull Jr. v. James Forten and Robert B. Forten trading under the firm of James and Robert B. Forten*, District Court, Appearance Docket, March 1844, p. 114. See also *James Maull, Jr. v. James Forten & Robert B. Forten defendants and John Graham Garnishee*, ibid., June 1844, p. 110, PCA; Philadelphia County Wills, Will Book 15, p. 445, no. 87 (1842); Philadelphia directory, 1843.

13. Philadelphia County Wills, Will Book 15, p. 445, no. 87 (1842); Philadelphia directories, 1842, 1847; *George H. Mecke, Christopher H. Plate and John Leppien trading under the firm of Mecke, Plate & Company v. James Forten and Robert B. Forten trading under the firm of J. and R. B. Forten*, District Court, Appearance Docket, March 1844, p. 127, PCA. Mecke himself had been declared insolvent in 1840. Moak, comp., *Insolvency Petitions*, 78.

14. Philadelphia County Wills, Will Book 15, p. 445, no. 87 (1842); *Robert Purvis v. James Forten and Robert B. Forten trading under the firm of J. and R. B. Forten defts. and John Martin, John Graham, P. L. and E. Laguerenne, Rinier Skaats, John Devereux, John McDermott, Charles I. Tully, William S. Smith, Adam Southern and J. C. Benedict, Garnishees*, District Court, Appearance Docket, March 1844, p. 161, PCA; Philadelphia directo-

ries, 1840–47; U.S. Census, 1850: Philadelphia, various wards. Martin had declared bankruptcy in 1841 and Graham in 1837. Moak, comp., *Insolvency Petitions*, 48, 74.

15. *Ramon de la Sierra v. James and Robert B. Forten, copartners as J. and R. B. Forten*, District Court, Appearance Docket, March 1844, pp. 163, 182; *Francis Harley Sr. v. James and Robert B. Forten, late copartners as J. and R. B. Forten*, ibid., 182; *Joseph W. Ham v. James Forten and Robert B. Forten trading under the firm of J. and R. B. Forten*, ibid., June 1844, p. 174, PCA; Philadelphia directory, 1842.

16. *William Harbeson v. James Forten & Robert B. Forten late trading as J. and R. B. Forten* and *William Harbeson v. Robert Purvis*, District Court, Appearance Docket, March 1844, p. 316; Philadelphia directories, 1842, 1847.

17. *William W. Smith v. James Forten & Robert B. Forten trading as J. and R. B. Forten* and *William W. Smith v. Robert Purvis*, District Court, Appearance Docket, June 1844, p. 95.

18. *Charlotte Forten et al. v. Peter Anderson*, District Court, Execution Docket, March Term 1845.

19. Philadelphia County Deeds, R.L.L., Book 18, p. 93.

20. Ibid., Book 19, pp. 238, 241.

21. Philadelphia County Sheriff's Deeds, Book A2, p. 526, PCA.

22. Philadelphia County Deeds, T.H. Book 129, p. 22, and Book 179, p. 251.

23. Minton, *Early History of Negroes in Business*, 16; PAS, *Register of the Trades of the Colored People*; U.S. Census, 1850: Philadelphia, Spruce Ward, 381; Moyamensing, Ward 2, p. 318.

24. King, "Sailmakers and Ship Chandlers," 221–22.

25. *NS*, May 4, 1849. She was still teaching at the school in 1851. Ibid., April 17, 1851. Along with several of her relatives, Jane Forten was active in antislavery circles in New York City. See, e.g., *NS*, April 26, 1850. She evidently lived apart from her husband and son. According to the 1850 census, she was boarding with confectioner John Lucien Esteve, his wife Clorice, and their daughter, Emina, in the city's Fifth Ward. Everyone in the household was described as white, but the Esteves were well-known members of the African-American community. John Esteve operated the highly successful Tivoli Garden, where he sold "Ice Cream of a superior quality." Esteve died in 1852, and in 1855 his widow married Charles L. Reason. Jane would have known quite a few of her neighbors. Her brother, Peter, lived nearby, as did his in-laws, the De Grasses, and James Forten, Jr.'s friend James McCune Smith. U.S. Census, 1850: New York City, Fifth Ward, 47–48, 62, 158; *CA*, August 26 and September 9, 1837; June 30, 1838; November 9, 1839; *FDP*, March 11, 1853; *ProvFree*, August 22, 1855; *PAppeal*, August 22, 1863.

26. *FDP*, September 15, 1854.

27. *New York Herald*, July 17, 1852.

28. Stevenson, ed., *Journals of Charlotte Forten Grimké*, 296, 306 (entries for March 28 and May 1, 1858); for another meeting between the cousins, see 230 (entry for June 18, 1857).

29. Rendezvous Reports (1863), 339, Record Group 24, Nat Arch.

30. Ibid. (1864), 713; Muster Roll, vol. 498, *Tuscarora* (1861–65), Record Group 24, Nat Arch.

31. Philadelphia County Deeds, G.G.P., Book 365, p. 83, and Book 599, p. 97.

32. James V. Forten Pension Application, Civil War Pension File 25551, Nat Arch. Philadelphia County Deeds, G.G.P., Book 365, p. 83. U.S. Census, 1900: Camden County, N.J., vol. 10, enumeration district 91, sheet 4. Researcher Reg Pitts kindly supplied the date of James V. Forten's death.

33. William Chew was a Philadelphia native. Hetty Chew had been born a slave in Maryland. Frederick A. Hinton had bought his way out of slavery in North Carolina. Philadelphia directory, 1844; Friends' Census (1847); Philadelphia Board of Health Records; U.S. Census, 1850: Philadelphia, Pine Ward, 321; Dock Ward, 503; Stevenson, ed. *Journals of Charlotte Forten Grimké*, 229, 234–35, 237, 240, 256, 260, 294, 296, 298–99, 302, 304, 310, 315, 322, 330–31, 354; Winch, ed., *The Elite of Our People*, 58–60, 63, 64, 150 n. 72.

34. In 1843, e.g., Robert Forten witnessed a deed for the Purvises. Bucks County, Misc. Book 9, p. 213, BCC.

35. Will of Thomas Hanscome, Charleston County Wills, vol. 39 (1826–34), p. 960, and Charleston County Inventories, Book G, p. 501. vol. 6, pp. 501–502, SCSA.

36. Like the Purvises, William Dacosta (1808–73) was probably of Jewish as well as African ancestry. The Dacostas had been prominent members of Charleston's Jewish community since the 1740s. Dacosta married Louisa Hanscome on February 12, 1833. John George Garden was the son of John (d. 1847) and Elizabeth Susan Garden (1784–1851). Mary Sophia Inglis (b. 1823) was the daughter of Thomas (1778–1835) and Martha Sophia Inglis (d. 1843). John Lee, Jr. (b. 1821), was the eldest son of John and Eliza Lee. Tracking James Hanscome and his wife or wives is no easy matter. He and Serena Elizabeth do not appear in the 1850 census. In 1860 he was living in Savannah, Georgia, married to Hetty Geary, a widow six years his senior. In 1870 he was back in Charleston. His third wife, Emma, was a South Carolinian, and they had one daughter, aged five. James had another daughter, twenty-two-year-old Sarah, presumably his and Serena's child. His family connections served him well. By 1872 he was a member of the city's police force. Pinckney, ed., *Register of St. Philip's Church, 1810–22*, 76. Register of St. Philip's Church, Charleston, 1823–1940, Caroliniana Collection, USC; "The Private Register of the Rev. Paul Trapier," 179; Charleston County Health Department, Death Records, CCL; U.S. Census, 1850: Charleston, St. Philip's, 218; 1860: Charleston, 297; 1870: Fifth Ward, 389; 1860: Savannah, Georgia, 198; Charleston directories, 1801, 1807, 1819, 1822, 1829, 1831, 1835–36, 1840–41, 1852, 1856, 1859, 1872–73; Charleston County Wills, vol. 40 (1834–39), p. 288; 42 (1839–45), p. 62; 43 (1839–45), p. 633; 44 (1845–51), p. 166; 66 (1851–56), p. 16; Marriage Settlements, vol. 14 (1837–40), pp. 249–53; 15 (1840–41), pp. 15, 302; Charleston Free Negro Capitation Tax Books, 1821–23, 1832–38, 1840–46, 1848–ca. 1852, 1855, 1857, 1860, SCSA; Koger, *Black Slaveowners*, 211–12; Powers, *Black Charlestonians*, 44, 59; Hagy, *This Happy Land*, 10, 11, 20, 91n, 92, 185, 304–5; Johnson and Roark, eds., *No Chariot Let Down*, 57–58, 62.

37. John Drayton Lee, the son of John and Mary (Hanscome) Lee, was born on April 25, 1844. Register of St. Philip's Church, 1823–1940.

38. "Tombstone Inscriptions Collected by the Late Joseph Ioor Waring," 36. The transcription says Ann Hanscome died on August 29, 1838, aged two years and three months. However, the register of St. Philip's Church gives her date of death as November 29, 1837. I have chosen to accept the date in the register. Ann is not mentioned

in her father's will and it seems unlikely that he would have failed to provide for her if she had been alive at the time of his death. Charleston County Wills, vol. 41 (1834–39), p. 809; Misc. Records, Secretary of State, Bills of Sale, Book 5T (1836–39), p. 473, SCSA; Koger, *Black Slaveowners*, 133–34.

39. Koger, *Black Slaveowners*, 20–21, 86–88, 96, 133–34; Misc. Records, Secretary of State, Bills of Sale, Book 5Z (1842–43), pp. 339–40, SCSA.

40. Bucks County Deeds, Book 72, p. 205; Bucks County Mortgages, Book 20, p. 453, BCC; Records of Neshaminy Presbyterian Church of Warwick, Hartsville, Bucks County, Pa., 1788–1879, pp. 165–66, HSP.

41. Bucks County Misc., Book 10, p. 133. The marriage settlement was also recorded in South Carolina. See Langdon, comp., *South Carolina Marriages*, 28, 131.

42. Bucks County Deeds, Book 74, p. 462; Book 79, p. 628; U.S. Census, 1850: Warminster Township, Bucks County, Pa., 123; U.S. agricultural census, Pennsylvania, 1850.

43. *PF*, April 2, 1846.

44. *NS*, March 16, 1849. However, Forten continued to support Douglass's newspaper. See ibid., February 8, 1850.

45. Ibid., June 13, 1850.

46. Bucks County Deeds, Book 135, p. 242.

47. Stevenson, ed., *Journals of Charlotte Forten Grimké*, 61–62, 67, 69 (entries for May 26–27, June 2 and 10, 1854).

48. Bucks County Deeds, Book 82, p. 709. Hanscome had difficulty disposing of his real estate in Philadelphia. He had to return from Toronto to revoke a deed of trust, sue his dishonest trustee, and appoint someone else. See Bucks County Misc. Book 12, p. 95; Philadelphia County Deeds, R.D.W., Book 77, p. 197; Book 80, p. 533; Book 81, p. 30.

49. U.S. Census, 1850: Warminster Township, Bucks County, Pa., 125; Canadian census, 1861: Toronto, Ontario, St. James Ward, Fifth District, 144, CNA. On her death in 1843, Martha Sophia Inglis named Thomas Hanscome guardian of her son, then a minor. Apparently Inglis remained on friendly terms with the Hanscomes long after he attained his majority. Charleston County Wills, vol. 43 (1839–45), p. 633.

50. Canadian census, 1871: Toronto, Ontario, St. James Ward, Fifth District, 33; 1861: 144.

51. Wilson and Wilson, comps., *Directory of the Province of Ontario, 1857*; *The Canada Directory for 1857–58*; Toronto directories, 1856, 1859–95, 1926; Canadian census, 1871: Toronto, Ontario, subdist. B, div. 6, p. 27; 1881: St. James, subdiv. E 2, pp. 146, 159; Index of Ontario Death Records, 1869–1921, NEHGS; *Toronto Telegram*, August 3, 1877; *Toronto Evening Telegram*, February 17, 1880; *Toronto Star*, October 2, 1894; *Toronto Globe*, October 2, 1894, and January 21, 1899.

52. Wilson and Wilson, comps., *Directory of the Province of Ontario* (where the name is given as Fortune), *The Canada Directory for 1857–58* (Robert B. "Fortune"), and *Railton's Directory for the City of London, C.W., for 1856–1857*, where the name was mangled as "Forsten." On antislavery activities in London, see Stouffer, *The Light of Nature*, 123.

53. Stevenson, ed., *Journals of Charlotte Forten Grimké*, 216–17, 272 (entries for May 4 and December 17, 1857).

54. According to the Philadelphia newspaper that William D. Kelley cited in his tribute to Robert Forten (*Congressional Record*, 38th Cong., 1st sess., 1998), the firm Forten worked for was in the Poultry, a street in the City of London close to the Bank of England. In the early 1860s there were two stationers in the Poultry. Richard Birchall, who sold stationery and account books, was at 8 Poultry. The much larger firm of Houghton Lucas and Co. had premises at 30 Poultry, where they made and sold envelopes and "fancy" stationery, and at nearby Chapel Place, where they sold legal stationery. *Kelly's Post Office Directory: Streets and Commercial* 61st ed. (1860); *Kelly's Post Office Directory: Streets and Commercial* 64th ed. (1863). Forten was unemployed in 1860, when he described himself on his son's death certificate as a "Gentleman." No occupation was listed for him in the 1861 census.

55. *Address of the London Emancipation Committee to the Rev. George B. Cheever* (London, 1860), BAP microfilm; Frederick W. Chesson Diary, May 24, 1859, Thompson Papers, John Rylands Library, Manchester University. I am grateful to Margot Melia of the University of Western Australia for sharing her research on the Chesson diary with me.

56. Wendell Phillips Forten's death certificate, Register of Deaths (July–September 1860), FRC.

57. Census of the United Kingdom (1861), Reel 124, Registration District 9, Sub-Dist. 6, folio 13, FRC.

58. Payne, *Recollections of Seventy Years*, 52–53.

59. *Lib*, February 19, 1864. I am grateful to Todd Gernes of the University of Michigan for bringing this poem to my attention.

60. *New York Tribune* in *Lib*, May 13, 1864.

61. Statement of J. W. Taggard, October 28, 1865, Robert B. Forten pension file, Civil War Pensions, file 99272, Nat Arch; *New York Tribune* in *Lib*, May 13, 1864.

62. Philadelphia Board of Health Records; Affidavit of Margaretta Forten and statement of George E. Heath, April 21, 1866, Robert B. Forten pension file.

63. *New York Tribune* in *Lib*, May 13, 1864.

64. Deposition of Mary Forten, May 3, 1865, in Robert B. Forten pension file; *Congressional Record*, 38th Cong., 1st sess., 1997–98.

65. Deposition of Mary Forten.

66. Samuel Preck to Commissioner of Pensions, August 5, 1865; J. W. Taggard to Commissioner, October 28, 1865; James R. Millikin to William D. Forten, January 8, 1866; affidavit of Jonathan DeLacy, M.D., March 2, 1866, all in Robert B. Forten pension file.

67. Margaretta Forten to Commissioner of Pensions, October 31, 1866, and "Brief in the Case of Mary Forten, Widow of Robert B. Forten, Sergt Maj 43 U.S.C. Inf.," Robert B. Forten pension file.

68. Mary Forten to Lockwood L. Dory, December 9, 1872; S. B. Dutetier to J. H. Baker, Commissioner of Pensions, December 26, 1872; note in file, May 6, 1876, and transfer letter, April 27, 1876, all in Robert B. Forten pension file.

69. Philadelphia County Deeds, G.G.P., Book 365, p. 83.

70. Her young aunt, Annie Wood, had already been sent to school in Salem. Ripley et al., eds., *Black Abolitionist Papers*, vol. 4, p. 183.

71. Stevenson, ed., *Journals of Charlotte Forten Grimké*, 181–82, 203 (entries for January 11 and March 17, 1857); Harriet Martineau to Charlotte Forten, February 18,

1857, in Cooper, ed., *Personal Recollections*, 39; Charlotte Forten to Charles Sumner, November 1856, Charles Sumner Papers, Houghton Library, Harvard.

72. Wendell Phillips to Charlotte Forten, January 18, 1857, in Cooper, ed., *Personal Recollections*, 17. Lydia Maria Child thought highly of Charlotte's ability as a writer. Child to William P. Cutler, July 10, 1862, in Meltzer and Holland, eds., *Lydia Maria Child*, 414.

73. Charlotte Forten to Charles Sumner, January 28, 1872; Sumner Papers.

74. Stevenson, ed., *Journals of Charlotte Forten Grimké*, 298 (entry for April 4, 1858); see also 300 (April 13, 1858).

75. Ibid., 156, 157 (entries for May 29 and June 18, 1856).

76. Ellen Wright to Martha Wright, December 13, 1858, Sophia Smith Collection, Smith College (copy in Black Abolitionist Archives); *Salem Register* in *Lib*, March 26, 1860.

77. On the initial antipathy of some of the freedpeople toward Charlotte Forten, whom they labeled "dat brown gal," see Thomas Wentworth Higginson to Mary Channing Higginson, October 25, 1863, in Looby, ed., *Civil War Journal*, 319. For Forten's account of her experiences, see "Life on the Sea Islands," *Atlantic Monthly* (May 1864): 587–96; (June 1864): 666–76.

78. Thomas Wentworth Higginson to Louisa Storrow Higginson, January 22, 1864, in Looby, ed., *Civil War Journal*, 350.

79. Whittier to Theodore Dwight Weld, July 28, 1865, and Whittier to James Thomas Fields, August 28, 1865, in Pickard, ed., *Letters of Whittier*, vol. 3, pp. 97–99.

80. U.S. Census, 1870: Philadelphia, Ward 4, dist. 14, p. 317.

81. Edmund Quincy to Richard D. Webb, April 7, 1870, in Taylor, ed., *British and American Abolitionists*, 543. Charlotte described it as "the intense longing of my life" to see other countries. Charlotte Forten to Charles Sumner, January 28, 1872, Sumner Papers.

82. Whittier to Sumner, September 10, 1870, in Pickard, ed., *Letters of Whittier*, vol. 3, pp. 233–34.

83. Charlotte Forten to Sumner, January 28, 1872, Sumner Papers.

84. Washington, D.C., directories, 1874, 1876.

85. For Charlotte's reflections on her forthcoming marriage, see Charlotte Forten to Ednah Dow Cheney, December 15, [1877], BPL.

86. Bruce, *Archibald Grimké*, 1–28.

87. Ibid., 18.

88. John G. Whittier to Cornelia M. Trimble, June 10, 1878, Whittier MSS., Friends' Historical Library, Swarthmore College.

89. Cooper, ed., *Personal Recollections*, 38.

90. PAS, *Statistics of the Colored People*, 8; Johnson and Roark, eds., *No Chariot Let Down*, 129–30. The girls were with Margaretta Forten for about two years. See Stevenson, ed., *Journals of Charlotte Forten Grimké*, 381 (entry for September 14, 1862). Other pupils included Julia and Miranda Venning, the daughters of Edward Y. and Julia Sanders Venning. The Vennings worshipped with the Fortens at St. Thomas's. Tuition receipt, October 20, 1871, Box 11, folder 11, Stevens–Cogdell, Sanders–Venning Collection, LCP.

91. On the sisters' role in organizing the annual fair, see *NASS*, April 25, 1844; December 20, 1849; January 10, 1857; *PF*, March 30, 1854; *ASA*, July 1858 and June 1859; *ASR*, June 1859.

92. *Thirty-Sixth Annual Report of the Philadelphia Female Anti-Slavery Society*, 37–38.

93. E.g., she helped found the Stephen Smith Home for Aged and Infirm Colored Persons. Pollard, "The Stephen Smith Home," 52.

94. Philadelphia Board of Health Records. A deed disposing of Forten family property gives January 28, 1875, as the date of her death. Philadelphia County Deeds, G.G.P., Book 365, p. 83. She died intestate. William Forten was named as her administrator.

95. However, there was one joyful event that year. On April 14, 1842, Harriet gave birth to a son, Charles Burleigh. McNeill, "Charles Burleigh Purvis," 79.

96. For an account of the 1842 riot, see Winch, *Philadelphia's Black Elite*, 148–50.

97. Lane, *Roots of Violence*, 136; *PL*, April 16, 1898; Henry C. Wright to Robert Purvis, August 11, 1842; Purvis to Wright, August 22, 1842, BPL.

98. Philadelphia County Deeds, R.L.L., Book 8, p. 351; *PL*, April 16, 1898.

99. U.S. agricultural census, Pennsylvania, 1850 and 1860; Stevenson, ed., *Journals of Charlotte Forten Grimké*, 305 (entry for April 28, 1858).

100. *NASS*, September 3, 1846; December 2, 1847; January 1, 1859; *Maryland Colonization Journal*, October 1846; Chadwick, ed., *A Life for Liberty*, 102; Sarah Pugh to Mary Estlin, November 29, 1853, Estlin Papers (microfilm), BPL; Martha Wright to David Wright, December 4, 1853, Sophia Smith Collection, Smith College (copy in Black Abolitionist Archives).

101. See, e.g., Stevenson, ed., *Journals of Charlotte Forten Grimké*, 300 (entries for April 11 and 13, 1858).

102. Chadwick, ed., *A Life for Liberty*, 102.

103. Siebert, *The Underground Railroad*, 346.

104. *NS*, October 20, 1848.

105. Robert Purvis to William Lloyd Garrison, September 12, 1853, BPL; *Lib*, September 16, 1853. On Purvis's occasional differences with white abolitionists, see *FDP*, May 19, 1854.

106. Philadelphia Female Anti-Slavery Society, Minute Book, 1839–44, entry for June 9, 1842; see also Minute Books, 1848–62, 1862–67, HSP. Winch, *Philadelphia's Black Elite*, 85.

107. Sarah Pugh to Mary Estlin, November 29, 1853, Estlin Papers.

108. *PF*, February 10, 1847, and November 10, 1853.

109. Ibid., November 10, 1853; Martha Wright to David Wright, December 4, 1853, Sophia Smith Collection, Smith College (copy in Black Abolitionist Archives).

110. *Lib*, June 13, 1856.

111. *ASB*, April 11, 1857, and American Antiquarian Society, Misc. Anti-Slavery Collection, both in BAP microfilm.

112. *Lib*, May 18, 1860.

113. See, e.g., entry for November 14, 1861, in Philadelphia Female Anti-Slavery Society Minute Book, 1848–62, HSP.

114. *Lib*, September 11, 1863.

115. Robert Purvis to ____, February 18, 1863, Cornell University Anti-Slavery Collection, in BAP microfilm.

116. Philadelphia Female Anti-Slavery Society, Minute Book, 1862–67, p. 80. On the campaign the Purvises and others mounted, see Foner, "Philadelphia Streetcars," 261–90, 353–79, and *Why Colored People Are Excluded from Streetcars*.

117. Robert Purvis to Wendell Phillips, September 9, 1867, Crawford Blagden Papers, Houghton Library, Harvard; see also Purvis to Phillips, November 8, 1867.

118. Wendell Phillips to Robert Purvis, September 13, 1867, and Purvis to Phillips, September 18, 1867, Crawford Blagden Papers. On Purvis's warm regard for Phillips, see *PL*, August 5, 1890.

119. Stanton et al., *History of Woman Suffrage*, vol. 2, p. 183.

120. Ibid., 265. On Stanton's sympathy for Purvis, see Matthews, "Race, Sex and Liberty," 278–79.

121. Stanton et al., *History of Woman Suffrage*, vol. 2, pp. 347, 358. Despite their ideological differences, father and son remained close. Charles and his family spent time at Byberry. In the mid-1870s, when Robert was a commissioner of the Freedman's Saving Bank, he was often in Washington, and he listed his address as 1118 Thirteenth Street, N.W., Charles's home. Charles B. Purvis to Gerrit Smith, May 29, 1871, Gerrit Smith Papers (microfilm), Sterling Library, Yale; Washington, D.C., directories, 1875–77.

122. Lane, *Roots of Violence*, 53.

123. Silcox, "The Black Better Class," 51.

124. *Press*, October 9, 1871, in Silcox, comp., "Newspaper Clippings About Blacks Taken from Philadelphia Newspapers, 1866–1900," Balch Institute. There is also evidence that the suggestion for the school's name came from individuals within the African-American community. Silcox, *Philadelphia Politics from the Bottom Up*, 73.

125. Silcox, "The Black Better Class," 52–53.

126. M. A. S. Carr to William Still, May 11, 1874, Leon Gardiner Collection, Box 9G, HSP.

127. Death Registers, Philadelphia County, 1875, PCA; *PL*, June 12, 1875; Friends' Fair Hill Burial Ground Records, vol. 1, p. 222, HSP.

128. Death Registers, Philadelphia County, 1877; Friends' Fair Hill Burial Ground Records, vol. 1, p. 238.

129. *Bucks County Intelligencer*, March 20, 1878; U.S. Census, 1900: Kennett Township, Chester County, Pa., vol. 60, enumeration district 79, p. 8.

130. Robert Purvis to John G. Whittier, August 27, 1880, George Whittier Pickard Papers, Houghton Library.

131. Lane, *Roots of Violence*, 62–66.

132. Lane, *William Dorsey's Philadelphia*, 204.

133. Ibid., 220.

134. Ibid., 217, 262.

135. Stanton et al., *History of Woman Suffrage*, vol. 4, pp. 136, 163. On Tacie Purvis's continued involvement, see *Thirty-Second Convention of the National American Woman Suffrage Association*, 97, 205.

136. *PL*, August 5, 1890; *New York Times*, April 16, 1898; *Sermon Preached at the Funeral of Robert Purvis*.

137. Philadelphia County Wills, Will Book 200, p. 291, no. 661 (1898).

138. U.S. Census, 1900: Chester County, Pa., vol. 60, enumeration district 79, sheet 8; Chester County Wills, Will Book 32, no. 26870, p. 348 (microfilm), PSA; *Friends' Intelligencer* 57 (1900): 759.

139. *PL*, May 15, 1851; *NASS*, May 29, 1851.

140. Stevenson, ed., *Journals of Charlotte Forten Grimké*, 85 (entry for July 11, 1854); *FDP*, June 26, 1851.

141. Philadelphia Board of Health Records.

142. Stevenson, ed., *Journals of Charlotte Forten Grimké*, 159 (entries for July 9 and 18, 1856).

143. On his activities as a member of the Junior Anti-Slavery Society of Philadelphia, see Robert Purvis, Jr., to C. A. Walbern, February 22, 1859, Charles F. Jenkins Papers, Friends' Historical Library, Swarthmore College. On his opposition to colonization, see *NASS*, February 16, 1854. On his brief career in business, see Philadelphia directories, 1859–61, and U.S. Census, 1860: Philadelphia, Ward 23, p. 975. On his problems finding employment, see Samuel Ringgold Ward to Frederick Douglass, March 1855, in Ripley et al., eds., *Black Abolitionist Papers*, vol. 1, p. 419.

144. Journal of Ellen Wright, entry for January 12, 1859, (microfilm) Schlesinger Library, Radcliffe College.

145. Ellen Wright to Martha Wright, December 13, 1858, Sophia Smith Collection, Smith College (copy in Black Abolitionist Archives); Journal of Ellen Wright, entry for February 3, 1859.

146. *Lib*, April 4, 1864.

147. Hattie Purvis to Ellen Wright, January 16, 1856, Sophia Smith Collection, Smith College, in BAP microfilm. Ellen eventually married William Lloyd Garrison's son, William Jr.

148. Harper, *Life of Susan B. Anthony*, vol. 3, p. 1132. For accounts of the Congress, see *Portrait Album of Who's Who at the International Congress of Women*. The Purvises were apparently present as observers. They were not included in the alphabetical list of those who were "to read papers, join in discussions, or in other capacities take part in the Congress."

149. Harriet died of meningitis. The death was registered twice, in Worcester, where she had been staying, and in Watertown, where she lived and where the funeral took place. Massachusetts Register of Deaths (1904), vol. 95, p. 240; vol. 100, p. 398, MSA; *Worcester Daily Telegraph*, April 6, 1904; *Watertown Tribune Enterprise*, April 8, 1904; Will Book 661, p. 533, and Probate 64527, Middlesex County Courthouse, Cambridge, Mass.; Alice H. Robie et al. release, Philadelphia County Deeds, W.S.V., Book 679, p. 523. Alice was her executrix. Harriet left her the house she owned in Philadelphia and $3000. Alice's brother received $500. Nieces Marie and Louisa Purvis, Henry's daughters, were left $100, while their father received $50. Brothers Charles and Granville were the residual legatees.

150. The *Alumni Register* of Oberlin College gives his date of birth as April 16, 1842. On his application for a pension for his Civil War services, Purvis gave 1841 as his birth year. However, this seems to be a mistake. Various other details on the pension application are wrong. Civil War Pension File 1337283, Nat Arch.

151. Simmons, *Men of Mark*, 690–93.

152. *NASS*, July 3, 1869; McNeill, "Charles Burleigh Purvis," 79, 81; *The Purvis Family, 1694–1988*, 227.

153. Purvis was highly critical of the government's funding and oversight of the hospital in his *Report of the Freedmen's Hospital . . . 1885*. For an account of his career as a physician and administrator, see McNeill, "Charles Burleigh Purvis," 79–82.

154. *People's Advocate*, June 23, 1883, in Abajian, comp., *Blacks in Selected Newspapers, Censuses, and Other Sources: A Supplement*, vol. 2, p. 263.

155. See *United States Congressional Hearings Index*.

156. Prior to his marriage, Purvis boarded with the family of Dennis Smallwood, a black government worker. McNeill, "Charles Burleigh Purvis," 80; Washington, D.C., directories, 1868–77; U.S. Census, 1870: Washington, D.C., Ward 2, p. 239; 1880: enumeration district 39, 41. In his pension application, Purvis gave the date of his marriage as April 18, 1871. Ann was some years older than him. According to the census there was an eight-year age difference; according to her death record, an eleven-year difference.

157. Ann's ashes were interred in the Purvis family plot at Fair Hill. Friends' Fair Hill Burial Ground Records, 390; Suffolk County Wills, estate 237961 (1929), Suffolk County Courthouse, Boston, Mass.

158. U.S. Census, 1900: Washington, D.C., vol. 7, enumeration district 16, sheet 14; Philadelphia Marriage License, 133702 (1901), PCA.

159. Massachusetts Marriages, 1904, vol. 547, p. 658, MSA. U.S. Census, 1900: Watertown, Middlesex County, Mass., vol. 53, sheet 8.

160. Boston directories, 1905, 1910; *Oberlin College Alumni Register, 1833–1960*, 377.

161. Charles Purvis was a prudent investor. In a letter to Francis J. Grimké, he noted: "I excelled my father in the art of saving" (Purvis to Grimké, January 14, 1921, Grimké Papers, Moorland-Spingarn Research Center, Howard University. (Historian Margaret Hope Bacon kindly shared her research notes with me.) His estate was worth over $145,000 in 1930. Suffolk County Wills, estate 237961 (1929).

162. Henry Purvis was in Oberlin's preparatory department from 1863 to 1866. *Oberlin College Alumni Register, Students, 1833–1909*, 791.

163. Ella Zenobia Barre (1852–1921) was the daughter of John Augustus Barre and Virginia Ann Ferrette. Barre was a native of Bordeaux. Virginia Ferrette had been born in South Carolina, but she was probably the daughter of John M. Ferrette, a white man who had fled to Charleston from Saint Domingue. When Barre died in 1856, he left Virginia and her six children his house, four slaves, the labor of three more for a term of years, and a substantial amount of cash. Charleston Death Certificate 6476. U.S. Census, 1850: Charleston, S.C., St. Philip's, 159, 277; 1860: Ward 4, 350; Ward 5, 393; 1870: Ward 4, 238; Charleston directories, 1860, 1866, 1872–73; Charleston County Wills, Book 47 (1851–56), p. 860; Koger, *Black Slaveowners*, 228; Holcomb, comp., *South Carolina Naturalizations*, 122.

164. For Henry Purvis's graphic account of the state of affairs in South Carolina in 1868, see *NASS*, August 22, 1868.

165. Philadelphia County Wills, Will Book 200, p. 291, no. 661 (1898).

166. He was also a notary public. Charleston directories, 1881–83, 1885–91, 1895, 1898–99, 1902. Henry was attacked in the Philadelphia press as a "shrewd and unscrupulous" man who had "dishonored an honored name." He "was a prominent leader in the House as chairman of a most important committee, and he did as much as any one to hasten the overthrow of negro rule. He now resides in Charleston and is a beneficiary of the national government." *The [Philadelphia] Times*, December 14, 1880.

167. Virginia Purvis died, age ten months, in 1880. Granville Purvis died in 1885 when he was three years old. Charleston County Death Records, CCL; U.S. Census, 1900: Charleston, S.C., enumeration district 113, vol. 113, sheet 25.

168. Augustus Glover Purvis was born in Charleston on June 22, 1884, and died in Hampton, Virginia. *The Alumni Record of Wesleyan University, 1831–1970* notes (138) that he died in March 1968. According to the Social Security Death Index, he died in March 1969.

169. *Oberlin College Alumni Register, 1833–1960*, 377; Charleston directories, 1885–91, 1895, 1898–99, 1902, 1940; Suffolk County, Massachusetts Wills, estate 237961 (1929); Wilkinson, ed., *Graduates of Howard University*, 301.

170. Wilkinson, ed., *Graduates of Howard University*, 301. Granville Purvis said on his application for a marriage license that he had been born on February 17, 1850. However, he is listed as four years old in the 1850 census and fourteen in the 1860 census. In 1900 he told the census-taker he had been born in July 1846.

171. *NASS*, March 4, 1871; Detroit directories, 1872–74, 1876–77, 1882, 1885, 1890–92, 1894, 1906–7; Katzman, *Before the Ghetto*, 161.

172. Ellen Wright to Martha Wright, December 13, 1858; Wright Family Correspondence, Sophia Smith Collection (in Black Abolitionist Archives). In the U.S. Census, 1900: Wayne County, Mich., vol. 33, enumeration district 142, sheet 2, Granville was listed as black. Philadelphia County Marriage License 123561 (1900).

173. U.S. Census, 1920: Los Angeles County, Calif., vol. 40, enumeration district 165, sheet 17.

174. *Oberlin College Alumni Register, Students, 1833–1909*, 791; Granville S. Purvis Death Certificate (1911), FRC. I am grateful to my brother, Roy Winch, for locating this certificate.

175. Los Angeles directories, 1921, 1925, 1930, 1935. Mother and daughter were living together as late as 1930.

176. For the purchase of Eddington Farm, see Bucks County Deeds, Book 60, 111.

177. See ibid., Book 64, p. 378; Book 70, p. 253; Book 76, p. 49. On his Philadelphia transactions, see Philadelphia County Deeds, R.L.L., Book 19, p. 241; Book 43, p. 191; Book 48, p. 267; A.W.M., Book 30, p. 70.

178. Delany, *Condition, Elevation, Emigration and Destiny*, 146; U.S. Agricultural Census (1850), Bucks County, Pa.

179. Bucks County Mortgages, Book 19, p. 300, and Book 20, p. 81.

180. Bucks County Deeds, Book 82, p. 469, and Bucks County Misc., Book 11, p. 413; see also Bucks County Deeds, Book 82, pp. 745, 749; Book 83, p. 488; Book 84, p. 454; Book 85, p. 251; Book 113, p. 473; Bucks County Mortgages, Book 25, p. 385.

181. Bucks County Deeds, Book 95, p. 296; Book 96, pp. 189, 346; Elk County Deeds (microfilm), Book K, 364, PSA; see also Bucks County Mortgages, Book 29, p. 503.

182. *PL*, January 24 and February 3, 1857; *NASS*, January 31, 1857.

183. Bucks County Orphans' Court, Book 13, p. 644, BCC.

184. Bucks County Administrations, file 10075, Adm. 8, no. 49; Bucks County Deeds, Book 100, pp. 53, 57; Bucks County Orphans' Court, Book 13, p. 678.

185. Bucks County Deeds, Book 100, pp. 472, 473; Book 106, p. 493; Elk County Deeds, Book K, 362; Bucks County Orphans' Court, Book 14, p. 488; Philadelphia County Orphans' Court, Book 49, pp. 240, 321.

186. Stevenson, ed., *Journals of Charlotte Forten Grimké*, 322–23 (entry for July 6, 1858).

187. Bucks County Orphans' Court, Book 15, p. 418.

188. Sarah L. Purvis to Theodore Dwight Weld, October 18, 1869; Weld–Grimké Papers, William L. Clements Library, University of Michigan (copy in Black Aboli-

tionist Archives). Eventually, Robert Purvis paid the "sacred obligation." He told Weld he had been shocked to learn from Margaretta Forten that the loan had not been repaid. Robert Purvis to Weld, June 6, 1871, Weld–Grimké Papers.

189. Bucks County Orphans' Court, Book 17, p. 517, see also p. 125.

190. *PL*, April 29, 1865; U.S. Mortality Census, 1870: Pa.

191. *PL*, August 13, 1869; Bucks County Deeds, Book 158, p. 462. In the 1865 Philadelphia directory, John Quincy Allen was listed as a "colored" teacher. That same year he attended the convention of the Pennsylvania State Equal Rights League as a delegate from Philadelphia County. Emily's uncle, William Forten, was a leading member of the organization, and her brother, William, was one of the Bucks County delegates. Philadelphia directory, 1865; Lane, *William Dorsey's Philadelphia*, 135–36; *Proceedings of the State Equal Rights Convention . . . 1865*, in Foner and Walker, eds., *Black State Conventions*, vol. 1, pp. 140, 150, 158. Emily Purvis Allen died on February 2, 1875. Her husband became the legal guardian of their only child, Annie. For John Q. Allen's dealings with the Purvis estate see Bucks County Deeds, Book 178, p. 397.

192. U.S. Census, 1850: New York, Rensselaer County, Troy, Seventh Ward, 258–59; Hine, "Dr. Benjamin A. Boseman," 335–62; *Catalog of Howard University for the Years 1871–72*, 45. On the Bosemans and their repeated challenges to segregation, see Mabee, *Black Education in New York State*, 104, 166–67, 193, 194. William Boseman eventually secured a government appointment as a clerk in the Treasury Department and spent some time in Washington in the 1880s. He returned to Kansas and died at Little Creek in 1889. Sarah and William had four children. William Jr., Eustace, and Bessie survived to adulthood, but daughter Elma died young. Sarah died on February 24, 1932. Washington, D.C., directories, 1869–72, 1884, 1885; U.S. Census, 1900: Anderson County, Kansas, vol. 1, enumeration district 17, sheet 3; Philadelphia County Deeds, G.G.P., Book 365, p. 83; *Iola (Kansas) Daily Register*, February 24, 1932 (photocopy supplied by Reg Pitts).

193. Bucks County Deeds, Book 168, p. 406. Sarah and Joseph Purvis's youngest daughter had actually been baptized Harriet, not Anne or Annie. She was probably called Annie by family members to avoid confusion with her cousin, Hattie or Harriet Purvis, Robert and Harriet's daughter. See U.S. Census, 1850: Bensalem, Bucks County, Pa., 73.

194. Ibid., Book 174, p. 143; Bucks County Misc. Book 18, p. 36.

195. *PL*, November 1, 1884; St. James the Less Episcopal Church, Philadelphia, Pennsylvania—Cemetery Records, lot 484, HSP. The entry in the Philadelphia Death Register gives the date of death as October 29.

196. Philadelphia directory, 1880, 1901, 1905; U.S. Census, 1900: Philadelphia County, vol. 186, enumeration district 832, sheet 2. Apparently, William tried to interest his well-to-do cousin, Charles, in investing in one of his projects, but to no avail. Charles B. Purvis to Francis J. Grimké, February 20, 1910, Grimké Papers, Howard University (copy supplied by Margaret Hope Bacon); Work, ed., *Negro Year Book, 1921–22*, 318; St. James the Less Cemetery Records, lot 484.

197. Joseph Purvis Pension Application, Civil War Pensions, file 281300; Nat Arch.

198. Ibid.

199. Ibid. Information on the date and place of Joseph Purvis's death kindly supplied by Reg Pitts.

200. Philadelphia directories, 1846–51, 1855–58, 1860–61, 1863, 1883–86, 1888, 1890, 1892–94, 1897; Friends' census, 1847, PAS MSS; U.S. Census, 1850: Philadelphia, New Market Ward, 384; 1860: Ward 5, 209; 1870: Ward 4, dist. 14, 317.

201. *FDP*, November 13, 1851; *VF*, January 15 and February 12, 1852; *WAA*, July 7, 1860.

202. *Memorial to the Senate and House of Representatives of Pennsylvania . . . from the "Colored Citizens,"* 15, 19. In fact, the petitioners were quoting verbatim from an article entitled "The Black Men of the Revolution and War of 1812," by John Greenleaf Whittier, that had appeared in the *National Era* of July 22, 1847.

203. William D. Forten to Charles Sumner, June 7, 1862; Sumner Papers.

204. "Men of Color! To Arms!" 1863 broadside, LCP.

205. William D. Forten to Charles Sumner, June 18, 1864, Sumner Papers.

206. *Proceedings of the State Equal Rights Convention . . . 1865*, in Foner and Walker, eds., *Black State Conventions*, vol. 1, pp. 141, 148, 157–58.

207. Silcox, "The Black Better Class," 47–48; *CR*, November 25, 1865; *Proceedings of the Annual Meeting of the Pennsylvania State Equal Rights' League, Held in . . . Harrisburg . . . 1865*, in Foner and Walker, eds., *Conventions, 1865–1900*, 136, 142, 146–47, 149, 150, 157.

208. NASS, March 24, 1866; *National Convention of Colored Soldiers and Sailors . . . 1867*, in Foner and Walker, eds., *Conventions, 1865–1900*, 295.

209. William D. Forten to Leonard Myers, March 23, 1868, Am. 1069, vol. 3, HSP.

210. William D. Forten to Charles Sumner, February 1, 1869, Sumner Papers.

211. Forten to Sumner, April 9, 1871, Sumner Papers.

212. Forten to Sumner, January 18, 1872, Sumner Papers.

213. Forten to Sumner, March 21, 1870, Sumner Papers.

214. Republican Congressional Committee, *Grant or Greeley*; Blackett, *Beating Against the Barriers*, 345–46.

215. *Elevator*, September 12, 1874; Silcox, "The Black Better Class," 53; *PAppeal*, May 20, 1876.

216. Silcox, *Philadelphia Politics from the Bottom Up*, 86.

217. Silcox, "The Black Better Class," 55; *Philadelphia Inquirer*, February 3, 1877.

218. On the factional in-fighting and Forten's role, see Blackett, *Beating Against the Barriers*, 359–60.

219. Silcox, "The Black Better Class," 46, 62–64.

220. Green Tree and Mutual Assurance policy 1917, HSP; Philadelphia directory, 1895. After the passage of Philadelphia's Consolidation Act of 1854, many homes in the city were renumbered. What had been 92 Lombard Street during James Forten's lifetime became 336 Lombard.

221. Pollard, "Stephen Smith Home," 50, 52; Home for Aged and Infirm Colored Persons, *Annual Report . . . 1897*, 21; *Thirty-Fourth Annual Report*, 15; Leon Gardiner to Orrin Evans, July 1, 1933, Leon Gardiner Collection, Box 10G, folder 20, HSP. Forten turned to an old friend, Democrat General Winfield Scott Hancock, to help him get a place in the Smith Home. Gardiner noted that three individuals signed Forten's application for admission to the Home: Hancock, Judge Ashman (probably William N. Ashman of the Orphans' Court), and a woman he identified as "Annie Bivens," of 3045 Fontain Street. "Annie Bivens" was in fact Forten's niece, Annie Purvis.

222. Pollard, "Stephen Smith Home," 132; U.S. Census, 1900: Philadelphia, enumeration district 879, p. 9; Philadelphia directory, 1905, 1908, 1909; Philadelphia Death Certificates, 1909, no. 6155, PCA; *PL*, March 10, 1909.

223. St. James the Less Cemetery Records, lot 484.

224. Stevenson, ed., *Journals of Charlotte Forten Grimké*, 208, 302, 306 (entries for April 4, 1857, and April 20 and April 29, 1858).

225. Philadelphia County Deeds, R.L.L., Book 18, p. 93; T.H., Book 129, p. 22; Book 179, p. 251.

226. U.S. Census, 1860: Bucks County, Bensalem Township, 47.

227. U.S. Census, 1870: Philadelphia, Ward 4, dist. 14, p. 317, and 1880: Ward 5, enumeration district 97, p. 7; Philadelphia directories, 1883–86, 1892, 1894.

228. Death Registers, Philadelphia County, 1897; St. James the Less Cemetery Records, lot 484.

229. It seems that the peripatetic James Forten, Jr., died before his mother. However, his family in Philadelphia may not have known for certain where and when he died.

230. Stevenson, ed., *Journals of Charlotte Forten Grimké*, 198 (entry for February 28, 1857).

231. See *NS*, October 13, 1848, where she is referred to as Mrs. James Foster.

232. Philadelphia County Deeds, R.D.W., Book 156, p. 506; A.D.B., Book 39, p. 424.

233. U.S. Census, 1850: Philadelphia, New Market Ward, 384, and 1870: Ward 4, dist. 14, p. 317; Philadelphia County Deeds, F.T.W., Book 186, p. 456; G.C.P., Book 562, p. 467, and Book 643, p. 531.

234. Cooper, ed., *Personal Recollections*, 10; Robert Purvis to John G. Whittier, August 27, 1880, George Whittier Pickard Papers.

235. Death Register, Philadelphia County, 1885. Charlotte died in the last week of 1884 but her death was not recorded until the first week of 1885.

236. Philadelphia Board of Health Records.

237. Ibid.

238. U.S. Census, 1860: San Francisco, Calif., Second District, 30.

239. Keys to Enlistment, vol. 2 (Boston, October 28, 1846, and September 28, 1848; New York, February 3, 1851); Rendezvous Reports, 1854, New York, February 2, 1854; 1855, p. 222; 1858, p. 33; 1859, p. 6; Record Group 24, Nat Arch.

240. Abby Dunbar died of consumption on November 18, 1844. James Dunbar died of a "bloody flux of the lungs" on May 29, 1848. Philadelphia Board of Health Records.

241. Rendezvous Reports, 1861, p. 60; 1862, p. 73; 1863, p. 306.

242. *Massachusetts Soldiers, Sailors, and Marines in the Civil War*, vol. 7, p. 851.

243. Rendezvous Reports, 1863, p. 363. For a discussion of the significance of sailors' tattoos, see Newman, "Reading the Bodies," 63, 69–70, 72, 79.

244. Reg Pitts tracked James Forten Dunbar to the Naval Asylum and generously supplied the information on his last years. Register of Admissions to United States Naval Asylum, Philadelphia, Pa., 1865–85; Record Group 52, Records of the Bureau of Medicine and Surgery, Department of the Navy; Monthly Muster Roll of Pensioners and Beneficiaries of the United States Naval Asylum, Philadelphia, Pa., for the month ending the 31st day of January 1870, Record Group 71, Records of the Bureau of Docks and Yards, Department of the Navy; and Records of United States Naval Asylum—Monthly Reports of Admissions, Deaths and Changes (1865–88), Record Group 181, Records of Naval Districts and Shore Establishments, Department of the Navy, Nat Arch., Mid-Atlantic Region, Philadelphia.

245. Walls, *The AMEZ Church*, 567; Philadelphia County Deeds, A.M. Book 29, p. 187; Philadelphia County Wills, Will Book 18, p. 170, no. 264 (1845); *PL*, December 17, 1845.

246. Education and Employment Statistics of the Colored People of Philadelphia, 1856, PAS MSS; U.S. Census, 1860: Philadelphia, Ward 13, p. 547. On the familial relationship between the two women, see Pinckney, ed., *Register of St. Philip's Church, 1810–22*, 53. Philadelphia County Wills, Will Book 66, p. 109, no. 639 (1869).

247. *Morning Press*, December 14, 1869; *Forney's Weekly Press*, December 18, 1869; *Sunday Dispatch*, December 19, 1869. (I am grateful to Margaret Hope Bacon for these references.) Sarah Vickers eventually returned to live with her family in Charleston. U.S. Census, 1870: Charleston, S.C., Fifth Ward, 378.

248. Confusing matters is the fact that there was another Annie Webb in Philadelphia in the 1870s and 1880s. Annie C. Webb was an unmarried white woman who lived with her brother, Charles, and his family. She described herself as an "authoress." She also operated a private school. She died in 1888. U.S. Census, 1860: Philadelphia, Ward 2, p. 296; 1870: Ward 2, dist. 7, p. 345; Philadelphia directories, 1869, 1870, 1875, 1880, 1881, 1885; Philadelphia County Wills, Will Book 141, p. 339, no. 1472 (1888).

249. She was in Philadelphia by February 1844, when she witnessed two deeds for her aunt and cousins. See Philadelphia County Deeds, R.L.L., Book 18, p. 93, and Book 19, p. 238; Charlotte Van Dine [*sic*] to the Board of Education of the Pennsylvania Society for Promoting the Abolition of Slavery, February 18, 1847, PAS Board of Education Correspondence, PAS MSS. Charlotte married Joseph C. West. *PL*, October 25, 1848; *PAppeal* February 27, 1864.

250. *Minutes of the State Convention . . . 1848*, in Foner and Walker, eds., *Black State Conventions*, vol. 1, pp. 128–29.

251. *ProvFree*, August 15, 1857; *CR*, February 9, 1861.

252. Robert Purvis to William Lloyd Garrison, Jr., July 4, 1882, Moorland-Spingarn Research Center, Howard University (copy in Black Abolitionist Archives).

253. *PL*, March 10, 1909.

254. Billington, "James Forten—Forgotten Abolitionist."

WORKS CITED

City Directories

Boston, Mass., 1905, 1910
Charleston, S.C., 1801–2, 1806–7, 1816, 1819, 1822, 1829, 1831, 1835–36, 1840–41,
    1852, 1856, 1859, 1881–83, 1885–91, 1895, 1898–99, 1902, 1940
Detroit, Mich., 1872–74, 1876–77, 1882, 1885, 1890–92, 1894, 1906–1907
London, England, 1860, 1863
London, Ontario, Canada, 1856–57
Los Angeles, Calif., 1906, 1908, 1910–18, 1920–21, 1925, 1930, 1935
New Orleans, La., 1823
Philadelphia, Pa., 1785–1910
Toronto, Ontario, Canada, 1856, 1859–95, 1926
Washington, D.C., 1866–80
Watertown, Mass., 1909

Manuscript Collections

American Philosophical Society, Philadelphia
    Stephen Girard Papers (microfilm), Ship Disbursements, 1797–1800, 1801–07, 1808–
        15, 1819–23
    Hannah Roach Card File: An Index of Names and Places, and Alphabetized Ab-
        stracts of Philadelphia Newspaper Items and Advertisements, ca. 1718 to 1795
Archives of the Episcopal Church, Austin, Tex.
    "Extract from the Minutes of St. Thomas's Episcopal Church"
    "Petition from members of St. Thomas' African Church, Phila. In favor of Jacob
        Oson & other testimonials in favor of the same"

Balch Institute for Ethnic Studies, Philadelphia
    Harry C. Silcox, comp., "Newspaper Clippings About Blacks Taken from Philadel-
        phia Newspapers, 1865–1900"
Black Abolitionist Archives, University of Detroit Mercy
    Weld–Grimké Papers (photocopies) from William L. Clements Library, Univer-
        sity of Michigan
    Wright Family Correspondence (photocopies) from Sophia Smith Collection, Smith
        College
Black Abolitionist Papers Microfilm, 17 reels, Ann Arbor, Mich.: University Micro-
        films, 1981–83
Blunt White Library, Mystic Seaport, Mystic, Conn.
    Pimer Papers
    Ship Registers of the Port of Philadelphia, Pa., A–D
        (Typescript, WPA, Philadelphia, 1942)
Boston Public Library
    ● American Colonization Society Papers (microfilm)
    Antislavery Manuscripts
    Buxton Papers (microfilm)
    Estlin Papers (microfilm)
Bucks County Courthouse, Doylestown, Pa.
    Administrations
    Deeds
    Miscellaneous Records
    Mortgages
    Orphans' Courts Records
Canadian National Archives, Ottawa
    Censuses of Canada West, 1861, 1871, and 1881
Caroliniana Collection, University of South Carolina, Columbia
    Register of St. Philip's Protestant Episcopal Church, Charleston, S.C., 1823–1940
Charleston County Library, Charleston, S.C.
    Charleston County Health Department, Death Records, 1821–1926
    Federal Naturalization Oaths, Charleston, S.C., 1790–1860
Christ Church Archives, Philadelphia
    Records of St. Thomas's Church Lottery
Church Missionary Society, London
    Misc. Letters, Church Missionary Society Archives
Family Record Centre, London
    Census of the United Kingdom, 1861
    Register of Deaths, 1860, 1911
Friends' Historical Library, Swarthmore College, Swarthmore, Pa.
    Charles F. Jenkins Papers
    "Minutes of the Committee's appointed by the Three Monthly Meetings of Friends
        of Philadelphia to the Oversight and Care of the School for Educating Afri-
        cans and Their Descendants Commencing the 28th of the 5th Month 1770"
    Whittier Manuscripts

Grand Lodge of Massachusetts, A. F. and A. M., Boston
    Minutes of the African Lodge, Philadelphia, 1797–1800 (microfilm)
    Prince Hall, Letters and Sermons (microfilm)
Haverhill Public Library, Haverhill, Mass.
    Whittier Collection, Diary of Elizabeth Whittier (1835–38)
Haverford College, Treasure Room
    Nathaniel P. Rogers Collection
Historical Society of Pennsylvania, Philadelphia
    Augustus Pleasonton, Manuscript Diary
    Breck Papers
    Burlington County, N.J., Deeds (microfilm)
    Cadwalader Papers
    Christ Church, Philadelphia: Baptisms, 1709–69, 1769–94, 1794–1819; Burials, 1709–85, 1785–1900; Marriages, Confirmations and Communicants, 1709–1800, 1800–1900
    Cox, Parrish, Wharton Papers
    Diary of Samuel Breck, 1832–33
    David Paul Brown Papers
    Dillwyn Manuscripts
    Dr. Benjamin Rush, Manuscript Correspondence
    Edward Carey Gardiner Collection
    Friends' Fair Hill Burial Grounds Records
    Green Tree and Mutual Assurance Company Papers
    Inscriptions in the Burying Ground of the Second Presbyterian Church, Philadelphia
    Leonard Myers Collection
    Leon Gardiner Collection
    McAllister Papers
    Maritime Records—Alphabetical—Masters and Crews, 1798–1880
    Misc. Legal Papers
    Notices of Marriages and Deaths in *Poulson's American Daily Advertiser*, 1791–1839
    (Old Swedes) Gloria Dei—Marriages, 1795–1816, 1816–73
    Pennsylvania Abolition Society Manuscripts
    Pennsylvania Misc. Papers, Penn and Baltimore, Penn Family, 1756–1768
    Philadelphia Board of Health Records, 1806–60
    Philadelphia Female Anti-Slavery Society, Minute Books, 1833–1870; Board of Managers' Minute Books, 1833–39; Correspondence Incoming
    Records of Darby Monthly Meeting, 1682–1891
    Records of Marriages from 1800–1851 Collected by Thompson Westcott
    Records of Neshaminy Presbyterian Church of Warwick, Hartsville, Bucks County, Pa., 1788–1879
    • Records of St. George's Methodist Episcopal Church, Philadelphia, 1785–1856
    Records of the Second Presbyterian Church, Philadelphia—Baptisms, Marriages and Burials, 1745–1823
    Register of Confirmations by Bishop White 1787 to 1836 inclusive
    St. James the Less Episcopal Church, Philadelphia—Cemetery Records
    St. Paul's Church, Philadelphia: Baptisms, 1782–1828; Marriages, 1759–1829; Burials, 1790–1852

Subscription Lists, 1744–1862
Vaux Papers
Yellow Fever Deaths in Philadelphia, 1793, 1797, 1798
Young Men's Anti-Slavery Society of Philadelphia, Committee Reports, 1836–37
Houghton Library, Harvard University, Cambridge, Mass.
Charles Sumner Papers
Crawford Blagden Papers
George Whittier Pickard Papers
Howard University, Moorland–Spingarn Research Center, Washington, D.C.
Francis J. Grimké Papers
Independence Seaport Museum, Philadelphia
Barry–Hayes Papers
Ships' Papers, *Fair American*
Vessel Registers, 1803–4
John Carter Brown Library, Brown University, Providence, R.I.
"Revolutions de Saint-Domingue"
John Rylands Library, Manchester University, Manchester, England
Frederick W. Chesson Diary, Thompson Papers
Library Company of Philadelphia
Album-Scrapbook of Martina Dickerson
Album-Scrapbook of Mary Ann Dickerson
"Original and Selected Poetry of Amy Matilda Cassey"
"Poulson's Scrapbook of American Biography"
"Poulson's Scrapbook of Philadelphia History"
Stevens–Cogdell, Sanders–Venning Collection
Massachusetts State Archives, Boston, Mass.
Massachusetts Deaths
Massachusetts Marriages
Middlesex County Courthouse, Cambridge, Mass.
Probate Records
National Archives, Mid-Atlantic Region, Philadelphia
Agricultural Censuses, Pennsylvania, 1850 and 1860
Monthly Muster Roll of Pensioners and Beneficiaries of the United States Naval
    Asylum, Philadelphia, Pa., for the Month ending the 31st Day of January
    1870
Passenger Lists, Arrivals in Philadelphia, 1800–1882
Records of the United States Naval Asylum—Monthly Reports of Admissions, Deaths
    and Changes (1865–88)
Register of Admissions to United States Naval Asylum, Philadelphia, Pa., 1865–85
National Archives, Washington, D.C.
Civil War Pension Applications: 25551 (James V. Forten), 99272 (Robert B. Forten),
    281300 (Joseph Purvis, Jr.), 1337283 (Charles B. Purvis)
Keys to Enlistment, U.S. Navy
Muster Rolls for USS *Tuscarora*
Rendezvous Reports, U.S. Navy
Seamen's Protection Certificates for the Port of Philadelphia

State Department, Index to Special Passports, 1829–87
  Index to Passport Applications, 1837
  Passports, January 4–December 31, 1834
United States Censuses, 1790–1920
  United States Mortality Census, Pennsylvania, 1870
New Bedford Free Public Library, New Bedford, Mass.
  Cuffe Papers
New England Historic Genealogical Society, Boston, Mass.
  Church of Jesus Christ of Latter-Day Saints, International Genealogical Index
  Index of Ontario Death Records, 1869–1921
  Records of Christ Church, New York City (microfilm)
Old Dartmouth Historical Society Library, New Bedford, Mass.
  Cuffe Letters
Pennsylvania State Archives, Harrisburg
  "A List of the Taxable Inhabitants residing within the County of Philadelphia, taken
      agreeably to an Act of the General Assembly, intitled 'An Act to provide for
      the enumeration of the taxable inhabitants, and Slaves, within this Common-
      wealth,' passed the 7th day of March 1800"   •
  Chester County Wills (microfilm)
  Elk County Deeds (microfilm)
  Record of Deaths in Philadelphia, 1791–1851
  Records of Pennsylvania's Revolutionary Governments, 1775–90
  Records of Pennsylvania Supreme Court, Eastern District: Appearance Dockets,
      1817–23; Continuance Dockets, 1818–25; DSB Papers, March Term 1822;
      Judgment Dockets, 1817–29
Philadelphia City Archives
  Administrations, Philadelphia County
  Board of Health, Cemetery Returns
  City Tax Duplicates: Southwark, 1795–98, 1800; New Market, 1833–42
  County Tax Assessment Ledger: Southwark, 1799, 1801–3, 1808; New Market,
      1809–11
  County Tax Duplicates: Blockley, 1822; New Market, 1810–13, 1816, 1818–19;
      Oxford, 1822; Southwark, 1773, 1775, 1793–94
  Court of Common Pleas: Appearance Dockets, March 1810–June 1844; Execution
      Dockets, March 1831–September 1835
  Death Certificates, Philadelphia County
  Death Registers, Philadelphia County
  Deed Books, Philadelphia County
  District Court: Appearance Dockets, March 1812–June 1844; Execution Dockets,
      June 1814–March 1845
  Effective Supply Tax, 1780
  Marriage Licenses, Philadelphia County
  Mortgage Books, Philadelphia County
  Orphans' Court Records
  Philadelphia County, Poor Tax Registers, New Market Ward, 1819–46
  Proprietary Tax, 1769

Provincial Tax Assessment Ledgers, 17th, 18th Penny Provincial Tax, City and County of Philadelphia, 1774

Sheriff's Deeds

State Personal Tax Assessment Ledger, New Market Ward, 1832

State Tax Assessment Ledgers: New Market Ward, 1841–43; Southwark, 1779

Tax of 1798

Wills, Philadelphia County

Presbyterian Historical Society, Philadelphia

Archives of the Episcopal Diocese of Pennsylvania

Public Record Office, London, England

Admiralty Records: Captain's Log of the *Amphion*, ADM 51/39, part 1; Captain's Log of *La Nymphe*, ADM 51/638; Master's Log of the *Amphion*, ADM 52/2133; Master's Log of *La Nymphe*, ADM 52/2427; Master's Log of the *Pomona*, ADM 52/2459; Muster of the *Amphion*, ADM 36/9561; Muster of the *Jersey*, ADM 36/9579

St. Thomas's African Episcopal Church, Philadelphia

Parish Registers

●Vestry Minutes, 1813–21 and 1821–31

Schlesinger Library, Radcliffe College, Cambridge, Mass.

Journal of Ellen Wright (microfilm)

South Carolina Department of Archives and History, Columbia

Charleston County, Court of Equity Bills

Charleston County Wills

Charleston County Inventories

Charleston District Court of Common Pleas, Judgment Rolls, 1791–1839

Charleston Free Negro Capitation Tax Books, 1821–23, 1832–38, 1840–46, 1848– ca. 1852, 1855, 1857, 1860

Marriage Settlements

Misc. Records, Secretary of State, Bills of Sale

Sterling Library, Yale University, New Haven, Conn.

Bacon Family Papers

Gerrit Smith Papers (microfilm)

Suffolk County Courthouse, Boston, Mass.

Probate Records

University of Pennsylvania Archives, Philadelphia

Nathan F. Mossell Papers

Newspapers and Periodicals

African Repository (Washington, D.C.)

Anglo-African Magazine (New York)

Anti-Slavery Advocate (London, England)

Anti-Slavery Bugle (Salem and New Lisbon, Ohio)

Anti-Slavery Reporter (London, England)

Atlantic Monthly (Boston, Mass.)

Aurora General Advertiser (Philadelphia)

Bucks County Intelligencer (Doylestown, Pa.)

Christian Recorder (Philadelphia)

Colored American (New York and Philadelphia)

Columbia Telescope (Columbia, S.C.)

Dunlap and Claypoole's American Daily Advertiser (Philadelphia)

Elevator (San Francisco, Calif.)

Emancipator (Boston, Mass. and New York)

Forney's Weekly Press (Philadelphia)

Frederick Douglass' Paper (Rochester, N.Y.)

Freedom's Journal (New York)

The Freeman's Journal (Philadelphia)

The Friend, a Religious and Literary Journal (Philadelphia)

Friends' Intelligencer (Philadelphia)

Genius of Universal Emancipation (Mount Pleasant, Ohio; Greenville, Tenn.; Baltimore, Md.; Washington, D.C.; Hennepin, Ill.)

Hazard's Register (Philadelphia)

Iola Daily Register (Iola, Kans.)

Liberator (Boston, Mass.)

London Chronicle (London, England)

Maryland Colonization Journal (Baltimore)

The Monthly Repository of Theology and General Literature (London, England)

The Morning Press (Philadelphia)

National Anti-Slavery Standard (New York)

National Era (Washington, D.C.)

National Enquirer and Constitutional Advocate of Universal Liberty (Philadelphia)

National Gazette (Philadelphia)

National Reformer (Philadelphia)

New Lloyd's List (London, England)

New-York Courier (New York)

New York Herald (New York)

New York Times (New York)

New Yorker (New York)

Niles' Weekly Register (Baltimore, Md., and Washington, D.C.)

North American (Philadelphia)

North Star (Rochester, N.Y.)

Pacific Appeal (San Francisco, Calif.)

Pennsylvania Evening Post, and Public Advertiser (Philadelphia)

Pennsylvania Freeman (Philadelphia)

Pennsylvania Gazette (Philadelphia)

Pennsylvania Packet (Philadelphia)

Pennsylvanian (Philadelphia)

Philadelphia Inquirer (Philadelphia)

Philadelphia Tribune (Philadelphia)

The Philanthropist (Mount Pleasant, Ohio)

Poulson's American Daily Advertiser (Philadelphia)

Provincial Freeman (Windsor, Toronto, and Chatham, Ontario, Canada)

Public Ledger (Philadelphia)

Relf's Gazette (Philadelphia)
The Sunday Dispatch (Philadelphia)
The Times (Philadelphia)
Toronto Evening Telegram (Toronto)
Toronto Globe (Toronto)
Toronto Star (Toronto)
Toronto Telegram (Toronto)
The True American Commercial Advertiser (Philadelphia)
Union United States Gazette and True American (Philadelphia)
United States Gazette (Philadelphia)
Voice of the Fugitive (Sandwich and Windsor, Ontario, Canada)
Watertown Tribune Enterprise (Watertown, Mass.)
Worcester Daily Telegraph (Worcester, Mass.)

Primary Sources

A Brief Sketch of the Schools for Black People, and Their Descendants, Established by the Religious Society of Friends, in 1770. Philadelphia: Friends' Book Store, 1867.

A List of Patents Granted by the United States, for the Encouragement of Arts and Sciences, Alphabetically Arranged, from 1790 to 1820; Containing the Names of Patentees, Their Places of Residence, and the Dates of the Patents; With an Alphabetical List of the Patentees: Also, All the Acts Passed by Congress on the Subject of Patents. Washington, D.C.: Alfred Elliott, 1820.

Abajian, James de T., comp. *Blacks in Selected Newspapers, Censuses, and Other Sources: An Index to Names and Subjects.* 3 vols. Boston: G. K. Hall, 1977.

———. *A Supplement.* 2 vols. Boston: G. K. Hall, 1985.

Abdy, Edward S. *Journal of a Residence and Tour in the United States of North America, from April 1833, to October 1834.* 3 vols. London: John Murray, 1835; rpt., New York: Negro Universities Press, 1969.

"Abstracts of Wills Recorded in the Administration Books, Register's Office, Philadelphia." *Publications of the Genealogical Society of Pennsylvania* 5 (March 1914): 271–322.

Account of the Grand Federal Procession, Philadelphia, July 4, 1788. Philadelphia: M. Carey, 1788.

Act of Incorporation, Causes and Motives, of the African Episcopal Church of Philadelphia. White-Hall: Printed for the Benefit of the Corporation, 1810.

Acts of the General Assembly of the Commonwealth of Pennsylvania, 1803–1804. Octoraro: Francis Bailey, 1804.

Adams, John Quincy. *An Oration Addressed to the Citizens of the Town of Quincy, on the Fourth of July, 1831, the Fifty-Fifth Anniversary of the Independence of the United States.* Boston: Richardson, Lord and Holbrook, 1831.

Addison, Joseph. *Cato: A Tragedy, in Five Acts.* London, 1713.

African Institution. *Tenth Report of the Directors of the African Institution.* London, 1816.

Allen, Richard. *The Life Experience and Gospel Labors of the Rt. Rev. Richard Allen.* Nashville: Abingdon Press, 1954.

Alumni Record of Wesleyan University, 1831–1970. Middletown, Conn., 1971.

America: A Poem, by Alexander Martin, Esq., To Which Is Added, Liberty, a poem, by Rusticus. Likewise Some Extracts from Mr. Addison, in Praise of Liberty. Philadelphia, 1769.

American Anti-Slavery Society. *First Annual Report*. New York, 1834.

_____. *Second Annual Report*. New York: 1835.

_____. *Third Annual Report*. New York: 1836.

_____. *Fourth Annual Report*. New York: 1837.

_____. *Fifth Annual Report*. New York: 1838.

_____. *Sixth Annual Report*. New York: 1839.

_____. *Seventh Annual Report*. New York: 1840.

American Colonization Society. *Fifth Annual Report*. Washington, D.C., 1822.

_____. *Seventh Annual Report*. Washington, D.C., 1824.

_____. *Eleventh Annual Report*. Washington, D.C. 1828.

_____. *Thirteenth Annual Report*. Washington, D.C., 1830.

An Appeal to the Women of the Nominally Free States, Issued by an Anti-Slavery Convention of American Women, Held by Adjournments from the 9th to the 12th of May, 1837. 2nd. ed. Boston: Isaac Knapp, 1838.

Baker, G. W. *A Review of the Relative Commercial Progress of the Cities of New-York and Philadelphia, Tracing the Decline of the Latter to State Development, and Shewing the Necessity of Trans-Atlantic Steamship Communication to Re-Establish Foreign Trade*. Philadelphia: Jackson, 1859.

Barnes, Gilbert H., and Dwight L. Dumond, eds. *Letters of Theodore Dwight Weld, Angelina Grimké Weld, and Sarah Grimké, 1822–1844*. 2 vols. New York: D. Appleton-Century, 1934.

Bell, Andrew. *Men and Things in America; Being the Experience of a Year's Residence in the United States*. London: W. Smith, 1838.

Benezet, Anthony. *The Pennsylvania Spelling-Book; or, Youth's Friendly Instructor and Monitor*. 6th ed. Dublin: John Gough, 1800.

Bergman, Peter M., and Jean McCarroll, comps. *The Negro in the Congressional Record, 1789–1801*. New York: Bergman, 1969.

_____. *The Negro in the Congressional Record, 1818–1819*. New York: Bergman, 1970.

Biddle, Craig, ed. *Autobiography of Charles Biddle, Vice-President of the Supreme Executive Council of Pennsylvania, 1745–1821*. Philadelphia: Privately printed for E. Claxton, 1883.

Biographie de Granville, par son fils. Paris: E. Brière, 1880.

Blatchford, John. *The Narrative of John Blatchford, Detailing His Sufferings in the Revolutionary War, While a Prisoner with the British, as Related by Himself*. New York: Privately printed, 1865; rpt., New York: Arno, 1971.

Bowers, John, and John B. Depee. *Memorial to the Honourable the Senate and House of Representatives, in General Assembly Met, the Memorial of the Subscribers, Free People of Colour, Residing in the City of Philadelphia*. Philadelphia, 1833.

Branagan, Thomas. *A Preliminary Essay on the Oppression of the Exiled Sons of Africa, Consisting of Animadversions on the Impolicy and Barbarity of the Deleterious Commerce and Subsequent Slavery of the Human Species*. Philadelphia: John W. Scott, 1804.

_____. *Avenia; or, a Tragical Poem on the Slavery and Commerce of the Human Species, Particularly the African; In Six Books, With Explanatory Notes on Each Book*. Philadelphia: S. Engles, 1805.

_____. *Serious Remonstrances, Addressed to the Citizens of the Northern States, and Their Representatives*. Philadelphia, 1805.

Branson, Ware, Jr. *The Art of Sailmaking, Illustrated by Rules and Examples for Cutting and Making Every Variety of Sails.* In I. R. Butts, *The Merchant's and Shipmaster's Manual and Shipbuilder's and Sailmaker's Assistant.* Boston: I. R. Butts, 1873.

Brothers, Thomas. *The United States of North America as They Are; Not as They Are Generally Described: Being a Cure for Radicalism.* London: Longman, Orme, Brown, Green and Longman, 1840.

Brown, Barbara W., and James M. Rose, comps. *Black Roots in Southeastern Connecticut, 1650–1900.* Detroit: Gale Research, 1980.

Brown, Isaac V. *Biography of the Rev. Robert Finley.* 2nd ed. Philadelphia: John W. Moore, 1857; rpt., New York: Arno, 1969.

_____. *Memoirs of the Rev. Robert Finley, D.D., Late Pastor of the Presbyterian Congregation of Basking Ridge, New Jersey.* New Brunswick, 1819.

Brown, William Wells. *The Black Man, His Antecedents, His Genius, and His Achievements.* 2nd ed. New York: Thomas Hamilton, 1863; rpt., New York: Johnson Reprint Corp., 1968.

Bruns, Roger, ed. *Am I Not a Man and a Brother: The Antislavery Crusade of Revolutionary America, 1688–1788.* New York: Chelsea House, 1977.

Butterfield, Lyman H., ed. *The Letters of Benjamin Rush.* 2 vols. Princeton: Princeton University Press for the American Philosophical Society, 1951.

The Canada Directory for 1857–58: Containing Names of Professional and Business Men, and of the Principal Inhabitants, in the Cities, Towns and Villages Throughout the Province. Montreal: John Lovell, 1857.

Carey, Mathew. *A Short Account of the Malignant Fever, Lately Prevalent in Philadelphia: With a Statement of the Proceedings That Took Place on the Subject in Different Parts of the United States.* 2nd ed. Philadelphia: The author, 1793.

_____. *Letters on the Colonization Society; and of Its Probable Results.* 4th ed. Philadelphia: Mathew Carey, 1832.

Catto, William W. *A Semi-Centenary Discourse Delivered in the First African Presbyterian Church, Philadelphia, on the Fourth Sabbath of May, 1857.* Philadelphia: Joseph M. Wilson, 1857.

Chadwick, French Ensor, ed. *The Graves Papers and Other Documents Relating to the Naval Operations of the Yorktown Campaign, July to October, 1781.* New York: For the Naval History Society, 1916.

Chadwick, John White, ed. *A Life for Liberty: Anti-Slavery and Other Letters of Sallie Holley.* New York and London: P. Putman's Sons, 1899.

Child, Lydia Maria. *The Freedmen's Book.* Boston: Ticknor and Fields, 1865.

Clarkson, Thomas. *History of the Rise, Progress, and Accomplishment of the Abolition of the Slave-Trade, by the British Parliament.* Philadelphia: James P. Parke, 1808.

Coil, Henry Wilson, Sr., and John MacDuffie Sherman, eds. *A Documentary Account of Prince Hall and Other Black Fraternal Orders.* St. Louis: Missouri Grand Lodge of Research, 1982.

Coker, Daniel. *A Dialogue between a Virginian and an African Minister.* Baltimore: Benjamin Edes for Joseph James, 1810.

Colledge, J. J. *Ships of the Royal Navy.* Annapolis: Naval Institute Press, 1987.

College for Colored Youth. An Account of the New-Haven City Meeting and Resolutions, With Recommendations of the College, and Strictures Upon the Doings of New-Haven. New York: 1831.

Congressional Record, 38th Congress, 1st. session (1864).

Constitution and Rules to Be Observed and Kept by the Friendly Society of St. Thomas's African Church. Philadelphia: W. W. Woodward, 1797. In Dorothy B. Porter, ed., *Early Negro Writing, 1760–1837*. Boston: Beacon Press, 1971.

Constitution, By-Laws, and List of Officers of the Young Men's Anti-Slavery Society of the City and County of Philadelphia, Instituted April, 1835. Philadelphia: M. Fithian, 1835.

* *Constitution of the American Society of Free Persons of Colour, For Improving Their Condition in the United States; For Purchasing Lands; and for the Establishment of a Settlement in Canada. Also the Proceedings of the Convention, With Their Address to the Free People of Colour in the United States*. Philadelphia: J. W. Allen, 1831.

Cooper, Anna Julia, ed. *Personal Recollections of the Grimké Family*. Washington, D.C.: For the author, 1951.

Corner, George W., ed. *The Autobiography of Benjamin Rush: His "Travels Through Life," Together With His Commonplace Book for 1789–1813*. Princeton, N.J.: American Philosophical Society, 1948.

. Cornish, Samuel E., and Theodore S. Wright. *The Colonization Scheme Considered, In Its Rejection by the Colored People—In Its Tendency to Uphold Caste—In Its Unfitness for Christianizing and Civilizing the Aborigines of Africa, and for Putting a * Stop to the African Slave Trade*. Newark, N.J.: Aaron Guest, 1840.

Cowan, Malcolm. *An Essay on the Construction of the Sails of Ships and Vessels, With Plans and Descriptions of the Patent Sails, Shewing the Many Dangers That May Be Avoided, and the Advantages Derived, from Adopting the Improved Sails*. London: J. Peck for the author, 1804.

Crane, Elizabeth Forman, ed. *The Diary of Elizabeth Drinker*. 3 vols. Boston: Northeastern University Press, 1991.

Cuffe, Paul, Jr. *Narrative of the Life and Adventures of Paul Cuffe, Jr., A Pequot Indian: During Thirty Years Spent at Sea, and in Travelling in Foreign Lands*. Vernon: Horace N. Bill, 1839.

Davies, Benjamin. *Some Account of the City of Philadelphia, the Capital of Pennsylvania, and Seat of the Federal Congress*. Philadelphia: Richard Folwell, 1794.

Delany, Martin R. *The Condition, Elevation, Emigration, and Destiny of the Colored People of the United States*. Philadelphia: The author, 1852; rpt., New York: Arno, 1968.

Denny, John F. *An Enquiry into the Political Grade of the Free Coloured Population, Under the Constitution of the United States, and the Constitution of Pennsylvania. In Three Parts. By a Member of the Chambersburg Bar*. Chambersburg, Pa.: J. Pritts, 1834.

. Dewey, Loring D. *Correspondence Relative to the Emigration to Hayti, of the Free People of Colour, in the United States. Together with the Instructions to the Agent Sent Out . by President Boyer*. New York: Mahlon Day, 1824.

Douglass, William. *Annals of the First African Church in the United States of America, Now Styled the African Episcopal Church of St. Thomas*. Philadelphia: King and Baird, 1862.

Dring, Thomas. *Recollections of the Jersey Prison-Ship; Taken and Prepared for Publication from the Original Manuscript of the Late Captain Thomas Dring, of Providence, R.I., One of the Prisoners, by Albert G. Green*. Providence: H. H. Brown, 1829; rpt., New York: Corinth Books, 1961.

Dunlap, William. *Diary of William Dunlap (1766–1839): The Memoirs of a Dramatist, Theatrical Manager, Painter, Critic, Novelist, and Historian.* Collections of the New York Historical Society for the Year 1929. New York: For the Society, 1930; rpt., Bronx, N.Y.: Benjamin Blom, 1969.

Early Unnumbered U.S. Patents, 1790–1836: Index and Guide to the Microfilm Edition. Woodbridge, Conn.: Research Publications, 1980.

"Effective Supply Tax, City of Philadelphia, 1780." *Pennsylvania Archives,* 3rd series, vol. 15 (1897): 189–367.

The Elements and Practice of Rigging, Seamanship, and Naval Tactics, Including Sail-Making, Mast-Making, and Gunnery. London: J. W. Morie, 1821.

Extract of a Letter from Dr. Benjamin Rush of Philadelphia, to Granville Sharp. London: Printed by James Phillips, 1792.

Finley, Robert. *Thoughts on the Colonization of Free Blacks.* Washington, D.C., 1816.

Forten, Charlotte. "Life on the Sea Islands." *Atlantic Monthly* 23 (May and June, 1864): 587–96 and 666–76.

Forten, James. *Letters from a Man of Colour on a Late Bill Before the Senate of Pennsylvania.* Philadelphia, 1813.

Forten, James, Robert Purvis, and William Whipper. *To the Honourable the Senate and House of Representatives of the Commonwealth of Pennsylvania.* Philadelphia, 1832.

Forten, James, Jr. *An Address Delivered Before the Ladies' Anti-Slavery Society of Philadelphia, on the Evening of the 14th of April, 1836.* Philadelphia: Merrihew and Gunn, 1836.

Fox, Ebenezer. *The Adventures of Ebenezer Fox in the Revolutionary War.* Boston: Charles Fox, 1838.

Garrison, William Lloyd. *An Address Delivered Before the Free People of Color, in Philadelphia, New York, and Other Cities, During the Month of June, 1831.* Boston: Stephen Foster, 1831.

———. *Thoughts on African Colonization; or, An Impartial Exhibition of the Doctrines, Principles and Purposes of the American Colonization Society, Together With the Resolutions, Addresses and Remonstrances of the Free People of Color.* Boston: Garrison and Knapp, 1832; rpt., New York: Arno, 1969.

Gilje, Paul A., and Howard B. Rock, eds. *Keepers of the Revolution: New Yorkers at Work in the Early Republic.* Ithaca: Cornell University Press, 1992.

Gloucester, Jeremiah. *An Oration, Delivered on January 1, 1823, in Bethel Church, on the Abolition of the Slave Trade.* Philadelphia: John Young, 1823.

Gloucester, John, Jr. *A Sermon, Delivered in the First African Presbyterian Church in Philadelphia, on the 1st of January, 1830, Before the Different Coloured Societies of Philadelphia.* Philadelphia, 1830.

Gloucester, Stephen H. *A Discourse Delivered on the Occasion of the Death of Mr. James Forten, Sr., in the Second Presbyterian Church of Colour of the City of Philadelphia, April 17, 1842, Before the Young Men of the Bible Association of Said Church.* Philadelphia: I. Ashmead, 1843.

Griggs, Earl Leslie, and Clifford H. Prator, eds. *Henry Christophe and Thomas Clarkson: A Correspondence.* Berkeley and Los Angeles: University of California Press, 1952.

Gurney, John Joseph. *A Visit to North America, Described in Familiar Leters to Amelia Opie.* Norwich, England: Josiah Fletcher, 1841.

Hallowell, Anna Davis, ed. *James and Lucretia Mott, Life and Letters*. Boston: Houghton Mifflin, 1884.

• Haytien Emigration Society of Philadelphia. *Information for the Free People of Colour, Who Are Inclined to Emigrate to Hayti*. Philadelphia: J. H. Cunningham, 1825.

Hildeburn, Charles E., ed. *The Inscriptions in St. Peter's Church Yard, Copied and Arranged by Rev. William White Bronson*. Camden, N.J.: Sinnickson Chew, 1879.

• Hinks, Peter P., ed. *David Walker's Appeal to the Coloured Citizens of the World*. University Park: Penn State University Press, 2000.

History of Pennsylvania Hall, Which was Destroyed by a Mob on the 17th of May, 1838. Philadelphia: Merrihew and Gunn, 1838; rpt., New York: Negro Universities Press, 1969.

Hoare, Prince. *Memoirs of Granville Sharp, Esq., Composed from His Own Manuscripts, and Other Authentic Documents in the Possession of His Family and of the African Institution*. 2 vols. 2nd ed. London, 1828.

Hodges, Graham Russell, ed. *The Black Loyalist Directory: African Americans in Exile after the American Revolution*. New York: Garland, 1996.

• Hodgkin, Thomas. *An Inquiry into the Merits of the American Colonization Society: And a Reply to Charges Brought Against It*. London: J. and A. Arch, 1833; rpt., London: African Publication Society, 1969.

Holcomb, Brent H., comp. *Marriage and Death Notices from the (Charleston) Times, 1800–1821*. Baltimore: Genealogical Publishing, 1979.

———. *South Carolina Naturalizations, 1783–1850*. Baltimore: Genealogical Publishing, 1985.

Home for Aged and Infirm Colored Persons. *Annual Report*. Philadelphia, 1897.

———. *Thirty-Fourth Report*. Philadelphia: Austin C. Leeds, 1898.

Horsmanden, Daniel. *The New-York Conspiracy; or, a History of the Negro Plot, With the Journal of the Proceedings Against the Conspirators at New-York in the Years 1741–42*. New York: Southwick and Pelsue, 1810. Edited with an introduction by T. J. Davis. Boston: Beacon Press, 1971.

Howard University. *Catalog for the Years 1871–72*. Washington, D.C., 1872.

Hunt, Benjamin. *Remarks on Hayti as a Place of Settlement for Afric-Americans; and on the Mulatto as a Race for the Tropics*. Philadelphia: T. B. Pugh, 1860.

Johnson, Michael P. and James L. Roark, eds. *No Chariot Let Down: Charleston's Free People of Color on the Eve of the Civil War*. Chapel Hill: University of North Carolina Press, 1984.

Jones, Absalom. *A Thanksgiving Sermon, Preached January 1, 1808, in St. Thomas's, or the African Episcopal Church, Philadelphia: On Account of the Abolition of the African Slave Trade, On That Day, By the Congress of the United States*. Philadelphia: Fry and Kammerer, 1808. In Porter, ed., *Early Negro Writing*.

Jones, Absalom, and Richard Allen. *A Narrative of the Proceedings of the Black People, During the Late Awful Calamity in Philadelphia, in the Year 1793: and a Refutation of Some Censures, Thrown upon Them in Some Late Publications*. Philadelphia: William W. Woodward for the authors, 1794.

Jones, Benjamin S. *Abolitionrieties; or, Remarks on Some of the Members of the Pennsylvania State Anti-Slavery Society for the Eastern District, and the American Anti-Slavery Society, Most of Whom Were Present at the Annual Meetings, Held in Philadelphia and New York in May 1840*. n.p., 1840.

Jones, Charles K., and Lorenzo K. Greenwich II, comps. *A Choice Collection of the Works of Francis Johnson.* 2 vols. New York: Point Two Publications, 1987.

Kaminkow, Marion, and Jack Kaminkow, comps. *Mariners of the American Revolution.* Baltimore: Magna Carta, 1967.

Kipping, Robert. *Elementary Treatise on Sails and Sailmaking.* 7th ed. London: Virtue Brothers, 1865.

Koelble, Susan S., and Kristin K. Bryson, comps. *Philadelphia Guardians of the Poor, Indenture Records 1791–1822.* Southampton, Pa.: Bare Roots, 1998.

Langdon, Barbara R., comp. *South Carolina Marriages Implied in the Miscellaneous Records and Marriage Settlements of South Carolina.* vol. 7. Aiken, S.C.: Langdon and Langdon Genealogical Research, 1999.

Laws of the General Assembly of the State of Pennsylvania Passed at the Session of 1828–29. Harrisburg, 1829.

Letter from the Secretary of State, Accompanied With a List of the Names of Persons Who Have Invented Any New and Useful Art, Machine, Manufacture or Composition of Matter, or Any Improvement Thereon, and to Whom Patents Have Been Issued for the Same from the Office of the Department of State. Washington, D.C.: Roger Chew Weightman, 1811.

Library of Congress. *Naval Records of the American Revolution, 1775–1788.* Washington, D.C.: Government Printing Office, 1906.

Lloyd's Register for the Year 1784. London, 1784.

Looby, Christopher, ed. *The Complete Civil War Journal and Selected Letters of Thomas Wentworth Higginson.* Chicago: University of Chicago Press, 2000.

Lyell, Sir Charles. *Travels in North America; With Geological Observations on the United States, Canada, and Nova Scotia.* London: John Murray, 1845.

Marryat, Frederick. *A Diary in America, With Remarks on Its Institutions.* 2 vols. London: Longman, Orme, Brown, Green and Longmans, 1839.

Massachusetts Soldiers, Sailors, and Marines in the Civil War. Norwood, Mass., 1933.

May, Samuel J. *Some Recollections of Our Anti-Slavery Conflict.* Boston: Fields, Osgood, 1869; rpt. New York: Arno, 1968.

McCrummill, James, and Jacob C. White. *Memorial to the Honourable the Senate and House of Representatives of the Commonwealth of Pennsylvania, in General Assembly Met, the Memorial of the Subscribers, Free People of Colour, Residing in the County of Philadelphia.* Philadelphia, n.d.

Meltzer, Milton and Patricia G. Holland, eds. *Lydia Maria Child, Selected Letters, 1817–1880.* Amherst: University of Massachusetts Press, 1982.

Memoir of Captain Paul Cuffee, a Man of Colour, Written Expressly for, and Originally Printed in, the Liverpool Mercury. Liverpool: Egerton Smith, 1811.

Memoirs and Autobiography of Some of the Wealthy Citizens of Philadelphia, by a Merchant of Philadelphia. Philadelphia, 1846.

Memorial to the Honorable the Senate and House of Representatives of the Commonwealth of Pennsylvania, in General Assembly Met, from the "Colored Citizens" of This State, Residents of the City of Philadelphia. Philadelphia, 1855.

Minutes and Proceedings of the First Annual Convention of the People of Colour, Held by Adjournments in the City of Philadelphia, from the Sixth to the Eleventh of June, Inclusive, 1831. Philadelphia: By Order of the Committee of Arrangements, 1831.

Minutes and Proceedings of the First Annual Meeting of the American Moral Reform Society, Held in Philadelphia from the 14th to the 19th of August, 1837. Philadelphia: Merrihew and Gunn, 1837. In Porter, ed., *Early Negro Writing*.

Minutes and Proceedings of the Second Annual Convention, for the Improvement of the Free People of Color in These United States, Held by Adjournments in the City of Philadelphia, from the 4th to the 13th of June Inclusive, 1832. Philadelphia: By Order of the Convention, 1832.

Minutes and Proceedings of the Third Annual Convention, for the Improvement of the Free People of Colour in These United States, Held by Adjournments in the City of Philadelphia, from the 3rd to the 13th of June Inclusive, 1833. New York: By Order of the Convention, 1833.

"Minutes of the Committee of Defense of Philadelphia, 1814–1815." *Memoirs of the Historical Society of Pennsylvania* 8. Philadelphia: J. B. Lippincott, 1867.

Minutes of the Fifth Annual Convention for the Improvement of the Free People of Colour in the United States, Held by Adjournments, in the Wesley Church, Philadelphia, from the First to the Fifth of June, Inclusive, 1835. Philadelphia: William P. Gibbons, 1835.

Minutes of the Fourteenth American Convention for Promoting the Abolition of Slavery, and Improving the Condition of the African Race: Assembled at Philadelphia, on the Ninth Day of January, 1815. Philadelphia: Printed by W. Brown, 1816.

Minutes of the Fourth Annual Convention, for the Improvement of the Free People of Colour, in the United States, Held by Adjournments in the Asbury Church, New York, from the 2nd to the 12th of June Inclusive, 1834. New York: By Order of the Convention, 1834.

Minutes of the Proceedings of a Special Meeting of the Fifteenth American Convention for Promoting the Abolition of Slavery and Improving the Condition of the African Race. Philadelphia: Hall and Atkinson for the Convention, 1818.

Minutes of the Proceedings of the Committee, Appointed on the 14th September, 1793, by the Citizens of Philadelphia, the Northern Liberties and the District of Southwark, to Attend to and Alleviate the Sufferings of Those Afflicted with the Malignant Fever, Prevalent in the City and its Vicinity. Philadelphia: R. Aitken and Son, 1794.

Minutes of the State Convention of the Colored Citizens of Pennsylvania, Convened in Harrisburg, December 13th and 14th, 1848. In Philip S. Foner and George E. Walker, eds., *Proceedings of the Black State Conventions, 1840–1865*. 2 vols. Philadelphia: Temple University Press, 1979–81.

"Minutes of the Supreme Executive Council of Pennsylvania." *Pennsylvania Colonial Records* 14 (1853).

Moak, Jefferson M., comp. *Insolvency Petitions and Bonds Filed in the Common Pleas Court of Philadelphia, 1790–1874*. Philadelphia: Philadelphia City Archives, 1992.

_____. *Philadelphia's Guardians of the Poor: Bonds for the Support of Illegitimate Children and Other Indigent Persons, 1811–1859*. Chestnut Hill, Pa.: Chestnut Hill Almanac, Genealogical Series, Publication no. 3, 1996.

Morrice, David. *The Young Midshipman's Instructor; With Useful Hints to Parents of Sea Youth, and to Captains and Schoolmasters in the Royal Navy*. London: Knight and Compton for the Author, 1801.

National Convention of Colored Soldiers and Sailors, Philadelphia, January 8, 1867. In Philip S. Foner and George E. Walker, eds., *Proceedings of the Black National and State Conventions, 1865–1900*. Philadelphia: Temple University Press, 1986.

The Negro Equalled by Few Europeans. Translated from the French. To Which Are Added, Poems on Various Subjects, Moral and Entertaining; by Phillis Wheatley, Negro Servant to Mr. John Wheatley, of Boston, in New England. Philadelphia: William W. Woodward, 1801.

Oberlin College, Alumni Register, Graduates and Former Students, Teaching and Administrative Staff, 1833–1960. Oberlin, 1960.

Oberlin College, Alumni Register, Students, 1833–1909. Oberlin, 1909.

Opinion of the Hon. John Fox, President Judge of the Judicial District Composed of the Counties of Bucks and Montgomery, Against the Exercise of Negro Suffrage in Pennsylvania. Harrisburg: Packer, Barrett and Parke, 1838.

Parrish, John. *Remarks on the Slavery of the Black People: Addressed to the Citizens of the United States, Particularly to Those Who Are in Legislative or Executive Stations in the General or State Governments: and Also to Such Individuals as Hold Them in Bondage*. Philadelphia: Kimber, Conrad, 1806.

Parrott, Russell. *An Oration on the Abolition of the Slave Trade, Delivered on the First of January, 1812, at the African Church of St. Thomas, Philadelphia*. Philadelphia: James Maxwell for the Different Societies, 1812.

_____. *An Oration on the Abolition of the Slave Trade, Delivered on the First of January, 1814*. Philadelphia: Thomas T. Stiles, 1814. In Porter, ed., *Early Negro Writing*.

———. *An Address on the Abolition of the Slave Trade, Delivered Before the Different African Benevolent Societies, on the 1st of January, 1816*. Philadelphia: T. S. Manning, 1816.

Payne, Daniel Alexander. *Recollections of Seventy Years*. Nashville: AME Sunday School Union, 1888; rpt., New York: Arno, 1968.

Pennsylvania Abolition Society. *The Present State and Condition of the Free People of Color of the City of Philadelphia and Adjoining Districts, as Exhibited by the Report of a Committee of the Pennsylvania Society for Promoting the Abolition of Slavery*. Philadelphia: Merrihew and Thompson, 1838.

_____. *Register of the Trades of the Colored People in the City of Philadelphia, and Adjoining Districts*. Philadelphia: Merrihew and Gunn, 1838.

_____. *Statistics of the Colored People of Philadelphia, Taken by Benjamin C. Bacon and Published by Order of the Board of Education of the Pennsylvania Society for Promoting the Abolition of Slavery*. Philadelphia: Merrihew and Thompson, 1856.

Pennsylvania, General Assembly. *Journal of the House, 1799–1832*.

_____. *Journal of the Senate, 1814–32*.

Philadelphia Female Anti-Slavery Society. *Thirty-Sixth and Final Annual Report*. Philadelphia, 1870.

Philadelphia in 1824. Philadelphia: H. C. Carey and I. Lea, 1824.

Pickard, John B., ed. *The Letters of John Greenleaf Whittier*. 3 vols. Cambridge, Mass.: Harvard University Press, 1975.

Pierson, George Wilson, ed. *Tocqueville and Beaumont in America*. New York: Oxford University Press, 1938.

Pinckney, Eliza, ed. *Register of St. Philip's Church, Charleston, South Carolina, 1810 through 1822*. Charleston: National Society of Colonial Dames of America in the State of South Carolina, 1973.

Portrait Album of Who's Who at the International Congress of Women, Held in London from June 26th to July 5th, 1899. London: The Gentlewoman, 1899.

Price, George R. and James Brewer Stewart, eds. *To Heal the Scourge of Oppression: The Life and Writings of Hosea Easton.* Amherst: University of Massachusetts Press, 1999.

"The Private Register of the Rev. Paul Trapier." *South Carolina Historical Magazine* 58 (July 1957): 163–82.

Proceedings and Debates of the Convention of the Commonwealth of Pennsylvania, to Propose Amendments to the Constitution, Commenced at Harrisburg, on the Second day of May, 1837. 13 vols. Harrisburg: Packer, Barrett and Parke, 1837–39.

Proceedings of the Annual Meeting of the Pennsylvania State Equal Rights' League, Held in the City of Harrisburg, August 9th and 10th, 1865. In Foner and Walker, eds., *Proceedings of the Black National and State Conventions, 1865–1900.*

Proceedings of the Anti-Slavery Convention of American Women, Held in Philadelphia, May 15th, 16th, 17th and 18th, 1838. Philadelphia: Merrihew and Gunn, 1838.

Proceedings of the Pennsylvania Convention, Assembled to Organize a State Anti-Slavery Society, at Harrisburg, on the 31st of January and 1st, 2nd and 3rd of February, 1837. Philadelphia: Merrihew and Gunn, 1837.

Proceedings of the State Convention of the Colored Freemen of Pennsylvania, Held in Pittsburgh, on the 23rd, 24th, and 25th of August, 1841, for the Purpose of Considering Their Condition, and the Means of Its Improvement. Pittsburgh, 1841.

Proceedings of the State Equal Rights Convention, of the Colored People of Pennsylvania, Held in the City of Harrisburg, February 8th, 9th and 10th, 1865, Together With a Few of the Arguments Presented Suggesting the Necessity for Holding the Convention, and an Address of the Colored State Convention to the People of Pennsylvania. In Foner and Walker, eds., *Proceedings of the Black State Conventions, 1840–1865.*

Proceedings of the Thirty-Second Annual Convention of the National American Woman Suffrage Association. Philadelphia: Alfred J. Ferris, 1900.

Protestant Episcopal Church, Diocese of Pennsylvania. *Journals of Five Conventions of the Protestant Episcopal Church, in the State of Pennsylvania, Held in Christ Church, in Philadelphia, Beginning With the Seventh Convention, in the Year 1791, and Ending With the Eleventh, in the Year 1795.* Philadelphia: Ormrod and Conrad, 1795.

_____. *Journal of the Thirty-Fourth Convention.* Philadelphia: S. Potter, 1818.

_____. *Journal of the Fortieth Convention.* Philadelphia: By Order of the Convention, 1824.

_____. *Journal of the Forty-Fourth Convention.* Philadelphia, 1828.

_____. *Journal of the Forty-Fifth Convention.* Philadelphia, 1829.

_____. *Journal of the Forty-Seventh Convention.* Philadelphia, 1831.

_____. *Journal of the Fifty-First Convention.* Philadelphia, 1835.

Purvis, Charles Burleigh. *Report of the Freedmen's Hospital to the Secretary of the Interior, 1885.* Washington, D.C., 1885.

Purvis, Robert. *Remarks on the Life and Character of James Forten, Delivered at Bethel Church, March 30, 1842.* Philadelphia: Merrihew and Thompson, 1842.

Purvis, Robert, et al. *Appeal of Forty Thousand Citizens, Threatened With Disfranchisement, to the People of Pennsylvania.* Philadelphia: Merrihew and Gunn, 1838.

"Record of Servants and Apprentices Bound and Assigned Before Hon. John Gibson, Mayor of Philadelphia, December 5, 1772–May 21, 1773." *Pennsylvania Magazine of History and Biography* 34 (1910): 99–121, 213–28.

"Registers Granted at the Port of Philadelphia in the Quarter Ending 5th January 1775." *Pennsylvania Magazine of History and Biography* 39 (1915): 192–95.

A Remonstrance Against the Proceedings of a Meeting, Held November 23rd, 1831, at Upton's, in Dock Street, Philadelphia. Philadelphia, 1832.

Reports of Cases Argued and Determined in the Supreme Court of Pennsylvania, by Frederick Watts, May to September 1837. Philadelphia: James King, Jr. and Brother, 1850.

Republican Congressional Committee. *Grant or Greeley—Which? Facts and Arguments for the Consideration of the Colored Citizens of the United States: Being Extracts from Letters, Speeches, and Editorials by Colored Men and Their Best Friends.* Washington, D.C., 1872.

* *Resolutions and Remonstrances of the People of Colour Against Colonization on the Coast of Africa.* Philadelphia, 1818.

Revill, Janie, comp. *Some South Carolina Genealogical Records.* Easley, S.C.: Southern Historical Press, 1986.

Ripley, C. Peter, et al., eds. *Black Abolitionist Papers.* 5 vols. Chapel Hill: University of North Carolina Press, 1989–91.

Ritter, Abraham. *Philadelphia and Her Merchants, as Constituted Fifty and Seventy Years Ago, Illustrated with Diagrams of the River Front, and Portraits of Some of Its Prominent Occupants, Together With Sketches of Character, and Incidents and Anecdotes of the Day.* Philadelphia: The author, 1860.

Roach, Hannah Benner, ed. "Taxables in the City of Philadelphia, 1756." *Pennsylvania Genealogical Magazine* 22 (1961): 3–41.

Rush, Benjamin. *An Account of the Bilious Remitting Yellow Fever, as It Appeared in the City of Philadelphia, in the Year 1793.* 2nd ed. Philadelphia: T. Dobson, 1794.

Saunders, Prince. *A Memoir Presented to the American Convention for Promoting the Abolition of Slavery, and Improving the Condition of the African Race, December 11th, 1818.* Philadelphia: Dennis Heartt, 1818. In Porter, ed., *Early Negro Writing.*

———. *An Address Delivered at Bethel Church, Philadelphia; on the 30th of September, 1818. Before the Pennsylvania Augustine Society, for the Education of People of Colour. To Which is Annexed the Constitution of the Society.* Philadelphia: Joseph Rakestraw, 1818.

Schultz, Ronald, ed. "Small Producer Thought in Early America, Part I: Philadelphia's Artisans and Price Control." *Pennsylvania History* 54 (April 1987): 115–47.

Shick, Tom W., comp. *Emigrants to Liberia, 1820 to 1843, an Alphabetical Listing.* Liberian Studies Research Working Paper, no. 2, Department of Anthropology, University of Delaware, 1971.

Ship Registers of New Bedford, Massachusetts, vol. 1: 1796–1850. Boston: National Archives Project, 1940.

Simmons, William J. *Men of Mark: Eminent, Progressive and Rising.* Cleveland: G. M. Rewell, 1887; rpt., New York: Arno, 1968.

Singleton, Arthur. *Letters from the South and West.* Boston: Richardson and Lord, 1824.

Smedley, Robert Clemens. *History of the Underground Railroad in Chester and the Neighboring Counties of Pennsylvania.* Lancaster, Pa.: Printed at the Office of the Journal, 1883; rpt., New York: Arno, 1969.

"Some Letters of Richard Allen and Absalom Jones to Dorothy Ripley." *Journal of Negro History* 1 (October 1916): 436–43.

Spring, Gardiner. *Memoir of Samuel John Mills.* 2nd ed. Boston: Perkins and Marvin, New York: J. Leavitt and J. P. Haven, 1829.

Steel, David. *The Art of Sail-Making, as Practised in the Royal Navy, and According to the Most Approved Methods in the Merchant-Service, Accompanied With the Parliamentary Regulations Relative to Sails and Sail-Cloth.* 2nd ed. London: P. Mason, 1809.

Stevenson, Brenda, ed. *The Journals of Charlotte Forten Grimké.* New York: Oxford University Press, 1988.

Stott, Richard B., ed. *William Otter, History of My Own Times.* Ithaca: Cornell University Press, 1995.

Sturge, Joseph. *A Visit to the United States in 1841.* London: Hamilton, Adams, 1842; rpt., New York: Augustus M. Kelley, 1969.

"Supply Tax, City of Philadelphia, 1782." *Pennsylvania Archives,* 3rd series, vol. 16 (1897): 277–521.

Sword of Truth; or, A Reply to Facts Relative to the Government of the African Methodist Episcopal Church Called Bethel, Which Facts Are Proved to Be No Facts at All, but a Tissue of Base and Unfounded Lies. By the Trustees of Bethel and Wesley Churches. Philadelphia: J. H. Cunningham for the Society, 1823.

Syrett, David, and R. L. DiNardo, eds. *The Commissioned Sea Officers of the Royal Navy 1660–1815.* Aldershot, England: Scolar Press for the Navy Records Society, 1994.

Tappan, Lewis. *The Life of Arthur Tappan.* New York: Hurd and Houghton, 1871; rpt., Westport, Conn.: Negro Universities Press, 1970.

Taylor, Clare, ed. *British and American Abolitionists: An Episode in Transatlantic Understanding.* Edinburgh: Edinburgh University Press, 1974.

"Tombstone Inscriptions Collected by the Late Joseph Ioor Waring, Esq." *South Carolina Historical and Genealogical Magazine* 27 (January 1926): 36–41.

Truxtun, Thomas. *Remarks, Instructions, and Examples Relating to the Latitude and Longitude; also the Variations of the Compass, &c, &c, &c, To Which Is Annexed a General Chart of the Globe, Together With a Short but General Account of Variable Winds, Monsoons, Hurricanes, Tornadoes, Tuffoons, Calms, Currents.* Philadelphia: T. Dobson, 1794.

United States. Office of Naval Records. *Naval Documents Related to the Quasi-War between the United States and France.* 7 vols. Washington, D.C.: Government Printing Office, 1935–38.

United States Congressional Committee Hearings Index, 23rd–64th Congress, December 1833–March 1917. Washington, D.C.: Congressional Information Service, 1985.

Van Horne, John C., ed. *Religious Philanthropy and Colonial Slavery: The American Correspondence of the Associates of Dr. Bray, 1717–1777.* Urbana: University of Illinois Press, 1985.

Vital Records of Westport, Massachusetts to the Year 1850. Boston: New England Historic Genealogical Society, 1918.

Wainwright, Nicholas B., ed. *A Philadelphia Perspective: The Diary of Sidney George Fisher Covering the Years 1834–1871.* Philadelphia: Historical Society of Pennsylvania, 1967.

———, ed. "The Diary of Samuel Breck, 1814–1822." *Pennsylvania Magazine of History and Biography* 102 (October 1978): 469–508.

———, ed. "The Diary of Samuel Breck, 1827–1833." *Pennsylvania Magazine of History and Biography* 103 (April 1979): 222–51.

Watson, John Fanning. *Annals of Philadelphia, Being a Collection of Memoirs, Anecdotes, & Incidents of the City and Its Inhabitants, from the Days of the Pilgrim Founders*. Philadelphia: E. L. Carey and A. Hart; New York: G. and C. and H. Carvill, 1830.

Wealth and Biography of the Wealthy Citizens of Philadelphia, Containing an Alphabetical Arrangement of Persons Estimated to Be Worth $50,000 and Upwards, With the Sums Appended to Each Name, by a Member of the Philadelphia Bar. Philadelphia: G. B. Zieber, 1845.

Whittier, John Greenleaf. "The Antislavery Convention of 1833." *Atlantic Monthly* 33 (February 1874): 166–72.

Why Colored People in Philadelphia Are Excluded from the Streetcars. Philadelphia: Merrihew and Son, 1866.

Wiggins, Rosalind Cobb, ed. *Captain Paul Cuffe's Logs and Letters, 1808–1817: A Black Quaker's "Voice from Within the Veil."* Washington, D.C.: Howard University Press, 1996.

Wilkinson, Frederick D., ed. *Directory of Graduates, Howard University, 1870–1963*. Washington, D.C.: Howard University Press, 1965.

Wilson, Thomas B., and Emily S. Wilson, comps. *Directory of the Province of Ontario, 1857, With a Gazetteer*. Lambertville, N.J.: Hunterdon House, 1987.

• Winch, Julie, ed. *The Elite of Our People: Joseph Willson's Sketches of Black Upper-Class Life in Antebellum Philadelphia*. University Park: Penn State University Press, 2000.

Yellin, Jean Fagan, ed. *Incidents in the Life of a Slave Girl Written by Herself*. Cambridge, Mass.: Harvard University Press, 1987.

Secondary Works

Books

Albion, Robert G. *Square-Riggers on Schedule: The New York Sailing Packets to England, France, and the Cotton Ports*. Princeton: Princeton University Press, 1938.

Ardouin, Beaubrun. *Géographie de l'île d'Haïti*. Port au Prince, 1832.

———. *Etudes sur l'histoire d'Haïti*. Paris, 1860.

Banbury, Philip. *Shipbuilders of the Thames and Medway*. Newton Abbot, England: David and Charles, 1971.

Banks, James Lenox. *David Sproat and Naval Prisoners in the War of the Revolution*. Boston: Knickerbocker Press, 1909.

Baughman, James P. *The Mallorys of Mystic: Six Generations of American Maritime Enterprise*. Middletown, Conn.: Wesleyan University Press, 1972.

Bay, Mia. *The White Image in the Black Mind: African-American Ideas about White People, 1830–1925*. New York: Oxford University Press, 2000.

Bell, Howard H. *A Survey of the Negro Convention Movement, 1830–1861*. New York: Arno, 1969.

Berlin, Ira. *Slaves Without Masters: The Free Negro in the Antebellum South*. New York: Pantheon, 1974.

———. *Many Thousands Gone: The First Two Centuries of Slavery in North America*. Cambridge, Mass.: Harvard University Press, 1998.

Bezanson, Anne, et al. *Prices and Inflation During the American Revolution—Pennsylvania, 1770–1790*. Philadelphia: University of Pennsylvania Press, 1951.

Birney, William. *James G. Birney and His Times*. New York: D. Appleton, 1890.

Blackett, R. J. M. *Beating Against the Barriers: Biographical Essays in Nineteenth-Century Afro-American History*. Baton Rouge: Louisiana State University Press, 1986.

Blackmar, Elizabeth. *Manhattan for Rent, 1785–1850*. Ithaca: Cornell University Press, 1989.

Bolster, W. Jeffrey. *Black Jacks: African American Seamen in the Age of Sail*. Cambridge, Mass.: Harvard University Press, 1997.

Bowman, Larry G. *Captive Americans: Prisoners During the American Revolution*. Athens: Ohio University Press, 1976.

Brown, Ira D. *The Negro in Pennsylvania History*. Gettysburg: Pennsylvania Historical Association, 1970.

Brown, Wallace. *The Good Americans: The Loyalists in the American Revolution*. New York: William Morrow, 1969.

Brown, Wallace, and Hereward Senior. *Victorious in Defeat: The American Loyalists in Exile*. New York: Facts on File, 1984.

Bruce, Dickson D., Jr. *Archibald Grimké: Portrait of a Black Independent*. Baton Rouge: Louisiana State University Press, 1993.

Bullock, Stephen C. *Revolutionary Brotherhood: Freemasonry and the Transformation of the American Social Order, 1730–1840*. Chapel Hill: University of North Carolina Press, 1996.

Burke, Sir Bernard. *Genealogical and Heraldic History of the Landed Gentry*. London: Burke's Peerage, 1939.

Clement, Priscilla Ferguson. *Welfare and the Poor in the Nineteenth-Century City: Philadelphia, 1800–1854*. London and Toronto: Associated University Press, 1985.

Coan, Josephus Roosevelt. *Daniel Alexander Payne, Christian Educator*. Philadelphia: AME Book Concern, 1935.

Cole, Hubert. *Christophe: King of Haiti*. London: Eyre and Spottiswoode, 1967.

Combe, George. *Notes on the United States of North America, During a Phrenological Visit in 1838-9-40*. Philadelphia: Carey and Hart, 1841.

Crisp, Frederick Arthur, ed. *Visitation of England and Wales*, vols. 16–17. N.p.: Privately printed, 1909–11.

Crosby, Alfred W., Jr. *America, Russia, Hemp and Napoleon: American Trade With Russia and the Baltic, 1783–1812*. Columbus: Ohio State University Press, 1965.

Cumming, William P., and Hugh Rankin. *The Fate of a Nation: The American Revolution Through Contemporary Eyes*. London: Phaidon, 1975.

Dabydeen, David. *Hogarth's Blacks: Images of Blacks in Eighteenth-Century English Art*. Kingston-upon-Thames: Dangaroo Press, 1985.

Dandridge, Danske. *American Prisoners of the Revolution*. Charlottesville, Va.: Michie, 1911.

Davis, Harry E. *A History of Freemasonry Among Negroes in America*. Cleveland, 1946.

Davis, Ralph. *The Rise of the English Shipping Industry in the Seventeenth and Eighteenth Centuries*. London: Macmillan, 1962.

Davis, T. J. *"A Rumor of Revolt": The "Great Negro Plot" in Colonial New York*. Amherst: University of Massachusetts Press, 1985.

DuBois, W. E. B. *The Philadelphia Negro, A Social History*. Philadelphia: For the University of Pennsylvania, 1899; rpt., New York: Shocken Books, 1967.

Eckhardt, Celia Morris. *Frances Wright—Rebel in America*. Cambridge, Mass.: Harvard University Press, 1984.

Edwards, Paul, and James Walvin. *Black Personalities in the Era of the Slave Trade*. Baton Rouge: Louisiana State University Press, 1983.

Ellison, Julie. *Cato's Tears and the Making of Anglo-American Emotion*. Chicago: University of Chicago Press, 1999.

Essah, Patience. *A House Divided: Slavery and Emancipation in Delaware, 1638–1865*. Charlottesville: University of Virginia Press, 1996.

Fabian, Ann. *Card Sharps, Dream Books and Bucket Shops: Gambling in 19th-Century America*. Ithaca: Cornell University Press, 1990.

Ferguson, Eugene S. *Truxtun of the Constellation: The Life of Commodore Thomas Truxtun, U.S. Navy, 1755–1822*. Baltimore: Johns Hopkins University Press, 1956.

Fladeland, Betty. *James Gillespie Birney: Slaveholder to Abolitionist*. Ithaca: Cornell University Press, 1955.

Fowler, William M. *Jack Tars and Commodores: The American Navy, 1783–1815*. Boston: Houghton Mifflin, 1984.

Fox, Early Lee. *The American Colonization Society, 1817–1840*. Baltimore: Johns Hopkins University Press, 1917; rpt., New York: AMS Press, 1971.

Garitee, Jerome R. *The Republic's Private Navy: The American Privateering Business as Practiced by Baltimore During the War of 1812*. Middletown, Conn.: Wesleyan University Press, 1977.

Garraty, John A., and Mark C. Carnes, eds. *American National Biography*. 24 vols. New York: Oxford University Press, 1999.

Garrison, Wendell Phillips, and Francis Jackson Garrison. *William Lloyd Garrison, 1805–1879: The Story of His Life Told by His Children*. 4 vols. New York: Century, 1899; rpt., New York: Arno, 1969.

Gerzina, Gretchen. *Black London: Life Before Emancipation*. New Brunswick: Rutgers University Press, 1995.

Goldenberg, Joseph A. *Shipbuilding in Colonial America*. Charlottesville: University of Virginia Press, 1976.

Goldstein, Jonathan. *Philadelphia and the China Trade, 1682–1846: Commercial, Cultural and Attitudinal Effects*. University Park: Penn State University Press, 1978.

Gough, Deborah Mathias. *Christ Church, Philadelphia: The Nation's Church in a Changing City*. Philadelphia: University of Pennsylvania Press, 1995.

Grimshaw, William Henry. *Official History of Freemasonry Among the Colored People in North America*. New York: Broadway, 1903; rpt., New York: Negro Universities Press, 1969.

Hagy, James William. *This Happy Land: The Jews of Colonial and Antebellum Charleston*. Tuscaloosa: University of Alabama Press, 1993.

Hansen, Debra Gold. *Strained Sisterhood: Gender and Class in the Boston Female Anti-Slavery Society*. Amherst: University of Massachusetts Press, 1993.

Harper, Ida Husted. *Life and Work of Susan B. Anthony*. Indianapolis: Hollenbeck Press, 1908; rpt., Salem, N.H.: Ayer, 1983.

Harris, Sheldon. *Paul Cuffe: Black America and the African Return*. New York: Simon and Schuster, 1972.

Hazard, Samuel. *Santo Domingo, Past and Present; With a Glance at Hayti*. New York: Harper, 1873.

Hickey, Donald R. *The War of 1812: A Forgotten Conflict*. Urbana: University of Illinois Press, 1989.

Hodges, Graham Russell. *Slavery and Freedom in the Rural North: African Americans in Monmouth County, New Jersey, 1665–1865*. Madison, Wisc.: Madison House, 1997.

Horsley, John E. *Tools of the Maritime Trades*. Camden, Me.: International Maritime Publishing, 1978.

Horton, James Oliver, and Lois E. Horton. *In Hope of Liberty: Culture, Community and Protest Among Northern Free Blacks, 1700–1860*. New York: Oxford University Press, 1996.

Hutchins, John G. B. *The American Maritime Industries and Public Policy, 1789–1914: An Economic History*. Cambridge, Mass.: Harvard University Press, 1941.

Jackson, John W. *The Pennsylvania Navy, 1775–1781—The Defense of the Delaware*. New Brunswick, N.J.: Rutgers University Press, 1974.

_____. *With the British Army in Philadelphia, 1777–1778*. San Rafael, Calif.: Presidio Press, 1979.

James, William Milburne. *The British Navy in Adversity: A Study of the War of American Independence*. London: Longmans, Green, 1926.

Jeffrey, Julie Roy. *The Great Silent Army of Abolitionism: Ordinary Women in the Antislavery Movement*. Chapel Hill: University of North Carolina Press, 1998.

Johnson, Paul E. *A Shopkeeper's Millennium: Society and Revivals in Rochester, New York, 1815–1837*. New York: Hill and Wang, 1978.

Jones, Howard. *Mutiny on the Amistad: The Saga of a Slave Revolt and Its Impact on American Abolition, Law, and Diplomacy*. New York: Oxford University Press, 1987.

Kaplan, Sidney, and Emma Nogrady Kaplan. *The Black Presence in the Era of the American Revolution*. Amherst: University of Massachusetts Press, 1989.

Katzman, David M. *Before the Ghetto: Black Detroit in the Nineteenth Century*. Urbana: University of Illinois Press, 1975.

Koger, Larry. *Black Slaveowners: Free Black Slave Masters in South Carolina, 1790–1860*. Columbia: University of South Carolina Press, 1989.

Lane, Roger. *Roots of Violence in Black Philadelphia, 1860–1900*. Cambridge, Mass.: Harvard University Press, 1986.

_____. *William Dorsey's Philadelphia and Ours: On the Past and Future of the Black City in America*. New York: Oxford University Press, 1993.

Lapsansky, Emma J. *Neighborhoods in Transition: William Penn's Dream and Urban Reality*. New York: Garland, 1994.

Larrabee, Harold A. *Decision at the Chesapeake*. New York: Clarkson N. Potter, 1964.

Lavery, Brian. *The Ship of the Line*. 2 vols. London: Conway Maritime Press, 1983.

_____. *The Arming and Fitting of English Ships of War, 1600–1815*. London: Conway Maritime Press, 1987.

Linebaugh, Peter. *The London Hanged: Crime and Civil Society in the Eighteenth Century*. Cambridge: Cambridge University Press, 1992.

Logan, Rayford W. *The Diplomatic Relations of the United States With Haiti, 1776–1891*. Chapel Hill: University of North Carolina Press, 1941.

Lutz, Alma. *Crusade for Freedom: Women of the Antislavery Movement*. Boston: Beacon Press, 1968.

Mabee, Carleton. *Black Education in New York State from Colonial to Modern Times*. Syracuse: Syracuse University Press, 1979.

MacGregor, David. *Merchant Sailing Ships, 1775–1815: Their Design and Construction*. Watford, England: Argus Books, 1980.

_____. *Merchant Sailing Ships, 1815–1850: Supremacy of Sail*. Annapolis: Naval Institute Press, 1984.

Mackenzie, Charles. *Notes on Haiti, Made During a Residence in That Republic*. London: Henry Colburn and Richard Bentley, 1830.

McManemin, John A. *Captains of the Privateers During the Revolutionary War*. Spring Lake, N.J.: Ho-Ho-Kus Publishing, 1985.

Major, Jerry, with Doris E. Saunders. *Black Society*. Chicago: Johnson Publishing, 1976.

Marino, Emiliano. *The Sailmaker's Apprentice: A Guide for the Self-Reliant Sailor*. Camden, Me.: International Marine, 1994.

Marshall, Dorothy. *Dr. Johnson's London*. New York and London: John Wiley and Sons, 1968.

Martin, John Hill. *Martin's Bench and Bar of Philadelphia*. Philadelphia: Rees Welsh, 1883.

Mayer, Henry. *All on Fire: William Lloyd Garrison and the Abolition of Slavery*. New York: St. Martin's Press, 1998.

Mead, Janet Cutler. *Bent Sails: A Sailmaking Saga Written in the Words of a New England Craftsman of Square Rigger Days*. Cincinnati: Mail It, 1962.

Miller, Floyd J. *The Search for a Black Nationality: Black Emigration and Colonization, 1787–1864*. Chicago: University of Illinois Press, 1975.

Miller, Nathan. *Sea of Glory: The Continental Navy Fights for Independence, 1775–1783*. New York: David McKay, 1974.

Minton, Henry M. *Early History of Negroes in Business in Philadelphia, Read Before the American Negro Historical Society, March 1913*. Nashville: AME Sunday School Union, 1913.

Mintz, Steven. *Moralists and Modernizers: America's Pre-Civil War Reformers*. Baltimore: Johns Hopkins University Press, 1995.

Montague, Ludwell Lee. *Haiti and the United States, 1714–1938*. Durham, N.C.: Duke University Press, 1940.

Moore, John Hammond. *Columbia and Richland County: A South Carolina Community, 1740–1999*. Columbia: University of South Carolina Press, 1993.

Nash, Gary B. *Forging Freedom: The Formation of Philadelphia's Black Community, 1720–1840*. Cambridge, Mass.: Harvard University Press, 1988.

_____. *Race and Revolution*. Madison, Wisc.: Madison House, 1990.

Nash, Gary B., and Jean R. Soderlund. *Freedom by Degrees: Emancipation in Pennsylvania and Its Aftermath*. New York: Oxford University Press, 1991.

Pease, William H., and Jane H. Pease. *Bound With Them in Chains: A Biographical History of the Antislavery Movement*. Westport, Conn.: Greenwood Press, 1972.

Pollock, Thomas Clark. *The Philadelphia Theatre in the Eighteenth Century Together With the Day Book of the Same Period*. Philadelphia: University of Pennsylvania Press, 1933.

Powell, John H. *Bring Out Your Dead: The Great Plague of Yellow Fever in Philadelphia in 1793*. Philadelphia: University of Pennsylvania Press, 1949.

Powers, Bernard E., Jr. *Black Charlestonians: A Social History, 1822–1885*. Fayetteville: University of Arkansas Press, 1994.

The Purvis Family, 1694–1988. Tillicoultry, Scotland: Privately printed, 1988.

Putney, Martha S. *Black Sailors: Afro-American Merchant Seamen and Whalemen Prior to the Civil War*. Westport, Conn.: Greenwood, 1987.

Quarles, Benjamin. *The Negro in the American Revolution*. Chapel Hill: University of North Carolina Press, 1961.

Rodger, N. A. M. *The Wooden World: An Anatomy of the Georgian Navy*. London: William Collins Sons, 1986.

Rosswurm, Steven. *Arms, Country and Class: The Philadelphia Militia and the "Lower Sort" During the American Revolution.* New Brunswick: Rutgers University Press, 1987.

Ruschenberger, W. S. W. *A Sketch of the Life of Dr. Robert Bridges, Read Before the American Philosophical Society, February 15, 1884.* Philadelphia: McCalla and Staveley, 1884.

Scharf, J. Thomas, and Thompson Westcott. *History of Philadelphia, 1609–1884.* 3 vols. Philadelphia: L. H. Everts, 1884.

Schultz, Ronald. *The Republic of Labor: Philadelphia Artisans and the Politics of Class, 1720–1830.* New York: Oxford University Press, 1993.

Scobie, Edward. *Black Britannia: A History of Blacks in Britain.* Chicago: Johnson Publishing, 1972.

Sermon Preached at the Funeral of Robert Purvis by Rev. Frederic A. Hinckley, of Philadelphia, Pa., on Friday, April 15, 1898, at Spring Garden Unitarian Church. Washington, D.C.: Judd and Detweiller, 1898.

Sernett, Milton C. *Black Religion and American Evangelism: White Protestants, Plantation Missions, and the Flowering of Negro Christianity, 1787–1865.* Metuchen, N.J.: Scarecrow Press, 1975.

———. *Abolition's Axe: Beriah Green, Oneida Institute, and the Black Freedom Struggle.* Syracuse: Syracuse University Press, 1986.

Shyllon, Folarin. *Black People in Britain, 1555–1833.* London: Oxford University Press, 1977.

Siebert, Wilbur H. *The Underground Railroad from Slavery to Freedom.* New York: Macmillan, 1898; rpt., New York: Arno, 1968.

Silcox, Harry C. *Philadelphia Politics from the Bottom Up: The Life of Irishman William McMullen, 1824–1901.* Philadelphia: Balch Institute Press, 1989.

Silverman, Jason H. *Unwelcome Guests: Canada West's Response to American Fugitive Slaves, 1800–1865.* Millwood, N.Y.: Associated Faculty Press, 1985.

Simmons, William J. *Men of Mark: Eminent, Progressive and Rising.* Cleveland: George R. Rewell, 1887; rpt., New York: Arno, 1968.

Southern, Eileen. *The Music of Black Americans: A History.* 2nd ed. New York: W. W. Norton, 1983.

Stanton, Elizabeth Cady, Susan B. Anthony, Matilda Joslyn Gage, and I. H. Harper. *History of Woman Suffrage.* 6 vols. New York: Fowler and Wells, 1881–1921; rpt., Salem, N.H.: Ayer, 1985.

Staudenraus, P. J. *The African Colonization Movement, 1816–1865.* New York: Columbia University Press, 1961.

Stouffer, Allen P. *The Light of Nature and the Law of God: Antislavery in Ontario, 1833–1877.* Baton Rouge: Louisiana State University Press, 1992.

Strane, Susan. *A Whole-Souled Woman: Prudence Crandall and the Education of Black Women.* New York: W. W. Norton, 1990.

Thomas, Lamont D. *Rise to Be a People: A Biography of Paul Cuffe.* Urbana: University of Illinois Press, 1986.

Tilley, John A. *The British Navy and the American Revolution.* Columbia: University of South Carolina Press, 1977.

Tise, Larry E. *The American Counterrevolution: A Retreat from Liberty, 1783–1800.* Mechanicsburg, Pa.: Stackpole Books, 1998.

Tooker, Elva. *Nathan Trotter, Philadelphia Merchant, 1787–1853*. Cambridge, Mass.: Harvard University Press, 1955.

Town of Hertford Bi-Centennial, 1758–1958, and Historical Data of Perquimans County, North Carolina. New Bern, N.C.: Owen G. Dunn, n.d.

Waldstreicher, David. *In the Midst of Perpetual Fetes: The Making of American Nationalism, 1776–1820*. Chapel Hill: University of North Carolina Press, 1997.

Walker, Juliet E. K. *The History of Black Business in America: Capitalism, Race, Entrepreneurship*. New York: Macmillan, 1998.

Walls, William J. *The African Methodist Episcopal Zion Church, Reality of the Black Church*. Charlotte, N.C.: AME Zion Publishing, 1974.

Walvin, James. *Black and White: The Negro and English Society, 1555–1954*. London: Allen Lane, 1973.

_____. *England, Slaves and Freedom, 1776–1838*. Jackson: University Press of Mississippi, 1986.

Wesley, Charles H. *Prince Hall, Life and Legacy*. Washington, D.C.: United Supreme Council, Southern Jurisdiction, Prince Hall Affiliation, 1983.

White, Shane. *Somewhat More Independent: The End of Slavery in New York City, 1770–1810*. Athens: University of Georgia Press, 1991.

Williams, William H. *Slavery and Freedom in Delaware, 1639–1865*. Wilmington, Del.: Scholarly Resources, 1996.

Williamson, James A. *The English Channel: A History*. Cleveland and New York: World Publishing, 1959.

Wilson, Carol. *Freedom at Risk: The Kidnapping of Free Blacks in America, 1780–1865*. Lexington: University Press of Kentucky, 1994.

Wilson, George. *Stephen Girard, America's First Tycoon*. Conshohocken, Pa.: Combined Books, 1995.

Winch, Julie. *Philadelphia's Black Elite: Activism, Accommodation, and the Struggle for Autonomy, 1787–1848*. Philadelphia: Temple University Press, 1988.

Winslow, Mary. *History of Perquimans County*. Raleigh, N.C.: Edwards and Broughton, 1931.

Work, Monroe N., ed. *Negro Year Book: An Annual Encyclopedia of the Negro, 1921–22*. Tuskegee, Ala.: Negro Year Book Publishing, 1922.

Yellin, Jean Fagan. *Women and Sisters: The Antislavery Feminists in American Culture*. New Haven: Yale University Press, 1989.

Zilversmit, Arthur. *The First Emancipation: The Abolition of Slavery in the North*. Chicago: University of Chicago Press, 1967.

Articles and Essays

Albion, Robert G. "New York Port and Its Disappointed Rivals." In Frank Otto Gatell, ed., *Essays on Jacksonian America*. New York: Holt, Rinehart and Winston, 1970, pp. 68–82.

Apperson, George M. "African Americans on the Tennessee Frontier: John Gloucester and His Contemporaries." *Tennessee Historical Quarterly* 59 (Spring 2000): 2–19.

Baily, Marilyn. "From Cincinnati, Ohio, to Wilberforce, Canada: A Note on Antebellum Colonization." *Journal of Negro History* 58 (October 1973): 427–40.

Bell, Howard H. "Free Negroes of the North, 1830–1835: A Study in National Cooperation." *Journal of Negro Education* 26 (Fall 1957): 447–53.

Billington, Ray Allen. "James Forten—Forgotten Abolitionist." *Negro History Bulletin* 13 (November 1949): 31–36, 45.

Blackson, Robert M. "Pennsylvania Banks and the Panic of 1819: A Reinterpretation." *Journal of the Early Republic* 9 (Fall 1989): 335–58.

Blight, David W. "In Search of Learning, Liberty, and Self-Definition: James McCune Smith and the Ordeal of the Antebellum Black Intellectual." *Afro-Americans in New York Life and History* 9 (July 1985): 7–25.

Boromé, Joseph A. "The Vigilant Committee of Philadelphia." *Pennsylvania Magazine of History and Biography* 92 (July 1968): 320–51.

Brewington, M. F. "The Sailmaker's Gear." *American Neptune* 9 (October 1949): 278–96.

Briggs, James Franklin. "Sails and Sailmakers." *Old Dartmouth Historical Sketches*, no. 65, in *Sketches of New Bedford's Early History* (1937).

Brown, Arthur Bevin. "A Philadelphia Merchant in 1768–1791." *Pennsylvania Magazine of History and Biography* 19 (1885): 397–402.

Brown, Ira V. "William D. Kelley and Radical Reconstruction." *Pennsylvania Magazine of History and Biography* 85 (July 1961): 316–29.

———. "Cradle of Feminism: The Philadelphia Female Anti-Slavery Society, 1833–1840." *Pennsylvania Magazine of History and Biography* 100 (April 1978): 143–66.

Brown, Wallace. "Negroes and the American Revolution." *History Today* 14 (August 1964): 556–63.

Bruns, Roger A. "Anthony Benezet and the Natural Rights of the Negro." *Pennsylvania Magazine of History and Biography* 96 (January 1972): 104–13.

Burnston, Sharon Ann. "Babies in the Well: An Underground Insight into Deviant Behavior in Eighteenth-Century Philadelphia." *Pennsylvania Magazine of History and Biography* 106 (April 1982): 151–86.

"Charles Ware, Sailmaker." *American Neptune* 3 (July 1943): 267–68.

Clark, William Bell. "That Mischievous *Holker*: The Story of a Privateer." *Pennsylvania Magazine of History and Biography* 79 (January 1955): 27–62.

———. "James Josiah, Master Mariner." *Pennsylvania Magazine of History and Biography* 79 (October 1955): 452–84.

———. "The Sea Captains' Club." *Pennsylvania Magazine of History and Biography* 81 (January 1957): 39–68.

Cleary, Patricia. "'She Will Be in the Shop': Women's Sphere of Trade in Eighteenth-Century Philadelphia and New York." *Pennsylvania Magazine of History and Biography* 119 (July 1995): 181–202.

Clement, Priscilla Ferguson. "The Philadelphia Welfare Crisis of the 1820s." *Pennsylvania Magazine of History and Biography* 105 (April 1981): 150–65.

Edwards, Paul. "Black Personalities in Georgian England." *History Today* 7 (September 1981): 39–44.

Egerton, Douglas R. "'Its Origin is Not a Little Curious': A New Look at the American Colonization Society." *Journal of the Early Republic* 5 (Winter 1985): 463–80.

Fisher, Barbara. "Maritime History of the Reading, 1833–1905." *Pennsylvania Magazine of History and Biography* 86 (April 1962): 160–80.

Foner, Philip S. "The Battle to End Discrimination Against Negroes on Philadelphia Street Cars." *Pennsylvania History* 40 (July and October 1973): 261–90, 355–79.

Geffen, Elizabeth M. "William Henry Furness, Philadelphia Antislavery Preacher." *Pennsylvania Magazine of History and Biography* 82 (July 1958): 259–92.

———. "Violence in Philadelphia in the 1840s and 1850s." *Pennsylvania History* 36 (October 1969): 381–410.

Gernes, Todd S. "Poetic Justice: Sarah Forten, Eliza Earle, and the Paradox of Intellectual Property." *New England Quarterly* 71 (June 1998): 229–65.

Gravely, William B. "The Dialectic of Double-Consciousness in Black American Freedom Celebrations, 1808–1863." *Journal of Negro History* 67 (Winter 1982): 302–17.

Hall, Elton W. "Sailcloth for American Vessels." *American Neptune* 31 (April 1971): 130–45.

Hine, William C. "Dr. Benjamin A. Boseman, Jr.: Charleston's Black Physician-Politician." In Howard N. Rabinowitz, ed., *Southern Black Leaders in the Reconstruction Era*. Urbana: University of Illinois Press, 1982: pp. 335–62.

Hoetink, H. "'Americans' in Samaná." *Caribbean Studies* 2 (April 1962): 3–22.

Hoff, Henry B. "Frans Abramse Van Salee and His Descendants: A Colonial Black Family in New York and New Jersey." *New York Genealogical and Biographical Record* 121 (April, July, and October 1990): 65–71, 157–61, 205–11.

Jable, J. Thomas. "Aspects of Moral Reform in Early Nineteenth-Century Pennsylvania." *Pennsylvania Magazine of History and Biography* 108 (July 1978): 344–63.

Jacobs, Donald M. "William Lloyd Garrison's *Liberator* and Boston's Blacks, 1830–1865." *New England Quarterly* 44 (June 1971): 259–77.

King, William F., Jr. "The Sailmakers and Ship Chandlers of 79 Commercial Street, Boston." *American Neptune* 15 (July 1955): 220–31.

Klepp, Susan E. "Zachariah Poulson's Bills of Mortality, 1788–1801." In Billy G. Smith, ed., *Life in Early Philadelphia: Documents from the Revolutionary and Early National Periods*. University Park: Penn State University Press, 1995, pp. 219–42.

Klepp, Susan E., and Billy G. Smith. "Marriage and Death: The Records of Gloria Dei Church." In Smith, ed., *Life in Early Philadelphia*, pp. 177–218.

Knight, Betsy. "Prisoner Exchange and Parole in the American Revolution." *William and Mary Quarterly* 48 (April 1991): 201–22.

Lammers, Ann C. "The Rev. Absalom Jones and the Episcopal Church: Christian Theology and Black Consciousness in a New Alliance." *Historical Magazine of the Protestant Episcopal Church* 51 (June 1982): 159–84.

Lapsansky, Emma J. "'Since They Got Those Separate Churches': Afro-Americans and Racism in Jacksonian Philadelphia." *American Quarterly* 32 (Spring 1980): 54–78.

Lapsansky, Phillip. "'Abigail, a Negress': The Role and the Legacy of African Americans in the Yellow Fever Epidemic." In J. Worth Estes and Billy G. Smith, eds., *A Melancholy Scene of Devastation: The Public Response to the 1793 Philadelphia Yellow Fever Epidemic*. Philadelphia: College of Physicians and Library Company of Philadelphia, 1997, pp. 61–78.

Leary, Lewis. "Thomas Branagan: Republican Rhetoric and Romanticism in America." *Pennsylvania Magazine of History and Biography* 77 (July 1953): 332–52.

Lindhorst, Marie. "Politics in a Box: Sarah Mapps Douglass and the Female Literary Association, 1831–1833." *Pennsylvania History* 65 (Summer 1998): 263–79.

Matthews, Jean. "Race, Sex, and the Dimensions of Liberty in Antebellum America." *Journal of the Early Republic* 6 (Fall 1986): 275–91.

McNeill, William. "Charles Burleigh Purvis." *Journal of the National Medical Association* 45 (January 1953): 79–82.

Miller, Richard G. "The Federal City, 1783–1800." In Russell F. Weigley, ed., *Philadelphia—A 300-Year History*. New York: W. W. Norton, 1982, pp. 155–205.

Mishoff, Willard O. "Business in Philadelphia During the British Occupation, 1777–1778." *Pennsylvania Magazine of History and Biography* 61 (1937): 165–81.

Morris, Charles Edward. "Panic and Reprisal: Reaction in North Carolina to the Nat Turner Insurrection, 1831." *North Carolina Historical Review* 62 (January 1985): 29–52.

Nash, Gary B. "Slaves and Slaveowners in Colonial Philadelphia." *William and Mary Quarterly* 30 (April 1973): 223–56.

_____. "Forging Freedom: The Emancipation Experience in Northern Seaport Cities, 1775–1820." In Ira Berlin and Ronald Hoffman, eds., *Slavery and Freedom in the Age of the American Revolution*. Charlottesville: University Press of Virginia, 1983, pp. 3–48.

_____. "Reverberations of Haiti in the American North: Black Saint Dominguans in Philadelphia." *Pennsylvania History* 65 (Special Supplement, 1998): 44–73.

Newman, Debra L. "Black Women in the Era of the American Revolution in Pennsylvania." *Journal of Negro History* 61 (July 1976): 276–89.

Newman, Simon P. "Reading the Bodies of Early American Seafarers." *William and Mary Quarterly* 55 (January 1998): 59–82.

Norton, Mary Beth. "The Fate of Some Black Loyalists of the American Revolution." *Journal of Negro History* 58 (October 1973): 402–26.

Oliver, Peter. "Travel by Water, To, From, Between and Within the United States in 1800." *American Neptune* 3 (October 1943): 292–313.

Pernick, Martin S. "Politics, Parties, and Pestilence: Epidemic Yellow Fever in Philadelphia and the Rise of the First Party System." *William and Mary Quarterly* 29 (October 1972): 559–86.

Price, Edward J., Jr. "School Segregation in Nineteenth-Century Pennsylvania." *Pennsylvania History* 43 (April 1976): 121–37.

Proctor, D. A. "Michael Fitton." *Mariner's Mirror* 79 (May 1993): 206–8.

Rowe, G. S., and Billy G. Smith. "The Prisoners for Trial Docket for Philadelphia County, 1795." *Pennsylvania History* 55 (October 1986): 289–319.

Runcie, John. "'Hunting the Nigs' in Philadelphia: The Race Riot of August, 1834." *Pennsylvania History* 39 (April 1972): 187–218.

Salinger, Sharon V. and Charles Wetherell. "Wealth and Renting in Prerevolutionary Philadelphia." *Journal of American History* 71 (March 1985): 826–40.

Salvucci, Linda K. "Supply, Demand, and the Making of a Market: Philadelphia and Havana at the Beginning of the Nineteenth Century." In Franklin W. Knight and Peggy K. Liss, eds., *Atlantic Port Cities: Economy, Culture, and Society in the Atlantic World, 1650–1850*. Knoxville: University of Tennessee Press, 1991, pp. 40–57.

Schroeder, John H. "Stephen Decatur: Heroic Ideal of the Young Navy." In James C. Bradford, ed., *Command Under Sail: Makers of the American Naval Tradition, 1775–1850*. Annapolis: United States Naval Institute Press, 1985, pp. 199–219.

Silcox, Harry C. "Delay and Neglect: Negro Education in Antebellum Philadelphia." *Pennsylvania Magazine of History and Biography* 97 (October 1978): 444–64.

_____. "The Black 'Better Class' Political Dilemma: Philadelphia Prototype Isaiah C. Wears." *Pennsylvania Magazine of History and Biography* 113 (January 1989): 45–66.

Slaski, Eugene R. "Thomas Willing: Loyalty Meant Commitment." *Pennsylvania History* 47 (July 1980): 235–52.

Smith, Mark A. "Andrew Brown's 'Earnest Endeavor': The *Federal Gazette's* Role in Philadelphia's Yellow Fever Epidemic of 1793." *Pennsylvania Magazine of History and Biography* 120 (October 1996): 321–42.

Soderlund, Jean R. "Black Women in Colonial Pennsylvania." *Pennsylvania Magazine of History and Biography* 107 (January 1983): 49–68.

Stewart, James Brewer. "The Emergence of Racial Modernity and the Rise of the White North, 1790–1840." *Journal of the Early Republic* 18 (Summer 1998): 181–236.

Tinkcom, Harry M. "The Revolutionary City, 1765–1783." In Russell F. Weigley, ed., *Philadelphia—A 300-Year History*. New York: W. W. Norton, 1982, pp. 109–54.

Turner, Edward R. "Slavery in Colonial Pennsylvania." *Pennsylvania Magazine of History and Biography* 35 (1911): 141–51.

Wade, Richard C. "The Negro in Cincinnati, 1800–1830." *Journal of Negro History* 39 (January 1954): 43–57.

Warner, Robert A. "Amos Gerry Beman—1812–1874: A Memoir on a Forgotten Leader." *Journal of Negro History* 22 (April 1937): 200–221.

Wax, Darold D. "The Demand for Slave Labor in Colonial Pennsylvania." *Pennsylvania History* 34 (October 1967): 331–45.

_____. "Africans on the Delaware: The Pennsylvania Slave Trade, 1759–1765." *Pennsylvania History* 50 (January 1983): 38–49.

Wesley, Charles H. "Negro Suffrage in the Period of Constitution-Making, 1787–1865." In Wesley, ed., *Neglected History: Essays in Negro History by a College President*. Washington, D.C.: Association for the Study of Negro Life and History, 1969, pp. 41–55.

White, Arthur O. "Prince Saunders: An Instance of Social Mobility among Antebellum New England Blacks." *Journal of Negro History* 60 (October 1975): 526–35.

White, Shane. "The Death of James Johnson." *American Quarterly* 51 (December 1999): 753–95.

Winch, Julie. "Philadelphia and the Other Underground Railroad." *Pennsylvania Magazine of History and Biography* 111 (January 1987): 3–35.

Wood, Peter H. "'Liberty Is Sweet': African-American Freedom Struggles in the Years Before White Independence." In Alfred F. Young, ed., *Beyond the American Revolution: Explorations in the History of American Radicalism*. DeKalb: Northern Illinois University Press, 1993, pp. 149–84.

Wright, Robert E. "Thomas Willing (1731–1821): Philadelphia Financier and Forgotten Founding Father." *Pennsylvania History* 63 (Autumn 1996): 525–60.

_____. "Artisans, Banks, Credit, and the Election of 1800." *Pennsylvania Magazine of History and Biography* 122 (July 1998): 211–40.

Zachary, Alan M. "Social Disorder and the Philadelphia Elite before Jackson." *Pennsylvania Magazine of History and Biography* 99 (July 1975), 288–308.

Dissertations and Theses

Adams, Donald R., Jr. "Wage Rates in Philadelphia, 1790–1830." Ph.D. diss., University of Pennsylvania, 1967.

Bauer, Carol Phillips. "Law, Slavery, and Sommersett's Case in Eighteenth-Century England: A Study of the Legal Status of Freedom." Ph.D. diss., New York University, 1973.

Brouwer, Merle Gerald. "The Negro as a Slave and a Free Black in Colonial Pennsylvania." Ph.D. diss., Wayne State University, 1973.

Eberly, Wayne J. "The Pennsylvania Abolition Society, 1775–1830." Ph.D. diss., Pennsylvania State University, 1973.

Hall, Elton Wayland. "Sailmaking in Connecticut Prior to 1860." M.A. thesis, University of Delaware, 1968.

Hornick, Nancy Slocum. "Anthony Benezet: Eighteenth Century Social Critic, Educator, and Abolitionist." Ph.D. diss., University of Maryland, 1974.

Jackson, James O'Dell. "The Origins of Pan-African Nationalism: Afro-American and Haytien Relations." Ph.D. diss., Northwestern University, 1976.

Luckett, Judith Ann. "Protest, Advancement and Identity: Organizational Strategies of Northern Free Blacks, 1830 to 1860." Ph.D. diss., Johns Hopkins University, 1992.

Manges, Frances May. "Women Shopkeepers, Tavernkeepers, and Artisans in Colonial Philadelphia." Ph.D. diss., University of Pennsylvania, 1958.

Nicholson, Wendy Ann. "Sober Frugality and Siren Luxury: The Transformation of Elite Culture in Philadelphia, 1750–1800." Ph.D. diss., University of California, Berkeley, 1994.

Opper, Peter Kent. "The Mind of the White Participant in the African Colonization Movement, 1816–1840." Ph.D. diss., University of North Carolina at Chapel Hill, 1972.

Pollard, Leslie James. "The Stephen Smith Home for the Aged: A Gerontological History of a Pioneer Venture in Caring for the Black Aged, 1864 to 1953." Ph.D. diss., Syracuse University, 1977.

Rasmussen, Ethel Elise. "Capital on the Delaware: The Philadelphia Upper Class in Transition, 1789–1801." Ph.D. diss., Brown University, 1962.

Rilling, Donna J. "Building Philadelphia: Real Estate Development in the City of Homes, 1790 to 1837." Ph.D. diss., University of Pennsylvania, 1993.

Scott, Julius S. "The Common Wind: Currents in Afro-American Communication in the Era of the Haitian Revolution." Ph.D. diss., Duke University, 1986.

Silcox, Harry Charles. "A Comparative Study in School Desegregation: The Boston and Philadelphia Experience, 1800–1881." Ed.D. diss., Temple University, 1971.

Ulle, Robert F. "A History of St. Thomas' African Episcopal Church." Ph.D. diss., University of Pennsylvania, 1986.

Unpublished Papers

Burkett, Randall K. "The Reverend Harry Croswell and Black Episcopalians in New Haven, 1820–1860."

INDEX

SEP - - 2002